EVERYDAY LIFE
in the German Book Trade

THE PENN STATE SERIES IN THE HISTORY OF THE BOOK

JAMES L. W. WEST III, GENERAL EDITOR

The series publishes books that employ a mixture of approaches: historical, archival, biographical, critical, sociological, and economic. Projected topics include professional authorship and the literary marketplace, the history of reading and book distribution, book-trade studies and publishing-house histories, and examinations of copyright and literary property.

Peter Burke, *The Fortunes of the "Courtier": The European Reception of Castiglione's "Cortegiano"*

James M. Hutchisson, *The Rise of Sinclair Lewis, 1920–1930*

Julie Bates Dock, ed., *Charlotte Perkins Gilman's "The Yellow Wall-paper" and the History of Its Publication and Reception: A Critical Edition and Documentary Casebook*

John Williams, ed., *Imaging the Early Medieval Bible*

James G. Nelson, *Publisher to the Decadents: Leonard Smithers in the Careers of Beardsley, Wilde, Dowson*

Ezra Greenspan, *George Palmer Putnam: Representative American Publisher*

PENN STATE REPRINTS IN BOOK HISTORY

James L. W. West III and Samuel S. Vaughan, Editors

Roger Burlingame, *Of Making Many Books: A Hundred Years of Reading, Writing, and Publishing*

EVERYDAY LIFE
in the German Book Trade

FRIEDRICH NICOLAI

AS BOOKSELLER AND PUBLISHER IN THE

AGE OF ENLIGHTENMENT

1750–1810

(Pamela E. Selwyn)

The Pennsylvania State University Press
University Park, Pennsylvania

Library of Congress Cataloging-in-Publication Data

Selwyn, Pamela Eve.
Everyday life in the German book trade :
Friedrich Nicolai as bookseller and publisher
in the age of enlightenment, 1750–1810 /
Pamela E. Selwyn.
    p.   cm.—(Penn State series in
the history of the book)
Includes bibliographical references and index.
ISBN 978-0-271-02797-5
1. Nicolai, Friedrich, 1733-1811. 2. Authors,
German—18th century—Biography.
3. Publishers and publishing—Germany—
Biography. 4. Publishers and publishing—
Germany—History—18th century. 5. Publishers
and publishing—Germany—History—19th century.
6. Enlightenment—Germany.
7. Germany—Intellectual life. I. Title. II. Series

PT2440.N4 Z875 2000
070.5′092—dc21
[B]   99-047076

Copyright © 2000
The Pennsylvania State University
All rights reserved
Printed in the United States of America
Published by
The Pennsylvania State University Press,
University Park, PA 16802-1003

It is the policy of The Pennsylvania State University
Press to use acid-free paper for the first printing of
all clothbound books. Publications on uncoated stock
satisfy the minimum requirements of American
National Standard for Information Sciences—
Permanence of Paper for Printed Library Materials,
ANSI Z39.48–1992.

FOR

Debs, Philip, *and* Steve

(contents)

Preface
ix

(1)
The Life and Opinions of Friedrich Nicolai,
Buchhändler and *Aufklärer*
1

(2)
The Nicolaische Buchhandlung, 1759–1811: A Publishing
Company in the Age of Enlightenment and Revolution
29

(3)
Everyday Life in the Book Trade
99

(4)
The Legal and Political Framework of the Eighteenth-Century
Book Trade: Privilege, Piracy, and Censorship
181

(5)
The *Allgemeine deutsche Bibliothek* as the Centerpiece
of Nicolai's Program of Enlightenment and of his Firm
251

(6)
Literary-Mercantile Relations: Nicolai and His Authors
299

Afterword
375

Appendix: Nicolai's Shop Employees
381

Bibliography
385

Index
403

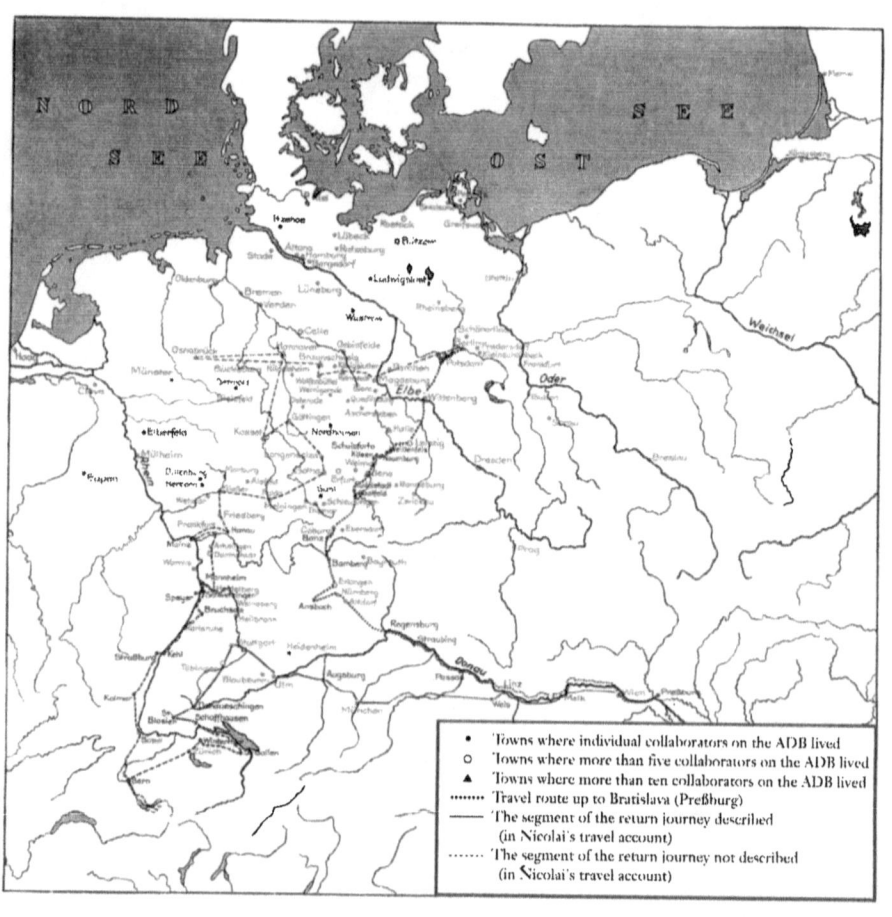

(preface)

The life of a wit is a warfare upon earth.

—*Alexander Pope, 1717*

Although Friedrich Nicolai could scarcely be called a neglected figure, he has been the subject of neither a scholarly biography[1] nor a study of his publishing and bookselling activities.[2] The new age of Nicolai, inaugurated in 1974 by Horst Möller's *Aufklärung in Preußen: Der Verleger, Publizist und Geschichtsschreiber Friedrich Nicolai*, continued in 1983 with various publications celebrating the 250th anniversary of Nicolai's birth. Major exhibitions in (West) Berlin and Wolfenbüttel and the accompanying catalogs,[3] as well as a volume of essays,[4] together with articles

---

1. Gustav Sichelschmidt's *Friedrich Nicolai: Geschichte seines Lebens* (Herford: Nicolai, 1971) is a popular biography composed chiefly of quotations from Nicolai's autobiographical writings and Leopold F. G. von Göckingk's *Friedrich Nicolais Leben und literarischer Nachlaß* (Berlin: Nicolai, 1820). Herbert Heckmann's contribution to the series "Preußische Köpfe," *Friedrich Nicolai* (Berlin: Stapp, 1984), is also more an introduction than a full-scale biography. Both Horst Möller's 1974 study of Nicolai's ideas and writings, *Aufklärung in Preußen: Der Verleger Publizist und Geschichtsschreiber Friedrich Nicolai* (which began life as a dissertation at the Freie Universität in Berlin), and Andreas M.G.H.-H. von Randow's "Öffentlichkeit Erfahrung und Beschreibung: Hausväterrepublik und Gelehrtenrepublik als Möglichkeiten kultureller Partizipation der Bürger Nicolai und Chodowiecki im friderizianischen Berlin" (Ph.D. diss., University of Bonn, 1984) contain useful biographical information, but neither is a biography in the usual sense. For an overview of the Nicolai literature up to 1970, see Möller, *Aufklärung in Preußen*, pp. 1–3, esp. nn. 2–6.

2. *Friedrich Nicolai: Verlegerbriefe*, selected and edited by Bernhard Fabian and Marie-Luise Spieckermann (Berlin: Nicolai, 1988), which presents some interesting, previously unpublished letters, was prepared for the 275th anniversary of the founding of the Nicolaische Buchhandlung.

3. *Friedrich Nicolai: Leben und Werk*, Ausstellung zum 250. Geburtstag, 7. Dezember 1983 bis 4. Februar 1984, Staatsbibliothek Preußischer Kulturbesitz (Berlin: Nicolai, 1983), compiled by Peter Jörg Becker, and *Friedrich Nicolai: Die Verlagswerke eines preußischen Buchhändlers der Aufklärung 1759–1811* (Wolfenbüttel: Herzog August Bibliothek, 1983), compiled by Paul Raabe.

4. *Friedrich Nicolai: Essays zum 250. Geburtstag*, ed. Bernhard Fabian (Berlin: Nicolai, 1983).

by Paul Raabe,[5] Bernhard Fabian,[6] Jochen Schulte-Sasse,[7] and Jonathon Knudsen,[8] have contributed to a more complex view of this much-maligned figure. Nicolai's own writings, long hard to come by, are being reprinted,[9] and an anthology, *Kritik ist überall, zumal in Deutschland nötig*, was published as part of the *Bibliothek des achtzehnten Jahrhunderts* (Leipzig, 1989). The novel *Leben und Meinungen des Herrn Magister Sebaldus Nothanker* (Frankfurt a. M.: Ullstein, 1986) is even available in paperback. A noteworthy curiosity is Jochen Beyse's *Der Aufklärungsmacher* (Munich: Piper, 1988), a novel in the Enlightenment-critical mode of the 1970s and 1980s[10] in which Nicolai's Romanticist son is oppressed by paternal pedantry during a voyage through Germany.

Occasional disparagements of Nicolai in works about the Romantics in particular notwithstanding,[11] the trend has thus long been toward a more balanced view of his virtues and vices. The revival of interest in Nicolai since the 1970s was part of the resurgence of studies on both the German Enlightenment and the literary market and book trade of the

---

5. "Die Aufklärung und das gedruckte Wort: Die Entfaltung neuer Ideen mit Hilfe Berliner Verleger," in *Digressionen: Wege zur Aufklärung*, Festgabe für Peter Michelsen, ed. G. Frühsorge, K. Manger, and Fr. Strack (Heidelberg: Winter, 1984), pp. 47–60; "Der Verleger Friedrich Nicolai, ein preussischer Buchhändler der Aufklärung," in *Bücherlust und Lesefreuden: Beiträge zur Geschichte des Buchwesens in Deutschland*, ed. Paul Raabe (Stuttgart: Metzler, 1984), pp. 141–64; and "Zum Bild des Verlagswesens in der Spätaufklärung: Dargestellt an hand von Friedrich Nicolais Lagerkatalog von 1787," in *Bücherlust und Lesefreuden*, pp. 66–88.

6. "Die erste Bibliographie der englischen Literatur des achtzehnten Jahrhunderts: Jeremias David Reuß' *Gelehrtes England*," in *Das Buch und sein Haus*, Fs. Gerhard Liebers, vol. 1., ed. Rolf Fuhlrott and Bertram Haller (Wiesbaden: Reichert, 1979), pp. 16–43.

7. "Friedrich Nicolai," in *Deutsche Dichter des 18. Jahrhunderts: Ihr Leben und Werk*, ed. Benno von Wiese (Berlin: Erich Schmidt, 1977), pp. 320–39.

8. "Friedrich Nicolai's 'wirkliche Welt': On Common Sense in the German Enlightenment," in *Mentalitäten und Lebensverhältnisse: Beispiele aus der Sozialgeschichte der Neuzeit*, Rudolf Vierhaus zum 60. Geburtstag (Göttingen: Vandenhoeck & Ruprecht, 1982), pp. 77–91.

9. A reprint series of Nicolai's collected works edited by Bernhard Fabian and Marie-Luise Spieckermann in Münster has been published, and an annotated version under the direction of Hans Roloff and Erhard Weidl in Berlin is under way. The latter will eventually include editions of parts of the unpublished correspondence.

10. The contributions to a lecture series on this issue sponsored by the Akademie der Künste in West Berlin are printed in *Der Traum der Vernunft. Vom Elend der Aufklärung* (Darmstadt: Luchterhand, 1985). For a collection of critical essays on the German Enlightenment in English, see *Impure Reason: Dialectic of Enlightenment in Germany*, ed. W. Daniel Wilson and Robert C. Holub (Detroit: Wayne State University Press, 1993). Although perhaps few people now seek the roots of fascism in the Enlightenment, as Max Horkheimer and Theodor W. Adorno did in their *Dialektik der Aufklärung* (1947; Frankfurt a. M.: Fischer, 1969), critiques of the Enlightenment from the perspectives of feminism and anti-racism are alive and well.

11. An example is *König der Romantik: Das Leben des Dichters Ludwig Tieck in Briefen, Selbstzeugnissen und Berichten*, ed. Klaus Gunzel, 2d ed. (Berlin: Verlag der Nation, 1986).

late eighteenth century. Even a popular English-language cultural history of Germany such as Gordon Craig's *The Germans* accords Nicolai a prominent place. Craig remarks that "when German intellectuals at the end of the eighteenth century talked of living in a Frederician age, they were sometimes referring not to the monarch in Sans Souci, but to his namesake, the Berlin bookseller Friedrich Nicolai."[12] The long (if not unbroken) denigration of the Enlightenment in favor of classicism and Romanticism as the founding traditions of modern German intellectual and cultural life, and of scholarly and practical literature in favor of works of imagination and speculation, which characterized much of German literary and cultural history throughout the nineteenth and well into the twentieth century, was not conducive to a balanced view of Nicolai. To be sure, monographs on Nicolai's early writings,[13] his theological ideas,[14] and on the psychology and nature of his relations with the *Sturm und Drang* authors[15] all provide important correctives to the caricature sketched in many standard literary histories of a shallow, arrogant philistine who failed to recognize Goethe's genius (along with that of Hamann, Herder, Kant, Fichte, and a host of others), and who ridiculed everything he did not understand (which included practically all important German literature and philosophy after 1770).[16] Goethe's and Schiller's assessment of Nicolai, expressed in the epigram "Little as you have done for the education of the Germans / Fritz Nicolai, you have earned a good deal in the process"[17] set the tone for many later authors. Even the more charitable older authors tended to admit that while Nicolai had accomplished something in his youth, under the salutary influence of his more profound friends G. E. Lessing and Moses Mendelssohn, and had been a central figure in the social and intellectual life of Berlin in his day, he had

---

12. *The Germans* (1982; New York: Meridian, 1983), p. 27.
13. Ernst Altenkrüger, *Friedrich Nicolais Jugendschriften* (Berlin: C. Heymann, 1894).
14. Karl Aner, *Der Aufklärer Friedrich Nicolai* (Giessen: A. Töpelmann, 1912).
15. Martin Sommerfeld, *Friedrich Nicolai und der Sturm und Drang* (Halle: M. Niemeyer, 1921).
16. Typical was the discussion in Robert Koenig's much reprinted *Deutsche Litteraturgeschichte* (twenty-nine editions by 1903), which describes Nicolai in terms of "the shallowest Enlightenment" and "crudely moralizing rationalism." *Deutsche Litteraturgeschichte*, 23d ed. (Bielefeld: Velhagen & Klasing, 1893), pp. 424–25; quoted in Becker, *Friedrich Nicolai: Leben und Werk*, p. 138.
17. "Hast du auch wenig verdient um die Bildung der Deutschen / Fritz Nicolai, sehr viel hast du dabey doch verdient." This epigram is one of a series of satirical epigrams in distichs or "Xenien" (many of them attacking Nicolai) that appeared in the *Musenalmanach für das Jahr 1797* (Tübingen: Cotta, 1796).

sadly outlived his time and usefulness.[18] In a 1788 letter to the author, translator, and (future) German Jacobin Georg Forster, the Göttingen *Aufklärer* Georg Christoph Lichtenberg wrote rather ambiguously that their mutual friend Nicolai had only to die "to be considered one of the finest minds of our century."[19] Nicolai, however, stubbornly persisted in breathing and writing for another twenty-three years, and many literary historians never forgave him for it.

For all the writings on Nicolai as author and critic, his main profession of bookseller and publisher has been relatively neglected. Moved perhaps by the need to rescue Nicolai's intellectual achievements from a century of scornful Germanists, Horst Möller devotes only some twenty pages of his book to this central aspect of Nicolai's career. The present study seeks to fill this lacuna and to illuminate Nicolai's career as a bookseller and publisher in the Enlightenment and as an *Aufklärer* in the book trade.

Given the state of eighteenth-century (German) bibliography, most studies of the period's publishers must begin with laborious compilations of their publishing lists from book fair and other catalog and inaccurate and incomplete bibliographical reference works. This circumstance, along with the relative scarcity of business archives, severe wartime losses particularly to the library and archives of the German book trade organization, the Börsenverein des Deutschen Buchhandels, and until rather recently, the difficulty of access to and information about holdings in the former German Democratic Republic has made it difficult to study individual German publishing houses in detail. These circumstances also explain why the remarkable *Geschichte des deutschen Buchhandels*, begun by Friedrich Kapp and Johann Goldfriedrich in the late nineteenth century, remains such a central source, based as it was on material either irrevocably lost or obtainable only through long and heroic interlibrary loan campaigns.

In the case of Friedrich Nicolai, the material remains unusually rich

---

18. This is the tenor, for example, of Jacob Minor's 1883 essay on Nicolai, which claims to be the first nonanecdotal survey of his life and works. "Scarcely any writer of the last century may claim as significant a place in the cultural history of his time as Friedrich Nicolai," Minor begins. This significance, however, was essentially negative; Nicolai embodied the "spirit of negation," was a "born enemy of beauty," and "the most narrowminded and consistent representative of the century of utility and Enlightenment." Jacob Minor, ed., *Lessings Jugendfreunde: Chr. Felix Weiße, Joh. Friedr. von Cronegk, Joach. Wilh. von Brawe, Friedrich Nicolai, Deutsche National-Litteratur*, vol. 72 (Berlin: W. Spemann [1883]), p. 277.

19. Lichtenberg to Forster, 18 February 1788, in Georg Christoph Lichtenberg, *Briefe*, vol. 4 of *Schriften und Briefe*, ed. Wolfgang Promies (Munich: Hanser, 1967), p. 724.

despite the loss of his account books. His prominence as an author and as a citizen of Berlin and the continued existence of his firm in family hands into the nineteenth century ensured the preservation of much of his correspondence. Although this correspondence is largely one-sided, his own letters being widely scattered or lost, it is frequently possible to reconstruct at least the outlines of Nicolai's own answers. His sometimes laconic, sometimes copious marginal notes, which indicate his spontaneous reactions (if not always his final, more diplomatic replies), and letters from his correspondents (filled though they may be with willful or unwitting misinterpretations of Nicolai's own words) provide the basis for such reconstructions. Paul Raabe's 1983 Wolfenbüttel catalog of Nicolai's production makes it possible to oversee the scope of his publishing activities.[20] I was most fortunate to have this excellent work as a starting point. In the course of research for this study, which was conducted between 1985 and 1990, Paul Raabe's catalog served as a key to unlock the formidable Nicolai papers, helping to locate the authors, translators, editors, and occasionally also printers among eighty-nine volumes of (partially) alphabetically ordered correspondence from some 2500 individuals housed in the Staatsbibliothek Preußischer Kulturbesitz in Berlin. The index of Kapp and Goldfriedrich's *Geschichte des deutschen Buchhandels* aided in the search for letters from members of the book trades. Each volume had to be scanned for letters from employees and jobseekers, customers, would-be authors, and other potentially relevant correspondents. I could read only some 20 percent of the circa 15,000 letters in detail, but since a large proportion of them chiefly treat reviews for the *Allgemeine deutsche Bibliothek*, many were of only limited interest for this study. In addition, I consulted the remaining fragments of the original three hundred or so volumes of Nicolai papers in the former Deutsche Staatsbibliothek (now united with the Staatsbibliothek Preußischer Kulturbesitz), along with letters and documents in the Landesarchiv and Archiv der Evangelischen Kirche der Union (Kirchenbuchstelle) in West Berlin; the Stadtarchiv, Buch- und Schriftmuseum and Universitätsbibliothek in Leipzig; the Haus-, Hof-, und Staatsarchiv in Vienna; and the Herzog August Bibliothek in Wolfenbüttel.

Although this study aims to present a rounded picture of Nicolai's life as a bookseller and publisher, it is more detailed in some respects than

20. Walter Eisenberg's 1977 Göttingen M.A. thesis, "Das Verlagsprogramm Friedrich Nicolais," represents the first attempt at cataloging Nicolai's publications and provided the basis for Raabe's more extensive project.

others. Three aspects of his life, in particular, deserve more extensive treatment. Future research on Nicolai's publishing company could focus on what I only touch on here, the physical appearance of books. Nicolai may have been less concerned than some of his contemporaries with the elegance of the works he published, but he was not oblivious to typographical and aesthetic issues and hired prominent illustrators such as Daniel Chodowiecki and Johann Wilhelm Meil to embellish novels in particular. The "look" of his books changed over the years, and it would be interesting to examine, for example, the extent to which format, layout, and typography reflected and determined the different uses and audiences for which books were intended. Using Raabe's Wolfenbüttel catalog as a guide to library holdings, one could analyze Nicolai's production for its place in what Nicolas Barker has called a revolution in the layout of books in the eighteenth century.[21] The dissemination and reception of the books Nicolai published is similarly deserving of greater attention than was possible here. A study of selected contemporary correspondences, of the catalogs of private and lending libraries and reading societies, and of reviews in the journals and *gelehrte Zeitungen* of different regions might give us a more precise picture of the social and geographical impact of Nicolai's publishing program. Finally, it would be interesting to know more about the sources and extent of Nicolai's capital. When he and his wife bought a house in the Brüderstraße in 1787 they paid over 30,000 taler in cash,[22] and despite all his complaints about devastating war contributions, Nicolai left a very considerable estate.[23] Tax records and scattered remarks in the correspondence about investments, borrowing, and lending might shed more light on this subject.

---

21. "Typography and the Meaning of Words: The Revolution in the Layout of Books in the Eighteenth Century," in *Buch und Buchhandel in Europa im achtzehnten Jahrhundert. The Book and the Book Trade in Eighteenth-Century Europe*, proceedings of the Fifth Wolfenbüttel Symposium November 1–3, 1977, ed. Giles Barber and Bernhard Fabian (Hamburg: Hauswedell, 1981), pp. 127–65.

22. Deed of sale between Carl Friedrich Dickow and Nicolai, dated 15 September 1787, copy of 1799. The price was 30,000 taler in Friedrich d'or, plus 500 taler "Schlüsselgeld" and 2000 taler for the furnishings, half in Friedrich d'or and half in Prussian courant (silver coins). The entire sum was due on 1 April. Berlin, Staatsbibliothek Preußischer Kulturbesitz Handschriftabteilung [hereafter cited as "SPKB"], Nachlaß Nicolai, vol. 285, no. 22 [hereafter cited as "NN" by volume number, and by item number when required]. Unlike most seventeenth- and eighteenth-century domestic structures in Berlin, this house is still standing, and lucky visitors who find the gates open may enter the courtyard and get some impression of how it must have looked in Nicolai's day.

23. Record of the duties on Nicolai's legacies, 31 March 1812, in NN 284.

Preface

Many people contributed to this study, whether directly or indirectly. Without the late William McClain, my inspiring teacher at Johns Hopkins, I would never have thought of studying the social history of German letters. Robert Darnton, who supervised the dissertation on which this book is based, first suggested that I might have a look at the Nicolai papers, and I thank him for his unflagging enthusiasm and helpful criticisms over the last fifteen years. The members of my Princeton dissertation committee, Natalie Davis, Anthony Grafton, and Walter Hinderer offered a number of helpful suggestions—a few of which I have managed to use. Paul Raabe of the Herzog August Bibliothek provided extremely valuable methodological advice, without which I would have been truly lost in the labyrinthine Nicolai papers. Hazel Rosenstrauch, Mark Lehmstedt, and Jeffrey Freedman have all shared their own research and ideas on the eighteenth-century book trade with me. I am also much indebted to Edoardo Tortarolo for his erudition on the Berlin Enlightenment and notes from a research trip to the former East German Zentralarchiv in Merseburg. The late Heinz Ischreyt generously provided me with parts of the manuscript of his now published edition of the correspondence between Friedrich Nicolai and Ludwig Heinrich von Nicolay. Erhard Weidl frequently asked me when I was finally going to publish my work.

The research for this book was supported by grants from the Germanistic Society of America (1984–85), the Herzog August Bibliothek in Wolfenbüttel (summer 1985), and the Institut für Europäische Geschichte in Mainz (1989–90). A position as research assistant to Reinhard Rürup at the Technische Universität from 1986 to 1989 afforded me the luxury of enough time in the archives to savor such pleasures as discovering two-hundred-year-old wildflowers pressed among the documents. The staff of the manuscript and rare book collection at the Staatsbibliothek Preußischer Kulturbesitz in Berlin, which houses Nicolai's papers, kindly put up with me as a seemingly permanent fixture for many years. I also thank the librarians and archivists of the Landesarchiv and Stadtarchiv in Berlin; the University of Leipzig; the Deutsches Buch- und Schrift Museum and the Stadtarchiv in Leipzig; the Haus-, Hof- und Staatsarchiv in Vienna; the Stadtarchiv of Frankfurt am Main; the Beinecke Library at Yale University; and the Herzog August Bibliothek in Wolfenbüttel.

Many individuals have offered advice on the project and support of various kinds over the years, and I would particularly like to thank my family, Hans-Erich Bödeker, John Borneman, John Carson, Ann Goldberg, Carla Hesse, Stefi Jersch-Wenzel, Philip Johnson and Deborah Ellinger, Jan Lambertz, Petra Olbrich, Lyndal Roper, and Stephen Shutt. Deborah Louise Cohen has saved me from several errors of judgment and taste. Without her encouragement, this book would still be an unfinished manuscript buried somewhere among the translation projects on my desk. Finally, I would like to thank my copyeditor, Andrew Lewis, for his meticulous and intelligent reading. Any remaining errors are, of course, my own.

The author would like to thank the Staatsbibliothek Preußischer Kulturbesitz zu Berlin for permission to reproduce the cover illustration.

Where not otherwise indicated, all translations from the German and the French are my own. Regrettably, space did not permit the inclusion of the original quotations in the notes, but I will be happy to supply them on request.

chapter

(1)

The Life and Opinions of Friedrich Nicolai, *Buchhändler* and *Aufklärer*

> Herr Nicolai is that rare creature, a learned bookseller, and
> follows in the footsteps of the Gessners, Elzevires, and others.
> There are, to be sure, those who believe this to be more
> detrimental than beneficial to literature.
>
> —*Büsten Berliner Gelehrten,* 1787

The German word *Aufklärer,* for which there is no English equivalent, literally means "one who enlightens." It is used in the literature on the German Enlightenment in much the same way as *philosophe*—described by Robert Darnton as an "ideal type—the man of letters committed to the cause of Enlightenment"[1]—is used in that on the French Enlightenment. Unlike "the Enlightenment" in English, *Aufklärer* and *Aufklärung* were contemporary terms in German (like *philosophe* in French). In this book, *Aufklärer* will be employed quite broadly to designate an intellectual, in this case Friedrich Nicolai, who was engaged in the collective enterprise of encouraging his or her fellow human beings to use their own minds critically in all areas of life, rather than to accept received doctrine and wisdom, and who believed that human existence and consciousness, and the improvement of human society, should be at the center of thought and expression.[2]

---

1. "Philosophers Trim the Tree of Knowledge: The Epistemological Strategy of the Encyclopédie," in *The Great Cat Massacre and Other Episodes in French Cultural History* (New York: Vintage, 1985), p. 208.

2. This is an extreme oversimplification of the German Enlightenment, which was a diverse movement, theologically, philosophically, and politically. A good introduction is Horst Möller, *Vernunft und Kritik: Deutsche Aufklärung im 17. und 18. Jahrhundert* (Frankfurt a. M. Suhrkamp, 1986). For a recent and concise comparative survey of the Enlightenment in Germany

When we think of the French *philosophes*, and of the French Enlightenment, we think first of anticlericalism and skepticism about the possibility of reforming the existing monarchical state. We also think of men (and a few women) who were alienated or excluded from the prevailing power structures. German *Aufklärer* like Nicolai, however, were mainly not anticlerical,[3] although most criticized religious intolerance, superstition, and oppressive orthodoxy. Depending upon where they lived and worked, they were more or less convinced that despotism, or milder forms of political repression, could be overcome by the gradual but growing influence of *Aufklärer*, and enlightened thought, upon monarchs. They came from a variety of mainly middle-class social backgrounds, but few were outsiders. They were generally firmly integrated into public office of some kind, whether as civil servants, university professors, pedagogues, or pastors, and thus had access to the resources of the state. Some even had the ears of monarchs. Given Frederick II of Prussia's notorious lack of interest in German writing, though, most of the men who had that particular royal ear were French *philosophes*. In 1785, however, he did invite Friedrich Nicolai to visit him, and the two chatted for an hour and a half, as Nicolai proudly recalled twenty years later.[4]

The German movement differed from the French in two other important ways. First, the universities, which played little role in France, were crucial centers in Germany (as they also were, for example, in Scotland). The second difference can be found in the area often known in the literature as "popular Enlightenment" (*Volksaufklärung*), or the attempt to process the main ideas of the Enlightenment in such a way as to reach and influence the uneducated, which played a much larger role in Germany than in France.[5]

---

and other countries, which emphasizes philosophical issues, see Werner Schneiders, *Das Zeitalter der Aufklärung* (Munich: C. H. Beck, 1997).

3. Naturally, there were exceptions. On the censorship of late-seventeenth and early-eighteenth-century atheist and deist texts in Saxony, for example, see Agatha Kobuch, *Zensur und Aufklärung in Kursachsen* (Weimar: Hermann Böhlaus Nachfolger, 1988). Christine Haug is currently engaged on a study of the production and distribution of clandestine literature, including radical theology, in the German-speaking lands at the end of the eighteenth century. See her "Geheimbündische Organisationsstrukturen und subversive Distributionssysteme zur Zeit der Französischen Revolution," *Leipziger Jahrbuch zur Buchgeschichte* 7 (1997): 51–74.

4. "Selbstbiographie," in *Bildnisse jetztlebender Berliner Gelehrten mit ihren Selbstbiographien*, 3. Sammlung (Berlin, 1806), pp. 45–46.

5. For overviews, see the review of the literature in H. Böning, "Der 'gemeine Mann' als Adressat aufklärerischen Gedankengutes," *Das 18. Jahrhundert*, 12, no. 1 (1989): 52–82, with a bibliography, and Wolfgang Ruppert, "Volksaufklärung im 18. Jahrhundert," in *Hansers*

Friedrich Nicolai, *Buchhändler and Aufklärer*

Many of these differences are explainable at least in part by the cultural and political dominance of Catholicism in France and Protestantism in Germany. German *Aufklärer*, who rarely embraced atheism publicly, nevertheless faced the dual enemies of the traditional Catholic Church and Protestant orthodoxy. The more liberal strands of Protestantism, which was being transformed during the eighteenth century by (among other things) new forms of biblical criticism, which regarded the stories of the Bible from a historical rather than a fundamentalist perspective, however, were allies of the Enlightenment.[6] Thus the pulpit was regarded by many not as a bastion of, but as a weapon in the struggle against intolerance and superstition. The German Enlightenment was a largely Protestant phenomenon, although there were certainly *Aufklärer* at work in the Catholic regions of Bavaria and Austria, in particular, and the reforms of Emperor Joseph II were strongly influenced by Enlightenment ideas. Readers in Catholic Germany were certainly aware of intellectual developments in the north, since many of the books they read (if often in pirated editions) were published in Leipzig or Berlin, among other publishing centers. However, for many German Protestants, Friedrich Nicolai prominent among them, the Catholic religion, and particularly the hierarchical structure of the church, was in itself incompatible with true Enlightenment. Nicolai shared a common, and by no means inaccurate, view of the Enlightenment as a continuation of the Protestant Reformation, a sort of extension of the priesthood of all believers to the realm of human life more generally. Only those in possession of all the facts, whether of religion, philosophy, or the natural world, could make sensible decisions and promote the common good. Yet just as the Lutheran Church did not dispense with ecclesiastical authority, so Nicolai and most other *Aufklärer* did not fully embrace the potentially democratic political implications of their ideas. Nicolai was militantly Protestant from a cultural, not a religious perspective, and theology, although not one of his own areas of expertise, was to play an important role in the review journal he founded, edited, and published, the *Allgemeine deutsche Bibliothek* (hereafter abbreviated *ADB*), as well as in his publishing list. Religious

---

Sozialgeschichte der deutschen Literatur, vol. 3, pt. 1, *Deutsche Aufklärung bis zur Französischer Revolution* (Munich: dtv, 1984), pp. 341–61.

6. For an introduction to German Enlightenment theology, see Walter Sparn, "Vernünftiges Christentum. Über die geschichtliche Aufgabe der theologischen Aufklärung im 18. Jahrhundert in Deutschland," in *Wissenschaften im Zeitalter der Aufklärung*, ed. Rudolf Vierhaus (Göttingen: Vandenhoeck & Ruprecht, 1985), pp. 18–57.

reform was a necessary part of, and indeed foundation for, the reform of social and intellectual life, of manners and morals, and ultimately of politics as well.

Nicolai was an atypical *Aufklärer* in that, like his close friend and fellow central figure in the Berlin Enlightenment, the philosopher Moses Mendelssohn, he neither had a university education nor held any kind of public office. By profession Nicolai was a *Buchhändler*, literally, someone who traded in books. In its eighteenth-century meaning, this word referred to both booksellers and publishers, since most *Buchhändler* of the time were both. Indeed, Nicolai asserted on several occasions that his position as a merchant, and more specifically as a merchant who produced and traded in books, afforded him a practical perspective on intellectual issues that was important to his notion of what it meant to be an *Aufklärer*. Abstract speculation was insufficient: one had to put one's ideas into practice (however defined) and express them in such a way that they were comprehensible to an audience wider than the so-called republic of letters. What one believed to be true required continual empirical scrutiny and submission to critical discussion with others, including the reading public at large.[7] Aside from the early-eighteenth-century German philosopher Christian Wolff, who exercised a massive influence over German Enlightenment thought before Kant, and whose works Nicolai read during his bookselling apprenticeship, one of Nicolai's most important early intellectual influences was the French Protestant scholar Pierre Bayle, whose 1697 *Historical and Critical Dictionary* he assigned a major place in his development. In many ways, however, his heart belonged to England, and the book with which he first stepped before the public was on Milton.

Nicolai's engagement with the Enlightenment cause went beyond merely writing, publishing, and selling books and journals. From 1783 until its dissolution in 1798, he was an active member of the Berlin Mittwochsgesellschaft or Society of Friends of Enlightenment, a secret group that met monthly on Wednesdays at a member's home to discuss the important social, philosophical, and political questions of the day. The members (mainly theologians, pedagogues, jurists, and higher civil servants—several of whom belonged to the commission engaged in drafting a new legal code for Prussia—with one physician and two merchants,

---

7. Since the focus here is on Nicolai as bookseller and publisher, I deal only tangentially with his own works. For more on Nicolai's ideas and writings, see the excellent and extensive account by Horst Möller, *Aufklärung in Preußen*.

Nicolai and Moses Mendelssohn) had the opportunity, by no means self-evident in Germany at that time, to affect state policy. Nicolai was thus able not only to influence public opinion but also to intervene quite concretely in policymaking, in his case in publishing law. Despite his almost religious belief in the necessity of public scrutiny, like many other *Aufklärer* he was also a Freemason, albeit an increasingly skeptical one.[8]

Although certainly no revolutionary or leveler, Nicolai did have an egalitarian streak, and he hoped that the progress of Enlightenment and education would gradually lessen differences of rank. He was, for example, an unwavering proponent of Jewish emancipation at a time when it was far from self-evident, even within the Enlightenment movement. An autodidact himself, he considered ability and hard work to weigh more heavily than birth or academic titles. He was a proud bourgeois, writing in later years that "culture and Enlightenment will soon spread from the middle class [*mittlere Klasse*] into the lower classes [*untern Klassen*] of the people ... and ... also into the higher ranks [*höhere Stände*]."[9] For Nicolai, the middle classes (*Bürgertum*) were the center and backbone of the state, and he believed that their social usefulness and moral and cultural leadership role gave them the right to be heard by monarchs. Typically for his time and place, however, he never openly called for direct political participation by these middle classes. As a prominent citizen of Berlin he possessed certain opportunities for influence, which he used, and professed satisfaction at this situation, since it was unlikely to change anytime soon. His growing skepticism during the reactionary years of the 1790s about the possibility of moving monarchs by mere argument led him to resignation rather than radicalism.

In his way Nicolai was a pioneer of liberalism, but unlike some of his more radical (and generally younger) contemporaries he restricted his engagement mainly to economic issues and freedom of the press. Perhaps

---

8. Nicolai was also a nominal member of the order of the Illuminati, a secret society that sought to reform society from the top down by creating an enlightened elite. The order, founded in 1776 by the Ingolstadt professor Adam Weishaupt, was persecuted by the Bavarian government in particular and, although officially dissolved in 1785, existed in secret until about 1793. Among its many illustrious members were Goethe, Herder, and Duke Carl August of Weimar. On Nicolai and secret societies, see Möller, *Aufklärung in Preußen*, pp. 238–45; for his views on the necessity of publicity, see esp. pp. 217–19. Nicolai published an account of his connection with the Illuminati, *Öffentliche Erklärung über seine geheime Verbindung mit dem Illuminatenorden; Nebst beyläufiger Digressionen betreffend Hrn. Johann August Stark und Hrn. Johann Kaspar Lavater* (Berlin: Nicolai, 1788).

9. *Beschreibung einer Reise durch Deutschland und die Schweiz im Jahre 1781* (Berlin: Nicolai, 1784), 4:924.

he was too tied down by material responsibilities to be willing to take risks and fight for a constitutional monarchy with its political guarantees of civil liberties. In 1788, he summarized his attitude to attempts to effect rapid political changes: "If I imagine the state to be a wagon pulled by swift horses, it appears to me foolish or foolhardy to try to stop it by its wheels. Nevertheless, I fear that the models devised by many learned men for a better organization of the state frequently resemble just such an undertaking. I will never imitate them, and I have neither the boldness nor the physical strength nor the necessary skill to grab the horses by the reins in order to interrupt or redirect their course."[10] Like many of his compatriots, he was convinced that a revolution such as had occurred in France would be unnecessary in Germany, particularly in Prussia. His objective, which he shared not merely with most of his fellow German *Aufklärer* but also with most of the French *philosophes*, was the reform, not the abolition, of the monarchy. In order to carry out reforms, however, the state needed an enlightened people prepared not merely to tolerate innovations but also to take an active part in their realization. A democratization of thinking and knowledge, in short, a general Enlightenment, was the prerequisite for true and lasting reform.

Young Nicolai on, and in, the Republic of Letters

In *Über meine gelehrte Bildung* (On My Learned Education), the 1799 defense of his autodidactic learning against his many enemies, Nicolai describes his preparation for his bookselling career in some detail. He received a rather rudimentary schooling, briefly attending both the Joachimthalische Gymnasium in Berlin and the Pietist-oriented Latin school of the Franckesche Stiftung in Halle, which left him permanently allergic to any kind of religious zealotry. The only part of his schooling that he recalled with any fondness was a year at the new and practically oriented Realschule in Berlin, where he bided his time until an apprenticeship in the book trade became available.[11]

In 1749, the sixteen-year-old Nicolai was sent to J. C. Kleyb's bookshop in Frankfurt an der Oder. Nicolai remembered his master with gratitude for having not merely instructed him in business matters but also indirectly furthered his general education by allowing him half of the

---

10. *Öffentliche Erklärung*, pp. 54ff.
11. Friedrich Nicolai, *Ueber meine gelehrte Bildung* (Berlin: Nicolai, 1799), p. 15.

day for his own studies.¹² An acquaintance of the Frankfurt days, however, the Schaffhausen preacher Johann Jacob Hoffmann, had rather different memories of the relations between the young Nicolai and Kleyb: "I was often in your shop and found you hidden away ... reading. You were at your ease, but Herr Kleyb wore a grim expression: 'You should be checking the books, not reading them!'"¹³ It is pleasant to imagine the efficient and officious adult Nicolai as one of those dreamy shop lads who allegedly only enter the book trade for the access to free reading material. Nicolai recounts his memories of this period in the best Protestant work ethic tradition. The eager young autodidact saved his breakfast pennies for lamp oil and, like Benjamin Franklin, another "bookish lad," studied late into the night and before the (unheated) shop opened in the mornings in his (equally unheated) apprentice's garret.¹⁴ A bookshop not being the worst place for an avid reader to find himself, in Nicolai's account he discovered inspiration in even his official activities, applying much industry to expanding his knowledge of books. His master set him to making an inventory of the entire shop, which had not existed up until that point. Having ample time for this task, he spent a good part of it looking through the shop's many "old and in some cases venerable books."¹⁵

One that made a particularly strong impression on him during this period of self-education was Pierre Bayle's *Dictionnaire historique et critique*. Bayle's work, which, like most books in the shop, he read in the unwieldy unbound state, must have had a formative influence on his notions of the republic of letters, the primacy of criticism, and religious toleration, all of which lay at the heart of his later interests and activities.¹⁶ Bayle's skepticism about the scope of reason, however, appears to have had less impact on him. Once acquired, there was no stopping the young Nicolai's thirst for "a knowledge of books." "Whenever I spied a book that I had not seen before, I picked it up, leafed through it, and tried to memorize its outward appearance. My good memory helped me here, but also received much practice thereby."¹⁷ Not satisfied with what he found

---

12. Ibid., pp. 25–26.
13. Hoffmann to Nicolai, Schaffhausen, 27 July 1786, in NN 88.
14. Nicolai, *Ueber meine gelehrte Bildung*, pp. 25–26. *Benjamin Franklin's Autobiography*, ed. J. A. Leo Lemay and P. M. Zall (New York: Norton, 1986), p. 8.
15. *Ueber meine gelehrte Bildung*, pp. 31–32.
16. Ibid., p. 32. On Bayle's ideas on criticism and the republic of letters, see Reinhard Koselleck, *Kritik und Krise: Zur Pathogenese der bürgerlichen Welt* (1959; Frankfurt a. M.: Suhrkamp, 1973), pp. 89–94.
17. *Ueber meine gelehrte Bildung*, p. 35.

in Kleyb's shop, Nicolai managed to gain access to the libraries of various professors, often spending Sundays poring over his finds.[18] When not in the shop or a professorial library, Nicolai could be found in the company of his friends Johann Joachim Ewald, a private tutor; Samuel Patzke, a theology student; and other young would-be literati such as the future Schaffhausen pastor J. J. Hoffmann who, over thirty years later, would remember the "happy hours we spent at Patzke's" and poetically compare the Nicolai of that time to "the bud ... that bears pleasing blooms and desirable fruits."[19] They organized a little learned society, reading and discussing one anothers' essays, poems, and translations. With Ewald in particular, Nicolai practiced his English, and it was perhaps then that he hatched his plan (never carried out) to travel to England, because in those days he, like many contemporaries all over Europe, "imagined that country to be the sole seat of liberty, tolerance, and magnanimity."[20]

At the end of his three-year apprenticeship, Nicolai, now eighteen, returned to Berlin to work in his father's bookshop, which, with changes of location, was to remain his base of operations for almost sixty years. Christoph Gottlieb Nicolai, a native of Wittenberg, had acquired his shop in typical old-regime fashion by marrying Maria Justina, the daughter of his employer Gottfried Zimmermann, a Wittenberg bookseller who had recently bought a shop in Berlin. In 1713, Zimmermann turned the establishment over to C. G. Nicolai for 3500 taler, payable in installments.[21] When Nicolai senior died soon after Friedrich's return in January 1752, his three sons inherited one of the most important bookshops in Berlin, with a stock of over 12,000 titles, including the latest works of the French Enlightenment. He also left them a solid if somewhat stuffy publishing list of some 400 works, rich in school texts and scientific treatises[22] and his Prussian royal privilege, which Friedrich Nicolai proudly

18. Ibid., pp. 36–37.
19. Hoffmann to Nicolai, 27 July 1786, in NN 88.
20. *Ueber meine gelehrte Bildung*, pp. 31–32; "Selbstbiographie," pp. 20–21. This optimistic view of English liberty and letters was shared by many foreigners. See John Brewer, *The Pleasures of the Imagination: English Culture in the Eighteenth Century* (London: Harper Collins, 1997), pp. xxviiff.
21. Sale contract dated 20 October 1713, in NN 285, no. 12. The final payment was made on 29 May 1731. The bookshop had formerly belonged to the firm of Johann Wilhelm Meyer.
22. Arthur Georgi, *Die Entwicklung des Berliner Buchhandels bis zur Gründung des Börsenvereins der deutschen Buchhändler 1825* (Berlin: Paul Parey, 1926), pp. 73, 103–4; on the French *philosophes* in the Nicolai family shop, see Martin Fontius, *Voltaire in Berlin* (Berlin: Rütten & Loening, 1966), pp. 11–12. Nicolai's father had published a complete stock catalog in 1737, the *Catalogus von Alten und Neuen Büchern welche vor beygesetzten billigen Preiß zu haben sind bey Christoph Gottlieb Nicolai Buchhändlern in Berlin*. SPKB Aq 8791a.

printed at the beginning of his three-volume *Description of the Royal Residences of Berlin and Potsdam* (1786), situating both himself and his father firmly in the city's history and emphasizing his protected position as an established bookseller and publisher.[23]

From Kleyb's small and rather sleepy shop in the university town of Frankfurt an der Oder, Nicolai found himself suddenly transported to a bustling business in the midst of Friderician Berlin, where the volume of activity required him to spend all day minding the store. Separated from his friends Ewald and Patzke, who wrote letters full of longing for the idyllic Frankfurt days and reminders to enjoy a bit of the springtime on his way to the Easter book fair,[24] Nicolai had only the "early morning and the late hours of the night, and often even the returning dawn" to devote to his books and reflections upon them.[25] During this time he apparently considered the idea of starting his own business in Halberstadt, where no bookshop existed, and where the officer-poet Ewald von Kleist offered to help him make the necessary literary contacts to flourish commercially.[26] It may be that the many years required for the settlement of his father's estate and the subsequent death of an elder brother kept Nicolai in Berlin and thwarted any ambitions he had of establishing himself elsewhere.

Nicolai recalled his time working under his brother as "three very difficult but also very happy years, for the labors of each day were sweetened by occasional hours of study."[27] Alongside his beloved classical and English authors, Nicolai also began to become aware of developments in the German literature of his day: "Unfamiliar ... with the world and human passions, the young man could not understand the state of a German literature that was at that time divided into two camps (by Gottsched and Bodmer). Both sides appeared to him to be wrong, albeit one somewhat less so than the other. In all of Berlin he had not a single acquaintance with whom he could have exchanged ideas about poetical or literary subjects, but rather had to seek everything within himself."[28] Nicolai overcame his isolation somewhat by corresponding with his friend J. J. Ewald,

---

23. *Beschreibung der königlichen Residenzstädte Berlin und Potsdam, aller daselbst befindlichen Merkwürdigkeiten, und der umliegenden Gegend*, 3 vols. (Berlin: Nicolai, 1786), vol. 1. When Nicolai's description of Berlin is mentioned in the text it refers to this work.

24. NN 20 and 56. Here, Ewald to Nicolai, Frankfurt an der Oder, May 1753, in NN 20.

25. "Selbstbiographie," p. 12.

26. Ewald to Nicolai, Frankfurt an der Oder, May 1753, in NN 20.

27. "Selbstbiographie," p. 12.

28. Ibid., p. 13.

now in nearby Potsdam, about contemporary literature, and sending him his essay on Milton (published by his old employer Kleyb in 1753) and poems and translations from his own pen.[29] Nicolai's solitary youthful ruminations on German letters culminated in his 1755 work, *Briefe über den itzigen Zustand der schönen Wissenschaften in Deutschland* (Letters on the Present Condition of Belles-Lettres in Germany). This book proved his entrée into the republic of letters and Berlin Enlightenment society. In 1756 he was admitted to the Montagsklub, a select local discussion society, and embarked on his important and fruitful friendships with Lessing and Mendelssohn. The *Briefe* also set the tone for his later career as writer, critic, and bookseller. They contain an astoundingly cocksure analysis and critique of the ills of the German republic of letters from a twenty-two-year-old who had never come any closer to university studies than eavesdropping at the door of lecture halls and borrowing students' notes. Contemporaries were impressed by this anonymously published work and curious about its author. The popular poet and fable-author Christian Fürchtegott Gellert informed the satirist Gottlieb Wilhelm Rabener in January 1756, "The author of the Letters on Taste is Nicolai, a young bookseller of eighteen years in Berlin, brother to the professor. He must have an excellent mind. I have not read anything like it in some time that appeared to me so correct and pleasant. I have this information from Lessing.... This same Nicolai is also said to be the author of the defense of Milton against Lawder."[30]

It was probably Nicolai's very lack of academic education, together with the brashness of youth, that gave him the courage to criticize the pedantry and unworldliness of German poets and scholars from the standpoint of a man of practical training and in daily contact with the marketplace of learning and letters. As a merchant, he also had a certain independence from the cabals of professional intellectuals. In any case, as Jochen Schulte-Sasse points out in a perceptive biographical essay, the *Briefe* contain notions that were to determine Nicolai's intellectual stance throughout his life[31] and that he echoed in many later pronouncements,

---

29. Ewald to Nicolai, May and 22 December 1753, in NN 20.
30. Gellert to Rabener, Leipzig, 24 January 1756, in C. F. Gellert, *Briefwechsel*, ed. John F. Reynolds (Berlin: De Gruyter, 1987), vol. 2, 1756–59, p. 15. Nicolai's first (anonymously) published work was a defense of Milton, *Untersuchung, ob Milton sein Verlohrnes Paradies aus neuern lateinischen Schriftstellern ausgeschrieben habe. Nebst einigen Anmerkungen über eine Rezension des Lauderischen Buchs von Miltons Nachahmung der neuern Schriftstellern* (Frankfurt and Leipzig, 1753). Gottsched had written an approving review of a book attacking Milton.
31. Schulte-Sasse, "Friedrich Nicolai," p. 322.

both in his correspondence and published writings.³² Since many of the ideas expressed in the *Briefe* were to become relevant for Nicolai's publishing activities and his sense of his role in the republic of letters, they are worth examining briefly here.

The central questions that Nicolai poses in the *Briefe* are: Why is German literature, on the whole, so mediocre, especially in comparison to that of the French and the English? and What can be done to improve the situation? His answers were, essentially, that German writers, because of their provincial experience and pedantic education, were less worldly than their French and English counterparts, who could look to the cultural capitals of Paris and London, with their sophisticated readers and writers, as arbiters of taste. The remedy he proposed was knowledge of the real and "very unpoetic world"³³ and good critical institutions that spared no author, no matter how famous or distinguished.

One may argue that Nicolai idealized French and English conditions, whether out of ignorance or for rhetorical purposes, or both. On the other hand, it is difficult to deny that there is no German equivalent of the "better" French and English literature of the early and mid-eighteenth century. At any rate—and this was particularly important to him—Nicolai felt that French and English writers were more attuned to their readers. He insisted that German writers, too, had to come to regard writing as part of a social process, taking care to acquaint themselves with their audience and to write in a manner comprehensible and pleasing to it. In his opinion, "A man of letters who seeks to introduce a new taste, a new manner of thinking, etc., from the depths of his study, and does not concern himself with the manner of thinking, indeed the prejudices of his compatriots, is like a naturalist who seeks to prove a doctrine by theoretical conclusion, without taking the trouble to undertake the experiments necessary for its demonstration."³⁴

It was not enough to know one's readers, however. Writers also had to abandon their overly elaborate, long-winded, and obscure means of

---

32. In later years Nicolai expressed dissatisfaction with some aspects of the *Briefe*, and he apparently intended to publish a new edition, but never did so. Nicolai first mentions a revised edition in a letter to Johann Peter Uz in March 1759. In a letter of 8 December 1766 he describes it as a mere "youthful effort" but fears reactions to a revised edition because he is now in a much more exposed position. See the Uz correspondence, in NN 76.

33. Friedrich Nicolai, *Briefe über den itzigen Zustand der schönen Wissenschaften in Teutschland* (Berlin: Kleyb, 1755), p. 194. For a discussion of the antipedantry debate of this period, see Wilhelm Kühlmann, *Gelehrtenrepublik und Fürstenstaat: Entwicklung und Kritik der deutschen Späthumanismus in der Literatur des Barockzeitalters* (Tübingen: Niemeyer, 1982), esp. pp. 456–73.

34. *Briefe über den itzigen Zustand*, p. 51.

expressing their ideas. "One of the foremost qualities of a language is clarity; in order to attain this, one must speak as other people do."[35] This was to remain a chief maxim of Nicolai's concept of popular Enlightenment, one he shared with many contemporaries all over Europe, and which he tried to impress upon his reviewers and authors. When Adam Ferguson worried some ten years later that "men at a distance from the objects of knowledge could produce only the jargon of a technical language and accumulate the impertinence of academical forms,"[36] he wrote as a man after Nicolai's own heart.

In the Eighteenth Letter, "On the Means of Promoting Belles-Lettres in Germany," Nicolai moved from the criticism of existing faults to suggestions for their correction, and in so doing provided a program for his own activities that led to the foundation of the aesthetic-critical journals *Bibliothek der Schönen Wissenschaften* and *Briefe, die neueste Litteratur betreffend*, and ultimately to his life's work, the *ADB*. What German literature needed most was more *Genie* (in the modest sense of talent, not in the more exalted sense of [divine] inspiration held by the Klopstockians, the *Stürmer und Dränger*, and the Romantics) and less stilted pedantry, more knowledge of the world beyond the scholar's study, and less dusty academic learning. Above all, the German republic of letters needed courageous critics who could provide at least some compensation for the lack of a capital city as a "Judgement Seat of Wit."[37] At present, Nicolai believed, German criticism did more harm than good. The greatest worry of an aspiring French or English writer might be the cabal of an older poet. A German author, in contrast, had more to fear from a cabal of his best friends. Through untimely and undeserved praise, these gave him (or her, as Nicolai and others were later to remark in the celebrated case of Anna Luisa Karschin, the "Prussian Sappho")[38] a puffed-up opinion of his

---

35. Ibid., p. 110. This notion places Nicolai firmly in the tradition of Christian Thomasius and Gottfried Wilhelm Leibniz. On their ideas about clarity in writing and the necessity of addressing the generally educated reader rather than merely scholars, see John A. McCarthy, *Crossing Boundaries: A Theory and History of Essay Writing in German, 1680–1815* (Philadelphia: University of Pennsylvania Press, 1989), pp. 177–89.

36. *An Essay on the History of Civil Society* (1766), quoted in Thomas Bender, *New York Intellect: A History of Intellectual Life in New York City, from 1750 to the Beginnings of Our Own Time* (New York: Knopf, 1987), p. 4.

37. See Nicolai, *Briefe über den itzigen Zustand*, pp. 196–200.

38. Anna Luisa Karsch[in] was an unlettered poet who excelled in extemporation. She was vigorously encouraged and supported by the poet Johann Wilhelm Gleim and his circle, who, as Nicolai's friend Patzke wrote in a telling but unflattering phrase, exhibited her at parties like some animal prodigy. Patzke to Nicolai, Magdeburg, 14 January 1762, in NN 56.

talents, hindering further development. "Nothing is easier in Germany than to be praised."[39] Criticism that provided a detailed judgment of a work's true faults and merits regardless of the author's identity and adherence to a literary party was, Nicolai believed, hard if not impossible to find.

Thus Nicolai rejected those explanations that traced the sorry state of German literature to a lack of patronage and remuneration for writers. He did not disapprove in principle of authors being well paid for their labors, particularly in the case of those engaged upon "larger works of poetry" who needed free time in order to create literature of excellence. Such payment alone would not help produce writers or works of genius, however. "How many obscure names do we not find among the well-paid members of the French Academy?" Nicolai remarked.[40] "A good mind who sees his genius oppressed by the laborious work that he is compelled to undertake in order to earn his living is, however, to be pitied; if I am not much mistaken, though, the riches and emoluments that appear so necessary to our poets might render them more lethargic than any financial worries; a German who was as rich as *Hr. de Voltaire* would consume his interest in peace and doubtless avoid at all costs endangering his reputation through tragedies, universal histories, and commemorative poems."[41] Given when he was writing, in the early 1750s, he was probably thinking more of sinecures and patronage than of publishers' honoraria and the literary marketplace. Nevertheless, even at the end of the century, Nicolai's authors were in no danger of buying chateaus or falling into pampered lassitude on the moderate honoraria he paid all but a few of them.

Like most of his midcentury contemporaries, the young Nicolai did not consider the writing of literature, especially poetry, to be a full-time occupation. Unlike painting, sculpture, and music, which require many years of formal training and much practice, a good *Genie* could learn the rules and practice of poetry without great effort, he thought. Poets were also only poets a few hours a day, he believed, so that "the republic may demand that they devote the rest of their time to its service."[42] In *Über meine gelehrte Bildung* he made a positive virtue out of the combination of practical and intellectual activities that characterized the life of bookseller and writer, which he was just beginning in 1755, believing that it might

39. *Briefe über den itzigen Zustand*, p. 200.
40. Ibid., p. 194.
41. Ibid., p. 195.
42. Ibid., pp. 192–94.

well be "more conducive to the health of the mind" than "living wholly in thought and imagination."[43] Despite frequent complaints about the dreariness of business and the lack of time to "live for himself" (*sich selbst leben*)[44] after he abandoned his brief career as a private scholar, Nicolai was proud of being at home in the counting house as well as in the library or the scholar's *cabinet*. In this he agreed with his many Enlightenment contemporaries (and their spiritual forbears), whose ideal was to combine the active with the contemplative life. As the Comte de Mirabeau put it in his book on Prussia under Frederick II, "A man does not fulfill the entire purpose of his existence if he only speculates; he must act."[45]

By education and training a merchant, by inclination an *Aufklärer* and a man of letters, Friedrich Nicolai made the best of his lot in life, which was to conduct his business in such a way that it furthered rather than hindered his loftier aspirations. He did consciously what many of his bookseller colleagues did unconsciously: he served as a vehicle for the spread of Enlightenment ideas. Nicolai was a man who thought it his business to enlighten his fellow Germans by giving them the tools to enlighten themselves. For many contemporaries, he took this business of Enlightenment far too seriously, or simply too far. Some objected to the Enlightenment, some to the business, and many to the alliance of the two. Nicolai's emphasis on opening the world of learning to those without academic training was central to his pedagogical conception of Enlightenment and informed his practice as author, critic, bookseller, and publisher. It was, however, precisely this quality of his life's work that opened him to the ridicule and scorn of the Romantic and Idealist philosophers and litterateurs in whose shadow he spent his final years. Fichte expressed this distaste for Nicolai's (and the popular philosophers')[46] eclecticism and alleged superficiality most pointedly in his 1801 *Friedrich Nicolai's Life and Curious Opinions: A Contribution to the Literary History of the Past Century and the Pedagogy of the Present One*. Hoisting Nicolai with the petard of his own book title, the 1798 *Life and Opinions*

---

43. *Ueber meine gelehrte Bildung*, pp. 38–39.

44. On 29 November 1756 Lessing had written to Nicolai of his decision to leave the bookshop "Blessed be your decision to live for yourself!" G. E. Lessing's *Sämtliche Schriften*, ed. Karl Lachmann, 3d ed., rev. Franz Muncker (Leipzig: Göschen, 1904), 17:76.

45. Honoré de Mirabeau, *De la monarchie prussienne sous Frédéric le Grand* (London, 1788), 5:160–61.

46. For an overview of popular philosophy in Germany, see Gert Ueding, "Popularphilosophie," in *Hansers Sozialgeschichte der deutschen Literatur*, vol. 3, pt. 2, pp. 605–34.

of Sempronius Gundibert, a satire on the new philosophy, Fichte proceeded in this pamphlet, which was edited by August Wilhelm Schlegel, to declare his subject dead and nevertheless to speak ill of him. In a scathing assessment, and caricature, of Nicolai's intellectual achievement Fichte asserted that nothing was more despicable "than the miserable treatment of learning which gathers up all the facts and opinions that one can get one's hands on without any context or purpose beyond that of throwing them all together and babbling on about them." He led the reader to understand that this was the intellectual method promoted by Nicolai and his ilk, who regarded all human knowledge as material for idle chatter, "whose chief requirement is that it be as understandable at the dressing-table as in the lecture hall."[47] Fichte's elitism and his infamous misogyny (he could imagine nothing lower than the boudoir) were combined here in the caricature of Nicolai and the ideals of much of the German Enlightenment. Richard Steele's idea, expressed in *The Spectator*, of bringing "Philosophy out of Closets and Libraries, Schools and Colleges ... to dwell in Clubs and Assemblies, at Tea-Tables, and in Coffee-Houses,"[48] was one that Nicolai wholeheartedly shared, and sought to put into practice.

Nicolai on Honor and Dishonor in the German Book Trade

The eighteenth-century book trade was no business for the timid or faint-hearted, as contemporaries were fond of remarking. Nicolai's Mannheim correspondent Christian Friedrich Schwan, for example, called it "a war of all against all."[49] This may be something of an exaggeration for the more sedate North German trade, but in the struggle to

47. Johann Gottlieb Fichte, *Friedrich Nicolais Leben und sonderbare Meinungen: Ein Beitrag zur Litteratur Geschichte des vergangenen und zur Pädagogik des angehenden Jahrhunderts*, ed. August Wilhelm Schlegel (Tübingen: Cotta, 1801), p. 2. This work was so extraordinarily vindictive, even by the standards of an age accustomed to scholarly mudslinging, that as Nicolai's grandson Gustav Parthey relates, the entire Berlin book trade refused to carry it. Upon hearing of his colleagues' resolve, Nicolai, ever the good businessman and the feisty veteran of many literary campaigns, reportedly let it be known that he would sell the book and order as many copies as the public required. Gustav Parthey, *Jugenderinnerungen: Handschrift für Freunde*, ed. Ernst Friedel (Berlin: Privatdruck-Ernst Frensdorff, 1907), p. 40.

48. Quoted in P. M. Mitchell, "Johann Christoph Gottsched," in *Deutsche Dichter des 18. Jahrhunderts. Ihr Leben und Werk*, ed. Benno von Wiese (Berlin: Erich Schmidt, 1977), pp. 35–61.

49. Quoted in Reinhard Wittmann, "Die frühen Buchhändlerzeitschriften als Spiegel des literarischen Lebens," *AGB* 13 (1973): col. 629.

spread Enlightenment and make a profit at the same time, booksellers like Friedrich Nicolai had to maneuver their way around expectations placed upon them by various groups in society—particularly other booksellers and that amorphous entity, the republic of letters, but also the reading public at large—and at the same time face the rigors of the market. Nicolai presented his own criticisms of the book trade, and his reactions to attacks on his honor as a bookseller, in his novel *Leben und Meinungen des Herrn Magister Sebaldus Nothanker* (Life and Opinions of Sebaldus Nothanker, M.A.), probably *the* literary bestseller of the German Enlightenment.

Booksellers' honor consisted of two main components, one referring more to their cultural, the other more to their economic role, although in practice the two were naturally intertwined. The bookseller's activities as cultural intermediary between author and public demanded a sense of responsibility for the content of works published and sold. Literary quality, good morals, respect for the reputation of persons, and factual accuracy (such as it was understood at the time) all belonged to the expectations placed upon the more respectable booksellers by the more demanding critics of the book trade and literary market in the second half of the eighteenth century.[50] The latter called upon the bookseller as merchant and manufacturer to engage in fair and honest relations with other booksellers, authors, and the reading public. These fair and honest dealings included respect for the property of others, especially when the publisher had an official privilege, refusal to sell pirate editions, particularly of the lawful editions of local booksellers, prompt payment of bills, fair remuneration of authors and respect for their wishes in regard to their texts, truth in advertising, and delivery of goods as promised. Needless to say, these were unattainable ideals, even among the upper ranks of the book trade, especially in a profession without a guild or other policing body, and under conditions of extreme political fragmentation.[51]

Friedrich Nicolai's depiction of the book trade in *Sebaldus Nothanker* illustrates the two components of honor in the book trade nicely. In the dialogues between the idealistic parson Sebaldus, who is deprived of his congregation by Lutheran zealots, and the Magister, a disillusioned hack writer, Nicolai satirizes the factory-like production of trivial literature,

---

50. See Otto Bettmann's extensive if rather idealized treatment in "Die Entstehung buchhändlerischer Berufsideale im Deutschland des XVIII. Jahrhunderts" (Ph. D. diss., Universität Leipzig, 1927).

51. See Wittmann, "Die frühen Buchhändlerzeitschriften," particularly cols. 628–32.

and in the relations between Sebaldus and Mynheer van der Kuit he criticizes a dishonest bookseller.

Sebaldus, the novel's innocent and unworldly hero, is shocked at what his neighbor, the more experienced Magister, who has served as a proofreader, translator, and pen-of-all-work for various Leipzig printers and publishers, has to say about writing and the book trade:

> Not a few booksellers commission their authors to write whatever they believe will sell: history, novels, tales of murder, reliable accounts of things they have not seen, demonstrations of things they do not believe, and thoughts on matters they do not understand. For such books publishers do not need authors with a name, but rather those who work by the yard. I know of one who has ten or twelve authors sitting at a long table in his house, each paid a daily wage to write so many lines. I do not deny it—why should I be ashamed of poverty?—I, too, have sat at that long table. I soon noticed, however, that I was ill-suited to this work, for I can read proofs without thinking, but I cannot write books without thinking.[52]

The worse the books, the Magister continued, to Sebaldus's growing dismay, the more profitable for publishers under the barter system (*Tausch* or *Changehandel*) at the book fair, because they increased the bookseller's chances of getting something better in exchange (p. 85). Horrified, Sebaldus turns to his friend and benefactor, the bookseller Hieronymus, whose character was (and is) often considered a self-portrait of Nicolai. Instead of the expected support for his indignation, Sebaldus meets with excuses for the publishers of unworthy books. Hieronymus, on hearing Sebaldus's quaint opinion that booksellers exist chiefly to aid scholarship, and thus should only print and sell good books, replies:

> My friend, the taste of great scholars is the taste of the very few; the bookseller, however, needs many buyers.... That is why author and publisher often cannot agree, despite mutual good will. The former wishes to sell the inner worth of his book, while the latter is interested only in the probability of sales.... The latter considers whether it is possible or probable that many people may want the book, without taking into account whether they are learned or unlearned, wise or foolish, desirous of edification or amusement. (p. 99).

52. Friedrich Nicolai, *Leben und Meinungen des Herrn Magister Sebaldus Nothanker* (Frankfurt a. M.: Ullstein, 1986), p. 84. All page numbers in the text that follows refer to this edition.

Hieronymus, the experienced bookseller, takes a pragmatic view of the book trade but, like his creator, is not without his idealistic moments: "When I speak as a merchant, I must certainly know what is to my own advantage, but I do not love my own advantage so much that I wish to obtain it at the expense of the whole world. I love the enlightenment of the human race, it is also beginning to show itself among us, but it is progressing by very small stages.... I have noticed for some time now in my home city that some bad books that once sold well now gather dust, and this pleases me" (p. 103). Hieronymus locates the German book trade's problems in the lack of demand for "good" books and the failings of German authors, who unlike their French and English counterparts, cannot write well for a wider audience, trapped as they are in provincialism and pedantry (pp. 104–12). This theme was to remain one of Nicolai's hobby-horses, from the 1755 *Briefe*, through his review journals, to his attacks on critical philosophy in the 1790s and beyond.

Later in the novel, Nicolai portrays a second bookseller, the Dutchman van der Kuit. Like Hieronymus, he takes a practical and unsentimental view of his business, but there the resemblance ends. Where Hieronymus is generous, honest, and interested in the welfare of humanity and learning, van der Kuit is a crafty skinflint. Quite apart from the quality of the books he publishes and sells, which is not really at issue in the novel, van der Kuit is an unscrupulous merchant and a bad human being. He shows the outside world a facade of honesty and humanitarianism, paying his debts promptly, always giving alms to the poor if anyone is watching, and never taking a debtor to court whom he was sure could not pay. Behind the veneer, though, he is utterly selfish. "Mynheer van der Kuit ... regarded a book as a thing to be sold, nothing more." His only interest was to maximize his profits, in the pursuit of which he went far beyond the usual little tricks of the trade such as thinking up catchy new titles for old books (which were also given new dates of publication) or securing translation rights by announcing the translation before the original had even appeared. He speculated on a grand scale, paying close attention to anything he could turn to his advantage, and acting "as if people he could not use, and books he did not own, did not exist. His cardinal principle was that other people had no business owning anything that might be useful to him" (pp. 402–3).

Van der Kuit's hard-heartedness and shady business practices are displayed to great effect in his treatment of the feckless Sebaldus. Sebaldus has the misfortune to have inherited the rights to a profitable scholarly journal that Mynheer van der Kuit has printed and long coveted. Every time he sold a copy it occurred to him that the work should have been his own property and not that of the author, who, after all, had merely written it (p. 404). Now that the rich and respected founder of the journal was dead, the bookseller saw no reason to allow the poor unknown foreigner Sebaldus to benefit from what should have been his. He finally achieves his end by convincing Sebaldus that he is about to be arrested for heresy because of a translation he had prepared and must flee the country at once to avoid imprisonment or worse. The terrified Sebaldus, recalling past persecutions, is only too happy to sell the rights to the journal to pay for his journey back to Germany (pp. 404–9).

To be sure, Mynheer van der Kuit violates the honor of more than just the book trade, and he is only one of a series of evil characters who seem to conspire to ruin Sebaldus's life. The description of his character and deeds, however, sketches the boundaries of honest dealings and emphasizes some of the practices and attitudes, the "normal little advantages" as well as the grand speculations, greed, and disrespect for authors and their books that appear often in criticisms of and among booksellers. When he behaves properly, paying bills promptly and giving alms to the poor, he does so purely in order to avoid social sanctions and appear to be what he is not. It is not the profit motive itself that discredits Mynheer van der Kuit—Hieronymus also admits the importance, even primacy, of financial considerations—but how he pursues profit that Nicolai condemns.

Nicolai, who certainly thought of himself as a "solid" and honest bookseller, and who had a general reputation as such, was nevertheless vulnerable to attacks on his own honor and business practices. Most public criticism of Nicolai relates to his powerful position as editor and publisher of the major review journal of the German Enlightenment, the *ADB*, or to his own writings, but there were also occasional attacks that focused on his behavior as a publisher. Two will be discussed here because Nicolai published replies to them that illuminate some of his own ideas about proper bookseller's conduct. His opponents in these two cases were none other than the novelist and journal editor Christoph Martin Wieland and the philosopher Immanuel Kant.

In a long sarcastic review of the novel *Johann Bunkel* that extended over several issues of his *Teutsche Merkur* in 1778–79, Wieland accuses Nicolai of false advertising and cheating subscribers. Nicolai had printed part of a glowing review of Thomas Amory's 1756 novel from the *Monthly Review* as an advertisement for the translation, but the seven hundred or so subscribers found not an original work, comparable to Shakespeare and Richardson, but rather one full of obscure and long-winded theological discussions. For Wieland, Nicolai had abused the trust the public placed in his good name.[53]

As was usual when he was attacked, Nicolai replied in full and tedious detail, both in the *ADB* and in a separate pamphlet, *A Few Words Concerning Johann Bunkel and Christoph Martin Wieland*. Wieland's insinuation that he had "sought, from spiteful motives, to burden the world with a book that was not merely bad but also the most tedious and crudest book imaginable and to rob the subscribers of their money" compelled him "to save my honest name and to show that I have, with the conscientious exactitude of an honest man, fulfilled all the promises I made to the public."[54] He calls upon all those who had read his printed advertisement to judge for themselves whether it was "quite simple and modest, or written in that braggardly and pompous tone with which so many other books are announced ... or in the self-satisfied arrogant tone with which Herr Wieland himself once presented his *Alceste* or his *Mercur* to the world."[55] As to his intentions in including part of the review from the English journal, Nicolai rather disingenuously remarked that "my intention was none other than to show how sensible men of letters in England, who are otherwise not much given to praise, assessed this work, without necessarily having to adopt every one of their judgments."[56] As a man who lived in a glass house, Nicolai continued, Wieland should not throw stones. He had his own shady dealings in the subscription business and was in no position to attack a bookseller who at least delivered the promised edition at the agreed price.[57] Thus Nicolai defended his practices

---

53. For a discussion of Wieland's attacks within the context of the translating and advertising practices of his day, see Helmut Knufmann, "Das deutsche Übersetzungswesen des 18. Jahrhunderts im Spiegel von Übersetzer- und Herausgebervorreden," *AGB* 9 (1969): cols. 557–59.

54. Friedrich Nicolai, *Ein paar Worte betreffend Johann Bunkel und Christoph Martin Wieland* (Berlin: Nicolai, 1779), pp. 11–12.

55. Ibid., pp. 12–13.

56. Ibid., p. 17n.

57. This was a reference to Wieland's *Alceste*, which had appeared later and at a higher price than subscribers had been promised. *Ein paar Worte*, pp. 25–26. Wieland did not let it rest there, but answered Nicolai's answer. See his letter of 1 February 1779 to Johann Georg Jacobi, in *Ungedruckte Briefe von und an Johann Georg Jacobi*, ed. Ernst Martin (Strasbourg: K. J. Trübner, 1874), p. 73. The whole matter was made even more piquant because *Johann Bunkel* was banned in Austria. Lessing, who thought little of *Bunkel* as a novel, told Nicolai that he thought that a book forbidden by the Imperial Book Commission should not be thus treated by a thinking man (i.e., if it aroused such ire in Vienna, the ideas it contained couldn't be completely worthless). Lessing to Nicolai, 30 March 1779, in Lessing's *Sämtliche Schriften*, 18:312.

less against some absolute standard than against that prevalent among other booksellers and authors. In comparison, he felt himself to be within the bounds of honesty and "conscientious exactitude."

Immanuel Kant's attack on Nicolai twenty years later was broader than Wieland's, embedded as it was in a critique of the contemporary book trade as such. His two open letters, "Über Buchmacherey" (On Bookmaking, 1798), were addressed to Nicolai "The Author" and Nicolai "The Publisher," respectively. The second letter would have been more properly addressed to both, because it dealt with Nicolai's own novel, *Sempronius Gundibert*, a satire on certain followers of Kant. The letter begins by emphasizing the importance of *Buchmacherey*, the production of books, as a branch of trade that gained much when carried out "industrially" (*fabrikenmäßig*) by clever publishers who cared little for the content or inner worth of their wares but much for their immediate market value. In a critique reminiscent of Nicolai's own in *Sebaldus Nothanker*, Kant sketches the behavior of the unscrupulous but businesslike publisher. An "experienced expert in bookmaking" will not wait for eager authors to send in their manuscripts. As the "director of a manufacture," he will devise the material and pattern most likely to arouse the curiosity of the reading public, "whether through its novelty or the quaintness of its wit." If the book is attacked, the blame falls on the author, not the publisher. The publisher, as a tradesman, is at least a useful citizen of the State, and there is no law against self-interest (*Eigennutz*). Thus in his attempt to cash in on public interest in Kant's philosophy Nicolai cuts a better figure as the publisher than as the author of *Sempronius Gundibert*.[58]

Nicolai took the double insult to his publishing and writing very seriously. In *Über meine gelehrte Bildung* Nicolai devoted several pages to refuting Kant's pamphlet. He challenges his readers (and Kant's) to consider his business undertakings of the past forty years and to ask themselves whether they had been respectable and useful to German literature or not. He defends his authors, in this case the author of a series of dialogues on Kantian philosophy, against the accusation of writing for hire[59]

---

58. Immanuel Kant, *Über die Buchmacherey. Zweiter Brief an Herrn Friedrich Nicolai, den Verleger* (1798), vol. 8 of *Kants Gesammelte Schriften* (Berlin: Reimer, 1912), pp. 436–37.

59. [Johann Christoph Schwab], *Neun Gespräche zwischen Christian Wolff und einem Kantianer über Kants metaphysische Anfangsgründe der Rechtslehre und der Tugendlehre* (Berlin: Nicolai, 1798). Nicolai wrote a preface to this anti-Kantian work. Schwab was privy councillor and director of the Geheimer Kanzlei in Stuttgart. Johann Jacob Gradmann, *Das gelehrte Schwaben* (Ravensburg, 1802). In *Ueber meine gelehrte Bildung* Nicolai tells the story of how he came to publish this work. "Quite coincidentally, when I had already completed the plan for the story of Gundibert

and asks rhetorically what designation the blackguard who claimed that Kant was a "hired bookmaker" in the service of Nicolovius would deserve.[60] According to Nicolai, Kant was seriously mistaken if he believed that there was any great demand for books on critical philosophy. Quite other books were in great demand, and many of these books Nicolai refused to publish. He takes Kant's accusation as an opportunity to criticize bitterly those of his fellow booksellers and writers who, popular in the negative sense of the word, pandered only to the worst of current taste and displayed no interest in the enlightenment of the public:

> If you wish to pursue bookmaking successfully, indulge the *genius saeculi*. Join the crowd, praise the idols of the great multitude, and you will be praised in turn by those who worship them. Write what people want to read, and say what people like to hear, claim what it is fashionable to claim, and praise threefold what the crowd praises.... Try to write about what everyone is talking about.... If an Empress Catherine has died, or a Countess Lichtenau fallen out of favor, describe the secret circumstances of her life, even if you know nothing of them. Even if all of your accounts are false, no one will doubt their veracity, your book will pass from hand to hand, it will be reprinted four times in three weeks, especially if you take care to invent a multitude of scandalous anecdotes. You will be thought a man in possession of secret information, and future historians will cite you as a source.[61]

Nicolai distanced himself from those who wrote and published *solely* for immediate commercial success, and he was wounded at being placed in this category. It was one thing to admit, as he had in *Sebaldus Nothanker*, that booksellers did not live by "good" books alone, but there were obviously different categories of "bad" books, and Nicolai generally drew the line at publishing scandal sheets and fictitious political accounts. The libelous *Histoire de la vie privée de Louis XV*, which Nicolai

---

and begun writing, a manuscript entitled *Nine Dialogues* was sent to me.... I found no reason not to publish it." As he had developed a number of ideas on the subject which did not fit into the novel *Sempronius Gundibert*, he decided to write a preface to the *Neun Gespräche*. *Ueber meine gelehrte Bildung*, pp. 103–4.

60. *Ueber meine gelehrte Bildung*, pp. 176–77. Friedrich Nicolovius was Kant's publisher in Königsberg.

61. Ibid., pp. 178–79. One detects here a certain bitterness of a man who was unwilling to praise the idols of the age and who was considered by many contemporaries to have fallen behind the times years before. Wilhelmine Enke, the countess of Lichtenau, was the mistress of Frederick William II of Prussia and the subject of numerous scandal-mongering pamphlets.

had translated the same year it was published in French (4 vols., 1781) represents something of a departure for him, and may have been just too tempting to pass up.[62] Whether it was a good investment is unclear. At any rate he sold or gave the remaining edition of the work to his former employee Georg Emanuel Beer in 1785 to help him establish his new Leipzig firm.[63] His oft-proclaimed "love of truth" and his passion for historical detail, as exemplified by his "corrected" versions of anecdotes about Frederick II, which led Thomas Carlyle to refer to him as "the irrefragible Nicolai,"[64] tended to keep him and the books he published from more heinous sins than self-satisfaction, longwindedness, and a tendency to see Jesuits under the bed.

The Bookseller's Role in the Republic of Letters and the State

In a letter written in November 1782 to reassure his family of his welfare (and to confuse them as to his whereabouts) the young Friedrich Schiller told his sister: "As soon as I arrive in Berlin I am assured of a secure income in the first weeks because I have excellent letters of introduction to Nicolai, who is, as it were, the sovereign of literature there, attracts all persons of wit, is already well-disposed toward me, and wields incredible influence throughout practically the entire realm of German letters."[65]

Schiller's description of Nicolai is a telling one. It was precisely this most unrepublican reputation that led many contemporaries to seek out Friedrich Nicolai whether by post or in person. He had become, and was to remain, a great tourist attraction for Berlin visitors with intellectual

---

62. *Geschichte des Privatlebens Ludwig XV,* 4 vols. (Berlin: Nicolai, 1781). I found no letters suggesting how Nicolai came to take on the project. He also intended to publish a translation of *Les Fastes de Louis XV* until he found out that it was not a continuation of the *Vie privée.* Karl Buchner, *Aus den Papieren der Weidmannischen Buchhandlung,* 2 vols. (Berlin: Weidmann, 1871–73), 1:27–28. The work was undertaken by Nicolai's main French translator of the 1780s, Karl Friedrich Trost, who also reviewed for the *ADB.* He worked at the Ober-Kriegs-Collegium in Berlin, which may explain the absence of correspondence.

63. The transfer of rights and privileges is announced in the Leipzig Easter Fair Catalog of 1785, p. 153. Beer published a fifth and final volume of the work at that fair.

64. Thomas Carlyle, *History of Friedrich II of Prussia Called Frederick the Great,* ed. John Clive (Chicago: University of Chicago Press, 1969), p. 193.

65. J.C.F. von Schiller to Christophine Schiller, 6 November 1782, [Oggersheim,] in Schiller, *Werke, Nationalausgabe,* vol. 23, *Schillers Briefe, 1772–1785* (Weimar: Hermann Böhlaus Nachfolger, 1956), p. 49. Schiller did not actually intend to go to Berlin but wanted people to think he was on his way there. See the notes on pages 273 through 276 of *Werke,* vol. 23. Nicolai had visited Schiller during his travels through Germany in 1781. Nicolai, *Beschreibung einer Reise,* 10:83.

interests or pretensions. Some twenty years after Schiller's letter Henry Crabb Robinson, an Englishman who did much to spread knowledge of and interest in German philosophy and literature in his native land, actually visited Nicolai. "I hastened upon my arrival to deliver a letter of introduction to one of the Berlin notabilities, and indeed one of the remarkable men of the day.... No one who has paid any attention to the German literature of the eighteenth century can be ignorant of the name of Frederick Nicolai, the Berlin publisher."[66] In the 1830s, Heinrich Heine could even look back on a Berlin where "Frederick the Great and the bookseller Nicolai reigned."[67]

As a financially independent bookseller and renowned writer, Nicolai exercised a double attraction for his contemporaries, especially for less well placed members of the republic of letters. He possessed not only the power that all established authors held in common—to praise or recommend other writers—but also the wherewithal to further their careers directly and materially through projects and authors' fees. With his critical journals, particularly the *ADB*, on the one hand, and his publishing program on the other, Nicolai early established a strategic position, which reached a high point during the 1770s and 1780s. In 1768, Christian Friedrich Daniel Schubart spoke of the time, not so long past, "when Nicolai's bookshop in Berlin became a colossal horse, out of whose belly armed critics sprang, teaching all authors to tremble."[68] The thousands of letters from some 2500 persons preserved in Nicolai's unpublished correspondence, rarely without a request for, or reference to, a favor of some kind are witness to Nicolai's importance and influence as a powerbroker in a period of transition.

Friedrich Nicolai's career would be unthinkable without the changes in the book trade and literary world that were beginning in the mid-eighteenth century when he was an apprentice bookseller. His father, Christoph Gottlieb Nicolai, was an active publisher of baroque learning and had one of the largest book inventories in Berlin,[69] but his name is as little remembered today as that of most other early eighteenth-century German booksellers. The spread of the Enlightenment movement, the

---

66. Henry Crabb Robinson, *Diary, Reminiscences and Correspondence*, ed. Thomas Sadler, 2 vols. (London: Macmillan, 1872), 1:84.

67. Heinrich Heine, *Beiträge zur deutschen Ideologie* (Frankfurt a. M.: Ullstein, 1971), p. 62.

68. Christian Friedrich Daniel Schubart to Christian Gottfried Böckh, 1 June 1768, in Schubart, *Briefe* (Leipzig: Dieterich, 1984), p. 85.

69. Georgi, *Die Entwicklung des Berliner Buchhandels*, pp. 103–4.

popularization of reading as a (middle-class) pastime,[70] the rise in German-language and the decline in Latin book production, and the transformation of the book trade from a service for school, church, and university into a broad-based market-oriented system of commodity production and distribution, together with the concomitant revaluation of the bookselling profession, form the preconditions and backdrop to Friedrich Nicolai's social position. To be sure, Friedrich Nicolai, unlike his father and most other booksellers, also published a major review journal and engaged with gusto in the intellectual debates of his day. But we must also take into account contemporary attitudes toward the book trade, which remained Nicolai's primary field of activity for over fifty years. Historians of the German book trade have often pointed out that the second half of the eighteenth century was a period of much reflection upon the role of the bookseller.[71] Paul Raabe has spoken of an "ideologization" of the profession.[72] Joseph II's much-quoted dictum that "one needs no more knowledge to sell books than to sell cheese," was certainly not representative of his age.[73] Yet ideas about the trade fluctuated between such extremes of economic pragmatism and ecstatic pronouncements like that of the journalist who in 1799 described booksellers as benefactors of humanity who promoted "all of the sciences useful to mankind, true enlightenment, and pure morals" as they dispersed "the fogs of prejudice, superstition, and ignorance."[74]

This high level of ideologization and idealization of the book trade was largely a phenomenon of the last quarter of the eighteenth century, perhaps only beginning in the 1790s. As Hazel Rosenstrauch has pointed out in the case of the Leipzig publisher Philipp Erasmus Reich, booksellers trained in the mid-eighteenth century did not tend to idealize their profession unduly or to emphasize cultural over economic values,[75] and

---

70. Rolf Engelsing uses the phrase "reading revolution" and discusses the phenomenon in his "Die Perioden der Lesergeschichte in der Neuzeit," *AGB* 10 (1970): cols. 981ff.

71. See esp. Bettmann, "Die Entstehung buchhändlerischer Berufsideale."

72. Paul Raabe, "Der Buchhändler im 18. Jahrhundert," in his *Bücherlust und Lesefreuden*, p. 32.

73. Joseph II's statement was made in the context of an anti-privilege campaign intended to vitalize the Austrian book trade by opening it up to more entrepreneurs. Quoted in Leslie Bodi, *Tauwetter in Wien. Zur Prosa der österreichischen Aufklärung 1781–1795* (Frankfurt a. M.: S. Fischer, 1977), p. 87.

74. Quoted from the *Allgemeine litterarischer Anzeiger*, 1799, in Raabe, "Der Buchhändler im 18. Jahrhundert," pp. 22–23.

75. Hazel Rosenstrauch, "Philipp Erasmus Reich—Bourgeois und Citoyen," *Karl-Marx-Universität Leipzig. Wissenschaftliche Zeitschrift*, Gesellschaftswissenschaftliche Reihe, 1 (1989): 98.

Friedrich Nicolai's conception of the role of bookseller and publisher likewise lay somewhere between the pedestrian and the heroic. Although fairly modest in his public appraisals of this role, and more interested in the practice than in the theory of the trade, he went far beyond the minimal requirements for running a solvent business. His enlightened self-interest led him to take an active role in the organization or *Policey* of the republic of letters and in the cultivation of the reading public, both as a retail bookseller and as a publisher.

As a retail bookseller, Friedrich Nicolai was not a mere supplier of books, but also an educator of taste and an adviser to his customers, some of whom lived in small towns or villages far from a good bookseller. Nicolai's position as a publisher was more complex, and more contradictory, than his position as a bookseller. He devoted the better part of his life, not to mention a vast amount of money, to the *ADB*, a project intended to criticize and thereby improve German letters. At the same time he confessed to publishing books he considered to be "bad."[76] Nicolai adhered to a traditional notion of authorship that emphasized a love of learning and poetry and denigrated the pursuit of gain, and like most of his contemporaries criticized those authors who regarded writing as a trade. Yet he paid authors by the sheet to carry out projects at least partially of his own devising and strongly emphasized the creative role of the publisher when it suited his purposes.

We need not speculate whether Nicolai accorded publishers more than a merely auxiliary role in the literary process, because he very conveniently stated his opinions in his 1790 suggestions for revisions to the articles concerning the book trade in the newly drafted Prussian legal code.[77] His testimony touches on many aspects of the book trade, but particularly interesting here are his remarks on the controversial topic of literary property and the rights of authors versus those of publishers. Not surprisingly, Nicolai defended the rights of publishers, since he was attempting—ultimately quite successfully—to influence legislation affecting his own business. He may have been a writer as well as a publisher,

---

76. It is not clear which books he meant. Nicolai may have been referring to reprints of old school texts he inherited from his father. In the 1790s he also published a series of translations of English novels that in most cases he had not even read, and which the translator did not consider to be of very great merit. See correspondence with F. H. Bothe, his translator and adviser at that period, in NN 7, and the discussion in Chapter 3.

77. These suggestions are printed in R. Voigtländer, "Das Verlagsrecht im Preußischen Landrecht und der Einfluß von Friedrich Nicolai darauf," *Archiv für die Geschichte des deutschen Buchhandels* [hereafter cited as "*AGDB*"] 20 (1898): 4–66.

but since he was his own publisher he experienced no economic conflict between his dual interests. As Wallace Kirsop has pointed out for French publishers, "The initiative in intellectual matters does not always come from the creators, and the role of the great bookseller-publisher is not that of a letter-box, a passive recipient."[78] This was Nicolai's position. He emphasized that the ideas for many useful books originated with their publishers, who usually understood public demand better than authors did. In such cases where they only used authors as "tools" to carry out their own projects, Nicolai believed that publishers' property rights took precedence.[79] The publisher also bore a greater financial risk. Thus he who generated the idea and owned the means of production also owned the rights to the end product.[80] In Nicolai's attitude we can see a strong connection between the two meanings of the German word *Verlag*: publishing company and putting-out enterprise. Publishing could be very much a "putting-out" industry.

Taking into account that Nicolai may well have overstated his case for the sake of persuasion, it remains clear that he accorded the bookseller and publisher a central place in the republic of letters as well as in the actual state. He may not have taken an active role in the book trade reforms of his time,[81] nor did he publish a book on the subject,[82] as did several of his colleagues. But he was firmly convinced of the utility of his profession and of its benefits to state and society. Whereas most authors, as he saw it, practiced their profession as a mere trade (as opposed to genuine *Gelehrte*, or men of letters) and would thus be better off serving their compatriots in state office or as craftsmen, booksellers were independent, economically productive citizens (even Immanuel Kant acknowledged this fact, if only ironically) whose enterprises the state should protect

78. Wallace Kirsop, "Les mécanismes éditoriaux," in *Le livre triomphant*, vol. 2 of *Histoire de l'édition française* (n. p: Promodis, 1984), p. 26.
79. Voigtländer, "Das Verlagsrecht," pp. 6–8. Nicolai was not the only one to emphasize this practice. See Bettmann, "Die Entstehung buchhändlerischer Berufsideale," p. 61, and J. C. Gädicke, *Der Buchhandel von mehreren Seiten betrachtet für solche Leser, die denselben näher kennen lernen, oder sich als Buchhändler etabliren wollen* (Weimar, 1803; 2d ed., Greiz, 1834), p. 14.
80. Voigtländer, "Das Verlagsrecht," pp. 6–8, 26.
81. Georgi, *Die Entwicklung des Berliner Buchhandels*, p. 108, mentions this in his characterization of Nicolai in the context of Berlin booksellers.
82. Nicolai apparently did write an essay on his bookselling career, now lost, at the request of the publisher J. C. Gädicke. It is mentioned in two letters to Gädicke of January 1801, in SPKB, Nachlaß 141, Kasten 3, and New Haven, Yale University, Beinecke Library, Speck Colln. N54b G801 1:26. For a discussion of works on the book trade written by booksellers, see Bettmann, "Die Entstehung buchhändlerischer Berufsideale."

from foreign competition, particularly from pirate publishers. As he portrayed it, the German book trade was fraught with particular risks and disadvantages—the book fairs, literary piracy,[83] the necessity of maintaining books in several languages in stock at all times, the high cost of travel and freight, the need to cater to the tastes of many provinces and not just of a capital city, and so on. In consistently maintaining a large inventory of books, at great expense, booksellers provided an important service.[84] They also brought a good deal of money into the public treasuries. Nicolai was only one of many Prussian booksellers to emphasize this point in 1794 in protest against stiffened theological censorship and the ban on the *ADB*. The local book trade, Nicolai argued in a petition to King Frederick William II, brought a significant amount of capital into circulation in Prussia; each year Nicolai's Berlin shop alone spent 1000–1200 taler on postage, a sum the state should not ignore.[85] Only with experience, order, and thrift could the bookseller make his business "solid,"[86] and it was incumbent upon the state to ensure that the laws regarding the book trade helped rather than hindered this process. Nicolai's sense of himself as a bookseller and publisher was thus scarcely heroic, but one based upon pride in a service to the state and society that united cultural and economic value.

---

83. Piracy was, of course, not a problem for the German book trade alone—London booksellers were faced with pirate editions, particularly from Ireland, and their colleagues in Paris saw the flourishing of illicit publishing enterprises along the eastern borders of France—but the issue was perhaps nowhere so hotly debated as in the German-speaking countries where political fragmentation made any central control of the book trade well-nigh impossible. For an account of the German discussion, see Reinhard Wittmann, "Der gerechtfertigte Nachdrucker," in his *Buchmarkt und Lektüre im 18. und 19. Jahrhundert* (Tübingen: Niemeyer, 1982), pp. 69–92.

84. Voigtländer, "Das Verlagsrecht," pp. 10–11, 28–30.

85. Nicolai to Friedrich Wilhelm II, 6 May 1794, in "Actenstücke zur Geschichte der preußischen Censur- und Preßverhältnisse unter dem Minister Wöllner," ed. Friedrich Kapp, part 2, 1794–96, *AGDB* 5 (1880): 269–70.

86. Voigtländer, "Das Verlagsrecht," pp. 11–12.

chapter

(2)

The Nicolaische Buchhandlung, 1759–1811

*A Publishing Company in the Age of
Enlightenment and Revolution*

The foremost concern of a publishing house is
to publish only good, new and consistently salable books. This
is the method by means of which Reich, Voß, Mylius, and
Nicolai made their firms profitable and flourishing.

—*Friedrich Johann Justin Bertuch, 1774*

Friedrich Nicolai's career as an independent bookseller-publisher began during the Seven Years' War. In 1758, the twenty-five-year-old reluctantly abandoned the career of a private man of letters and returned to the dry world of business. His joy at having escaped the daily bookshop routine in 1757 (when the belated settlement of his father's estate provided him with a small income) was thus short-lived. An older brother's early death left him with full responsibility for the firm during a time of inflation, bad coinage, and risky transportation.[1] Many years later, Nicolai recalled some of the perils of business in wartime:

> In October 1760 ... Leipzig was occupied by Austrian troops during the Michaelmas fair.... Wittenberg, where N[icolai] had the main depot for his publishing company in those days, was being bombarded by the Imperial army, so that a great part of the city went up in flames; ... the man whom he had sent to the Leipzig fair was unfortunately trapped in Wittenberg with a large sum of money and the account books, and had to await the end of the siege. At the very same time Berlin came under Austrian and Russian fire, and was subsequently occupied. Thus the

---

1. Nicolai, "Selbstbiographie," pp. 50–51.

three main sites of his business were imperiled by war, but he had the good fortune to lose nothing of substance in any of these places.[2]

The German book trade was, as he was fond of reminding his contemporaries, a "laborious, complicated and under certain circumstances exceedingly awkward business."[3] Unlike their counterparts in Paris or London, who might get away with merely selling books over the counter for cash, Germans could never rely on customers in only one city for their livelihood. Without a guild, strictly prescribed training, or clear corporative character, the book trade that Nicolai entered demanded much of its practitioners. In 1769, after some twenty years in the business, he summarized the requirements as follows: an unusually broad knowledge of existing books, of the best manner of procuring them, and their relative value as commodities; a strict sense of order—not merely in mundane matters such as the tying up of packages[4] or the treatment of individual books, and their proper placement so that they can be readily found in large shops or depots—but also in bookkeeping; tireless industry in selling, correspondence, the speedy dispatch of book orders, and visiting the book fairs; great care in printing, acquisition, exchange, and so on.[5] The six or seven years of training informally agreed upon in the

---

2. Ibid., pp. 21–22. Nicolai's poor *Diener* August Mylius described his terror when a cannonball flew into his room in Wittenberg, almost crushing him in his bed. The church next to the house where he was staying was engulfed in flames. Nicolai to Philipp Erasmus Reich, 21 October 1760, quoted in F. H. Meyer, "Die geschäftlichen Verhältnisse des deutschen Buchhandels im achtzehnten Jahrhundert," *AGDB* 5 (1880): 233.

3. Nicolai's "Review" of Lessing's *Hamburgische Dramaturgie* and of the pirate edition of it in *ADB* 10, no. 2 (1769): 5. He makes very similar arguments in his *Beschreibung einer Reise*, 8:56–47. Others at the time also emphasized the particular difficulties of the German book trade and contrasted the plight of booksellers in German cities with their supposedly luckier brethren in London and Paris. See, for example, Philipp Erasmus Reich in his notes to *Des Herrn [Simon Nicolas Henri] Linguets Betrachtungen über die Rechte des Schriftstellers und seines Verlegers, aus dem Französischen mit einigen Anmerkungen* (n. p. = Leipzig: Weidmanns Erben und Reich, 1778), pp. 44–45n. In London and Paris, "it is easier for the book trade to make a profit, since each of these cities is home to more than one million largely well-off [sic] persons, such that the sales of a good book are rapid, sure, and large; while, in contrast, the book trade in Germany is subject to endless detail, unspeakable efforts, and many a danger and uncertainty."

4. Lessing had questioned the qualities necessary for a bookseller which Dodsley and Company had claimed should preclude authors publishing their own works. "What sort of necessary qualities are these? That one must spend five years learning how to bind packages from a man who also can do nothing but bind packages?... Since when has the book trade been a guild? What are its exclusive privileges?" *Hamburgische Dramaturgie*, nos. 101–4 (1769).

5. "Review" of G. E. Lessing's *Hamburgische Dramaturgie*, pp. 5–6. That knowledge of business practices, such as dual-column bookkeeping, was by no means universal among booksellers is demonstrated by Nicolai's comments about his own son, Carl August: "He understands neither dual-column bookkeeping nor merchandise, nor bills of exchange." Nicolai to his

book trade were only the beginning, and booksellers needed "diligence and experience" to perfect their knowledge and skills.[6] In an 1806 autobiographical essay, Nicolai looked back on the early period of his life when "without any inclination toward trade, or any experience in running such a business, he was compelled to manage an extensive enterprise that was in many respects in need of reorganization."[7]

When Friedrich Nicolai inherited the family business upon his brother's death in 1758, he had the good fortune to inherit its creditworthiness as well. He may have begun with debts, as he told Friedrich Perthes, but he never had to struggle, as other young booksellers did, to establish a reputation and gain the confidence of his colleagues. When, at the Easter book fair of 1759, the first catalog appeared under the imprint of "Friedrich Nicolai, Buchhändler in Berlin. In der Brüder Strasse im du Fourschen Hause," Nicolai had already been in the business for nearly ten years. While still occupying a subordinate position in the shop under his brother Gottfried Wilhelm, he began to dabble in publishing, arranging for the plays of Neric Destouches (1755–63) and Jean-François Regnard (1757) to be translated into German by his old friend Samuel Patzke and published by the family firm.[8]

The financial and other hardships of wartime notwithstanding, the early years of Nicolai's career were ones of risk-taking and innovation, and he embarked on several enterprises aimed at rejuvenating and consolidating the family firm. Along with establishing two journals, the *Briefe, die neueste Litteratur betreffend* and later the *ADB*, which made his company known all over Germany, Nicolai also experimented, albeit not always successfully, with other novel means of seizing public attention and serving his customers. In the early 1760s, he conceived the grandiose plan of reprinting the best works of English literature to make them available at lower prices than the expensive imports. Although the project began and ended with the ten-volume works of Alexander Pope (1762–64), since few Germans could read English in the 1760s, it was a highly innovative idea that won Nicolai praise at the time. In 1765, the Leipzig *Neue Zeitungen von gelehrten Sachen* reported, "The printing is so beautiful, and carried out so correctly, that one will gladly dispense with

---

daughter Wilhelmine, Klein Schönebeck, 7 February 1794, in Berlin, Landesarchiv Berlin [hereafter cited as "LAB"], Rep. 200 Acc 450 vol. 9.

6. "Review," of G. E. Lessing's *Hamburgische Dramaturgie*, p. 6.
7. Nicolai, "Selbstbiographie," p. 21.
8. See Patzke to Nicolai, Frankfurt an der Oder, 29 March 1755, 4 February 1757, and 3 February 1763, in NN 56.

the English edition. This work honors its publisher and may encourage him to render the other excellent works of the English better known and more widely disseminated among us."[9]

Around the same time, Nicolai devised a less lofty but more lucrative idea. At the end of the Seven Years' War, the firm produced the "Berlockenbücher," a series of seven miniature books that could be worn as watch fobs or pendants. These dainty objects, decorated with a fine gold braid ordered especially from Nuremberg and bearing such titles as "Die Freude beim Frieden" (or for francophones, "La Joye sur la retour de la paix"), "Dänemarks Friedensfreude, " and "Rußlands Glückseligkeit," found favor not only in Berlin.[10] As a Magdeburg correspondent commented in March 1763, the "little peace books" had sold out there in one day and people were clamoring for more.[11] "Every patriotic Prussian had to possess one of these miniature calendars; thousands were sold," reported Nicolai's grandson Gustav Parthey. According to him, the *Berlockenbücher* published in 1763/64 brought in more than 6000 taler, a handsome sum indeed.[12] In the summer of 1763, in the midst of the postwar credit crisis and bankruptcies, Moses Mendelssohn remarked wryly: "Long live the *Berlokenbüchlin*! However bad they may be, they are better than many letters of exchange ... at least they are harmless papers."[13]

9. *Neue Zeitungen von gelehrten Sachen auf das Jahr 1765*, no. 44 (3 June 1765), p. 351. Nicolai had hoped to publish Shakespeare's works next. Nicolai to Uz, 5 October 1762, in NN 76. In 1765, Nicolai offered the Pope edition at a reduced price, for 5, instead of the usual 8 taler. *ADB* 1, no. 2 (1765): 313–14. On English-language publishing at the period in Germany, see Bernhard Fabian, "English Books and their 18th-Century German Readers," in *The Widening Circle: Essays on the Circulation of Literature in Eighteenth-Century Europe*, ed. Paul J. Korshin (Philadelphia: University of Pennsylvania Press, 1976), pp. 126–37.

10. Parthey, *Jugenderinnerungen*, p. 54. See also Raabe, Nicolai catalog, p. 35.

11. Patzke to Nicolai, 13 March 1763, in NN 56. Patzke sold the works at first through Daniel Christian Hechtel, the local publisher of his own journal *Der Greis*. Realizing that Nicolai would not want much to do with Hechtel, who was not only a pirate (including, sometime later, of one of Nicolai's own publications) but a purveyor of some racy "livres philosophiques," Patzke ended up giving the commission to a dealer in fancy goods (*Galanterienhändler*) named Schmidt. He turned out to be a reluctant payer, however, and Patzke came close to taking him to court. Patzke to Nicolai, 5 November 1763, in NN 56. On Hechtel, see Johann Goldfriedrich, *Geschichte des deutschen Buchhandels*, vol. 3 (Leipzig: Börsenverein, 1909), p. 427. It appears that the "Berlockenbücher" were sold by non-booksellers outside Prussia as well. In 1764 the poet Johann Jakob Dusch in Altona ordered and received fifty copies on consignment for a relative of his, a local merchant called Grävesmühlen. Dusch to Nicolai, 11 December 1764 and 14 January 1765, in NN 15.

12. Parthey, *Jugenderinnerungen*, p. 54.

13. Berlin, 10 August 1763, printed in Moses Mendelssohn, *Neuerschlossene Briefe Moses Mendelssohns an Friedrich Nicolai*, ed. Alexander Altmann and Werner Vogel (Stuttgart: Frommann-Holzboog, 1973), pp. 15–16. Mendelssohn himself used the English term "harmless papers."

In 1759, the first year in which books appeared under his own name, Nicolai published only a few titles, but these represent several important strands in his list. He began the review journal *Briefe, die neueste Litteratur betreffend* and the *Sammlung vermischter Schriften zur Beförderung der schönen Wissenschaften und der freyen Künste*, a collection of translations of important aesthetic texts. He also published a theological polemic and a new edition of one of his father's school texts, Friedrich Muzell's 1726 collection of models of Latin epistolary style. Working together with his new friends Lessing and Mendelssohn, among others, Nicolai began to realize his ideals of enlightened criticism in his journals. With his initial interest in improving German taste and style, Nicolai focused at first on foreign literatures. He considered, but never published, an edition of Shakespeare's works.[14] Translations of Salomon Gessner's poetry into French were intended to introduce the German-Swiss writer (and fellow publisher) to a wider audience. The project of a series of biographies of Greek and Roman authors, which however never went beyond the first volume, arose from Nicolai's interest in introducing classical literature to the literate but unlearned public.

While establishing his reputation as a publisher and bookseller, Nicolai also solidified his position in Berlin society by marrying Elisabeth Macaria, daughter of the late royal physician Samuel Schaarschmidt in December 1760. In June 1762 their first child, Samuel Friedrich, was born, and six months later, on 22 January 1763, Nicolai attained full adult male status by becoming a citizen of Berlin.[15] Three weeks later the Treaty of Hubertusburg was signed, ending the Seven Years' War and inaugurating a relatively long period of peace that allowed for the gradual economic recovery that benefited Nicolai, among others.

The unedifying spectacle of Prussian and imperial troops slaughtering each other in their thousands gave way to new hopes for German cultural unity, hopes that helped fuel the initial success of the *ADB*. The founding of this review journal soon after the war ended initiated a new stage in Nicolai's career, and the mid to late 1760s were a period of consolidation for the publishing company. It published fewer titles between 1765 and

14. Nicolai to Uz, 5 October 1762, in NN 76. Nicolai feared, however, that Shakespeare was at once untranslatable and and incomprehensible, in any language, to those without a solid grounding in English language and manners.

15. Rodenberg quotes from the Berliner Bürgerbuch, in Julius Rodenberg, "Die Nicolaische Buchhandlung," in *Beiträge zur Kulturgeschichte von Berlin. Fs. zur Feier des fünfzigjährigen Bestehens der Korporation der Berliner Buchhändler* (Berlin: Korporation der Berliner Buchhändler, 1898), p. 232n.

1769 than in the previous half decade, and almost one-third of these were reprints. The range of new titles was narrow but distinguished, dominated by the much-discussed *Vom Verdienste* (On Merit, 1765) by Thomas Abbt and *Phädon, oder über die Unsterblichkeit der Seele*, Moses Mendelssohn's 1767 set of Socratic dialogues on immortality.[16] Having recognized with the failure of his Alexander Pope venture that the German public was not yet ready for English literature in the original, Nicolai now hoped to promote German writing in an English mode, characterized by clear writing and a practical approach to philosophical issues. The *ADB* occupied much of Nicolai's attention from 1764 on, as did the founding of a lending library in Berlin and a new shop in Stettin in 1765. The births of three more children (five in all survived to young adulthood) in 1765, 1767, and 1769 may have strengthened Nicolai's tendency to emphasize projects that would stabilize the firm's finances and pull it out of debt.[17]

During the 1770s, when *ADB* circulation was at an all-time high (over 2500 copies of each issue were printed in 1777) the number and variety of other titles Nicolai published also rose steadily. The *ADB* provided both the capital and the personnel for this expansion. Literary feuds with Goethe, Herder, Lavater, Wieland, and others, as well as numerous writing projects of his own, such the satirical novels *Sebaldus Nothanker* and *Die Freuden des jungen Werthers*, the controversial analysis of the scandal surrounding an alleged poisoning of the communion wine in Zurich,[18] or the *Almanach* of folk songs kept Nicolai busy, and in the public eye, for much of the decade. At that time he contemplated publishing an annotated bibliography for self-tuition, about which we will hear more later, and a series of German dictionaries, but neither of these projects came to fruition.[19] In the late 1770s, he frequently had to contend with the Austrian censors, particularly in regard to the *ADB*, which, together with the Unitarian polemic-cum-novel *Johann Bunkel*, was banned outright in

---

16. Mendelssohn's work was translated into English by Charles Cullen, as *Phaedon; or, The Death of Socrates* (London, 1789).

17. Nicolai mentions his debts in a letter to Lessing of October 1769. Lessing, *Sämtliche Schriften*, 19:318.

18. *Einige Zweifel über die Geschichte der Vergiftung des Nachtmahlweins welcher zu Zürich 1776 geschehen seyn soll. Nebst einigen Anmerkungen betreffend Herrn Ulrichs und Herrn Lavaters Predigten über diesen Vorfall* (Berlin: Nicolai, 1778). This pamphlet first appeared as a review in the *ADB*. This case, which occurred in September 1776 and had broad political, scientific, and religious implications, was a hot topic in the German periodical press. Jeffrey Freedman is currently preparing a study of the affair.

19. The dictionaries are mentioned in a letter of 25 July 1773 from Johann Beckmann in Göttingen, in NN 3.

1778. Piracy lawsuits were the outward sign of the success of many of his titles.

With the *ADB* as a secure financial basis and the late Enlightenment in full swing, Nicolai was at the height of his prestige, making the 1780s his most productive decade as a publisher. The first half of the 1780s was, in the main, a period of prosperity and expansion for him. The firm's production boomed, with ninety-one new titles between 1780 and 1784. At the beginning of the decade Nicolai and his son were able to undertake a costly five-month journey through Germany, the Habsburg lands, and Switzerland in their own private carriage. Poor sales, for example at the 1783 Easter book fair in Leipzig,[20] were at least partially compensated for by rich commissions from Catherine II at the same period.

The second half of the decade was more mixed in its blessings. Book production began to decline, a trend that was to continue until Nicolai's death in 1811. Still, the seventy-six new titles he published between 1785 and 1789, not including continuations of works begun earlier, far outpaced the fifty-two titles he brought out during the 1770s. Nicolai was plagued by frequent illnesses and overwork, and his feuds with the so-called crypto-Catholics and their supporters, which gave rise to numerous polemical works from his own pen as well as those of the Baltic noblewoman-turned-*Aufklärer* and born-again opponent of *Schwärmerei* Elisa von der Recke, among others.[21] Seventeen eighty-six saw the death of his beloved friend Moses Mendelssohn and his beloved sovereign Frederick II. In 1788 and 1789 Nicolai's worst fears seemed realized in the new Prussian edicts concerning religion and censorship. As we will see, he even considered for a time moving his base of operations from Berlin to Braunschweig so that his two eldest sons, whom he hoped would someday run the business jointly, could be assured of a more liberal atmosphere than that prevailing in the Prussian capital. On the more

---

20. Nicolai to Eschenburg, Leipzig, March 1783, in the Herzog August Bibliothek Cod. Guelph 622 Nov [hereafter cited as "HAB"], no. 50.

21. Elisa von der Recke, *Etwas über des Herrn Oberhofpredigers Johann August Stark Vertheidigungsschrift nebst einigen andern nöthigen Erläuterungen* (Berlin: Nicolai, 1788). Rather unusually for a (noble)woman, she published this work under her own name. The pamphlet was directed against Darmstadt court preacher Johann August Starck, who was accused by various members of the Berlin Enlightenment of being a crypto-Catholic (which he vehemently denied in polemics of his own). On her conversion from religious enthusiasm and superstition to the Enlightenment, in which both her encounter with the adventurer Cagliostro (who promised her contact with the spirit of her dead child) and a reading around the same time of Lessing's play *Nathan the Wise* played a central role, see her account in Elisa von der Recke, *Tagebücher und Selbstzeugnisse*, ed. Christine Träger (Munich: C. H. Beck, 1984), esp. pp. 353ff. and 396–97.

positive side, in 1787–88 Nicolai and his wife bought and renovated a large house and shop premises in Berlin's elegant Brüderstraße, which soon became an important center of sociability for local and visiting intellectuals.[22] In 1788 Samuel Friedrich Nicolai, the heir apparent, married Juliane Sophie Eleonore, daughter of Ernst Ferdinand Klein, one of the authors of the new Prussian legal code, thus cementing the family's already friendly relations with the Prussian administrative elite.

An inquiry into the direct impact of the events of the French Revolution on Nicolai's publishing list yields conspicuously meager results. The most important work Nicolai published was also the earliest, Ernst Ferdinand Klein's 1790 *Freiheit und Eigenthum*, a dialogue on property and civil and political liberties that contrasted unreconstructed French absolutism with the reformist Prussian version. According to Horst Möller, the work was based on actual discussions in the Mittwochsgesellschaft, although Klein himself claimed that he had merely based the characters on fellow members of an unnamed society, inventing what he thought the different men would have said on the subject.[23] Georg Heinrich Behn's memoirs of Paris "written for physicians" (1799); the Comte de Mirabeau's discourse on national education, with notes and a preface by the Prussian educational reformer Friedrich von Rochow (1792); and Johann Wilhelm von Steck's *Essais sur divers sujets relatifs à la navigation et au commerce pendant la guerre* (1794) were more peripheral titles. While debates about the French Revolution raged elsewhere, Nicolai published works on more German "revolutions": in favor of Prussian legal and administrative reform and against Idealist philosophy.

As Heinrich Heine was to note with characteristic irony after another French revolution in 1831:

22. According to Elisa von der Recke, buying the house was Elisabeth Nicolai's idea, because she wanted a larger home where they could invite friends from out of town to stay. When Nicolai complained of the expense, she said, "Why should we amass money every year without enjoying it, now that we are growing old? We can live simply in a beautiful large house, too, without being crowded together like a pile of ants." *Tagebücher und Selbstzeugnisse*, p. 139. Elisa vonder Recke always returned to the house in the Brüderstraße during her peripatetic life, and the Nicolais became a family she vastly preferred to the court circles in which she was compelled to move.

23. Möller, *Aufklärung in Preußen*, p. 286 n. 122. Ernst Ferdinand Klein, "Selbstbiographie," in *Bildnisse jetztlebender Berliner Gelehrten mit ihren Selbstbiographien*, ed. M. S. Lowe, 3d collection (Berlin, 1806). On Klein's work in its contemporary context, see Günter Birtsch, "Freiheit und Eigentum: Zur Erörterung von Verfassungsfragen in der deutschen Publizistik der Französischen Revolution," in *Eigentum und Verfassung: Zur Eigentumsdiskussion im ausgehenden 18. Jahrhundert*, ed. Rudolf Vierhaus (Göttingen: Vandenhoeck & Ruprecht 1972), pp. 179–92.

It is curious that the practical doings of our neighbors beyond the Rhine nonetheless share some elective affinity with our philosophical dreams in peaceful Germany.... If one compares the history of the French Revolution with the history of German philosophy, one might be tempted to believe that the French, who were responsible for so much genuine business that required them to remain wide awake at all times, asked us Germans to sleep and dream in their stead, and that our German philosophy was nothing other than the dream of the French Revolution. Thus our break with the status quo and tradition occurred in the realm of ideas, just as the French had theirs in the realm of society.... Kant was our Robespierre ... [and] Fichte with his ego the Napoleon of philosophy.[24]

Nicolai was certainly a vociferous opponent of the dreamers Heine describes; the mention of Kant and Fichte in this context is particularly apposite, since they, or more particularly the excesses of their followers, were far more important targets of Nicolai's pen in the 1790s than anything occurring in France. Nicolai and his friends were neither Jacobins nor arch-reactionaries. Accused as he was, together with all *Aufklärer*, of having brought about the Revolution, and with the fate of the *ADB* in the balance, Nicolai may have decided to avoid even a whiff of political controversy elsewhere in the publishing company. Still, the paucity of books dealing even tangentially or critically with the French Revolution is striking. Skeptical as he was about the Revolution from the beginning, Nicolai failed utterly to recognize its epochal significance "because it could not be grasped with his categories," as Horst Möller convincingly argues.[25] Thus the most important political event of Nicolai's lifetime left only a minor visible mark on his publishing program. In the 1790s, Nicolai's attention was focused far more on events in Germany, and more particularly in Prussia, than on happenings in France. In fact, he rather neglected all things French in the 1790s, publishing only three translations from the French during those years, as opposed to fifteen in the 1780s. He apparently received few manuscripts or outlines for books on France, let alone on the Revolution. In 1791, an author did offer him a *Gelehrtes Frankreich*, a biographical and bibliographical dictionary on

---

24. Heinrich Heine, "Einleitung zu 'Kahldorf über den Adel'" (1831), in *Historisch-kritische Gesamtausgabe*, ed. Manfred Windfuhr (Hamburg: Hoffmann & Campe, 1978), vol. 11, ed. Helmut Koopmann, p. 134.

25. Möller, *Aufklärung in Preußen*, p. 40.

the model of Johann Georg Meusel's work on Germany and Jeremias David Reuß's on England, and Nicolai seriously considered accepting it, but in the end thought better of the idea.[26]

The year 1790 inaugurated a more precipitous decline in fortunes for both family and business. In March of that year, Nicolai returned from a journey to find his son Samuel Friedrich dead by his own hand.[27] With the second son Carl August too young and immature to take over the firm, Nicolai's dreams of retirement evaporated. The growing threat—and reality—of censorship in Prussia, which caused Nicolai to sell the *ADB* in 1792, the frightening turn of events in France, the growing scarcity of cash at the book fairs, exacerbated by the wars that continued for most of the rest of Nicolai's life, all contributed to his sense of gloom. When his wife died in 1793 and the *ADB* was banned, if only temporarily, in 1794, Nicolai's pessimism deepened. Constant conflicts with his independent and rebellious son Carl August added to his malaise.[28] Carl August Nicolai's disinclination to work, at least under his father's watchful eye, was partially resolved when Nicolai set him up in his own firm in 1795, from which he published works by Romantics such as Ludwig Tieck. In November 1799, however, he died at the age of thirty, leaving his father with disorganized account books, a host of creditors, and a Leipzig storeroom to clear out because none of his siblings was interested in inheriting his business.[29] He also left him with support payments for his illegitimate child.[30]

---

26. Nicolai's annotations on a letter of 9 June 1791 from Esch in Jena, in NN 19.

27. He and his wife and daughter Minna had been at Rekahn, visiting the pedagogical author Friedrich von Rochow. Nicolai discusses the event in letters of 3 April 1790 to J. J. Eschenburg (in HAB, no. 102) and 30 April 1790 to Uz (in NN 76). Throughout 1790 his letters are full of references to his deep sadness at his son's death. Nicolai's grandson Gustav Parthey mentions that Samuel Friedrich's death was a suicide. *Jugenderinnerungen*, p. 41.

28. Nicolai's friend L. G. von Göckingk reported to a correspondent that Nicolai had spent three hours weeping and complaining about troubles with his son, "a dissolute lad, quite full of himself, who incurs debts behind his father's back, spends his time in coffee houses, theaters, and ridottos, and yet wants to be a solid man." Göckingk to Benzler, 3 December 1793, postscript of 17 January 1794, in Heinrich Pröhle, "Der Dichter Günther von Göckingk über Berlin und Preußen unter Friedrich Wilhelm II und Friedrich Wilhelm III," *Zeitschrift für preußische Geschichte und Landeskunde* (1877): 26.

29. Nicolai to Heinrich Beumner, Carl August Nicolai's Leipzig landlord, 16 February 1800, in Leipzig, Universitätsbibliothek, Ms 01321.

30. The mother of the child, a Frau Gottleber née Gross, was apparently trying to obtain retroactive payments beyond the child support that Nicolai had paid voluntarily until April 1800. In order to do so she had to take an oath swearing that she had had sexual intercourse (*fleischlich vermischt*) with C. A. Nicolai in the period between 28 November 1798 and 11 February 1799. Henneberg to Nicolai, Berlin, 11 March 1803, with Nicolai's marginal annotations, in NN 32.

The Nicolaische Buchhandlung, 1759–1811

While Prussian censorship released its stranglehold somewhat toward the end of the century, economic conditions worsened and Nicolai further reduced the firm's output. He had often remarked that he could replace the *ADB* with twenty other titles and do better financially, but his output actually dropped, rather than rose, when he stopped publishing the journal. The number of new titles fell from fifty-five in the first half of the decade to forty-two in the second. The number of larger works (comprising two or more volumes) begun but not necessarily completed fell from fifty-two in the 1780s to thirty-two in the 1790s. Large projects had become a greater risk. Of the fifteen multivolume works Nicolai began publishing between 1795 and 1799, eleven were novels, including two by the very popular author Johann Gottwerth Müller and two by Nicolai himself. Expensive large-scale works were to be undertaken only under extraordinary circumstances. Nicolai lamented in March 1799 that the prices of printing and paper had become exorbitant, gold was all but unattainable, and the book trade was in a sorrier state than he had ever seen it. His prognostications for the upcoming Easter book fair were dire indeed; it was likely, he wrote, that most booksellers would simply stay away because they lacked the money to settle accounts. The war provided them with an all-too-plausible excuse, and pirate editions were once again taking over the market.[31] Nicolai was certainly not alone in his gloomy pronouncements. The "Meß-Relationen," reports made by Leipzig officials on each book fair based upon booksellers' testimony, attest to a general mood of discontent through much of the 1790s and early 1800s. As early as Michaelmas 1789 (around 29 September), some booksellers reported that war was presenting obstacles to trade. In 1794, Austrian censorship was blamed for falling sales there. The restrictions on book imports to Russia in 1798–99 virtually closed a lucrative market to German booksellers. In 1800, publishers complained that inflation was causing scholars to buy fewer books. In 1801, they claimed that cash was virtually unattainable and that Swiss and southwest German booksellers were avoiding the fair, buying less, and returning works they had ordered on consignment. At the Easter fair of 1803, despite some improvement in the economic situation, the report stated that "solid booksellers claim that there is little money to be earned in the book trade at present, and that the larger the trade becomes, the more it loses its inner value." Rising paper and printing costs, the rising number of (frequently untrained)

---

31. Nicolai to Eschenburg, Berlin, March 1799, in HAB, no. 199.

new booksellers (about which there had, however, been complaints since the 1730s),[32] and continuing piracy were "dragging this once lucrative trade down further every day." The lack of cash, lamented once again in the 1804 reports, was causing a return to barter, forcing booksellers to accept books they did not want in order to secure at least some payment. The same complaints were repeated in 1805, 1806, and 1807, with the addition of worsening inflation and obstacles to transport caused by the war in southern Germany.[33]

In 1800, the unfavorable economic situation notwithstanding, Nicolai resumed publication of the foundering *ADB*, much to the relief of Carl Ernst Bohn, the Hamburg publisher who had taken it over. In 1799 he had begun publishing the *Neue Berlinische Monatschrift* (which his son Carl August had published under the title *Berlinische Blätter*), thus uniting under his imprint the two major organs of the declining late Enlightenment. Otherwise, he reduced his book production still further. Although his overall production rose slightly in the final half-decade of his life (from 47 titles to 52), this was a result largely of reprints of old works, which accounted for over a third of his list from 1805 to 1811. It was, thus, not a particularly productive period for the firm, although the number of titles published still exceeded that of all half-decades before 1780. The most interesting feature of Nicolai's list at the period is perhaps the substantial proportion of theological works, which comprised 20.6 percent of new titles and 17.3 percent of total titles, the largest percentage of any period since the early 1770s. This percentage greatly exceeded the 13.55 percent of titles represented by theology at the Leipzig Easter fair of 1800.[34] With politics such a hot topic, theology was apparently safe once again. The last years of Nicolai's career were overshadowed by the loss of his eyesight, and of his three remaining children, the defeat of Prussia, and the occupation of Berlin. The continuing economic constraints of wartime saw the number of new publications drop slightly

32. See "Charlatanry in the Book Trade," a baroque pamphlet decrying newfangled forms of entrepreneurship introduced by "rotten *magistri*, half or completely unstudied students and quacks, ambitious and greedy printers, journeymen expelled from their guilds, runaway apprentices..., dissolute clerks, incompetent engravers, miserable tailors, master- and honorless lackeys" who sought their fortune as booksellers, quoted in Reinhard Wittmann, *Geschichte des deutschen Buchhandels* (Munich: C. H. Beck, 1991), pp. 94–96.

33. F. H. Meyer, "Die Leipziger Büchermesse von 1780 bis 1837," *AGDB* 14 (1891): 309–10, 292–97.

34. Rudolf Jentzsch, *Der deutsch-lateinische Büchermarkt nach den Leipziger Ostermeßkatalogen von 1740, 1770 und 1800 in seiner Gliederung und Wandlung*, Beiträge zur Kultur- und Universalgeschichte, 22 (Leipzig: R. Voigtländer, 1912), table 1.

from thirty-six to thirty-four. In a period of economic hardship, Nicolai stayed with the tried and true: sermons and schoolbooks. His main bow to the *Zeitgeist* was Johann Wilhelm Lombard's 1808 *Matériaux pour servir à l'histoire des années 1805, 1806 et 1807. Dédié aux Prussiens par un ancien compatriote*, which also appeared in a German translation, and apparently met with warm interest and approval in Berlin.[35] In an 1809 letter to a friend, Nicolai lamented not only the dire state of the book trade but also of "my poor country."[36] He also complained bitterly, some friends thought excessively, of the burdens he incurred during the French occupation. From the winter of 1806 on he was billeting troops in his house almost constantly, and he claimed in 1809 to have lost nearly one-half of his property through contributions and other effects of the war.[37]

Despite bitterness and gloom during the last few years of his life, Nicolai still hoped to undertake a number of book projects, including a "History of the Enlightenment of the German Nation."[38] When his faithful friend and biographer Leopold von Göckingk went through the publisher's voluminous notes after his death, he found a sheet, dated May 1810, with ideas for various other works Nicolai would like to have written. Among the projected essays on Celtic languages, ancient Greek music, and the potential uses of physiognomy and tales of adventurers he had known, there were also a number of biographical works on figures of the Prussian Enlightenment, a history of German literature since 1750, and the story of the *ADB*—subjects about which he, more than most of his contemporaries, was equipped to give an eyewitness account.

Friedrich Nicolai had begun his publishing career in 1759 as a hopeful reformer of twenty-six, eager to shake up the German republic of letters. Some fifty years later, sadder if, according to many, not wiser, he could

---

35. Berlin publisher Johann Daniel Sander to Carl August Böttiger, 12 December 1809, in *Die Briefe Johann Daniel Sanders an Carl August Böttiger*, ed. Bernd Maurach (Berne: Peter Lang, 1993), 4:188. On Nicolai's own contributions as a historian, see the very thorough discussion in Möller, *Aufklärung in Preußen*, pp. 322–517.

36. Nicolai to L. H. von Nicolay, Berlin, 12 December 1809, in *Die beiden Nicolai. Briefwechsel zwischen Ludwig Heinrich Nicolay in St. Petersburg und Friedrich Nicolai in Berlin (1776–1811)*, ed. Heinz Ischreyt (Lüneburg: Nordostdeutsches Kulturwerk, 1989), pp. 544–46.

37. Nicolai to Eschenburg, 1 January 1808, in HAB, no. 218, and to L. H. von Nicolay, 12 December 1809, in *Die beiden Nicolai*, pp. 544–46. L. G. von Göckingk reported to his friend Benzler that Nicolai believed that billeting troops was ruining him financially, a ridiculous fear considering his wealth. In fact, he appeared to be more concerned about his money than about the impending death of his one remaining child. Göckingk to Benzler, 13 January 1807, in Pröhle, "Der Dichter Günther von Göckingk," p. 77.

38. Nicolai's annotations on Ouvrier to Nicolai, Leipzig, 17 October 1808, in NN 55.

look back on a long and financially successful life. He had contributed over 420 new titles, including many from his own pen, and over 540 works to the German reading public. The more than 1100 volumes he published, including 199 volumes of the *ADB*, represent a little library of Enlightenment thought on a multitude of subjects. As Paul Raabe, author of the excellent catalog-bibliography of Nicolai's firm has noted, his publishing program, particularly beginning in the 1770s, reflected "the universality that was also the underlying concept of the *Allgemeine deutsche Bibliothek*."[39] Nevertheless, when Nicolai died in January 1811 at the age of seventy-seven, mourned by his few surviving friends and relations and by a host of Berliners who remembered his charitable deeds, many people thought it was high time. The *enfant terrible* of the 1750s had become a curmudgeon who, ill-pleased with the new age, consoled himself by satirizing the present and immersing himself in the ancients.[40] In the years between those two poles of hope and resignation, amid the friendships and feuds of the German republic of letters, Nicolai built his reputation as a publisher, launching bestsellers and bombs (*Läufer* and *Ladenhüter*), and everything in between.

When Nicolai first started attending the Leipzig book fairs, most publishers bartered their wares sheet for sheet. By the time he died, many booksellers not only paid cash for the printed sheets they took home from the fair, but no longer published any works of their own at all. The number of publishers, and of the works they printed, had expanded beyond the imagination of their predecessors just a generation before. The size of editions and the shelf-life of books had contracted accordingly, as Nicolai and many contemporaries lamented at the end of the eighteenth and the beginning of the nineteenth century. Whereas novels, for example, had frequently appeared in editions of 1500 in the 1770s, a contemporary author reported that the average edition had fallen to 500 copies by 1800.[41] As early as 1783, Nicolai noted that a book that would have warranted an edition of 1500 twenty or thirty years previously was now good for only 300, 500, or 750 copies.[42] The implication was that an

---

39. "Der Verleger Friedrich Nicolai," p. 151.
40. Nicolai to Uz, 27 April 1793, in NN 76.
41. *Ueber Buchhandel und Romanen-Fabricatur* (Eisleben: O. G. Verdion, 1804).
42. Nicolai to Graf Görtz, in Regensburg, 23 September 1783, in NN 25. According to Reinhard Wittmann, the average edition for literary works, presumably novels and poetry together, in the late eighteenth century was 1000 copies. Only works by particularly famous authors like Wieland, or those published by subscription, had substantially larger editions. "Zur Verlegertypologie der Goethezeit," *Jahrbuch für internationale Germanistik* 8, no. 1 (1976): 113.

overcrowded market had made it more difficult to sell large numbers of any given work. An analysis of the figures for Nicolai's own firm, albeit from a small sample of sixty-six editions or ca. 12 percent of his output, does show a downward trend in edition size in the latter part of his career for all works other than schoolbooks. Over the period 1773 to 1809 the average edition size was about 1100, or 900 if we exclude textbooks. In the period before 1790, however, the average edition size was nearly 1400. Thereafter the average dropped to 960. For books other than school texts the drop was even more precipitous, from 1280 to 670. The usual press run for a novel in the 1790s was 750. Edition sizes ranged from 300 and 225 for the two volumes of W.F.H. Reinwald's *Hennebergisches Idiotikon* (1793, 1801), a scholarly linguistic work of obviously limited appeal, to 5000 for editions of Hilmar Curas's French grammar (1780) and J. M. Schröckh's textbook of world history (1805).[43] Of seventeen titles published before 1785 for which edition figures could be found only one, a special 500-copy excerpt on fables from Johann Joachim Eschenburg's 1783 handbook of classical literature, had a press run under 1000.[44] Of forty-nine titles printed in or after 1785, thirty, or some 60 percent, had printings smaller than 1000.

Trends in Nicolai's Production:
A Quantitative, Thematic and Chronological Overview

Before proceeding to the material aspects of Nicolai's publishing activities, a survey of his production over the years may be in order.[45] The output of Nicolai's firm increased greatly over his lifetime, but it did not develop in a simple upward curve from year to year. In some years he

---

43. Nicolai's annotations on Reinwald to Nicolai, Meiningen, 1 February 1796 and 16 October 1800, in NN 60; note of December 1779 from Walch to the Schleusingen printer Müller on printing Curas's grammar, in NN 79; bill of 12 May 1805 from the printer Johann Chr. Görling in Erfurt, in NN 25.
44. When the *Grundzüge* was reprinted in 1787, the edition was increased to 1000. Scrap of paper (28 May 1805?) in Nicolai's hand, listing the sizes of the various editions of Eschenburg's *Handbuch* (in NN 19). See also the letter of 30 November 1782 from the printer Carl Christian Dürr in Wittenberg to Nicolai, in NN 15.
45. The figures that follow are based on the catalog of Nicolai's publications compiled by Paul Raabe, *Friedrich Nicolai: Die Verlagswerke eines preußischen Buchhändlers der Aufklärung 1759–1811*. In what follows I have frequently translated titles of works into English, since my main interest was to indicate the range of topics of books Nicolai published rather than to document the works themselves. Readers interested in specific titles should consult Raabe's catalog for bibliographical details.

published only two new titles, in others ten. This contrasts, for example, with the figures for the firm of Weidmanns Erben und Reich, which rose steadily from 1760 until 1785.[46] Rather, Nicolai's production fluctuated according to various economic, political, and personal factors. Viewed decade-by-decade, his publications show a growing diversification, and then a narrowing of scope toward the end of his career.

If we look at the number of titles published in 1759–1811, we see a general upward trend from 1759 to 1784, and then a steady decline thereafter, with a slight rise during the final period of his career, 1805–11. Within the upward trend, however, there was a decline in numbers for the years 1765–69. This may be explained by Nicolai's emphasis on developing the *ADB* in that half-decade, which tied up capital that he might otherwise have spent on book projects. During that period Nicolai published ten volumes of the *ADB*, the equivalent of twenty books of 320 pages each in octavo, or a much larger number of pamphlets. Since Nicolai believed religiously in balancing publishing with retail sales, it is probable that he reduced the number of titles he published alongside the *ADB* in order not to create an imbalance, but this is impossible to verify without knowing the volume of sales for the period. The period from 1785 to 1789 represents the beginning of a precipitous and continuing decline in the number of books published, which is mitigated however by the thirty volumes of the *ADB* printed in that period. The 1792 sale of the *ADB* to Bohn meant that for the period 1793–1800 the decline in titles was not compensated for by publication of volumes of the *ADB*, making the fall in numbers all the more striking. The Easter book fair of 1793 was, Nicolai reported, "indescribably bad," with little hope of immediate improvement. He attributed the situation to the excessive number of booksellers and books, the war, and the restriction of press freedom. Nicolai believed that too many books were flooding a tight market, and he apparently followed his conviction, and his business sense, and published less.[47] Despite the downward trend, though, the number of titles Nicolai published during the final six years of his life still exceeded that for the pre-1780 period.

---

46. Mark Lehmstedt, "Struktur und Arbeitsweise eines Verlages der deutschen Aufklärung: Die Weidmannsche Buchhandlung in Leipzig unter der Leitung von Philipp Erasmus Reich zwischen 1745 und 1787" (Ph. D. diss., Karl-Marx-Universität, Leipzig, 1989), p. 9.

47. Nicolai to Eschenburg, Leipzig, 7 May 1793, in HAB, no. 146. In a letter of 10 May 1790 Nicolai had already complained to Eschenburg that business at the fair was bad, and that, considering the direction the book trade was taking, and the "incredible number of books," matters could not be otherwise. In HAB, no. 103.

The development of Nicolai's publication of new titles, and thus of the most dynamic and creative element of his list, largely follows that for publications as a whole. New title publication dropped very slightly in the 1775–79 and 1805–11 periods, rather than rising along with general production in those years. As a percentage of total production, new titles reached a peak in 1780–84, when they comprised some 86 percent of the books Nicolai published. New titles outweighed reprints at all periods of Nicolai's career.

Reprints and revised editions followed a slightly different trend. The figures here may be somewhat low because of the difficulty of tracing later editions without the firm's account books. Although it mirrors the overall pattern of declining numbers in 1765–69, the reprinting of older works (including those taken over from Christoph Gottlieb Nicolai's list) peaked earlier, in both numbers and percentages, in 1775–79, fell slightly in 1780–84 in absolute numbers, but sharply as a percentage of total titles, rose very slowly until 1790–94, fell in the period 1795–99, and climbed to its highest level in absolute numbers in 1805–11. At the end of his career (as at the beginning) Nicolai relied on reprints of older works on his list for more than one-third of his production, a measure perhaps both of his own gradual withdrawal from active publishing and of the need to rely on perennials in times of heightened economic uncertainty.

Nicolai was essentially a German-language publisher. Over the years, French titles made up some 4.6 percent of his total production, a figure similar to the 5 percent Mark Lehmstedt has calculated for Weidmanns Erben und Reich, another major firm of the period.[48] In both absolute (five) and relative numbers (20 percent of new titles), 1759–64 was the period when French titles were most prominent on Nicolai's list. Of these five titles, three bore the imprint "et se vend à Berlin chez Frédéric Nicolai." What actual role Nicolai played in their publication is unclear. The works were Thomas Abbt's translation of Moses Mendelssohn's *Über die Empfindung* (Berlin: Voss, 1755) and two works by the Zurich poet, artist, and publisher Salomon Gessner (Paris 1761 and 1762). In the same period, Nicolai published the dramatic works of Denis Diderot (2 vols., 1763) and the Berlin academician Samuel Henri Formey's translation from the Greek of Claudius Aelianus's *Varia historia* (1764). Nicolai also published a collection of *Pièces fugitives* by Voltaire in 1773.[49] Almost half

---

48. Lehmstedt, *Struktur und Arbeitsweise*, p. 11.
49. This work is mentioned in a letter of 3 May 1773 from Springer in Erfurt (in NN 72), who was making the selection and overseeing the printing. It is not mentioned in Raabe's

of the French titles Nicolai published were translations from the German, which were presumably intended for both the local aristocratic and Huguenot markets and those in Russia and the Baltic region. The French translations of the 1769 and 1793 versions of Nicolai's own description of Berlin and Potsdam were directed at those many visitors to the city, whether from western or eastern Europe, who were more at home in French than in German. One of the few of Nicolai's German authors who preferred to write in French was Johann Christoph Wilhelm von Steck, whose essays of 1790 and 1794 on legal and political aspects of international commerce and navigation were probably directed at a European rather than a German audience in the first place.[50]

Latin titles (twelve in all, including reprints) were an insignificant factor in Nicolai's publishing, as befits a publisher more concerned with a general than a scholarly audience. Almost all of the Latin works he published were school texts. The three exceptions were two medical works, one of which was published simultaneously in German translation, and a 1787 ode to the late Frederick II, which was also accompanied by a German translation.[51] After 1790–94 the only Latin work Nicolai published was a new edition of a school grammar. Numerous studies emphasize the waning importance of Latin in the German book trade throughout the eighteenth century, but there is some disagreement over percentages, not surprisingly, given the difficulty of accurately estimating total German book production. While Johann Goldfriedrich sees the proportion of Latin books declining from 18.6 percent of total titles in 1765 to 13.6 in 1775 and 8.8 in 1785 and Rudolf Jentzsch gives figures of 27.68 percent in 1740, 14.25 in 1770, and 3.97 in 1800, Reinhard Wittmann

---

catalog. The Leipzig Easter Fair Catalog of 1773 lists only "Jean Hennuyer, Eveque de Lizieux, Drame par Mr. Voltaire 8º à Paris et à Berlin, en commiss. chez Fr. Nicolai," which was actually by Louis-Sébastien Mercier. *Bibliothèque Nationale. Catalogue générale des livres imprimés*, vol. 214, no. 2 (Paris, 1978).

50. *Essai sur les consuls; on y joint les traités de commerce et de navigation les plus récents comme aussi l'Ordonnance du Roi de France pour les consulats du Lévant, du 3me Mars 1781* (1790) and *Essais sur divers sujets relatifs à la navigation et au commerce pendant la guerre* (1794).

51. Johann Friedrich Meckel, *Tractatus de morbo hernioso congenito singulari et complicato feliciter curato*, translated by E. G. Baldinger as *Beschreibung der Krankheit des Herrn Leibarzt Zimmermann, und der dabey glücklich angewandten Operation und Cur*, and *Nova experimenta et observationes de finibus venarum ac vasorum lymphaticorum in ductus visceraque excretoria corporis humani, ejusdemque structurae utilitate*, both of which were published in Berlin in 1772; Johann Melchior von Birkenstock, *D. M. FREDERICI. II. Dem abgeschiedenen Geiste Friedrichs des Zweiten geheiligt* (Berlin, 1787).

more recently estimated that Latin titles still comprised 17.3 percent of the market in the early 1780s, or 10.7 percent without university and school texts.[52] Only in the period 1770–74 did Nicolai's publication of Latin titles approximate almost exactly the figure mentioned by Jentzsch, 14.25 percent, and this represents the highest percentage of Latin books the firm produced in any period. Otherwise Nicolai's Latin production was low when compared to any of these estimates. In the early 1780s, for example, fewer than 1 percent of Nicolai's titles were in Latin, compared to Wittmann's overall figure of 17.3 percent. Weidmanns Erben und Reich, also a very German-oriented firm, published 8.4 percent of its titles in Latin during the period 1748–87.[53] Even if we exclude, for purposes of comparison with Reich, those titles Nicolai published after 1784, Latin works represent a mere 5.59 percent of total titles. The figure for Nicolai in the years 1759 to 1794, the last year he published a Latin title, is 4.5 percent, or 2.2 percent over his publishing career.

Translations from the French and more particularly from the English were important factors in Nicolai's publishing program. The proportion of translations in Nicolai's list fluctuated greatly, from 23 percent of new titles in 1795–99 to less than 2 percent in 1805–11. Viewed as a proportion of total titles over the years, translations comprised nearly 12 percent of Nicolai's production. This was a far smaller percentage than the 48 percent of titles published by Weidmanns Erben und Reich (1745–87), but greater than the German average of 6.6 percent calculated by Goldfriedrich for the period 1765–85.[54] Over the years Nicolai published twenty-seven translations from the French and thirty-six from the English. While the number of translations from the French peaked in 1780–84, that from the English peaked in the decade of the 1780s and again in the second half of the 1790s. Translations reached a height of 22 percent of new titles in the years 1795–99. Translations from other languages were few: four from the Greek,[55] two from the Hebrew,[56] and

---

52. Goldfriedrich, *Geschichte des deutschen Buchhandels*, 3:305; Jentzsch, *Der deutsch-lateinische Büchermarkt*, p. 333; Wittmann, "Die frühen Buchhändlerzeitschriften," cols. 828f.

53. Lehmstedt, *Struktur und Arbeitsweise*, p. 11.

54. Ibid., p. 18. The figure of 6.6 percent for Goldfriedrich is an average of the three figures he gives for 1765, 1775, and 1785.

55. The 1762 edition of Xenophon, Köhler's 1778 *Iphigenia in Aulis*, a 1781 edition of the Greco-Egyptian theological-philosophical treatise *Poimandres*, attributed to Hermes Trismegistus, and F. H. Bothe's 1800–1803 translations of the works of Euripides.

56. Moses Mendelssohn's abovementioned translation of the Pentateuch and his 1787 treatise on the immortality of the soul.

one each from Arabic,[57] Italian,[58] Swedish,[59] Turkish,[60] and Old Frisian.[61] Nicolai also published several translations into foreign languages, including an edition of Carl Gottlieb Svarez and Christoph Goßler's layperson's guide to the new Prussian legal code for Polish-speaking Prussian subjects.

Numerically speaking, the most important categories of books on Nicolai's list were, in descending order, belles-lettres; theology; pedagogical works and school textbooks; science and mathematics; medicine; technology, military science, and agriculture; geography and travel; and jurisprudence and administration. Let us take a brief look at his production in some of these categories.

Although not known as a literary publisher, Nicolai published more literary titles than any other category of books. In comparison to Philipp Erasmus Reich, 36.5 percent of whose titles between 1745 and 1787 consisted of literary works, in Nicolai's firm such works made up only 15.2 percent of all new titles.[62] This was within the normal range for the period, according to Rudolf Jentzsch's figures of 13.37 percent for the Easter fair of 1770 and 16.5 percent for the Easter fair of 1800.[63] With one interruption in the second half of the 1780s, the number of novels Nicolai published rose consistently from the 1770s onward. Nicolai himself was his firm's most prolific novelist, so that the 1780s, when he abandoned fiction for historical studies and his travel account, coincide with a decline in numbers. The few novels and stories on Nicolai's list in

---

57. *Der Naturmensch, oder Geschichte des Hassan Ebn Yoktan*, Johann Gottfried Eichhorn's 1782 translation of Abu-Bakr Muhammad Ibn-Tufail's *Risalat Hajj Ibn Jaqzan*.

58. F. H. Bothe's 1798 translation of F. Grosse's essay on the Greek epigram.

59. A new edition of Johann Gottschalk Wallerius's *Mineralogie* in 1763.

60. *Gesandtschaftsberichte bey seinen Gesandtschaften in Wien im Jahre 1757 und in Berlin im Jahre 1763* (Berlin and Stettin, 1809), Joseph von Hammer-Purgstall's translation of Ahmed Resmi Efendi's account of his tenure as Ottoman ambassador to Vienna in 1757 and Berlin in 1763.

61. Tileman Wiarda's transcription and translation of the *Asega-Buch*, a collection of medieval legal texts.

62. It makes sense to speak of new titles here because the vast majority of literary works Nicolai published were first and only editions. Only *Sebaldus Nothanker* was successful enough to warrant multiple editions, although Nicolai did publish a new edition of Ludwig Heinrich von Nicolay's works out of friendship, as he said, although sales were extremely poor. See Nicolai to Elisa von der Recke, Berlin, 30 December (?) 1794, in NN 288. The figures on Reich are in Lehmstedt, *Struktur und Arbeitsweise*, p. 13.

63. Jentzsch, "Der deutsch-lateinische Büchermarkt," table 3.

the 1780s were all translations.[64] Novels and short fiction were most prominent in the period 1795–99 when they represented nearly 29 percent of all new titles. In 1800–1804, novels comprised some 14.3 percent of all new works Nicolai published. In 1780–84, in contrast, the period with the second largest number of novels, they made up only 7.6 percent of new titles. The particular prominence of novels in the late 1790s was not simply a peculiarity of Nicolai's firm. In this economically and politically difficult period Nicolai went over more and more to publishing novels he hoped, somewhat vainly as it turned out, would meet current tastes. These included books by the already-popular Johann Gottwerth Müller as well as translations from the English. Other publishers were apparently doing the same, and at Easter 1797 a special rubric for novels appeared for the first time in the Leipzig book fair catalog. In the 1800 Easter fair catalog novels made up a substantial 11.68 percent of all titles.[65] Nicolai's production thus lay somewhat above the trade-wide figures for the period around 1800. After 1804, however, he no longer published novels at all.

Poetry and drama were quantitatively less important in Nicolai's list than novels, reflecting their place in the book trade more generally.[66] They also represent a rather haphazard collection of titles, underlining Nicolai's waning taste for contemporary German literature. The largest number of poetic and dramatic works in any half-decade, five, was published in each of the periods 1759–64 and 1785–89. The first peak is accounted for by publication of the works of Salomon Geßner and Denis Diderot in French and Alexander Pope in English, the second by the comedies of the Empress Catherine of Russia (1788–89), a long (and long-forgotten) poem on the youth and visions of St. Blasius by the Braunschweig classicist and theologian Konrad Arnold Schmid (1786), and the 1788 "rational Christian poems" by the dramatist and theorist of

---

64. J. J. Cointreau's *Salamander, ein Liebhaber. Oder desto schlimmer für ihn* (1781, trans. Johann Daniel Kluge), *Der Naturmensch, oder Geschichte des Hassan Ebn Joktan. Ein morgenländischer Roman des Abu Dschafar Ebn Tofail* (1782, trans. Johann Gottfried Eichhorn), the anonymous *Fräulein Julie von Rosenbaum* (1785, trans. Karl Friedrich Trost), the *Straußfedern, oder Sammlung unterhaltender Geschichten*, a collection of translations and adaptations of French stories by Johann Karl August Musäus and Johann Gottwerth Müller (1787–98), and a late English addition to the Werther literature, William James's *Lottens Briefe an eine Freundinn, während ihrer Bekanntschaft mit Werthern* (1788, trans. W.F.H. Reinwald).

65. Jentzsch, "Der deutsch-lateinische Büchermarkt," p. 250.

66. See Lehmstedt, *Struktur und Arbeitsweise*, p. 14.

tragedy Johann Friedrich Schink. Nicolai's most important poetic author was his friend Ludwig Heinrich von Nicolay, whose collected works he published in 1778–86 and 1792–1810. Although he was keenly interested in the development of the German theater, the dramas he did publish were mainly by foreign authors. The only German dramatic authors Nicolai published were the eccentrics Johann Karl Wezel (*Die komische Familie*, 1780) and Christian Leberecht Heyne, who used the pseudonym Anton-Wall (*Die Expedition oder die Hochzeit nach dem Tode*, 1781, an adaptation of a French play).

Theological and religious works were at all times a significant component of Nicolai's list, but he published little scholarly theology, doubtless viewing the many reviews in the *ADB* to be sufficient contribution in this area. Not only were some of his closest friends and collaborators pastors, but like many other German *Aufklärer* he considered the pulpit one of the chief instruments for enlightening broad strata of the population, particularly those who could or did not read. Sermons were thus one of the most important genres among his theological publications. Devotional works and books for the religious education of children also played a central role in Nicolai's list.[67] More topical works were an anonymous critique of religious fanaticism and superstition, *Betrachtungen über Wunderglauben, Schwärmerey, Toleranz, Spott- und Predigtwesen* (1777),[68] Friedrich Germanus Lüdke's dialogues on the abolition of the clerical estate, with a consideration of whether it was beneficial or harmful to the state (1784), and Heinrich Corrodi's book on the famous and controversial Zurich theologian and author Johann Caspar Lavater (1786). The theological authors were mainly Lutheran pastors from Berlin and the surrounding region.[69] Theology was probably the most German

---

67. For example, Johann Samuel Diterich's *Unterweisung zur Glückseligkeit nach der Lehre Jesu*, which went into three editions (1772, 1776, 1781) and was also published in an abridged version (2 eds., 1774, 1782) or his hymnal for household devotions (1787).

Books for the Christian education of children included Diterich's *Entwurf zum Gespräch mit Kindern über die Hauptstücke der christlichen Lehre* (1787) and Georg Friedrich Treumann's *Unterricht in der christlichen Religion* (3 eds., 1783–1811) and *Katechisationen* (1787–88; 2d ed., 1805).

68. Paul Raabe attributes the pamphlet to Johann August Eberhard. He was, however, apparently not the sole author of this work, which was directed at least in part against the Zurich pastor J. K. Lavater. Nicolai and unnamed others also contributed. See the letters from J. E. Springer, who was supervising the printing of the work in Erfurt, to Nicolai, 23 and 28 April and 4 May 1777, in NN 72.

69. They included J. S. Diterich and G. H. Treumann, Raymund Dapp, Friedrich Germanus Lüdke, Jakob Elias Troschel, Johann Friedrich Zöllner, and Johann August Eberhard. Theological authors from outside Nicolai's Berlin orbit were Hermann Andreas Pistorius,

segment of Nicolai's production, with translations accounting for a miniscule proportion of all titles. After the 1759 translation of John Conybeare's 1732 defense of revealed religion against Mathew Tindal's deist *Christianity as old as the Creation*, Nicolai published only one further translation of an explicitly theological work, the Unitarian Joseph Priestley's liturgy and prayers for public worship among Christians of all denominations, including a preface on the in those days radical notion of ecumenical Christian worship (1786), although Thomas Amory's novel *Leben, Bemerkungen und Meinungen Johann Bunkels* (1778) was certainly treated by many (including the work's reviewer in the *ADB*), as a Unitarian tract.

While Nicolai's overall production reached its apogee in 1780–84 and declined steadily thereafter, the publication of new theological titles peaked, in absolute numbers, a half-decade later. It declined precipitously in the period 1790–94, remained constant in 1795–99, and dipped still further in 1800–1804, only to rise again in 1805–11. Thus while Nicolai brought out twenty-two new theological works in the 1780s, he only published eight in the years between 1790 and 1804. It does not seem far-fetched to see the explanation in the 1788 and 1789 Prussian edicts concerning religion and censorship and the ensuing severe crackdown on unorthodox theology in the 1790s, which will be discussed in more depth below. In 1792, Nicolai explicitly mentioned the prohibition on writing anything against the Lutheran church's "symbolic books" as his reason for postponing a new edition of his 1774 novel *Sebaldus Nothanker*, which criticized Lutheran orthodoxy and intolerance, among other things.[70]

In terms of relative production, the proportion of theological works fluctuated greatly, declining from some 25 percent of new publications at the beginning of Nicolai's career, in 1759–64, to 13 percent in 1765–69, when his attention was focused on the *ADB*, rising again to over 28 percent in 1770–74, only to fall to 8 percent in 1775–79. Percentages rose again to around 11 percent in 1780–84, then to 16 percent in 1785–89, then fell to some 7.4 percent in 1790–94. There was a slight increase to almost 9 percent in 1795–99. In 1800–1804 Nicolai published no new theological titles at all, but in the final years of his life, in 1805–11, they

---

pastor on Rügen Island; Johann Moritz Schwager, pastor in Jöllenbeck in northwest Germany; Johann August Hermes, pastor of St. Nicholas and consistorial councillor in Quedlinburg; and Heinrich Corrodi, professor of ethics at the Gymnasium in Zurich, all of them also *ADB* reviewers.

70. Nicolai to Uz, 12 May 1792, in NN 76. The new edition of *Sebaldus Nothanker* appeared in 1799.

again comprised over 20 percent of new titles. For comparison, Rudolf Jentzsch calculated that theological works made up 24.47 percent of all titles at the 1770 book fair and 13.55 percent in 1800.[71] In the earlier period, Nicolai's production—25.7 percent of total titles in 1770–74—approximated the German trend, but in later years it diverged markedly. In 1800–1804, theology made up a scant 2.13 percent of his total production, but in 1805–11 over 17 percent.

Surveying the theological titles that Nicolai did publish during the period of strictest censorship, 1790–94, we find that they were mainly sermons or other practically oriented works, rather than polemical or critical texts. Among these were new editions of works by two of Nicolai's most prolific theological authors, a fourth edition of Friedrich Germanus Lüdke's 1772 *Communionbuch* and a second edition of Georg Heinrich Treumann's explanation of the Lutheran catechism for the schools, both published in 1793. The new titles included Raymund Dapp's popular book of sermons, particularly for countryfolk and country pastors (6 vols., 1793–1806)[72] and Johann Moritz Schwager's 1792 sermon on the horrors of premature burial.

In both ideological and economic terms, pedagogical works and school books were a central element of Nicolai's publishing program from the very beginning. Nicolai began with a strong list of schoolbooks from his father's firm and, in the form of reprints and revised editions, they represented a mainstay of his own publishing program through the years. The publishing company was essentially aimed at the educated middle and upper classes, but certain works in the pedagogical realm, along with those in theology, sought to reach a wider audience. Although he did not publish books directly addressing the popular classes, Nicolai saw works directed at educating both pastors and schoolteachers, particularly those in the countryside, as an essential instrument in the struggle against superstition and ignorance. His travel account frequently lamented the abysmal state of the schools in various parts of Germany and Austria, particularly those for poorer children, pronouncing it "very sad to see the children of middling and commen men, who are not destined for [university] studies, and yet who represent the genuine components of the nation, almost everywhere so miserably taught."[73] The works of Friedrich Eberhard von

---

71. Jentzsch, *Der deutsch-lateinische Büchermarkt*, table 1.

72. According to Paul Raabe's catalog, the first three volumes of Dapp's sermons went through three editions each, p. 66.

73. Nicolai, *Beschreibung einer Reise*, 8:127.

Rochow, Georg Friedrich Treumann, and Friedrich Gabriel Resewitz, bearing titles such as "Attempt at a School Book for the Children of Country Folk, or Instruction for Teachers in Lower and Rural Schools" (*Versuch eines Schulbuchs für die Kinder der Landleute, oder Unterricht für Lehrer in niedern und Landschulen*), a work by the reform pedagogue Rochow that went into four editions between 1772 and 1810, were attempts to meet this need. Nicolai also published more general works on education, such as Ernst Christian Trapp's 1781 *Versuch einer Pädagogik*, and textbooks on all subjects, from Latin and French grammar to world history, epistolary style, and mathematics. Johann Joachim Eschenburg's very successful series of handbooks and anthologies, although not written strictly as textbooks, represent a coherent curriculum in literary and aesthetic studies for the academic schools, like Braunschweig's Carolinum where he himself taught, and the universities. The firm's only contribution to the popular new genre of literature specifically written for children, however, appears to have been the 1793 "New Pocketbook for Youth, or Anecdotes from the Childhoods of Famous and Good People," compiled by the Berlin pedagogues Johann Georg Philipp Müchler and Karl Friedrich Splittegarb.[74]

Educational works always comprised more than 10 percent of total titles at any given period, ranging from 11.5 percent in 1795–99 to 25 percent in 1805–11. They made up 9.6 percent of new titles, and 17.8 percent of total titles, over the years. While the early period saw mainly reprints of textbooks from his father's firm, Nicolai soon began to publish works by Prussian educational reformers. Local Berlin pedagogues also found a place on his list.[75] The firm published a journal for schoolteachers, the *Neue teutsche Schulfreund*, edited by Heinrich Gottlob Zerrenner from 1801 to 1814. Alongside German educational thinkers Nicolai also published a translation/edition (1781, by E. C. Trapp) of David Williams's *Treatise on Education*, which examined the methods used in Europe and more particularly England, considered the methods recommended by Milton, Locke, Rousseau, and Helvetius, and suggested a "more practicable and useful" approach, and a translation (1792, by F. E. von Rochow) of the Comte de Mirabeau's discourse on national education.

---

74. The book's German title was *Neues Taschenbuch für die Jugend oder Anekdoten aus der Jugendgeschichte berühmter und guter Menschen*. Splittegarb was director of a school in the Brüderstraße that Nicolai's son Carl August attended from 1778 to 1781. See his letters in NN 87.

75. These included Peter Villaume, Johann Albrecht Friedrich August Meinecke, Johann Georg Philipp Müchler, Johann Heinrich Ludwig Meierotto, and Friedrich Rambach.

Nicolai's increasing interest in practical reforms, heightened both by his voyage through Germany in 1781 and subsequent participation in discussions in the Mittwochsgesellschaft and by his ever-broadening circle of correspondents, fostered the diversification of his publishing program as it expanded in the 1780s. "Technology" was a new discipline in the second half of the eighteenth century founded by Johann Beckmann, professor in Göttingen and an *ADB* reviewer. It was, essentially, the study of the technical aspects of the crafts and manufactures. As a good *Aufklärer*, a public-spirited citizen, and an avid amateur gardener Nicolai took a keen interest in new inventions, scientific experiments, and the improvement of both agriculture and manufacturing on the basis of rational and scientific methods. One of the most important works Nicolai published in this eminently practical vein was Johann Karl Gottfried Jacobsson's *Technologisches Wörterbuch* (1781–84, supplements 1793–95), which will be discussed at some length below. Parts of Georg Simon Klügel's *Encyclopedia of Useful Knowledge* (3 eds., 1782–84, 1792–94, 1806–9) also fall into this category. Books on brewing, soapmaking, and dyeing took their place alongside those on forestry, navigation, land reclamation, horticulture, and sugar production. Many of these works were translations from the English. Among the home-grown products were the accounts by Prussian agricultural reformer Karl Friedrich von Benekendorf of his experiments in new methods of management and production on own estate (3 vols., 1781–84) and by the cameralist Karl August Nöldechen on the planting of and experiments with root vegetables for sugar extraction (3 vols., 1799–1803). The Berlin chemist Sigismund Friedrich Hermbstädt, who also reviewed for the *ADB* and translated chemical texts, provided works on dyeing, printing, and bleaching fabrics "on physical-chemical principles" for the instruction of local calico manufacturers, dyers, and bleachers and on the "science of soapmaking" for "soapmakers and housekeepers who wish to exercise this art with understanding."[76] These last two titles in particular, with their application of the terms "science," "rational," and "understanding" to dyeing and soapmaking, make clear the Enlightenment impulse to provide a new, more

76. *Grundriß der Färberkunst oder allgemeine theoretische und praktische Anleitung zur rationellen Ausübung der Wollen-, Seiden-, Baumwollen- und Leinenfärberey; so wie der damit verbundenen Kunst, Zeuge zu drucken und zu bleichen. Nach physikalisch-chemischen Grundsätzen und als Leitfaden zu dem Unterrichte der inländischen Kattun-Fabrikanten, Färber und Bleicher auf allerhöchsten Befehl entworfen* (2 eds., 1802, 1807) and *Die Wissenschaft des Seifensiedens, oder chemische Grundsätze der Kunst, alle Arten Seife zu fabriciren. Für Seifensieder oder Hauswirtinnen, welche diese Kunst verständig ausüben wollen* (1808).

scientific basis for all facets of human endeavor. The most popular, and largest, scientific work Nicolai published was *Natürliche Magie* (twenty volumes from 1779–1805). Begun by the Langensalza apothecary and chemical author Johann Christian Wiegleb (who wrote the first two volumes) as a collection of home experiments and demonstrations involving electricity, magnetism, optics, chemistry, and mechanics, the work was so successful that it went into a second edition and was continued at Nicolai's instigation by Gottfried Erich Rosenthal, who from 1789 to 1805 provided a volume almost every year, using the work as a vehicle for expounding upon the latest discoveries in physics and chemistry, thus teaching the reader basic science and parlor tricks at the same time.[77] As a Prussian patriot and friend to many officers, especially in his early years, Nicolai was also concerned with improvements in military science. The works he published in this field included one on the military applications of the recently invented hot-air balloon.[78] As a percentage of total new titles, works on technology and agriculture were most prominent in the periods 1780–84 and 1800–1804. Except for two early military titles and Johann Christoph Erich von Springer's 1771 statistical *Ökonomische und kameralische Tabellen*, with a preface on the fate of the cameral sciences, these fields were a new addition to Nicolai's list in the 1780s.

Travel accounts and geographical/statistical works were also very much a phenomenon of the 1780s and 1790s in Nicolai's list. Of the twenty-five new titles in these fields, twenty were published in those decades. Only three were published before 1780, and only one after 1800. It is probably no coincidence that Nicolai published the greatest number of travel accounts and works on geography, both physical and political, during the period when he was writing an account of his own 1781 journey through Germany, Austria, and Switzerland (12 vols., 1783–96). He was preoccupied with similar topics and problems and entertained correspondences with like-minded individuals, many of whom he met during his voyages. Interestingly, the great majority of travel accounts and geographical/statistical studies dealt with Europe, rather than more exotic locales. The exceptions were accounts by Aubry de Lamottraye of his journeys in the

---

77. John Ferguson, *Bibliotheca Chemica*, 2 vols. (London: Derek Verschoyle, 1954), 2:548.

78. The military works included two French works, Robert de Lo Looz's *Recherches sur l'art militaire, ou essai d'application de la fortification à la tactique* (1768) and a translation by a Prussian artillery officer of an anonymous 1773 essay on artillery, and Johann Karl G. Hayne's *Versuch über die neuerfundene Luftmaschine des Hrn. von Montgolfier, besonders in wie fern solche in der Kriegskunst eine Änderung machen und einem Staate nüzlich und nachtheilig seyn könne* (1784).

Near East (1781), Johann Christoph Wolf's of a journey to Ceylon (1782–84), and an excerpt from Captain Cook's voyages in 1776–80 (1794).[79] These works, though describing far-away and potentially romantic places, nevertheless reflected Nicolai's own chiefly practical interest in travel accounts; they were intended to be informative for the general public and for governments, not escapist literature or journeys of self-discovery.

This is also evident in the economic and/or scientific focus of most European travel accounts he published, whether they described German locales (e.g., Franz von Beroldingen's 1788 *Remarks on a Journey through the Quicksilver Mines of the Palatinate and Zweibrücken*) or other parts of Europe (e.g., Johann Andreas Engelbrecht's 1789 translation of James Anderson's account of the Hebrides and the west coast of Scotland, "chiefly containing recommendations on the improvement of fisheries and the prosperity of the land"). Other works dealt with current politics as much as geography. Johann Anton Ludwig Seidensticker's work on legal and political conditions in Italy and the Habsburg states, particularly Vienna (1792), and Karl Friedrich Trost's 1782 translation of Carlo Antonio Pilati di Tassulo's *Letters on the Present Situation in Holland* were examples of the kinds of political geography, then known as *Statistik*, which Nicolai published.

One of the most striking phenomena in the development of Nicolai's list is the very late appearance of books in the fields of law and administration. His father's firm had published the Brandenburg Criminal Code in 1717, but Nicolai himself showed little interest in matters of jurisprudence, aside from reviews for the *ADB*, until political and legal issues assumed a central place in Prussian public discourse in the late 1780s.[80] The crisis of leadership in Prussia after the death of Frederick II in 1786 intensified debate around political, administrative, and legal questions. The largely Prussian emphasis of the works Nicolai published in the field reflects this atmosphere. Strengthened contacts with Prussian officials in the Mittwochsgesellschaft and participation in debates there around the drafting of the new Prussian legal code were decisive personal factors as, perhaps, were the marriages of three of his children into the Prussian

---

79. It seems that the translator/editor added this excerpt chiefly in order to make the small astronomical/nautical work to which it was appended more appealing to the public. Kirchhof to Nicolai, Hamburg, 11 June 1793, in NN 38.

80. Jonathon Knudsen discusses this phenomenon for Germany more generally in the introduction to his *Justus Möser and the German Enlightenment* (Cambridge: Cambridge University Press, 1986), esp. pp. 7–11.

bureaucracy in the 1780s and 1790s.[81] Nicolai's main legal authors were, in fact, his fellow members of the Mittwochsgesellschaft, Ernst Ferdinand Klein (his son's father-in-law) and Carl Gottlieb Svarez, who were also among the drafters of the Allgemeines Preußisches Landrecht. Klein's major undertakings for Nicolai were the *Annals of Legislation and Jurisprudence in the Prussian States* (24 vols., 1788–1807) and the *Noteworthy Legal Opinions of the Halle University Faculty of Law* (5 vols., 1796–1802), but he also published a number of smaller mainly polemical and theoretical works.[82] Svarez and Christoph Goßler, also a member of the legal code commission, published three legal guides for laypersons, one on Prussian laws,[83] one on court procedures,[84] and one on law for businessmen.[85] In the last twenty years of his career Nicolai also published a number of legal and administrative handbooks for Prussian civil servants.[86]

Other characteristic areas of Nicolai's list, although numerically less significant, are also worth mentioning. The interlocking fields of history, biography, and works on Berlin and Brandenburg were all of particular interest to Nicolai. While his firm was known neither for the sweeping "pragmatic" histories we usually associate with Enlightenment historiography, nor for the philosophical history developed by Herder, Nicolai published a number of historically oriented works. He was himself an avid and ambitious amateur historian who burrowed through centuries of archives to write the introduction to his description of Berlin, a study of the Knights Templar (1782), and a cultural history of wigs (1801).

---

81. In 1788 Samuel Friedrich Nicolai married the daughter of the jurist Ernst Ferdinand Klein, his third son David married the daughter of Geheimer Oberfinanzrat Eichmann, and his eldest daughter Minna married Hofrat Friedrich Parthey, who was employed in the financial administration.

82. These included an account of the legal dispute between Voltaire and Abraham Hirsch (1790), "Three Essays on the Spirit of the Laws and Judicial Administration in the Prussian Monarchy" (1802), "On Extraordinary Punishments Owing to Incomplete Evidence and on Prisons" (1805), and "On the Legal and Judicial Advancement of the Peasant Estate, with reference to the Royal Prussian Edict of 9 October 1807" (1808).

83. *Unterricht über die Gesetze für die Einwohner der Preussischen Staaten von zwey Preussischen Rechtsgelehrten* (1793).

84. *Unterweisung für die Parteien zu ihrem Verhalten bei Prozessen und andern gerichtlichen Angelegenheiten, nach Anleitung der allgemeinen Gerichtsordnung für die Preußischen Staaten* (1796).

85. *Handbuch gemeinnütziger Rechtswahrheiten für Geschäftsmänner nach Anleitung des allgemeinen Gesetzbuchs entworfen* (1793), by Goßler alone.

86. These included Eberhard Julius Wilhelm Ernst von Massow's *Anleitung zum praktischen Dienst der Königl. Preußischen Regierungen, Landes- und Unterjustizkollegien und Justizcommissarien, für Referendarien und Justizbediente entworfen* (1792) and Carl Appelius's *Handbuch zur praktischen Kenntniß des Accisewesens, der Acciseverfassung und Accisegesetze von der Kurmark Brandenburg* (1800), among others.

Nicolai's other historical publications ranged from an essay on the history of the Crusades and their consequences (1780) to a study of feudal services in Franconia (1803). While Johann Matthias Schröckh's much-pirated textbook, *Lehrbuch der allgemeinen Weltgeschichte zum Gebrauche der ersten Unterricht der Jugend* (5 eds., 1774–95) was one of Nicolai's most popular titles, Justus Möser's *Osnabrückische Geschichte* (1780), was one of which he was particularly proud, even if it did not sell as well.[87]

The proper study of mankind being man, biographical and autobiographical works were a small but important component of the publishing program. Nearly all of the works Nicolai published were on his contemporaries or near-contemporaries. They ranged from the highly serious biography of the composer Handel by Dr. Charles Burney (1785) to the highly irreverent history of the private life of Louis XV (1781) attributed to Barthélemy-François-Joseph Moufle d'Angerville.[88] Nicolai himself contributed several essays on the lives, character, and works of his departed friends Ewald von Kleist (1760), Thomas Abbt (1767), Justus Möser (1797), Johann Jakob Engel (1806), Wilhelm Abraham Teller (1807), and Johann August Eberhard (1810), which Horst Möller has aptly characterized collectively as a "necrology of the *Aufklärung*."[89] Aside from the memoirs of the physician Melchior Adam Weickard (1784; 2d ed., 1787) and the English actor Tate Wilkinson (1795), Nicolai also published two interesting correspondences, Johann Joachim Winckelmann's letters to one of his closest friends during the years 1756–68 (with an appendix of letters to various other persons, 1781) and Gotthold Ephraim Lessing's correspondence with Karl Wilhelm Ramler, Johann Joachim Eschenburg, and Friedrich Nicolai, with some remarks on Lessing's correspondence with Moses Mendelssohn (1794).

Nicolai's collection of (historically corrected) anecdotes on Frederick II (1788–92) and his *Frank Remarks on Herr von Zimmermann's Fragments on Frederick the Great by Some Brandenburg Patriots* (1791–92) were critical

---

87. On Möser, see Knudsen, *Justus Möser and the German Enlightenment*.

88. According to Robert Darnton, the author of this work may also have been Arnoux Laffrey. *The Corpus of Clandestine Literature in France 1769–1789* (New York: W. W. Norton, 1995), p. 185.

89. On Nicolai as a biographer, see Möller, *Aufklärung in Preußen*, pp. 149–85. Although he did not publish it himself, Nicolai also wrote an "Ehrengedächtniß Ramlers," which is printed in the *Sammlung der deutschen Abhandlungen, welche in der Königlichen Akademie der Wissenschaften zu Berlin vorgelesen worden in den Jahren 1798–1800* (Berlin: Decker, 1803), pp. 1–8. He also wrote an introduction to the 1810 autobiography of the Berlin popular philosopher and academician Johann Georg Sulzer and published his own *Ueber meine gelehrte Bildung* (1799).

contributions to recent Prussian politics and history as well as to the explosion of Frederician literature after the king's death in 1786.[90] The works on Frederick bring together the fields of history, biography, and Brandenburgiana, as do the various versions of Nicolai's very popular description of Berlin, the *Beschreibung der Königlichen Residenzstädte Berlin and Potsdam* (1769, 1779, 1786, abridged editions 1793, 1799). Other works Nicolai published on Berlin and Brandenburg include Karl Wilhelm Hennert's description of the palace and gardens at Rheinsberg (1778), Carl Martin Plümicke's sketch of a history of theater in Berlin (1781), and Heinrich Ludwig Manger's architectural history of Potsdam, particularly under the reign of Frederick II (1789–90).

The Everyday Life of a Publishing Company

While Nicolai himself, aided by his authors and other friends, handled what modern parlance describes as editing and marketing, the physical production of books occurred at a further remove. Like most German booksellers of the period, Nicolai had no printing shop of his own. Nor did he have a single regular printer or paper supplier, so that the production of each book had to be negotiated anew. Here, as in other aspects of his business, authors, *ADB* reviewers, and other helpers played a vital role.

The Material Framework: Paper and Printing

Paper was an item of far greater concern to eighteenth-century printers and publishers than it was to their twentieth-century counterparts. It not only made up a higher proportion of production costs but was frequently difficult to procure in the necessary quantity, dependent as it was on weather conditions, water quality, and a steady supply of raw materials, particularly linen rags.[91] "The importance of paper manufactures and the paper trade is greater than commonly assumed," Nicolai noted in *Beschreibung einer Reise* (2:382), and the enormous sums spent by Germans on imported Dutch, French, and Swiss paper seemed to prove that Germany

---

90. More minor items of Fredericiana that Nicolai published after his death included a Latin ode by the Austrian statesman Johann Melchior von Birkenstock (1787), a memorial sermon (1786), and the Prussian army chaplain Karl Daniel Küster's "Letters on Various Character Traits of Frederick the Only" (1791).

91. The eighteenth century witnessed numerous attempts to produce paper from other more plentiful materials, such as straw, wood, and old paper, with some success, but the products were not of the quality necessary for writing and printing. For some examples, see Wisso Weiß, *Zeittafel zur Papiergeschichte* (Leipzig: VEB Fachbuchverlag, 1983).

needed more paper mills of her own. The printing and publishing boom only exacerbated the situation. In some regions, including Brandenburg, the shortage of high-quality rags and the sharp increase in demand from the burgeoning book trade encouraged papermakers to produce poor quality paper, since they could immediately sell anything they made for a good price (ibid., pp. 76–77).

The quality and availability of paper, particularly for the printing trade, was a subject of lively interest for all European governments in the eighteenth century. The case of paper manufactures well illustrates the inability of many absolutist states to enforce their mercantilist policies satisfactorily, as well as the limited effectiveness of the policies themselves in generating local prosperity. Paper shortages existed at one time or another in most countries, but the situation in northern Germany seems to have been particularly grave.[92] The paper industry, so essential to the book trade, was woefully underdeveloped in the Prussian lands throughout Friedrich Nicolai's career. Not only were the finer-quality (white linen or hemp) rags in short supply, but few paper mills were equipped with the newest methods and highly skilled workers.[93]

As a result, most Prussian publishers and printers had to import paper from abroad at great expense. Many booksellers, including Nicolai, chose to give their custom to non-Prussian printers, sending their manuscripts to neighboring German states such as Saxony where paper supplies were more plentiful, cheaper, and often of better quality. According to its own principles, the Prussian government could not help but be displeased with this state of affairs. Yet to critical observers, it appeared to consider the problem a mere bagatelle.[94] Although various measures were taken over the years to solve the paper problem there was little willingness to invest the capital necessary to put paper manufactures on a sound footing.

Essentially, there were three main tactics for supporting the domestic

---

92. Austria, for example, prohibited the export of rags in 1768 in order to ensure a supply for the domestic paper mills, and France took similar action in 1771. See Weiß, *Zeittafel*, pp. 190–91 and passim, on measures taken by various European governments to secure their paper supply.

93. Georgi, *Die Entwicklung des Berliner Buchhandels*, p. 101 n. 3. On this problem in (northern) Germany more generally, see Victor-L. Siemers, "Die Förderung der Papiermühlen durch Herzog Karl I. (1735–80) von Braunschweig. Ein Beispiel für merkantilistische Wirtschaftspolitik in einem deutschen Kleinstaat des 18. Jahrhunderts," *Leipziger Jahrbuch zur Buchgeschichte* 8 (1998): 79–113, esp. 79–81.

94. *Schattenriß von Berlin* (1788; reprint, Berlin: Berliner Handpresse, 1975), 2:31–32.

paper industry, and all were tried at one time or another with varying degrees of failure. These were the prohibition of the export of rags,[95] the prohibition of the use of foreign paper by domestic printers,[96] and the foundation of new paper mills which were intended to set a higher standard of quality and eventually make paper imports unnecessary altogether.[97]

The only really effective measure, but one that was a perfect example of "too little, too late" was the foundation in fits and starts of a paper mill at Spechthausen near Eberswalde in the 1780s. It was capable of producing paper to international standards but only in small quantities.[98] One successful venture could not solve the whole Prussian paper problem, though. In its 1780 recommendation to lift the ban on paper imports, the General-Ober-Finanz-Kriegs- und Domänendirektorium (generally known as the Generaldirektorium, which functioned as a department of internal, especially financial affairs) questioned the wisdom of this mercantilist initiative. The excise taxes generated by paper imports were not insignificant, and since Prussia could not produce the necessary paper, the import ban only served to take bread out of the mouths of Prussian printers and their workers. The fact that the increasing trade in books published in Prussia more than compensated for the sums spent on imported paper made it senseless to continue the ban.[99] Frederick II was convinced by this argument and agreed that imports of paper (except

---

95. On Prussian efforts in this area, see *Acta Borussica. Die Handels, Zoll- und Akzisepolitik Preußens 1740–1786*, vol. 3, pt. 1 (Berlin: Paul Parey, 1928), pp. 639–41. The government kept a close watch on rags until 1803 when, in the name of freedom of trade, the official rag-collecting districts were abolished. This did not solve the problem, and in 1805 a certain Herr Weber was using a report by Nicolai that he found in the archive of the Manufactur und Commerz Collegio as the basis for articles in the Berlin gazettes encouraging people not to waste linen rags. Weber to Nicolai, Berlin, 11 June 1805, in NN 80.

96. These prohibitions of paper imports were doomed to failure because there was not enough Prussian paper to fill local needs. In 1780, for example, local printers complained that the ban would only force Prussian publishers to send their manuscripts abroad to be printed. See *Acta Borussica*, vol. 3, pt. 1, pp. 640, 642–43; Weiß, *Zeittafel*, p. 180.

97. As early as 1756 the Department of Manufactures seems to have consulted a Swabian papermaker on the building and organization of paper mills in Prussia but no more serious efforts were made for twenty years. There was also the ever-popular tactic of offering a prize for the best paper produced by a Prussian mill. Such a contest was announced in 1765. See Weiß, *Zeittafel*, pp. 181, 187.

98. On the checkered history of this paper mill and other efforts to improve paper quality in Prussia, see *Acta Borussica*, vol. 3, pt. 1, p. 642; Weiß, *Zeittafel*, pp. 195, 200; and Hugo Rachel, *Das Berliner Wirtschaftsleben im Zeitalter des Frühkapitalismus* (Berlin: Rembrandt, 1931), pp. 184–85.

99. *Acta Borussica*, vol. 3, pt. 1, pp. 642–43.

from Bohemia) should be allowed until Prussian mills could fill the local demand.[100] Neither he nor Friedrich Nicolai lived to see that day.

The debate over how the state could raise its revenues from the book trade and keep money in Prussia continued after the death of Frederick II.[101] As became clear in discussions of paper imports, the Prussian paper shortage brought with it a second, related problem, that of printing abroad. A conflict of interest had arisen between Prussian printers and publishers. Whereas the former wished to see a prohibition on Prussian booksellers having their works printed abroad, the latter rejected the suggestion vehemently. On several occasions the Prussian government considered the possibility of requiring local publishers to print in Prussia. Each time, though, it came to the conclusion that the mercantilist advantages were outweighed by the possible harm to the book trade in the form of higher prices and vengeful actions on the part of foreign powers (most likely Saxony).[102] In June 1787, Friedrich Nicolai entered the fray with a long written testimony outlining his opinions on the subject of paper and printing problems in Prussia. It had all begun some six months earlier when Privy Secretary Friedrich Ludwig Joseph Fischbach suggested to King Frederick William II the establishment of new paper mills and a ban on printing abroad for Prussian publishers. The latter recommendation in particular met with sharp opposition when Fischbach's report was circulated to interested government departments, printers, and bookseller-publishers, and a lively discussion ensued. Minister of State Karl Abraham von Zedlitz expressed fears that books might become even more expensive if they could not be printed abroad, and that some authors might withdraw their works from Prussian publishers if they could no longer oversee printing and proofreading in their home towns. Berlin printers were so busy that they could take on no additional work. The best way to diminish printing abroad would be to encourage the establishment of new printing shops in small towns along the road to Leipzig by offering "special premiums, immunities and privileges."[103]

---

100. Ibid.

101. On the more general issue of conflicts over Prussian economic policy at this period, see Ingrid Mittenzwei, *Preußen nach dem Siebenjährigen Krieg. Auseinandersetzungen zwischen Bürgertum und Staat um die Wirtschaftspolitik* (Berlin: Akademie, 1979).

102. Georgi, *Die Entwicklung des Berliner Buchhandels*, pp. 102–3. A ban on printing abroad was considered in the years 1748, 1756, 1767–68, and 1787.

103. Freiherr von Zedlitz to the Generaldirektorium, 8 February 1787. All quotations in the following are from a manuscript copy in the Deutsche Bücherei: Deutsches Buch und Schrift Museum [hereafter cited as "DBSM"] in Leipzig, BöV Archivalien 95/2, of originals in the former Preußisches Geheimes Staatsarchiv (Tit. XXXI, Buchhandlung No. 1).

Fearing competition, the Halle printers vehemently rejected this suggestion. They sent along a table showing the number of presses standing idle in each of the eleven Halle printing shops—twenty-two out of a total of forty-three. Their own capacities should be exhausted, they argued, before any new printing shops were established. The printers saw several factors as responsible for their plight, which show nicely the interconnectedness of official policy and the various branches of the book trades: (1) fear of piracy caused publishers to prefer smaller editions, which meant less work for printers; (2) the strict censorship exercised by the University of Halle frightened off authors and publishers who otherwise might have printed there; and (3) some of the most capable printers were beginning to lose the desire to exercise their craft because of the threatened loss of their collective status and privileges, in particular exemption from military service.[104] The Halle printers received support from their provincial administration, which reiterated the printers' criticism of the "untimely and strict censorship" in Halle.[105] It also emphasized the contribution of the inflated prices of other materials in Prussia to high printing costs: Prussian type-foundries could scarcely be expected to match the low prices of their foreign rivals if they had to pay so much for iron, antimony, copper, lead, and bismuth.[106] The Prussian government would have to rethink its excise taxation as well as its censorship policies if the printing trade were to flourish.

Friedrich Nicolai was asked for the bookseller's view on Fischbach's controversial recommendations and answered at length. The points he made are worth quoting in some detail, since they tell us something about his own practice as well as his attitudes toward the problem. So far as the book trade was concerned, Privy Secretary Fischbach was an ignoramus who had no conception of the actual situation. Nicolai defended the good will of his colleagues to employ Prussian printers where feasible, but these were often not in a position to have books ready in time for the book fairs. He outlined the economic reasons why Prussian booksellers had to print abroad and the benefits the state derived from the present state of affairs:

1. Prussia produced less than one-third of the paper needed for printing. Most books were sold at the Leipzig fairs, however, and the costs of

---

104. Halle printers to the Prussian king, 26 March 1787, in DBSM, BöV Archivalien 95/1.

105. Years before, the cameralist J. H. G. von Justi had blamed the fact that the Halle printers did less business than those in Leipzig on the strict censorship there. Quoted in Goldfriedrich, *Geschichte des deutschen Buchhandels*, 3:412.

106. Magdeburg Kammer to the Prussian king, 10 April 1787, in DBSM, BöV Archivalien 95/2.

sending paper to Berlin and the printed books back to Leipzig were prohibitive. In the case of books such as school texts, whose price had to be kept low, high freight costs for paper ordered from distant mills could have a deleterious effect. Thus it was often necessary to print books in the vicinity of Leipzig or in towns where living costs and wages were lower than in Prussia and where the printers delivered postage-free to Leipzig.

2. Almost no Prussian printer could keep quantities of paper in stock because it was so expensive and difficult to procure. Especially around book fair time it was often impossible to find a Prussian printer with sufficient paper. One way to alleviate this situation would be to lift the ban on imports of Bohemian paper, which was one of the contributing factors in the shortage and inflated price of paper in Prussia. If the king were to reinstate the complete freedom of paper imports the number of printing shops would increase steadily, benefiting Prussian publishers. The establishment of more paper mills was also desirable, but experience showed that the shortage of rags was still a major obstacle.[107] Whatever it did, the government must not require publishers to print in Prussia. A prohibition on printing abroad would give an unfair advantage to the Saxons, "who would then have more liberties than we do." The Prussian booksellers, he asserted, constituted a substantial factor in Prussian foreign trade, even when they printed abroad. It was not true, as Fischbach maintained, that Prussian booksellers only bartered at the book fairs, and thus had to take money out of Prussia to pay foreign printers. Almost all Prussian publishers now also sold for cash at the fairs, and this "foreign" cash paid the "foreign" printers. With the books Prussian booksellers did take in exchange for their own products "we engage in lucrative trade with foreigners in Mecklenburg, Anhalt, Poland etc. and here, too, the state attains an advantageous balance through the book trade." His own business, like that of many Prussian booksellers, was mainly in other states. "Through these very laborious efforts, which are supported by the freedoms granted to the book trade by Your Majesty, we enrich the country as far as our trade extends, increase the revenues of the Royal Post and ourselves amass fortunes which we could not amass from our compatriots alone."[108]

In keeping with the statements in his 1787 report, Friedrich Nicolai's firm employed at least twenty-six printers in Berlin and eleven other

---

107. Nicolai also suggested that the government might investigate Schäffer's method of making paper from plants grown on sandy wasteland.

108. Report of 27 June 1787, in DBSM, BöV Archivalien 95/2.

cities over the years.¹⁰⁹ Compared to correspondences with authors, editors, and prenumeration collectors, those between Nicolai and printers and especially papermakers are rather thin. This may be attributed in part to the opportunities for personal meetings between Nicolai and printers at the Leipzig fairs. Many authors also sent or took their manuscripts directly to the printing shop, with some of them negotiating with printers and overseeing the printing process on Nicolai's behalf. Thus he may have been somewhat less directly involved in the production process than he was in other facets of the publishing business. In those cases where the author insisted on reading the proofs personally, the printer's proximity to the author's home was a decisive factor. As Nicolai emphasized in his reply to Fischbach, places of printing were generally chosen on the basis of their convenience to Leipzig, though, because the printed sheets were usually dispatched first to the book fair and only later to Berlin. As Nicolai remarked in 1785 when his friend Friedrich Gabriel Resewitz asked him to give some work to the Widow Pansa in Magdeburg, whose presses were standing idle, Magdeburg was too inconvenient to Leipzig unless an author specifically requested that his work be printed there.¹¹⁰ A Herr Will in Darmstadt, whom Nicolai hired to print a book in 1789, had previously worked only for Frankfurt and Heidelberg publishers and had no experience in organizing freight to Leipzig. Thus Nicolai had to arrange for transport through one of his Frankfurt colleagues, reason enough not to print in Darmstadt again.¹¹¹

The availability of adequate supplies of appropriate type, and more important, of the sort and amount of paper required, preferably at a low price, were also very significant considerations when choosing a printer. With paper the most expensive and variable element in production costs, Nicolai might prefer to pay more for printing if the printer had access to cheaper paper.¹¹² Each printing shop had its own local paper suppliers, so

---

109. Nicolai's printers included Christian Ludwig Kunst, Christian Müller, Petsch, Johann Friedrich Unger, Friedrich Vieweg, and Winter in Berlin; Christian Friedrich Solbrig and Ulrich Christian Saalbach in Leipzig; C. P. Franke, Johann Jacob Gebauer, Grunert, and J. G. Heller in Halle; Johann Chr. Görling and Josef Jacob Friedrich Straube in Erfurt; Fickelscher and Johann Michael Mauke in Jena; Rudolf A. W. Ahl in Coburg; Johann Georg Rosenbusch in Göttingen; Peter Elias Schirach in Rudolstadt; Carl Christian Dürr, Carl Gottfried Giese, and Chr. Wilhelm Melzer in Wittenberg; C. S. Ife in Weissenfels; Christoph Günther and Johann Georg Müller in Schleusingen; and Will in Darmstadt.

110. Nicolai's annotations on Resewitz to Nicolai, Kloster Bergen, 1 October 1785, in NN 60.

111. Klipstein to Nicolai, Darmstadt, 30 November 1789, in NN 39.

112. In his annotations on a letter of 7 July 1789 from Friedrich August Müller, who was overseeing the printing of his poem *Richard Löwenherz* in Halle, Nicolai records that the paper

that it was usually the printer rather than Nicolai who ordered paper. Not all printers enjoyed good credit with papermakers, however. Christoph Günther in Schleusingen, for example, who for many years printed the *ADB*, could only buy paper when Nicolai's friend Albrecht Georg Walch co-signed the bills of exchange.[113] A lack of credit made it very difficult to order well in advance, the prerequisite for ensuring a steady supply of paper.[114]

Nicolai's delegation of responsibility for overseeing printing to authors or other intermediaries is particularly striking in the case of the *ADB*, whose appearance was made possible only by the unflagging efforts of a few loyal correspondents who paid the printing shop and often the paper mill as well, saw to the proofreading, kept Nicolai informed when problems arose, and conveyed his desires and concerns to the printers. Throughout the periods 1765–92 and 1801–6, the *ADB* represented Nicolai's chief printing problem. As a large periodical project whose publication could not simply be postponed until the next book fair if paper was unavailable or the printer or proofreader too busy, parts of the *ADB* were usually printed in more than one place at any given time. Of course, this caused some confusion, and those correspondents who supervised the printing understandably tried to convince Nicolai to have all the work done in a single shop.[115] It was also a matter of local patriotism to attract and keep a large, steady commission like the *ADB*, and Nicolai's agents saw themselves under considerable pressure to maintain his custom. As Walch reported from the Thuringian town of Schleusingen in 1777, when Nicolai had temporarily stopped printing there, "There are people who are firmly convinced that it is up to me whether the *ADB* continues to be printed here. People in high places have also intervened and are asking me to give this work, if at all possible, to the local printer Müller."[116]

Nicolai apparently entertained some hope of locating a truly reliable printer for the *ADB* but never managed to find all the necessary qualities

---

the printer Grunert offered was very expensive (18½ taler per bale at 2 taler 4 groschen printing costs) and that they would have done better to accept Hendel's higher printing fee of 2 taler 16 groschen, since his paper only cost 15 taler per bale. See also Müller's letter of 24 June 1789 laying out the printers' initial offers, in NN 51.

113. Walch to Nicolai, Schleusingen, 25 (?) November 1782, in NN 79.
114. Walch to Nicolai, Schleusingen, 27 January 1776, in NN 79.
115. Walch to Nicolai, Schleusingen, 15 November 1775, in NN 79, and Springer to Nicolai, Erfurt, 20 April 1777, in NN 72.
116. Walch to Nicolai, Schleusingen, 11 October 1777, in NN 79.

in one place.[117] Nine printers in the towns of Schleusingen, Erfurt, Coburg, Wittenberg, and Weissenfels participated in the production of the *ADB* over the years.[118] The firms seem to have been chosen chiefly for their cheapness, convenience to Leipzig, availability at the necessary times, and the presence of a correspondent who was willing to oversee the work for Nicolai. Quality was secondary. In fact, some of them caused a good deal of trouble over the years through incompetent proofreading,[119] slow or slovenly distribution,[120] lack of credit with papermakers, or various forms of dishonesty such as charging Nicolai extra for proofreading but not paying the proofreader.[121] The image of printers in the letters of those Nicolai correspondents—chiefly Walch in Schleusingen and Springer in Erfurt—who oversaw printing for him is of poor devils begging for work, plagued by disloyal employees, hypersensitive to any criticism, beset by creditors, and thus constantly harassing authors or other intermediaries for payment. "[Josef Jacob Friedrich] Straube and his journeymen bombard me daily with requests for money," wrote Springer in 1773.[122] Nicolai could consider himself fortunate that he did not have to face most of these people personally, except for occasional stand-offs at the Leipzig fair. His loyal helpers, on the other hand, might see the printers almost daily, plying them with cash advances for the papermaker and listening to their endless complaints about illegible manuscripts, last-minute corrections, or problems with journeymen such as the typesetter who quit in disgust after three weeks of working nights, including Sundays, to get out an issue of the *ADB*.[123] Springer even gave Straube's journeymen little presents "to keep them cheerful, but only when the work is finished."[124] For his part, Nicolai kept abreast of the progress of

---

117. In 1776, for example, Nicolai had written to his friend Wilhelm Heinrich Bucholz in Weimar for information about Peter Elias Schirach in Rudolstadt as a potential *ADB* printer. Nothing seems to have come of this, despite Bucholz's favorable reports. Bucholz to Nicolai, Weimar, 23 January 1776, in NN 11. Schirach did print several works for Nicolai in later years.

118. Rennsperger (later Günther) and Müller in Schleusingen; Dürr, Giese, and Melzer in Wittenberg; Straube and Görling in Erfurt; Ahl in Coburg; and Ife in Weissenfels.

119. Letters from Walch in Schleusingen regarding Dürr in Wittenberg, 28 June 1785 to Samuel Friedrich Nicolai, and 21 April 1787 to Friedrich Nicolai, in NN 79.

120. Nicolai's note on Walch to Nicolai, Schleusingen, 28 November 1783, in NN 79, regarding Günther in Schleusingen, and Walch to Nicolai, Schleusingen, 3 October 1785, in NN 79, on negligent distribution by the other *ADB* printers. Walch also complained that Dürr in Wittenberg was a very poor packer. Walch to Nicolai, Schleusingen, 27 December 1786, in NN 79.

121. Walch to Nicolai, Schleusingen, 2 September 1775, in NN 79.

122. Springer to Nicolai, Erfurt, 21 January 1773, in NN 72.

123. Walch to Nicolai, Schleusingen, 30 September 1780, in NN 79.

124. Springer to Nicolai, Erfurt, 4 May 1773, in NN 72.

his publications through his correspondents and occasional letters from the printers themselves. When he was particularly interested in a work, he had the printer send him the page proofs directly.[125] When it came to his own novels, or those whose appearance was particularly important to him, such as works by friends (e.g., Ludwig Heinrich von Nicolay's *Vermischte Gedichte*, Heinrich Gottfried von Bretschneider's novel *Georg Waller*), or Friedrich Heinrich Bothe's translation of Euripides, he oversaw production himself, choosing good and expensive printers like Johann Friedrich Unger in Berlin who possessed a collection of handsome fonts and the contacts and wherewithal to purchase high quality paper. In Unger's case, at least, Nicolai was generous with advances, either in the form of cash or allowing him to write a bill of exchange in Nicolai's name,[126] and in 1802 Unger expressed warm gratitude for Nicolai's support of his business over the years, and his "benevolent conduct."[127] There was a definite hierarchy of printing shops, and the printers knew it. Christoph Günther in Schleusingen, for example, had no such flattery for Nicolai and complained that he was only good enough when other printers were too busy to take on work.[128]

Nicolai had frequent occasion for dissatisfaction with his printers, and they with him. Excessive typographical errors and poor proofreading were his chief complaints. In 1772, for example, Nicolai addressed some sharp words to the Erfurt printer Straube regarding flagrant departures from a manuscript, and ordered him to reprint large sections of the work. These accusations had deeply wounded Straube, Nicolai's Erfurt correspondent Springer reported. Straube was as innocent as a babe in arms, the victim of an author who could not tell the difference between the dative and accusative and a proofreader who had corrected his Berlin dialect in some cases but not in others. What were the poor typesetter and proofreader to do, "who ... know no German but High German?"[129]

Just as Nicolai chided his printers, so they expressed their annoyance with him and his authors for the execrable state of many manuscripts. In 1776, for example, Rudolf Ahl in Coburg found the index to the *ADB* appendix so hopelessly muddled that he had to stop printing and coax

---

125. Examples were E. F. Klein's *Annalen der Preußischen Gesetzgebung* and G. S. Klügel's *Encyklopädie*. Gebauer to Nicolai, Halle, 12 January 1793, in NN 24.
126. Unger to Nicolai, Berlin, March 1786 and 29 March 1787, in NN 87.
127. Unger to Nicolai, Berlin, 12 June 1802, in NN 87.
128. Walch to Nicolai, Schleusingen, 27 December 1786, in NN 79.
129. Springer to Nicolai, Erfurt, 22 November 1772, in NN 72. When Straube fell seriously ill soon thereafter, his employees blamed it on the shock of having to reprint the book! Springer to Nicolai, Erfurt, 10 December 1772, in NN 72.

his proofreader into checking it against all twelve volumes of the journal. Carl Christian Dürr in Wittenberg reported that the manuscript of Jacobsson's *Technologisches Wörterbuch* was so confusing that his typesetters were threatening to quit. He also had to raise their wages twice before they would consent to work further on the *ADB*.[130] Even the manuscript of Nicolai's own book on the Knights Templar was chaotic, as he had made frequent additions and changes, and the Berlin printer Christian Ludwig Kunst complained that "each correction cost my typesetters as much effort as if they had had to set the text anew."[131]

The acquisition of paper was the thorniest production problem Nicolai and his helpers faced, though, and one that they never managed to solve satisfactorily. The paper dilemma involved two problems: payments and local paper supplies. In 1773, Johann Gustav Dauling in Schleusingen wrote that since lack of paper had been the main cause of disorder in producing the *ADB*, he had decided to help both Nicolai and the printer Rennsperger by contracting with a good local papermaker, a certain Herr Schwarz, to provide prompt delivery of paper for regular cash payments.[132] When the printer failed to pay the papermaker on time, however, they had a falling out, and the presses stood still for weeks until the printer found another, inferior, paper source. Both Dauling in Schleusingen and Springer in Erfurt (who oversaw the work of the printer Straube) appear to have had difficulty getting regular cash payments in order to pay the local printer and lay in a stock of paper.[133] Why it was so difficult to keep steady sums of money flowing to the papermakers is unclear. One problem was that cash transfers themselves could be difficult. Nicolai sometimes used his bookseller colleagues to pay printers, but apparently they were often negligent.[134] These examples underline the

---

130. Ahl to Nicolai, Coburg, 29 August 1776, in NN 1, and Dürr to Nicolai, Wittenberg, 8 March 1781 and 14 February 1782, in NN 15.

131. Kunst to Nicolai, Berlin, 14 August 1782, in NN 42. Unger, too, cited problems with his employees because of Nicolai's works. They were so upset at having to reset numerous pages of the travel account that only assiduous wheedling and extra pay—costs that had to be passed on to Nicolai—had showed any effect. Unger to Nicolai, Berlin, 4 June 1795, 2 and 9 February 1796, and 20 January 1797, in NN 87.

132. The papermaker required such regular cash payments in order to pay for rags. Johann Georg Dauling to Nicolai, Schleusingen, 1 May and 26 June 1773 and 29 January and 20 April 1774, in NN 14.

133. Springer to Nicolai, Erfurt, 30 January 1773 and 5 January 1774, in NN 72.

134. As Walch reported in 1779, the bookseller Carl Wilhelm Ettinger had placed him in an unpleasant situation by not paying Günther the money from a bill of exchange made out to him as promised. Günther had already told various creditors that he would soon have cash and pressured the unfortunate Walch for the money, since he was accustomed to dealing with him. Walch to Nicolai, Schleusingen, 24 November and 18 December 1779, in NN 79. Ettinger sent

interconnectedness of all branches of the book trade. If the booksellers did not pay their debts on time, the printers did not get their money and could not pay the papermakers, who could not buy rags. Certainly, the fact that Nicolai used so many printers and papermakers made it difficult to build up solid relations with any one mill, and the overseeing of the production process by several individuals in different towns made it harder to maintain an overview.

Nicolai was no friend of luxury papers, but neither was he wholly indifferent to quality. He was dedicated to relatively low prices both for the prevention of piracy and the accessibility of books to a wide range of customers, but when he used grayish papers it was also a concession to the difficulty of acquiring good paper. As he said of the paper for his travel account, "It was difficult enough to find paper as uniform as I did. For such a large work it is truly impossible to find a sufficient quantity of good paper unless one was able to collect it several years before."[135] He frequently complained of the nonuniformity of paper for the *ADB*, but again, the problem could only have been solved by purchasing paper in advance, since the Schleusingen mills only produced to order. The printer Günther could not afford to pay in advance, so that he was unable to keep paper in stock and had to take whatever was available at printing time, although he *did* give the journeyman at the mill little presents to ensure that they used better rags.[136]

Even with ready cash, however, paper was not always available when and where it was needed. In 1788, the Rudolstadt printer Peter Elias Schirach complained to Nicolai that "paper is becoming ever dearer ... and despite advance payments and begging one seldom receives the number of bales ordered." Fortunately he always made sure to lay in a good supply, otherwise "I would often share the fate of many printers hereabouts and have to buy paper sheet by sheet and bale by bale."[137] When the weather was bad, production slowed or stopped altogether. "Our paper mills have been under water for several weeks and could not work

---

part of the money in December, apparently at an unfavorable exchange rate. In 1781, Ettinger was again behind in his payments, and Walch suggests that his thirst for social prestige caused him to spend his money on other things first. Nicolai also had problems with payments to the Darmstadt printer Will via Frankfurt booksellers, as the author Philipp Engel Klipstein, who organized the printing of his own works, reported in 1790. Klipstein ended up advancing the money to the printer himself. Klipstein to Nicolai, Darmstadt, 12 September 1790, in NN 39.

135. Nicolai to Lüdke, Berlin, 18 May 1783, in NN 60 [Resewitz correspondence].
136. Walch to Nicolai, Schleusingen, 14 March 1781, in NN 79.
137. Schirach to Nicolai, Rudolstadt, 18 July and 25 August 1788, in NN 66.

at all," reported Walch from Schleusingen in February 1783. In order to keep the presses running, he had helped the printer Günther to buy paper from elsewhere, at a higher price and lower quality than usual.[138]

When Nicolai did want better-quality paper, presumably for presentation or authors' copies, it came from abroad. In 1777 he requested and received samples of fine Dutch paper from his correspondent Theodor Gülcher in Amsterdam, and in the 1790s the Berlin printer Unger ordered paper from Basel for the new edition of L. H. von Nicolay's works.[139] Nicolai may also have used the services of paper merchants for some printing projects. The correspondence, at any rate, contains a communication from the Hamburg firm of Haupt & Grisson which accompanied samples of French and Dutch papers, noting that they kept all sorts of English, French, Dutch, and German papers in stock. "Through our close connections with many mills we are in a position to provide the fairest prices and we believe that we may claim with justification that it is not easy to equal us," they assured him, adding that various Berlin publishers and printers would give a good account of their services.[140]

Considering all the trouble Nicolai encountered during the production process, both with printers and with the acquisition of paper, it may seem strange that he never acquired his own printing shop. To be sure, other large German publishers, such as Weidmanns Erben und Reich, also farmed out their printing work. Reich, however, had almost all of his books printed in Leipzig, where he could oversee the process personally, if necessary, and avoid the costs and risks of transportation.[141] Nicolai

---

138. Walch to Nicolai, Schleusingen, 8 February 1783, in NN 79. The winter of 1784/85 was also wet, and the paper mills again fell behind. Günther to Nicolai, Schleusingen, 22 December 1784, in NN 28. Too much frost rather than too little could also cause problems; on 30 December 1774 the Coburg printer Rudolf Ahl had reported that the local paper mills were all frozen in and he had had to buy paper wherever he could find it. He was now almost out of paper. "But who can command nature?" he notes philosophically, in NN 1. Similarly, when J. J. Eschenburg ordered paper for his latest book at Nicolai's request, the local Braunschweig paper mill refused, pleading unfavorable weather conditions and too many orders. Eschenburg to Nicolai, Braunschweig, 15 January 1782, in NN 19. Nicolai noted that they would have to print the book in Wittenberg or Halle, where he had printers with paper and good proofreaders. Nicolai to Eschenburg, Berlin, 12 February 1782, in HAB, no. 41.

139. Gülcher to Nicolai, Amsterdam, 9 July 1777, and Unger to Nicolai, Berlin, 18 May 1793, in NN 59 [Ramler correspondence]. The paper from Basel was held up for some time because of French obstruction of traffic on the Rhine, which necessitated the use of slower overland transport.

140. Haupt und Grisson, paper merchants in Hamburg, to Nicolai, 13 August 1788, in NN 30. The Berlin firms mentioned in the letter are Voß, Decker, Vieweg, Pauli, Siegmund, and Schlecker.

141. Lehmstedt, *Struktur und Arbeitsweise*, p. 45.

could doubtless have afforded to buy a printing shop, but despite several offers never did so. Johann Erich Springer, who oversaw the printing of the *ADB* and other works in Erfurt in the early 1770s, suggested in 1773 that Nicolai open a printing shop there. Several were available at modest prices of a few hundred taler and he received assurances that the governor or *Statthalter* would support the project.[142] A few years later, Johann Gottlieb Stöckner, who had printed the *ADB* in Rennsperger's Schleusingen shop for five years, informed Nicolai that the shop was up for sale for 5–6000 taler. Stöckner, who had since worked in the famous shops of Johann Gottlob Immanuel Breitkopf in Leipzig and Johann Christoph Dieterich in Göttingen, suggested that Nicolai buy the Schleusingen shop and hire him to run it, citing the town's advantages of lenient censorship, low rents and prices for other necessities, easy access to Leipzig, good and cheap paper (if one had the ready cash), and surrounding villages full of wagoners who transported goods all over Germany.[143] The prospect of potential savings on printing costs and of "greater correctness and beauty of printing"[144] was apparently not enough to convince Nicolai to add printing to his publishing business, however, and he continued to muddle along.

Marketing: Advertising and Subscription

While modern publishing companies have special departments for marketing, eighteenth-century booksellers depended upon their own personal efforts and those of their friends to make titles known to the public. Larger works and more particularly those published by subscription called for genuine marketing campaigns, which included a combination of advertisements in newspapers and journals, distribution of leaflets through the book trade, *ADB*, and friendship networks, and the petitioning of powerful individuals. Book catalogs, newspaper and journal advertisements and reviews, announcements of related titles at the back of books, advertising brochures sent to private individuals and booksellers, and the judicious distribution of free copies of books to strategic and influential people were the methods, then as now, that booksellers employed

---

142. Springer to Nicolai, Erfurt, 21 January 1773, in NN 72.
143. Stöckner to Nicolai, Göttingen, 2 August 1777, in NN 73.
144. Letter of 5 February 1793 from an anonymous printer in Berlin who said that he had learned the trade in his uncle's shop, then perfected his skills in Vienna, Prague, Leipzig, and Berlin, in NN 2. Nicolai's author Carl Martin Plümicke, who had bought a printing shop in Sagan but no longer had time to run it, offered it to the publisher for ca. 1700 taler. Plümicke to Nicolai, Sagan, 22 October 1794, in NN 58.

most frequently to make their publications known, entice the public to buy them, and tell them where and how to acquire the books in question. The power of personal persuasion was also put to good use in the case of pre-paid subscriptions or "prenumeration," where the publisher or author employed collectors in different regions to drum up financial support among their friends and neighbors for a book that none of them had ever seen.[145]

As the publisher of influential and widely read journals, Nicolai was well placed to disseminate information about his own publications and other books he offered for sale. The *ADB* printed his subscription brochures as well as notices of new books and special offers.[146] A less common advertising method at that time, and one that Nicolai apparently only adopted in later years, was to print ads at the back of books.[147] Hoping to reach beyond the readership of his own publications, Nicolai also advertised in numerous other journals, newspapers, and *gelehrte Zeitungen*. Here he was aided by his large network of correspondents all over Germany who placed advertisements or reviews for him in their local periodicals, saving him time and postage. The line between an advertisement and a review could be extremely fine, since advertisements sometimes quoted reviews (as, of course, they still do today), and most reviews merely noted the work's contents. When Johann Hermann

---

145. For a discussion of the rewards and perils of research on subscription, see Reinhard Wittmann, "Subskribenten- und Pränumerantenverzeichnisse als Quellen zur Lesergeschichte," in his *Buchmarkt und Lektüre im 18. und 19. Jahrhundert*, pp. 46–68.

146. One such notice, announcing reduced prices, was headed "Nachricht: Der Buchhändler Friedrich Nicolai in Berlin, erbiethet sich von itzt bis zur Ostermesse 1766 inclusive folgende nützliche Bücher, den Bücherliebhabern um sehr billige Preise, und zum Theil um die Hälfte des bisherigen Verkaufspreises gegen baare Bezahlung in wichtigen Louisd'or a 5 Rthl. gerechnet, oder in Münzen von gleichen Werth zu verlassen." Printed in *ADB* 1, no. 2 (1765) and 2, no. 2 (1766). Another, titled "Verzeichniß der Bücher welche Friedrich Nikolai Buchhändler in Berlin und Stettin auf seine Kosten hat drucken lassen oder bey ihm in Menge zu haben sind," was printed in the *ADB* 86, no. 1 (1789): 286–310. The list contained older works as well as new; copies of the "Berlockenbücher" from the period of the Seven Years' War were still available, for example.

147. Arriving at the end of the 1809 *Des türkischen Gesandten Resmi Ahmet Efendi Gesandtschaftliche Briefe*, for example, the reader finds a notice of three other works from Nicolai's firm chosen to appeal to devotees of Prussian politics: Johann Wilhelm Lombard's *Materialien zur Geschichte der Jahre 1805, 1806 und 1807* (also available in French), Friedrich von Bülow's *Bemerkungen, veranlasst durch des Hrn. Hofraths Rehberg Beurtheilung der Königlich Preußischen Staatsverwaltung und Staatsdienerschaft*, and Heinrich Wilhelm Heerwagen's *Anleitung zur richtigen Kenntniß der Preußischen Staatswirtschaft. Veranlasst durch die Schrift des Herrn Hofraths Rehberg zu Hannover*. All were offered either unbound or, for an additional 2 groschen, in paper wrappers (*geheftet*).

Stöver, editor of a Hamburg newspaper, asked Nicolai to send in reviews of his own publications in order to ensure their prompt appearance, he asked that they be as concise as possible because the newspaper public "merely desires brief information on the existence and content of a book."[148] The German word *Anzeige*, which today indicates an advertisement, was used fairly interchangeably with *Rezension* to mean a book review, while an advertisement was generally called either an *Ankundigung*, *Bekanntmachung*, or *Avertissement*.

The regional dissemination of newspaper and journal advertisements for Nicolai's publishing company was broad but still focused on the northern and central regions of the German-speaking world and those other areas where he had good contacts, such as Switzerland and Vienna. Thus at one time or another Nicolai's publications were advertised, among other places, in the newspapers of Altona, Braunschweig, Erfurt, Erlangen, Frankfurt am Main, Göttingen, Gotha, Greifswald, Hamburg, Hanau, Leipzig, Magdeburg, Mannheim, Mitau, Nordhausen, Schaffhausen, Vienna, Wesel, and Wittenberg as well as in important journals such as the *Teutsche Merkur* and the *Deutsches Museum*.[149]

The distribution of free copies could also be part of an advertising strategy. For example, when Nicolai sent Prussian Minister for Silesia Karl Georg Heinrich von Hoym a copy of Jacobsson's *Technologisches Wörterbuch*, the latter wrote back asking the price of this "useful book" and informed the publisher that "in order to make this good work more generally useful in this province" he had ordered the Silesian departments of war and finance (Kriegs- und Domainen-Cammern) and the local magistrates and finance bodies to purchase the book for their own internal use. Nicolai continued to send Hoym gifts, including the supplements to the *Technologisches Wörterbuch*, which the minister also recommended for acquisition.[150] Similarly, Eschenburg suggested that it would help promote his *Handbuch der klassischen Litteratur* if Nicolai were to send a copy to Minister von Zedlitz; "perhaps he will have the book introduced as a school text, which could greatly benefit sales."[151] The addressees did not

---

148. Johann Hermann Stöver to Nicolai, Hamburg, 23 February 1796, in NN 73.

149. For citations of the correspondents in various cities who placed advertisements for Nicolai in local papers and journals, see Pamela Selwyn, *Philosophy in the Comptoir: The Berlin Bookseller-Publisher Friedrich Nicolai 1733–1811* (Ann Arbor: Michigan: University Microfilms, 1992), chap. 6, nn. 312-31.

150. Karl Georg Heinrich von Hoym to Nicolai, Breslau, 16 May 1785, 20 March 1793, and 29 August 1795, in NN 87.

151. Eschenburg to Nicolai, Braunschweig, 9 June 1783, in NN 19.

even have to be illustrious personages, but only individuals with influence in their own circles. When Nicolai sent his *ADB* reviewer and faithful helper, the Schleusingen school director Walch, a copy of Schröckh's *Allgemeine Weltgeschichte* in 1775, Walch replied "I will try to get it introduced here instead of the silly Zopf, although such a change is always difficult." Nicolai noted in the margin, "I wish it for the good of the young," but he doubtless wished it for financial reasons as well.[152]

Direct petitions to persons in power were also common. In June 1793, Nicolai contacted Minister Karl August von Hardenberg in Ansbach regarding the distribution to various government agencies of Svarez and Goßler's guide to the new Prussian legal code. In August, Hardenberg assured Nicolai that the necessary steps had already been taken in the Franconian provinces to recommend the acquisition of this work to "civil servants, magistrates and the clerical estate."[153] Nicolai also used his authors' influence to promote their works. He asked Ernst Ferdinand Klein to see to it that Großkanzler Heinrich Casimir von Carmer in Berlin recommended acquisition of the *Annalen der Preussischen Gesetzgebung* to the Prussian provincial administrative bodies (*Regierungen* and *Landeskollegien*), whether in his official capacity or by private letter. Nicolai also wanted to be able to refer publicly to Carmer's recommendation in order to further promote the work. Nicolai, Klein, the latter's collaborator Eisenberg, and apparently Svarez as well put their heads together about whom else they might contact in other cities to get the work adopted for more government offices.[154] In the case of Klügel's *Vernunftkenntnisse*, a school book, the author applied to the school authorities (Oberschulkollegium) in Halle to suggest the book for use in the higher grades. He also sent copies of the book, accompanied by letters, to various men with influence over the schools. Klügel also drafted the formal petition that Nicolai then submitted.[155]

Prepaid subscription was an extremely popular method among both publishers and self-publishing authors in the last quarter of the eighteenth century. The subscriber paid the requested price to a collector appointed by the author or bookseller and received a receipt that could later be

---

152. Walch to Nicolai, Schleusingen, 19 July 1775, in NN 79.
153. Hardenberg to Nicolai, Ansbach, 12 August 1793, in NN 30.
154. Klein to Nicolai, Berlin, 14 July and 21 October 1787 and undated, and Nicolai's marginal annotations on the first, in NN 39.
155. Klügel to Nicolai, Halle, 26 February, 12 March, 14 May, 11 June, and 25 June 1791, in NN 40.

redeemed for a copy of the book. According to Reinhard Wittmann, at the height of its popularity between 1770 and 1810, at least one-sixth of advertised works were sold by this method.[156] The exact number of books Nicolai published by prenumeration is unclear, but the figure is probably smaller than the one Wittmann gives. Nicolai collected money for at least fifteen titles in advance of their publication. Twelve were published in the period 1778–88 and three thereafter.[157] Many of the titles were multivolume works, which were particularly costly to produce because large quantities of paper had to be ordered and paid for in advance in order to assure a sufficient and uniform supply. Others, like the novel *Johann Bunkel* or J. E. Bode's map of the world, were rendered expensive by the costs of engraving and printing the plates. The smaller works, such as sermons, were presumably directed at audiences who might not learn of the work unless addressed directly, such as country parsons who could not afford to buy journals regularly and often lacked access to reading clubs or lending libraries. Thus "prenumeration" for the publisher might mean opening up new markets as well as securing the capital for paper and printing costs.

The subscription process involved the collaboration of four parties: authors, publishers, subscribers, and collectors. The last were either booksellers or friends of the author or publisher. They acted as additional intermediaries in the literary process, organizing a more or less broadly dispersed patronage system within an increasingly anonymous book market. In Nicolai's case, the *ADB* was the prime recruiting ground for collectors and, alongside the bookshops themselves, an effective network for distributing subscription leaflets. At one time or another, though, Nicolai called upon most of his friends and authors to solicit subscribers. From Schaffhausen to Stockholm they pleaded and persuaded, hoping to

---

156. "Subskribenten-und Pränumerationsverzeichnisse," p. 51. Perhaps the figure of one-sixth is high for the book trade as a whole, because books printed by (pre-paid) subscription were more likely than others to be advertised in the journals?

157. The works included only one novel (Thomas Amory's *Johann Bunkel* in 1778), four religious works (J. A. Hermes's and R. Dapp's sermons in 1781 and 1787, G. F. Treumann's *Katechisationen* in 1787/88, and H. Corrodi's *Versuch Über Gott, die Welt und die menschliche Seele* in 1788), three legal works (E. F. Klein's *Annalen der Preußischen Gesetzgebung* [1788–1807] and *Merkwürdige Rechtssprüche der Hallischen Juristen Facultät* [1796–1802], and Massow's *Anleitung zum praktischen Dienst* [1791]), Nicolai's travel account (1783–97) and history of the Knights Templar (2d ed., 1783), Klügel's *Encyklopädie* (1781–83), Jacobsson and Rosenthal's *Technologisches Wörterbuch* (1781–84, 1793–95), J. E. Bode's map of the world (1781), J. J. Ferber's *Physikalisch-Metallurgische Abhandlungen* (1780), and K. D. Küster's *Briefe eines preußischen Feldpredigers* (1791).

find seven "prenumerants" in order to earn an eighth bonus copy for themselves. Thus they had the satisfaction not only of promoting useful knowledge and helping their friends but also of a small emolument. Particularly efficient collectors could turn the free copies into a tidy little income by selling them.

Subscribers also benefited in several ways. They received the book earlier than those who purchased it from the shops, and at a lower price, and had a chance at good illustrations before the copperplates were worn out. They could also appear publicly as patrons of the arts and sciences, with their names printed for all present and future readers of the book to see, which might or might not boost their status, depending upon the work itself and local habits.

Once a publisher or self-publishing author had decided to print a work by subscription, an advertising leaflet was printed up and sent around to booksellers and other potential collectors as well as to journals and newspapers to be printed in full or as an excerpt. Advertisements were generally divided into two sections. In the first, the author gave a more or less detailed sketch of the work, often also describing his aims in writing it and the intended audience. In the second, Nicolai briefly laid out the practical conditions of subscription: when the work was expected to appear, how many volumes it would contain, the price, when payment was due, how subscribers could get their copies, and some description of the paper, typeface, and illustrations if any, as well as the conditions for collectors.

In the case of Georg Simon Klügel's *Encyklopädie*, for example, the author, a professor in Helmstedt, began by explaining that the idea for the book had come from a once-useful but now outdated work on Nicolai's list. He intended to produce a completely new work, suited to the new age, from which unlearned (*ungelehrte*) readers could gain an up-to-date overview of the branches of scholarship and knowledge to aid them in self-tuition. He emphasized that the work could also be useful to scholars interested in fields outside their own and for the instruction of the young "in order to make them aware at an early age of various useful facts, to accustom them through the method applied to order, clarity and precision of terms, and also to provide them with an overview which will aid in their future study of the individual parts." He then proceeded to give an outline of each of the work's fifteen sections, which covered topics ranging from Linnaeus's system of classification to physiognomy, ethics, and German grammar. Despite this breadth, he hoped to keep to four alphabets (96 sheets or 1536 pages) in two large octavo volumes, with sixteen plates at the most, including a new map of the world. Nicolai added a brief note on the size of the work, the typeface and (good quality white) paper, and the price, 1 ducat or 2 taler 20 groschen *Conventionsmünze*, a considerable savings over the projected shop price of 4 taler–4 taler 8 groschen.[158]

The potential advantages to subscribers notwithstanding, by the late 1770s at the latest readers had begun to grow suspicious of this method of publication. Many publishers promised books and then delivered them after only five or six years, by which time many subscribers had lost their payment slips. Others never published the books at all. People were also annoyed to find that the books they had subscribed to were being sold in the shops for the same price or even less. In Copenhagen, Nicolai's correspondent reported, prenumerants had also been outraged when a publisher sent them water-damaged copies. A collector who had recruited twenty subscribers had also never received the free copies he had earned. Given these experiences, he said, no one in the city was interested in either collecting or subscribing anymore.[159]

The novelist and *ADB* reviewer Johann Karl August Musäus accused Nicolai himself of promising more than he delivered and disappointing the public. Advertising leaflets all too often offered buyers "the raptures of Paradise ... and when they subscribe they receive nothing but rubbish ... and are deceived in a displeasing manner, as the prenumerants to [Klopstock's] *Gelehrtenrepublik* and *Bunkels Leben und Meinungen* experienced."[160] The complaint that the books could often be had for the

---

158. Printed in *Buchhändlerzeitung auf das Jahr 1781*, no. 13.

159. Carsten Niebuhr to Nicolai, Copenhagen, 2 December 1777, in NN 53. Similarly, a certain Möller in Greifswald told Nicolai that experiences with Wieland's and Klopstock's prenumeration projects had turned people there against the practice. Möller to Nicolai, Greifswald, 28 April 1778, in NN 50. Other collectors who complained of the distaste for prenumeration included Johann Beckmann in Göttingen (9 March 1781, in NN 3), Walch in Schleusingen (25 November 1782 and 8 February 1783, in NN 79), and J. E. Springer in Bückeburg (16 March 1783, in NN 72).

160. Musäus to his niece Amalie Gildemeister, late summer 1778, quoted in Barbara Maria Carvill, *Der verführte Leser: Johann Karl August Musäus' Romane und Romankritiken*, Canadian Studies in German Language and Literature, no. 31 (New York: Peter Lang, 1985), p. 288 n. 3. Around the same time, the novelist Johann Timotheus Hermes also railed against *Bunkel* in a letter to Daniel Chodowiecki: "Nicolai must be a sorceror if he gains Germany's forgiveness for having besmirched us with Bunkel, a book so unutterably dull and badly written that even the ever-popular demolition of religion could not lend it any interest." Hermes to Chodowiecki, 31 July 1778, in Daniel Chodowiecki, *Briefwechsel zwischen ihm und seinen Zeitgenossen*, ed. Charlotte Steinbrucker, vol. 1, *1736–86* (Berlin: Carl Duncker, 1919), p. 223.

prenumeration price in the shops was also justified; Nicolai himself even went so far as to offer the *Technologisches Wörterbuch* to any Brandenburg cleric at the prenumeration price long after the prenumeration period was over.[161] Equally well founded were complaints that books appeared years late, or in more volumes, and thus at far greater expense, than had been announced. A relatively harmless example was Klügel's *Encyklopädie*, which appeared in three instead of two volumes and was completed two years late.[162] Jacobsson's *Technologisches Wörterbuch*, which grew from the announced two volumes to four, plus four supplements, was a more serious instance. Nicolai's travel account, admired as it was by many, became notorious both for boring many subscribers with its dry recitals of statistics and for outgrowing its original plan by many volumes. Reinhard Wittmann echoes contemporary complaints in his characterization of Nicolai's advertising leaflet as arrogant and irresponsible toward a public with high expectations of a work from the author of *Sebaldus Nothanker*. Not only did he do nothing to make his book sound particularly enticing, believing his name to be advertisement enough; he also left open the number of volumes and the time when they would appear, which was particularly inexcusable from an experienced publisher.[163] The more charitable interpretation of Nicolai's relentlessly dry, matter-of-fact advertisement is that, having been violently attacked two years earlier for overpraising the novel *Johann Bunkel*, he now intended to leave himself open to no such criticisms. However convinced Nicolai was that his travel account would contribute to national self-knowledge among Germans, "since one part of Germany is still little known in the other," he avoided any too-rapturous tone in announcing this. A work which Nicolai originally supposed might comprise six to eight volumes, with two appearing at each book fair, grew to twelve volumes over a period of fourteen years. From the beginning, Nicolai promised prenumerants only that they could have each alphabet (24 sheets or 384 pages) for a fixed price of 14 groschen *Conventionsmünze*, plus engravings at an unnamed "reasonable" price with delivery postage-paid to Berlin, Stettin, or Leipzig. Upon the completion of the work, he would settle with subscribers based on the

---

161. Uz to Nicolai, Ansbach, 29 January 1789, in NN 76.
162. When the work grew to three instead of two volumes, and was delayed, Klügel and Nicolai notified the prenumerants through the journals, apologized, explained the reasons for the delay and announced an as yet unnamed supplementary payment for the third volume. *Buchhändlerzeitung auf das Jahr 1782*, p. 219, and *Buchhändlerzeitung auf das Jahr 1783*, pp. 247–49.
163. Wittmann, "Die frühen Buchhändlerzeitschriften," cols. 892–94.

number of sheets he had published. He promised, and actually delivered, the first two volumes at the Easter fair of 1783.[164] This arrangement seemed perfectly fair to him, and he became distinctly sensitive to criticism of it in later years. From 1787 on he no longer accepted prenumerations for the work, which had grown to eight volumes, with no end in sight. He explained to subscribers in the preface to volume 8 that since he could no longer promise to deliver the next two volumes on schedule (volume 10 did not appear until 1795!), he would wait until he was ready to print to announce his readiness to accept pre-payment, or even merely send copies to subscribers after the book fair at the prenumeration price. He would also refund money to the impatient. Contrary to what some malcontents might think, he noted defensively, he had given good value for money, not charging prenumerants at all for the twenty-five-and-a-half sheets of polemic that he had incorporated into the travel account. He had actually provided more, rather than less, than initially promised, at least in quantity, and hoped that people would thus agree that they had no right to complain![165] Nicolai's defensiveness, expressed in exact calculations of the number of sheets he had sent his subscribers to date, was a partial answer to the travel account's numerous critics, the first and most vociferous of whom had been the Viennese author Alois Blumauer. Like Wieland's Bunkeliads of the late 1770s, Blumauer's 1783/84 pamphlet launched a double attack on both Nicolai's ideas (particularly his anti-Catholic and anti-Austrian bias) and his publishing practices.[166] Nicolai answered, however, as a publisher only. He had fulfilled his promises, vague though they were, and felt that he owed his subscribers no more.

Despite such disappointments and the public's increasing reluctance to pay in advance for books they had not seen, prenumeration campaigns could still be successful. People in Berlin or other large cities might consider it laughably provincial to collect prenumerations, or to ask one's friends to subscribe, but those elsewhere might be all too happy to see their names in print or to support the work of an admired author.[167]

164. Leaflet dated 24 Herbstmonat (September) 1782.
165. *Beschreibung einer Reise*, 13:xxiii.
166. *Prozeß zwischen Herrn Friedrich Nikolai, Buchhändlern in Berlin, an einem, dann denen 797 Pränumeranten, die auf besagten Herrn Nikolai neuesten Reisebeschreibung für baares Geld vornhinein bezahlten, andern Theils. . . . Allen Buchhändlern, die auf so eine Art reich werden wollen, zum schrecklichsten Beyspiel theilweis herausgegeben* (Leipzig [=Vienna], 1783–84).
167. As early as 1773, Nicolai had remarked upon Berliners' reluctance to subscribe. Nicolai's annotations on a letter of 9 June 1773 from Johann Christian Wolf in Vienna, who was trying to

When the Ulm bookseller Konrad Friedrich Koehler sent in four subscriptions for Raymund Dapp's sermons in 1786, he asked Nicolai to make sure that the names appeared on the subscription list printed in the book.[168] Some people were willing to lend their cash but not their names to a controversial work. Baron Franz Karl Kresel von Guatenberg in Vienna, for example, subscribed to Nicolai's travel account but asked that his name be left off the printed list. "You know, my dear fellow, how this worthy man seeks to avoid any sensation," wrote Nicolai's Austrian lawyer Bernhard Samuel Matolay.[169]

Enthusiastic and influential local collectors could work wonders. At the instigation of Nicolai's friend and reviewer Bretschneider, then university librarian in Ofen, *ADB* reader Gabriel von Pronay managed to get sixteen of the nineteen Protestant pastors in his jurisdiction in rural Hungary to subscribe to Johann August Hermes's sermons. Bretschneider and Pronay devised a campaign that included sending an advertising leaflet accompanied by a Latin letter to each of the pastors.[170] One can imagine their sense of flattery at such attention, unlikely as they were to have been overrun with subscription offers, and the feeling of belonging to a community of reformist theologians stretching to Berlin and beyond. Even in the smallest Hungarian hamlet they could be patrons in a small way of enlightened Protestantism.

There are works that, by virtue of the sensational topic or the author's fame, all but sell themselves. Nicolai's travel account had been one of these. There are others whose desirability is less obvious, and thus has to be established through dedicated advertising. Jacobsson's *Technologisches Wörterbuch* belonged to the second category. The subject matter was, as one correspondent put it "not for many," and the author a rather obscure, noncommissioned officer who had published only one previous book.[171] Nicolai campaigned successfully to have the *Technologisches Wörterbuch* adopted for Prussian government offices. He also made good use of the

---

enlist Nicolai's aid in collecting pre-paid subscriptions for a book on dual-column bookkeeping published by Trattner, in NN 83. A 1784 article in the *Berlinische Monatschrift* also remarks upon this phenomenon, saying that it had long been considered ridiculous in good society to carry around subscription leaflets, and no sensible person did so anymore. Cited in Wittmann, "Subskribenten- und Pränumerationsverzeichnisse," p. 66.

168. Konrad Friedrich Koehler to Nicolai, Ulm, 20 September 1786, in NN 42.
169. Matolay to Nicolai, Vienna, 19 March 1783, in NN 48.
170. Pronay to Nicolai, Atsa, 17 December 1781, in NN 58; Bretschneider to Nicolai, Ofen, 12 April and 29 December 1781, in NN 9. Hermes was Consistorialrat in Quedlinburg.
171. Uz to Nicolai, Ansbach, 16 September 1780, in NN 76.

pages of the *ADB* and of his reviewers' network, as well as advertisements in other journals, such as the Hamburg *Buchhändlerzeitung*,[172] and personal letters to many friends. Nicolai asked Johann Peter Uz in Ansbach "to make Jacobson's [sic] dictionary as widely known as possible. It is a useful work, which however is causing me much expense."[173] Georg Forster in Kassel, whom he had sent a batch of prenumeration notices, requested an additional twenty to thirty copies to distribute. The book sounded most promising, and "I would be glad to earn a copy."[174]

The book's addressees were, as the author said "not only ... scholars ... but also ... people who as yet know nothing whatsoever of the subject, and are thus desirous to learn."[175] The work was indispensable for the "cameralist, merchant, manufacturer, and mechanic," boasted an announcement for the supplements in the *ADB* (109, no. 1 [1792]: 309). Gottfried Erich Rosenthal, the author of the supplements, also hoped to reach "jurists ... town councillors, civil servants and practical men of affairs of all kinds."[176] As a contribution to the formalization of craft knowledge and terminology, making them more transparent to outsiders—particularly government officials bent on improving and encouraging manufactures—the work, or at least the prenumeration campaign, seems to have been more successful at reaching officials than artisans. At a subscription price of 1 ducat per quarto volume, the work was probably too expensive for most craftsmen and the only artisan subscribers listed as such were a surgeon in Durlach, two apothecaries in Riga and Bernburg, a tanner in the canton of Berne, and a leather manufacturer in Breslau. Two printers, in Halle and Schleusingen, and a bookbinder in Anclam may have been ordering either for themselves or for customers. The 365 names listed as prenumerants to the *Wörterbuch* also include numerous merchants, military officers, mining overseers, pastors, teachers, professors, physicians, and government and court officials of all descriptions, among them a certain "Herr Geheimerath Göthe [sic] in Weimar," subscriber number 207. The bulk of people subscribed from volume 1 on, with 33 joining the list in volume 2, 10 each in volumes 3 and 4, 22 in volume 5, and 65 in volume 6. The twelve (mainly minor) crowned heads

---

172. The twelve-page subscription notice, written in two parts by the author and publisher, was printed in the *Buchhändlerzeitung auf das Jahr 1780*, pp. 239–50.
173. Nicolai to Uz, Leipzig, 26 April 1780, in NN 76.
174. Forster to Nicolai, Kassel, 3 April 1780, in NN 22.
175. Author's preface to *Technologisches Wörterbuch* (Berlin: Nicolai, 1781–84), 1:14.
176. Preface to *Technologisches Wörterbuch*, supplements, 5:viii.

who prenumerated[177] were joined by 241 other individuals and a number of corporate subscribers[178] as well as 31 government and municipal offices all over the Prussian provinces and beyond.[179] Despite the usual reluctance of Berliners to subscribe, the major center in this case was Berlin (24 copies,) followed at some distance by Lübeck (9), Mitau (8), Bayreuth (8), Hannover (8), Breslau (7), Bernburg (7), and Gotha (7). Copies were sent abroad as far as Milan and St. Petersburg. Fourteen booksellers dispersed across north-central Europe prenumerated a total of twenty copies,[180] so that most people appear to have subscribed via collectors rather than the regular book trade. From the standpoint of publishers, prepaid subscription was mainly a way of financing large or expensive projects, and of reaching specially targeted audiences. For readers, however, it was not merely a means of access to crisper illustrations or lower prices. It also gave them a more personal connection to the world of literature or learning, and in small towns and villages in particular, it was connected to a wider sociability around books.

The Editorial Process: Advisers, Editors, and Proofreaders

Professional (copy) editors are a relatively recent phenomenon in the publishing business, but we can trace their roots to those numerous members

177. The princes of Hohenlohe-Langenburg, Hohenlohe-Kirchberg, and Hohenlohe-Neuenstein, the crown prince of Hohenlohe-Schillingsfürst, the markgräfin of Baden, Dowager Duchess Amalia of Saxe-Weimar, Duke Carl-August of Saxe-Weimar, Prince Heinrich, the abbot of Fulda, Prince August of Saxe-Gotha, Prince Friedrich Erdmann of Anhalt-Köthen, and Duke Friedrich August of Braunschweig-Lüneburg.
178. These included the Litterarische Gesellschaft, Stadtbibliothek, and Kommerzbibliothek in Hamburg; the princely library in Gotha; the Electoral library in Dresden; and the libraries of the University of Ofen, the Philanthropin (a reform-pedagogical boy's school in Dessau), the Kloster Bergen school near Magdeburg (where Nicolai's friend Resewitz was abbot), the school in Buchsweiler, the St. Nicholas Church in Stettin, the Physikalische Gesellschaft in Zurich, the Oberlausitzsche Gesellschaft in Görlitz, the masonic lodge Zu den drey Degen in Halle, and the office of the *Deutsche Zeitung* in Gotha.
179. Copies went to Berlin and nearby Spandau, Marienwerder, Minden, Beeskow, Elbing, Gumbinnen, Neumarkt, Treuenbrietzen, Aschersleben, Bellgardt, Demmin, Filse, Ober-Glogau, Lenzen, Löbechun, Oderberg in the Neumark, Osterburg in the Altmark, Reichenbach, Soest and Wetter in Westphalia, Salzwedel, Stendal, Küstrin, Gotha, Gorz, Stettin, Dresden, Gleiwitz, Darmstadt, Buchsweiler, Blankenburg, Karlsruhe, Hannover, and Magdeburg.
180. The booksellers included Abraham ter Meer in Krefeld, Voß, Hesse, and August Mylius in Berlin (2 copies each); Orell, Geßner, and Füßli in Zurich (4 copies); Heinrich Steiner in Winterthur, Varrentrapp und Wenner in Frankfurt am Main, and Friedrich David Wagner in Marienwerder (3 copies each); Weingand und Köpf in Pest; M. J. Bauer in Nuremberg; Isaac van Cleef in The Hague; Lanx in Bachy; A. D. Sellschor's Widow und P. Huart in Amsterdam; and Johann Friedrich Korn Senior in Breslau.

of the republic of letters, who, paid and unpaid, performed many of the same tasks. While Philipp Erasmus Reich, for example, depended heavily on a group of literary advisers,[181] Nicolai usually made his own decisions on whether or not to publish manuscripts. On an informal level, though, Nicolai's reviewers, friends and authors formed a network of advisers and literary assistants. They recommended manuscripts and authors, edited for grammar and style, supervised printing in their towns, and took on the tedious task of reading the final proofs when the author could not do so. Much of this work was done free of charge, at most for a copy of the book in question. It was apparently a normal part of membership in the republic of letters and the society of *Aufklärer*.[182] Sometimes these friends and helpers were hired specifically to do a job and were paid for their services, however.

Nicolai did occasionally submit potential works to authors or friends for their opinion before deciding whether or not to publish.[183] In at least two cases, Nicolai used the more regular services of an adviser, in both cases for popular literary works. Wilhelm Heinrich Brömel, a playwright who worked at the Forestry Department in Berlin and reviewed for the

---

181. See Lehmstedt, *Struktur und Arbeitsweise*. Another Leipzig publisher, Adam Friedrich Böhme, submitted potential manuscripts to "an aged antiquary, who summer and winter presided at an open bookstall at the corner of the Grimmaer- and Ritter-strasse" for his opinion. As Perthes informed a correspondent, "All the MSS. that he receives are submitted to the old antiquary, and then whether they treat of the three bread-earning studies—reading writing or arithmetic, or of mathematics, philology, paedagogy, farriery, or polite literature, if the oracle declares 'it will do,' the thing is settled ... does he say, 'it will not do,' it is as certainly rejected." Clemens Theodor Perthes, *Memoirs of Frederick Perthes*, 2 vols. (Edinburgh: Constable, 1856), 1:18 and 20.

182. Wolfgang von Ungern-Sternberg speaks of these activities as part of the prehistory of the editorial profession (*Lektorat*). "Schriftstelleremanzipation und Buchkultur im 18. Jahrhundert," *Jahrbuch für internationale Germanistik* 8 (1976): 80.

183. One such case was a plan for a collection of minnesongs submitted to him by a Dr. Johann Ludwig Kulmus in Danzig. As he explained to J. J. Eschenburg, whose advice he solicited, such a collection was unlikely to be lucrative because of the small audience. On the other hand, if some of the songs really were unpublished, he might decide to go ahead, "for the sake of a good cause." He asked Eschenburg for a sort of reader's report, setting down his views (anonymously if he preferred) on a separate sheet of paper which he could send on to Kulmus. Nicolai to Eschenburg, Berlin, 14 January 1788, in HAB, no. 76. He never published the work. Eschenburg also submitted his opinion regarding a translation of V. Knox's *Practical Treatise on the methods of acquiring useful and polite learning* when Nicolai was considering publication in 1787. The English teacher Friedrich Ernst Ruhkopf in Neu-Rüppin encouraged Nicolai to publish the work and offered to translate and edit it himself if Eschenburg was not interested. Ruhkopf to Nicolai, Neu-Rüppin, 26 October 1787, in NN 64. Once Ruhkopf had actually read the book, though, he agreed with Eschenburg that it would need too much revision for a German audience. Ruhkopf to Nicolai, 26 October, 19 November, and 31 December 1787, in NN 64.

ADB, read plays and novels for Nicolai in 1785 and 1786. His acerbic remarks are reminiscent of the scathing, short *ADB* reviews of trivial literature. Of one comedy he remarked, "Its poetic value is so slight that one must seek it with a lantern, and still one finds nothing."[184] Similarly, in the late 1790s, the translator Friedrich Heinrich Bothe read English novels for Nicolai and suggested which were worth publishing and had good sales potential. Nicolai often followed his advice. In 1797, Nicolai gave him *Man as He Is*, a novel by Robert Bage, a member of William Godwin's circle, to read. Bothe thought it worth translating and went to work.[185] *The Orphan*, on the other hand, contained scarcely eight or ten passable sheets, he said, and thus was not worth their trouble. Nicolai continued to solicit his opinion of English novels, and he returned another two in 1798. *The Little Family*, by Charlotte Sanders, director of a girls' boarding school in Bath, was "written not without knowledge and feeling, quite natural and unadorned, and yet pleasing." The nuances of some of the children's characters betrayed the observant teacher. As a whole, however, it was not up to the standard of "our better books for children." Nicolai decided to publish it anyway. A novel referred to simply as *Fragments* evoked nothing but scorn. "The man must have a curious idea of the Manner of Sterne [English in the original]. Almost everything trivial, frosty, forcedly witty and ... garrulous." Bothe cited a passage to show just how pretentious and badly written it was: "O Pity! thy tear is a diamond of the mind—polished by Humanity, which sparkles in the eye, but beams throughout the soul."[186] A year later, in 1799, Nicolai sent Bothe a whole stack of English novels, of which *The Jesuit* was apparently the most interesting. *The Stranger* and *Men and Manners* were too English to be successfully transplanted to Germany, Bothe believed.[187] In 1800, after translating some six English novels for Nicolai in three years, and reading many more, Bothe was heartily sick of adapting these works for the German market and hoped that Nicolai felt the same way.

184. Brömel to Nicolai, Berlin, 19 April 1785, in NN 10.
185. Bothe to Nicolai, Berlin, 31 October 1797, in NN 7. Bothe, who is mainly known as the translator of Euripides, also penned a satire on contemporary literary feuds, in which he lampooned Nicolai and other *Aufklärer* as well as the Romantics. In *Gigantomachia, das ist heilloser Krieg einer gewaltigen Riesenkorporation gegen den Olympus* (Leipzig, 1800), Nicolai appears as a giant with fifty heads and a hundred arms who helps to defend the gods against the Romantic ogres (*Giganten*).
186. Bothe to Nicolai, Berlin, February 1798, in NN 7.
187. Bothe to Nicolai, Berlin, 7 November 1799, in NN 7. On other potential translation projects, see Bothe's letters of 15 June and 23 November 1798 and 21 May 1799, in NN 7.

He had long believed that "alas! almost all of the ephemeral à la mode novels that come here from England little deserve the efforts we invest in them." Even the best ones had to be heavily abridged and adapted "if they are to be made bearable!" Sometimes he had had to jettison forty or fifty pages at a time of *Walsingham*, and *Man as He Is* had shrunk from four sturdy English volumes to two small German ones. "Let us put these little books aside," he suggested,[188] and Nicolai assented. Bothe's hopes that Nicolai would publish his novels instead were thwarted, though, by the publisher's decision to cut back drastically on novels.[189]

Nicolai also submitted some manuscripts to other authors for a final editorial polish. The "German Horace," Berlin poet Karl Wilhelm Ramler, who was known at the time as much for collecting and correcting the verse of others as for his own works, was the most prominent of these copy editors. In 1773, Nicolai entrusted him with revisions to his own novel *Sebaldus Nothanker*. Ramler noted that he had done nothing more than "brush the dust from a handsome book," the "little mechanical task" of reading each page three times for grammar, spelling, and punctuation. He prepared a separate sheet with his preferred spelling for the proofreader, reminding us that orthography was still subject to debate in the late eighteenth century. He recommended a certain Herr Heynitz as a proofreader "because he has thoroughly studied period and comma, and never overlooks such mistakes."[190] Ramler also looked through the edition of Lessing's letters that Nicolai published in 1794 as part of the edition of Lessing's works undertaken by the Berlin publisher Christian Friedrich Voß.[191]

The main project that Ramler took on for Nicolai, however, was the editing of Ludwig Heinrich von Nicolay's various literary works from the 1770s to the 1790s. In 1776, Nicolay had given his publisher carte blanche to "suppress, publish, trim, tailor, change anything not to your taste, or which you deem in need of alteration."[192] He believed that his works required "severe revision in regard to language"[193] and was happy

188. Bothe to Nicolai, Berlin, 26 April 1800, in NN 7.
189. Nicolai only published three novels after 1800, all by the Prussian jurist E. F. W. E. Follenius.
190. Ramler to Nicolai, Kerstin, 12 July 1773, in NN 59.
191. Ramler to Nicolai, Berlin, 18 February 1793, in NN 59.
192. Nicolay to Nicolai, St. Petersburg, 24 October 1776, in NN 52. Printed in *Die beiden Nicolai*, p. 26.
193. Nicolay to Nicolai, St. Petersburg, 30 December 1776, in NN 52. Printed in *Die beiden Nicolai*, p. 30.

to accept Ramler's offer to go through his poems before publication.[194] As he remarked in a letter to his publisher, he had noted the "happy influence of Herr Ramler's masterly hand." His elegies had "truly gained much by his changes."[195] Ramler was gratified and thanked him for his "kind reception of the little alterations that I dared to make to your excellent poems," calling his editorial work a "labor of love."[196] Ramler suggested that Nicolai the publisher give Nicolay the author the final say on whether his revisions stood or fell. Nicolay soon began to send his works directly to Ramler.[197]

Ramler's labors were not the mere services of a friend, however. He was paid for his work, although the rate is unclear. He received three copies on fine paper of each volume and, in 1793, fifty taler for editing volumes 3 and 4 of Nicolay's *Vermischte Gedichte*.[198] Ramler gave his seal of approval to the poems and stories sent to him and recommended which ones should be included in which volume. He also chose the frontispiece illustrations. His editorial authority ranged from correcting Nicolay's erratic spelling, to changing rhymes that might offend North German pronunciation ("readers often trip over such pebbles," he explained),[199] to suggesting revisions of entire works. For example, he felt that the fable "Pluto und Proserpine" needed so much polishing that it should be saved for a new edition of Nicolay's works. It also contained impolite remarks about the female sex, such as, "that once married to them we are eager to be rid of them," a thought which "I have suppressed for the sake of gallantry, and which, as a poet, I will not take up again until I find a way to clothe it with perfection."[200]

When it came to proofreading, those friends who oversaw the printing of some of Nicolai's publications, such as Walch in Schleusingen,

---

194. Nicolay to Nicolai, St. Petersburg, [21 June] 1777, in NN 52. Printed in *Die beiden Nicolai*, p. 36.
195. Nicolay to Nicolai, St. Petersburg, 18 (29) April 1778, in NN 52. Printed in *Die beiden Nicolai*, p. 50.
196. Ramler to Nicolay, Berlin, 22 September and 26 December 1778, in *Die beiden Nicolai*, pp. 54 and 62.
197. Nicolay to Nicolai, St. Petersburg, 4/15 April 1779, in NN 52, and Ramler to Nicolai, Berlin, 24 April 1781 and 20 September 1782, in NN 59.
198. Ramler to Nicolai, Berlin, 12 April 1793, in NN 59.
199. Ramler to Nicolay, Berlin, 25 March 1783, in *Die beiden Nicolai*, p. 136; Ramler to Nicolai, Berlin, undated, probably 1793, regretting that Nicolay did not stick to Adelung's dictionary for his spelling, in NN 59; Ramler to Nicolai, Berlin, 17 October 1777, in NN 59.
200. Ramler to Nicolai, Berlin, 21 December 1779, in NN 59.

frequently also undertook the arduous office of *Corrector*.²⁰¹ A certain Herr Wetzel in Berlin was apparently hired specifically as a proofreader for several works printed in Berlin, including Nicolai's own anecdotes on Frederick II of Prussia (1788–92).²⁰² He also compiled the index to the first eight volumes of Nicolai's travel account and did some writing for an unnamed project.²⁰³ Wetzel was only one of many men in Berlin, Leipzig, and other cities who, like the Magister in *Sebaldus Nothanker*, made their living from or supplemented insufficient incomes with proofreading and compilation work.²⁰⁴ Thus both members of the republic of letters who provided services out of friendship and what we would call freelancers played an essential role in book publishing at this period.

The Publisher as *Aufklärer*, the *Aufklärer* as Publisher

When it came to the many controversies within the Enlightenment movement, what set Nicolai apart from most of his bookseller colleagues, including many of those discussed in the literature as *Aufklärungsverleger*,²⁰⁵ was his personal involvement. He both helped to create controversies and reflected them. Nicolai's publishing program was nevertheless

---

201. See Walch to Nicolai, Schleusingen, 17 January 1781, 28 June, and 28 November 1783, in NN 79.

202. Bill for proofreading services, dated 5 April 1788 and paid on 12 April, in NN 82. Wetzel charged between 6 and 9 groschen per sheet for proofreading the various works. The total bill for proofreading 102 1/2 sheets was 28 taler 13 groschen and for compiling a five-sheet index to the *Anecdotes* 20 groschen.

203. Wetzel to Nicolai, Berlin, 16 November 1788, 30 January 1789, and 10 February 1790, in NN 82. Wetzel charged 10 taler for the index, hoping that Nicolai would not consider this exorbitant.

204. Another, the young Dr. Wolbrecht, told Nicolai that he had worked as a proofreader for Latin, Greek, and French books for the firm of Ruprecht in Göttingen during his studies there. Recently admitted to the practice of medicine in Prussia, he needed to support himself during the remainder of his stay in Berlin and asked Nicolai for proofreading work. Wolbrecht to Nicolai, Berlin, 2 June 1798, in NN 83. The proofreader for the *Neue Allgemeine Deutsche Bibliothek* was Magister Heinrich Ludwig Leopold. An inheritance had given him hopes of devoting himself to the academic life, but his plans had been foiled, he said, by the chicaneries of lawyers and his fellow heirs. While waiting for a position as tutor or private secretary, he ferreted out the frequent egregious errors occasioned by reviewers' illegible (and sometimes less than literate) manuscripts. Leopold to Nicolai, Wittenberg, 16 April 1803 and 5 February 1805, in NN 45.

205. Wolfgang von Ungern-Sternberg uses the term *Aufklärungsverleger* to describe Nicolai and such colleagues as Johann Gottlob Immanuel Breitkopf, Johann Gottfried Dyck, Johann Christian Gädicke, Johann Jakob Kanter, Johann Friedrich Hartknoch, Lagarde und Friedrich, Johann Jakob Korn, and the notorious Viennese pirate publisher Johann Thomas Edler von Trattner. "Schriftsteller und literarischer Markt," in *Hansers Sozialgeschichte der deutschen Literatur*, vol. 3/2, pp. 148–49.

far from being a grand design or carefully planned enterprise, and in this he was doubtless typical of his era.

Nicolai's status as an Enlightenment publisher should be measured not simply by the particular subjects or the ideological bents of his publications but also by their nature as intended contributions to the *process* of Enlightenment through informed criticism and debate. His desire to recreate on a (linguistically) national level his own opportunities for discussion in Berlin's urban setting was embodied not only in his review journals, which by their very nature commented upon recent works and debates, but also in a multitude of books and pamphlets that engaged in dialogue with the works of others. While books always form part of a chain reaction, for Nicolai and his comrades-in-arms this was a central, intended effect, and one of much more than merely academic interest. Some of the most important books in this context were concerned with the situation of Jews and with Jewish-Christian relations. Moses Mendelssohn's *Schreiben an den Herrn Diaconus Lavater zu Zürich*, printed together with Johann Caspar Lavater's *Antwort an den Herrn Moses Mendelssohn zu Berlin* (1770) and Christian Wilhelm Dohm's 1781 *Ueber die bürgerliche Verbesserung der Juden* (new edition, 1783) are particularly noteworthy contributions. The first contained the results of the Zurich theologian Johann Kaspar Lavater's unfortunate challenge to the Berlin philosopher Moses Mendelssohn either to refute a recent "proof" of the truth of Christianity or convert.[206] The controversy aroused heated emotions among adherents of enlightened religious toleration and Christian orthodoxy alike, and Nicolai's firm's documentation of the dispute allowed the interested public to judge which of the two men was the more enlightened and humanitarian, the Christian Lavater or the Jew Mendelssohn. Dohm's treatise, which was in turn greatly influenced by Moses Mendelssohn, focused on the controversial topic of measures for "reforming" the Jews (whom Dohm regarded as corrupted by too much participation in trade) and integrating them into German society, based on legal equality and a separation of church and state. In a second volume, Dohm documented the debate unleashed by his work. Other significant publications in this area were a translation of the seventeenth-century Dutch rabbi

---

206. This "proof" appeared in Charles Bonnet, *La Palingénésie philosophique, ou Idées sur l'Etat futur des êtres vivans* (Geneva: Philibert, 1769). Lavater translated a section into German as *Herrn Carl Bonnets, verschiedener Akademien Mitglieds, philosophische Untersuchung der Beweise für das Christentum. Samt denselben Ideen von der künftigen Glückseligkeit der Menschen* (Zurich: Füssli, 1769). Lavater dedicated his translation to Mendelssohn.

Menasse Ben Israel's appeal to Oliver Cromwell to abandon his prejudices against the Jews and allow them to settle in England (*Rettung der Juden*, 1782, with a preface by Moses Mendelssohn refuting Prussian objections to Dohm's polemic),[207] and Mendelssohn's pioneering 1780 German translation (in Hebrew characters) of the first five books of the Bible, which was instrumental in introducing Yiddish-speaking Jews to German as a written language, thus fostering their integration into German society.[208]

Such works were the teething rings of the infant body politic, continuing and stimulating ongoing discussions on a wide range of topics of public interest. Even in those cases where the polemical nature of a book was not immediately apparent, as in the case of many literary works, current controversies had an extraordinary impact on Nicolai's production. This is, of course, not surprising, since several of the novels he published (and wrote) were satires. The bestseller *Sebaldus Nothanker* ranged widely from a satire on sentimentalism to a critique of clerical intolerance and the state of the book trade, taking on any number of contemporary ills and foibles along the way. *Die Freuden des jungen Werther* (The Joys of Young Werther) was, of course, a contribution to the massive Werther literature of the mid-1770s, in which the eponymous hero survives his suicide attempt and marries his beloved Lotte. *Eyn feyner kleyner Almanach Vol schönerr echterr liblicherr Volckslieder, lustigerr Reyen unndt kleglicherr Mordsgeschichte* (A Fine Little Almanac Full of Beautiful Genuine Lovely Folk Songs, Jolly Rounds and Piteous Tales of Murder, 2 vols., 1777–78) was at once an ironic commentary on the *Sturm und Drang* idealization of the folk song—and of those who sang them—complete with deliberately quaint archaic spellings, and a serious collection of songs compiled by Nicolai with the help of friends. Nicolai's novels of the 1790s, *Sempronius Gundibert* and *Geschichte eines Dicken Mannes*, were literary salvos in his battle against what he saw as the excesses of Idealist philosophy.

Eclectic though they may have been, there are patterns in the subjects of the books Nicolai published, with the nature of his list reflecting changes in his own intellectual interests as well as those of the times in

---

207. This work was published both as an appendix to the second volume of Dohm's book and as a separate work. The translation was by the Berlin Jewish physician and *Aufklärer* Markus Herz (husband of the famous salonnière Henriette Herz). Herz had studied with Kant in Königsberg and gave public lectures on Kantian philosophy in Berlin.

208. *Die fünf Bücher Mose, zum Gebrauch der jüdischdeutschen Nation*, ed. Josia Friedrich Christian Löffler (Berlin: Nicolai, 1780).

which he lived. Theoretically, at least, Nicolai had the means at his disposal to realize his ideals for the improvement of literary taste and writing. After the early period of his career in the late 1750s and 1760s, when he was intensely involved in German and European literary and aesthetic debates, literary works per se, although they remained numerous, began to play a less central role in Nicolai's publishing program. Unlike his colleagues Philipp Erasmus Reich or Georg Joachim Göschen, Nicolai's firm left no lasting mark on poetry, fiction, or drama. Admiring though he was of the talents of many of its practitioners, Nicolai was disappointed at the direction German literature took in the 1770s and began to follow its development less avidly. What he saw as the extravagances and mania for originality of the *Sturm und Drang* and the ill-placed admiration of Klopstock's followers for everything Germanic turned him away from many new authors.[209] In the winter of 1773/74, for example, his reading apparently contained no new fiction or poetry at all, although he did re-read his favorite novel, Alain-René Lesage's *Gil Blas*, for about the twenty-fifth time, as he reported to J. K. Lavater (proof, if any were necessary, that intensive reading persisted even as people began to consume larger numbers of books).[210] He by no means abandoned his interest in German style, but shifted his focus to nonliterary writing. For example, he greatly admired the style of his authors Moses Mendelssohn and the Osnabrück historian Justus Möser, praising the simplicity, grace, and clarity of the former's writing and calling the latter an original and one of "the foremost German prose authors."[211]

The novels, poems, and plays Nicolai published from the 1770s on, other than those from his own pen, were acquired in an apparently haphazard manner. If an author offered a manuscript at a good moment, and Nicolai liked it, he published it. The translations he commissioned were determined in part by the selection left over after more enterprising literary publishers such as Philipp Erasmus Reich had already staked out the most promising English and French titles. An exception was the four-volume *Dramatische Werke* of Samuel Foote, the "English Aristophanes," which Nicolai seems to have commissioned out of his own admiration

---

209. See the correspondence between Nicolai and the Swiss writer and artist Salomon Gessner, esp. Nicolai's letter of November 1770 and Gessner's letters of 9 April 1770 and 12 February 1775 on trends in contemporary German literature, in NN 86. See also Sommerfeld, *Friedrich Nicolai und der Sturm und Drang*.

210. Nicolai to Lavater, 25 April 1774, quoted in Sommerfeld, *Friedrich Nicolai und der Sturm und Drang*, p. 361.

211. Quoted in Möller, *Aufklärung in Preußen*, pp. 160 and 163.

for the playwright. Even if they are largely forgotten today, the English works Nicolai published in the 1790s were perhaps a cut above the much-lamented yard goods of the period. The novelists form an interesting group and provide something of a contrast to Nicolai's more staid German authors. Among them were Robert Bage, a radical Quaker papermaker much admired by Sir Walter Scott; William Beckford (under the pseudonym Harriet Marlow), the eccentric author of gothic novels and oriental fantasies; and Mary Darby Robinson, whose checkered career proceeded from Shakespearean actress to mistress of the future George IV and, finally, prolific writer for the circulating libraries. Fanny Burney, whose last major novel, *Camilla* (1796), Nicolai published in translation, is the best known of Nicolai's English authors today. Although Nicolai put little active effort into scouting out promising new German literary authors, he did publish early works by a few largely forgotten young litterateurs, including the poet Friedrich August Müller and novelists Sophie Singer and Emmanuel Friedrich Wilhelm Ernst Follenius. He also has the distinction of having published the early works of Ludwig Tieck as part of the *Strausfedern* collection.[212]

Practical works on the one hand and polemics on contemporary topics on the other increasingly came to dominate the publishing company. As a good *Aufklärer*, Nicolai was concerned with practical pedagogy, and school textbooks represented an important and lucrative component of his list throughout his career. Handbooks aimed at the self-education of adults on a variety of subjects ranging from agricultural improvements to the new Prussian legal code were also prominent. Religion and reform theology, from sermons, catechisms, and devotional works to pamphlets directed against religious fanaticism and enthusiasm (*Schwärmerei*), crypto-Catholicism, and superstition also belonged to his stock-in-trade.

Nicolai's publishing program frequently emphasized the mediation between scholars and interested laypersons. His location in Berlin and his own autodidactic education were significant here. Although he corresponded with many university professors in his function as editor and publisher of the *ADB*, his own day-to-day life was lived in a major urban center among people from all walks of life. The city had no university during Nicolai's lifetime and the intellectuals he knew best were either government officials, physicians, clergymen, or teachers in the secondary

---

212. His more adventurous, and less scrupulous son Carl August even printed the first, unauthorized, edition of Tieck's collected works, for which the incensed author took him to court. On the relations between Tieck and the Nicolais, see *König der Romantik*.

schools, with a sprinkling of self-educated merchants such as himself and Moses Mendelssohn.[213] Their foremost needs, as well as his own, were for practical rather than theoretical works.

The new and expanded editions of the work of Benjamin Hederich, whose *Guide to the Primary Historical Sciences* and *Brief Guide to the Primary Languages and Sciences for Future Citizens and Others Who Do Not Intend to Study* had been published by Christoph Gottlieb Nicolai, are only one example of the genre of learning for the unlearned.[214] Another interesting project in this vein, which like so many others never got past the planning stages, was an introduction to logic for the "unlearned classes." Nicolai had publicly announced his intention to publish such a work, whereupon the popular philosopher Johann August Eberhard sent him some ideas on the subject that he had developed during a solitary carriage ride. Nicolai applauded his novel plan of getting country parsons of his acquaintance to note and collect their parishioners' prejudices, rules, proverbs, and methods of reasoning, and to use these to fashion a textbook on logic tailored to the needs of the "lowest classes."[215] This surely, would have been the *Volksaufklärung* (popular Enlightenment) in action. Nicolai's zeal for the edification of the general reader is also evident in another unrealized pet project, an annotated bibliography for readers seeking instruction and entertainment. For over fifteen years he tried to convince his prolific author and reviewer J. J. Eschenburg to provide this "Library for Amateurs of Learning" (Bibliothek für Liebhaber der Wissenschaften), "for it is incredible how little people know about books, the best of which go unread because so few are aware of their existence." Readers could inform themselves about the best poetry, classical

---

213. The city had, of course, the Academy of Sciences as well, but the Berlin academicians during much of Nicolai's lifetime were mainly French speakers and belonged to quite different circles from the German *Aufklärer*. Of the twenty-seven new members admitted in the period 1764–86, only one was a German. Horst Möller, *Fürstenstaat oder Bürgernation: Deutschland 1763–1815* (Berlin: Siedler, 1989), p. 374. By the 1780s, though, the divisions had begun to break down. Nicolai, who finally became a regular member of the academy in 1804 (he was voted an extraordinary member in 1799), was in contact with such academicians as Samuel Henri Formey and Johann Georg Sulzer (one of the few German speakers to be elected by Frederick II), and even published some of their works.

214. Hederich's books, of which Nicolai published revised editions in 1760 and 1762, later served as the springboard for several new, updated works for self-tuition: Georg Simon Klügel's *Encyklopädie, oder zusammenhängender Vortrag der gemeinnützigsten Kenntnisse* (1782–84; 3d ed., 1806–9), Johann Joachim Eschenburg's *Handbuch der klassischen Literatur* (1787; 5th ed., 1808), and Christoph von Schmidt-Phiseldek's *Handbuch der vornehmsten historischen Wissenschaften* (1782).

215. Eberhard to Nicolai, Halle, 13 January 1784, in NN 16.

literature,[216] novels, history, politics and perhaps also agriculture, and the liberal and mechanical arts in a convenient one-volume handbook. Descriptions of the books would be bibliographically precise, "intelligent and edifying."[217] Over the years the plan was expanded considerably to include French, English, and Italian periodicals and a complete list of the German literary-scholarly gazettes, which were often little known outside regional circles. Nicolai later envisioned a special section for philosophy, particularly for ethics, the philosophy of life, and popular philosophy, and one for travel accounts.[218] The category of theology remained notably absent.[219] Despite initial interest, Eschenburg had neither time nor inclination for this eminently patriotic task, however, and Nicolai had to abandon the idea, but it typifies his pedagogical aspirations.

Nicolai was also a "no-frills" publisher, eschewing the luxury editions many contemporaries favored. Although his arguments were largely economic, there may have been some principle involved as well, since

216. Nicolai, who began studying Greek as an adult in order to read his beloved Homer, was also interested in the problem of providing editions of classical literature for those who knew neither Greek nor Latin. Translations of Greek and Roman authors held a prominent place in his selective book catalogs of 1787 and 1795; and although his publishing in this field was modest (German translations of Euripides' *Iphigenia in Aulis* in 1778 and of his collected works in 1800–1803, as well as handbooks on mythology and classical literature by Martin Gottfried Hermann and J. J. Eschenburg, respectively, and an essay on the Greek epigram by Eduard Romeo Count Vargas = Friedrich Grosse), he encouraged his friends to gear their editions of the classics to a broad readership. In a letter to Uz, who had recently sent him his Horace translation, for example, Nicolai notes the necessity of explanatory notes tailored to the needs of readers without a classical education. His wife Elisabeth Macaria had read and enjoyed Uz's translation, but had discovered numerous unfamiliar expressions that neither she nor Nicolai could interpret. Echoing one of his favorite themes, Nicolai tells Uz that "the German scholar rarely understands the needs of this class [of readers], which is very numerous and very worthy." Authors all too often fear the scorn of the critics, whom he ironically dubs "so astonishingly learned and wise men," who despise anything they saw as written for the "common horde." But one can scarcely expect women, or men who were either unfamiliar with Latin and Greek but eager for edification, or too busy to look up references or dust off their schoolboy learning, to understand every allusion in a classical author. Nicolai to Uz, Leipzig, 1 May 1773, in NN 76.
217. Nicolai to Eschenburg, Berlin, 7 July 1779, in HAB, no. 35.
218. Nicolai to Eschenburg, Berlin, 11 October 1779, in HAB, no. 36.
219. Over the next several years Nicolai ventured periodic queries about the progress of the *Lesebibliothek*. Nicolai to Eschenburg, Berlin, 4 November 1780, 8 February 1783 and 8 November 1786, in HAB, nos. 38, 48, 66. When nothing had materialized by 1786, he suggested that Eschenburg commission someone to compile the work under his supervision, and then give the work its final polish himself. He reminded Eschenburg of how imperative it was "to guide the reading of so many, and to get them away from bad and mediocre works and point out good and useful ones." Nicolai to Eschenburg, Berlin, 8 November 1786, in HAB, no. 66. In 1795, he broached the subject again to Eschenburg, who again declined. Another candidate whom he had sent the old plan lacked access to the necessary libraries. Nicolai to Eschenburg, Berlin, 26 September and 17 December 1795, in HAB, nos. 179 and 181.

Nicolai tended to emphasize books as objects of use rather than aesthetic contemplation. As he said of one of his own works, "No one who understands anything of the matter can argue that I should have printed my Travels on fine paper. I have copies on writing paper for the very few gentlemen of such dainty tastes if they are willing to pay extra.... Nowadays one must look to the general public, who need to save money. It is easy to go on about typographical beauty but there are few people indeed prepared to pay for it."[220] With few exceptions, Nicolai printed in median octavo format and on plain paper. Of 238 works for which Paul Raabe's catalog of Nicolai's production lists a format, 219 were in median octavo, 6 in small octavo, one in large octavo, one in duodecimo, and only 11 in quarto format. Only authors' copies were printed on fine paper, contrary to the common practice at the time of printing separate fine and plain paper editions (occasionally even in different formats) for smaller and larger purses.[221]

In 1796, surveying his efforts of the previous forty years to mediate between authors and readers, Friedrich Nicolai remarked: "It has frequently been my intention to bring the two elements closer together and, as far as my meager powers permit, to offer our men of letters hints on how to render our literature more useful and pleasant for the broad public. I have the most immediate motivation to do so since I myself received no scholarly education but instead, my constant love for all literature notwithstanding, have been involved with practical business from my earliest youth until the present day."[222]

A long excursus on Schiller and Goethe's journal *Die Horen* in the penultimate volume of his travel account prompted Nicolai to reiterate his ideas on the relationship between German authors and the German

---

220. Nicolai to Lüdke, Berlin, 18 May 1783, in NN 60.

221. Exceptions were Friedrich August Müller's epic poem on Richard the Lionheart (*Richard Löwenherz*), all four hundred copies of which were sent out into the world on high-quality writing paper, and J. J. Eschenburg's *Entwurf einer Theorie und Literatur der schönen Wissenschaften*, which was printed on "Herren Papier" at the author's request. On Müller, see Nicolai's annotations on Müller to Nicolai, Halle, 13 June 1789, in NN 51. In this case, the authors' copies were printed on fine Holland paper rather than the usual writing paper. Nicolai mentions the paper for Eschenburg's *Entwurf* in a letter of 18 May 1783 to Pastor Lüdke, in NN 60 [Resewitz correspondence].

Philipp Erasmus Reich often published both luxury and cheap paper editions, and as the century wore on more and more booksellers took up this practice. Hazel Rosenstrauch, "Buchhandelsmanufaktur und Aufklärung. Die Reformen des Buchhändlers und Verlegers Ph. E. Reich (1717–1787). Sozialgeschichtliche Studie zur Entwicklung des literarischen Marktes," *AGB* 26 (1986): 44 n. 72; von Ungern Sternberg, "Schriftstelleremanzipation und Buchkultur," p. 82.

222. *Beschreibung einer Reise*, 11:xxiv–xxv. All page numbers in parentheses refer to this work.

public, a favorite theme of his since the 1750s. He regarded the new trends in literature, as exemplified by Goethe and Schiller's journals of this period, as well as the writings of such Romantic philosophers and litterateurs as Fichte and the brothers Schlegel, as a dangerous return to the disregard for the public against which he had warned forty years previously. Now, instead of dry pedantry, convoluted and obscure scholarly prose, and stiff piety, his targets fed the public the—in his eyes equally non-nutritive—"raw transcendental deductions of formal figments of the imagination or ... subtle and inward images of heightened imagination" on which they themselves thrived. Both approaches to writing were "wholly removed from the real workaday world" and would always remain so. In either case, the presumptuousness "of proclaiming themselves the overseers of the thirty million [German speakers]" was equally misguided (p. xxii). He did not, however, expect gratitude from authors, describing his role as as thankless as that of a man who placed himself between a quarreling husband and wife in the hope of reconciling them (p. xxv).

Nicolai described the German public as divided into two distinct groups: the legion of 8,000 authors (as counted by the industrious Johann Georg Meusel)[223] and their potential readers, the 30 million German speakers. Each group was valuable in its own right, but they were separated by a great chasm, knowing and understanding little of each other. The authors, many of them worthy contributors to German literature, were all too frequently blinded by allegiance to their separate disciplines. Among the millions, thousands, or only hundreds who read any given work there might be any number of worthy persons who had honed their analytical powers—"whether scholastically or not is of little consequence" (p. xix). These readers, however, having gained and tested their knowledge through practical experience with people from many walks of life, and through observations "which only the complicated collisions of life itself can provide," had a very different way of viewing the world from those who saw it only from the scholar's study (p. xx). The unfortunate gulf of understanding between the learned and unlearned segments of the public prevented German literature from exerting the influence it should "upon the broad expanse of Germany" (p. xx). Many of the most

---

223. Meusel was an *ADB* reviewer and took over the compilation of the biographical and bibliographic lexicon *Das gelehrte Teutschland* from its founder, Georg Christoph Hamberger (also an *ADB* contributor). The lexicon, which was begun in 1767 and continued with supplements into the nineteenth century, is still an important source of information, particularly for minor eighteenth-century German writers.

important ideas and discoveries, if they reached the unlearned public at all, did so only after they had already been superseded by new ideas. The great public often remained in ignorance "because they lacked the receptivity for certain information, which would however be useful to them" (p. xxi), while authors often failed to understand the needs of the multitude. The solution Nicolai proposed is one that recalls his earliest critical works: scholars who wished to write for a "large, mixed public" needed to become better acquainted with their audience, from its requirements and peculiarities to its "peccadillos and prejudices" (p. xxi). They ignored this injunction at their peril. If the public lost its taste for reading (and here he meant serious literature), "crude sensuality and disdain for any cultivation of the intellect ... could easily become, once again, the lot of the masses and often of the distinguished masses as well" (p. xxii). Philosophy and imagination, properly applied, could have such a salutary effect in cultivating and improving the inhabitants of Germany, but if authors did not soon learn to recapture their public and "to influence their minds successfully," educated persons of both sexes might abandon German literature altogether and return to foreign, particularly French writers. Quite the opposite occurred, but in 1796 Nicolai neither foresaw the fervent nationalism that would inflame his compatriots during the struggle against Napoleon, nor did he realize that the seemingly ephemeral literary and philosophical trends he decried would dominate German cultural life for more than a century.

However much (non-bookseller) contemporaries may have scorned the combination of business and Enlightenment, and however much Nicolai himself may have complained of the tedium of trade, his work as a publisher and his vocation of *Aufklärer* were closely intertwined. By publishing his own works, which represented a significant proportion of his production in both quantitative and financial terms, he pulled his two roles even more closely together. No matter what he did, he would be identified with the works he published in a way that simple publishers were not. This had both positive and negative consequences. Interest in and admiration for Nicolai's own works generated excitement and anticipation that extended to his firm's other titles. Precisely because expectations were so high, however, the disappointment and bitterness could also be great, as in the backlash against Nicolai's own travel account.

Nicolai never lost sight of publishing's essential nature as a business, in which one must sell books or face bankruptcy. He was willing to take risks for projects he believed in, and to oppose state repression up to a point, but never so far as seriously to endanger his business. His large family, with three sons and two daughters to educate,[224] and solid bourgeois life of fine wines, frequent entertaining, summers at Bad Pyrmont, and charitable deeds, required a steady cash flow. Good planning and good fortune allowed him to make a living without greatly compromising his principles. The successes of his own works, of the *ADB* (at least until the mid-1780s) and of sermons and school books supported the publication of less popular projects. Nicolai did not need to publish the sort of chivalric romances that received scathing one-line critiques in the ADB; his own *Sebaldus Nothanker* sold quite enough copies. The multiple editions of Johann August Eberhard's *Apologie des Sokrates*, Moses Mendelssohn's *Phädon*, or Klügel's *Encyklopädie*, to name just a few, proved that the Enlightenment sold.

---

224. Even his daughters were sent away from home for at least part of their schooling.

chapter

(3)

Everyday Life in the Book Trade

> Imagine a man who must manage the daily business
> of three bookshops (in Berlin, Stettin, und Danzig) with all
> of the accompanying annoyances and worries, who is forced
> to spend eight weeks visiting two Leipzig fairs and
> occasionally the Danzig fair as well, who writes and
> signs some 400 letters a year concerning the d[eu]tsche
> Bibl[iothek], not counting other correspondence, [and]
> who is not safe from interruption at any hour of the
> day, because anyone may enter a public shop.
>
> —*Friedrich Nicolai, 1774*

Friedrich Nicolai took a rather dim—and fatalistic—view of developments in the book trade during his lifetime. He was especially pessimistic about the possibility (and unsure of the desirability) of organizing booksellers to regulate the trade centrally from Leipzig.[1] In 1769, when his friend Lessing expressed concerns about a possible booksellers' cabal against authors' self-publication projects, Nicolai replied that he need not worry; German booksellers would never succeed in uniting over anything.[2] Perhaps because he was so busy spreading Enlightenment and "proper ways of thinking" in the republic of letters and the wider reading public, Nicolai seems to have been less concerned with reforming his business colleagues. Although he took part in various joint efforts to prosecute pirate publishers, he did not join his friend and colleague Philipp Erasmus Reich's Buchhandlungsgesellschaft, whose chief aim was to stop pirates, and he opposed various other of Reich's reforms in the 1760s, especially his price increases and insistence on cash payments

---

1. See F. H. Meyer, "Der deutsche Buchhandel gegen Ende des 18. und zu Anfang des 19. Jahrhunderts," *AGDB* 7 (1882): 221–23.

2. Nicolai to Lessing, Berlin, 8 November 1769, in Lessing, *Sämtliche Schriften*, 19:324.

in Saxon currency at the imperial exchange rate, which gave Leipzig publishers even more of an advantage than they already enjoyed.[3] Men who in Nicolai's eyes did not possess "correct notions" of the book trade were unsuited to reform it. Even Reich, whom Nicolai entrusted for some twenty years with his Leipzig commissions, was not immune to criticism of his practices. Nicolai spoke often of the advantages of moderation in business and of the necessity of a careful balance between publishing and retail selling (*Verlag* and *Sortiment*), the neglect of which, he believed, could bring only misfortune. In a letter to Lessing, he rather smugly cited Reich as an example: "He works very hard to maintain the reputation of the house of Weidmann as the largest publisher in Germany. This does not benefit him, however; he admits as much himself, and knows not why this is the case. I can explain it easily enough according to my principles, though. He should publish only one-third of what he does at present; his life would be simpler, and he would go farther than he does now."[4]

Nicolai enunciated his principles and practices in more detail in a reply to a letter from the young bookseller Friedrich Perthes in 1808. Hard work, good bookkeeping, and self-reflection were the keys to success in the risky German book trade.

> Probably very few booksellers will do what I have done.... I have balanced my accounts every year from January 1, 1762 ... always adding notes on the business of the past year, with an impartial assessment of the same, not failing to mention my own mistakes.[5] This has made many matters regarding the book trade much clearer to me than to those who simply carry on without proper reflection ... doing much business without calculating what capital remains, or how much their firm's capital is worth. The rightness of the principles upon which I set up my business, at least for me, is demonstrated by the fact that, although I had debts for the first seventeen years, had a large family to support and live in a city where rents and other necessities are very dear, I managed in the subsequent fifty years to multiply my initial capital several times over....
> A rational merchant must organize his way of doing business in such a

---

3. See Meyer, "Die geschäftliche Verhältnisse," pp. 195–200; Georgi, *Die Entwicklung des Berliner Buchhandels*, p. 166; on Reich's reforms, see Rosenstrauch, "Buchhandelsmanufaktur und Aufklärung."

4. Nicolai to Lessing, Berlin, 8 November 1769, in Lessing, *Sämtliche Schriften*, 19:325–26.

5. These yearly notes on the state of the business have apparently not survived.

way that he can, if possible, at least hold his own even in case of great misfortune.[6]

To a great extent, Nicolai clung to the ideals of "solid trade" prevalent in his youth. If he did not precisely *glorify* past conditions in the book trade, he did agree with the many contemporaries who registered decline and saw chaos on the march. Rather than conceive of new possibilities for organization, such as eventually led to the foundation in 1825 of the book trade organization Börsenverein der Deutschen Buchhändler, Nicolai imagined salvation (however unlikely) in the guise of a return to older principles and practices. Thus he informed Perthes that he had seen "the best era of the book trade ... in which fewer books came to the fairs, booksellers had to pay little and most of them nothing at the fairs, and thus each was able to keep his money. A few old booksellers such as old Herold and old Bohn in Hamburg had very proper notions of the book trade such as, I fear, are rarely to be found today."[7] Far from being an advantage to the German book trade, the book fair had always been at best a necessary evil because few German cities, with the exception of Vienna, were rich enough to support a bookseller who did business only there. But it had become a more precarious business than ever, and the German book trade had been ruined by those booksellers who went to the fair "only to sell their own publications, among whom [the Leipzig publisher Johann Friedrich] Weygand provided the first bad example." Such booksellers "have ruined the German book trade so that now at the book fairs one finds many sellers, and the buyers naturally have no money." Nicolai does not mention it here, but the fact that buyers had less (or less valuable) money at the book fairs of that period had as much to do with the Napoleonic wars and the occupation of Prussia and Saxony as it did with the rise of pure publishing enterprises.[8] The only hope, as he saw it, was to trade in "fewer and greater books," which retained their

---

6. Nicolai to Perthes, Berlin, 4 May 1808, in NN 56. This letter and Perthes's letter, which it answers, are printed in "Ein Generationskonflikt unter Buchhändlern? Der deutsche Buchhandel im Briefwechsel zwischen Friedrich Perthes und Friedrich Nicolai im Frühjahr 1808," ed. Pamela E. Selwyn, *Börsenblatt für den deutschen Buchhandel* (Leipzig ed.), no. 24 (1990), Beiheft 2, pp. 13–17.

7. Nicolai to Perthes, Berlin, 4 May 1808, in NN 56, and in "Generationskonflikt unter Buchhandlern?" Christian Herold and Johann Carl Bohn were both Hamburg booksellers.

8. Nicolai complained increasingly from 1790 on of the decline of business at the fairs and lack of currency, especially gold. See, for example, Nicolai to Eschenburg, Berlin, 10 May 1790, in HAB, no. 103, and Nicolai to Nicolay, Berlin, 12 December 1809, in *Die beiden Nicolai*, pp. 544–46.

value longer, making possible larger editions. In addition, he envisioned a return to a modified barter system. The "most solid firms" would trade with each other on an exchange basis, with as little cash as possible changing hands, as had been the case sixty years before.[9]

In a certain sense, Nicolai was bemoaning the results of those very developments that he himself had fostered during his long career as *Aufklärer* and bookseller. The development of a national literature (even if it was one he didn't always approve of), the growing reading public, and new organs for disseminating information about books, such as the *ADB*, had all contributed to the flood of material at the book fairs. Nicolai's own behavior and writings inspired countless polemical pamphlets. Enlightenment, anti-Enlightenment, and anti-anti-Enlightenment works all vied for their share of the market along with the many books that took little notice of the intellectual struggles of the day. The more the book trade became a potential vehicle for the broad dissemination of new ideas and trends, the more it became a competitive business, with all the possibilities for rapid successes and equally rapid failures that entails.

Nicolai Among the Booksellers

However controversial Nicolai may have been as an author and as the editor and publisher of the *ADB*, and however much authors such as Kant may have maligned his publishing activities, he was respected by his colleagues in the book trade, both in Berlin and elsewhere. They frequently sought his advice on business matters, employees, and printers, as well as assistance of various kinds. N. G. Frommann in Züllichau, for example, one of Nicolai's best friends in the book trade and a good customer as well, not only discussed and exchanged *Diener* with him and solicited recommendations of printers, but also turned to him for suggestions on such questions as how much to offer for the bookshop of the Züllichau orphanage, which he intended to purchase, and how to deal with the shop's creditors.[10] Nicolai was also a financial resource, lending

---

9. Nicolai to Perthes, Berlin, 4 May 1808, in NN 56, in "Generationskonflikt unter Buchhändlern?" p. 16.

10. Frommann to Nicolai, Züllichau, 27 January, 17 February, and 8 October 1785, in NN 23. Their business dealings included a request from Frommann for five hundred copies of Nicolai's book on the Knights Templar on consignment. He had read the book, he said, was sure there would be great interest in it, and wanted to help it become better known in his area. Frommann to Nicolai, Züllichau, 13 March 1782, in NN 23. He also asks Nicolai's advice on how to avoid the dire consequences of inadvertently infringing on the Berlin Academy's calendar monopoly. Frommann to Nicolai, Züllichau, 15 and 20 January 1781, in NN 23.

a large sum of money to at least one young bookseller just beginning his career.[11]

With his many valuable publications, including his own works and the *ADB*, Nicolai was in a good position to trade with other publishers, so he probably only rarely had to pay much cash to settle accounts, except to those, like Philipp Erasmus Reich, who insisted on it. To what extent he continued to engage in barter with his more trusted customers, those who offered works of similar value to his, and with foreign booksellers in order to avoid currency problems, is unclear. Sadly, there is little mention of accounts in the correspondence, since much was discussed at the Leipzig fairs or relegated to the columns of account books rather than letters.

The Book Trade in Berlin and Prussia: Structure and Conflicts

In Berlin, as in many other German cities, bookselling and publishing, on the one hand, and printing, on the other, were quite distinct trades, with separate traditions and legal rights.[12] There was a hierarchy in status among those authorized to sell books, with the privileged booksellers at the top. Those highest on the scale were naturally anxious to protect their prerogatives, and without a guild the booksellers used both personal influence and legal action to control access to their trade, correct what they saw as abuses, and make their collective and individual voices heard.

The city in which Nicolai began his career in 1752 had advanced from a publishing backwater in the seventeenth century to the fourth-largest publishing center in Germany.[13] Berlin in 1752 could boast of seven bookseller-publishers and six retail bookshops.[14] By 1786, there were seventeen bookseller-publishers in Berlin, and by 1792 the number had jumped to twenty-three.[15] In the second half of the eighteenth century, Berlin rose to second place in German publishing, gaining particular

---

11. In 1792, Ferdinand Troschel, son of Nicolai's Berlin acquaintance C. L. Troschel, borrowed 7100 taler at 4 percent interest to open a shop in Danzig. For an account, see chap. 6, pp. 417–18 and n. 532, of Selwyn, *Philosophy in the Comptoir*. The Troschel correspondence of 1792–1804 regarding the loan is in NN 75.

12. According to Arthur Georgi, only 13.7 percent of books appearing in Berlin between 1751 and 1825 were printed by their publishers. *Die Entwicklung des Berliner Buchhandels*, p. 62.

13. The largest center was Leipzig, followed by Frankfurt am Main and the university town of Halle. Georgi, *Die Entwicklung des Berliner Buchhandels*, p. 97.

14. The numbers in 1700 had been three and two, respectively. Georgi, *Die Entwicklung des Berliner Buchhandels*, p. 74. Between 1754 and 1766 most of these purely retail shops, all but one of them French, had closed their doors. In a book trade dominated by the Leipzig fair it was difficult to acquire books with nothing but scarce cash to give in exchange.

15. Nicolai, *Beschreibung der königlichen Residenzstädte*, 2:588; Georgi, *Die Entwicklung des Berliner Buchhandels*, p. 186.

significance for the trade in books between Germany and northeastern Europe.[16]

In Berlin, the men and women authorized to deal in books fell into three categories: bookseller-publishers (*Buchhändler*), printers, and bookbinders. Unlike Leipzig, where booksellers had their own separate category within the citizenry, Berlin booksellers belonged to the *Kaufmannschaft* and within that group to those merchants with royal privileges. This put them in the same category as the stationers, flour and butter merchants, print sellers, apothecaries, and purveyors of Italian delicacies. Unlike the flour and butter merchants, they had no guild or corporation to regulate entry into the trade and set standards of behavior. Printers, of whom sixteen masters were in business in Berlin in 1786, had no guild either, but rather belonged to a so-called *unzünftiges Gewerk* (non-guild trade). In contrast, Berlin's thirty-nine bookbinders (including six widows) were members of a guild with a corporate privilege.[17] *Buchhändler* in general both published and sold (but did not print) books, but each activity had a distinct legal status. Anyone could *publish* books, but only those in possession of a privilege were authorized to sell them to the public, and only those lucky enough to hold a general privilege (*General-Privilegium*) were allowed both to publish and to sell books of all kinds.[18] Friedrich Nicolai inherited his father's 1713 general privilege, which he proudly printed in full at the front of his 1786 description of Berlin and Potsdam.[19] The privilege not only authorized Christoph Gottlieb Nicolai and his heirs to keep a bookshop "in the place he shall deem most convenient" and, like other privileged booksellers, to buy and sell "all manner of good, useful and permissible books and materials in all of the faculties, liberal arts and languages, old and new, bound and unbound, engravings, maps, plain and illustrated." It also permitted him to publish and trade in the above-mentioned items and promised protection against piracy by all those persons not privileged as booksellers in Berlin and Potsdam who dared to sell Nicolai's publications "in our lands, secretly or openly."[20] This was

---

16. Leipzig remained by far the most important publishing center in the Holy Roman Empire. Georgi, *Die Entwicklung des Berliner Buchhandels*, pp. 143–45.

17. Nicolai, *Beschreibung der königlichen Residenzstädte*, 2:582, 588.

18. August Schürmann, *Der deutsche Buchhandel der Neuzeit und seine Krisis* (Halle: Buchhandlung des Waisenhauses, 1895), pp. 20–21. This was true not only for Berlin and Prussia.

19. As he later recalled, "My father came to our country as a foreigner [from Saxony], and thus received a general privilege for himself and his heirs for all of the works he published." Quoted in Voigtländer, "Das Verlagsrecht," p. 36.

20. Nicolai, *Beschreibung der königlichen Residenzstädte*, vol. 1.

the highest form of privilege a bookseller could attain and, together with his local and national reputation, helped to make him a leading member of the Berlin book trade.

The *General-Privilegium* represented at once the right to engage in bookselling and the favored position of the holder vis-à-vis those who tried to engage in the book trade without the benefit of royal permission. This type of privilege, bestowed for the lifetime of the holder and heritable, could also be transferred with official permission. Those seeking a general privilege applied to the Generaldirektorium. No particular qualifications were necessary until 1801 when, in order to alleviate the overcrowding of the book trade, the granting of a *Geschäftsprivilegium* or privilege to do business (as it was then called) was made contingent upon a six-year apprenticeship, two years as a *Diener*, a capital of 5000 taler for Berlin and 2000 for the provinces, and evidence of a local need for an additional bookseller.[21] Even without a guild, booksellers were never wholly without influence on the government and did their best to intervene when newcomers applied for general privileges.[22] Before bestowing a general privilege in the king's name, the Generaldirektorium commissioned a report from the Kurmark Kammer (the regional administrative authority for Berlin), which requested the opinion of the Berlin Magistrat or municipal council, which in turn asked the privileged Berlin booksellers to evaluate the application.[23] A letter from a colleague to Nicolai illustrates this process. In November 1800, the bookseller J. C. Belitz received an anonymous tip informing him that a bookseller's assistant named Müller had applied for a new general privilege. The sender had enclosed copies of Müller's application and a rescript from the Generaldirektorium to the Kurmark Kammer. Belitz felt it his duty to send the

---

21. Georgi, *Die Entwicklung des Berliner Buchhandels*, p. 178; Schürmann, *Der deutsche Buchhandel*, p. 23; Martin Vogel, "Deutsche Urheber- und Verlagsrechtsgeschichte zwischen 1450 und 1850. Sozial- und Methodengeschichtliche Entwicklungsstufen der Rechte von Schriftsteller und Verleger," *AGB* 19 (1978): col. 118. Luckily for Nicolai, he did not have to meet these prerequisites; he had only absolved a three-year apprenticeship!

22. Reinhard Wittmann emphasizes the helplessness of booksellers in the face of growing competition and dubious practices because they did not have a guild or other professional organization. "Die frühen Buchhändlerzeitschriften," cols. 628–29. Although this may have been true in terms of the book trade as a *national* entity (and certainly the booksellers complained loudly and bitterly of their plight), it may underestimate the influence booksellers were able to exert over their own governments. The Berlin and Prussian governments at least asked for the opinions of booksellers. In 1796, for example, Town Councillor Lieder wrote to Nicolai (among other booksellers) for his suggestions on how to combat the piracy of Prussian publications in Austria. Letters of 2 and 20 May 1796, Berlin, in NN 45.

23. Georgi, *Die Entwicklung des Berliner Buchhandels*, p. 181.

copies on to Nicolai, "because it seems advisable on this occasion that all of the booksellers oppose the petition of... Müller under your advice and leadership." The chances of success were good because as one could see from the rescript, the Generaldirektorium was disinclined to bestow a new privilege and would certainly seek the opinion of all local booksellers first.[24] Of course, the king was not obliged to follow the booksellers' advice, and according to the historian of the Berlin book trade Arthur Georgi, privilege applications were often approved regardless of whether a new bookseller was "needed" or not, the argument being that booksellers' "monopolies" led to high prices.[25] Booksellers' opinions were at least integrated into the decision-making process, though, and sometimes proved influential: Müller was denied the coveted privilege.[26]

Privileged booksellers were equally intolerant of people from outside the book trades invading their "turf." In January 1784, for example, the bookseller S. F. Hesse informed Nicolai of the progress of the case of a Jew named Simon who was accused of selling unbound books. Hesse had recently been called as a witness before the Berlin municipal council, which was handling the case after it had been referred from the Generaldirektorium. The case came to nothing,[27] but in order to deter potential

---

24. Belitz to Nicolai, Berlin, 12 November 1800, in NN 3.
25. Georgi, *Die Entwicklung des Berliner Buchhandels*, p. 181.
26. Ibid., pp. 180–82. Several others shared this fate, although some were successful in the end.

   In addition to general privileges, the Prussian state also issued special privileges, usually for the publication of a specific book or journal, but sometimes also for a certain class of book (e.g., school primers). Special privileges were issued by the Lehnsdepartment (department of feudalities in the Ministry of Justice). Printers, for example, held only special privileges, and their publishing activities were generally limited to Bibles, sermons, hymnals, school texts, pamphlets, and the like. Before the introduction of freedom of trade in 1810 they were usually only permitted to sell books at local fairs (*Jahrmärkte*). There were, of course, exceptions, notably Johann Friedrich Unger and the royal printer Georg Jacob Decker, who were both also important publishers in Berlin. Similar regulations applied to the bookselling activities of bookbinders. Behind such regulations was the idea of preventing *doppelte Nahrung*, the practice of two trades at the same time. Georgi, *Die Entwicklung des Berliner Buchhandels*, pp. 179–80 and 162. On attempts to control the bookselling activities of bookbinders in Prussia, see pp. 189–90. See also the stipulations in the Prussian legal code of 1794, which threatened bookbinders with the confiscation of any unbound books they were offering for sale, as well as a fine. *Allgemeines Landrecht für die Preußischen Staaten von 1794 (ALR)*, Textausgabe (Frankfurt a. M.: Alfred Metzner, 1970), pt. 2, title 20, sec. 15, "Von Beschädigungen des Vermögens durch strafbaren Eigennutz und Betrug," §1297.

27. Hesse attended the interrogation of Simon's thirteen-year-old son who, according to his father, had actually sold the books in question. The boy denied having taken the books on commission for sale, insisting instead that they had been a gift for which he had no use. There was no proof of any criminal intent, and a search unearthed no further unbound books. The boy was

miscreants, Hesse applied in the name of all Berlin booksellers to the Generaldirektorium to announce in the newspapers that no person without a royal privilege was authorized to sell books unbound. His petition was registered and sent to a higher instance for approval. Hesse was asked to present his privilege for this purpose, but apparently not all royal privileges were created equal and he thought Nicolai's might be more convincing: "Since it [Hesse's privilege] is only a general one, and I hear from Herr Voß that yours is much more exact and incomparably more useful for this purpose ... it would surely be more advantageous for us."[28] Thus did Berlin booksellers, including Nicolai, use collective channels to close ranks against interlopers.

Book Fairs, Commissionaires, and Trading Partners

The Frankfurt and Leipzig book fairs were at once the distinguishing feature of the German book trade and the central events of the bookseller-publisher's year. They reflected the decentralized nature of bookselling and publishing and promoted the relatively rapid dissemination of new books throughout the German-speaking region. The system of barter at the fairs, introduced during a period of cash shortages and debased currency after the Thirty Years' War, also determined the continuing predominance of combined publishing-bookselling enterprises in Germany until the late eighteenth century. Few booksellers had enough ready money to pay for the books they needed in cash rather than kind, and publishers were loath to offer credit to purely retail booksellers. Thus most were compelled to publish titles of their own.[29] The Frankfurt fair had been declining in importance vis-à-vis Leipzig since the seventeenth century, a process that Philipp Erasmus Reich saw fit to declare complete in 1764 with an announcement that he would no longer attend the Frankfurt fair. Nicolai himself never went to the Frankfurt fair. The Leipzig fair was originally held for one week three times a year (at Michaelmas in late September, Christmas, and Easter). By the time Nicolai began attending, however, it was reduced to two weeks in the early autumn and spring. Of these, the Easter fair was far better attended and thus offered

---

released with a warning to refrain from further trade in unbound books. Perhaps this was the precocious start of the B. Simonsohn who appears as an antiquarian bookseller and commissionaire in Berlin in 1797? He is mentioned by Georgi, *Die Entwicklung des Berliner Buchhandels*, p. 132.

28. Hesse to Nicolai, Berlin, 6 January 1784, in NN 34.
29. Meyer, "Die geschäftlichen Verhältnisse," pp. 176–82.

wider opportunities for exchange and sales as well as for making contacts with authors, customers, and printers. Most new titles appeared at the Easter fair and only continuations at Michaelmas. By the late eighteenth century, accounts were settled only once a year, at the Easter fair.[30] The second week of the fair, which booksellers devoted to financial dealings, was known as payment week (*Zahlwoche*).[31]

The system of trade fairs, once widespread throughout Western Europe, declined in the sixteenth and seventeenth centuries as new credit institutions and stock exchanges were founded and major cities took on the function of permanent fairs.[32] In the German book trade, the eighteenth century brought the expansion of selling between the fairs and the development of a system of commissionaires, which enabled more booksellers to conduct business from their own cities. Despite these developments, however, the German book fairs, like the other trade fairs of Central and Eastern Europe, retained their importance throughout most of the eighteenth century.[33] The book trade may, as Reinhard Wittmann has argued, have been growing more anonymous as cash payments replaced the old barter system, but Nicolai knew most of his business partners personally and met them frequently during his lifetime.

Nicolai's life revolved around preparations for and journeys to and from the book fairs. He considered Leipzig, where he spent some eight weeks of every year, to be his second home.[34] He used midwinter and midsummer, the slowest periods of the bookseller's year because the most distant from fair time, to recuperate. Almost every summer he took the waters, in earlier years at Bad Freyenwalde and later at Bad Pyrmont, where he was joined by numerous friends and authors. After Christmas he often retreated to the country, staying with friend and author Pastor Raymund Dapp at Klein Schönebeck near Berlin, and devoted himself to writing. It was there, for example, that he composed most of *Sebaldus Nothanker* in a few weeks of intense activity.

30. Goldfriedrich, *Geschichte des deutschen Buchhandels*, 2:268–69.

31. This term is mentioned in Walch to Nicolai, Schleusingen, 30 September 1780, in NN 79.

32. Geoffrey Parker, "The Emergence of Modern Finance in Europe, 1500–1730," *The Fontana Economic History of Europe: The Sixteenth and Seventeenth Centuries*, ed. Carlo M. Cipolla (Glasgow: Collins/Fontana, 1974), p. 548.

33. Hermann Kellenbenz emphasizes the continued importance of trade fairs for the economies of Eastern and Central Europe in *The Rise of the European Economy. An Economic History of Continental Europe from the Fifteenth to the Eighteenth Century*, ed. Gerhard Benecke (London: Weidenfeld & Nicolson, 1976), p. 302.

34. Nicolai, *Beschreibung einer Reise*, 2:37.

Although war or poor health prevented Nicolai from attending several Michaelmas fairs, it was not until 1798, when he was seriously ill, that Nicolai missed an Easter fair. Such constancy was by no means universal. Some booksellers lived too far away to attend the fairs regularly, and instead used the services of a Leipzig commissionaire or another bookseller who went to the fair and attended to business for them. They saved time and expense, but missed the opportunity of meeting their fellow booksellers personally.[35] A visit to the book fair could be quite costly. When Benjamin Gottlob Hoffmann of Hamburg visited the 1782 Easter fair, for example, he spent some 150 taler for the journey, lodgings, and food. The price of Leipzig shop and warehouse premises could run an additional 50 to 200 taler annually.[36] Once in Leipzig, the bookseller was also faced with printers, papermakers, and sometimes authors, as well as fellow booksellers clamoring for payment. The Langensalza bookseller Johann Siegmund Zolling told Nicolai he was avoiding the 1790 Easter fair because he could not confront his creditors there.[37] Similarly, in 1801 Koehler of Ulm decided that with business as miserable as it was, he would do better to save the money for a journey to Leipzig and pay off his "hardhearted" creditors instead.[38]

Since he almost invariably traveled to the fairs, or sent representatives on the rare occasions when he could not attend himself, business remained a matter Nicolai conducted personally. The many years of editing the *ADB* made it particularly important that Nicolai knew exactly which new books were appearing, and acquired them at the source for his reviewers, which he could best accomplish by attending the fairs. He had a large enough volume of trade to need two *Diener* and two *Markthelfer* (at least in the early 1790s), and to maintain double sets of fair account books.[39]

35. The Mannheim bookseller Christian Friedrich Schwan, who was represented in Leipzig by his father-in-law Johann Georg Esslinger of Frankfurt am Main, mentions the valuable opportunities for personal contact with other booksellers afforded by the fair in a letter of 22 June 1773 to the printer Georg Jacob Decker, in SPKB, Nachlaß Decker, vol. 9, no. 210.

36. Gert Ueding and Bernd Steinbrink, *Hoffmann und Campe: Ein deutscher Verlag* (Hamburg: Hoffmann & Campe, 1981), p. 77.

37. Zolling apologized to Nicolai for not being able to meet his obligations and asked if he would be interested in taking over a work he could not afford to continue publishing. Zolling to Nicolai, Langensalza, 2 May 1790, in NN 84.

38. Koehler to Nicolai, Ulm, 2 April 1801, in NN 42. Koehler and Nicolai corresponded from at least 1783 on literary and political conditions in Swabia. Koehler published the *Schwäbisches Magazin*. He collected prenumerations for Nicolai. In 1803 lack of funds once again kept him away from Leipzig. Koehler to Nicolai, Ulm, 22 April 1803, in NN 42.

39. Nicolai to P. G. Kummer, Berlin, 13 April 1792, in DBSM, BöV Archivalien, Kummersches Archiv, Kasten 1, no. 3a. 6.

With a wide range of customers of differing tastes, he was obliged to do business with many publishers in different cities, which was more convenient at the fair than through extensive correspondence. Leipzig was also the place to discuss those topics, from actions against pirates to intricate financial negotiations or censorship problems, which might be difficult or dangerous to treat by letter. Finally, the book fair also gave Nicolai the opportunity to meet personally with authors and reviewers from the surrounding region, and to visit friends and correspondents on the way to and from Leipzig.[40]

In his memoirs Friedrich Perthes characterizes meeting Nicolai at the Leipzig fair as "one of the most memorable incidents of my life." As he recalls the event, "I spoke to F. Nicolai; he is just as I had pictured him to myself, tall and stout, and a most extraordinary swaggerer; I thought he would have carried himself proudly to the booksellers, but he stood in a doorway for half-an-hour chatting with them."[41] Nicolai had many friends in Leipzig, and numerous people not directly connected with the book trade gathered during the fair to meet acquaintances or publishers and to inform themselves about new titles.[42] A visit to the Leipzig fair combined business with pleasure, and Nicolai sometimes took his wife and daughters along.[43] During the less hectic first week of the fair, while the *Markthelfer* and *Diener* unpacked and got the shop in order, the booksellers and their friends and families attended balls, dinners, and the theater or made pleasure trips to the surrounding countryside.[44] Thus the fairs, although primarily commercial occasions, also formed part of

---

40. After the 1773 Easter fair, for example, Nicolai and his former *Diener*, the Berlin bookseller August Mylius, went to Weimar to meet Wieland and others. In Leipzig, he had met with the *ADB* reviewer Johann Heinrich Merck. Nicolai to Ludwig Julius Friedrich Höpfner, Leipzig, 26 June 1773, in *Briefe aus dem Freundeskreis von Goethe, Herder, Höpfner und Merck*, ed. Karl Wagner (Leipzig: Ernst Fleischer, 1847). Other booksellers also used their journeys to and from the book fairs for social and business calls. Ueding and Steinbrink, *Hoffmann und Campe*, p. 78.

41. *Memoirs of Frederick Perthes*, 1:14.

42. One of Nicolai's customers, Fräulein Westfeld, for example, informed him that she would be visiting the fair to look for interesting new books. Westfeld to Nicolai, Lauterburg, 5 January 1775, in NN 82.

43. At Easter 1764, for example, Nicolai was accompanied by his wife, and at Easter 1791 by his wife and daughters. C. F. Weiße to Nicolai, Leipzig, 5 July 1764, in NN 81; Nicolai to Eschenburg, Leipzig, 27 April 1791, in HAB, no. 114.

44. Ueding and Steinbrink, *Hoffmann und Campe*, p. 77. In 1796, Nicolai informed his daughter Wilhelmine, who was contemplating a visit to Leipzig to see Elisa von der Recke, that she would first have to make the round of "Diners and Soupers" before she could spend time with her friend. Nicolai to Wilhelmine Nicolai, Leipzig, 23 April 1796, in LAB, Rep. 200 Acc 450, vol. 9, no. 44.

the wide range of sociability that came to revolve around books in the latter half of the eighteenth century.

At the fair, booksellers gathered in a few streets around the university, the St. Nicholas churchyard, and the two Neumärkte (old and new) where the Leipzigers had their bookshops. In the 1760s, Nicolai's Leipzig premises were located, appropriately enough, in the Nicolaistraße, "at the sign of the golden ring."[45] At Michaelmas 1776 he moved to the house of A. F. Schott on the Alter Neumarkt where he remained until at least 1792. His space there was substantial, consisting of six rooms, including two on the ground floor facing the street. From 1782 on Nicolai also had the use of an attic year round and an "auditorium" equipped with tables, chairs, and benches during fair time. From 1801 on he leased smaller premises from the university off the courtyard of the Collegium Paulinum, and apparently lodged separately.[46]

Until 1780 Nicolai was represented in Leipzig by Philipp Erasmus Reich, the city's most prominent publisher, and thereafter by P. G. Kummer. A number of Nicolai's mainly quite brief letters to Reich from the 1770s have survived, allowing us to reconstruct at least some of their dealings. Sums of money are only rarely mentioned in the correspondence, and there is no indication of what fee Reich received for his services. They may have worked on a basis of reciprocal services; for example, Reich made payments to the Berlin illustrator Daniel Chodowiecki via Nicolai and Nicolai helped find a French translator for a work Reich was publishing.[47] Reich's services included locating rooms in Leipzig for Nicolai, placing advertisements for him in the local papers, registering his new titles with the Book Commission, dispatching letters and packages, and distributing copies of the *ADB* and other books to Leipzig

---

45. *Leipziger Stadtadreßbuch* (Leipzig, 1764), p. 163.

46. Contract between Nicolai and A. F. Schott, dated 16 May 1776, with additions from 22 October 1782, which lists the annual rent as 80 and 100 taler (in louis d'ors, to be paid in two installments), respectively, and contract dated 11 December 1800 between Nicolai and Leipzig University, mentioning a rent of 50 taler. In NN 285, nos. 19 and 20. A letter of 31 March 1801 from Christiane Haasin (in NN 29) offers him two rooms, one large and one small at 12 and 4 taler respectively, plus 2 taler each for feather quilts for the coming Easter fair.

47. Nicolai to Reich, Berlin, 18 November and 2 December 1775, in SPKB, Autogr. I/1590 15 and 16, which refer to sending money to Nicolai for Chodowiecki. Nicolai also acted as intermediary between Reich and the Berlin artist Bernhard Rode, perhaps for the illustrations to J. M. Schroeckh's *Weltgeschichte für Kinder*. Nicolai to Reich, Berlin, 14 April 1778, in SPKB Autogr. I/1590–20. Nicolai arranged for the French Reformed pastor P.C.F. Reclam in Berlin to translate Hirschfeld's *Theorie der Gartenkunst*. Nicolai to Reich, Berlin, 10 October 1778, in SPKB Autogr. I/1590-22.

customers between the fairs.[48] Nicolai sent Reich bales of printed sheets to store for him,[49] and printers closer to Leipzig than Berlin often sent works they had printed for Nicolai to Reich, who then sent on the copies needed in Berlin by wagon (*zur Fuhre*) and retained the rest for Nicolai's Leipzig storeroom,[50] to which he held the keys. Thus he could distribute books, when requested, to other booksellers or to Nicolai himself.[51] It was Reich who in 1775 advised Nicolai to establish a warehouse (*Niederlage*) for his publications in Frankfurt am Main, probably in order to make them more cheaply and readily available there and thus discourage pirates. Nicolai agreed that it was a good idea, noting "the only trick is to find a reliable and meticulous commissionaire."[52] There were also limits to his services; Nicolai emphasized repeatedly that Reich was not obliged to dispatch books from the storeroom to booksellers outside Leipzig if it was inconvenient. Only occasionally, when a book was not in stock in Berlin, or when a customer requested transport by wagon of a package that local regulations deemed too small (but which would have been too costly to send by post), should Reich dispatch it from Leipzig.[53]

Eventually, Nicolai decided (or agreed?) to relieve Reich of his commissionaire duties, as they were causing his already busy colleague too much trouble. He thanked Reich "for the many favors and kindnesses" he had shown him and promised that he would be happy to reciprocate.[54] Reich apparently accepted the change in their relations with relief or at

---

48. Nicolai to Reich, Berlin, 27 January and 26 December 1770, 11 February, 18 February, 15 March, 17 June, and 7 November 1775, in SPKB Autogr. I/1590-2, 7, 8, 9, 10, 11, 12, 14.

49. For example, in 1775 Nicolai sent Reich two bales of volume 1 of *Sebaldus Nothanker* on two different kinds of paper by wagoner. Nicolai to Reich, Berlin, 12 December 1775, in SPKB Autogr. I/1590-18.

50. This was the case, for example, when the *ADB* was printed by Ahl in Coburg. Nicolai to Reich, Berlin, 26 September 1775, in SPKB Autogr. I/1590-13.

51. Sometimes Nicolai asked Reich to send packages right away by post, and other times to wait until he had enough to give a wagoner bound for Berlin. A letter of 3 June 1772 from Nicolai mentions waiting until Reich had amassed half a hundredweight. In Staats- und Universitätsbibliothek Hamburg, Handschriftenabteilung [hereafter cited as "SUB Hamburg"]. I thank Mark Lehmstedt for a copy of his transcription of this letter. For a more detailed account of the letter's contents, see Selwyn, *Philosophy in the Comptoir*, pp. 397–400.

52. Nicolai to Reich, Berlin, 17 June 1775, in SPKB Autogr. I/1590-12.

53. Nicolai to Reich, Berlin, 9 December 1775 and 15 September 1778, in SPKB Autogr. I/1590-17 and 1590-21. He repeated this request in a letter of 25 January 1780, in SPKB Autogr. I/1590-23. In September 1778, for example, Nicolai asked Reich to send some books to bookseller customers in Basel and Breslau. Nicolai to Reich, Berlin, 15 September 1778, in SPKB Autogr. I/1590-21.

54. Nicolai to Reich, Berlin, 25 January and 1 May 1780, in SPKB Autogr. I/1590-23 and -26.

least equanimity. "I thank you, dearest friend," wrote Nicolai, "for taking the change in my commission ... in the spirit in which it was intended."[55]

Reich was not only Nicolai's commissionaire but also an important business partner. A letter of 1772 outlining Nicolai's dissatisfaction with aspects of their accounts gives us some idea of their trade and underlines the problem, experienced not only by South German booksellers, of the financial advantages enjoyed by Leipzig publishers. The main bone of contention was the 25 percent discount Reich accorded Nicolai, which Nicolai found inadequate given what he saw as their special relationship and the imbalance of trade between them now that Reich was publishing so many more books a year than he was. Nicolai complained that their dealings were financially disadvantageous to him, since he lost an average of 6 percent on freight (from Leipzig to Berlin, then often from Berlin to Stettin or Danzig) and 6 percent on currency exchange. He could not simply compensate for these losses by raising prices, because, in the case of Reich's publications, he had to compete with the Berlin bookseller Voß, to whom Reich accorded a larger discount,[56] and who thus advertised (and sold) the books at the lower original prices. Reich's discount left no buffer to protect him against all the books that sat on the shelves or his losses from bad debts. Nicolai felt that his own conduct toward Reich entitled him to better conditions; he paid his annual bills punctually and was one of Reich's more substantial customers. At the previous Easter fair alone he had ordered 300 taler worth of books, which he had to pay for in cash rather than kind. Out of friendship for Reich, and for the sake of German literature, he had made sure that these books were well publicized, including reviews in the Stettin papers. For all these reasons he believed he deserved a 33 percent discount, which all other firms whose prices he could not raise granted him, he said. If Reich could not offer him this discount for both *Netto* and *Sortiment* books (i.e., books from his own firm and from other firms), he should bill him separately for the latter at the 25 percent discount customary at the time for *Sortiment*.[57] If Reich agreed to his terms Nicolai promised to continue to

---

55. Nicolai to Reich, Berlin, 9 (?) May 1780, in SPKB Autogr. I/1590-25.

56. Voß apparently took a large quantity of Gellert's works on consignment from Reich to sell to other booksellers—perhaps as a means of discouraging the piracies of the Berliner Joachim Pauli—in exchange for a larger discount. Nicolai mentions a discrepancy in price between the copies of Gellert's *Moral* he received from Reich and those from Voß, which went under the title of Gellert's *Schriften*, vols. 6 and 7. Voß's copies cost 4 groschen less than Reich's. Nicolai to Reich, Berlin, 31 October 1770, in SPKB Autogr. I/1590-5.

57. Meyer, "Die geschäftlichen Verhältnisse," p. 211.

promote Reich's books to the best of his ability. Otherwise, for his own "self-preservation" he would have to order only the books he absolutely needed and expend less effort in advertising Reich's products. Nothing obliged him to keep such a large stock of Reich's titles if they brought so little profit. In short, if Reich sought his own advantage he could not fault Nicolai for doing the same. It went without saying, Nicolai assured him, that any larger discount afforded him would remain their secret.[58] Whether Nicolai got the desired 33 percent discount is not recorded. Reich apparently only rarely granted more than 25 percent.[59] Despite their close ties and the high value of Nicolai's publications, Reich also required from him as he did from others cash payments (as opposed to sheet-for-sheet barter). He did, however, make the apparent concession of doing some consignment trade with Nicolai, at least by 1780.[60]

Most booksellers offered their colleagues discounts of one-third on those books sold for cash only (*Netto*) but discounts of 20, 25, or 30 percent were not uncommon. Greater discounts were frequently available for bulk orders.[61] Self-publishing authors or editors were sometimes willing to give larger discounts than those customary in the book trade. Wilhelm von Archenholtz, for example, offered Nicolai a 40 percent discount on his journals (*British Mercury* and *English Lyceum*), asking that he keep the offer secret. He knew that the Hamburg booksellers Hoffmann and Bohn could not afford to offer discounts of one-third after what they paid him.[62] Nicolai himself was not averse to offering substantial discounts for large orders. When Gebrüder Hahn in Hannover requested 200 copies of a single title on consignment, Nicolai offered them 40 percent off, which he asked them to keep to themselves.[63] On the other hand, Nicolai granted some booksellers, such as the Bamberg pirate Tobias Goebhard, only 25 percent discounts. Goebhard's lawyer used this fact as part of his defense strategy in Nicolai's piracy suit against his client.[64] Presumably, Nicolai gave a one-third discount to his better customers,

---

58. Nicolai to Reich, Berlin, 3 June 1772, in SUB Hamburg.
59. Lehmstedt, *Struktur und Arbeitsweise*, p. 56.
60. Thus in May of that year Nicolai ordered thirty copies of J. G. Sulzer's *Tagebuch* on consignment, and Reich in turn asked to return unsold copies of the *ADB* in exchange for other books from Nicolai's firm. Nicolai to Reich, Berlin, 9 (?) May 1780, in SPKB, Autogr. I/1590-25.
61. Meyer, "Die geschäftlichen Verhältnisse," pp. 188–90.
62. Archenholtz to Nicolai, Hamburg, 19 February 1788, in NN 2.
63. Nicolai's annotations on a letter of 19 November 1807 from the author of the work in question, Friedrich von Bülow in Berlin, in NN 11.
64. See Chapter 5.

since he expected that in return, as is revealed not only in his exchange with Reich but also in an 1800 conflict with the Berlin bookseller Johann Daniel Sander over discounts.[65]

Nicolai's letter to Reich also raises a second important topic, that of *Sortiment*. *Sortiment* books were ordered between the fairs and often from a single bookseller, like Nicolai, who maintained a large stock of titles from many firms and acted as a wholesaler. This was more convenient than ordering from several publishers and saved on postage. The procedure was for the bookseller who wanted to buy to send a letter or a handwritten list of desired titles, called a *Memorial*, to the *Sortimenter*. If the latter did not have all the titles, he or she procured the missing books from other local bookshops.[66] Nicolai had many *Sortiment* customers, although few orders have survived, perhaps because they were copied into the account books and then returned with shipments as invoices. One substantial customer was the Riga bookseller J. F. Hartknoch. His *Memorial* of 23 January 1774 listed books from ten Berlin firms as well

---

65. On Sander, see Uwe Hentschel, "'Wäre ich Ramler, so könnte ich mir Antheil an manchem Lafontainschen Buch zuschreiben!' Der Verleger Johann Daniel Sander und sein Erfolgsautor August Lafontaine," *Leipziger Jahrbuch zur Buchgeschichte* 7 (1997): 75–106. Sander had bought the business of the Berlin publisher/bookseller Arnold Wever in 1798 and refused to accord Nicolai the 33⅓ percent that his predecessor had, explaining that he had almost totally abandoned the retail trade. The exchange, of which we unfortunately only have Sander's side, presents the image of a powerful and somewhat menacing Nicolai as he must have appeared to a younger Berlin bookseller just getting started in a difficult period. As Sander noted, Nicolai was a rich man with grown children, while he was a mere beginner. For him, the additional 8 percent Nicolai demanded was no bagatelle, particularly if, as he hoped, they would do several hundred taler worth of business a year with each other. He found a 25 percent discount quite adequate among Berlin booksellers because they enjoyed the advantage of immediate delivery, and other booksellers were satisfied with that amount. To show his respect, however, Sander was willing to give him the old discount on Wever's titles. Soon after, though, matters took an unpleasant turn. Sander's books were left out of Nicolai's latest shop catalog, whether deliberately or not, and he was ready to believe the worst. Someone in Nicolai's shop had apparently told Sander that he would be left out of the catalog again if he did not raise his discount. He had also heard a rumor that Nicolai's firm had threatened another Berlin bookseller, Sander's old employer Voß, with the same treatment if he did not come up with a 33⅓ percent discount in exchange for monthly payment. Now Sander was willing to accord Nicolai the requested discount under the condition that he tell nobody, not buy his books for third-party booksellers, and grant him 33⅓ percent as well. Nicolai must have written quite a conciliatory letter to Sander, because the latter agreed to forget recent events and give him a 33⅓ discount from then on. Sander to Nicolai, Berlin, 19 and 22 April, 28 October, and 1 November 1800, in NN 65. Apparently Nicolai also asked the Widow Mylius to grant him a larger discount, but she refused, saying that all the other firms would expect 33 percent as well, and she could not afford it, what with the low price of school texts and rising production costs. Madame Mylius to Nicolai, Berlin, 16 May 1808, in NN 51.

66. Meyer, "Die geschäftlichen Verhältnisse," pp. 209–12.

as Nicolai's company. His largest orders were for a hundred copies of a work on geography and twenty-five of *Sebaldus Nothanker*.[67] Other *Sortiment* customers whose orders have survived include Johann Joachim Christoph Bode in Hamburg (later Weimar), W. G. Korn in Breslau, Johann Schweighauser in Basel, Pierre Gosse in The Hague, and J. H. Schneider in Amsterdam.[68] Nicolai himself ordered his *Sortiment* from Reich in Leipzig and Johann Christian Gebhard in Frankfurt am Main, among others.[69]

Cooperation and Competition among Booksellers: The Case of Translations

Although the book trade certainly had its share of unscrupulous characters, they were by no means the majority. In his 1808 letter to Friedrich Perthes, Nicolai looked back with some nostalgia on the book trade of his youth, seeing it as a time of order compared to the chaos of the present, with its dog-eat-dog struggles for economic survival. The ideal of an enterprise among gentlemen and equals who adhered to the principles of "solid trade" was one that he clung to, out of both moral conviction and the belief that it represented the soundest economic practice. Respectable publishers not only made a point of keeping each other informed of pirate editions and joined together to fight their less law-abiding colleagues, or members of other branches of the book trade who overstepped legal or customary boundaries, but also took other measures to ensure a certain degree of peace within the trade.

Booksellers or authors who wished to publish translations were, for example, under no obligation to deal with the publisher of the original work, since purchasing translation rights was unheard of. Where contacts did exist, they involved either the mere physical acquisition of the work to be translated (sometimes even before publication in the original language),[70] or orders for illustrations. *Sebaldus Nothanker*, Nicolai's

---

67. The other publishers on Hartknoch's list were Mylius, Birnstiel, Boßi, Decker, Haude und Spener, Himburg, Lange, Pauli, Voß, and the Realschule. Hartknoch, *Memorial* to Nicolai, 23 January 1774, in NN 30 [Hartknoch correspondence].

68. Bode to Nicolai, Hamburg, 17 January 1772, 8 May 1781, and October 1782, in NN 6; Korn to Nicolai, Breslau, 15 March 1767, in NN 42; Schweighauser to Nicolai, Basel, 20 April 1772, in NN 70; Gosse to Nicolai, The Hague, 18 February 1777, in NN 26; and Schneider to Nicolai, Amsterdam, 27 March 1778, in NN 68.

69. Nicolai, undated *Memorial* to Weidmanns Erben and Reich, 1770s, in SPKB Autogr. I-1590-1, and Gebhard to Nicolai, Frankfurt am Main, 1 March 1765, in NN 84.

70. See the example, mentioned below, of J. H. Munnikhuisen, who was publishing a Dutch translation of the German translation/adaptation of *Johann Bunkel* (originally an *English* novel) and awaited the text from Nicolai.

Everyday Life in the Book Trade

most-translated publication,⁷¹ furnishes two examples. In 1777, the Société typographique de Neuchâtel wrote to request copies of Daniel Chodowiecki's engravings for *Nothanker*, but Nicolai regretted that he could not oblige because, he said, the plates were worn out from the large German printings.⁷² In 1796, however, when the Gothenburg publisher Samuel Norberg made a similar request, he consented. Perhaps he believed that *Nothanker*'s Swedish readers would be less exacting than the Société's sophisticated clients? He did warn Norberg, who had apparently lost all of his 1788 Swedish translation in a fire, that the impressions would be very weak, but did not refuse his request for 1000 copies of each plate. The price he set—about 40 taler for 1000 copies of sixteen illustrations—was some 6 taler above his estimate of the cost. Perhaps he was touched by the sad story of the complete destruction of Norberg's printing shop and house or by his wistful remarks about Gothenburg not being the kind of place "where one man can offer another many pleasant services in the literary line.... One has little to do with the scientific enlightenment of the soul here. One is a merchant and nothing more."⁷³

Among respectable booksellers, at least within the same city, it was considered proper to inquire whether one was intruding on any territory before undertaking a project involving works from another publisher's firm. This was both polite and prudent, if one wished to avoid unpleasant and sometimes all-too-public conflicts. In 1780, when Rudolph Zacharias Becker offered Nicolai an expanded German version of his answer to the Berlin Academy's essay competition Nicolai refused, as he said, because his Berlin colleague Voß printed all the prize essays and it would be improper to publish a revised version at the same time. He would, however, be happy to publish it in a year or two.⁷⁴ In 1791, the Königsberg

---

71. *Sebaldus Nothanker* was also translated into Danish, Dutch, English, and French.
72. Nicolai to the Société typographique de Neuchâtel [hereafter cited as "STN"], Berlin, 20 August 1777, in STN MS 1187 fols. 98–105. I thank Jeffrey Freedman for providing a transcription of this letter.
73. Norberg to Nicolai, Gothenburg, 28 December 1796, in NN 54. Despite his misfortunes, Norberg had managed to rebuild and even expand his business. He owned ten presses and two paper mills and was in the process of acquiring a type foundry.
74. Nicolai's annotations on Becker's letter of 14 September 1780, quoted in Reinhard Siegert, "Aufklärung und Volkslektüre: Exemplarisch dargestellt an Rudolph Zacharias Becker und seinem 'Noth-und Hülfsbüchlein,'" *AGB* 19 (1978): col. 634. In the event, the work was published not by Nicolai but by Siegfried Lebrecht Crusius in Leipzig. The competition question, one of the most important and controversial of the period, was "Est-il utile au peuple d'être trompé?" (Is it useful to the people to be duped [by their government]?), which Becker, known as a proponent of the popular Enlightenment, naturally answered in the negative.

publisher Friedrich Nicolovius asked Nicolai whether he had any objection to his printing an excerpt from Jacobsson's *Technologisches Wörterbuch*. The compiler had assured him that Nicolai did not wish to publish it himself, but Nicolovius wanted Nicolai's written permission and would respect his wishes if he refused to grant it.[75] When Nicolai asked the publisher Christian Gottlieb Rabenhorst for permission to reprint some writings by Justus Möser, the rights to which Rabenhorst had acquired from the firm of Cramer, for his edition of the collected works, the bookseller admitted "that it pains me to relinquish my publishing rights [*Verlags Recht*]" but recognizing Nicolai's "noble intentions in the new edition," he would not try to thwart him. He asked only that Nicolai allow him to sell the remaining stock of some thirty copies, to which Nicolai noted in the margin "most certainly."[76]

When Nicolai found himself in a similar position, however, he acted rather differently. Rather than ceding his rights, he suggested a division of labor. The Berlin bookseller Voß, who was planning an edition of Lessing's works in the 1790s, requested Nicolai's permission to include the *Antiquarische Briefe*. He promised not to sell these volumes separately, so that they would not compete with Nicolai's older edition, and expressed his willingness to do any service Nicolai asked of him to show his gratitude. Rather than either cede the rights or refuse to do so, Nicolai's solution in this case was to publish the work himself in the same format as Voß's edition and to provide Voß with as many presentation copies on French paper as he wished, free of charge. Voß agreed and gave Nicolai instructions on the paper and printing. Nicolai, in turn, offered Voß advice on the order in which some of Lessing's essays should be printed, and on whether all of the essays were really his work, and the like. In February 1794, when Nicolai was in the country visiting friends, Voß even sent him the *Berliner Zeitung* for the years 1751–53 (when Lessing had written for the paper), asking him to choose some articles to fill out volume 23. Nicolai was the only person who could help him, Voß said, because of his close early friendship with Lessing. "Even small fragments of Lessing are of interest to the nation," Voß assured him.[77]

Ordinarily, Nicolai appears to have preferred to avoid competing with other booksellers over publishing rights. In the case of Baumgart and

---

75. Nicolovius to Nicolai, Königsberg, 3 February 1791, in NN 52.
76. Rabenhorst to Nicolai, Leipzig, 17 September 1796, in NN 59.
77. Voß to Nicolai, Berlin, 17 November 1791, 19 June 1792, 1 July and 6 September 1793, and 5 and 8 February 1794, and Nicolai's annotations, in NN 77.

Svarez's *Briefen-Wechsel über die Justitz Reform in den Königlich Preußischen Staaten*, which both Nicolai and the royal printer Georg Jacob Decker were interested in, Nicolai noted "In order to avoid all conflict I will withdraw voluntarily." The fact that Großkanzler Carmer told the authors not to accept a fee of less than 3 louis d'or or about 15 taler per sheet may have strengthened his resolve to avoid a collision with Decker.[78]

Translations of well-known literary works and books on hot topics were doubtless a frequent source of conflicts over rights, but Nicolai, at least, seems to have found amicable solutions. In 1767, for example, he apparently ceded the rights to a translation of the Marquis d'Argens's *Lettres chinoises* to Heinrich Ludwig Brönner in Frankfurt am Main. The first volume of the translation, which Nicolai had commissioned from a certain Herr Jünger, the translator of his edition of d'Argens's *Lettres juives*, was already finished. Presumably, Brönner had also been planning a translation. Although Brönner published the work and paid the translator, Nicolai permitted his own name to appear as publisher on the title page, probably because it would not have passed the strict imperial censors in Frankfurt.[79] In a later case of 1782, Nicolai and Philipp Erasmus Reich also found that they were both having the same work translated. In this instance, Nicolai's response was not to retreat, but to deny that any conflict existed. The book in question was an alleged sequel to Moufle d'Angerville et Bouffonidor's *Vie privée de Louis XV*, which Nicolai had published in four volumes in 1781, as Reich well knew. When his correspondent Isaak van Cleef in The Hague announced a forthcoming fifth volume, Nicolai was naturally interested and again engaged the translator Karl Friedrich Trost. Meanwhile, Philipp Erasmus Reich had hired Christian Friedrich Blankenburg to translate the same work and staked his claim as rightful publisher with an entry in the protocol book of the Leipzig Book Commission. According to the Mandate of Electoral Saxony of 1773, this gave him preference as publisher.[80] Nicolai claimed that Reich had known of his planned translation at the Easter book fair, but had gone ahead nevertheless and hired a translator. By the time Nicolai

78. Nicolai's annotations on Baumgart to Nicolai, Berlin, 10 October 1780, in NN 87.
79. Brönner to Nicolai, Frankfurt am Main, 17 January and 6 February 1767, in NN 10. The book, originally published in 1739–40, appeared in five volumes as *Chinesische Briefe, oder philosophischer, historischer und kritischer Briefwechsel, zwischen einem reisenden Chinesen in Paris und seinen guten Freunden in China, Moscau, Persien und Japan* (1768–71).
80. For more on conflicts over translations, see Mark Lehmstedt, "Die Geschichte einer Übersetzung. William Robertsons 'Geschichte von Amerika' (1777)," *Leipziger Jahrbuch für Buchgeschichte* 1 (1991): 265–97, esp. 279–80.

heard of Reich's translation in the summer, it was already half-completed, and Reich demanded that he withdraw. Nicolai, however, insisted that each should continue with his plans, given their obligations to their translators and the fact that no bookseller could forbid another from publishing a translation. The entry in the protocol book, he insisted, was designed only to protect Reich against a piracy, not a separate translation. By the time a third publisher, Joachim Pauli in Berlin, entered the fray, Nicolai had made the interesting discovery that the book in question was not a continuation of the *Vie privée*. Thus he decided to drop his translation (despite his obligation to the translator), but not without a somewhat disingenuous word to Reich on the nature of translation rights: "Certainly, several translations may exist alongside each other, and this competition is even useful. If I ever commission a translation again, I cannot and will not prevent anyone from having another translation made, even if mine were already registered ... since two different translations are two entirely separate pieces of property."[81] To be sure, Nicolai did not try to prevent others from publishing translations, but he was himself extremely unlikely to accept a translation for publication if there was any danger of its being duplicated, knowing that its economic value could only be diminished.

Buying and Selling Abroad

Bernhard Fabian has described the eighteenth-century German book trade as "well organized internally," but "provincial and not sufficiently well connected in England, France, Italy, and other countries,"[82] and this certainly applies to Nicolai's business. A few firms were well connected with foreign booksellers or even maintained agents abroad,[83] but they were the exception rather than the rule. German booksellers depended heavily upon the Leipzig fairs for business contacts, and very few foreigners visited the fairs after the middle of the eighteenth century, relying

---

81. Nicolai to Reich, Berlin, 21 September 1782, quoted in Buchner, *Aus den Papieren der Weidmannischen Buchhandlung*, 1:26–29. See also Nicolai's letters of 16 July and 20 August 1782 to Reich's translator Blankenburg, in NN 5.
82. Bernhard Fabian, "The Beginnings of English-Language Publishing in Germany in the Eighteenth Century," in *Books and Society in History* (New York and London: Bowker, 1983), p. 128.
83. Philipp Erasmus Reich and the Berlin firm of Haude and Spener, for example, used the services of Johann Friedrich Schiller as a scout and correspondent in London. An agent on the spot provided not only the advantage of up-to-date information but also the opportunity to acquire freshly printed sheets of works for translation before the original work had even appeared. In the very competitive translation market this was an important factor. Lehmstedt, "Die Geschichte einer Übersetzung," pp. 272–74.

instead on commissionaires.[84] When he did need books from abroad, Nicolai frequently used intermediaries, including many who were not members of the book trade, to help locate books and to put pressure on recalcitrant payers in far-off places. It can be difficult to gauge the volume of trade among booksellers because they did not necessarily, or primarily, engage in direct correspondence. The expense of postage meant that foreign booksellers frequently sent their letters to Germany via a correspondent who was attending the Leipzig fair. Thus even when they did not attend the fair themselves, their business may have been conducted in Leipzig without a written record being left behind. Nevertheless, Nicolai's correspondence contains a number of references to relations with foreign booksellers, as well as to the problems of obtaining books from abroad. These, together with the foreign publishers whose books are listed in Nicolai's 1787 selective catalog,[85] give us some idea of the breadth of Nicolai's bookseller contacts outside of Germany, and of the different problems of trade with various countries.

Although Nicolai dealt primarily in German books for German readers, he was keenly interested in literary developments in France and England in particular, and, depending upon the ease of trade with the various countries involved, used a variety of methods for obtaining foreign-language books. He most frequently sold French titles, but did not need to deal directly with French publishers, since the books, even if published in France, were more readily obtained from the Netherlands or Switzerland, or from German booksellers such as Heinrich Ludwig Brönner[86] or Johann Christian Gebhard[87] in Frankfurt, Weidmanns Erben und Reich

---

84. Most of the foreign booksellers who attended the Leipzig book fairs regularly came from the Low Countries, and they were instrumental in the dissemination of French literature in Germany. Albrecht Kirchhoff refers to Johann Schreuder of Amsterdam and J. F. Bassompierre of Liège. After the 1770s Dutch booksellers apparently no longer attended the fairs personally. Kirchhoff, "Der ausländische Buchhandel in Leipzig," *AGDB* 14 (1891): 171, 186–87. Only one French publisher, J. M. Bruyset of Lyon, is listed in the "Alphabetical list of all booksellers and printers who visit the Leipzig fairs or whose products may be purchased there," printed in *Buchhändlerzeitung*, no. 15 (1779): 224.

85. Paul Raabe lists all the publishers mentioned in Nicolai's *Verzeichniß einer Handbibliothek* in "Zum Bild des Verlagswesens in der Spätaufklärung," pp. 66–88.

86. C. F. Weiße mentions a packet of new French books, which he had received from Paris via Brönner in Frankfurt. Weiße to Nicolai, Leipzig, 21 July 1762, in NN 81. The books included St. Foix's new plays, a new edition of Marmontel's *Contes moraux*, four recent numbers of the *Journal Etranger*, several comic operas by Favart, a new volume of Descamps's *Histoire des peintres flamands*, one volume of the *Annales typographiques*, and several "Critiques et Reflexions sur les tableaux du dernier Salon."

87. Gebhard, for example, provided sixteen copies of the Abbé Prevôt's *Mémoires d'un homme de qualité* in 1765. Gebhard to Nicolai, Frankfurt am Main, 1 March 1765, in NN 84.

in Leipzig, or in later years, Pierre-François Fauche in Hamburg.[88] Berlin, with its substantial Huguenot population, also had several French bookshops of its own. During the second half of the eighteenth century, at least one-half of French-language books were published outside France.[89] Many were printed in Germany, the most famous example being the editions of Voltaire's works published by Walther in Dresden. Nicolai's 1761 *Catalogue de plusieurs livres françois latins italiens et anglais* listed 21 books printed in Paris and five other French cities,[90] but these were far outnumbered by the 176 French-language[91] titles published in Switzerland, the Low Countries, and the ubiquitous but fictitious place of publication, "Londres."[92] Among German cities, the catalog named Frankfurt am Main with 11 titles; Cologne, Dresden, Göttingen, and Hamburg with 2 titles each; and Berlin, Halle, Nuremberg, Regensburg, Strasbourg, Tübingen, and Vienna with one title each.

For those booksellers without a large volume of trade with France, simply dispatching packages could be difficult. When in 1757 Friedrich Nicolai asked Johann Gottfried Dyck in Leipzig, who was publishing his *Bibliothek der schönen Wissenschaften*, to send something to Paris for him, the latter replied, "I cannot yet say by what means I will be able to send a package to Paris."[93] Johann Goldfriedrich asserted that direct trade between Germany and France, particularly Paris, was difficult, mainly because of the practices of French booksellers. The French, he said, gave only short-term credit, discounts of 16 or at most 25 percent, and wanted to pay their bills in books only, while expecting cash in return. Tariffs

---

88. Fauche to Nicolai, Hamburg, 21 August 1794, mentioning an order of Nicolai's, in NN 21.

89. Henri-Jean Martin, Roger Chartier, et al., *Le livre triomphant 1660–1830*, vol. 2 of *Histoire de l'édition française* (n. p. : Promodis, 1984), pp. 302–3.

90. The Parisian publishers mentioned are Durand, Bassompierre, d'Houry, and Briasson. Fourteen of the twenty-one titles are listed as published in Paris, three in Lyon (all by J. M. Bruyset), and one each in Besançon, Montpellier, Nancy, and Rouen (no publisher given).

91. Many of these were French translations of works from the Latin or English, such as Richard Cumberland's *Traité philosophique des Loix naturelles* (Lausanne: Bousquet, 1744); David Hume's *Discours politiques* in 5 vols. (Amsterdam, 1755); Alexander Pope's *Oeuvres diverses* in 7 vols. (Vienna: Trattner, 1761); or Jonathon Swift's *Conte du Tonneau* (Lausanne: Bousquet, 1756).

92. Amsterdam provided 29 titles (this may also be a false place of publication; 14 titles list no publisher. Those mentioned are Wetstein, Chatelain, Rey, l'Honoré, the Compagnie, Schreuder, Bernard, and Changuion). The ever-popular "Londres" was next with 16 titles, followed by The Hague with 15 (Gosse, de Hondt, Scheurler, Swart, Moetjens), Lausanne with 11 (d'Arnay, Bousquet), Basel with 9 (Thurneysen), Berne with 4 (Société typographique), Leiden (Elie Luzac) and Brussels with 3 titles each, and Geneva (Cramer and Barillot) and Liège (Bassompierre) with 2 each.

93. Dyck to Nicolai, Leipzig, 10 July 1757, in NN 15.

increased expenses even more.⁹⁴ At least two documents in the Nicolai correspondence tend to contradict this gloomy picture, however. In a 1772 letter to Philipp Erasmus Reich, Nicolai noted that the conditions offered by the booksellers of Paris and Louvain were very favorable as to both price and time allowed for payment, and that they even sent books on consignment.⁹⁵ Returning a number of copies of Nicolai's (French) edition of Voltaire's *Pièces fugitives* in 1773, the Frankfurt am Main bookseller Johann Konrad Deinet explained that he was currently deluged with price catalogs from Parisian booksellers, who, to spite the Swiss, were selling for half the price.⁹⁶ The problem then, may have been more the expenses of currency exchange, tariffs, and postage, which made it cheaper to buy French books from firms in Switzerland or the Low Countries who visited the Leipzig fairs or had representatives there.⁹⁷

In the 1770s, at least, Nicolai ordered French books from several firms in the Netherlands, using the Amsterdam merchant and *ADB* reviewer Theodor Gülcher as an intermediary and adviser. The German Gülcher apparently thought better of the Dutch than of the Huguenot booksellers. He believed Nicolai would never get along with the arch-boor (*Erzgrobian*) Marc-Michel Rey, for instance, and that the other French booksellers were not sufficiently meticulous (*accurat*).⁹⁸ Thus Gülcher recommended Dutch booksellers and tried to smooth over problems when they arose, which appears to have happened quite frequently. Johann Schreuder, in his opinion, was "honest and upright; but his business has fallen off a good deal,"⁹⁹ which was the reason why he had not been able to pay for the books Nicolai sent him. Gülcher suggested that Nicolai not send him any new books, take back what he could, and accept books in exchange rather than cash so that they could settle up. Jan Doll,

---

94. Goldfriedrich, *Geschichte des deutschen Buchhandels*, 3:532–33.
95. Nicolai remarks upon this in his letter of 3 June 1772 to Reich, in SUB Hamburg.
96. Deinet to Nicolai, Frankfurt am Main, 20 December 1773, in NN 14.
97. One bookseller who at least tried to interest Nicolai in a trade in French books was the Liège pirate publisher Bassompierre, who attended the Frankfurt book fairs. Bassompierre's daughter, writing on her father's behalf, explained that he had sent Nicolai one of their catalogs via their Frankfurt commissionaire Kiefhaber and hoped that they could do business together. She particularly drew Nicolai's attention to the *Dictionnaire d'histoire naturelle*, in six volumes, printed in Berne, and listed the firm's latest publications. Mlle. Bassompierre to Nicolai, Liège, 20 March 1769, in NN 3. Whether anything ever came of this connection is not indicated by the correspondence.
98. Gülcher to Nicolai, Amsterdam, 31 January 1777, in NN 28.
99. Gülcher to Nicolai, Amsterdam, 6 May 1777, in NN 28. Schreuder was one of the leading Amsterdam booksellers. Hans Furstner, *Geschichte des Niederländischen Buchhandels* (Wiesbaden: Otto Harrassowitz, 1985), p. 67.

on the other hand, was "a poor payer, so be careful with him."[100] Another business partner, Munnikhuisen, was a chicaner; he refused to accept Nicolai's bill, saying that he had already sent him books to the value of half the amount and would not pay the remainder until he received the complete *Johann Bunkel* (of which he was publishing a translation) because, as Gülcher noted sarcastically, "if it was not completely finished and you died, or he died (or the sky fell down and we all died), his money would be lost."[101] When E. van Harreweld, who also supplied Nicolai with French books, became angry because he thought Nicolai was ordering from other firms to his disadvantage, Gülcher mollified him and arranged for Harreweld to provide the French journals Nicolai needed and order a number of copies of Nicolai's forthcoming description of Berlin for his shop.[102]

Nicolai also dealt with some booksellers in the Netherlands on his own. In the 1770s, he had both cash and exchange trade with Pierre Gosse in The Hague.[103] Apparently, Nicolai also approached J. H. Schneider in Amsterdam around this time, hoping to do business with him, perhaps because he was having trouble with other Amsterdam booksellers. Schneider replied that he could not enter into trade with Nicolai without knowing more about his business and asked for several copies of a new work he was publishing, and a copy of his catalog, if possible postage-paid.[104] In the 1780s, Nicolai corresponded with the bookseller Isaac van Cleef in The Hague, who kept him informed of new French titles.[105]

100. Gülcher to Nicolai, Amsterdam, 2 December 1777, in NN 28. Almost a year later Doll had still not paid his bill. Gülcher asked Nicolai to enclose a note in his next letter telling Doll that he had ordered Gülcher to take him to court for the money. Gülcher to Nicolai, Amsterdam, 3 November 1778, in NN 28. Doll published the Dutch translation of *Sebaldus Nothanker* in 1775–76.

101. A few months later, Gülcher delivered the sheets and accepted a three-month bill of exchange from Munnikhuisen, who asked him to put in a good word with Nicolai. More than half a year later, however, Munnikhuisen still had not paid up. Gülcher to Nicolai, Amsterdam, 2 December 1777 and 17 March and 3 November 1778, in NN 28.

102. Gülcher to Nicolai, Amsterdam, 31 January 1777, in NN 28.

103. Gosse asked for twelve copies of the *Mémoires pour servir à la connoissance des affaires politiques et oeconomiques du Royaume de Suède jusqu'à la fin de 1775*, published in Dresden, to be sent by the first available post coach. As for their exchange account, Gosse was determined not to maintain open exchange accounts and promised as soon as the waters were navigable to send 108 taler 12 groschen. worth of "Livres de Change," including four *Bibliothèque des sciences*. Gosse to Nicolai, The Hague, 18 February 1778, in NN 26.

104. Schneider to Nicolai, Amsterdam, 27 March 1778, in NN 68.

105. Nicolai mentions van Cleef in Nicolai to Blankenburg, Berlin, 20 August 1782, in NN 5. Van Cleef was one of the prenumerants to Johann Karl Gottfried Jacobsson's *Technologisches Wörterbuch*. "Ferneres Verzeichniß der Pränumeranten," in *Technologisches Wörterbuch*, vol. 2 (Berlin, 1782).

Nicolai's contacts in Switzerland were better established and more personal because many of the Swiss booksellers visited the Leipzig fairs. His main business partners were German-Swiss colleagues. As Nicolas Beguélin, a correspondent of the Société typographique de Neuchâtel who had tried unsuccessfully to interest Nicolai in trading with that company reported in 1776, French books were only a sideline for the Berliner, and his needs were generally met by what he found in Leipzig, making trade with the STN more trouble and expense than it was worth.[106] Another French-Swiss publisher who tried unsuccessfully to establish an exchange trade with Nicolai was Jean Abraham Nouffer of Geneva. In 1778, Nouffer sent him a little catalog containing the most scandalous "philosophical" books, including the notorious *Histoire du Dom Bougre*, and *Les Aventures monacales, ou la Vie scandaleuse du Frère Maurice parmi les religieuses*.[107] He may have assumed that Berlin would be a good market for spicy French books, but he clearly knew little about Nicolai's trade if he offered him political pornography, and one wonders whether his own customers would have been much interested in the kind of German literature that was Nicolai's stock-in-trade.

The firms from the German-speaking part of Switzerland mentioned in Nicolai's correspondence include the booksellers Heidegger and Orell, Geßner, and Füßli in Zurich; the Société typographique de Berne and Albrecht Emmanuel Haller in Berne; the firms of Johann Rudolph Im Hof and Son, Emmanuel Thurneysen, and Johann Schweighauser in Basel; Heinrich Steiner in Winterthur; and Reutiner Junior in St. Gallen.[108] He mentioned in letters to his Basel *ADB* correspondent Isaak

---

106. Beguélin to the STN, Berlin, 25 May 1776, in STN MS 11–19. I thank Jeff Freedman for providing a transcription of this letter.
 Nicolai emphasized on several occasions that he dealt little in French books, usually when he was politely refusing to do business with someone. In 1795, for example, when a certain C. Zeller of Hamburg sent him two anti-Revolutionary brochures, saying he could furnish up to five hundred copies of each at 5 Friedrich d'or per hundred, Nicolai replied that he couldn't use them "because I do not trade in French books." The brochures were "Atrocités commises envers les citoyens" and "Angoisses de la Mort." Zeller to Nicolai, Hamburg, 13 July 1795, and Nicolai's notes to a reply, in NN 84.

107. Nouffer was active as a printer and bookseller in Geneva from 1775 to 1783. John R. Kleinschmidt, "Les imprimeurs et libraires de la République de Génève 1700–1798" (Ph.D. diss., University of Geneva, 1948), pp. 146–48. On "livres philosophiques" as a genre, see Robert Darnton, "Livres philosophiques," in *Enlightenment Essays in Memory of Robert Shackleton*, ed. Giles Barber and C. P. Courtney (Oxford: The Voltaire Foundation, 1988), pp. 89–108, and *Édition et sédition. L'univers de la littérature clandestine au XVIIIe siècle* (Paris: Gallimard, 1991).

108. On the bizarre case of the bad debtor Reutiner, who was not only divorced by his wife, apparently for homosexual activities, but also became a Catholic and put himself under the

Iselin that he had no correspondence with either Johann Rudolph Im Hof or Emanuel Thurneysen between the fairs, which implies that he did deal with them at the fairs.[109] His main Basel correspondent appears to have been Johann Schweighauser, with whom he dealt at least from 1767 until 1784.[110] Schweighauser's Leipzig commissionaire Christian Gottlob Hilscher acted as intermediary in transactions between the Basel and Berlin colleagues. They may have engaged in exchange trade, since no prices are mentioned in Schweighauser's order for eighteen titles (forty-six copies in all) from Nicolai's catalog in 1772.[111] Schweighauser also ordered books for Nicolai from other Basel firms, including the Société typographique de Bâle and Thurneysen. In one instance, at least, he tried to obtain the requested books from Thurneysen, only to give up, "because it is very difficult to get anything from that gentleman."[112]

While Nicolai ordered his French books from Swiss, Dutch, and German booksellers, his access to English-language works tended to be organized through contacts in Germany, usually non-booksellers. English literature and philosophy had an enormous and early impact on Nicolai, and his reputation as an expert on English books led the Altenburg publisher Richter to ask Nicolai's advice when planning his own series of English-language books in 1786.[113] Aside from publishing a number of translations of English novels, Nicolai's English publishing projects ranged from the 1762 pocket edition of Pope's works in English[114] and

---

protection of the prince of St. Gallen in order to escape his creditors and the authorities of the town of St. Gallen, see the letters of 24 May 1787 to 28 May 1792 from Dr. Wartmann in St. Gallen to Nicolai, in NN 89. Reutiner later reconverted to Protestantism, then tried to become a Catholic again. His trail disappears from Nicolai's correspondence in 1792.

109. Im Hof und Sohn accepted payment from Nicolai at the Leipzig Easter Fair for Isaak Iselin's *ADB* reviews, at least between 1767 and 1771. Nicolai to Im Hof und Sohn, Berlin, 19 March and 20 October 1767, receipt dated Leipzig, 7 May 1771, from Im Hof, in NN 86 [Iselin correspondence].

110. Schweighauser is mentioned in Nicolai to Iselin, Berlin, 20 October 1767, in NN 86; and there is a letter from him dated 7 May 1784, in NN 89.

111. Schweighauser to Nicolai, Basel, 20 April 1772, in NN 70.

112. Ibid.

113. Richter refers in his letter to a suggestion in the *ADB* that someone should undertake an edition of English prose authors and says that he had had the same idea for some time but lacked a good selection of works. Nicolai suggested Hume's *History of England*, Robertson's *History of Charles V* and *History of America*, Shaftesbury's Works, Samuel Richardson's *Pamela, Clarissa*, and *History of Sir Charles Grandison* and the journals *The Connoisseur, The Idler*, and *The Rambler*. Nicolai's annotations on Richter to Nicolai, Altenburg, 8 March 1785, in NN 61.

114. He dropped his planned editions of Milton, Addison, James Thomson, Shakespeare, Edward Young, Prior, Mark Akenside, and others when Pope's works proved a dismal miscalculation. Numerous copies of the 1762 edition were still available in the firm's 1846 catalog! See Bernhard Fabian, "Nicolai und England," in *Friedrich Nicolai. Essays zum 250. Geburtstag*, pp. 174–97.

the 1785 translation of Charles Burney's biography of Handel to Jeremias David Reuß's 1791 *Gelehrtes England*. Despite all this interest and activity, Nicolai never established firm connections with his English colleagues. According to Bernhard Fabian, this was typical of German-English book trade relations at the time: "The almost conspicuous absence of English booksellers from the Leipzig fairs suggests that although trade relations existed, the British interest in the German market was anything but intense."[115] The higher price of English books relative to German ones, together with the difficulty and expense of acquiring books from England, fostered the phenomenon of German reprints of English-language works, such as Nicolai's own edition of Pope. None of this prevented Nicolai from ordering books from England, but he did so through intermediaries with good contacts in London. In the 1770s, his chief connections seem to have been Heinrich Christian Boie in Hannover and the Göttingen bookseller Johann Christian Dieterich, who were aided by the dynastic connections of Hannover (to which the city of Göttingen belonged) to England. In March 1770, for example, Boie sent Nicolai an English book catalog belonging to Dieterich and told him that the latter could deliver any of the works at the prices listed within two months.[116] Boie also ordered books from England for Nicolai and arranged for them to be delivered by the London-Hannover government courier. He asked Nicolai not to publicize this fact, since he did not wish to appear to be abusing the great privilege of receiving books via courier.[117] In receiving books by courier, Nicolai not only benefited from rapid delivery but also avoided customs duties. Another intermediary in things English was the scientist Johann Reinhold Forster (father of the more famous Georg), an *ADB* reviewer in Halle, whose fourteen-year sojourn in England had left him with good connections there.[118] In 1784, Nicolai apparently asked Forster's advice on how to go about establishing business contacts in England. Forster sent Nicolai numerous English booksellers' catalogs so that he might learn how they were organized and how they set prices,

---

115. Fabian, "Beginnings of English-Language Publishing in Germany," pp. 128–29.
116. Boie to Nicolai, Hannover, 18 March and 17 April 1770, in NN 7.
117. Boie to Nicolai, Hannover, 9 December 1776, in NN 7. The courier, who left Hannover after New Years, returned in February. The university library in Göttingen obtained its English books by diplomatic post, a service organized by the *Legationsrat* in London. I thank Graham Jefcoate of the British Library for this information.
118. Forster and his son had accompanied Captain Cook on his second expedition to the South Seas, of which the son, Georg, published an account, *A Voyage Round the World, in His Britannic Majesty's Sloop, Resolution, Commanded by Capt. James T. Cook, during the Years 1772, 3, 4 and 5* (London, 1777).

but given the modesty of the Berliner's needs and the lack of an English market for German books, he was not optimistic. Peter Elmsley, for example, was an excellent and honest fellow, "but since your publications can scarcely be of interest to him, and what you require from England could not amount to sums substantial enough to overcome the indolence of a wealthy English bookseller, it will be difficult to find an English bookseller willing to trade with you under these conditions."[119] He recommended that Nicolai use the services of a young German in Halle, Henry Zumbrock, who carried on a little consignment trade in English books alongside his position as bookkeeper. For a small fee, Zumbrock would provide booksellers' catalogs,[120] order any titles Nicolai wished, pay for the books, arrange for them to be shipped to a Hamburg commissionaire of Nicolai's choice, and bill him at either Berlin or Leipzig. Whether or not Nicolai took Forster's advice about Zumbrock, in 1785 he was dealing with a certain Everth in London. The latter, who wrote in German and was apparently not a bookseller, sent him a shipment of books via a young man traveling to Amsterdam who dispatched them from there by post to Berlin.[121] Other people who ordered books from England for Nicolai, both in the 1790s, were Friedrich Wilhelm Utrecht of the Seehandlungssocietät (overseas trading company) in Berlin[122] and the future Cambridge theologian and bishop of Peterborough, Herbert Marsh, who lived for many years in Leipzig.[123] In 1799, Nicolai had hoped that Marsh could provide him with a steady supply of English journals, but this was apparently a complicated proposition. Marsh himself had no regular method of obtaining them, he wrote, and only received the

119. Forster to Nicolai, Halle, 21 September 1784, in NN 22.

120. Forster suggested those of Benjamin White, Lockyer Davies, Thomas Payne, Henry Payne, James Robson, Samuel Hayes, Leigh and Sotheby, and Thomas Cadell.

121. One of the books, *Chambers' Dictionary*, was sent by ship to the bookseller Bohn in Hamburg (with whom Nicolai frequently did business) with instructions to dispatch it to Nicolai. Nicolai had originally requested that the books be posted from London, but this would have been too costly. The order was a large one, costing £20.8.4 inclusive or more than 100 taler. The titles were a mixed bag: Priestley's *Unitarian Prayers*, Smith's *Use and Abuse of Freemasonry*, "Inanimate Reason," Chef's "Player detected," "Antidote to Journey to Siberia," "Theoretic hints on brewing," "Statistical essays on brewing," "Suits for Crim. Con. ," "Bibliotheca Topog. Britan.," and the abovementioned *Chambers' Dictionary*. Nicolai apparently also asked Everth for information on other books, including the *Encyclopædia Britannica*. Everth to Nicolai, London, 5 July 1785, in NN 20.

122. Utrecht to Nicolai, Berlin, 18 April 1793, with no details beyond a promise to acquire the books in question from England, in NN 76.

123. Marsh to Nicolai, Leipzig, 23 September 1799, in NN 48. The books included Ben Jonson's works, biographies of Elias Ashmole and William Lilly, and Colley Cibber's *Apology*.

Monthly Review two or three times a year as the opportunity arose. He knew an English merchant in Hamburg, however, who took on all manner of transport business and could order the journals for a small commission fee.[124] The merchant J. M. Durand proposed to subscribe to *The European Magazine* and *Monthly Review* for Nicolai during his winter sojourn in London. He could not promise to send the issues every month, however, "because that will depend entirely upon the opportunities that arise."[125] Nicolai's experience with English booksellers, limited as it was, did not leave him with a very good impression. "I know of no less businesslike people than English booksellers," he told Jeremias David Reuß in 1802.[126] The acquisition of English books may have been simplified by W. Möller's establishment in Hamburg in 1799 of the first English bookshop in Germany, but we have no evidence that Nicolai took up his offer of doing business together.[127]

Italian and Spanish books were even more difficult to procure, since Nicolai had no business contacts in either country. Of the nine Italian-language titles in Nicolai's 1761 foreign-language book catalog, only one was actually published in Italy. The rest came from Switzerland, with one title each bearing the imprint "Londra" and Leipzig. The demand for Italian and Spanish books was apparently only sporadic among Nicolai's customers, so that he was never forced to find a permanent solution to his acquisition problems. In some cases, at least, Nicolai did manage to obtain Italian books through normal channels, using the better connections of other German booksellers such as Weidmanns Erben und Reich in Leipzig.[128] More commonly, however, he had to rely on contacts from outside the book trade. In 1767, he asked Isaak Iselin in Basel, "Do you know a way to receive books from Italy? I have orders for about twelve Italian books and nobody wants to have them sent to them."[129] Iselin replied that Nicolai might be able to order via the Basel bookseller

124. Marsh to Nicolai, Leipzig, 2 October 1799, in NN 48.
125. Durand to Nicolai, Hamburg, 3 December 1799, in NN 15. He promises to write from London with further details but there is no other letter from him in the correspondence.
126. Nicolai also felt that his beloved English were in decline; he noted that there was no public library in London where a scholar could find a book he needed, and Oxford and Cambridge were in a sorry state, eclipsed by the Scottish universities. Nicolai to Reuß, Berlin, 23 October 1802, quoted in Fabian, "Die erste Bibliographie," p. 39 n. 63.
127. On 30 April 1799, Möller wrote to Nicolai announcing the founding of his shop and offering to procure any English titles he desired (in NN 50).
128. Nicolai mentions ordering Italian books from this firm in his annotations to Eschenburg's letter of 29 December 1790, in NN 19.
129. Nicolai to Iselin, Berlin, 20 October 1767, in NN 86 [Iselin correspondence].

Schweighauser. The engraver Christian von Mechel, who had recently returned from Italy and had good connections with J. J. Winckelmann in Rome, would be a better intermediary, though.[130] In 1775, when J. J. Eschenburg asked for a copy of Jagemann's Italian translation of Büsching's geography, Nicolai noted, "Despite all my efforts, I still do not know how to manage it."[131] He was similarly pessimistic in 1782, when Eschenburg ordered the Livorno edition of Count Algarotti's works for the abbess of Gandersheim:[132] "Experience has taught me how difficult it is to acquire books from Italy. One waits for years, incurs high costs, and still does not receive what one wants." Success was likely only with assistance from outside the book trade, in this case from a Hamburg merchant with trade in Livorno, who could ask a correspondent there to purchase the book and enclose it with a regular shipment of goods. "If something like this is done out of friendship," he told Eschenburg, "one might receive it, but in the normal course of trade it is impossible."[133] Ordering books from Spain presented similar problems, and an instance from 1799 illustrates the roundabout methods that might prove necessary. When Nicolai received a request for a copy of *Don Quixote* in Spanish, he again turned to the Seehandlungssocietät in Berlin, which he hoped had some correspondence with Madrid. His correspondent in that organization, a certain Herr Heiniccius, replied that they did not, but that he had written to an acquaintance in Paris and asked him to purchase the book there. Unable to find the book in Paris, the man had a friend order it from Madrid.[134]

In contrast to his dealings in western and southern Europe, Nicolai's bookselling contacts in the East and the Scandinavian countries tended to be more those of a seller than a buyer. Via his branch in Danzig, and later in Stettin, he was well placed to sell to the northeastern European market. Poland was, nevertheless, something of a *terra incognita* for Nicolai. Although he published one Polish-language book, a translation of Svarez and Goßler's guide to the new Prussian legal code for laymen, Nicolai

---

130. Iselin to Nicolai, Basel, 5 November 1767, in NN 86.

131. Nicolai's annotations on Eschenburg to Nicolai, Braunschweig, 9 January 1775, in NN 19.

132. Eschenburg to Nicolai, Braunschweig, 22 June 1782, in NN 19.

133. Nicolai to Eschenburg, Berlin, 20 August 1782, in HAB, no. 44. Together with Genoa, Livorno was the chief center of sea trade between Italy and northern Germany. Kellenbenz, *The Rise of the European Economy*, p. 289.

134. Heiniccius to Nicolai, Berlin, 20 December 1799, in NN 31. The friend in Paris was a certain Le Content.

apparently had few bookseller customers in Poland. When a journal editor asked for his help in soliciting subscribers for *Le Nord littéraire, physique, politique et morale,* "Since your business ventures must extend to Poland and Russia," Nicolai replied, "I have no correspondence with Poland, because they are the worst payers there."[135] The Polish market, such as it existed for Nicolai's purposes, appears to have been handled via the Breslau booksellers Friedrich and Wilhelm Gottfried Korn. His contacts in Russia and the Baltic were more extensive. Nicolai had several very lucrative customers there, chief among them Catherine II (who used the Petersburg bookseller Johann Jakob Weitbrecht as her intermediary), Friedrich Albrecht von Koch, and the duchess of Courland. Although within Russia proper he seems to have corresponded only with J. J. Weitbrecht,[136] Nicolai did a good deal of business with Johann Friedrich Hartknoch in Riga as well as with Johann Jakob Kanter of Königsberg and Mitau (with whom he had traveled to the Easter book fair of 1763), and Friedrich Nicolovius in Königsberg, all of them well-connected in the Russian and Baltic trade.[137] For a time in the early 1790s, he enjoyed the assistance of a certain "von Maltzow" (probably Petr Malcev of the Russian embassy), who dispatched packets from Berlin to Russia for him via diplomatic post.[138] In Scandinavia, Nicolai's main book trade contact appears to have been the Stockholm publisher and royal librarian Carl Christoffer Gjörwell. As a fellow scholar-publisher and vigorous anti-Catholic, Gjörwell professed great admiration for Nicolai, comparing him to Pierre Bayle, which must have flattered the other man no end.[139] Gjörwell ordered books from Nicolai[140] and adapted one of his firm's books for the local schools.[141]

135. Olivarius to Nicolai, Kiel, and Nicolai's marginal annotations, 10 October 1797, in NN 55.
136. Nicolai to Weitbrecht, Berlin, draft letter of 15 November 1782, and Weitbrecht to Nicolai, St. Petersburg, 22 November 1782, both in in NN 81.
137. Heinz Ischreyt mentions Kanter and Nicolai's journey in his "Die Königsberger Freimaurerloge und die Anfänge des modernen Verlagswesens in Rußland (1760–1763)," in *Rußland und Deutschland,* Festschrift für Georg von Rauch, ed. Uwe Liszkowski, Kieler Historische Studien, 22 (Stuttgart: Klett, 1974), p. 118. See also his "Buchhandel und Buchhändler im nordosteuropäischen Kommunikationssystem (1762–1797)," in *Buch and Buchhandel,* pp. 249–69.
138. Maltzow to Nicolai, Berlin, 18 February 1791, in NN 47.
139. Gjörwell to Nicolai, Stockholm, 4 March 1785, in NN 25.
140. He mentions Klügel's *Encyklopädie,* Bode's *Weltcharte,* and Nicolai's *Reisebeschreibung* in Gjörwell to Nicolai, Stockholm, 4 March 1785, in NN 25.
141. Gjörwell published a version of the "kurzer inbegrif aller Wissenschaften," Benjamin Hederich's *Kurze Anleitung zu den vornehmsten, einem zukünftigen Bürger und andern, so nicht eben*

These often anecdotal fragments raise three points of particular interest: first, that barter continued to play a significant role in international contacts; second, that as in many aspects of Nicolai's work, individuals outside the book trade often played important roles in his business; and third, that when it came to acquiring books from abroad, even one of the foremost publishers and figures of the German Enlightenment was rather provincial and frequently at a loss. In this he may well have been typical of all but a handful of the German bookseller-publishers of his day. As a well-known writer and journal editor in his own right, however, he had both a name outside Germany and an extensive network of contacts to compensate at least in part for his lack of solid and continuous international book trade connections. Although never a major figure in the international trade in books, as a publisher and purveyor of mainly German-language titles Nicolai was an important link in a chain of communication running across northern Europe.

Bookshops, Customers, and Employees

Paul Raabe has argued that bookselling was more important than publishing to Friedrich Nicolai,[142] and given his often haphazard approach to shaping his list there may well be some truth in this. Certainly, Nicolai devoted himself with enthusiasm to the retail trade and to the task of making good books published by others better known to the public.

Nicolai began and ended his career as an independent bookseller in the Brüderstraße, a short busy street about ten minutes by foot from the political and cultural center of Berlin. The presence of the city's first-class

---

studiren wollen, dienlichen Sprachen und Wissenschaften (1st ed., 1743). He also offered suggestions for such future projects as an account of the final illness and death of Moses Mendelssohn and a biographical lexicon modeled on Bayle's *Dictionnaire historique et critique* (9th ed., 1774). Gjörwell to Nicolai, Stockholm, 4 March 1785 and 13 June 1786, in NN 25.

As for Denmark, in 1767 Nicolai noted that Copenhagen firms accepted no books between the fairs, which would indicate that he dealt with them only in Leipzig (whether personally or through commissionaires), and explain the absence of correspondence with Danish publishers. In a letter that does mention dealings with a Danish bookseller, Nicolai wrote that he preferred to have nothing further to do with Hansen in Schleswig "since he is so disorderly that he either answers my business letters not at all, or only half-way, and I fear that he is likely to mislay the packages altogether." Nicolai to Heinrich Wilhelm von Gerstenberg in Copenhagen, Berlin, 21 March 1767, in "Gerstenbergs Briefe an Nicolai nebst einer Antwort Nicolais," ed. R. M. Werner, *Zeitschrift für deutsche Philologie* 23 (1891): 53.

142. Paul Raabe, "Der Buchhändler im achtzehnten Jahrhundert in Deutschland," in *Buch und Buchhandel*, 4:286.

hostelries, the Hotel Stadt Paris and the König von England, must have brought wealthy out-of-town customers into the street's three bookshops, those of Etienne de Bourdeaux and August Mylius in addition to Nicolai's.[143] The royal printer Georg Jacob Decker also had his shop in the Brüderstraße, and Berlin's most famous illustrator, Daniel Chodowiecki, made his home there. It was, thus, an important street for the production and sale of books.[144] In 1763, after his marriage, Nicolai moved his shop from the Brüderstraße to his mother-in-law's house Auf der Stechbahn (or "sous les Arcades"), on the edge of the royal palace.[145] At some point in the 1780s Nicolai moved to what was known as Audibert's house "auf der Schloßfreiheit,"[146] where his neighbor was the venerable firm of Haude and Spener, a Berlin publishing house that still exists. The shop remained there until he bought his own house in the Brüderstraße in 1787.[147]

143. One of the illustrious guests of the Hotel Stadt Paris was the Comte de Mirabeau, who lived there during his sojourn in Berlin. In 1788 he asked an acquaintance, a certain Herr Zahn, subrector of the Friedrichswerder Gymnasium, to have Nicolai send him a copy of the new edition of his description of Berlin. Zahn also informed Nicolai that Mirabeau wanted to meet him. Zahn to Nicolai, Berlin, 5 February 1788, in NN 84. In the late eighteenth century, the area around the Brüderstraße was one of the most fashionable in Berlin. Rodenberg "Die Nicolaische Buchhandlung," p. 235.

144. Other major concentrations of booksellers were in the Breite Straße (Gottlieb August Lange, Christian Friedrich Voß, and the French bookseller Samuel Pitra) and the area around the royal palace (Haude und Spener, Joachim Pauli, Johann Heinrich Rüdiger, Arnold Wever). Nicolai lists the addresses of booksellers and printers in the 1769 edition of his *Beschreibung der königlichen Residenzstädte*, pp. 282–83.

145. Not in 1765 as stated in *275 Jahre Nicolaische Verlagsbuchhandlung. Eine Chronik* (Berlin: Nicolai, 1988), p. 16. In the autumn of 1763 Nicolai listed his address as "Auf der Stechbahn im Schaarschmidschen Hause." *Catalogus von allerhand Büchern*, Continuatio LIII (Michaelmas 1763). In a letter of 3 December 1763 to Uz he mentions having moved into a new house and shop (in NN 76). There is some confusion about the locations of Nicolai's bookshops. Hugo Rachel, for example, says that Nicolai moved from the Poststraße (the street where he was born) to the Stechbahn in 1765. *Das Berliner Wirtschaftsleben*, p. 182. Dora Duncker claims that he stayed in the Heilige Geist Straße until 1765. "Zweihundert Jahre Nicolaische Buchhandlung, 1713–1913," in *Festschrift zur Zweihundert-Jahr-Feier zum 3. Mai 1913* (Berlin: Nicolai'sche Buchhandlung Borstell & Reimarus, 1913), p. 10. The shop's correct addresses, as far as could be ascertained, are Heilige Geist Straße (1715–57), Brüderstraße (1757–63), Auf der Stechbahn (1763–8?), Schloßfreiheit (178?–88), and Brüderstraße (1788–1892?). Nicolai was married on 12 December 1760. Marriage Register of the Sophiengemeinde, Berlin 1742–63 39/105, *Archiv der Evangelischen Kirche der Union, Berlin*, Kirchenbuchstelle. Madame Schaarschmidt, the widow of a royal physician, also moved to the Brüderstraße and continued to live with her son-in-law and grandchildren after her daughter's death in 1794.

146. He gives this address on the title page of his 1787 *Verzeichniß einer Handbibliothek*.

147. Deed of sale between Nicolai and Carl Friedrich Dickow, 15 September 1787 (copy of 1799), in NN 285, no. 22. Presumably he did not move the shop until the following year.

Aside from his Berlin shop, Friedrich Nicolai had some kind of branch in Danzig and, from 1765 on, a shop in Stettin. He regularly sold books at the summer Dominicus fair in Danzig, attending personally at least until the early 1760s and occasionally thereafter as well. A commissionaire named Gronau saw to Nicolai's Danzig affairs.[148] Although the new Stettin shop may have taken over from that in Danzig to some extent in handling the northeast European market, there is no indication of when or if Nicolai closed the latter, or what its function may have been in his business. In 1808, Nicolai claimed to have founded the Stettin shop because of the *ADB*'s success and all of the extra trade it brought in. The title-page of the first issue of the *ADB* reads "Berlin und Stettin," however, so that he was either prescient or forgetful.

Stettin, although not directly on the coast, as Danzig was, was situated near the mouth of the Oder River. It was much closer to Berlin, yet well placed for shipping to the Baltic region as well as to cities on the Oder River, such as Breslau. Furthermore, since 1668 the Oder had been connected by canal with the Spree, which ran through Berlin. Stettin had yet another advantage over Danzig: it was a Prussian city. The Stettin shop, which Nicolai's troublesome uncle by marriage, Daniel August Gohl managed for many years, was located first in the house of a Widow Schulz and later in "Sander's house" in the Große Domstraße.[149] Nicolai sometimes saw to business there in the summer, perhaps in combination with visits to Bad Freyenwalde, a spa town between Berlin and Stettin.[150]

---

148. Nicolai reported to Uz in letters of 15 September 1759 and 13 December 1763 that he had spent much of the summer in Danzig. In NN 76 [Uz correspondence]. A letter of 6 July 1770 to Isaak Iselin mentions sending a *Diener* to the Danzig Dominicus fair, in NN 86. In 1773 Nicolai sent his *Diener* Müller to the Danzig fair, as is mentioned in a letter of 20 August 1773 from another *Diener*, C. G. Amende, to Nicolai in Bad Freyenwalde, in NN 1. Gronau is mentioned as Nicolai's commissionaire in a letter of 11 May 1771 from Johann Adam Tritt (in NN 75) and one of 30 March 1790 from Wilhelm Paul Verpoorten (in NN 77), both of Danzig.

149. The title page of Nicolai's 1787 *Verzeichniß einer Handbibliothek* mentions the address in the Große Domstraße. Nicolai refers to his "Oncle *OberCommissarius* Gohl, who manages my shop in Stettin." Nicolai's annotations to F. G. Resewitz to Nicolai, Copenhagen, 14 January 1775, in NN 60. The widow Schulzin complained on 7 August 1768 that Gohl was most reluctant to pay the rent on time, in NN 70. Likewise the Stettin wine merchants J. J. Vanselow and Company wrote to Berlin on 20 March 1772 (in NN 77) that Gohl had failed to pay Nicolai's wine bills and had outstanding debts of his own with them going back to 1764. Despite this behavior, which included not only reluctance to pay debts but also rude letters signed with Friedrich Nicolai's name (J. C. Sinapius to Nicolai, Hamburg, 24 May 1782, in NN 71), Nicolai appears to have kept Gohl on until his death in 1784. Afterwards Nicolai also supported his "poor cousin Mlle. Gohlinn" with a small pension. Nicolai to Eschenburg, Berlin, 18 December 1788, in HAB, no. 84.

150. In a letter of 23 August 1777 to Isaak Iselin (in NN 86), Nicolai mentions having just

Everyday Life in the Book Trade

In 1764, Nicolai founded a lending library.[151] An advertising leaflet dated 14 October 1763 announced the establishment of the new institution, motivated, Nicolai wrote, by numerous requests.[152] He promised potential members a wide range of general-interest books: "histories both true and fabulous, fine arts and literature, criticism and the pleasing parts of natural history." Each book fair would add new works, as well as older ones not yet in the collection, "so that we hope within a short time to assemble everything of this type that is available in the German language." If there was a demand for a particular work, he would do his best to make it available. He was also building up a library of French books, which he would endeavor to make as complete as the German one. For a monthly fee of 1 taler (later he stipulated 16 groschen),[153] to be paid in advance, readers might borrow as many titles as they pleased. Those who wished to borrow only occasionally would pay 2 to 8 groschen per volume depending on the format, and could borrow up to three volumes. The further conditions for the library hint at problems that he had already encountered when lending books more informally. A deposit of 5 taler was required for each title (this applied to friends and acquaintances as well, he noted); unbound books from his shop were not available for borrowing, although he would endeavor to provide a bound copy of any book requested, and customers would have to pay for any books damaged or lost.

At the Michaelmas fair of 1764, Nicolai announced the imminent appearance of a catalog for the lending library. He also informed the interested public that six months' reading would cost them 3 taler 12 groschen in advance (as opposed to 4 if they paid monthly) and one year, 6 taler (as opposed to 8 if they paid monthly). We unfortunately know nothing more about the library.[154] At some point, disappointed with the

---

returned from a business trip to Stettin. In the 1760s and 1770s Nicolai frequently went to Freyenwalde, just as he recuperated from the rigors of business at Bad Pyrmont in the 1780s and 1790s.

151. Nicolai's establishment is not mentioned in the literature. According to Johann Goldfriedrich's *Geschichte des deutschen Buchhandels*, the first Berlin lending libraries were founded around 1704. See vol. 2, p. 354, and vol. 3, p. 257.

152. "Auserlesene Bibliothek von allerhand zur Ergötzlichkeit und zum Unterricht dienlichen Büchern in deutscher und französischer Sprache welche unter nachstehenden Bedingungen dem Publico zum Gebrauch dargebothen wird von Friedrich Nicolai Buchhändlern in Berlin auf der Stechbahne im Schaarschmidschen Hause."

153. Continuatio LIV (Easter 1764) of Nicolai's book fair catalog, *Catalogus von allerhand Büchern*. One Reichstaler = 24 groschen.

154. After 1764, the trail becomes lost, and the lending library catalog could not be located.

meager returns for so much work, Nicolai abandoned the project and returned to loaning out books gratis to good customers, mainly in Berlin, who requested them. A typical case was that of the duchess of Courland, who was visiting Berlin and asked to borrow a copy of Voltaire's *Nanine* for a few days.[155] In 1776, however, he sent a copy of Johann Kaspar Lavater's *Physiognomik* all the way to Colberg where a certain Herr Madeweiß and his friends were eager to see this expensive work illustrated by Daniel Chodowiecki, which they said they could not afford to purchase.[156]

Nicolai's catalogs, printed at Easter and Michaelmas, of the books he had acquired at the Leipzig fairs, and his selective general bibliographies, a new genre among booksellers' catalogs, kept readers and booksellers in even the most remote towns and villages informed of a wide range of available literature while providing excellent advertising for his own business.[157] So useful were the firm's twice-yearly fair catalogs that people collected them for bibliographical reference. In 1778, for example, Johann Christian Wiegleb ordered two complete sets of the fair catalogs for several book lovers in the town of Langensalza near Gotha.[158] Nicolai inherited the firm's 1737 stock catalog comprising 576 pages and some 11,000 titles, the *Catalogus von Alten und Neuen Büchern welche vor beygesetztem billigen Preiß zu haben sind bey Christoph Gottlieb Nicolai Buchhändlern in Berlin*. He began revising this inventory as soon as he took over the business, intending to publish a new catalog at the end of 1760, but his plans were thwarted by the wartime volatility of prices. He postponed the project

---

If not for a 1787 exchange of letters with J. J. Eschenburg, one might be tempted to believe that the lending library came to nothing. Eschenburg requested information on Nicolai's experience because the Waisenhaus Buchhandlung in Braunschweig was reorganizing its lending library. Eschenburg to Nicolai, Braunschweig, 21 May 1787, in NN 19. Nicolai replied that he had long since given up his lending library and no longer possessed the corresponding notices and book catalogs. Nicolai to Eschenburg, Berlin, 6 June 1787, in HAB, no. 71.

155. Dorothea, duchess of Courland, to Nicolai, Berlin, 27 January 1786, in NN 13. The duchess was the sister of Nicolai's good friend and author Elisa von der Recke and a frequent customer at this period.

156. Madeweiß to Nicolai, Colberg, 14 December 1776, in NN 47.

157. On the various types of booksellers' catalogs in eighteenth-century Germany, see Ernst Weber, "Sortimentskataloge des 18. Jahrhunderts als literatur- und buchhandelsgeschichtliche Quellen," *Bücherkataloge als buchgeschichtliche Quellen in der frühen Neuzeit*, ed. Reinhard Wittmann (Wiesbaden: Harrassowitz, 1984), pp. 209–46. Weber follows his essay with a selected bibliography of booksellers' catalogs, indicating library holdings. See also Goldfriedrich, *Geschichte des deutschen Buchhandels*, 3:542–43.

158. Wiegleb to Nicolai, Langensalza, 17 April 1778, in NN 82. Another correspondent noted in 1792 that he had saved these catalogs for twenty years because of their accuracy and completeness. Walch to Nicolai, Schleusingen, 6 June 1792, in NN 79.

indefinitely,[159] contenting himself with occasional smaller efforts, such as the 215-item *Catalogue de plusieurs livres françois latins italiens et anglais qui se vendent au prix marque à Berlin chez Frederic Nicolai libraire rue des Freres dans la maison de Mr. Du Four* published in 1761.[160] When he returned to the idea of a large catalog, it was a selective rather than a "universal" one, not surprising given the boom in publishing during those years. Nicolai's first selective catalog with prices, the 1772 *Verzeichnis einer Auswahl nützlicher Bücher,* proved a great success. Rather than merely list the books on a particular subject, he made a personal choice of worthwhile books in all disciplines and branches of literature.[161] Nicolai asserted in 1773 that he printed and distributed more copies of the catalog than he did of the *ADB*, which at its height in the 1770s appeared in an edition of 2500.[162] The *Verzeichniß einer Handbibilothek der nützlichsten deutschen Schriften zum Vergnügen und Unterricht*, as the work was called in the editions of 1780, 1787, 1795, and 1811, was greeted enthusiastically.[163] Gabriel von Pronay, who lived far off the beaten path of literature in Atsa, Hungary, for example, eagerly awaited his copy.[164] Johann Joachim Eschenburg liked to keep a few copies of the *Verzeichniß* on hand to give away to people who asked him for advice on books,[165] and Heinrich Gottfried von Bretschneider found the work essential in his office as university librarian.[166] Nicolai sent free catalogs to his better customers.[167]

So successful and popular was the *Verzeichnis* that it was pirated by Nicolai's Berlin colleague Christian Friedrich Himburg in 1782, and the 1787 edition was translated into English.[168] As the *ADB* reviewer remarked, it

159. Nicolai to Uz, Berlin, 22 July 1760 and 13 October 1761, in NN 76.
160. The catalog was published as part of the regular book fair catalogs that the firm printed twice a year.
161. Nicolai mentions in a letter of 6 June 1787 to J. J. Eschenburg that the *Handbibliothek* was mainly the work of his son Samuel Friedrich. In HAB, no. 71.
162. Nicolai to Tobias von Gebler in Vienna, Berlin, 10 March 1773, in *Aus dem Josephinischen Wien. Geblers und Nicolais Briefwechsel während der Jahre 1771–1786*, ed. R. M. Werner (Berlin: Hertz, 1888), p. 40.
163. Unfortunately, only the editions of 1787 and 1795 could be located. For a detailed description of the 1787 *Verzeichniß*, see Raabe, "Zum Bild des Verlagswesens in der Spätaufklärung," pp. 66–88.
164. Pronay to Nicolai, Atsa, 17 December 1781, in NN 58. Their mutual friend in Ofen was H. G. von Bretschneider.
165. Eschenburg to Nicolai, Braunschweig, 19 July 1783, in NN 19.
166. Bretschneider to Nicolai, Ofen, 21 April 1789, in NN 9.
167. Mentioned in Nicolai to Eschenburg, 26 September 1795, in HAB, no. 179.
168. The pirate edition is mentioned on the verso of the title page of the 1787 edition, as well as in *Aus dem Josephinischen Wien*, p. 139 n. 33. The translation was titled *A select Catalogue of German Books, with the Subject of each in English, and an Appendix of the best Editions of the Classics,*

was not often that a bookseller's catalog had the honor of being translated into a foreign language,[169] and it was a particularly unusual move at a time when there was as yet little market for German books in England. The *Verzeichniß* also influenced other German-language catalogs. When Martin Hochmeister, a bookseller in Transylvania, printed his own catalog, he invoked Nicolai's example to explain why he had not organized it alphabetically, as many other booksellers did, but had instead followed the "scholarly categories" introduced by Nicolai.[170] Nicolai organized his 1787 catalog into twenty-four categories, and the 1795 edition into twenty-nine. This stands in stark contrast to the three "Fakultäten" of his father's 1737 stock catalog, where all books not belonging to the disciplines of theology (with a small appendix of Catholic books), jurisprudence, or medicine were designated either *libri peregrini idiomatis* (various foreign language works) or *libri miscellanei*. The last category contained such disparate items as letter-writing manuals, poems, biographies, travel accounts, German dictionaries, and love stories; books on alchemy, the Plague, cooking, gardening, and housekeeping; musicalia; and writings published on the occasion of the arrival of Protestant refugees from Salzburg.[171] Although the 1787 *Verzeichniß* contained only half as many titles as that of 1737, doubtless jettisoning much ballast of baroque learning along the way,[172] an astounding differentiation had taken place. Rubrics that might have surprised Christoph Gottlieb Nicolai, such as "books on education and for the entertainment of children" (1787), "Freemasonry,

---

and some French Books, published in Germany, and printed in 1789 for the Oxford booksellers Daniel Prince and Joshua Cooke. According to the title page, it was sold in London by John, Francis, and Charles Rivington in St. Paul's Church Yard and by Peter Elmsley in the Strand. Short review in the *ADB* 93, no. 1 (1790): 202. The fact that the work was published by an Oxford firm may reflect the greater likelihood of interest in German books among academic circles than the general reading public in England.

169. *ADB* 93, no. 1 (1790): 202. Apparently, the English translation left out some works considered to be of lesser interest, such as those on Brandenburg local history.

170. Heinz Stanescu, "Vertriebsformen der Hochmeisterschen Buchhandlung in Hermannstadt im letzten Viertel des 18. Jahrhunderts," in *Buch- und Verlagswesen im 18. und 19. Jahrhundert*, ed. Herbert G. Göpfert, Gerard Kozielek, and Reinhard Wittmann (Berlin: Camen, 1977), p. 280.

171. "An den Bücherliebenden Leser," preface to *Catalogus von Alten und Neuen Büchern*, 1737.

172. Ernst Weber has pointed out the tendency of booksellers' catalogs in the latter part of the eighteenth century to feature fewer and fewer old titles. "Sortimentskataloge," p. 223. The 1788 reviewer of Nicolai's *Verzeichniß einer Handbibliothek* remarked upon the relative newness of the titles contained therein: "We found products of the previous century in only a few rubrics, such as the history of Prussia and Brandenburg." *ADB* 82, no. 1 (1788): 239.

Rosicrucians, Illuminati, Knights Templar and secret societies," "Books for town-dwellers, country folk, and the people more generally," or "Books for ladies" (added in 1795) had become the meat and potatoes of late-eighteenth-century booksellers. "Love stories" now styled themselves "novels," and "German dictionaries" were elevated to "Writings treating the German language." Law and medicine receded into the background, and theology, which had taken up the first 219 pages of the old Nicolai's *Catalogus*, occupies a mere fifteen in his son's 1787 and 1795 *Verzeichnisse*, about the same number of pages as books on "Housekeeping, agriculture, forestry, and gardening." Theology is also no longer the first rubric, but the second, preceded, significantly, by "Moral and philosophical writings." These were new categories for a new world of readers and writers, one in which the three original faculties represented but a fraction of human knowledge and interests. Nicolai set a standard not only for a more systematic and finely tuned organization of catalogs, but also for greater bibliographical exactitude. As the *ADB* reviewer of the 1787 edition put it, Nicolai deserved the thanks, not merely of the general public, but also of "true scholars ... because this *Handbibliothek* provides both an overview of recent literature in the fields treated by Herr Nic[olai] and precise and correct information on the editions, volumes, publishers and prices of the books listed. Herr Nic[olai] has even named those authors who are not mentioned [in the books themselves]."[173] Thus the catalogs could also be of great assistance to booksellers and librarians. At the same time, they saved Nicolai the trouble of answering every request for advice or information individually.[174]

Nicolai and His Customers

In his study of eighteenth-century booksellers' catalogs, Ernst Weber has emphasized the still-rudimentary nature of our knowledge of book distribution.[175] Without an account book, list of customers, or anything approaching a complete set of catalogs, and with book orders scattered randomly throughout the correspondence, an exact reconstruction of Nicolai's bookselling activities is impossible. Still, it is possible to indicate

---

173. *ADB* 82, no. 1 (1788): 238–39.
174. He mentions this factor in his publisher's note to the 1787 catalog.
175. Weber, "Sortimentskataloge," pp. 209–10. "The subject of retail bookselling in the eighteenth century remains unexplored," wrote Paul Raabe in "Der Buchhändler im achtzehnten Jahrhundert in Deutschland," p. 274.

something of the range and nature of Nicolai's retail business and of his customers, based largely on the orders of some sixty, mainly private, customers, for a total of 520 titles.

In contrast to Leipzig publishers like Philipp Erasmus Reich, who lived mainly from publishing and commissionaire activities,[176] Friedrich Nicolai's business depended on the retail sale of books from his Berlin and Stettin shops and, even more, on a wide range of correspondence customers throughout Germany and beyond.[177] As a late-seventeenth-century author on the book trade had noted, bookselling was a territorial trade (*Land-Handel*), and customers in the bookseller's own city made up only a fraction of his business.[178] While members of the popular classes satisfied their much-lamented "reading mania" with penny pamphlets acquired from country fairs, bookbinders, peddlers, or the vendors (*Krämer*) who set up book-tables on Berlin's Mühlendamm or other urban thoroughfares,[179] more prosperous readers took their trade to respectable, privileged booksellers like Nicolai. Among his more illustrious customers were Catherine II and Grand Duke Paul of Russia,[180] Duchess Dorothea of Courland, the dowager duchess of Braunschweig[181] and Prince Ferdinand[182] (sister and brother of Frederick II), Prince George of Waldeck-Pyrmont,[183] Frederick Augustus Hervey, fourth earl of Bristol

---

176. The very large number of booksellers in Leipzig, a city with about one-fifth the population of Berlin, may have precluded many of them building up a substantial retail business. As Friedrich Perthes recalled of his master Böhme, who had a large commission business, "He had only two private customers—the princely library of Rudolfstadt and the historian Anton; but the principal booksellers of Germany were his correspondents." *Memoirs of Frederick Perthes*, 1:18.

177. Nicolai noted in a letter of 31 October 1770 to Philipp Erasmus Reich that he lived mainly from correspondence customers. In SPKB Autogr. I/1590-5.

178. Adrian Beier, quoted in Johann Goldfriedrich, *Geschichte des deutschen Buchhandels*, 2:279.

179. The geographer Anton Friedrich Büsching deplored the cheap little histories, songs, dream-books, and the like that he found for sale on the Mühlendamm in 1775 and called for more enlightened and useful reading matter for the common folk. *Beschreibung seiner Reise von Berlin über Potsdam nach Rekahn unweit Brandenburg, welche er vom dritten bis achten Junius 1775 gethan hat*, 2d ed. (Frankfurt and Leipzig, 1780), pp. 12–13, quoted in Rudolf Schenda, *Volk ohne Buch. Studien zur Sozialgeschichte der populären Lesestoffe 1770–1910* (Munich: dtv, 1977), p. 67.

180. Ludwig Heinrich von Nicolay and the librarian Johann Chr. von Malthé both placed orders for Grand Duke Paul. Nicolay to Nicolai, St. Petersburg, 18 June 1778, in NN 52; Malthé to Nicolai, St. Petersburg, 25 July (5 August) 1785, in NN 47.

181. Via J. J. Eschenburg she ordered Anton Yves Goguet's *De l'origine des loix, des arts et des sciences* (Paris, 1758). Eschenburg to Nicolai, Braunschweig, 3 May 1792, in NN 19.

182. On 23 November 1787 Prince Ferdinand ordered six copies of the *Geheime Briefe über die preussische Staatsverfassung seit der Thronbesteigung Friedrich Wilhelm des IIten* (Utrecht, 1787). Letter from Berlin, asking that the copies be sent by post from Leipzig, in NN 58.

183. A letter of 1 April 1806 from Bunsen in Arolsen (in NN 11) refers to the prince's debt with Nicolai. Since the prince lived in Pyrmont where Nicolai frequently took the waters, they probably met there.

Everyday Life in the Book Trade

and bishop of Derry,[184] the Comte de Mirabeau,[185] and Prussian ministers Karl August von Hardenberg[186] and Julius August Friedrich von der Horst.[187] Nicolai's customers also included less famous aristocrats—some of whom he had met during his summer sojourns at the fashionable spa Bad Pyrmont, where bourgeois and nobles mingled somewhat more freely than they did at home[188]—as well as Prussian military officers,[189] merchants, pedagogues,[190] medical men, professors, librarians, government

184. Lord Bristol ordered Homer's *Iliad* and a work he referred to as the epic of Dionysius the Areopagite in the edition of Eustathius (bishop of Antioch, 324–27), as well as the *Gazette française de Berlin*. Bristol to Nicolai, Berlin, 31 October 1795, and Bad Pyrmont, 25 August 1796, in NN 10.

185. In a letter of 5 February 1788 Zahn, subrector of the Friedrichswerder Gymnasium, ordered a copy of the new edition of Nicolai's description of Berlin for the Comte de Mirabeau (in NN 84). Two years before, von Nolde had inquired on Mirabeau's behalf about several books on Prussian history and politics, and whether it would be worthwhile to purchase them. Nolde to Nicolai, Berlin, 21 November 1786, in NN 54.

186. The librarian Johann Gottlieb Albrecht in Ansbach ordered a copy of Nicolai's *Verzeichniß einer Handbibliothek* on Hardenberg's behalf. Albrecht to Nicolai, Ansbach, 9 September 1792, in NN 30.

187. Minister Julius August Friedrich von der Horst asked Johann August Eberhard, then pastor in Charlottenburg near Berlin, to order two copies of the forbidden *Briefe des Prinzen von Preußen*. Eberhard, to Nicolai at the Easter book fair, Charlottenburg, 1772, in NN 16.

188. On the social atmosphere in Pyrmont, see the interesting account in Reinhold P. Kuhnert, *Urbanität auf dem Lande. Badereisen nach Pyrmont im 18. Jahrhundert* (Göttingen: Vandenhoeck & Ruprecht, 1984). Elisa von der Recke's journals also contain references to Nicolai's stays in Bad Pyrmont. On 23 August 1791, for example, Nicolai gave a dinner party for Elisa von der Recke and a Frau von Grävemeyer to which Prince Friedrich Christian von Augustenburg practically invited himself. On 25 August Nicolai went on an outing with Elisa von der Recke and her sister the duchess of Courland, the princess von Augustenburg, Leipzig professor Ernst Paul Platner, Amalie von Goeckingk, the count von Hoffmannsegg, Julie von Vietinghoff, Lisette von Rutenberg, Fräulein von Behr, Frau von Watzdorf, and *Kammerjunker* Döring. Recke, *Tagebücher und Selbstzeugnisse*, pp. 122–24.

189. In the 1760s and early 1770s a group of Potsdam officers, surnamed Gensau, Goltz, and Knobloch, ordered books from Nicolai. The last-mentioned also reviewed military works for the *ADB*. Gensau, for example, ordered Le Blond's *Lagerkunst*, translated by Moritz von Brühl, the *Lebensbeschreibung eines patriotischen Kaufmanns*, and Gautier's work on highway construction, 8 September 1764 (in NN 87). Knobloch ordered Home's *Versuch über die Sittlichkeit*, Johann Elert Bode's *Vom gestirnten Himmel*, Roehl's *Astronomische Wissenschaften*, and Gerard's *Redekunst*. Receipt acknowledged in Knobloch to Nicolai, Potsdam, 18 December 1768, in NN 41.

190. The well-known pedagogical author Joachim Heinrich Campe, for example, frequently ordered books from Nicolai during his years in Potsdam. In 1774 he even apologized for not having ordered much lately; he had sold a manuscript to August Mylius and was receiving his honorarium in books. Campe to Nicolai, Potsdam, 13 March 1774, in NN 12. His orders included Weiße's *Bibliothek der schönen Wissenschaften*, "A Collection of new Plays by several Hands ," the works of Ossian, a map of Poland after the recent partition, and Leonhard Euler's *Lettres à une princesse d'Allemagne sur divers sujets* and three copies of *Télémaque* in French as well as three subscriptions to Wieland's journal, *Teutsche Merkur*. Campe to Nicolai, Potsdam, 24 November 1775 and 17 January 1776, in NN 12.

officials,[191] Protestant pastors,[192] learned women,[193] and even the occasional Catholic cleric.[194]

Just as they came from many professions, Nicolai's customers were also spread over a wide geographical area, in villages, small towns, and cities from London to Yekaterinenburg. Indeed, his most lucrative customers were often those who lived farthest from Berlin. The geographical distribution of his customers seems largely to follow that of the *ADB*. Nicolai thus had many customers in northern and central Germany, and few in Austria and southern Germany. A number of them lived outside the German-speaking region, particularly in Russia. The geographical range of Nicolai's customers probably widened with the advent of the *ADB*, as he became better known outside his usual orbit of Prussia and Saxony. Nicolai's correspondence customers were, by definition, those who thought in supra-regional terms. The very act of writing to a far-off bookseller indicated a certain breadth of horizon and knowledge of literary events in other parts of the German-speaking world. Nicolai's customers thus took part, at least marginally, in the society of *Aufklärer*,[195] an intellectual culture linked across state borders by books, journals, and (epistolary) friendships.

Nicolai offered his customers more than mere delivery of the latest

---

191. For example, Freiherr Tobias von Gebler in Vienna; Samuel Gottfried Baumeister in Reibersdorf, Saxony; Hanns Ernst von Teubern in Dresden; and Johann Erich Springer in Erfurt.

192. Nicolai had many friends, and presumably customers, among the Berlin clergy. The proverbial poverty of Protestant clerics in the countryside, however, did not make for lucrative customers. This problem is addressed in an interesting letter from a certain Herr Stemler in Wehernbrück near Wittenberg who suggests that the solution to the pastors' lack of access to books, and thus to new and useful ideas they could pass on to their parishioners, might be a system of lending libraries especially for country parsons. Stemler to Nicolai, Webernbrück, 26 January 1788, in NN 73. One order from a country pastor near Ansbach was relayed by Nicolai's friend Johann Peter Uz. It was for the *Technologisches Wörterbuch*. Uz to Nicolai, Ansbach, 29 January 1789, in NN 76. A Pastor Bensel in Groß Küssow near Stargard, requested a (free) defective copy of Wilhelm Abraham Teller's sermons. Letter of 17 June 1788, in NN 4.

193. The abbess of Gandersheim favored Italian literature, and Friederike von Radecke Enlightenment polemic. The latter ordered Nicolai's description of Berlin, his travel account, and his pamphlet against Pastor Starck, as well as Lavater's journals (she professed to being an opponent of his overheated imagination). Radecke to Nicolai, Constadt in Silesia, 25 January 1790, in NN 59.

194. Father Romanus Lerchberger was the Benedictine chaplain of the convent in Seeba in the Tyrol. He read the *ADB* and ordered the very heterodox novel *Johann Bunkel*. Lerchberger to Nicolai, Seeba, 5 May 1778, in NN 45.

195. The phrase comes from the title of Richard van Dülmen's *Gesellschaft der Aufklärer: Zur bürgerlichen Emanzipation und aufklärerischen Kultur in Deutschland* (Frankfurt a. M.: Fischer, 1986), which discusses clubs and societies as organizational forms of the Enlightenment.

titles. As a man knowledgeable about all branches of literature, he provided advice on books to buy and even sent out books for customers to choose from. When in January 1787 a certain Herr Mencken did not feel like braving Berlin's icy streets to reach Nicolai's shop, he asked him to send "some of the most useful books on botany more generally, as well as pomology, kitchen gardens, and hardy foreign plants ... so that I may choose what I need."[196] Some correspondents entrusted Nicolai himself with the choice of books. In 1769, for example, Nicolai received a request to put together "a select library" for a military officer in Mecklenburg at the price of 100 taler a year.[197]

Customers frequently called upon his prodigious memory and detective skills when they did not know a title or author, or garbled them beyond the recognition of latter-day researchers. One customer, a certain Herr von Rothe, said that Nicolai might know the books he wanted "if I say that one was in French and against religion, reviewed quite poisonously, though described as beautifully written, in the French newspaper in Cleve in 1768–69.... The other contains historical tables by an Englishman whose name, I believe, begins with L."[198]

Nicolai was thought to have access to books other booksellers could not find, although in the case of foreign works, as we have seen, this was frequently not the case. Thus after Friedrich Wilhelm von Veltheim had scoured Kassel and environs in vain for Augustin Barruel's *Abrégé des mémoires pour servir à l'histoire du jacobinisme*, he turned to his Berlin friend, saying that if Nicolai could not find it, nobody could.[199] He also ferreted out antiquarian titles for his customers or bought for them at auctions.[200] Although he usually sold books "raw" or unbound, Nicolai sent copies

196. Mencken to Nicolai, Berlin, 23 January 1787, in NN 49. Nicolai noted that he had sent Mencken a few books and his garden bibliography on the twenty-fourth.
197. The request came from a brother officer in the Ziethen Hussars, Lieutenant D. F. von Lück. Lück to Nicolai, Berlin, undated [1769] and 23 May 1769, in NN 46. Rittmeister von Wolfradt requested, among other things, a German translation of Voltaire's *Zadig*, "and any other excellent moral writings that have appeared recently." Lück to Nicolai, Berlin, 23 May 1769, in NN 46. Prince Moritz of Isenburg in Birstein also asked Nicolai to send him interesting new books for up to 20 ducats per book fair (letter of 24 March 1779, Birstein, in NN 37). Similarly, Theodor Gülcher, an Amsterdam merchant and loyal customer, told Nicolai to send him the "most important and beautiful" new books from the Michaelmas fair. Letters of 20 September and 12 October 1773 and 3 November 1778, in NN 28.
198. Rothe to Nicolai, Rundeweise, 12 December 1769, in NN 64.
199. Veltheim to Nicolai, Kassel, 10 June 1798, in NN 77.
200. Bretschneider to Nicolai, Lemberg, 9 October 1794, in NN 9; Madeweiß to Nicolai, Königsberg, 17 December 1810, in NN 87; and Wiegleb to Nicolai, Langensalza 4 April 1783, in NN 82.

out to be bound in the customer's usual style when they requested this service. Benedict Maria Hermann in Siberia ordered all of his books *broschiert*, or bound in paper covers, because there were no bookbinders for miles around.[201] Others requested this service only occasionally.[202]

Nicolai had not only private but also a number of corporate customers. These included the Prussian legal code commission,[203] the university libraries at Ofen and Halle, the Electoral library in Dresden, the British Museum, and some of the lending libraries and reading societies that were such a prominent feature of eighteenth-century German literary and social life. Nicolai had drawn up a plan for the establishment of reading societies, which, as he told a correspondent in 1787, had served as the basis for the founding of some twenty such institutions. This was a far more lucrative, and less onerous undertaking, he asserted, than a lending library. Sadly, there is no indication of which societies were founded according to his plan, which is all the more regrettable since they probably ordered their books from Nicolai and may have been a substantial factor in his business in the 1780s. Letters referring to reading societies, and to their commercial counterparts, the lending libraries, are rare in the correspondence. Those societies that ordered from Nicolai may have done so through local booksellers whom he met at the Leipzig fairs. Theodor Gülcher in Amsterdam relayed an order for the *ADB* for an "unnamed reading society."[204] An examination of the catalogs of several Swiss and Southwest German reading societies[205] reveals that six of the eight owned at least one Nicolai publication, but it is unclear whether he supplied them directly. In all they possessed twenty-nine copies of twenty-one

---

201. Weikard to Nicolai, Weichers, 2 November and 6 December 1784, in NN 81; Hermann to Nicolai, Yekaterinburg, 1787 and 1788, in NN 33. Another customer who ordered her books bound was Dorothea, duchess of Courland (letter of 3 December 1785, in NN 13).

202. Walch to Nicolai, Schleusingen, 2 January 1788, in NN 79; Rothe to Nicolai, Rundewiese, 28 January 1770, in NN 64; Wiarda to Nicolai, Aurich, 27 December 1799, in NN 82.

203. Baumgarten ordered "as soon as possible, all of the changes [to the law] ... published during Joseph's reign ... particularly any changes regarding marriage" for the legal code commission. Baumgarten to Nicolai, Berlin, 16 April 1783, in NN 87. Nicolai ordered the laws by post apparently from the Vienna bookseller Lucas Hohenleiter on 22 April (annotations to Baumgarten's letter).

204. Gülcher to Nicolai, Amsterdam, 17 March 1778, in NN 28. Gülcher took three copies of the *ADB*; one for himself on fine paper, one for a friend, and one for the reading society.

205. The catalogs are printed in Barney M. Milstein's *Eight Eighteenth-Century Reading Societies: A Sociological Contribution to the History of German Literature* (Bern: Herbert Lang, 1972). Milstein publishes the membership lists and catalogs of the reading societies as appendices, pp. 166–311.

titles.²⁰⁶ The "first" Schaffhausen society had the largest holdings of Nicolai's products. Nicolai's *ADB* reviewer in Schaffhausen, the historian Johannes von Müller, a probable member of the society from 1771 to 1782,²⁰⁷ may have been instrumental in establishing a connection between the society and Nicolai, or at least in choosing books from Nicolai's list.²⁰⁸ As to lending libraries, there are occasional allusions to them in the correspondence, but no actual orders. A perusal of the published catalogs of three lending libraries, however, yields a number of Nicolai titles, even as late as the 1830s.²⁰⁹ Among these, not surprisingly, works of fiction dominate, with a sprinkling of popular philosophy.²¹⁰ Thus even some of

206. The Basel reading society owned J. J. Eschenburg's *Beispielsammlung zur Theorie und Litteratur der schönen Wissenschaften* (8 vols., 1788–95) and Nicolai's own novel *Geschichte eines Dicken Mannes* (2 vols., 1794). The society in Zug, founded on the basis of an existing civic library in 1806, listed the 1765 edition of Thomas Abbt's *Vom Verdienste*, Moses Mendelssohn's *Phädon*, and Raymund Dapp's *Kurze Predigten und Predigtentwürfe über die gewöhnlichen Sonn-und Festtags-Evangelien . . . besonders für Landleute und Landprediger* (1793–1806), a somewhat curious choice for a Catholic society. The journal reading society in Ludwigsburg took the *ADB* from 1769 on as their only work from Nicolai's firm, as did the Trier society from 1783 to 1793. Their copy of Moses Mendelssohn's *Phaedon* was, not surprisingly, a pirate edition ("Leipzig, 1778"), since they ordered most of their books from the reprint catalog of the infamous Christian Gottlob Schmieder in Karlsruhe. Milstein, *Eight Eighteenth-Century Reading Societies*, p. 62.

207. Milstein, *Eight Eighteenth-Century Reading Societies*, p. 109.

208. These included the *Briefe, die neueste Litteratur betreffend* (1759–66), the *ADB* from 1765 on (acquired after 1789), Diderot's *Oeuvres de théâtre* (2 vols., 1763), Thomas Abbt's *Vom Tode für das Vaterland* (1761) and *Vom Verdienste* (1768 ed.), Mendelssohn's *Phädon* (1769 ed.) and *Schreiben an den Herrn Diaconus Lavater zu Zürich* (1770), Justus Möser's *Patriotische Phantasien* (4 vols., 1775–86), Ludwig Heinrich von Nicolay's *Vermischte Gedichte* (1778–86), Johann Gottwerth Müller's novels *Friedrich Brack* (1795) and *Sara Reinert* (1796), Eberhard Friedrich von Rochow's *Versuch eines Schulbuches für Kinder auf der Landleute* (1776 ed.), and, last but not least, Friedrich Nicolai's *Sebaldus Nothanker* (3 vols., 1773–76), *Beschreibung der königlichen Residenzstädte* (3 vols., 1786), *Beschreibung einer Reise* (first 8 vols., 1783–87), and *Geschichte eines Dicken Mannes* (1794). The "second" Schaffhausen society, which existed alongside the first, also acquired Nicolai's *Reisebeschreibung* (first 10 vols., 1783–95) and Johann Gottwerth Müller's *Friedrich Brack* (1795) and *Sara Reinert* (1796), as well as his *Selim der Glückliche* (1792), Friedrich Gabriel Resewitz's *Gedanken, Vorschläge und Wünsche zur Verbesserung der öffentlichen Erziehung als Materialien zur Pädagogick* (5 vols., 1778–86), and the story collection *Strausfedern* (from 1797 on). It sold a copy of Thomas Abbt's *Vom Verdienste* together with other books at auction in 1797 in anticipation of a new edition of the collected works. Milstein, *Eight Eighteenth-Century Reading Societies*, p. 130.

209. The catalogs discussed here are reprinted in *Die Leihbibliothek der Goethezeit: Exemplarische Kataloge zwischen 1790 und 1830*, ed. Georg Jäger, Alberto Martino, and Reinhard Wittmann (Hildesheim: Gerstenberg, 1979).

210. The 1790 catalog of J. M. Zehetmayer and B. Kiermayr in Vienna, for example, which boasted that its titles had been chosen according to "the judgments of men of taste, the Allgemeine deutsche Litteraturzeitung, and the Allgemeine deutsche Bibliothek of Berlin," features nine titles from Nicolai's firm, plus pirate editions of two Nicolai titles, Thomas Abbt's *Vermischte*

Nicolai's seemingly most ephemeral publications survived well into the next century via lending libraries.

One institution that did deal directly with Nicolai was the "Casino" club library in Berlin.[211] Carl Christoph Goßler, a Nicolai author and member of the Prussian legal code commission (which Nicolai had supplied with books in the 1780s) requested Nicolai's assistance in selecting a broad range of journals for the library, which had a diverse membership.[212] Nicolai's suggested list of journals is dominated by politics, history, travel, and current events, with nods to the ladies and enthusiasts of pomology and philosophy. Six of the seventeen titles were published in Berlin, but only one by Nicolai's firm.[213]

Werke (Frankfurt a. M., 1783) and Moses Mendelssohn's *Phädon* (Reutlingen, 1789). Franz Roßnagel's little lending library in Dillingen, whose 1815 catalog features mainly anonymous novels, possessed only Thomas Abbt's *Vermischte Werke* and, as a more obvious choice, one volume of the story collection *Strausfedern*. The *Verzeichniß der Lese-Bücher, welche in der Franz Roßnagel'schen Leih-Bibliothek zu haben sind* is a bibliographical nightmare, organized neither alphabetically nor chronologically and without dates or places of publication. Thus, it is impossible to know whether the editions of Abbt and the *Strausfedern* were piracies or original editions. An 1833 catalog put out by David Raphael Marx in Karlsruhe, and intended as a model for other lending libraries, yields an unexpectedly large number of Nicolai titles, including twelve of the twenty-nine novels the firm published. See *Handbuch für Leih-Bibliotheken oder Anleitung zur Bearbeitung eines Catalogs sowohl nach den Verfassern als nach den Titeln* (Karlsruhe and Baden, 1833). The lending library was established in 1801 by Marx's father, thus the books could have been acquired from Nicolai himself, although there is no evidence for this. "Zur Geschichte der Leihbibliotheken im 18. und 19. Jahrhundert," in *Die Leihbibliothek der Goethezeit*, p. 501.

211. In the latter part of the eighteenth century, "casino" was one of several designations for a club combining sociability and reading. Marlies Stützel-Prüsener, "Die deutschen Lesegesellschaften im Zeitalter der Aufklärung," in *Lesegesellschaften und bürgerliche Emanzipation: Ein europäischer Vergleich*, ed. Otto Dann (Munich: C. H. Beck, 1981), p. 71.

212. Goßler to Nicolai, Berlin, 24 December 1795, in NN 26. This was not the first time Nicolai had been asked to recommend titles for a club. In 1778, a Herr Richter in Potsdam wrote to say that he and some friends had arranged with the bookseller Carl Christian Horvath to start a "Gelehrte Zeitungs Societät." They intended to subscribe to the Göttingen and Berlin journals as well as Büsching's magazine and were looking for two more titles. Richter asked Nicolai to suggest the "most interesting and solid." They and Horvath would also appreciate any other "information [to aid] in the fruitful establishment of this literary commerce." Richter to Nicolai, Potsdam, 20 December 1778, in NN 61. Richter provided Nicolai with documents and research assistance for his guide to Berlin and Potsdam. Goßler to Nicolai, Berlin, 24 December 1795, in NN 26.

213. Undated list, in NN 26 [Goßler correspondence]. Nicolai's terms, as indicated by a marginal note, were that he would furnish the journals at an unnamed discount plus a flat rate for postage, with a 10 percent discount for books.

The largest library order mentioned in Nicolai's correspondence was one that never came to fruition. Over the years, Heinrich Gottfried Bretschneider did his best as librarian of the University of Ofen in Hungary to order as many as possible of the books he needed from his Berlin friend. In 1780, Maria Theresa allocated 12,000 fl. for the improvement of the Ofen

Everyday Life in the Book Trade

The bookseller Hieronymus may have deplored to Sebaldus Nothanker the public's preference for bad books over good, but a sample of Nicolai's own customers substantiates his claim that tastes were improving. We will never know the extent of trivial literature that Nicolai sold from his bookshops, but his correspondence customers showed great interest in the literature of the Enlightenment. Among them von Koch of St. Petersburg stands out not only for the sheer volume of his book order of 1790, but also for the high quality of the works he chose. Koch was a customer from at least 1788 until his death in 1800. The 1790 order, in the form of a simple list or *Memorial*,[214] is striking as an attempt to acquire all at once a library of recent German literature, aesthetics, history, and philosophy. The order reads like a *Who's Who* of the Enlightenment and Sturm und Drang.[215] Koch also ordered translations of the works of Spinoza, the eighteenth-century Italian playwright Carlo Gozzi, and "Ossian," the fictional Celtic bard. He ordered sixty-seven titles unbound

---

Library, with a promised 1500 fl. yearly for further acquisitions. Apprising Nicolai of the situation, Bretschneider suggested he send him a list of academic treatises and large works on medicine and natural history at reasonable prices, accompanied by a letter asking whether he knew of any interested buyers. In this way, they could avoid the appearance of collusion. Nicolai needed to act quickly before the local booksellers got wind of the project. Unfortunately, Maria Theresa died just as they were about to close the deal. As Bretschneider reported, he had been in Vienna with Nicolai's book list and presented it to the faculties of medicine and philosophy at the university, who had approved the acquisition of most titles. With the death of the empress, however, the availability of funds for the library at the appointed date of Easter 1781 was uncertain. By March of the next year, Bretschneider had not abandoned hope of money for the library, but the subject thereafter disappears from the correspondence. Bretschneider did make two large orders in the spring and summer of 1785, which may have been for the university library, but they were certainly not worth the hoped-for 12,000 fl. Bretschneider to Nicolai, Ofen, 22 January, 2 July, 16 August, and 9 December 1780, 9 March 1781, and March or April 1785, in NN 9.

214. Since Koch ordered two or three copies of some titles, he may have been ordering for friends or for some institution as well as himself. The book list is in the correspondence of G. F. Hoffmann in Erlangen, in NN 36. Koch's bill was paid by a Herr Ott of the Russian embassy in Vienna. Ott to Nicolai, Vienna, 4 September 1790, in NN 58. A note on the back from someone in Nicolai's shop indicates that Koch owed 190 taler 18 groschen including postage.

215. Koch ordered works by Thomas Abbt, Johann Christoph Adelung, J. W. von Archenholz, Alois Blumauer, Gottfried August Bürger, Salomon Geßner, Johann Wolfgang von Goethe, Albrecht von Haller, Johann Jacob Wilhelm Heinse, Johann Gottfried Herder, August Wilhelm Iffland, Immanuel Kant, Friedrich Maximilian von Klinger, Friedrich Gottlieb Klopstock, Sophie von La Roche, Johann Kaspar Lavater, Gotthold Ephraim Lessing, Christoph Meiners, Moses Mendelssohn, Anton Raphael Mengs, Justus Möser, Johann Gottwerth Müller, Johannes von Müller, Johann Karl August Musäus, Gottlieb Wilhelm Rabener, Karl Wilhelm Ramler, Friedrich Schiller, Johann Georg Schlosser, Johann Gottlieb Schummel, Christian Gottlob Selle, Friedrich Leopold von Stolberg, Johann Georg Sulzer, Johann Peter Uz, Johann Heinrich Voß, Christoph Martin Wieland, Johann Joachim Winckelmann, and Johann Georg Zimmermann, among others. Koch also ordered the *Berlinische Monatschrift* beginning with December 1789.

and eighty-one bound in a simple brown "English binding," with author and title stamped on the spine. The book order ended with a request that the books not only be original editions (i.e. no pirate editions) but also the best and newest ones available. Money was apparently no object.

Koch was by no means a typical customer, though he was one of several buyers who sent in long order lists. Despite the cost and dangers of transport, those customers who ordered the most books tended to be those who lived far from Nicolai, presumably without access to a good German-language bookshop. Many of them lived in Russia or elsewhere in northeastern Europe. Thus Melchior Adam Weikard, for example, who had recently moved from Fulda to St. Petersburg, complained that the bookshops there were both expensive and poorly stocked, and he continued to order books from Nicolai, including the new French edition of Tissot's works, and any other good new French books "philosophical or otherwise."[216] Dorothea, duchess of Courland, sister of Nicolai's friend and author Elisa von der Recke, frequently made quite substantial orders of books both for herself and friends.[217]

216. Weikard to Nicolai, St. Petersburg, 9 (20) August and 22 October 1784 and 31 December 1784 (11 January 1785), in NN 81. Other customers in Russia were Zenovieff (a Russian nobleman who had made the acquaintance of J. J. Eschenburg during a sojourn in Braunschweig), who ordered a long list of German books, mostly gleaned from the *Verzeichnis einer Handbibliothek* (Eschenburg to Nicolai, Braunschweig, to Nicolai, 13 September 1784, in NN 88), and Benedict Franz Hermann, an Austrian who became director of the Siberian salt mines. The latter ordered over three hundred titles from Nicolai during his 1787–88 sojourn in Yekaterinburg. Hermann to Nicolai, Yekaterinburg, 1787 and 1788, in NN 33. Nicolai published three titles by Hermann: *Beyträge zur Physik, Oekonomie, Mineralogie, Chemie, Technologie und Statistik besonders der russischen und angränzenden Länder* (3 vols., 1786–89); *Versuch einer mineralogischen Beschreibung des uralischen Erzgebürges* (2 vols., 1789); and a revised and annotated edition of Johann von Hornegk's *Bemerkungen über die österreichische Staatsökonomie* (1784). The author took his honorarium in books.

217. On 13 June 1786, she paid Nicolai 340 taler for books. Dorothea, duchess of Courland to Nicolai, Friedrichsfelde, 13 June 1786, in NN 13. One of the friends she ordered for was Count Ludovico Aurelio Savioli, who had been sent back to Italy during the Illuminati purges of 1785 after a period in Bavarian government service. Along with another Italian aristocrat, Count Costanzo, Savioli had been one of the most active Illuminati in Munich. See Mirabeau, *De la monarchie prussienne*, 5:100, and van Dülmen, *Gesellschaft der Aufklärer*, p. 110. Back in Bologna, Savioli was anxious to keep up with German literature. In 1785, the duchess ordered for Savioli Lessing's pamphlets against the Hamburg pastor Johann Melchior Goeze, *Ernst und Falk*, *Fragmente*, and *Nathan der Weise*; Elisa von der Recke's *Geistliche Lieder*; Friedrich Heinrich Jacobi's works; the *Berlinische Monatsschrift* for 1785; Johann August Eberhard's *Apologie der Vernunft in Beziehung auf die christliche Versöhnungslehre*; and Nicolai's own history of the Knights Templar. Courland to Nicolai, Berlin, 3 December 1785, in NN 13. Later she ordered Frederick II's and Goethe's complete works to be sent to Savioli via George Wachter in Augsburg. Courland to Nicolai, Wirzau, 28 November 1787, in NN 13. Dorothea's orders for herself included the *Berlinische Monatsschrift*, the *Storia della vita e tragica morte di Bianca Capello*, and Rousseau's works. Courland to Nicolai, Berlin, 27 January 1786, and Sagan, 15 July 1786, and undated, in NN 13.

Nicolai's most lucrative customer in Russia was none other than the Empress Catherine, who informed herself about German literature by reading the *ADB*.[218] Having admired the novel *Sebaldus Nothanker*, Catherine sent Nicolai, via the Petersburg bookseller J. J. Weitbrecht, a golden commemorative medal with her own likeness on one side and that of a statue of Peter I on the other.[219] She not only asked him to send on all his other writings, but also entrusted him with two major book orders over the next few years. First, in May 1783, she asked Nicolai to compile a list of all historical works in French and German concerning all the countries of the world! Nicolai had accomplished this bibliographical feat by September of that year. Then she asked him to buy all the books on the list for her. In what must have been a mammoth undertaking, Nicolai acquired and dispatched the books over a period of several years.[220] At the end of 1784, Catherine asked Nicolai to send her all the reference books she would need for a comparative lexicon of all languages, living and dead. Aided by a friend, in January 1785 he sent her a manuscript bibliography titled "Tableau général de toutes les langues du monde, avec un Catalogue des principaux Dictionnaires de leur étymologie, de leur origine et de leur affinité." So pleased was Catherine with Nicolai's efforts that she sent him the manuscript of her historical essays, translated into German,[221]

218. The Petersburg bookseller J. J. Weitbrecht mentions in a letter of 10 January 1783 that Catherine read the *ADB*. Melchior Adam Weikard, Catherine's physician, also mentions in a letter of 9 (20) April 1784 that she thought very highly of the *ADB* and had asked after Nicolai. Both letters are in NN 81.

219. The event was exciting enough to be reported in the *Buchhändlerzeitung auf das Jahr 1782*, pp. 721–22. Nicolai probably submitted the notice himself.

220. We can only guess at how Nicolai procured all the books on the list. One, at least, he ordered directly from its author. On 21 November 1784, he wrote to Jeremias Jakob Oberlin (1735–1806) in Strasbourg to subscribe for the empress to his latest work "on the handsomest paper." Nicolai to Oberlin, Berlin, in Bibliothèque National Ms. allem. tome VIII (199) No. 218, Corresp. Oberlin.

221. Nicolai's first biographer Leopold von Göckingk recounts the story of Catherine's book orders in his *Friedrich Nicolais Leben und literarischer Nachlaß*, pp. 41–43. Weitbrecht sent Nicolai the medal and note from Catherine in early autumn 1782, and Nicolai replied in November. Draft letters to Catherine and Weitbrecht, dated 15 November 1782, in NN 81 [Weitbrecht correspondence]. Nicolai sent Catherine copies of his *Freuden des jungen Werthers* and *Versuch über die Beschuldigungen welche dem Tempelherrenorden gemacht worden, und über dessen Geheimniß* with a rather maladroit letter in French that caused some hilarity at court, as Weitbrecht recounts in his own letter of 6 December 1782 (in NN 81). The courtiers misquoted Nicolai somewhat, saying he had written "Je vous adore, Madame," and referred to "Votre divine main qui distribue des graces." Weitbrecht was bemused, to say the least, to hear that Nicolai had used such language to write to an empress and hoped that the courtiers had been mistaken. What he actually wrote, according to the much crossed-out draft, was "J'ai toujours adoré Votre M. T." He also referred to her "main divine qui sait d'un coup de plume fixer le destin de l'Europe et de l'Asie, et manier en même tems le Bureau des Graces." Nicolai was clearly not experienced in

which he published as *Bibliothek der Großfürsten Alexander und Konstantin* (9 vols., 1784–88).²²²

Other major customers from outside the German-speaking region included a Mr. Hawkins in London, apparently an acquaintance of Nicolai's friend and author J. J. Eschenburg, who made a substantial order for over 360 taler in 1791, and the young Scottish physician Alexander Crichton.²²³ Theodor Gülcher was a faithful customer from the early 1770s on; in 1773 alone he bought over 60 taler worth of books.²²⁴ He appears to have had a standing order with Nicolai for anything new and interesting appearing at the Leipzig fairs. In 1775, for example, Nicolai sent him Johann Kaspar Lavater's new *Physiognomische Fragmente* from the Leipzig Easter Fair, but Gülcher returned it several months later, saying that the subject was not important enough to him to justify the book's exorbitant price, although he appreciated having had a chance to peruse it.²²⁵ He complained of the meager pickings of one fair, reporting that he had enjoyed only the *ADB*, "otherwise the brochures from the last fair which I leafed through ... contain only bland stuff and precious

---

writing to female heads of state. Weitbrecht believed that Nicolai could smooth over any embarassment by reviewing Catherine's works in the *ADB* and sending copies on fine paper to her in future. He would make sure that she knew they came from Nicolai. Weitbrecht to Nicolai, St. Petersburg, 10 January 1783, in NN 81.

222. Later, at the suggestion of J. G. Zimmermann in Hannover, Nicolai published Catherine's three plays on superstition, *Der Betrüger*, *Der Verblendete*, and *Der Schaman von Sibirien*. Zimmermann to Nicolai, Hannover, 30 May and 6 June 1787, in NN 84; Zimmermann to Catherine, Hannover, 12 June and 4 September 1787, and Catherine to Zimmermann, St. Petersburg, 1 July 1787 and 4 September 1787, in *Der Briefwechsel zwischen der Kaiserin Katharina II. von Russland und Joh. Georg Zimmermann*, ed. Eduard Bodemann (Hannover: Hahn, 1906), pp. 46–56. Catherine expressed some surprise that Nicolai would publish these plays in the current climate in Berlin: "Je pense que ces pièces sont de la contrebande dans l'esprit du tems présent." Catherine to Zimmermann, Moscow, 1 July 1787, in *Briefwechsel*, p. 49. Zimmermann, however, assured her that the work was in production. Nicolai had shown him the first sheets at Bad Pyrmont where they were both taking the waters. Zimmermann to Catherine, Hannover, 4 September 1787, in *Briefwechsel*, p. 52.

223. Hawkins's order, which sadly has not survived, is mentioned in a letter of 15 August 1791 from Nicolai's Berlin bookshop to Eschenburg, in HAB, no. 117. The shop employee informs Eschenburg that the crate of books was being sent to Hamburg and would be on the first available ship to England. The bill was for 363 taler 20 groschen. The Edinburgh native Crichton, who had studied medicine in Leiden, Paris, Stuttgart, Vienna, and Halle, traveled to Berlin with a letter of introduction from Nicolai's friend and author Johann August Eberhard and the intention of assembling, with Nicolai's assistance, a collection of good German authors. Eberhard referred to him as an enthusiastic friend of German literature. Eberhard to Nicolai, Halle, 1 December 1787, in NN 16.

224. Gülcher to Nicolai, Amsterdam, 28 June and 29 July 1774 and 15 August 1775, in NN 28.

225. Gülcher to Nicolai, Amsterdam, 15 August 1775, in NN 28.

little Roast Beef."²²⁶ On another occasion he asked Nicolai to spare him the modish literary trivia (*MusenAlmanache, Blumenlesen, Taschenbuch für Dichter*, and the like) and send him only the most excellent poetry. Anything else was unbearable.²²⁷ Nicolai supplied Gülcher with the Leipzig fair catalogs, and before the book fair Gülcher usually ordered specific titles. He was a local resource for German literature in Amsterdam and once chided Nicolai for not having sent the latest from Leipzig yet because "certain translation manufacturers knock on my door daily to learn whether anything has yet appeared for which it would be worth their while to set up chairs."²²⁸ Nicolai was probably his main supplier of German books, at least in the 1770s. He was particularly interested in periodicals and works on history, travel, and politics but also ordered literary titles such as Johann Timotheus Hermes's *Sophiens Reise nach Memel*, Johann Gottlieb Schummel's *Empfindsame Reisen durch Deutschland*, Just Friedrich Wilhelm Zachariä's *Auserlesene Stücke aus den besten deutschen Dichter*, Klopstock's *Messias*²²⁹ and *Gelehrtenrepublik*, and Goethe's *Leiden des jungen Werthers* and, later, *Faust*.²³⁰

Nicolai had substantial customers in Germany as well. Von Rothe, for example, ordered over a hundred titles between 1769 and 1773. These ranged from literature and aesthetics (such as a German translation of William Hogarth's *Anatomy of Beauty*, the fables of La Fontaine in French, and Samuel Richardson's *Clarissa* and *Sir Charles Grandison*, and Shakespeare's works in English), to philosophical, mathematical, and scientific texts (such as Newton's *Philosophiae naturalis, Principia mathematica*, and *Arithmetica universalis*; Madame de Châtelet's *Institution de physique*; and the works of Locke, Descartes, and Leibniz) and works on politics and history (such as Frederick II's *Anti-Machiavel*, Johann Christoph Gatterer's *Synopsis historiae universalis* and *Handbuch der neuesten Genealogie und Heraldik*, and the Austrian reformer Joseph von Sonnenfels's *Grundsätze der Polizey, Handlung und Finanz*).²³¹ Another large customer

226. Gülcher to Nicolai, Amsterdam, 31 January 1777, in NN 28. "Roast beef" is in English in the original.
227. Gülcher to Nicolai, Amsterdam, 3 November 1778, in NN 28.
228. Gülcher to Nicolai, Amsterdam, 24 October 1775, in NN 28.
229. Gülcher to Nicolai, Amsterdam, 28 February 1772, in NN 28.
230. Gülcher to Nicolai, Amsterdam, 20 September and 12 October 1773; March 1773 (?); November 1774 (?); 28 March, 15 August, 26 September, 24 October, and 27 December 1775; 31 January 1777; and 7 November 1788, in NN 28. For a complete list of authors and titles ordered by Gülcher, see Selwyn, *Philosophy in the Comptoir*, pp. 336–37.
231. Rothe to Nicolai, Rundewiese, 12 December 1769, 28 January 1770, and 4 November 1773, in NN 64.

was a certain Madeweiß in Colberg on the Baltic. His surviving book orders are almost exclusively for literary works, including J.J.C. Bode's influential translations of Laurence Sterne's *Tristram Shandy* and *Sentimental Journey*, Goethe's *Leiden des jungen Werthers*, and all available items of Wertheriana. At Easter 1776, the 110 taler he owed Nicolai for books were more than balanced out by the 118 taler worth of geese, salmon, and other local delicacies he sent to Berlin.[232]

Of course, many of Nicolai's customers could not afford to order books at will. An important category of book customers was Nicolai's more modestly situated authors and *ADB* reviewers. Although he frequently sent them the books for free, men like Heinrich Gottfried von Bretschneider, Johann August Eberhard, and Johann Joachim Eschenburg, to name just a few, were significant customers. Walch, who oversaw the printing of the *ADB* in Schleusingen, frequently ordered books "for my account" (*auf Rechnung*). At least in the case of his own titles, however, Nicolai provided the books gratis.[233]

Discounts for non-book trade customers were something of a sore point in the late-eighteenth-century book trade. The more established and prosperous booksellers considered discounts of 20 percent and more to private customers to be *Schleuderei*, or throwaway pricing, which was defined by the bookseller Georg Joachim Göschen as "selling more cheaply than one can if one wishes to continue in trade as an honest man."[234] Without fixed retail prices, and with growing competition among booksellers for public favor as the century wore on, discounts became increasingly extreme, and many customers expected to be able to negotiate prices.[235]

---

232. Madeweiß to Nicolai, Colberg, 2 April 1776, in NN 47.

233. Walch to Nicolai, Schleusingen, 16 July 1783, in NN 79. Nicolai had noted "Gratis" on Walch's order of 20 January 1782 for volume 3 of Johann Georg Sulzer's *Vorübungen zur Beförderung der Aufmerksamkeit und des Nachdenkens*, in NN 79. Similarly, when J. J. Eschenburg asked for Jacobsson's *Technologisches Wörterbuch* at the prenumeration price Nicolai sent him a copy for free. Nicolai's annotations on Eschenburg to Nicolai, Braunschweig, 7 May 1784, in NN 19.

234. Quoted in Hans Widmann, *Geschichte des Buchhandels: Vom Altertum bis Gegenwart*, 2d ed. (Wiesbaden: Harrassowitz, 1975), p. 119. The practice of offering discounts to private customers had begun as an incentive for prompt or cash payments. Philipp Erasmus Reich was rumored to have offered scholars a 10 percent discount. Later in the century, as competition for customers increased, some booksellers offered discounts of 20 percent and more. Leipzig and Berlin publishers like Wilhelm Oemigke delivered books postage-paid with a 20 percent discount even to the far North. Schürmann, *Der deutsche Buchhandel*, pp. 13–14. See also the mention of Oemigke's discounts in a letter from Nicolai's own shop manager in Stettin below.

235. Wittmann, *Geschichte des deutschen Buchhandels*, pp. 131ff. Teubern in Dresden, for example, asked Nicolai to lower the price of the 1761 edition of Goldoni's comedies, which he had

Johann Erich Springer, for example, asked Nicolai what discount he would be willing to offer, remarking that all the booksellers and publishers he had dealt with so far had obliged him with either 12½, 18¾, or even 26¼ percent. He promised that nobody need know of their agreement.[236] J. J. Eschenburg inquired on behalf of a Russian customer what discount Nicolai might accord him on his large book order.[237] Nicolai did accord Ernst Theodor Langer, librarian in Wolfenbüttel, a 20 percent discount.[238] When A. M. Scherer had the temerity in 1803 to ask for several titles from Nicolai's own company at the trade price, however, Nicolai scribbled in the margin that it was "against the elementary principles of business."[239] Nicolai was not generally in the habit of according discounts to individuals, except in the cases of extra author's copies and works he had decided to discount himself, as well as back issues of the *ADB*.[240] He granted discounts on the *ADB* to a number of customers,[241] and when one who had lost much of his library in the great fire of 1781 in Gera asked the bookseller to replace the destroyed volumes of the *ADB*, as well as Nicolai's history of the Knights Templar at a 50 percent discount, he received the books without a bill.[242] It was also not unheard of for correspondents to request free books. A Halle theology student whose family library had apparently also been lost in a fire asked Nicolai for the page proofs, now mere waste paper, of recent volumes of the *ADB*, and of Anton Friedrich Büsching's *Magazin für die neue Historie und Geographie* and his *Neue Erdbeschreibung*. He hoped that, however outrageous his

---

noticed in his latest catalog, to 12 taler. Teubern to Nicolai, Dresden, 30 January 1767, in NN 74. An acquaintance of the poet Ramler wanted to know if he could have 11 taler worth of books for 10 taler. to Nicolai, Berlin, 8 December 1772, in NN 59.
    236. Springer to Nicolai, Erfurt, 28 April 1776, in NN 72.
    237. Eschenburg to Nicolai, Braunschweig, 13 September 1784, in NN 88.
    238. Langer to Nicolai, Wolfenbüttel, 27 September 1803, in NN 43.
    239. Nicolai's annotations on Scherer to Nicolai, Leipzig, 16 May 1803, in NN 66.
    240. In volume 1, no. 1 (Michaelmas 1765): 313–14 of the *ADB*, Nicolai announced a temporary special offer on Johann Leonhard Frisch's *Deutschlateinisches Wörterbuch*, the *Sammlung vermischter Schriften zur Beförderung der schönen Wissenschaften und der freyen Künste*, the complete works of Alexander Pope, and Nathanael Lardner's *Glaubwürdigkeit der evangelischen Geschichte*. Customers had to pay cash in louis d'or or coin of equal value in order to take advantage of the discounts of up to 50 percent. He offered an additional 8 percent discount for orders of ten or more copies. The advertisement was repeated in volume 2, no. 2 (New Year 1766).
    241. Boie to Nicolai, Hannover, 28 January and 30 May 1778, in NN 7. Nicolai noted on Weikard's letter of 2 November 1784 that he had offered him a price of 90 taler for the *ADB* up to volume 58, including the ten supplements, in NN 81.
    242. Carl Friedrich Uhrlandt to Nicolai, Gera, 17 January and 21 May 1783, in NN 76. Uhrlandt, however, insisted on paying for the books.

query might seem, Nicolai's well-known "philanthropy" would not allow him to think ill of one so devoted to learning.[243] Nicolai's answer is not recorded, but when an elderly and impecunious country pastor in Mecklenburg made a similar request for a defective copy of Wilhelm Abraham Teller's sermons, erroneously believing it to be one of Nicolai's publications, he was astonished at Nicolai's response: "What would another man, who was not a Nicolai, have done in this case? He would have answered that he regretted that since the sermons had not been published by his firm ... he could not send me such a copy.... And what did you do? You were so kind and made me so happy with your splendid gift that I feel several years younger already. I cannot express in words how well pleased I am with Hermes's sermons and the two books by von Rochow."[244] A somewhat bolder request for books came from the wife of a poor military officer who, in order to support her family, had founded a lending library, which she apparently stocked in part by writing to various authors for free copies of their works. As thanks, she wrote, Nicolai would know that he had helped to save her "almost sinking family."[245]

It was common to expect a discount when ordering a large number of a single title, particularly when the work was intended for educational purposes. In such cases, the fear that customers might otherwise prefer to purchase—or even instigate—pirate editions also played a role, and it was in Nicolai's own interest to oblige with quite substantial discounts. In 1787, Nicolai was approached by Johann Georg Scheffner, a poet and former civil servant who leased a small estate in East Prussia and took an interest in rural education in his neighborhood. Having received the permission of the provincial church and school commission to order the books, he asked whether Nicolai would be willing to provide special editions of 600 copies each of Friedrich Eberhard von Rochow's *Versuch eines Schulbuchs für Kinder der Landleute, oder Unterricht für Lehrer in niedern und Landschulen* and Carl Friedrich Riemann's *Versuch einer Beschreibung der Reckahnschen Schuleinrichtung* (an account of Rochow's model school) with an appendix containing excerpts from two other pedagogical works, Johann Bernhard Basedow's *Geschenk an Bürgerschulen* and Johann Gotthilf Lorenz's *Kurze Anleitung für Lehrer, wie der Kinderfreund des Herrn von*

---

243. Chr. Friedrich Wendland to Nicolai, Zanzmühle near Landsberg, 18 August 1782, in NN 81. Wendland apparently believed that Büsching's works were published by Nicolai. Both were published in Hamburg.

244. Bensel to Nicolai, Groß Kussow near Stargard, 17 June 1788, in NN 4.

245. Louise Thilo, née Lots to Nicolai, Zerbst, 3 April 1786, in NN 74. Nicolai notes on the letter that he answered from Leipzig, but does not indicate the content of his response.

Rochow und jeder andere gute lesebuch in Bürger- und Landschulen mit Nutzen und Vergnügen könne gebraucht werden, for a total price of 250 taler. He had all but convinced the penurious local authorities to adopt Rochow and Riemann for free distribution to village schoolmasters, but the price of the regular editions was too high. He was certain that Nicolai, with his "world-famous ambition to destroy the reign of ignorance," would approve of the idea; particularly with such a reasonable publisher, it would be improper to engage in a local reprint. Nicolai took his time in answering Scheffner's query, probably because it arrived during preparations for the Michaelmas book fair, and when he did write his tone was somewhat unfriendly. Apparently, Nicolai resented what he, not surprisingly, perceived as Scheffner's veiled threat to pirate the works in question. He considered Scheffner's request presumptuous and offered instead to sell his regular editions of Rochow and Riemann at a 50 percent discount. He had, however, only 300 rather than the desired 600 copies of the latter and did not wish to print more at present because the book was selling slowly. He could not agree to Scheffner's suggestion to allow him to have the missing copies printed in Königsberg, which would be tantamount to condoning piracy, as would permitting him to print excerpts from Basedow and Lorenz. After some contentious correspondence back and forth, Scheffner agreed to Nicolai's conditions but was disappointed in the publisher who, at their meeting in Nicolai's Berlin garden, had seemed such a kind, obliging, and friendly fellow. He was sure that they could clear up any misunderstandings if only given the opportunity to do so in person. Mollified, Nicolai then offered to reprint the Riemann after all, provided the author had time to revise his work. Scheffner, however, could not wait that long and feared that the local authorities would balk at the higher price of the new edition. They finally agreed that Nicolai would provide 600 copies of the Rochow and 300 of the Riemann, plus 12 copies of Rochow's *Katechismus der gesunden Vernunft* for 175 taler in gold, which was less than half of the original price. This earned Nicolai Scheffner's gratitude as a "true promoter of Enlightenment." The Königsberg school authorities, however, refused to pay for the catechism because, as Scheffner noted with irony, they could not approve of "Vernunft" (reason) in such close proximity to "Katechismus" (catechism).[246]

246. Scheffner to Nicolai, Sprintlack, 8 September, 2 October, 15 November and 3 December 1787, and 29 January 1788, and Nicolai's marginal annotations on each, in NN 66. The actual price Scheffner paid, 175 taler, was less than 50 percent of the original, which would have been 375 taler without the twelve copies of the catechism. Scheffner had originally asked the

Lacking Nicolai's account books, it is hard to say which of the works he sold were the most popular. The correspondence orders provide at least some idea of which titles were in demand. School books from Nicolai's firm (particularly those by Eschenburg, Muzell, Rochow, Schröckh, and Curas), Nicolai's own works (especially his description of Berlin and Potsdam, his travel account, the history of the Knights Templar, the *Verzeichnis einer Handbibliothek*, and the novel *Sebaldus Nothanker*), the *ADB*, the "Berlockenbücher," Ernst Ferdinand Klein's *Annalen der Gesetzgebung und der Rechtsgelehrsamkeit in den Preussischen Staaten*, Thomas Abbt's *Vermischte Werke*, Friedrich Germanus Lüdke's *Communionbuch*, Jakobsson's *Technologisches Wörterbuch*, and Amory's *Johann Bunkel* all seem to have done well. Of the 520 titles ordered in the sample analyzed, the most popular categories of books were belles-lettres (142); philosophy, psychology, and pedagogy (57); periodicals (41); history and politics (40); classics (35); theology (30); biography and correspondences (20); school and children's books (19); geography and travel, dictionaries and encyclopedias, natural sciences, agriculture, and technology (13 each); and polemical literature (12). Although the figures for classics, philosophy, and belles-lettres are inflated by von Koch's large book order of 1790, belles-lettres was the largest category overall, as it was in Nicolai's own publishing program. Medicine and law (4 and 7 titles, respectively) are both underrepresented in the orders in contrast to Nicolai's own list, probably because few of the customers in the sample happened to belong to those professions and thus did not purchase this largely technical literature. German titles far outweighed those in other languages. There were 67 French titles, 37 Latin (including grammars and school texts), 17 English, 6 Italian, 5 Greek, 4 Arabic-Latin, and two Danish. What is striking, however, is the broad range of these 520 titles, most of which occur only once or twice. From Christina Warg's Swedish cookery and housekeeping book, ordered by Göttingen professor Johann Beckmann, to Francesco di Algarotti's works for the abbess of Gandersheim, from the *Secret Letters on the Prussian State since the Coronation of Frederick William II* for Prince Ferdinand of Prussia to Johann Samuel Diterich's hymnal

---

school commission to provide seven pedagogical titles, plus Wilhelm Abraham Teller's *Wörterbuch des neuen Testaments* (for pastors only) free of charge to all country parsons and local schoolmasters. In the end he compiled his own excerpts from the books not acquired and the commission had 3000 copies of the volume printed. On Scheffner, see Arthur Plehne, "Johann Georg Scheffner" (Ph.D. diss., University of Königsberg, 1934). Scheffner is remembered today, if at all, chiefly for his (anonymously published) erotic poetry, such as the 1771 *Gedichte im Geschmack des Grécourt*. Wolfgang Promies, "Lyrik in der zweiten Hälfte des 18. Jahrhunderts," in *Hansers Sozialgeschichte der deutschen Literatur*, vol. 3, pt. 2, p. 901 n. 94.

for household devotions for the Schleusingen pedagogue Walch, the orders cover most genres of literature for entertainment and edification.

As far as we can tell, Nicolai dealt mainly, if not exclusively, in the more respectable sorts of literature from the legal book trade. He was willing at times to supply books forbidden for political reasons, such as the *Letters of the Prince of Prussia* or the *Authentic and Highly Remarkable Revelations on the History of Counts Struensee and Brandt* (prohibited in Prussia and Hamburg, respectively),[247] but appears to have drawn the line at pornography, or books that he considered to be such. The closest Nicolai's customers in our sample seem to have come to requesting "livres philosophiques" was an order by the Halle professor Johann August Eberhard for *Vituline, ou la courtisane insolente*. This book, published in Berlin in French and German in 1782, at least had a racy title. Eberhard looked forward to it as "a pretty lampoon [*Pasquill*]."[248] According to Nicolai's own account, he had declined to sell Johann Friedel's 1784 *Briefe über die Galanterien von Berlin*, an account of the seamy side of morals and manners in the city (including a rare mention of male prostitution) because he never knowingly sold any book "that contains crude indecencies [*Unsittlichkeiten*] and obscenities [*Zoten*].... I believe that I have only done my common duty as an honest man by not dealing in such books."[249]

Just as we have nothing approaching a full record of the titles that Nicolai actually sold, we also know little about the demand among his customers for different formats and paper qualities. Nicolai himself thought little of fancy paper and quarto editions and believed that most German book buyers likewise valued thrift over splendor. When he printed on fine paper, it was usually only for the author and his friends or patrons. He did have better-heeled customers, however, who specifically requested their books on fine paper. Hanns Ernst von Teubern, a Saxon official in Dresden, invariably ordered books printed on fine, or "writing," paper (*Schreibpapier*), and when he requested the 1760 edition of Ewald von Kleist's poetical works he asked specifically for the large octavo

247. Eberhard to Nicolai, Charlottenburg, Easter 1772, ordering two copies of the *Letters* for Horst, in NN 16, and Valentin August Heinze to Nicolai, Kiel, 12 May 1788, ordering six copies of the *Revelations* for himself and friends, in NN 31.

248. Eberhard to Nicolai, Halle, 1 December 1781, in NN 16. The anonymous title also appeared as *Vituline oder die übermüthige Kokette*. No publisher is mentioned. *Bibliotheca Germanorum Erotica & Curiosa*, ed. Hugo Hayn and Alfred N. Gotendorf, vol. 7, 3d ed. (Hanau: Müller and Kiepenheuer, n.d.; reprint, 1968), p. 134.

249. Nicolai is quoted in an *ADB* review of Friedel's book. *ADB* 59, no. 1 (1784): 237. Friedel had accused Nicolai of being his enemy, and Nicolai replied in a letter dated 6 June 1784 that he had no particular animosity toward Friedel or his book; he simply did not sell such works. The publisher had sent him 100 copies, and he had "put them away."

edition with German type, on writing paper, and with good impressions of the vignettes.²⁵⁰ The reasons for ordering a particular paper or format could also be practical rather than aesthetic (or financial), though. J. J. Eschenburg, for example, had a very particular reason for requesting Johann Georg Sulzer's *Vorübungen zur Beförderung der Aufmerksamkeit und des Nachdenkens* on fine paper: he wanted it for English students of German who found Gothic type daunting enough without the often blurry printing on cheap paper.²⁵¹ When Prince Moritz of Isenburg ordered the cheaper octavo edition of Frederick II's *Oeuvres du Philosophe de Sans Souci* rather than the finer quarto edition he would have preferred, he apparently did so because his bookshelves were built for the smaller format.²⁵²

What we can say from looking at a sample of Nicolai's correspondence customers, is that they ran the gamut from people who ordered only a few books within their own fields of study or occupation to those widely interested in the most up-to-date literature, philosophy, and current affairs. They included both intensive and extensive readers,²⁵³ often in personal union. Although it would be a gargantuan task to sift through the entire correspondence for accounts of reading experience, the Nicolai papers could doubtless be an interesting source for a history of reading in the German Enlightenment as well, a topic that exceeds the bounds of the present study.

Employees and Their Work

Naturally, Friedrich Nicolai could not keep up with such a large and far-flung circle of customers on his own. With his bookshops and the twice-yearly book fairs in Leipzig he depended upon a number of employees in

---

250. Teubern to Nicolai, Dresden, 22 January 1768, in NN 74. The Kleist edition was published by Voß in Berlin. Teubern noted that since he did not know Voß, he hoped Nicolai would do him the favor of acquiring the desired edition. Teubern worked at the Department of Justice and for Lower Lusatia, translated from French and English, and published a novel, *Dubois und Gioconda. Eine corsische Geschichte*, in 1766. He also wrote for several journals. Johann Gottlieb August Kläbe, ed., *Neuestes gelehrtes Dresden* (Dresden, 1796). Teubern also asked for his copies of Nicolai's own publications on writing paper. On 7 April 1769, for example, he requested volume 2 of Thomas Abbt's works and the newest edition of Moses Mendelssohn's *Phädon* on writing paper (in NN 74). All eleven Amsterdam subscribers to the novel *Johann Bunkel* requested it on writing paper. Theodor Gülcher to Nicolai, Amsterdam, 17 March 1778, in NN 28.

251. Eschenburg to Nicolai, Braunschweig, 14 May 1784, in NN 19. As a popular pedagogical work, the *Vorübungen* were printed on cheap paper to keep the price low.

252. Prince Moritz of Isenberg to Nicolai, Birstein, 24 March 1779, in NN 37.

253. The standard work on this phenomenon remains Rolf Engelsing, *Der Bürger als Leser: Lesergeschichte in Deutschland, 1500–1800* (Stuttgart: Metzler, 1971).

several places to keep his business running smoothly. Employment in the book trade, like that in other commercial sectors in eighteenth-century Germany, is a little-explored subject.[254] Many details of everyday practice that might interest us now were considered too banal to record, so that we must guess at them from off-hand remarks and isolated references. The information we have on work in the book trade in Nicolai's correspondence comes from letters from his fellow booksellers, his employees, and applicants for positions in his shops.

Except for a few unusual enterprises, such as Trattner's in Vienna, which united type-foundry, bindery, printing shop, bookshop, reading room, and publishing company, most eighteenth-century bookseller-publishers ran small operations indeed.[255] A shop, a storeroom, and a *comptoir* or office were all that was necessary in the publisher's hometown, and shop premises in Leipzig, perhaps with sleeping quarters attached, if the bookseller visited the fairs regularly. The employees would consist of one to four clerks (*Diener, Gehilfen*), plus a manager (*Factor, Geschäftsführer*) if the business was large enough, and one or at most two apprentices (*Bursche, Lehrling*) to wrap packages, deliver books to customers in town, and perform similar unskilled tasks while learning the business. For the book fair, publishers also engaged *Markthelfer* to pick up and deliver books and do other chores, which freed them and their *Diener* to discuss business and settle accounts with other booksellers. Philipp Erasmus Reich, despite the impressive size of the publishing operation he managed on behalf of the firm's owner Marie Louise Weidmann, and his extensive activities as Leipzig commissionare for many booksellers, including Nicolai, apparently kept only one apprentice, one *Diener*, and a *Markthelfer*. A later *Diener*, Johann Christian Benjamin Reim, who acted as a

---

254. This is in marked contrast to the attention paid to artisans and proto-industrial laborers of the same period, and to commercial employees in the nineteenth and twentieth centuries. A notable exception is Rolf Engelsing's article, "Die wirtschaftliche und soziale Differenzierung der deutschen kaufmännischen Angestellten im In- und Ausland 1690-1900," in *Zur Sozialgeschichte deutscher Mittel- und Unterschichten* (Göttingen: Vandenhoeck & Ruprecht, 1973), pp. 51–111, which however has nothing specific to say about the book trade. Even the indefatigable Goldfriedrich is very sketchy on this topic, devoting a small amount of space to booksellers' training in the early eighteenth century. *Geschichte des deutschen Buchhandels*, 2:414–15. The memoirs of booksellers and their unpublished letters could doubtless provide more information about the everyday work of employees.

255. Nicolai visited Trattner and greatly admired his industry and career as a self-made man, much as he disapproved of his piracies: "Nowhere in Germany does one find such important institutions of this kind together ... and it must be noted that he ... created all of this himself, albeit with strong support from the late empress." *Beschreibung einer Reise*, 4:454–57.

sort of deputy manager, took over the business upon his death in 1787.[256] This small number of employees is probably explained by the unimportance of the retail trade to Reich's business, which rendered shop assistants less necessary. With a much higher ratio of booksellers to population than any other German city, local retail sales in Leipzig would have been a relatively minor factor for any one firm. Nicolai, although he published less than Reich, had many private customers and a flourishing retail business both inside and outside Berlin, and thus required a larger staff.

Bookshop employees were in the difficult position of being expected to display a level of education and knowledge that they often had had no opportunity to acquire. Those who followed the traditional route started as apprentices at the age of fourteen or fifteen and served for about six years. Frequently their conditions stipulated that they serve their master for an additional year as *Diener* before applying for a position in another firm. If they were lucky, as Nicolai said he had been during his apprenticeship to Kleyb in Frankfurt an der Oder, they had the opportunity for some literary self-education and to improve their language skills before entering the next stage of their careers. Those less fortunate spent much time fetching and carrying, and in some cases also cleaning the house and shop, a fate they shared with many craft apprentices. Apprentices lived a spartan life, and some, contemporaries reported, were treated little better than slaves.[257] Friedrich Perthes, who entered the service of the pious Leipzig bookseller Adam Friedrich Böhme at the Michaelmas fair of 1787, describes typical conditions in his memoirs. As something between sons and servants, the two apprentices accompanied their master to church on Sunday, after which they were allowed out for a few hours in the afternoon. They shared a tiny attic room, had to ask permission to leave the house, and were always hungry. Twenty years later, apprentices still had modest expectations. Apparently in response to a query of Nicolai's, his Stettin shop manager Hane described the conditions to which the apprentice Johann Wilhelm Richardi, who was going to work in the

---

256. Reich's attachment to his *Markthelfer*, Johann Samuel Nagel (d. 1775), is demonstrated by the 1774 portrait of him that he commissioned from the famous artist Anton Graff. The portrait is reproduced in the exhibition catalog *Philipp Erasmus Reich (1717–1787): Verleger der Aufklärung und Reformer des deutschen Buchhandels* (Leipzig, 1989), p. 82. On Reich's other employees, see pp. 103–4.

257. The Züllichau bookseller Frommann explained that Schneider, a young *Diener* he was sending to work for Nicolai, was very timid because his first master had treated him like a slave. It would be necessary to boost his self-confidence, Frommann believed. Frommann to Nicolai, 17 September 1778, in NN 23.

Berlin shop in 1808, was accustomed. During the week, Hane gave Richardi tea and rolls for breakfast but on Sundays only coffee. Hane and Richardi always ate dinner together, but now that hard times had come with the French occupation, Hane himself usually only ate bread and butter in the evening. He had the housekeeper make a soup or heat leftovers from lunch for Richardi, who would doubtless become accustomed to whatever he received in Berlin: "If you give him bread and butter that will suffice, and doubtless there will be an occasional warm meal for him from your kitchen."[258]

With no fixed standards for training, some unfortunates reached their twenties with only rudimentary skills and little prospect of managing a shop, let alone of becoming booksellers in their own right someday, the dream of all ambitious *Diener*. Those who set their sights high tried to educate themselves as best they could. Friedrich Perthes, whose skill and diligence earned him the respect of his master, was frustrated at the limited scope offered him. "My principal, indeed, teaches me all that is necessary for one who is to continue a servant, but very little suffices for that; a special knowledge of the trade I certainly do not learn from him, for he conducts his business in the most mechanical manner—he does everything in the way that first occurs to him, without being guided by any principle; if a question is asked, he replies, 'We will do it in this way,' but can never give a reason why it is done so, and not otherwise, for if the same thing occur again, he will do it in some other way." Like Nicolai, Perthes improved his education at night, and he often fell asleep over his French or English grammar.[259] One future independent bookseller, Wilhelm Fleischer, who, however, was well beyond the apprenticeship stage, even tried to make free mornings for his studies a condition of his employment.[260]

---

258. Hane to Nicolai, Stettin, 1 October 1808, in NN 87.
259. On Perthes's apprenticeship, see *Memoirs of Frederick Perthes*, pp. 6–21.
260. On 27 December 1789 Fleischer wrote to Nicolai from Göttingen asking for a position in his shop. He had left the book trade for a time to study in Göttingen but was disappointed with university life and missed the hustle and bustle of the bookshop. He sought a position in a large city and asked Nicolai under what conditions he would be prepared "to take me on if I were to devote my knowledge and abilities to your shop in the afternoon, but have the mornings for myself?" (in NN 22). Nicolai's answer is not recorded, but in the 1790s Fleischer became a well-known bookseller and proponent of the popular Enlightenment in Frankfurt am Main. He wrote *Die Wichtigkeit des Buchhandels* (Frankfurt 1791) and *Über bildende Künste, Kunsthandel und Buchhandel in Hinsicht auf Menschenwohl. Glaubensbekenntniß eines Kunst-und Buchhändlers* (Frankfurt 1792) and in 1795 opened an extensive lending library and reading room. See Goldfriedrich, *Geschichte des deutschen Buchhandels*, 3:262, 285ff.

Book trade employees were quite mobile. There were no formal journeyman years for booksellers, but it was taken for granted that a young man who had completed his apprenticeship would want to work for several booksellers before settling down. The more ambitious tried to see the insides of as many shops as possible, particularly in the more important cities, in order both to learn from different booksellers and to make useful connections for the future when they might need credit for their own businesses. Nicolas Himmes, *Diener* to Himmes and Esslinger in Koblenz, wished "to expand my knowledge of the book trade, and ... to work in the foremost bookshops in Germany in order to learn how business is truly done."[261] Franz Christian Friedrich Francke decided to leave J. G. Hanisch in Hildburghausen "since ... I see that I cannot make my fortune here nor do I have any future prospects."[262] Although satisfied with his next job working for Johann Jacob Stahel, he found Würzburg too pious for his taste.[263] Similarly, Johann Wilhelm Güth was most anxious to escape Liège where he felt uncomfortable as a Protestant among fervent Catholics "whose character is not the best."[264] Although most of his own employees were trained by a small number of booksellers in a handful of cities—Erfurt, Jena, Stendal, Züllichau, Breslau, Frankfurt am Main—Nicolai also received applications from farther afield: Koblenz, Strasbourg, Liège, Münster, Regensburg, Nuremberg, Winterthur, Würzburg, and Vienna.

The hiring and firing of *Diener* was a major topic of booksellers' correspondence between the fairs. Some thirty letters on this subject survive in Nicolai's correspondence. Because standards of training, for example, the point at which an apprentice was ready to become a *Diener*, were ill-defined and formally nonexistent, and the quality of employees varied accordingly, personal correspondence and exchange of information were essential. While some booksellers were apparently seriously committed to turning out useful members of the book trade, others (mis)used their apprentices as cheap labor. Members of the book trade apparently knew which masters made an effort to train their apprentices, and which shops presented opportunities for gaining a good knowledge of the business.

261. Himmes to Nicolai, Koblenz, 4 October 1788, in NN 35. In a similar vein, see the letters from Friedrich Wilhelm Martiny, who worked for Korn Senior in Breslau (16 November 1788, in NN 48) and C. W. Lohmann of Hannover (December 1792, in NN 46).

262. Francke to Keyser, Erfurt, 15 January 1789, in NN 22. Keyser apparently passed the letter on to Nicolai because he knew he was looking for a *Diener*.

263. Francke to Nicolai, Würzburg, 27 June 1789, in NN 22.

264. Loyalty to his boss, Plomteux, who had paid for his expensive journey, however, forced him to stay a bit longer. Güth to Nicolai, Liège, 27 October 1769, in NN 28.

Everyday Life in the Book Trade

When P. G. Kummer wrote to Nicolai about three potential candidates, he suggested that a recommendation from the Prague bookseller Johann Gottfried Calve was a reliable one, "since Calve is undeniably a skilled and hardworking bookseller." A *Diener* trained by Carl Christian Kümmel in Halle, however highly recommended, might not be a good prospect. Kummer feared that "he will have acquired very little knowledge of books in Kümmel's shop."[265] Booksellers asked each other to keep an eye out for likely candidates and also shared accounts of dishonest or negligent workers. Nicolai corresponded with at least twenty booksellers on the subject of employees.[266] They were, for the most part, those with whom he otherwise had strong business ties.[267] Sixteen of the twenty are represented in his 1787 selective book catalog, thirteen of them with twenty or more titles.[268] Appeals for apprentices often went to non-book trade acquaintances as well, since the main requirements were a rudimentary knowledge of Latin or French, a legible hand, and a desire to learn the trade. On the other side of the equation book trade employees, who often knew each other from the fairs, exchanged information about employers and vacancies.[269] The actual arrangements for hiring an

---

265. Kummer to Nicolai, Leipzig, 4 September 1790, in NN 42.

266. The booksellers were Johann Georg Esslinger (1764), Johann Christian Gebhard (1765), Heinrich Ludwig Brönner (1767), and Johann Benjamin Andreä (1788) in Frankfurt am Main; J. C. Brandt (1765) and Carl Ernst Bohn (1773) in Hamburg; Franz Heinsius (1768) in Gotha; J. J. Hartknoch (1773) in Riga; C. G. Günther (1775) in Groß Glogau; Crusius (1775) and Johann Samuel Heinsius (1783, 1791) in Leipzig; Christian Friedrich Schwan (1779) in Mannheim; N. G. Frommann (1778, 1781, 1783, 1784) in Züllichau; W. G. Korn (1783) and J. Friedrich Korn (1787) in Breslau; J. Kurzböck in Vienna (1784); P. G. Kummer in Leipzig (1790); Johann Siegmund Zolling (1794, 1795) in Langensalza; the Gebrüder Pfähler (1795) in Heidelberg; and Georg Adam Keyser (1796, 1802) in Erfurt.

267. For example, they also took care of his commissions in Leipzig (Kummer), ordered books from him between the fairs (Hartknoch in Riga, Frommann in Züllichau, Schwan in Mannheim), solicited business advice (Frommann in Züllichau), placed advertisements for him in local papers and discussed problems of piracy (Schwan in Mannheim).

268. Crusius 136 titles, Bohn 83, Hartknoch 62, W. G. Korn 47, Schwan 43, Brönner 33, J. F. Korn 29, Kurzböck 29, Esslinger 27, J. S. Heinsius 23, Frommann 23, Keyser 20, Kummer 20, Andreä 14, Pfähler 7, and Günther 4. Figures from Raabe, "Zum Bild des Verlagswesens in der Spätaufklärung, table 6, pp. 84–88.

269. Rostock, for example, who worked for Korn and Gampert in Breslau, heard of an opening in Nicolai's shop from an employee of Meyer, another Breslau firm (Rostock to Nicolai, 4 June 1764, in NN 51); Carl Christian Friedrich Schweppe, an employee of Fleischer in Frankfurt am Main, learned of the same opening from Kochendorster there (Schweppe to Nicolai, 9 August 1764, in NN 70); Carl Friedrich Raspe, *Diener* to W. G. Korn Junior in Breslau, was informed that Nicolai needed a new *Diener* by his colleague Steinfurt (Raspe to Nicolai, Michaelmas 1783, in NN 59); and Friedrich Wilhelm Martiny learned from Nicolai's own *Diener* Lotter that Bube was vacating a position in Berlin (Martiny to Nicolai, Breslau, 16 November 1788, in NN 48).

employee were usually made at the Leipzig fairs, but contact was often initiated in letters. The hiring process normally involved correspondence between the prospective employer and the employee, as well as the current employer.

Although booksellers were often at a loss for suitable employees, the public advertising of vacancies was uncommon until the end of the century. Nor did the book trade make use of employment brokers, who helped to place commercial employees in other trades.[270] When the trade journal *Neues Archiv für Gelehrte, Buchhändler und Antiquare* began printing advertisements from *Diener* seeking employment, as well as from booksellers offering positions in 1795, the innovation stirred up controversy. Certain employees worried that this apparent move from the old patronage system to an open market in labor would invite comparisons between them and domestics. Ludwig Christian Kehr, *Diener* to Friedrich Eßlinger in Frankfurt am Main, composed an outraged letter to the editor expressing his and some of his colleagues' injured sense of honor upon reading the journal's "Persons seeking employment" rubric. They had, he said, nothing but contempt for colleagues who thus put themselves on public display, offering their services to the highest bidder like scullery maids. Professional pride and honor forbade such groveling, and it was no wonder that some employers treated their *Diener* as glorified errand boys. The man of honor, he concluded, would only apply for a position through a private letter—if, that is, he were capable of penning a decent one.[271] Thus Kehr sought emphatically to distance the *Diener* (which, nevertheless, means "one who serves") from the servant, and to assert a measure of occupational pride. In a society painfully conscious of every gradation in the social hierarchy, and in a situation in which the book trade was becoming crowded with untrained independent booksellers, men like Kehr feared for their status. If *Diener* did not act like servants, he implied, they would not be treated as such. What Kehr's response obscures is the fact that it was not *Diener* themselves who placed the ads, but their employers. In most cases they sought positions for

---

270. Marperger provides a sample letter from a *Diener* to such a *Mäckler* or broker in *Getreuer und Geschickter Handels-Diener, In welchem vornehmlich Was ein Handels-Diener sey, was derselbe vor Qualitäten und Wissenschaften an sich haben müsse* ... (Nuremberg: Peter Conrad Monath, 1715), p. 114.

271. *Neues Archiv für Gelehrte, Buchhändler und Antiquare*, vol. 1, no. 35 (Erlangen: Palm, 1795), pp. 547–49. Kehr, who was trained by Weiß und Brede in Offenbach and went to work for Eßlinger in 1795, later became an independent bookseller in Kreuznach and wrote his memoirs, *Selbstbiographie von Ludwig Christian Kehr, Buchhändler in Kreuznach. Zunächst für angehende Buchhändler geschrieben* (Kreuznach, 1834).

young men who had just completed their apprenticeships. Kehr's emphatic letter may also reflect a struggle between *Diener* and booksellers for control of the application process and thus also of the employment market. In a reply to Kehr, Johann Jakob Palm, publisher of the *Neues Archiv*, remarked that he saw nothing dishonorable in publicly seeking employment. Kehr displayed a prejudice that colleagues in England, France, and the Netherlands had long since jettisoned, he said. Palm believed, in the spirit of the Enlightenment, that the openness of publicity was healthy; the applicant's claims were laid bare to scrutiny and dispute. The *Neues Archiv* was also not a general gazette, but a journal directed solely at the book trade. No bookseller in his right mind would compare the services of a *Diener* to those of a scullery maid just because both were offered publicly, nor assume that either was incompetent simply because he or she advertised. The purpose of the employment advertisement, Palm emphasized, was simply to make it easier for worthy employees (*brauchbare Subjekte*) to find positions, and to make it more difficult for the worthless ones. With so many booksellers, how was a *Diener* looking for a new employer to find out about openings? He might have to send out many letters. By advertising publicly, he became known to a greater number of potential employers and might be able to choose among several offers. More importantly, the bookseller seeking a *Diener* could investigate the candidates before dealing with them directly. A jobseeker whose name was publicly advertised was under more pressure not to lie about his accomplishments or promise more than he could deliver.[272]

As far as we can tell from the correspondence and other scattered sources, Nicolai employed some twenty-three persons in his shops over the years, including his sons Samuel Friedrich and Carl August.[273] Of these, twenty-two had undergone apprenticeships, five of them in Nicolai's own Stettin shop. As a bookseller of old-fashioned principles, he preferred *Diener* with formal training in the book trade. The sole exception was Christian Friedrich Schneider, who was already an experienced commercial clerk when he went to work in the Stettin shop. At least two educated men with literary interests offered him their services,[274] but

272. *Neues Archiv*, 1, no. 35 (1795): 549–62, esp. 551–56.
273. For the names and origins of Nicolai's shop employees, see the Appendix.
274. Pauli, a law graduate, to Nicolai, Stettin, 28 September 1784, in NN 56, and Philippi, a former postal employee who had worked as a proofreader and in other capacities for Trattner in Vienna, to Nicolai, Strasbourg, 5 July 1781, in NN 57. It became more common toward the end of the eighteenth century for men without book trade training to set up as independent booksellers. See Wittmann, *Geschichte des deutschen Buchhandels*, pp. 130ff.

Nicolai thought too highly of the specialized knowledge needed for the book trade to take a risk with outsiders, including his own son-in-law, Friedrich Parthey. In the terminology of the time, he preferred *gelernte* (trained) to *gelehrte* (scholarly) booksellers.[275] Of Nicolai's employees whose fates are known, five (including his son Carl August) became independent booksellers, two went on to serve in other bookshops, and one left the book trade altogether. Four died while working for Nicolai. Nicolai remembered the four who were still working for him at his death in his will. Nicolai's staff included one apprentice each in Berlin and Stettin and a manager in Stettin. The number of *Diener* varied over time, reaching a height of four in the Berlin shop in the 1790s.[276]

With four *Diener*, Nicolai's shop was a fairly substantial enterprise in the context of local commerce at the period, although smaller than most of the Berlin printing shops, which employed an average of seven workers.[277] In 1784, the 561 members of the Berlin merchant guild employed only 321 *Diener* in all, and in 1801, 877 merchants had only 368 *Diener*.[278] One of the city's most important firms, the banking and manufacturing house of Splitgerber und Daum, had 10 *Diener* in 1781.[279]

The shop hierarchy was clearly expressed in salary. In the Stettin shop around 1790—the only instance where comparison among employees is possible—the manager earned 300 taler yearly, the two *Diener* 200 and 72 taler, and the housekeeper 24 taler.[280] Less information is available for the Berlin shop. The *Diener* Carl Gottfried Amende and J.C.D. Schneider each received 60 taler as a starting salary in the 1770s, while F.C.F.

---

275. On these two terms, see Gädicke, *Der Buchhandel von mehreren Seiten betrachtet*.

276. Around the same time, another important firm, the Frankfurt bookshop of Friedrich Eßlinger, employed five *Diener*. Meyer, "Die geschäftlichen Verhältnisse," p. 226.

277. Berlin had twenty-one printing shops in 1805. The two largest, those of Decker and Unger, employed 66 and 58 people, respectively. Geheimes Staatsarchiv Preußischer Kulturbesitz Berlin-Dahlem, General-Direktorium, Fabrikendepartement, Tit. XCVI, No. 50, General-Fabriquen-Tabelle von Berlin pro 1805/06, Abschnitt II: Fabriken-Anstalten außer den Webereyen, fol. 27. Reproduced in Helga Eichler, "Berliner Buchdrucker, Buchhändler und Verleger am Ende des 18. Jahrhunderts," typescript, p. 20.

278. Hugo Rachel and Paul Wallich, *Berliner Großkaufleute und Kapitalisten*, vol. 2, *Die Zeit des Merkantilismus 1648–1806* (Berlin: privately printed, 1938), p. 520 n. 1.

279. Ibid., p. 224.

280. Undated scrap of paper, possibly December 1791, from Hane in Stettin to Nicolai, listing expenses for the Stettin shop, in NN 87. According to Nicolai's handwritten additions to the note he was paying Hane 300 taler a year. In 1797, Hane requested a raise of 50 taler and Nicolai accorded him 60. Hane remarked that profits had been rising because of his efforts and he hoped to reap some benefit from this. Hane to Nicolai, Stettin, 13 January 1797, and Nicolai's annotations, in NN 87.

Everyday Life in the Book Trade

Francke was paid 80 taler for the shop's lowest position, as fourth *Diener*, in 1791. Johann Wilhelm Richardi, however, who completed his apprenticeship in Stettin and went to work in Berlin in 1808, was earning 100 taler by 1810. Precisely what benefits, such as room and board, went along with these salaries is unclear. A letter of 1778 mentions only that the employee in question had been promised breakfast, tea, and sugar,[281] but these may have been considered extra because master and employees took their midday meal together. The thirty-one-year-old Francke, who went to work for Nicolai at Easter 1790, spoke of certain necessary but unspecified services and conveniences he hoped to receive.[282] Those employees who spent a long time in Nicolai's service were apparently treated well; Nicolai paid expensive medical bills for Hane, the manager of his Stettin shop, for example.[283] The Berlin *Diener* Johann Christophe Kraehe was invited to stay with Nicolai's old friend and collaborator Pastor Dapp in the country and to take the waters in the summer of 1796.[284] Booksellers' employees were better paid than many artisanal workers and some pastors and schoolmasters as well. However, when compared to the salaries of bank clerks, for example, their remuneration was hardly princely.[285] In the book trade, what high salaries there were were reserved for the independent managers of shops. Philipp Erasmus Reich, for example, was paid 2000 taler per year for running the Weidmannische Buchhandlung in Leipzig from 1766 on. He had started at the substantial sum of 800 taler.[286] Reich's own *Diener* earned between 50 and 125 taler per year.[287]

281. Frommann, who was sending an employee to work for Nicolai in Berlin, to Nicolai, Züllichau, 9 July 1778, in NN 68.
282. Franz Christian Friedrich Francke to Nicolai, Würzburg, 13 August 1789, in NN 22.
283. Nicolai corresponded with Hane's physician, who asked him to encourage Hane not to overexert himself. The bills amounted to the substantial sum of 100 taler for twelve weeks. Dr. Kölpin to Nicolai, Stettin, 6 and 26 September 1809, in NN 87. During Hane's illness, business was handled by the apprentice. Hane to Nicolai, Stettin, 12 and 21 September 1809, in NN 87.
284. Kraehe to Nicolai, Klein Schönebeck, June 1796, in NN 42.
285. In Berlin, for example, the banking firm of Splitgerber und Daum paid out 5000 taler in salaries to its seven clerks in 1745. A nineteen-year-old who started at 50 taler in 1748 could double his salary in a year and was earning 500 taler by 1758. In 1745, the firm's best-paid *Diener* earned 1000 taler. Rachel and Wallich, *Berliner Großkaufleute*, p. 224.
286. Lehmstedt, *Struktur und Arbeitsweise*, p. 39.
287. Mark Lehmstedt, *Philipp Erasmus Reich, 1717–1787: Verleger der Aufklärung und Reformer des deutschen Buchhandels*, exhibition catalog (Leipzig: Karl Marx Universität, 1989), pp. 103–4, and *Struktur und Arbeitsweise*, p. 39. The *Markthelfer* at the firm's Warsaw branch earned 50 taler per year, as did Leipzig *Diener* Johann Christoph Ernst Klopstock (1760/61), who had just finished his apprenticeship. Gottlieb Christian Götz, *Diener* from 1775 to 1780 received 80 taler, the Warsaw manager 100 taler, and Johann Christian Benjamin Reim 70 and later 125 taler.

While in many other branches of commerce salaries improved greatly over the course of the eighteenth century, Nicolai and many of his fellow booksellers at the end of the century were paying what other merchants had already paid their employees at the beginning of the century.[288] It is not surprising that book trade *Diener*, who considered themselves among the elite of commercial employees, complained of the comparatively low pay they received for rather demanding work. Among them was the L. C. Kehr we encountered above, who remarked that many excellent employees in the book trade could barely survive on their incomes if they wished to live in a style appropriate to their station in life and to indulge in the occasional pleasure.[289] The publisher of the *Neues Archiv*, however, felt that *Diener* had become too extravagant and demanding. According to Palm, there had been a time when new employees fresh from their apprenticeship had been satisfied with 30–40 taler, but now they expected up to 100 taler a year.[290] Johann Matthias Ensslin, an employee of the Regensburg firm of Montag, whom Nicolai offered the position of fourth

---

288. See the figures for commercial employees, taken from a 1715 publication, in Engelsing, "Die wirtschaftliche und soziale Differenzierung," pp. 65–66. An unnamed bookseller in a middle-sized city, for example, offered 80 taler a year plus room and board (breakfast, lunch, dinner, and coffee) and a yearly bonus for a *Diener* who was expected to run the shop in his master's absence and to train an apprentice. He promised to treat the employee not as an inferior but as a friend and helper, should his work be satisfactory. Rubric "Subjecte, so gesucht werden," *Neues Archiv* 1, no. 43 (1795): 688–89. The youngest son of the Hamburg bookseller Christian Herold, who had worked as a *Diener* for two years, received a salary of 50 taler from the firm of Walther in Dresden in 1773. Bohn to Nicolai, Hamburg, 30 July 1773, in NN 7. In 1787, the Altenburg bookseller Richter was likewise willing to pay his future employee 50 taler. Meyer, "Die geschäftlichen Verhältnisse," p. 226. Karl Friedrich Treuttel, *Diener* in Leipzig, mentioned in a letter applying for a vacant position in Nicolai's shop that his current employer, Crusius, paid him 100 taler plus room and board, 1 November 1789, in NN 74. In some cases, employees seem to have been paid a specific sum for board (*Kostgeld*) beyond their salary. Meyer, "Die geschäftlichen Verhältnisse," p. 226.

289. Letter to the editor, *Neues Archiv* 1, no. 37–38 (1795): 599–600. Kehr mentions in his memoirs that he received 80 fl. (ca. 53 taler) in salary and 180 fl. (ca. 120 taler) for board during his first year in Eßlinger's employ (1795). The next year he received 150 fl (ca. 100 taler) salary and 330 fl (ca. 220 taler) board, and the third year 200 fl (ca. 130 taler) salary. Meyer, "Die geschäftlichen Verhältnisse," p. 226.

290. Footnote to Kehr's letter, *Neues Archiv* 1, no. 37–38 (1795): 601. Palm considered that the large Leipzig firms were at least partly at fault for the inflation of *Diener*s' salary expectations. It had reached a point, he said, where many smaller firms could no longer afford a qualified *Diener* and had to make do with apprentices who were so busy that they had no time to educate themselves. He does not say at what period *Diener* had been satisfied with 30–40 taler a year, nor when they had ceased to be so. In 1775, the bookseller C. G. Günther in Groß Glogau promised his inefficient apprentice Johann Zacharias Logan 40 taler for his first year as *Diener*, plus 20 taler for new clothes, "because he has been with me for so long." Günther to Nicolai, 15 February 1775, in NN 28.

Diener in his Berlin shop in 1790, requested a salary of 200 taler for the first year, plus room and board. Nicolai, who set aside 80 taler for this job, noted in the margin of Ensslin's letter, "He isn't in his right mind. It is the 4th position." Needless to say, Nicolai did not hire him.[291]

What were the social origins of *Diener* and what qualities and abilities were expected of them for 60 to 300 taler a year? Judging by those who wrote to Nicolai, booksellers' *Diener* often came from bookselling families, but were just as likely to be the sons of merchants or other members of the urban middle classes.[292] What they seem to have shared was basic Latin education without the desire, aptitude, or means to pursue the university studies for which some may initially have been intended. Friedrich Nicolai himself had been one of those boys. Although a passionate reader, he had had no desire to follow in the footsteps of his elder brother, who became a professor in Frankfurt an der Oder, or so he recalled in his memoirs. Under such circumstances, the book trade could appear to be a logical alternative, strengthened in cases such as Nicolai's by family tradition and pressure. Thus for example, C. W. Lohmann, whose late uncle (an *ADB* reviewer) had groomed him for classical studies, explained that various circumstances had made him change this plan and devote himself to the book trade.[293]

That the book trade involved much more tedious work than reading manuscripts and chatting with customers about books was something that apprentices learned early on, though not early enough for many employers, who frequently lamented that they had only entered the business for access to books. Contemporary debates about reading mania (*Lesesucht, Lesewut*)[294] found an echo in tales of absent-minded *Diener* who preferred reading to keeping the books. The bookseller Frommann mused that one might be better off with solid, quiet employees, even if

---

291. Ensslin to Nicolai, Regensburg, 27 September 1790, in NN 18. Ensslin had also written to the Leipzig bookseller Kummer, as the latter mentioned to Nicolai in a letter of 4 September 1790, in NN 42. Ensslin had apprenticed under Widow Klett.

292. Holle and Karl Friedrich Treuttel were, respectively, the nephews of the booksellers Johann Samuel Heinsius in Leipzig and Treuttel in Strasbourg. Heinsius to Nicolai, Leipzig, 6 July 1791, in NN 31; and Treuttel to Nicolai, Leipzig, November 1789, in NN 74. Friedrich Wilhelm Martiny was "related to considerable merchant houses," in Breslau. E. D. Schumann to Nicolai, recommending Martiny, Breslau, 17 December 1788, in NN 70. Friedrich Osterloh was the son of a Halle merchant. Osterloh to Nicolai, Halle, 31 October 1786, in NN 55. C. W. Lohmann was the nephew of Rector Köppen, an *ADB* reviewer, and Johannes Ritter was the stepson of Pastor Zerrenner, a pedagogical author whom Nicolai published.

293. Lohmann to Nicolai, Hannover, 10 November 1791, in NN 46.

294. See Wittmann, *Geschichte des deutschen Buchhandels*, pp. 186ff.

they possessed no great talents, than with those "who thought themselves geniuses."²⁹⁵ The qualities expected of a *Diener* were both practical and moral. A good general education, knowledge of languages, bookkeeping, and currency exchange were all desirable, while a legible hand, the ability to compose a business letter, and a respectful manner were well-nigh essential. Honesty, diligence, attention to detail, loyalty, and discretion were the qualities most frequently mentioned by employers and employees alike. Only aspiring *Diener* without book trade experience believed that a passion for literature was sufficient or necessary preparation for their duties. Johann Andreas Schäfer, who entered Nicolai's firm in the autumn of 1768, promised to devote himself to the business with "tireless work, loyalty, enthusiasm and honesty, as well as discretion."²⁹⁶ The goal of all training was "to become a useful member of the book trade."²⁹⁷ G. Pfähler, bookseller in Heidelberg, described an ideal employee in a 1795 letter to Nicolai: "A well-bred young man of twenty-one years who has learned the trade properly in my shop.... Apart from writing a pretty hand he speaks and writes French, knows a good deal about books, is well-mannered, handsome, hardworking and energetic, understands bookkeeping, which I have allowed him to do almost wholly on his own for many years, and which I expect to be done very cleanly and exactly. He is eminently suited to the retail trade and with some guidance is capable of managing a shop on his own."²⁹⁸ A less ideal, but still adequate candidate was Harrer, whom Nicolai, perhaps for lack of anyone better, actually hired in 1784 to run his Stettin shop. Frommann, who had trained Harrer from his fourteenth to his twentieth year in Züllichau, wrote:

> I can recommend him from the standpoint of absolute honesty, good will, and industriousness. I have found that he has become ever more attentive to business over the years and I hope that he will strive to become ever more useful, particularly since he knows that his future fortunes depend entirely upon his skill and conduct. He is, to be sure,

---

295. Frommann to Nicolai, Züllichau, 8 January 1781, regarding an employee Nicolai had promised to send him, in NN 23.

296. Schäfer to Nicolai, Gotha, 12 October 1768, in NN 65.

297. This typical phrase was used by Carl Gottfried Amende, whom Nicolai had just hired for the Berlin shop at Michaelmas 1769. Amende to Nicolai, Breslau, 25 November 1769, in NN 1.

298. Pfähler to Nicolai, Heidelberg, 25 April 1795, in NN 57. Nicolai noted on the letter that he had no position open but would think of the young man in future. At the 1796 Easter fair he made a note to ask Pfähler for the *Diener*'s name.

not very quick-witted, but his attentiveness makes up for this lack and I have always wished to see him placed in a good house.... My pupil would not, however, be capable of running your Stettin shop. He still lacks the insight that is necessary to supervise such a business.[299]

Unsupervised, Harrer indeed became a problem. Although "a hardworking and meticulous man," if somewhat absentminded, life in Stettin apparently went to his head after the quiet of Züllichau. He attended masked balls, picnics, and promenades and gambled unluckily with officers in smoking shops (*Tabagien*). He told another *Diener* that he had gone through some 500 taler during his two years in the city, which probably exceeded his salary.[300] Such stories must have been common at the time, for another *Diener*, Franz Christian Friedrich Francke, emphasized in a letter of 1789 accepting Nicolai's offer of employment that he was no spendthrift or man-about-town: "I am not given to gaming, or only for entertainment. I am also no friend of large parties, and am accustomed always to live within my means."[301]

Many aspiring members of the book trade offered Nicolai their services over the years. Some had heard from a friend along the *Diener* grapevine that a position was open. Others simply tried their luck in the hope that Nicolai would remember them in future.[302] When Nicolai received a promising letter, he consulted the *Diener's* current employer for further information about the applicant's qualifications and character. Johann Zacharias Logan, for example, wrote several enthusiastic letters

---

299. Frommann to Nicolai, Züllichau, 26 August 1784, in NN 23.

300. Harrer apparently spent 20 taler alone on his sailor's costume for the local commercial clerks' procession, where all dressed as mariners. As head *Diener* in the shop he also played up his favored status with Nicolai and dissuaded his underlings from asking Nicolai for raises and thanking him for a New Years' gift. Then, in late August 1786, he suddenly embarked, without luggage, on an urgent journey which he said would only last a few days and disappeared for several weeks at least. Probably not coincidentally, he had met a young lady with no money but an ambitious mother at his dancing class and apparently promised to become engaged to her on 3 September. Harrer to the Stettin shop, Anclam, 30 August 1786, in NN 67; Schmidt to Nicolai, Stettin, 3, 4, 7, 11 and (received) 20 September 1786, in NN 67.

301. Francke to Nicolai, Würzburg, 13 August 1789, in NN 22.

302. *Diener* who offered Nicolai their services on the chance that he might have (or know of) a vacant position were F. C. L. Lange, of the firm of Meyer in Braunschweig (September 1768, in NN 43), Friedrich August Leo, of Breitkopf in Dresden (7 March 1785, in NN 45), P. J. N. Thorn of Huber in Koblenz (29 December 1788, in NN 74), Frans Ludwig Kaebelmann in Königsberg (2 September 1791, in NN 38), C. W. Lohmann of Ritscher in Hannover (10 November 1791, December 1792, in NN 46), and Johann Leonhard Kießling of Grattenauer in Nuremberg (24 September 1792, in NN 38).

to Nicolai, full of eagerness to widen his horizons in the famous Berlin firm.[303] His letters were literate and his hand elegant. The bookseller Christian Friedrich Günther, though clearly fond of the young man who had served as his apprentice for six-and-a-half years, spoke of Logan's qualities in less than glowing terms, however. Although (or perhaps because) Logan was well educated, he was absent-minded in the extreme. He was too fond of reading to pay sufficient attention to his work and had probably only chosen the book trade in order to have a constant supply of books. He wasted time pondering things that were none of his business "and with which he will also earn no money." All in all he thought rather too much of himself and needed constant supervision.[304] Nicolai decided not to hire Logan.

Once hired for a term of service usually commencing at either Easter or Michaelmas, the prospective employee made his way, at his new master's expense,[305] either to the bookseller's home town or to Leipzig. The new employee was frequently needed to help with business at the fair, and it was thus a great disappointment to Nicolai in 1765 when a new *Diener* was unavailable at Easter because he had to mind his current employer's Frankfurt shop while the bookseller was in Leipzig.[306]

Apart from the shop employees in Berlin and Stettin, but equally necessary to the running of the business, there was also a lower echelon of workers. The Leipzig *Markthelfer*, a sort of porter, opened and helped set

303. Logan to Nicolai, Groß Glogau, 12 February, 5 March, and 9 April 1775, in NN 46.
304. Günther to Nicolai, Groß Glogau, 15 February 1775, in NN 28. The case of a certain Seyberth illustrates another common bookseller's complaint. In January 1778, the Leipzig bookseller Crusius wrote to Nicolai regarding a former employee who had applied for a position in the Berlin shop. Crusius had been forced to dismiss him for lovesickness, the same infirmity that had apparently hastened his departure from Varrentrapp und Wenner in Frankfurt. Apparently Seyberth had an all-too-understandable penchant for the daughters of booksellers, but he was unlucky in his choices and useless at his work once smitten. Crusius noted that Seyberth's love was always mixed with pride and the prospect of making his fortune. Since marriage was the simplest, and for many the only, route to independence in the book trade, Seyberth's behavior may not have been uncommon. At any rate, Crusius was not the only employer to note the dire effects of love on employee performance. See Crusius to Nicolai, Leipzig, 2 and 13 January 1778, in NN 13, and J. F. Korn to Nicolai, Breslau, 12 January and 20 October 1787, in NN 42.
305. Occasionally, a prospective employee offered to pay his own travel expenses. P. J. N. Thorn and Nicolas Himmes, both of Koblenz, may have feared that the cost of such a long journey from the far west of Germany to Berlin might dissuade Nicolai from considering them. Thorn to Nicolai, Koblenz, 29 December 1788, in NN 74; Himmes to Nicolai, Koblenz, 4 October 1788, in NN 75.
306. Johann Eberhard Zehe, who worked for Gebhard in Frankfurt am Main, to Nicolai, 2 and 9 February and 1 March 1765, in NN 84.

Everyday Life in the Book Trade

up the bookseller's storeroom before the fair began, unpacked the bales of books to be sold and picked up and delivered during the fairs, assuring the smooth running of booksellers' exchanges of unbound printed sheets. House servants provided for the material well-being of the bookseller and his shop employees. Unlike Philipp Erasmus Reich, Nicolai did not commission any fine portraits of his market helpers. We know only that he paid him one of them 6 taler 8 groschen at the Leipzig book fair in 1760,[307] and that in 1792 he was looking for a second, "who is loyal and sober and good at finding people."[308] A servant in Stettin left a more lasting impression. The Widow Gerhardtin, who had been hired as housekeeper by Nicolai's cousin, wrote a letter to Nicolai complaining of her treatment at the hands of the shop's manager, Hane.[309] Frau Gerhardtin's exact duties are unclear; she may have waited on customers in the shop as well as cooked and cleaned for the *Diener* and apprentice. Her letter attests to a high degree of literacy and suggests that she was one of those respectable middle-class widows whose main employment opportunities at the time were as housekeepers. To her nameless successor fell the thankless and onerous task of looking after the numerous soldiers billeted in the house during the French occupation of Stettin, as well as the manager and apprentice. C. F. Schmidt's letters from the late 1780s and early 1790s and Hane's from the period around 1800 give some impression of everyday life for the members of Nicolai's Stettin establishment. Certainly they enjoyed greater independence than their Berlin counterparts, who lived and worked directly under their principal's nose. They would have seen Nicolai once a year at most, in the late summer. By today's standards Stettin (Szczecin) is not far from Berlin, but the 170 kilometers or so that lay between it and Berlin (which was about the same distance

307. Meyer, "Die geschäftlichen Verhältnisse," p. 237.
308. Nicolai to P. G. Kummer, Berlin, 13 April 1792, in DBSM Böv Archivalien, Kummersches Archiv, Kasten 1, No. 3a. 6. I thank Mark Lehmstedt for sending me a transcription of this document.
309. Gerhardtin to Nicolai, Stettin, 29 March 1788, in NN 24. Frau Gerhardtin had been working at the bookshop for three years when Hane dismissed her without the proper three months notice stipulated in the *Gesindeordnung*, the law regulating relations between servants and their employers. She believed he was annoyed with her because she had criticized him for leaving the shop unattended on many occasions and demanded that she receive the salary due her for the full period of her contract or be given three months' notice. Hane's version of matters was rather different. On 27 March 1788 he wrote merely, "The Widow Gerhartin has served Nicolai's Bookshop loyally and honestly for three years, but now has permission to enter other employment at the end of next month." Note under Gerhardtin to Nicolai, in NN 24.

as Leipzig in the opposite direction), was a substantial journey in the eighteenth century. The Berlin employees, by contrast, saw Nicolai not only in the shop but also at meals.[310]

The tasks of the *Diener* in Berlin and Stettin varied. In Stettin, the employees were responsible for all aspects of running the shop, including waiting on customers, ordering stock, inventory and bookkeeping, local advertising, pursuing reluctant payers, and if necessary taking them to court. The Berlin employees had to deal with some aspects at least of the publishing as well as the retail side of the business, handling authors and printers during Nicolai's absence and even ordering emergency reprints when piracy threatened. Two of the Berlin *Diener* also visited the Leipzig fairs with Nicolai. In order to expedite matters, one of them stayed at his shop there to accommodate booksellers who came to settle their accounts while the other went out to the shops of other booksellers. Each had to keep an account book.[311] At Michaelmas 1794, for example, Nicolai took his son Carl August and the *Diener* Steckmesser with him to Leipzig and left Kraehe to mind the shop in Berlin.[312] As Nicolai grew older and his eyesight, which had been declining since the 1770s, failed, he delegated more and more correspondence to his employees. The death of his eldest son Samuel Friedrich, however, thwarted his plan to withdraw from business in the 1790s. Despite announcing his retirement in May 1807,[313] he continued to take an active role in the business until shortly before his death in January 1811.

None of Nicolai's account books has survived, so that we can only surmise from the experience of other booksellers and occasional references in employees' letters how this essential aspect of everyday work was organized. A mid-eighteenth-century description of the German book trade lists ten separate registers and account books used in the shop, and

---

310. Nicolai's grandson Gustav Parthey mentions that, although he often spent the day in his (Berlin) garden house during the summer, Nicolai went home to the Brüderstraße for lunch with his employees and family. *Jugenderinnerungen*, pp. 130–31. Whether the shop employees lived in his house is unclear.

311. Nicolai to P. G. Kummer, Berlin, 13 April 1792, in DBSM, Böv Archivalien, Kummersches Archiv, Kasten 1, No. 3a. 6.

312. Nicolai to his daughter Minna, Leipzig, 11 October 1794, in LAB, Rep. 200 Acc 450 vol. 9.

313. A circular dated 25 May 1807 and addressed to his friends and correspondents announced that illness and the loss of his eyesight made it impossible to answer letters anymore or take part in his business. He asked them to direct any necessary correspondence either to the bookshop or to his son-in-law Friedrich Parthey. The circular is reproduced in Nicolai, *Verlegerbriefe*, pp. 198–200.

Everyday Life in the Book Trade

Nicolai and his employees presumably kept similar records. These were (1) the inventory, organized by (academic) discipline with one volume for each and a separate volume for foreign-language books; (2) an alphabetical subject catalog so that books on a particular topic could be readily found for customers; (3) an order book; (4) a register of so-called defect sheets needed from all out-of-town booksellers, arranged alphabetically, so that missing sheets could be ordered between the fairs as the opportunity arose; (5) the daily journal, listing all books loaned out, or sent to customers in other cities; (6) the main account book (*Hauptbuch*), containing the bills from the individual account books, so that one could survey all accounts at once; (7) the book fair register, recording all transactions, whether for cash (*Contant*) or exchange (*Change*), made at the book fairs; (8) the booksellers' main register, a neater version of the book fair register made upon returning home so that one could survey transactions from fair to fair; (9) the cash book (*Cassabuch*), listing all income and outlays; and (10) the copy book, noting the essential contents of incoming and outgoing correspondence to provide a record when mistakes or disputes arose.[314] Those records which the Stettin managers mentioned sending periodically to Berlin were the monthly and yearly *Manual*, the *Extracte der Einnahmen* (extract of cash receipts), the *Meßmemorial* (presumably a list of books received from the fairs), the *Continuations Buch* (probably a record of continuations of multivolume works),[315] the *Schuldenextract* (extract of debts), *Ballen Ausmessung* (measurement of bales of printed paper received), the monthly financial statement or *Cassen-Abschluß*, and the main account book, the *Haupt Cassen Conto* or *General Cassen Conto*. Nicolai also kept a separate account book for printers who did work for the firm, the *Buchdrucker Register*.[316]

Not surprisingly, little correspondence has survived between Nicolai and his Berlin employees. The exceptions are the occasional letter sent

---

314. *Hardi's Mittheilungen über Buchhandel und Buchdruck vor 140 Jahren: Neudruck aus Hilarius Goldsteins Leben und Reisen* (Frankfurt a. M., 1885), pp. 30ff. Quoted in Raabe, "Der Buchhändler im achtzehnten Jahrhundert in Deutschland," pp. 277–78. Hardi was a bookseller in Frankfurt am Main.

315. Schmidt to Nicolai, Stettin, 3 September, 7 September, 11 September, and 20 September (received) 1786, in NN 67. The other account books are mentioned in Johann Wilhelm Richardi to Friedrich Parthey, Stettin, 4 May 1811, in LAB, Rep. 200 Acc 450 vol. 11, no. 30, and Hane to Nicolai, Stettin, December 1791 (?, received 4 January 1792) and 13 January 1797, in NN 87.

316. Nicolai mentions it in a marginal note on Walch to Nicolai, Schleusingen, 30 April 1784, in NN 79, saying that an entry should be made under Günther, whose printing of the *ADB* Walch was overseeing.

to Nicolai during the book fair, his summer visits to spas, or his May to November 1781 journey with his son through Germany, Austria, and Switzerland. During his absence the shop forwarded important correspondence, informed him of problems with customers, such as reluctance to pay bills, and sought his advice on matters such as extending credit to new customers.[317] They also sent on the galleys of his own works for proofreading and kept him apprised of relations with authors and printers, of manuscripts they had rejected out of hand for publication, and of the state of accounts with other booksellers.[318] Nicolai's wife Elisabeth Macaria Schaarschmidt had power of attorney to carry out financial dealings during his absence. Although there is no evidence that she was directly involved in the business on a regular basis, she did take over some of Nicolai's functions when he left Berlin for six months in 1781.[319]

The Stettin employees, in contrast, were compelled to write Nicolai regularly, and a number of letters have survived for the period from 1786 to 1810 that offer some idea of how the shop was run. The manager in Stettin ordered books from the Berlin shop and from Leipzig, apparently making his own choices as to what would interest local customers. None of these orders survive in the correspondence, but in 1806 the shop manager Hane referred to the subject, assuring Nicolai that he had never knowingly ordered offensive (*anstößig*) books and always refused customers who requested them.[320] At book fair time, the shop employees were busy sorting the books they received from Leipzig and distributing them to customers, a process that took several weeks, at least in later years, when the manager had only an apprentice to help him.[321] He also regularly sent Nicolai the Stettin newspapers, bills and receipts, lists of

317. *Diener* J. G. Amende in Berlin to Nicolai, who was taking the waters at Bad Freyenwalde, 17 and 20 August 1773, in NN 1. Amende also forwarded letters and reviews from *ADB* contributors.
318. Kraehe to Nicolai in Ulm, Berlin, 26 June 1781, in NN 89, and Carl Zolling to Nicolai in Leipzig, Berlin, 21 April 1796, in NN 84.
319. On 30 April 1781, before leaving on his extended journey, Nicolai made out power-of-attorney forms naming his wife and Moses Mendelssohn as his representatives. The forms were witnessed by his two *Diener* Johann Christoph Kraehe and Georg Emmanuel Beer, in NN 292. Madame Nicolai sent the Berlin *ADB* reviewer Mayer "the Viennese books in question" in July 1781. Madame Nicolai to Mayer, Berlin, 1 August 1781, in NN 87. In a letter to her, Moses Mendelssohn also mentions a work published by "your publishing company" and asks her to send the author fifty copies. Mendelssohn to Madame Nicolai, Berlin, 4 September 1781, in Mendelssohn, *Neuerschlossene Briefe*, p. 63.
320. Hane to Nicolai, Stettin, 13 November 1806, in NN 87. This letter was apparently answering some query of Nicolai's. There may have been a problem with the censors in Stettin.
321. Hane to Nicolai, Stettin, 3 June 1806, in NN 87.

maculature,³²² and the various account books mentioned above. During the mysterious disappearance of the shop manager Harrer in 1786, the *Diener* Schmidt took on all these tasks and more, assuring Nicolai that he was opening and answering the mail and making copies of the answers, "so that one can see at a glance how each friend of the shop has been served. I did this in the belief that I owed it to you and the good reputation of the firm." Nicolai, obviously pleased, noted "Good lad" in the margin. Suddenly faced with so much responsibility in Harrer's absence, though, the overworked Schmidt was terrified of making a mistake. "The thought that you might be dissatisfied with my conduct oppresses me terribly, and tears of distress often roll down my face," he confessed.³²³ In December or January, the manager sent Nicolai the annual financial statement so that he could survey the state of the business. Of course he also sent the shop's profits to Berlin, part in cash and part in bills of exchange (*Anweisung*).³²⁴

When it came to business practices, the Stettin manager was apparently on his own and acted much as an independent bookseller would. He possessed a power of attorney to act on Nicolai's behalf in legal matters, notably in cases of bad debts.³²⁵ Hane explained to Nicolai that he held on to tried-and-true methods and refused to woo customers with the newfangled practices introduced by certain Berlin booksellers: "Herr Oemigke, in particular, with his peddling and 20 percent discounts along with free postage, has taken away some of my good customers even here in town.... How he does it, and even more, how his business survives it, is a mystery to me." Like many other booksellers in the financially troubled period of the Napoleonic wars, Wilhelm Oemigke attempted to win new customers with enticements that traditional members of the trade considered dishonorable.³²⁶ Hane regretted the loss of good customers, he wrote, but refused to stoop to such methods, telling people that he

322. In a letter of 9 February 1800 Hane mentions having begun his maculature list on 31 January and only being at the letter H in the ordinary (octavo?) format, in NN 87.
323. Schmidt to Nicolai, Stettin, 7 September 1786, in NN 67.
324. Hane to Nicolai, Stettin, 13 January 1797 and 30 December 1805, in NN 87.
325. In an extensive letter received in Berlin on 4 January 1792, the Stettin *Factor* Hane asked Nicolai to execute a new power of attorney for him which gave him more leeway to settle out of court, to stop lawsuits in progress, and to transfer power of attorney to a third party so that he would no longer have to travel in person to Stargard or other cities, in NN 87. Readers interested in cases of bad debts may consult the section "Debts and Debtors," in chap. 6 of Selwyn, *Philosophy in the Comptoir*.
326. These innovations may not have done Oemigke much good, since that same year he asked Nicolai for a loan of 2000 taler. Oemigke to Nicolai, Berlin, 3 December 1806, in NN 55.

could not blame them for going elsewhere if the prices were better.[327] In this atmosphere it became more important than ever to satisfy customers promptly in order to compete with the Berlin booksellers. This was particularly the case with journals, which Hane could deliver on every post day. The Berliners, on the other hand, had to wait until they had enough items to make a shipment to Stettin worth their while, which made some customers think twice about taking up a seemingly good offer. Hane's own practice was to charge a bit more for the journals but deliver them on time, he reported.[328]

Although Hane was only the manager, and apparently received no share of profits except in the indirect form of gifts or occasional raises, he appears to have identified strongly with the Stettin shop's fortunes. During the French occupation of the city, which began in October 1806, he professed to being deeply depressed every time he sat in the shop and no customers came because they could no longer afford to buy books. His military customers disappeared, postal service was suspended, and money became scarce. To add insult to injury, he had to billet rude hungry soldiers in the living room of his cramped lodgings and move into a little chamber with his servant and apprentice. To be sure, the year 1807 was not as bad, financially, as it could have been, "but it has often wounded me deeply to see the shop for whose advancement I ... have enjoyed working for so many years suddenly sunk so low, and many a good customer ... forced to bid me farewell."[329] All of this devotion notwithstanding, when he died, Nicolai bequeathed Hane a mere 75 taler, far less than he gave his longtime Berlin shop employees.[330] Whether this reflected his sentiments toward Hane or the relative importance of his Berlin and Stettin businesses is unclear.

Between Tradition and Innovation

Friedrich Nicolai's bookselling career illustrates the union of traditional and innovative elements in the late-eighteenth-century German book trade. He remained a lifelong champion of the combination of retail

---

327. Hane to Nicolai, Stettin, 13 November 1806, in NN 87. He raised the subject again in a letter of 3 January 1807.
328. Hane to Nicolai, Stettin, 3 January 1807, in NN 87.
329. Hane to Nicolai, Stettin, 31 December 1807, in NN 87.
330. Johannes Ritter received 500 taler, while Kraehe, clearly Nicolai's favorite, was left an annuity of 300 taler. Nicolai also left the young *Diener* Richardt 100 taler and his manservant Gransee 300 taler. Record of the taxes due on Nicolai's legacies, 31 March 1812, in NN 284.

bookselling and publishing that had been a virtual necessity in the era of barter. He emphasized the balance of *Verlag* and *Sortiment* at every opportunity and claimed to long for the good old days of the mid-century book fairs, viewing many new practices with suspicion. Yet he experimented fairly early with a lending library and initiated an influential new type of book catalog. He collaborated with other booksellers in Berlin and beyond to petition for their collective rights and to oppose pirates and interlopers. At the same time, he was reluctant to join any booksellers' organization, and skeptical of the efficacy of the various reforms and reform attempts made during his lifetime, particularly his commissionaire P. G. Kummer's idea of a central booksellers' exchange in Leipzig. Not only would taking part in the new arrangement inconvenience his long-established ways of doing business, but such a place, he thought, would also give rise to loud and uncivilized behavior, since people could so easily overhear what others said and often did not possess "the capacity to curb their passions."[331]

His own chief idea for reform of the book trade was a small and practicable one; he asked first Philipp Erasmus Reich and later Reich's successor Ernst Martin Gräff to change the structure of the book fair catalog. Arrangement by publisher rather than book title would make it easier both for the compiler of the catalog and for booksellers at the fair, and an alphabetical author index could be added for the general reading public. In answer to Nicolai's letter of early 1795, Gräff pointed out that he sent the catalog to more members of the public than to the trade, and that many booksellers apparently preferred the arrangement, since they modeled their own catalogs after it.[332] At the Easter fair of 1795, however, a compromise solution was introduced: a publishers' index. Thus Nicolai left no legacy of sweeping reforms like Philipp Erasmus Reich in his own day or Friedrich Perthes in the next generation. He did not change the way booksellers did business with each other. His innovations were in the field of retail book sales, in the works he published, and in his particular combination of intellectual and business pursuits.

---

331. Nicolai to Kummer, Berlin, 13 April 1792, in answer to the latter's printed circular of 4 April 1792, in DBSM, Böv Archivalien, Kummersches Archiv, Kasten 1 No. 3a. 6.

332. Gräff to Nicolai, Leipzig, 28 February 1795, in NN 26. Karl Buchner reports that Nicolai had also made this suggestion twenty years earlier in the name of several booksellers, including Steiner, Voß, and Mylius. *Aus den Papieren der Weidmannischen Buchhandlung*, 1:25.

chapter

(4)

The Legal and Political Framework of the Eighteenth-Century Book Trade

Privilege, Piracy, and Censorship

> Any author who has the good of his country and the
> enlightenment of his age at heart should resist ... ignorant
> censors when their judicial authority degenerates through
> abuse into tyranny.
>
> —*Friedrich Nicolai, 1777*

> If literary piracy is proof of patriotic sentiment,
> then highway robbery, by means of which strangers' goods
> are acquired by violence rather than payment, is no less so.
> Both spare the state the outflow of cash and the only difference
> lies in the formalities of comportment.
>
> —*Joseph von Sonnenfels, 1784*

State control of the book trade and the printed word during the eighteenth century represented both a threat and a promise: the threat of punishment, the promise of protection. Neither was wholly effective, mirroring the incomplete nature of absolutist authority and economic measures in an age without effective surveillance techniques, swift communications, or centralized enforcement of either laws or standards. Control of the book trade in the Holy Roman Empire consisted of a loose, decentralized, but interlocking system of regulations. There was no Code de Librairie or Director of the Book Trade as existed in France until the Revolution.[1] Instead, contemporaries faced a daunting labyrinth

---

1. On these institutions, see Martin, Chartier, et al., *Le livre triomphant 1660–1830*.

of edicts, decrees, ordinances, and offices on various levels of government in different states. The immediate political situation and the bookseller's connections determined his or her chances of emerging from the labyrinth relatively unscathed and prosperous. Censorship decisions were especially sensitive to current politics, particularly during the war years of the second half of the eighteenth century and the French Revolution.

What all the laws and authorities regulating the book trade held in common was their organization around the principles of privilege and censorship.[2] "Privilege," one of the pillars of the old regime legal system, will be used here mainly in the narrower sense of the *privilegium impressorium*. The jurist J. J. Moser described its function in 1772 as prohibiting "certain books from being reprinted within a certain period of time against the will and to the detriment of the privilege holder, or copies reprinted elsewhere from being sold within the German empire."[3] Privileges of this kind, issued to authors, printers, or publishers, represented the only (if often inadequate) protection available for literary property before the advent of copyright law.[4] Censorship will be used here in the sense of state control of the products of the printing press through administrative or criminal sanctions, whether as preventative (pre-publication) or prohibitive (post-publication) censorship.[5] In the eighteenth century, censorship was not synonymous with banning books. Censors controlled (read and reported upon) but usually did not forbid the works presented to them. The proportion of books banned to those allowed (with or without changes) depended upon many factors, from the current political situation to personal antipathy or scholarly feuds.[6]

Governments' interest in the book trade was both an interest in *books* and an interest in *trade*. The authorities viewed books essentially from three angles: first, books were commodities and thus sources of wealth,

---

2. For a study of the legal underpinnings of book trade regulations in the Holy Roman Empire, see Ulrich Eisenhardt, *Die kaiserliche Aufsicht über Buchdruck, Buchhandel und Presse im heiligen Römischen Reich Deutscher Nation (1496–1806). Ein Beitrag zur Geschichte der Bücher- und Pressezensur*, Studien und Quellen zur Geschichte des deutschen Verfassungsrechts, Series A, vol. 3 (Karlsruhe: C. F. Müller, 1970).

3. *Von den Kayserlichen Regierungs-Rechten und Pflichten*, quoted in Eisenhardt, *Die kaiserliche Aufsicht*, p. 10.

4. See Vogel, "Deutsche Urheber- und Verlagsrechtsgeschichte."

5. For a discussion of these categories of censorship, see Dieter Breuer, *Geschichte der literarischen Zensur in Deutschland* (Heidelberg: Quelle & Meyer, 1982), pp. 19–20.

6. See Grete Klingenstein, *Staatsverwaltung und kirchliche Autorität im 18. Jahrhundert. Das Problem der Zensur in der theresianischen Reform* (Munich: Oldenbourg, 1970), chap. 1, "Über die Zensur als geschichtliches Problem."

or loss of wealth, for the state. From this standpoint arose regulations regarding the import and export of books, of paper, and of the raw materials for making paper. Privilege and censorship also represented sources of revenue, and measures taken to encourage the domestic book trade, including pirate publishing, formed part of the mercantilist economic policies of many German states. Second, books were potential sources of dangerous ideas and information, whether religious, moral ("die guten Sitten"), or political, whereby (generally speaking) the emphasis of state vigilance shifted in the second half of the eighteenth century, especially after the French Revolution, from the religious to the explicitly political.[7] This viewpoint shaped both preventative and prohibitive censorship policies. Third, books could also be regarded as sources of education and useful knowledge. The censorship system implied not only official disapproval of those books which were banned but also approval of those which were allowed.[8] In Austria, for example, the positive benefits for the state of increased reading were emphasized in attempts to revitalize the book trade and reform the censorship system in the service of educational and religious reform.[9]

The eighteenth-century German book trade operated within the fragmented political and economic context of the Holy Roman Empire. In theory, imperial regulations applied everywhere in the empire, but the laws and policies of the individual cities and territories had a much greater impact on everyday practice. Between states, matters affecting the book trade, from the violation of privileges to disagreements over censorship decisions, were objects of foreign policy and diplomacy. This had both negative and positive consequences for the book trade. On the one hand, it made the pursuit by "lawful" publishers of pirate publishers and printers across frontiers slow, difficult, and sometimes impossible because most governments supported their own subjects. Financial dealings in a plethora of currencies were burdensome and complicated, and the negotiation of tariff and postal regulations confusing and costly. On the other hand, the patchwork of censorship laws and policies allowed clever authors and booksellers to evade the preventative censorship of their draconian local authorities by printing a work within the nearby jurisdiction

---

7. See Eisenhardt, *Die kaiserliche Aufsicht*, p. 130.

8. On censors as literary critics, see Wolfram Siemann's stimulating "Ideenschmuggel: Probleme der Meinungskontrolle und das Los der deutschen Zensoren im 19. Jahrhundert," *Historische Zeitschrift* 245 (1987): 101–2.

9. See Klingenstein, *Staatsverwaltung und kirchliche Autorität*, and Bodi, *Tauwetter in Wien*.

of more lenient governments. While Parisian authors might have to send their books to the relatively far-off Netherlands or Switzerland to be published, the Saxon bookseller Richter in Altenburg could, when denied permission to print a manuscript there, offer it to Nicolai in Berlin "because I know that they are not so strict in your city."[10] Of course, the book could be banned after publication anyway, but the "damage" would have already been done and few governments had the wherewithal for anything approaching thorough controls of the many books coming from the Leipzig fair. A further consequence of the dispersal of censorship authority across so many states and cities was that writers and professors all over Germany came to know the pleasures and pains of censorship from both sides. The experience of *being a censor* as well as *being censored* was widespread in the German republic of letters and affected both proponents and opponents of the Enlightenment.[11]

The Bookseller at Home:
The State and the Book Trade in Prussia and Berlin

As in the Holy Roman Empire more generally, Prussia had no centralized institution to control the book trade, but rather a series of offices and regulations, often applying only to certain cities or provinces.[12] The dominant character of Prussian regulations was mercantilist and thus strongly concerned to see that Prussian money was spent in Prussia. As it affected the book trade, this mercantilism frequently operated in a repressive sense only, for example, in attempts to stop the export of rags (as a raw material necessary for making paper and thus for printing books) and the import of paper (as a finished good). Prussia engaged in little such concerted financial encouragement of its book trade as was attempted for example in Austria under Maria Theresa and Joseph II in the course of their reform programs.[13] Nevertheless, and despite Frederick II's much-lamented lack of interest in German literature, Berlin

---

10. Richter to Nicolai, Altenburg, 24 November 1776, in NN 61.

11. It is interesting to contemplate the consequences this had for ideas on writing and freedom of the press in Germany. A study of this phenomenon, which to my knowledge does not yet exist, might shed new light on the famous loyalty to state institutions characteristic of many members of the German Enlightenment.

12. The most informative sources on the eighteenth-century Prussian book trade remain Georgi, *Die Entwicklung des Berliner Buchhandels*, and Goldfriedrich, *Geschichte des deutschen Buchhandels*, vol. 3.

13. See Bodi, *Tauwetter in Wien*.

became the second city in German publishing during his reign. This is attributable at least in part to the relative liberality of censorship during his reign, which helped foster the burgeoning of intellectual life in the city during those years.

The Prussian Government and Piracy

If Nicolai's experiences are representative, the Prussian government was generally quite willing to intervene with foreign powers on behalf of Prussian publishers whose books had been pirated. When Prussian publishers themselves engaged in pirating, however, the authorities, like those elsewhere, seem to have turned a blind eye. Joseph II enunciated a widespread attitude when he declared in 1784 that he would surely not be the last to suppress piracy as soon as other princes and cities were ready to do so collectively. However, he had no inclination to take the first step in forbidding his subjects to engage in such a lucrative business.[14] Only the *Allgemeines Preußisches Landrecht* of 1794 gave all foreign and Prussian booksellers clear protection against privileged Prussian pirates.

In his *Testament politique* of 1752, Frederick II had toyed with the mercantilist advantages of actively supporting the book trade, including "reprinting" as one of the manufactures to be encouraged.[15] Prussia never actively promoted piracy on the grand scale that Austria and certain southern German governments did, though, and produced no book entrepreneur comparable to Johann Thomas Edler von Trattner in Vienna.[16] But the ambiguous position of the Prussian authorities and their frequent unwillingness to punish pirates gave both foreign and local publishers some cause for exasperation. At least in the 1750s and 1760s, the Prussian government had the lamentable habit of bestowing privileges on local publishers for only slightly altered versions of already privileged works, and alteration in such cases could mean a mere change of format from quarto to octavo. What mattered was the lower price of the new edition, which was easy enough to manage when one did not have to pay the author and used smaller type and cheaper paper. This was a seemingly contradictory policy, reducing as it did the value of Prussian

---

14. Quoted in Bodi, *Tauwetter in Wien*, pp. 85–86.
15. *Acta Borussica. Die Behördenorganisation und die allgemeine Staatsverwaltung Preußens im 18. Jahrhundert*, vols. 7–12 (Berlin: Paul Parey, 1904–26), 9:355.
16. On Trattner, who owned bookshops, paper mills, a type foundry, and printing shops in Vienna and other cities and became rich through a methodical program of pirating North German bestsellers, with the encouragement of the Austrian government, see Ursula Giese, "Johann Thomas Edler von Trattner," *AGB* 3 (1961): cols. 1013–1454.

privileges.[17] In effect, without abandoning the system of privileges, the state instituted a mild form of free trade in books. This combination of traditional and laissez-faire economics led in 1765, for example, to the Berlin bookseller Joachim Pauli receiving a royal privilege for a reprint of Gellert's works. Only three years before, Gellert's Leipzig publishers Reich and Fritsch had acquired a Prussian privilege, which was good for another seven years. The government's argument for this blatant violation of its own promise of protection was that the price of the original was excessive, causing Prussian subjects to send too much money out of the country. Pauli had to promise to sell his edition for one-half the price of the original.[18]

In 1776, when the bookseller Brönner in Frankfurt am Main argued that the local town council should not pursue the pirate publisher of Friedrich Nicolai's novel *Sebaldus Nothanker*, he cited the lack of assistance he had received in Prussia when the notorious pirate Daniel Christoph Hechtel had reprinted seven of his books.[19] But Nicolai, himself a Prussian publisher, was no safer from Hechtel's activities. The latter reprinted Moses Mendelssohn's *Phädon* and Thomas Abbt's *Vom Verdienste*.[20] Curas's French grammar, the most frequently pirated of all of Nicolai's publications, was also reprinted by a Prussian, L. G. Faber, in Halle. The edition was confiscated, to be sure, but Faber was never required to pay the fine stipulated in Nicolai's general privilege.[21]

The 1765 plans of the Buchhandlungsgesellschaft,[22] the first bookseller's association in Germany, to fight piracy with piracy were the

17. Georgi, *Die Entwicklung des Berliner Buchhandels*, p. 182.
18. Ibid., pp. 164–65.
19. Brönner to Nicolai, Bretschneider, 8 March 1776, in NN 9. Similarly, a Hamburg bookseller accused of selling pirated editions of Berlin publishers' works in November 1784 countered that he himself had suffered from the piracies of Berlin colleague Christian Friedrich Stahlbaum. The case is mentioned in Henri Brunschwig, *La Crise de l'état prussien à la fin du XIIIe siècle et la genèse de la mentalité romantique* (Paris: Presses Universitaires, 1947), p. 173. On Hechtel, see Ernst Weber, "J. G. Müllers Wochenschrift 'Der Deutsche': Ein Modell aufklärerischer Publizistik," in *J. G. Müller von Itzehoe und die deutsche Spätaufklärung*, ed. Alexander Ritter (Heide in Holstein: Boyens, 1978), pp. 207–8. Hechtel operated out of Magdeburg and Helmstedt.
20. Nicolai's Pro Memoria to the Bücher-Commission in Leipzig, 5 October 1769, in Stadtarchiv Leipzig, Tit. XLVI (Feud.) No. 144.
21. Faber had protested his innocence of any wrongdoing, and Nicolai tried in vain to have the pirate edition turned over to him. His lawyer suggested he might get the copies of Faber's edition if he offered to reimburse him for the printing and paper costs. Glück to Nicolai, Halle, 14 February 1767, in NN 25.
22. On the *Buchhandlungsgesellschaft*, see Rosenstrauch, "Buchhandelsmanufaktur und Aufklärung," esp. pp. 59–61.

subject of some controversy, not only within the Prussian government. The "Departments" of Foreign Affairs and Justice and the Generaldirektorium regarded the association's planned activities as an unlawful intervention in the government's distribution of privileges because it sought to harm *privileged* booksellers who engaged in piracy. For this reason they followed General-Fiskal Friedrich Benjamin d'Anières's suggestion to forbid Prussian booksellers to become members. The Buchhandlungsgesellschaft, it was argued, should be opposed on the basic principle that "a book is no more the property of a publisher because he printed it first than a pattern was the property of a manufacturer because he was the first to fabricate something using it." In addition, d'Anières found that "such associations of merchants are always dangerous because they imply a veritable monopoly and inhibit all industry by others" and, finally, "that the public, which has an interest in the abundant and cheap availability of useful and excellent works (others are not reprinted) is most harmed by such institutions."[23] The intervention of the Marquis d'Argens, a leading member of the Berlin Academy of Sciences, on behalf of the Leipzig publisher Philipp Erasmus Reich, however, convinced Frederick II to allow Berlin booksellers to become members of the Buchhandlungsgesellschaft after all. One of those who did not join was Friedrich Nicolai. Ever the pragmatist, he told a correspondent that the new organization was "well-intentioned, but I have not wished to join thus far because it establishes principles that are mere chimeras and will never be put into practice."[24] In 1766, the Prussian government forbade its booksellers to pirate privileged books, but Pauli continued to pirate, including titles belonging to the Berlin firms of Christian Friedrich Voß and Hande und Spener. In response, the Berlin booksellers, led by Voß, requested on 21 April 1767 both that Pauli be forbidden further reprints and that the piracy of all foreign and domestic books, whether or not they held Prussian privileges, be prohibited everywhere in Prussia. According to Johann Goldfriedrich, this was the first such sweeping request in the history of the German book trade. The government refused, claiming that such a general prohibition could have negative consequences in cases where the

---

23. Report to the Foreign Ministry, 6 May 1766; quoted in Goldfriedrich, *Geschichte des deutschen Buchhandels*, 3:30. The Saxon government also had its misgivings about the *Buchhandlungsgesellschaft* and only officially recognized it in 1769. Rosenstrauch, "Buchhandelsmanufaktur und Aufklärung," p. 61.

24. Nicolai to Johann Georg Zimmermann, Berlin, 18 February 1766, in Nicolai, *Verlegerbriefe*, p. 36.

original publisher was unable to print a needed new edition, where the books had become *res communes*, or where prices were inflated. As long as Pauli had a general privilege as a Prussian bookseller, the Prussian government would protect him against foreign powers. Only his pirate editions of *Prussian* original works would be considered unlawful.[25]

Some ten years later, though, the Prussian government claimed that the 1766 prohibition of the piracy of Prussian works could be construed as applying to Saxon works as well. After long and drawn out negotiations beginning in December 1774, the Prussian and Saxon governments eventually reached an agreement regulating the recognition of their respective *privilegia impressoria* and the protection of their subjects against pirates.[26] Nevertheless, the Prussian government again refused to forbid all piracy outright, stating that every sovereign had the right to permit local publishers and printers to reprint books, and to grant them privileges for such works, when the spread of useful knowledge and the interests of printers and booksellers demanded it.[27] The Saxons answered that henceforth the products of Prussian booksellers would be protected against piracy in Saxony even if the books were not printed, privileged, or registered in Saxony, on the condition of legitimate ownership, Prussian reciprocity, and Prussian acceptance of the stipulations of the Saxon mandate that pirate editions, where tolerated, had to meet certain requirements (sufficient copies, correct printing, good paper, reasonable price).

By November 1780 the matter seems to have been settled between Prussia and Saxony, if not to their complete mutual satisfaction. The Prussian government began to consider possible imperial regulations against piracy while the Saxons preferred the more easily realizable method of anti-piracy agreements between states, in the hope that accords among Brunswick, Saxony, and Prussia could form the basis of a larger association of the most important North German book-producing

---

25. Goldfriedrich, *Geschichte des deutschen Buchhandels*, 3:32; Georgi, *Die Entwicklung des Berliner Buchhandels*, p. 167.

26. See Vogel, "Deutsche Urheber- und Verlagsrechtsgeschichte," cols. 82–83. The whole affair began as a dispute between Erfurt and Brandenburg publishers over the property rights to and sales of a title that both firms had published. The Prussian government intervened on behalf of the Brandenburgers, whose property had been pirated in Erfurt with a Saxon privilege. Minister Ewald Friedrich von Hertzberg argued that Saxon books were covered by the 1766 Prussian piracy regulation, provided the publisher could prove ownership of the rights. Thus Saxony should extend similar protection to Prussian booksellers. On the Saxon mandate and piracy policy more generally, see Rosenstrauch, "Buchhandelsmanufaktur und Aufklärung," and Vogel, "Deutsche Urheber- und Verlagsrechtsgeschichte."

27. Goldfriedrich, *Geschichte des deutschen Buchhandels*, 3:436–37.

states.[28] Neither vision was to be realized, and anti-piracy laws continued to exist above all to protect the citizens of each individual state first. Prussia and Saxony were outvoted at the election of the new emperor in 1790 when they supported an imperial prohibition of all piracies (introduced by the Prussian Legationsrat Johann Friedrich Ganz).[29] The 1794 Prussian legal code, the *Allgemeines Preußisches Landrecht*, whose strict regulation of piracy owed much to Friedrich Nicolai's written suggestions for changes, continued to allow Prussian subjects to reprint books published by foreigners, "to the extent that foreign states permit piracy to the detriment of our publishers."[30] Inspired no doubt by his own experiences, Nicolai had insisted that it was in the financial interest of the Prussian government to follow the practice in other countries and consider its own subjects first "even at the expense of [violating] strict legality."[31]

Censorship and Censors in Friderician Prussia

Leslie Bodi's concept of a dialectic of "enlightened" and "absolutist" components in Austrian censorship policies under Joseph II applies to Prussia as well. In the light of events after 1788, and especially after 1792, the reign of Frederick II often appeared in a golden glow of press freedom. Even the Jacobin Georg Friedrich Rebmann chided those of his contemporaries in 1793 who in their criticisms of Frederick forgot "to take into consideration the freedom that every writer in Prussia enjoyed in Frederick's day to speak and write freely upon any topic."[32] In comparison to the often draconian theological censorship in Catholic countries or those where Lutheran orthodoxy held sway, or to the violent methods of the duke of Württemberg, who had the journalist Christian Friedrich Daniel Schubart kidnapped and imprisoned without trial for ten years for

28. Ibid., pp. 440–41.
29. Vogel, "Deutsche Urheber- und Verlagsrechtsgeschichte," cols. 84–85; Goldfriedrich, *Geschichte des deutschen Buchhandels*, 3:442–47. Ganz had begun a campaign of garnering support from booksellers before the imperial election, writing to Nicolai among others, for advice. His letters and handwritten circulars are in NN 24.
30. *ALR*, "Von Verträgen, wodurch Sachen gegen Handlungen versprochen werden," pt. 1, title 11, sec. 8, "Verlagsverträge," p. 164. On Nicolai's suggestions on piracy law, see Voigtländer, "Das Verlagsrecht," pp. 29–36. It is a measure of Nicolai's standing and influence that his corrections to the *ALR*'s book trade regulations were so closely followed, because his remarks arrived at the very last moment, when that section of the legal code was already being typeset. See Ernst Ferdinand Klein's letter of 1 December 1790 admonishing Nicolai to hurry with his comments, in NN 39.
31. Nicolai's comments on §725 of the draft *ALR*, in Voigtländer, "Das Verlagsrecht," pp. 31–32.
32. Cited in Möller, *Vernunft und Kritik*, p. 282.

articles in his *Deutsche Chronik*,[33] Prussian conditions under Frederick II seemed very liberal. Seen close up, however, they gave even dyed-in-the-wool patriots like Friedrich Nicolai cause for occasional alarm. Nicolai never had to fear a Berlin Bastille,[34] but censorship was a time-consuming and at times depressing part of his everyday life as a writer, bookseller, and publisher. If his censorship problems during Frederick's reign seem fairly tame, it is useful to remember that he was a pillar of social, intellectual, and economic life in Berlin,[35] personally acquainted with numerous members of the bureaucracy, and that he produced books and journals mainly, if not exclusively, for the consumption of the educated and respectable. Publishers of newspapers and popular pamphlets doubtless faced rather different conditions.[36]

Before proceeding to an account of Nicolai's experiences with the Prussian censors, we may find it useful to examine the laws underpinning the censorship system he faced during his career. The censorship edicts

33. On Schubart and his imprisonment, see the biographical afterword to his *Briefe*.

34. According to Daniel Roche, 183 persons were imprisoned in the Bastille in the years 1760–89 for offenses connected with publishing, printing, and selling books. See "Censorship and the Publishing Industry," in *Revolution in Print: The Press in France 1775–1800*, ed. Robert Darnton and Daniel Roche (Berkeley and Los Angeles: University of California Press, 1989), table 1, p. 24.

35. On Nicolai's active participation in Berlin's social and organizational life, see Möller, *Aufklärung in Preußen*, esp. pp. 226–54.

36. The work of Ernst Consentius on the situation of newspapers, both printed and manuscript, points to fairly strict attempts at control. See his "Friedrich der Grosse und die Zeitungs-Zensur," *Preußische Jahrbücher* 115 (1904): 220ff., and "Die Berliner Zeitungen während der Französischen Revolution," *Preußische Jahrbücher* 117 (1904): 449–88. The older literature on Prussian censorship tends to portray it in terms of the contrast between theological and philosophical liberty on the one hand and political repression on the other (the Berlin printer Johann Heinrich Rüdiger was nevertheless sentenced to prison in 1748 for a work attacking the Christian religion; see Franz Hugo Hesse, *Die Preußische Preßgesetzgebung, ihre Vergangenheit und Zukunft* [Berlin: E. H. Schroeder, 1843], p. 11). More recent authors, however, have emphasized a division along the lines of the intended readership. Eckhart Hellmuth emphasizes that *ancien régime* censorship practice oriented itself "towards the dichotomy between enlightened elite and irrational masses"—hence the strict censorship of widely disseminated literature and greater leniency toward publications intended for the learned. This partial tolerance for works for the educated public made the system appear more liberal than it was and helped mask the lack of scope for fundamental political debate. See his "Zur Diskussion um Presse- und Meinungsfreiheit in England, Frankreich und Preußen im Zeitalter der Französischen Revolution," in *Grund-und Freiheitsrechte im Wandel von Gesellschaft und Geschichte*, ed. Günter Birtsch (Göttingen: Vandenhoeck & Ruprecht, 1981), p. 212, and "Aufklärung und Pressefreiheit. Zur Debatte der Berliner Mittwochsgesellschaft während der Jahre 1783 und 1784," *Zeitschrift für historische Forschung* 9 (1982): 315–45. A detailed study of Prussian book and journal censorship in the eighteenth century against which one could compare Nicolai's experiences remains to be written. For a recent overview of Prussian censorship, see Bodo Plachta, *Damnatur, Toleratur, Admittitur. Studien und Dokumente zur literarischen Zensur im 18. Jahrhundert* (Tübingen: Niemeyer, 1994), pp. 84–115.

of 1749, 1772, and 1788 formed the framework of censorship practice during Nicolai's lifetime. While the edict of 1772 mainly reaffirmed the stipulations of its predecessor, the edict of 1788 differs in interesting ways from earlier laws, reflecting both a new political situation and new conditions of and ideas about authorship.

The censorship edict of 1749 for Prussia excluding Silesia and Pomerania followed a series of regulations in the 1740s that had attempted unsuccessfully both to centralize the exercise of censorship and to ensure that all works printed in Prussia were actually seen by a censor before publication. Special emphasis was placed on books "that touched on public affairs" but also "scandalous writings contrary to religion or morals." On 7 March 1749, Ministers Samuel von Cocceji, Levin Friedrich von Bismarck, and Karl Ludolph Danckelmann brought the lack of a censorship authority to the king's attention. He agreed to the need for action but stressed that a censor should be a rational man "who does not make a fuss over every trifle."[37] In order to clarify and regulate the somewhat muddled situation, the 1749 edict declared that *all* books, wherever they were printed, had to be submitted to a censor before publication. It named a four-member censorship commission,[38] which was to be responsible for censoring all books other than those emanating from the Academy and universities (who censored themselves), political works (the province of the Department of Foreign Affairs), and occasional writings (relegated to the provincial departments or municipal authorities). Thus centralization of censorship was only partial. The edict also forbade the sale of "scandalous" and "offensive" books printed outside Prussia and laid down penalties for the violation of its stipulations: a hefty 100 taler for printers or publishers who failed to submit manuscripts to the censors and 10 taler for booksellers who knowingly traded in books of which the government disapproved (or would be likely to disapprove; Prussia had no catalog of forbidden books). There is no mention whatever of the responsibility of authors.[39]

In 1772, the 1749 edict was renewed with a few minor changes. The reasons given for the renewal were both the deaths of some of the censors

---

37. Quoted in *Acta Borussica. Die Behördenorganisation*, 8:315–16.

38. The commission's original members were Academy members Simon Pelloutier (for historical works), Johann Peter Süßmilch (for theology), Jakob Elsner (for philosophy), and Privy Councillor Buchholtz (for juridical works).

39. The 1749 edict is printed in Hesse, *Die Preußische Preßgesetzgebung*, pp. 217–18. See also *Acta Borussica. Die Behördenorganisation*, 8:315–16.

named in the earlier law and the disregard for some of its stipulations in various instances. For the first time, censors were to be paid for their onerous duties: 2 groschen per printed sheet. Potential delinquents were reminded that all works referring to the *Statum publicum* of the Holy Roman Empire or of "our House and the rights of our domains" or "foreign powers and imperial estates," whether published in Berlin or Potsdam, one of the university towns, or elsewhere in Prussia were, without exception, to be presented to the Department of Foreign Affairs. This also applied to university censors, who were to await the Department's decision on a manuscript before issuing their own reports. The king saw fit to reassure his subjects that his intention in setting down these censorship regulations was by no means to inhibit "a seemly and serious investigation of truth," but rather to restrict anything "directed against the general principles of religion and the moral or social order." The penalties remained the same as in the edict of 1749.[40]

The 1788 Renewed Censorship Edict for the Prussian States excluding Silesia[41] was to be quite a different matter altogether, both in the letter and the spirit. Nearly three times as long as the 1772 edict, and thus far more detailed, the text begins with a long explanation of the necessity for censorship. The very existence of this explanation reflects fundamental critiques of the practice and institution of censorship in the 1780s. Ernst Ferdinand Klein's essay "On Freedom of Thought and the Press" (Über Denk- und Druckfreyheit) in the April 1784 *Berlinische Monatsschrift* and Carl Friedrich Bahrdt's more radical critique of censorship in his 1787 pamphlet *On Freedom of the Press* are but two examples of an extensive debate on press freedom and its limits.[42] What is also striking about the 1788 edict is its shift of focus from (bad) *books* to (bad) *authors* . In this respect the otherwise traditionally oriented censorship edict of 1788 represents a transitional phase on the way to the emphasis on legal measures against authors and vendors of already published seditious and libelous works in the 1794 *Allgemeines Preußisches Landrecht*. The *Allgemeines Preußisches Landrecht* was ahead of its time in containing no stipulations on pre-publication censorship. Crimes related to writing and publishing

---

40. Hesse reproduces the edict of 1772, in *Die Preußische Preßgesetzgebung*, pp. 219–22. The new censorship commission consisted of Geh. Finanzrat Ludwig Martin Kahle (historical works), Geheimer Tribunalrat Johann Christoph Wilhelm von Steck (juridical writings), Ober-Consistorial Rat Wilhelm Abraham Teller (theology), and Johann Georg Sulzer (philosophy).

41. Hesse reproduces the edict of 1788, in *Die Preußische Preßgesetzgebung*, pp. 223–31.

42. On this discussion in Prussia, see Hellmuth, "Zur Diskussion um Presse- und Meinungsfreiheit," esp. pp. 210–19.

are placed under the rubrics "Offenses against the Internal Peace and Security of the State," "Insults to Religious Communities," and "Insults to Honor."[43]

This emphasis on authors in the 1788 edict emerges in its adoption of contemporary discussions about the commercialization of writing and the resulting decay of literature, morals, and social order (from a greed for gain or *Gewinnsucht* to reading mania or *Lesesucht*) in order to justify the need for censorship. As long as writing was dominated not by those men (female authors being either unforeseen or undesirable) whose chief aims were the search for and spread of truth, but rather by those who pursued it as "a mere trade to satisfy their greed for gain and other secondary objectives," this trade would require the supervision of the state in order to prevent abuses, and censorship legislation would have to be adapted to new conditions. Here, for the first time in Prussian law, writing, not publishing and bookselling, was addressed as a trade requiring state surveillance.

In contrast to earlier censorship edicts, authors were now explicitly accorded full responsibility for their works. The responsibility of printers and publishers ended with the censorship and approbation of the manuscript, unless the author was anonymous and they refused to divulge his identity. If a book was subsequently banned, the author could be punished. Nevertheless, Johann Erich Biester, editor of the *Berlinische Monatsschrift*, could remark optimistically that the new censorship edict contained oppressive stipulations for publishers and printers in formal terms only, "but actually nothing for the author."[44] Perhaps he felt so sanguine because, although the edict foresaw stricter penalties, the censorship guidelines themselves were not particularly ominous. In fact, the edict did not set down clear guidelines for the censors at all (as censor Christian Wilhelm Dohm had demanded in 1784).[45] Only in conjunction with the Edict Concerning Religion, to be discussed later, did it produce stricter censorship categories.

Taken as a whole, the censorship edict of 1788 contains ambiguous regulations both for authors and their printers, publishers, and booksellers.

43. *ALR*, pt. 2, title 20, pp. 672–91. On the lack of censorship measures in the *ALR*, see Hesse, *Die Preußische Preßgesetzgebung*, pp. 25–26.

44. He made this statement in a 1789 letter to Frederik Munter, quoted in Edoardo Tortarolo, *La ragione sulla Sprea. Coscienza storica e cultura politica nell'illuminismo berlinese* (Bologna: il Mulino, 1989), p. 307n.

45. On Dohm's call for clear censorship guidelines, see Hellmuth, "Zur Diskussion um Presse- und Meinungsfreiheit," p. 214.

Along with a (negative) responsibility, the new edict also explicitly afforded authors (as well as publishers) the possibility of formally appealing censorship decisions. They merely had to apply "with appropriate modesty" and present the manuscript and censor's report for review. At the same time, the publisher now had the right to take author and censor to court to recover printing expenses if a book was subsequently banned.[46]

In order to better distribute censorship duties and ensure more rapid handling of manuscripts, these duties were spread out among a larger number of institutions. Clearly, the four members of the Berlin Censorship Commission could not keep up with the flood of new publications. Now, for example, instead of a single theological censor, the review of theological and philosophical works was delegated to the Supreme Consistorial Council in Berlin, and to the provincial consistorial councils. Juridical works became the responsibility of the Berlin Kammer-Gericht and the provincial departments and Landes-Justiz-Collegia. Universities became responsible for periodicals and economic and belletristic works printed in their cities. Procedures were also laid down for collegial censorship decisions. The printer or publisher was to send the manuscript to the institution's president or head, who then could approve the work himself if its topic, contents, and author were unobjectionable or its treatment of the subject comprehensible only to specialists. If he had misgivings about the manuscript, however, he was to submit it to a colleague, and if the case were still unclear, to the entire institution for its opinion.

The penalties laid down for violations of the censorship edict of 1788 were both stricter and more detailed than those indicated in the edicts of 1749 and 1772, which mentioned monetary fines only. New, for example, was the stipulation that repeat offenders who failed to submit manuscripts to the censors could lose their bookseller's privileges or printer's permits. Authors who published their own works without having them censored beforehand faced prison or confinement in a fortress (*Festungsstrafe*). Booksellers were admonished to report at once to the censorship authorities any suspicious books they had unwittingly ordered. If caught knowingly selling objectionable books, booksellers were threatened with fines of twice the retail price of all copies in their shop and the possible loss of their privileges. For the first time, the edict also regulated the

---

46. The Berlin bookseller Unger actually took advantage of this possibility when one of his publications was forbidden after the theological censor had passed it with no objections. See Hesse, *Die Preußische Preßgesetzgebung*, pp. 19–23.

lending libraries that had recently become popular. Library directors as well as booksellers could be punished for lending out "improper books." Even those who merely delivered books, the "so-called colporteurs [*Herumträger*] ... who knowingly distributed forbidden books to others" faced punishment of eight days' to six weeks' imprisonment.

As a member of both the privileged *Kaufmannschaft* and the cultural elite of Friderician Berlin, Friedrich Nicolai presents a good case study of the delicate and tenuous status of even the best-placed booksellerpublishers vis-à-vis state authority. Nicolai was either a particularly lawabiding bookseller, or skeptical of the apparent liberality of the authorities. In 1759 he paid a call on the censor for philosophical works, Dr. Heinius, and requested that he take on the censorship of his new critical journal, the *Briefe, die neuesten Litteratur betreffend*. The censor expressed surprise that anybody would solicit his services, "which had not happened for quite some time."[47]

This caution stood Nicolai in good stead three years later, in March 1762, when the journal was forbidden after a denunciation by Johann Heinrich Gottlob von Justi, who had felt insulted by a book review.[48] A few months later, after the affair had died down, Nicolai joked to his friend Johann Peter Uz, quoting from Justi's attacks. "You are really quite wrong to defend so vigorously such an ungodly work.... You should know 'that the *Briefe* are written by a Jew and thoroughly curse Christians and the Christian religion' and that they denigrate the king of Prussia and all things respectable and honorable." On the basis of these accusations, and without listening to Nicolai's self-defense or even informing him of the proceedings, the Ministry of State had prohibited the sale of the *Litteraturbriefe*, setting a penalty of 100 taler per printed sheet for violations. Fortunately, Nicolai was able to produce the original censor's report, and the ban was lifted as quickly as it had been imposed. "What do you think of this story?" Nicolai asked Uz, "and of the freedom of the

---

47. Quoted by Goldfriedrich, *Geschichte des deutschen Buchhandels*, 3:411. According to Franz Hugo Hesse, the 1749 requirement that all books be presented to the appointed censors before publication was rarely observed. Those who were found to have contravened the law were released from payment of the fine by the king, but warned that the law would be applied strictly in future. *Die Preußische Preßgesetzgebung*, p. 13.

48. Justi himself had been a censor in Vienna, and—ironically in light of his 1762 denunciation of the *Litteraturbriefe*—in 1761 had stated his conviction that censorship must "not suppress rational liberty of thought or obstruct the book trade." Quoted in Eisenhardt, *Die kaiserliche Aufsicht*, p. 150.

press in Berlin, which is so highly praised abroad? Mightn't an author lose all desire to write anything?"[49] Here, as in other cases, the problem was not a strict censor, but another government office altogether. Post-publication (prohibitive) censorship was a matter for the General-Fiskal, "a public person who oversees the princely revenues and the enforcement of the laws and takes action against the violation of both in the ruler's name."[50] Nicolai encountered a similar problem a few years later when a book he sold in his shop was banned. "On His Royal Majesty's Most Gracious Specific Command," the Ministers Friedrich Ludwig Karl von Finckenstein and Ewald Friedrich von Hertzberg informed General-Fiskal Friedrich Benjamin d'Anières that they had received his report together with eighteen copies of the work in question, the so-called *Anecdotes on Brandenburg History*,[51] and were well satisfied with the measures taken to suppress sales of this book. They also approved of the fine of 10 taler imposed on Nicolai.[52] This was not the last Nicolai was to hear from the punctilious General-Fiskal. In 1775, for reasons that are not clear from the sources, d'Anières asked him to submit two volumes of the *ADB*. Ideological disapproval of some review may have been lurking in the background, but d'Anières's own zeal seems to have been more for the letter of the law than the letters of the press. When Nicolai did not immediately oblige, d'Anières wrote again, ordering him to reply within three days and to explain why he had published and sold the *ADB* without having it censored beforehand, which contravened the explicit stipulations of the censorship edict of 1749. He added "if, however, the work has already been censored, the censor's approbation should be produced." D'Anières was not satisfied with Nicolai's excuses for not submitting the journal to formal censorship procedures. "I have received the approbation

---

49. Nicolai to Uz, Berlin, 1 July 1762, in NN 76. With the help of the censor, Dr. Heinius, and the son of General-Fiskal Johann Christian von Uhden, Nicolai managed to get the Ministry of State to reverse the ban after only four days. Nicolai published an account of the affair in the *Neue Berlinische Monatsschrift*, December1807, pp. 340–59.

50. Johann Christoph Adelung, *Grammatisch-kritisches Wörterbuch der hochdeutschen Mundart*, 4 vols. (Leipzig: Breitkopf, 1775).

51. Presumably the *Anekdoten zur Erläuterung der brandenburgischen Geschichte, und des letzten Krieges*, printed without a place of publication in 1769 (the Michaelmas book fair catalog gave its place of publication as Amsterdam, always a rather suspicious imprint for political works). The work contains correspondence between Frederick II and Prince August William and Baron de la Motte-Fouqué. It may have been forbidden in the wake of the 1763 circular reinforcing the ban on the printing and sale of all works referring to affairs of state ("die in die Publica einschlagen") unless approved by the Foreign Ministry. *Acta Borussica. Die Behördenorganisation*, 12:615–17.

52. D'Anières to Nicolai, Berlin, 15 November 1769, in NN 1.

certificate of Consistorial Councillor Teller, which the bookseller Nicolai sent me, but the question is not whether this or that censor approved of such a work after publication, but rather whether the work was censored before it was printed, and I await further information on this matter."[53] Not to be intimidated, Nicolai appealed to a higher authority. "The bookseller Nicolai complained to us that you have troubled him concerning the censorship of the Allgemeine Bibliothek," d'Anières was informed by royal order of 4 December 1775.[54] On 1 December, Nicolai filed a petition with Frederick II regarding the censorship of the *ADB*. Since the journal's inception, he reported, Supreme Consistorial Councillor Wilhelm Abraham Teller, one of the Berlin censors, had been a regular contributor, and Nicolai had often submitted manuscripts of reviews to him, as well as the page proofs as they arrived from the printer. "I did not request written approval from him, in part because I believed ... that a work to which a royal censor also contributes receives sufficient legitimation thereby." In his many years as a bookseller, the local censors had been heard from rarely, even in regard to books printed in Berlin. Thus Berlin booksellers were of the general opinion that books printed abroad did not need to be censored in Berlin. Most, including himself, had not even been familiar with the stipulations of the 1749 edict until the 1772 edict reactivated censorship, he wrote. This free atmosphere had made the *ADB* the work it was, and he feared that stricter censorship might scare off reviewers. "Authors," he remarked, "fear the restriction of their freedom of thought more than anything."[55] The king instructed d'Anières to drop his proceedings against Nicolai, arguing that to require the *ADB* to be censored in Berlin might prove not merely inconvenient but even harmful to the work itself.

Nicolai succeeded not only in getting d'Anières called off, and in having the *ADB* officially recognized as a "work conducive to the public benefit."[56] The king's order also explicitly stated that henceforth books

---

53. D'Anières to Nicolai, Berlin, 3, 16, and 20 November 1775, in NN 1. It is unclear from the sources why d'Anières decided to check up on the censorship status of the *ADB* in November 1775. The journal was printed outside Prussia from at least 1770 on.

54. Hesse, *Die Preußische Preßgesetzgebung*, p. 14n.

55. Friedrich Nicolai, "Eingabe an Friedrich II wegen Zensur der AdB in Berlin," 1 December 1775, Geheimes Staatsarchiv Preußischer Kulturbesitz Berlin-Dahlem, Rep. 9 F 2a Fasc. 14. I thank Edoardo Tortarolo for his transcription of this document.

56. When the *ADB* was banned in 1794, Nicolai reminded the king that in 1775 the entire Council of State had declared it "a work conducive to the public benefit," a declaration published on page 366 of the 1775 collection of edicts. "I am thus all the more rightfully dismayed at this strict prohibition." Nicolai's petition of 6 May 1794, printed in "Actenstücke," pt. 2, p. 269.

printed abroad would not have to be censored twice, first in the place where they were printed and then in Berlin. The publisher, of course, remained responsible for any content that contradicted religious principles or the moral and social order.[57] Despite the comparative ease and success with which the matter was settled, Nicolai complained to a friend that the "damned censorship affair" had taken up the better part of the winter.[58]

In comparison to the annoyance caused him on several occasions by the General-Fiskal, Friedrich Nicolai's relations with the Prussian censors seem to have been quite friendly, perhaps because many of them *were* his friends. He could bargain with them and speak with them as fellow men of letters, not merely as servants of the state interested in upholding edicts and, where possible, collecting fines.[59] These censors were not the anonymous functionaries we often associate with the word in this century. Eighteenth-century Berlin censors were Enlightenment theologians (members of the Oberkonsistorium such as Wilhelm Abraham Teller), members of the Academy of Sciences such as Johann Georg Sulzer, or of the Collegium Medicum, civil servants who also wrote books such as Christian Wilhelm von Dohm and Ludwig Martin Kahle. Several of them were Nicolai's fellow members in the Mittwochsgesellschaft. All exercised their censorship functions in addition to their other official duties. They were known by name and often personally to writers and booksellers. They went in and out of each others' homes, shops, and offices. They shared a common worldview and values.[60] The main difference

---

57. The document is printed in Hesse, *Die Preußische Preßgesetzgebung*, p. 14n. This was not the first time the king chided d'Anières for overzealousness. See Goldfriedrich, *Geschichte des deutschen Buchhandels*, 3:411. Ingrid Mittenzwei argues that the legend of Prussian press freedom could be maintained precisely because of a "division of labor" between the king and the censors (here perhaps more the king and the General-Fiskal). While the censors could be strict, the king exercised tolerance and allowed for frequent exceptions when he felt that the censors had judged philosophical or theological works too harshly. His tolerance stopped at mentions of Prussian politics, however. *Friedrich II. von Preußen*, 2d ed. (Berlin: Deutscher Verlag der Wissenschaften, 1987), p. 206.

58. Nicolai to Höpfner, Berlin, 19 September 1776, in *Briefe aus dem Freundeskreis*, p. 141.

59. This seems to be something of a difference from the Parisian structure. Daniel Roche emphasizes that the censors represented both ideological and financial interests. In Berlin, although the policy of censorship of course was both ideological and financial, there seems to have been a division of labor between the censors and the General-Fiskal. The censors had some financial interest, however, being paid a small fee for their work (before 1772, a free copy of each work, thereafter, 2 groschen per printed sheet as a "douceur"). "Circulare ... betreffend die Censur," dated 1 June 1772, in Hesse, *Die Preußische Preßgesetzgebung*, pp. 219–22.

60. On the close relations between censors and censored in the Berlin Enlightenment, see Tortarolo, *La ragione sulla Sprea*, pp. 239–42.

between these censors and other intellectuals was that they were experts on which ideas and information, particularly about religion and the state, could safely be expressed in print. It was part of their role to educate authors and publishers to express themselves within the allowed limits.[61] Daniel Roche's description of relations between authors/booksellers and censors in Paris during C.-G. de Lamoignon de Malesherbes's tenure as director of the Book Trade (1750–63) applies as well to relations between authors/booksellers and censors in Berlin throughout most of the reign of Frederick II. Roche notes that "suppression was carried out by negotiation and by tacit agreement between writers/publishers on the one hand, and by royal officials on the other hand.... Authors, recognizing the state's tactic of qualified tolerance, acquired the habit of visiting the censors and accommodating themselves to their requirements."[62]

Friedrich Nicolai's correspondence provides evidence of this practice. Particularly in cases of potentially controversial works (in the Friderician period, this mainly meant those dealing with the Prussian state or "foreign" powers), he was careful to observe the necessary formalities. According to the royal circular of 28 January 1763, all works published in Prussia referring to affairs of state, whether of the Holy Roman Empire, Brandenburg-Prussia, or "foreign powers and imperial estates," had to be censored by the Foreign Ministry.[63] When Nicolai inquired in 1767 whether he needed to submit his forthcoming *Description of Berlin* to the ministry for censorship, he received the answer that this would only be required if the book contained "political information or anecdotes from the history of Brandenburg."[64]

Nicolai dealt most frequently with the political censors when he received reviews for the *ADB* that touched on foreign governments. Although officially the *ADB* itself did not have to be censored in Berlin, Nicolai was anxious to avoid trouble and submitted potentially controversial review manuscripts with a brief note to the censor.[65] In December 1775, just after his run-in with d'Anières, he agreed to remove the offending passages from a review at the censor's request.[66] In 1778, in light of

---

61. See Siemann, "Ideenschmuggel," pp. 101–2.
62. Roche, "Censorship," p. 9.
63. Repeated in Circular of 1 June 1772, in Hesse, *Die Preußische Preßgesetzgebung*, pp. 219–22.
64. Conrad to Nicolai, Berlin, 28 October 1767, in NN 12.
65. See, for example, Nicolai to Councillor of War von Steck, Berlin, 12 August 1778, in NN 72, and to Councillor of War Schlüter, Berlin, 6 April 1779, in NN 87.
66. Nicolai to Hertzberg, Berlin, 9 December 1775, in NN 34.

the imperial authorities' threat to ban the *ADB*, Nicolai was concerned about the possible repercussions of reviews of books concerning the War of the Bavarian Succession. In circulars of April, June, and November 1778, he reminded his reviewers to refrain from remarks upon public affairs that might legitimately cause offense in any province of Germany.[67] The *ADB* or Nicolai might otherwise encounter difficulties, since certain people in Vienna were working against the journal.[68] In order to avoid unpleasant surprises, he submitted the reviews to the censor for juridical writings, Johann Christoph Wilhelm von Steck. The censor, with whom Nicolai seems to have been on very good terms, passed the reviews on to the ministry in order to play it safe at this critical juncture.[69] In the hope of averting the ban of the *ADB* in the Habsburg lands, Steck also offered Nicolai some friendly advice on possible changes to a review to avoid further provoking the ire of the Austrian government. Nicolai could protect himself by noting at the beginning or end that the review had been sent in from southern Germany (*aus dem Reiche*), that the reviewer refrained from passing political judgment, and that one must mention the pros and cons when discussing affairs of state.[70]

Where the Prussian monarch was concerned, particular caution was also necessary, as Nicolai discovered when he submitted the manuscript of a translation of *La Vie privée de Louis XV* in 1780. The scandalous remarks about Louis XV appear to have caused no problems; those regarding his Prussian counterpart were another matter. The censor, Schlüter, informed him that the (highlighted) passages regarding the king of Prussia

---

67. Circular dated 20 June 1778, in HAB, no. 34. Here he mentions that he had already admonished reviewers to be cautious in his April circular.

68. Circular dated 10 Wintermonat (November) 1778, in NN 86 [Iselin correspondence].

69. Steck to Nicolai, Berlin, 2 (?) June 1778, in NN 72. Steck's thirty-odd letters to Nicolai from the years 1776–97 contain not only censorship business but also requests for information and anecdotes from Vienna, and requests to review books in the *ADB*, as well as personal matters. In another case of reviews regarding the Bavarian succession, Steck took personal responsibility for censorship, although he was not officially allowed to authorize works on public affairs in the absence of the ministers, since the reviews did not contain anything offensive. Steck to Nicolai, Berlin, 13 August 1778, in NN 72.

70. Steck to Nicolai, Berlin, 10 June 1778, in NN 72. The Cabinet Ministry approved the reviews. Steck to Nicolai, Berlin, 20 (?) June 1778, in NN 72. The *ADB* was actually banned in Austria in the summer of 1778. The first issue of 1778 still had Nicolai's imperial privilege printed in it. Nicolai took action as soon as he heard of the impending ban but only managed to get a stay of execution. He petitioned Frederick II, who on 14 March 1778 ordered the Prussian ambassador in Vienna to announce that he would not take kindly to a ban of the *ADB* in the empire, which represented a presumptuous and inadmissible attack on Protestant books. Frederick II to Freiherr von Gebler, Leipzig, 9 May 1778, in *Aus dem Josephinischen Wien*, pp. 93–95.

could not be published unaltered in a city under Prussian rule and left it to Nicolai's own discretion to make the needed changes.[71] The relative press freedom in Frederick's Prussia was anchored more in custom than in law and was highly dependent upon the liberality of the men filling its positions. The authors and publishers who met with sympathetic officials were lucky, for they at least made the process of censorship, which Nicolai opposed on principle, more bearable and more predictable.

As far as Nicolai was concerned, the practice of pre-publication censorship on his home turf consisted mainly of altering a few passages of books and articles upon the advice of the censor. Only in one case does the publication of a book seem to have been prevented altogether, and it was in Breslau rather than Berlin. In 1774 Count Hoym, Prussian minister for Silesia, stopped the publication of Johann Christian Sinapius's book on Silesian manufactures and trade, whose forthcoming appearance Nicolai had already announced in the book fair catalog for Michaelmas of that year. Minister von der Horst in Berlin had expressed no objections to the work, so Sinapius had not anticipated any problems.[72] It seems, however, that he had not followed the proper formalities for a work touching on the economy of Silesia. Minister von Hoym, with whom he was otherwise on good terms, he wrote, had been annoyed that he was not consulted about the book before Sinapius traveled to Berlin, and asked him to do him the favor of not publishing the book. He had even refused to return the manuscript.

Sinapius possessed a rough draft of his manuscript and thus might still have published it. He noted that he preferred to avoid a falling out with Hoym for the sake of his friends, however. As he remarked in a letter to Nicolai, he should have left well enough alone (i.e., not shown the manuscript to Hoym) and taken the risk upon his own shoulders; there was, after all, "nothing in it against the Prussian political system." If only Nicolai had simply sent the manuscript to Leipzig to be printed, it would now be selling in Silesia. After this experience he had lost any desire to

---

71. Schlüter to Nicolai, Berlin, 13 November 1780, in NN 87. The book was *Geschichte des Privatlebens Ludwig XV*, trans. Karl Friedrich Trost, 4 vols. (Berlin: Nicolai, 1781).

72. Nicolai's friend, author, and sometime copy editor J. A. Eberhard had dined with von der Horst in the Tiergarten and had given him the manuscript upon the minister's promise to set his imprimature on it. Eberhard to Nicolai, from Charlottenburg, where he was pastor, 22 July 1774, in NN 16. The manuscript was then returned to Sinapius in Breslau where the misfortune occurred. Count Hoym distinguished himself in later years by calling in 1794 for the arrest of anyone who *talked* about the French Revolution. See Klaus Epstein, *The Genesis of German Conservatism* (Princeton, N. J.: Princeton University Press, 1966), p. 369.

write about trade, since the minister could quite easily decide to confiscate his further works, he noted bitterly.[73] Thus, depending on the circumstances, the relative informality, and personalization of censorship, decisions could also produce harsher and more restrictive outcomes than the law required.

"A Terrible Blow": The Censorship Edict of 1788 and the Banning of the *Allgemeine deutsche Bibliothek*

The Edict Concerning Religion and the Censorship Edict of 1788 enacted to aid in its enforcement and stifle criticism of its harsh stipulations were intended to combat "freethinking" among Prussia's Protestant clergy. These edicts, along with similar censorship regulations introduced elsewhere in Germany to increase state control over religious expression and the printed word in the 1780s, such as the laws of 1782 in Ulm and 1788 in Bavaria, were reactions to the increasingly political (and theologically more radical) manifestations of the Enlightenment in the years preceding the French Revolution. In the 1790s, the French Revolution put the fear of godlessness into the crowned heads of Germany. Freethinking became potentially even more dangerous because of its connection not just with moral depravity but also with political upheaval and violence. Those who propagated unorthodox religion were seen as at least indirectly responsible for the French Revolution, and it seemed best to silence them before the contagion spread too far. As Nicolai remarked in the account of his travels through Germany, certain people had accused him and other members of the Berlin "Enlightenment synagogue" of having caused the French Revolution![74]

As the new laws were put into action in the years that followed, they succeeded in fostering disunity in the upper echelons of the bureaucracy and the censorship system and brought on a conflict between the king and the Kurmark Kammer. They also frightened a number of booksellers

---

73. Sinapius to Nicolai, Breslau, 9 November 1774, in NN 71.

74. Foreword to *Beschreibung einer Reise*, 10:179. One of those who accused the central representatives of the Berlin Enlightenment of fomenting rebellion was Johann August Starck, court preacher in Darmstadt and archenemy of the "philosophic conspiracy" that he saw spreading over Germany like a fungus. In April 1789, Nicolai's friend J. A. Eberhard, now a professor and censor in Halle, wrote that he had just censored one of Starck's works, which contained an attack on the Berlin deists, Nicolai himself, and the editors of the *Berlinische Monatsschrift* because of whom "rulers find themselves compelled to restrict the freedom of the press because they spread principles whereby kings are no longer safe on their thrones." Eberhard to Nicolai, Halle, 13 April 1789, in NN 16. On Starck, see Epstein, *The Genesis of German Conservatism*, pp. 506–17.

and authors into action and helped sharpen many Prussian authors' and bureaucrats' growing sense of the contradictions between Enlightenment and absolutist practice after the death of Frederick II in 1786.[75] In the late 1780s and 1790s, enlightened Prussian officials—a category that included most of the Berlin censors—were confronted with an increasing tension between their ideals and the requirements of office.

Among these enlightened officials were the members of the Supreme Consistorial Council (Oberkonsistorium) in Berlin. When the pious Frederick William II ascended the throne, he was disturbed to find that all but one of the six clerical members adhered to the rationalist variant of Enlightenment theology—clearly not an auspicious basis for reestablishing religious orthodoxy in Prussia. On 3 July 1788, less than two years after the death of his religiously indifferent predecessor, the new king appointed the former pastor and fellow Rosicrucian Johann Christoph Wöllner minister of justice and head of the Department of Ecclesiastical Affairs. Six days later the Edict Concerning Religion was promulgated, to be followed on 10 September 1788 by the Censorship Edict, which took effect on 19 December.

In his years as adviser and tutor to the then crown prince, Wöllner had already convinced Frederick William of the need for religious and moral renewal in Prussia. He viewed Berlin in particular as a city corrupted by the irreligious example of Frederick II and his French *philosophes*, as well as the pernicious example of those local intellectuals centered around the *Berlinische Monatsschrift*. Wöllner, who had once been an *ADB* reviewer, referred to the *Monatsschrift* editors, Friedrich Gedike and Johann Erich Biester, as "apostles of unbelief."[76] Wöllner's main interest lay in reestablishing Protestant orthodoxy. Private individuals could retain freedom of conscience and religious expression *in private*, but "freethinking" was henceforth to be banished from the pulpit and the classroom. Thus according to the new law, which proclaimed the return of the Christian

---

75. See Möller, *Aufklärung in Preußen*, chap. 7, "Die politische Dimension in der Zeitkritik Nicolais," esp. p. 560.

76. Quoted in Günter Birtsch, "Religions- und Gewissensfreiheit in Preußen von 1780 bis 1817," *Zeitschrift für historische Forschung* 11 (1984): 189. My discussion of the edict up to now follows Birtsch's account, pp. 186–89. On the Edict Concerning Religion and Prussian policy during Frederick William II's reign, see also Paul Schwartz, *Der erste Kulturkampf in Preußen um Kirche und Schule 1788–1798* (Berlin: Weidmann, 1925). Contemporary pamphlets and articles concerning the edict have been published in a microfiche edition with an accompanying text volume as *Mißbrauchte Aufklärung? Schriften zum preußischen Religionsedikt vom 9. Juli 1788*, ed. Dirk Kemper (Hildesheim: Olms, 1994).

religion to its "original purity and authenticity," nobody was to be subjected to "moral constraint" at any time "as long as each fulfills his duties but keeps his particular opinions to himself."[77]

The Edict Concerning Religion and the Censorship Edict gave Friedrich Nicolai a mighty jolt. As a Prussian patriot, he had spent most of his adult life publicly praising local press freedom in comparison to conditions prevailing in other German states.[78] He had had occasion to grumble from time to time, but the general tenor had remained positive. Now he found himself confronted with the unpleasant choice between muzzling himself and his authors or breaking the law. In the summer of 1788, soon after the Edict Concerning Religion was enacted, Nicolai even began to look for an escape route from Prussia and asked his friend and author Johann Joachim Eschenburg to investigate the possibility of buying a business in Braunschweig.[79] On 24 January 1789, a month after the Censorship Edict went into effect, the situation had clearly become more acute. He wrote to Eschenburg with the rather bizarre request to make discreet inquiries about a possible (unpaid) position for him with the duke of Brunswick. He sought princely protection against the uncertain situation in his own country and a quieter old age, yet his business and family kept him tied to Berlin, so that he could not quit the city altogether "if I do not wish to cause a scene at my departure." Nicolai assured Eschenburg that he would never abuse his position to attack the Prussian government. He blamed the author Andreas Riem for having aroused the wrath of the Prussian authorities and thus occasioning the Censorship Edict, "which indeed places the book trade in the gravest predicament and which, if strictly enforced—which I hope it will not be—could destroy it."[80] The stipulations of the new edict, especially as regarded the extension of booksellers' responsibility for the contents of the works they published and sold, worried him. "These formalities oppress me indescribably, for I do not wish to break the law and am most sensitive to

77. Quoted in Birtsch, "Religions- und Gewissensfreiheit in Preußen," p. 192.

78. See, for example, Nicolai's comparison of Prussian and Austrian censorship in his pamphlet on the banning of the *ADB* and other works in the Habsburg lands in *Bescheidene und freymüthige Erklärung an das Deutsche Publikum betreffend das Verbot der allgemeinen deutschen Bibliothek und vieler sonst allgemein erlaubten Bücher in den Kaiserlichen Königlichen Erblanden* (Berlin: Nicolai, 1780).

79. Nicolai to Eschenburg, Berlin, 6 September and 18 December 1788, in HAB, nos. 81 and 84.

80. Andreas Riem was the author of the two "fragments" on Enlightenment *Über Aufklärung. Ob die dem Staate- der Religion- oder überhaupt gefährlich sey, und seyn könne?* and *Über Aufklärung. Was hat der Staat zu erwarten- was die Wissenschaften, wo man sie unterdrückt?* (Berlin, 1788).

unpleasant regulations that I do not deserve. As long as there is no end to scribbling against people in authority [*gens en place*], it is impossible for a local bookseller, however cautious, to avoid unpleasant predicaments." He intended to observe the requisite caution. "If I were to write candidly in such a situation, I would always take care to broach certain topics either not at all or only gently. This would be quite easy for me, as I have long believed that one should use candor only when it *serves some clear purpose*.... Thus I have long remained silent upon many matters because I know full well how far our famous German liberty extends."[81]

Friedrich Nicolai did not leave Berlin or end his days as *lecteur* to the duke of Brunswick, but the fact that he considered doing so for even a moment shows how much the new Prussian climate distressed him. In a letter to a friend, his wife ventured the opinion that he would more easily survive the loss of her, their children, and everything else dear to him than the demise of the *ADB*, which was his chief concern at the time of the new edict.[82] After the sudden death of his eldest son and heir-apparent Samuel Friedrich early in 1790 the plans he had discussed with Eschenburg for withdrawing from business and establishing his sons as booksellers outside Prussia could no longer be realized. When the Immediat-Examinations-Kommission was created in 1791 to enforce religious orthodoxy Nicolai solved his most pressing problem by selling the *ADB* to Carl Ernst Bohn, whose Kiel bookshop enjoyed the freer air of Danish rule.[83]

Nicolai's relationship with the Berlin censors seems to have continued much as usual in the first years after the enactment of the new law.[84] Even

---

81. Nicolai to Eschenburg, Berlin, 24 January 1789, in HAB, no. 86.

82. Elisabeth Macaria Nicolai to Elisa von der Recke, Berlin, 19 September 1789, in LAB, Rep. 200 Acc. 450, vol. 1, no. 16.

83. Bohn lived and had his main business in Hamburg, but maintained a convenient branch in Kiel. See Nicolai's extensive correspondence with Bohn during these years, in NN 7, and Günter Ost, *Friedrich Nicolais Allgemeine Deutsche Bibliothek*, Germanistische Studien 63 (Berlin: E. Ebering, 1928), pp. 87–89. The *Berlinische Monatsschrift* also moved its place of publication outside Prussia, to Jena.

84. See, for example, the letters of 27 January and 9 March 1789 (in NN 71) from fellow *Mittwochsgesellschaft* member Christian Ludwig Siebmann regarding the censorship of Nicolai's *Anekdoten von Friedrich II* by the Foreign Ministry. In the second letter, Siebmann mentions giving the book to Minister von Hertzberg. "He did not mention the censorship, and neither did I. He merely asked whether the Anecdotes contained anything particularly noteworthy." On 26 June 1789, Siebmann informs Nicolai (see NN 71): "The minister wishes to read the little book first and then say whether the passage against the Commission should be removed altogether or toned down. I believe it will have to be left out altogether." See also a letter of 9 January 1791 from the historical censor Schlüter (in NN 87) regarding *ADB* reviews which he had looked through "and found nothing offensive therein."

so, he admonished his *ADB* reviewers not to tempt fate in matters regarding the Edict Concerning Religion and the Censorship Edict or ecclesiastical politics. In a July 1791 circular he repeated an earlier request that they refrain from mentioning the edicts or related matters in the journal and exercise prudence when discussing catechisms and the like.[85]

His real troubles began, however, during his negotiations with Bohn for the sale of the *ADB*. At that time the censorship of theological works was removed from the hands of his friends in the Supreme Consistorial Council and turned over to the religious zealots Gottlob Friedrich Hillmer and Hermann Daniel Hermes. The two leading members of the newly founded Immediat-Examinations-Commission were appointed theological censors in September 1791 because the "previous book censors care nothing for the Censorship Edict, treating it far too frivolously."[86] They were also made the censors of monthly journals, periodicals and occasional writings, works on education, and brochures of philosophical and moral content "because such writings often contain matters touching on theology."[87] In February 1792, the king decided to order a tightening of censorship practice. He tried to impress upon his ministers the necessity of greater vigilance and admonished them "as loyal servants of the state, to treat this matter with mature reflection, and not take it lightly." All printers and bookshops were to be placed under surveillance and no book sold without passing the censors, no matter where it came from, "even if it should mean the ruin of the book trade." Thus rhetorically, at least, the king placed ideological purity above the economic interests of the state. Booksellers or printers who sold or produced seditious writings were threatened with a draconian sentence of ten years imprisonment with hard labor, instead of the fines previously deemed sufficient in most cases. If the censors and the General-Fiskal neglected their duties, the ministers would henceforth be held responsible.[88] Ill pleased with this additional responsibility, the ministers informed His Majesty that the

---

85. Circular dated 2 July 1791, in HAB, no. 116. The sentencing of Heinrich Würzer to six weeks' imprisonment in 1789 for criticizing the Edict Concerning Religion had doubtless not been forgotten. See the account in *Annalen der Gesetzgebung und Rechtsgelehrsamkeit in den Preußischen Staaten*, ed. Ernst Ferdinand Klein (Berlin: Nicolai, 1789), 4:135–58.

86. Ost, *Friedrich Nicolais Allgemeine Deutsche Bibliothek*, p. 87.

87. Georgi, *Die Entwicklung des Berliner Buchhandels*, pp. 204–5. As a result, the *Gothaer gelehrten Zeitung* was forbidden in Prussia, as was the Jena *Allgemeine Literaturzeitung*. Ost, *Friedrich Nicolais Allgemeine Deutsche Bibliothek*, p. 87.

88. Consentius, "Die Berliner Zeitungen," p. 456; Goldfriedrich, *Geschichte des deutschen Buchhandels*, 3:414–15.

proposed measures were neither desirable nor enforceable. Indeed, the only effect would be to ruin the book trade "a branch of commerce so useful to the state."[89] Under the circumstances, Nicolai was glad of his decision to get rid of the *ADB* and even claimed to have lost the desire to write, "except, perhaps, something on botany or astronomy," which would not interest the censors. "Truly, if one cannot write quite freely, it is better to write nothing. I have long wished to publish a new ... edition of *Sebaldus Nothanker*, but that would be high treason against the Holy Roman Empire of the German Nation, since the electoral capitulation[90] states that nothing may be printed against the dogmatic symbols, and surely neither *Sebaldus Nothanker* nor I would write anything in their favor." He ended the letter to his old friend Johann Peter Uz with the remark that he was glad that the greater part of his life was finished.[91]

The long-feared disaster did not befall the *ADB* until 1794, however. On 17 April of that year the king informed Großkanzler Heinrich Casimir von Carmer that the Immediat-Examinations-Kommission had demanded the prohibition of the *ADB* "as a dangerous book opposed to the Christian religion."[92] "The banning of the Bibl[iothek] is ... a terrible blow," admitted Nicolai in a letter of 23 May 1794 to his collaborator Ludwig Julius Friedrich Höpfner. "Certainly the review of the writings on the Religious Edict is the true cause, but they did not see fit to mention it."[93] The immediate, if not the officially acknowledged, impetus to the prohibition of sales of the *ADB* in Prussia was a series of reviews of books and pamphlets on the Edict Concerning Religion. In two 1793 issues of the journal (114, no. 2, and 115, no. 1), the Helmstedt professor of theology Heinrich Philipp Conrad Henke, a reviewer of many years standing, discussed ninety-two books and pamphlets written in response to the Edict Concerning Religion. He also devoted seventy-five pages to a "review" of the edict itself.[94] Sandwiched, if not quite hidden, in the midst of almost six-hundred pages were eight on the Censorship Edict.

89. Quoted in Goldfriedrich, *Geschichte des deutschen Buchhandels*, 3:415.
90. Of the new Emperor Franz II in 1792. With a bow to events in France, the electoral capitulation of his predecessor Leopold II had already stated in Article II § 8 that no works would be tolerated that "promoted the overthrow of the present system or the disturbance of public peace." The so-called dogmatic symbols (*symbolische Bücher*) consisted of the official doctrinal statements of the church.
91. Nicolai to Uz, Leipzig, 12 May 1792, in NN 76. The new edition of *Sebaldus Nothanker* was not published until 1799, the Edict Concerning Religion having been lifted in 1797.
92. Quoted in Ost, *Friedrich Nicolais Allgemeine Deutsche Bibliothek*, p. 87.
93. *Briefe aus dem Freundeskreis*, pp. 328–29.
94. Henke appears to have begun reviewing for the *ADB* in 1783. In 1788, Nicolai published

This series of reviews catapulted the *ADB* into the center of contemporary political controversy. Quoting from Friedrich Wilhelm II's Cabinet Order of 10 September 1788, in which he had expressed epigrammatically his concern "that freedom of the press [*Preßfreyheit*] is degenerating into the impudence of the press [*Preßfrechheit*],"[95] Henke proceeded to agree that state and monarch had a legitimate interest in protecting themselves and their subjects from libel, licentiousness, and serious error. Censorship was neither an adequate nor a sensible method to this end, though. Thus he tried to balance on the tightrope separating legitimate theoretical reflection upon censorship in general from presumptuous criticism of Prussian law and policy in particular. In a rather weak attempt to imply that he was *not* criticizing the Prussian law itself, or the king, which could easily have been construed as *Preßfrechheit*, he remarked that the Prussian censorship edict was neither harsher nor milder than other similar laws.[96] If authors, booksellers, or printers complained about the new law, it was not because the law itself was so much stricter than previous Prussian legislation, or that of other German states, but because they were accustomed to a good deal of freedom in practice, "and ... the government appeared intent on pursuing its measures for restricting press freedom in earnest and strictly."[97] What was alarming was the change in censorship practice, particularly the role of the zealous Hillmer and Hermes. Hillmer managed to convince the king to let him censor a wider variety of writings in order to stamp out the truly dangerous sorts of periodical and popular literature. He suggested to the king that monthlies and occasional writings in particular were read by people of all classes, and that such works did more harm to religion, peace, and good order—in Germany as in France—than larger theological and moral works.[98] Hillmer's increased censorship jurisdiction was announced to all Berlin booksellers in a circular of 10 November 1791; and as *ADB* reviewer Henke cautiously formulated it, these new measures *were said to have* caused much trouble for the local printing shops.[99]

---

his pamphlet, *Ueber J. M. Sailers vollständiges Gebetbuch für Katholische Christen*. The Bavarian Jesuit Johann Michael Sailer, a proponent of Catholic reform and religious awakening, was extremely influential in the field of pastoral theology.

95. *ADB* 114, no. 2 (1793): 124.
96. Ibid., pp. 130–31.
97. Ibid., p. 131.
98. Ibid., pp. 131–32.
99. Ibid., p. 132.

Henke, at least, was convinced that he had remained within the boundaries of good sense and of the law. He considered Nicolai's suggestions for changes to his review overcautious and tried to calm Nicolai's fears about the official reaction to his piece, emphasizing that his language was careful and sufficiently qualified to pass the censors.[100] He seriously misjudged the situation, though. His strategic use of the subjunctive and the conditional and claims to condemn censorship and religious intolerance in general but not the Prussian laws in particular did not impress the suspicious and vigilant theological censors. Nicolai sighed in retrospect over Henke's overconfidence. "Had Henke only believed me and couched his assessment quite briefly and in a different tone.... But writers always believe that when they write a little book, the great must change their minds. I predicted the outcome to Henke in person in August.... But he thought it impossible."[101] Nicolai was pessimistic about the new regime in Berlin as only a man could be whose pet hatred and professional enemy was religious orthodoxy. Because the *ADB* was neither printed nor published in Prussia, Hillmer had no means of preventing its production, but he could and did make it illegal to sell the journal within the jurisdiction of the Censorship Edict.

The ban of the *ADB* in Prussia by an order of 17 April 1794 thus came as a blow to Nicolai and his colleagues but hardly as a surprise. Even Henke, who had to pay for his sins by putting his name publicly to the reviews in a special foreword to the *ADB* (reviews were otherwise almost always published anonymously), could not have been too astonished anymore.[102] The long-time reviewer Walch told Nicolai that he had long feared such an outcome, especially since the appearance of the "masterly review" of the writings on the religious edict.[103] Numerous letters of sympathy arrived, and many Prussian publishers, including Friedrich Vieweg in Berlin and all of the Halle booksellers, petitioned the king. They protested the banning of such a useful work and lamented the probable financial decline of the Prussian book trade as a result of overzealous censorship.[104] Nicolai reported that he had wasted some three weeks of

100. Henke to Nicolai, Helmstedt, 18 September 1793, in NN 31.
101. Nicolai to Eschenburg, Berlin, 29 May 1794, in HAB, no. 165.
102. In his letter of 26 September 1793, Henke admits to some unwise phrasing. More than the censors, though, he feared the wrath of those fellow authors whose works he had criticized under his own name, in NN 31.
103. Walch to Nicolai, Schleusingen, 11 May 1794, in NN 79. He had read the news in a Hamburg paper.
104. Several of these petitions are published in "Actenstücke," pt. 2, pp. 265ff.

his life vainly applying for the lifting of the ban. As he told a friend, "Everyone agrees that it is unjust, and nobody knows how to put things right again."[105] Minister Wöllner remarked firmly and laconically in response to Nicolai's query, that he had neither ordered the ban nor did he possess the power to have it lifted.[106] Nicolai apparently also appealed to the University of Halle to contest Hillmer's ban, but to no avail. As the jurist and Halle professor Ernst Ferdinand Klein, Nicolai's in-law, friend, and author regretfully explained, the university had turned down the request "with the admonition that we must provide academic youth with an example of submission to His Majesty's will."[107] Local students, less obsequious, prepared a warm welcome for Hillmer and his crony Hermes when they visited Halle at the end of May 1794. Instead of the "sprinkling with incense" their visits elsewhere had led them to expect, the two men found their lodgings surrounded by a crowd of irate students. According to Klein, this only stiffened their resolve. The next day, while making visits, Hermes complained of the insults he had suffered and declared that the king would *never* unban the *ADB*—to which Klein and his allies had replied "that we will not cease to ask most obediently for its free import."[108]

Meanwhile, the Kurmark Kammer composed a report based on the submitted petitions and, doubtless influenced by the economic arguments put forward by the Prussian booksellers (including Nicolai himself) regarding the decline since 1788 in the number of printing presses in operation, and the probable by-passing of Prussia in trade between northeastern Europe and the Leipzig fair, as well as the large sums they spent on postage, recommended that the ban on the *ADB* be lifted. Ignorance did not appear to them "the proper way to lead the nations to order and obedience."[109] The ban was formally lifted on 1 April 1795 (some eight months after the report suggested the measure), but Friedrich Nicolai was to be held responsible for any attacks on religion contained in the journal, despite the fact that he no longer published it, with the argument that he still benefited from it financially. Nicolai protested in a petition, arguing that while Bohn still owed him a sizable sum, he had nothing whatsoever to do with the editing of the *ADB* and never saw the articles before they

105. Nicolai to Eschenburg, Berlin, 29 May 1794, in HAB, no. 165.
106. Wöllner to Nicolai, Berlin, 7 May 1794, in NN 83.
107. Klein to Nicolai, Halle, 25 May 1794, in NN 39.
108. Klein to Nicolai, Halle, undated letter, received 1 June 1794, in NN 39.
109. Quoted in Ost, *Friedrich Nicolais Allgemeine Deutsche Bibliothek*, pp. 88–89.

were printed, and therefore could not possibly assume responsibility for the contents. The authorities rejected Nicolai's (only partially truthful) statements.[110]

The *ADB* censor in Wittenberg, Johann Matthias Schröckh, took this circumstance greatly to heart and asked Nicolai to see that the reviewers were more careful, for both their sakes and for the journal. As a censor, he lamented the recklessness of authors who refused to take into account both the altered political situation and his own delicate position, torn between his loyalties to the republic of letters and to his official post. "Some of these gentlemen believe that everything they discuss among themselves can and must also be printed in every land." Henke, whose review had been most responsible for the ban, had been very angry at Schröckh for toning down the most scathing passages in his reviews and had even complained publicly in the gazetteer of the competition, the *Allgemeine Litteratur Zeitung*, of the liberties taken by his censor.

Schröckh remarked that he was not a censor by choice (as a professor of history in Wittenberg he was obliged to censor the writings printed there in his field) and would gladly relinquish his duties, all the more so in light of the possible repercussions of excessive leniency. "If I could follow my inclinations, I would not censor at all, and according to my way of thinking there should be no religious oath whatsoever. Since, however, I must follow the law of the land, I cannot incur difficulties merely in order to please a few reviewers." He recommended that Nicolai send Bohn some appropriate remarks for the next printed circular to the reviewers, advising greater prudence if they did not wish to see the journal banned again, or to cause unpleasantness for the poor censor who, after all, did not live in England or France! Enlightenment, he concluded, could not be introduced "by thrusting burning torches under people's noses."[111]

Schröckh's redoubled caution could not save Nicolai from further conflicts with the Berlin censorship authorities, however. In December 1796, a royal rescript from the plume of Hillmer, countersigned by Wöllner, reminded him of his continuing responsibilty for the contents of the *ADB*, which had been the precondition for lifting the ban on the journal. It complained "that the theological reviewers therein continue to make some

---

110. "Actenstücke," pt. 2, pp. 300–302.

111. Schröckh to Nicolai, Wittenberg, 26 April 1795, in NN 69. To justify his caution, Schröckh cited the case of a fellow Wittenberg censor who had suffered investigations and fines because of a single passage he had failed to strike from a pamphlet.

disrespectful and improper statements and judgments of biblical dictums and central tenets of Christianity more generally and the Lutheran denomination more particularly," in clear violation of the Edict Concerning Religion. If Nicolai incurred difficulties, he would have no one but himself to blame.[112] These remained empty threats, however; and when Frederick William II died in 1797, Hillmer and Wöllner fell from power with the edict they had so zealously tried to enforce.[113]

In 1798, Nicolai's friends were back in their old positions. Prefect Adolf Friedrich von Scheve, whom Nicolai had sent a manuscript, promised that he would set his imprimature on the work as soon as Wilhelm Abraham Teller returned it. "It would be overly punctilious of me to expect such a well known writer as yourself to give me a new copy of the manuscript, and it is thus unnecessary for you to present the galleys to the censor" (a reference to the practice of requiring the galleys as well as the manuscript to ensure that no changes had been made without the censor's knowledge). He assured Nicolai that he would expedite matters as much as possible, although it would be impossible to do as Nicolai requested and appoint permanent censors, "since the Supreme Consistorial Council is inclined to rotate censorship duties as much as possible among its clerical members." The procedure from now on would be as follows: Nicolai would send Scheve the manuscript, he would have it delivered to the appointed censor and, when it was returned to him, to the official who kept a record of the censorship fees. After a few days Nicolai could send someone for the manuscript, or have it delivered by the messenger of the Supreme Consistorial Council, who would, however, expect a gratuity.[114] Thus by 1798 censorship activities, at least for the more respectable and prudent publishers like Nicolai, had almost returned to the "normality" of the 1770s and 1780s.[115] Nicolai's friend Walch in Schleusingen

---

112. The rescript of 23 December 1796 is printed in "Actenstücke," pt. 2, p. 305.

113. One of Frederick William III's first acts as monarch, on 27 December 1797, was to abolish the Immediat-Examinations-Kommission. Wöllner was dismissed a few months later in March 1798. Georgi, *Die Entwicklung des Berliner Buchhandels*, pp. 208–9.

114. Scheve to Nicolai, Berlin, 23 February 1798, in NN 66.

115. See letters of 8 March 1799 from Scheve (in NN 66), and of 30 October 1799, 17 June 1800, and 11 July 1800 from Lüderitz (in NN 46). In Prussia, newspapers in particular continued to be strictly censored. In other countries, the late 1790s were a time of very strict censorship. The Russian tsar, for example, banned the *Berlinische Monatsschrift* (along with all of the Berlin and Königsberg newspapers), and the Saxon government banned Fichte's *Philosophisches Journal* and unsuccessfully tried to get Prussia to do the same. See Consentius, "Die Berliner Zeitungen," p. 477, and H. H. Houben, *Der ewige Zensor. Längs- und Querschnitte durch die Geschichte der Buch-und Theaterzensur* (1926; Kronberg/Ts.: Athenäum, 1978), p. 35.

congratulated him "and all noble Berliners on the freer air that the fortunate change has allowed you to breathe!"[116] As the old *Aufklärer* (Nicolai was sixty-five in 1798) began to breathe more easily, though, they were rapidly becoming dinosaurs in a changing intellectual climate where political debate took on unheard-of (and unthought-of) forms. The *Allgemeines Preußisches Landrecht*, published as subsidiary law in 1794, no longer even mentioned pre-publication censorship, focusing instead on libel and sedition law. This development, which had taken place in Britain in the late seventeenth century, represented the beginning of an irrevocable shift of emphasis from the book to its creator that would characterize nineteenth-century German censorship practice.[117]

The censorship process in Friedrich Nicolai's lifetime represented both a threat from the state and a link between booksellers and the government. Under Frederick II, Nicolai could usually count upon the basic solidarity of the censors with his plight as author, publisher, and fellow member of the Enlightenment elite in Berlin. Under Frederick William II, Nicolai lost a good deal of his influence because of a drastic change in censorship attitudes and personnel. The system itself was fragile and dependent upon the liberality and sympathies of its representatives. Even at the worst of times, however, Berlin booksellers and authors were not completely at the mercy of the king and his new censors' zealousness. The ministers and the Kurmark Kammer retained an open ear for rational argument and appeals to their responsibility for the financial well-being of the state and were able at least in some cases to press their opinions on the monarch. Absolutism was never absolute, and Prussian censorship practice is a case in point.

The Bookseller Abroad:
Friedrich Nicolai and Book Trade Policy outside Prussia

As a Prussian bookseller-publisher who did business all over the German-speaking world, Friedrich Nicolai was naturally far from indifferent to the book trade policies of other states. He was dependent on imperial privileges as well as privileges issued by the Elector of Saxony—and on the Reichshofrat and Leipzig Book Commission that enforced them—to

---

116. Walch to Nicolai, Schleusingen, 12 May 1798, in NN 79.

117. Siemann discusses this as a process both of the growing juridification of censorship (*Verrechtlichung*) and its shift to the orbit of criminal law (*Verstrafrechtlichung*). See "Ideenschmuggel," pp. 105–6.

protect his more lucrative titles from the ubiquitous pirates, and he sold books as far afield as Ofen and St. Petersburg. Thus his publications were subject to banning and confiscation in a number of states. As we have seen, Nicolai also frequently had works printed outside Prussia and faced pre-publication censorship particularly in Electoral Saxony where theological censorship, his main worry, was stricter than in Prussia.[118]

Privilege: Broken Promises

By issuing a privilege, Simon Nicolas Henri Linguet notes in his work on the rights of authors and publishers, the monarch was acting as "a powerful and armed witness who, by testifying to the production of this work or agreement [the transfer of rights] declares himself prepared to defend them."[119] From Nicolai's perspective, the most relevant privileges, apart from his own Prussian *Generalprivilegium*, were those issued by Electoral Saxony and the imperial government.[120] Although the Prussian and Saxon governments agreed in 1776 to recognize each other's *privilegia impressoria*, Prussian publishers continued for some time to apply for Saxon privileges, which were considered a more effective protection against pirates because having one made it easier to prove ownership of a title when disputes came before the Leipzig Book Commission.

---

118. On Saxon censorship, see Kobuch, *Zensur und Aufklärung in Kursachsen*.

119. *Des Herrn Linguets Betrachtungen*, pp. 40–41.

120. Of course, other states also issued privileges, but they were often of little use to foreign publishers. As Mannheim bookseller Christian Friedrich Schwan, one of the most respectable South German booksellers, wrote Nicolai in 1777, "It would not be difficult to acquire a Palatine privilege for anything you wish, but I am convinced that it would be of no use for any foreigner." Given the geographical position of the Electoral Palatinate, with a different sovereign every few miles, only an imperial privilege was of any significance. Schwan suggested that Nicolai might want to try the method of printing title pages for the books he wished to sell in the Palatinate with "Berlin und Mannheim bei Nicolai und Schwan," which would discourage at least some pirates. Schwan to Nicolai, Mannheim, 18 October 1777, in NN 70. In December 1778, the government of the Elector Palatine announced measures to protect the property of foreign booksellers and encourage them to sell their editions locally. The new regulations, which followed some suggestions Schwan mentions in his letter to Nicolai, permitted local booksellers to keep a stock of "foreign" books in Mannheim, and stated that all foreign booksellers "who sent their publications to such a depot would enjoy our particular protection" and advantageous treatment. The Elector also promised to found a special commercial court to handle book trade disputes. Schwan was to be one of its permanent members. Finally, booksellers registered with the Mannheim commercial court who sold their books via a Mannheim representative were assured that piracies of their works would be forbidden in the Palatinate. They were also offered duty-free import and export of their books. This was announced in the Hamburg *Buchhändlerzeitung* of 25 February 1779 (no. 7, pp. 113–17) in a letter to the editor signed "von Sr. Churfürstl. Durchlaucht gnädigst verordnetes Handlungsgericht."

How did Nicolai and other booksellers acquire privileges? In the case of imperial privileges, Nicolai's lawyer in Vienna addressed his official request to the emperor, asking for a certain book to be privileged to protect his client against pirates. Typically, the application would contain a statement such as "Since there is reason to fear that other profit-hungry publishers might dare to pirate this work and my client could suffer substantial damage thereby, the latter feels compelled to apply most humbly to Your Imperial Majesty for a most gracious privilege of ten years in order to protect himself."[121] Along with such a request, the petitioner sent five copies of the work in question—eighteen if the work was a periodical, one for each member of the Reichshofrat (Imperial Aulic Council)—and, from the 1760s on, a censors' report clearing the work.[122] Nicolai generally sent a Prussian censor's report but his applications for imperial privileges also include reports from the Leipzig and Helmstedt (university) censors.[123] Once the privilege was granted, a formal certificate was issued explaining its conditions and the penalties for violations. The letter of privilege forbade the reprinting and sale of the work in question anywhere in the Holy Roman Empire without the holder's knowledge and consent for ten years from the date of issue. Theoretically, this encompassed the publication of abridged versions and editions in different formats, an issue we will return to presently.[124] A fine of "6 marks in fine gold," half to the imperial treasury and half to the lawful publisher, was set for violations.[125] Finally, the Imperial Book Commission in Frankfurt am Main was informed that the privilege had been granted, and it registered the work. The privilege was renewable. Each new volume of ongoing works also had to be submitted in quintuplicate.

The process of applying for a Saxon privilege was less formal but more expensive. The bookseller merely requested the privilege from the book inspector in Leipzig and sent along the book's title to be registered in the Book Commission's protocol book.[126] Twenty copies of each volume (or

---

121. Application for an imperial privilege for Nicolai's *Sebaldus Nothanker*, signed Erasmus von Gretzmiller, undated (June 1776), in ÖHHStA, Bestände Reichshofrat, Impressoria, Fasc. 53.
122. Eisenhardt, *Die kaiserliche Aufsicht*, pp. 11–12, 14, 135.
123. See ÖHHStA, Bestände Reichshofrat, Impressoria, Fasc. 53.
124. Ibid.
125. Ibid.
126. On the Leipzig Book Commission and its activities, see Kobuch, *Zensur und Aufklärung in Kursachsen*, pp. 34–38, and A. Kirchhoff, "Die kurfürstliche Bücherkommission zu Leipzig," *AGDB* 9 (1884): 47ff.

fifteen of very long works) had to be sent to the Supreme Consistorial Council of Electoral Saxony. The privilege letter was signed by several officials: the book inspector, the senior town clerk (Ober Stadt Schreiber), and representatives of the Ecclesiastical Council and Supreme Consistorial Council, as well as by the booksellers attending the fair. With this signature, they expressed their recognition of the privilege and, by extension, their agreement to abide by it. In cases where a privilege was issued outside the time of the book fair booksellers were notified of it at the next fair. The Saxon privilege was also issued for ten years and renewable.

Friedrich Nicolai by no means requested privileges for all of the books he published, which would have been a waste of time and above all money. Logically enough, he seems to have taken out privileges only for those books likely to be successful and therefore attractive to potential pirates. Before the liberalization of censorship in Austria under Joseph II, many of Nicolai's most important titles (for example the works of Thomas Abbt and Moses Mendelssohn) were on the index of forbidden books. Even under the new, more favorable conditions several works such as the *ADB* and Nicolai's travel account were available only "by ticket" (*auf Zettel*), that is, to holders of written authorization. They were merely tolerated (*toleratur*) rather than actually permitted (*admittitur*) and thus could be sold only to those deemed respectable and well known enough to withstand the temptations of heterodox literature. Thus it is not surprising that in the early years of his career Nicolai took out an imperial privilege for one book only, Hilmar Curas's French grammar text, a perennial from his father's list. He renewed its 1751 privilege every ten years until 1801.[127] Despite his assiduous renewals, however, the work was reprinted numerous times between 1769 and 1798 by the Vienna book entrepreneur Johann Thomas Edler von Trattner.[128] Other titles for which Nicolai sought (and received) imperial privileges confirm this pattern. They included, between 1776 and 1783, Johann Matthias Schröckh's *Lehrbuch der allgemeinen Weltgeschichte*, a popular school text; Nicolai's own best-selling novel *Leben und Meinungen des Herrn Magister Sebaldus Nothanker* and his travel account, the *ADB*, *Leben, Bemerkungen und Meinungen Johann Bunkels nebst den Leben verschiedener merkwürdiger Frauenzimmer*;

---

127. See the privileges in ÖHHStA, Bestände Reichshofrat, Impressoria, Fasc. 53, 1751, 1760, 1771, 1780, 1791, 1801.

128. On 2 August 1769, an anonymous correspondent in Vienna informed Nicolai of Trattner's pirate edition of Curas, in NN 2. For a list of further Trattner editions, see the bibliography in Giese, "Johann Thomas Edler von Trattner."

Georg Simon Klügel's encyclopedia; and Johann August Hermes's sermons.[129] In Saxony, Nicolai took out privileges for Thomas Abbt's *Vom Verdienste*, Hilmar Curas's *Universal Historie*, Moses Mendelssohn's *Phädon*, and his own description of Berlin and Potsdam, among other works.[130] Even after the agreement between the Saxon and Prussian governments Nicolai continued to seek Saxon privileges for certain books, an example being Johann Jakob Engel's introduction to poetics, *Anfangsgründe einer Theorie der Dichtungsarten*.[131] In 1788, however, he decided not to renew the Saxon privilege for the *ADB* for a second time because of the expense of submitting twenty free copies, which, he said, often found their way into the hands of Saxon booksellers, as he informed Book Inspector Mechau.[132] Perhaps by 1788 the danger of piracies of the *ADB* had already passed, either because potential publishers had been frightened off by Nicolai's disputes with *ADB* pirates in the 1770s (e.g., Carl Friedrich Bahrdt) or because the journal was no longer the lucrative proposition it had once been.

The granting of a privilege did not necessarily indicate approval of a work's contents, nor did it protect the book from later banning and confiscation. The censor's report merely stated that the work contained nothing "contrary to religion and good morals, or to the laws of the empire."[133] Once granted, a privilege could be just as easily rescinded if serious complaints reached the Reichshofrat contesting the original censor's opinion,[134] as Nicolai discovered from bitter experience in the cases of the *ADB* and the novel *Johann Bunkel*, whose 1777 imperial privileges could not save them.[135]

---

129. The applications and privileges are in ÖHHStA, Bestände Reichshofrat, Impressoria, Fasc. 53.

130. See StA Leipzig, Tit. XLVI (Feud.) Nos. 144, 388.

131. Nicolai to the Leipzig Book Inspector Mechau, 15 November 1777, in Leipzig, Universitätsbibliothek [hereafter cited as "UB Leipzig"], 25 zh 7. On 27 November 1781, he again asked Mechau to request a privilege for several books (the list of titles is now lost). Letters in UB Leipzig 25 zh 7.

132. Nicolai to Mechau, 24 October 1788, in UB Leipzig 25 zh 7. Nicolai first took out a Saxon privilege for the *ADB* in 1766, and renewed it in 1777 after letting it lapse for a year. Ost, *Friedrich Nicolais Allgemeine Deutsche Bibliothek*, p. 67.

133. Quoted from Leipzig Book Commissioner and Professor Carl Andreas Bel's censor's report to the imperial government concerning *Sebaldus Nothanker* and *Johann Bunkel*, dated Leipzig 14 May 1776, in ÖHHStA, Bestände Reichshofrat, Impressoria, Fasc. 53.

134. Eisenhardt, *Die kaiserliche Aufsicht*, p. 61.

135. The fact that the *ADB* bore no imperial privilege in the twelve years before 1777, when it was a major factor on the German intellectual scene, probably indicates both the strict censorship situation in Austria and the lack of a strong market for the journal in Austria and the

When Nicolai applied for an imperial privilege for *Johann Bunkel* in 1777, he submitted censor's reports from his Berlin friends Wilhelm Abraham Teller and Johann Georg Sulzer. The theologian Teller declared laconically that as royal censor he had "found nothing in it that is contrary to religion and good morals" and that it was therefore worthy of publication. Sulzer merely added a brief note stating that he agreed with his colleague's assessment.[136] Their "report" was dated 11 April 1777, and the privilege was issued in August. A year later, the Imperial Book Commissioner Franz Xaver van Scheben, suffragan bishop of Worms, launched a scathing attack on *Johann Bunkel* in a letter addressed to the emperor.[137] Far from being worthy of publication, as Teller and Sulzer had testified, the novel was "one of the most offensive, vexatious books attacking the three accepted [Christian] religions in the Holy Roman Empire." As evidence, he submitted the damning report of Mainz theological censor Hermann Goldhagen, a reactionary former Jesuit.[138] According to this report, the author of *Johann Bunkel* not only denied the Holy Trinity and the divinity of Jesus Christ and the Holy Spirit, but also the Redemption, the eternity of hellfire, and all mysteries of the Christian religion. In their stead the book preached Arian, Socinian, and even deist ideas "which may by no means be tolerated."[139] The "highly malicious and dangerous book" contained numerous insults to the Catholic religion. What is more, the author "extols reason in relation to religion" and implies that "one can reach Heaven without the Christian religion.... Socrates, Zeno, Cicero ... and similar moral heathens can even ascend with the Christian sons of light and be closer to the Throne."[140] Under the circumstances, the privilege must be considered to have been obtained under false pretenses.

Catholic South during those years. Until there was a clear danger of piracy, a privilege was a needless expense, especially when five copies of each issue had to make the long and expensive journey to Vienna. Nicolai's Vienna lawyer Bernhard Samuel Matolay mentions the problems of delivering the necessary copies of each issue on time in several (undated) letters to the *Reichshofrat*, in ÖHHStA, Bestände Reichshofrat, Impressoria, Fasc. 53.

136. See ÖHHStA, Bestände Reichshofrat, Impressoria, Fasc. 53.
137. On F. X. van Scheben, see Eisenhardt, *Die kaiserliche Aufsicht*, p. 81. Eisenhardt mentions this case as an example of the withdrawal of an imperial privilege without naming Nicolai, p. 62n.
138. On Goldhagen, see F. G. Dreyfus, *Sociétés et mentalités à Mayence dans la seconde moitié du dix-huitième siècle* (Paris: Armand Colin, 1968), pp. 487–88.
139. Van Scheben to Joseph II, Worms, 19 September 1778, in ÖHHStA, Bestände Reichshofrat, Impressoria, Fasc. 53.
140. Extracts from censor's report by Goldhagen, Mainz, dated 18 September 1778, in ÖHHStA, Bestände Reichshofrat, Impressoria, Fasc. 53.

Privilege, Piracy, and Censorship

The Imperial Book Commission asked that it be rescinded and the godless and blasphemous work forbidden. The princes and estates should be instructed to confiscate and suppress all copies.[141] The privilege was duly withdrawn on 29 September 1778 with a *rescriptum* to the Imperial Book Commission.[142] Nicolai was incensed and sent a copy of the Reichhofrat's "sentence against honest Bunkel" to his friend Isaak Iselin in Basel in the hope that he would treat the case in his journal, *Ephemeriden der Menschheit*. "It matters not," wrote Nicolai, "whether one agrees with Bunkel's opinions, but it belongs to the history of our century that the Reichshofrat has declared a book that Sulzer and Teller deemed worthy of publication to be blasphemous on the basis of a mere complaint without hearing the other side. I believe that it is the business of all men of letters to resist firmly the efforts of hypocrites to enlist secular government in support of stupidity." Nicolai feared that if the War of the Bavarian Succession continued, the imperial government would become even bolder, and the Prussian king would not be in a position to intervene on his behalf. "It would be a true misfortune for German literature if the Austrian dynasty were to attain more influence in Germany," he told Iselin.[143] Fortunately, at least as far as censorship was concerned, these fears proved largely unfounded.

Piracy

Nicolai's attitude toward piracy was a pragmatic one. Although he spent a good deal of time and money pursuing pirate publishers with varying degrees of success, the campaign against illicit reprinting (*Nachdruck*) was never his chief concern in life. He even professed admiration for the infamous pirate Johann Thomas Edler von Trattner as a man who had overcome obscure origins to become a major entrepreneur. He only regretted that such an industrious fellow "had fallen into piracy, thus gaining himself a bad reputation abroad."[144] He expressed his sense of the complicated

141. Scheben to Joseph II, Worms, 19 September 1778, in ÖHHStA, Bestände Reichshofrat, Impressoria, Fasc. 53.
142. In ÖHHStA, Bestände Reichshofrat, Impressoria, Fasc. 53. This must not have come as a complete surprise to Nicolai. In January 1778, his friend Heinrich Gottfried von Bretschneider, who was one of many collecting prenumerations for *Johann Bunkel*, mentioned the possibility that the novel might be banned altogether in the Austrian lands. Bretschneider to Nicolai, Werschez, 14 January 1778, in NN 9.
143. Nicolai to Iselin, Berlin, undated, probably January or February 1779, in NN 86 [Iselin correspondence].
144. Trattner was not merely a publisher and a printer of books and engravings but also owned a bookbindery, type foundry, and paper mill. Nicolai was mightily impressed by all this

nature of the subject in a 1766 letter to Johann Georg Zimmermann, who had reviewed various Swiss books for the *ADB*. He could not, he wrote, use the review of the Berne/Vienna pirate edition of the best German authors. "I am a publisher," he told Zimmermann, "and must take my colleagues into consideration." Admittedly, this piracy could be of great use in spreading good literary taste among readers in the southern German provinces and Switzerland, but it was equally true that the legitimate publishers would suffer.[145] Under the circumstances, given his recent refusal to join the Buchhandlungsgesellschaft, this was probably the least Nicolai could do to reassure his respectable colleagues that he had not defected to the other side.

When it came to enforcement and protection against pirates, not all privileges were equal. While an imperial privilege theoretically protected the publisher against pirates everywhere in the Holy Roman Empire, the difficulty and slowness of enforcement often rendered it practically useless. As the Mannheim bookseller Christian Friedrich Schwan observed to Nicolai in 1777, "Probably no printer has ever benefited more from the imperial privileges than the pirates of Karlsruhe and Reutlingen."[146] A Saxon privilege, on the other hand, although more limited in scope, offered much quicker results in the case of disputes. Thus Nicolai's experiences in the piracy wars differed greatly depending on whether the battlefield was Leipzig, Vienna, or Tübingen.[147] In Electoral Saxony, where the government had been the first to enact strict laws against piracy to protect its citizens' leading position in the German book trade, Nicolai seems to have been consistently successful.[148] When he wrote to the

---

when he visited Trattner's works in Vienna, marveling at the separate room where three proofreaders were constantly occupied with correcting the proofs as they came from the printing shop, and at the technology that pumped water into the second story from a well in the garden. *Beschreibung einer Reise*, 4:456–57.

145. Nicolai to Zimmermann, Berlin, 18 February 1766, in Nicolai, *Verlegerbriefe*, p. 36.

146. Schwan to Nicolai, Mannheim, 18 October 1777, in NN 70.

147. Nicolai was one of forty-one booksellers who petitioned the duke of Württemberg in 1779, protesting the activities of the Tübingen pirates Christian Gottlieb Franck and Wilhelm Heinrich Schramm and asking that piracies of works already legally owned by a publisher be denied censorship approval in Tübingen. See "Collectiveingabe an Herzog Karl Eugen von Würtemberg gegen die Tübinger Nachdrucker vom 10. Februar 1779," *AGDB* 14 (1891): 150–54. Local Tübingen booksellers Jacob Friedrich Heerbrandt and Johann Georg Cotta also brought a lawsuit against Franke and Schramm for their audacious activities. See Brigitte Riethmüller, "1596–1971. Die Geschichte der Osianderschen Buchhandlung," in *Osiander 1596–1971. Buchhandlung in Tübingen* (Tübingen: Osiander, 1971), p. 39.

148. In 1769, even before the Saxon Mandate, Saxon Book Commissioner Bel had acted quickly on Nicolai's complaint against Daniel Christoph Hechtel in Sangershausen, who sent an

Leipzig Book Commissioner Carl Andreas Bel in February 1775 complaining of a fake second volume to his novel *Sebaldus Nothanker*, which the Widow Dramburg from Hamburg was selling, he did not even have to lodge a formal complaint. Bel was quick to offer his assistance, promising, "I shall soon put a stop to her activities."[149] Bel was as good as his word. Only one week after writing to Nicolai he issued an order to all Leipzig booksellers and printers to shun the false Nothanker or risk the penalty stipulated in Nicolai's privilege. The fact that the work was not even a piracy in the usual sense but "an unauthorized continuation of a privileged work against the will and to the detriment of the rightful author and publisher" seems to have made no difference in this case.[150]

In Austria and the South German states, which were busy building up their own book trades to compete with those of the dominant North, and where most piracies of Nicolai's publications occurred, he had less success. Unlike Philipp Erasmus Reich, he does not even appear to have *tried* to prosecute Thomas Edler von Trattner, who reprinted several of his more lucrative school textbooks under the protection of the government in Vienna.[151] The differences in Nicolai's experiences with the Saxon and imperial authorities were a function both of the system of dealing with piracy cases in Saxony, which was far less bureaucratic than the unwieldy (and distant) machinery of imperial justice, and of the more obliging attitude of the Leipzig Book Commission to him as a familiar North German (Protestant) publisher.

Nicolai's experience of trying to pursue the Würzburg printer-publisher J. J. Stahel before three different bodies—the Leipzig Book Commission, the government of the prince-bishopric of Würzburg, and the Reichshofrat in Vienna—illustrates these differences nicely. Stahel had printed a catholicized version of a lucrative textbook, the *Lehrbuch der Allgemeinen Weltgeschichte* by Johann Matthias Schröckh, for which Nicolai possessed

---

apprentice around on horseback selling pirate editions of Moses Mendelssohn's *Phädon* and Thomas Abbt's *Vom Verdienste* (for both of which Nicolai had Saxon privileges), among other books. Bel agreed immediately that the Town Council of Sangershausen should be notified and asked to confiscate copies of the piracies and send them to Leipzig. Nicolai's Pro Memoria to the Book Commission of 5 October 1769, and Bel's reply of 9 October 1769, in StA Leipzig, Tit. XLVI (Feud.) No. 144.

149. Bel to Nicolai, Leipzig, 18 February 1775, in NN 3.
150. Leipzig, 25 February 1775, in StA Leipzig Tit. XLVI (Feud.) No. 190.
151. Reich, a more perspicacious opponent of piracy than Nicolai, took Trattner to court in 1765 for his editions of the works of Christian Fürchtegott Gellert. Lehmstedt, *Philipp Erasmus Reich*, p. 101.

both Saxon and imperial privileges.[152] When Stahel's edition appeared at the Easter fair in Leipzig in 1777, Nicolai reported it to the Leipzig Book Commission, asking that all copies be confiscated, the stipulated fine levied, and sales of the book forbidden. The Book Commissioner took immediate action, visiting Stahel's stand, confiscating sixty-five copies of the work, and ordering him to appear before the Book Commission the next day. Stahel and Nicolai gave their statements and the former was fined 50 taler, which was advanced by Stahel's (and Nicolai's) Leipzig commissionaire Philipp Erasmus Reich, pending appeal. Stahel lost the appeal at the following Michaelmas book fair.[153]

How different were the reactions of the authorities in Würzburg and Vienna! In August 1777, the Prussian ambassador Christian Karl Ludwig von Pfeil presented the prince-bishop of Würzburg with Nicolai's written complaint against Stahel, in which he announced his suit before the Reichshofrat. Nicolai asked the king of Prussia to intervene on his behalf with the government of the prince-bishop, fearing that without the support of Stahel's sovereign the case before the Reichshofrat would move very slowly indeed. Stahel was asked to answer Nicolai's accusations and managed to convince his government that the edition was not a piracy at all. He argued that the original work for which Nicolai held an imperial privilege was intended for a Protestant market only, and clearly inappropriate for Catholic schools. The Würzburg authorities politely but firmly informed the Prussian ambassador that they could not intervene now that the case was already before the Reichshofrat.[154] After five years of legal disputes and bitter recriminations, the Reichshofrat also ruled in Stahel's favor. One of the chief arguments in the numerous briefs submitted by Stahel's lawyers remained that the Protestant and Catholic editions of a historical school text could, by definition, never be identical. Thus a Catholic work could not be a piracy of a Protestant one. By emphasizing

---

152. This work was so popular that it was not merely pirated several times, but also expanded into a six-volume *Weltgeschichte für Kinder*, illustrated with more than 100 full-page copperplate engravings after designs by the well-known artist Bernhard Rode, and published from 1779 to 1784 by Weidmanns Erben und Reich in Leipzig. See Mark Lehmstedt, "*Ich bin nicht gewohnt, mit Künstlern zu dingen ...*" *Philipp Erasmus Reich und die Buchillustration im 18. Jahrhundert* (Leipzig: Deutsche Bücherei, 1990), pp. 33–35.

153. Acta Herr Friedrich Nicolai Buchhändler zu Berlin contra Herr Johann Jacob Staheln, Buchdrucker in Würzburg, das von letzterm nachgedruckte Schröckhische Lehrbuch der allgemeinen Weltgeschichte betr. Anno 1777, in StA Leipzig Tit. XLVI (Feud.) No. 388.

154. The documents in the case are partially reproduced in Adolf Koch, "Nicolai in Berlin contra Stahel in Würzburg. Ein Nachdruckstreit aus dem Jahre 1777, nach Papieren des Königlichen Kreisarchivs in Würzburg," *AGDB* 13 (1890): 264–68.

the irreconcilable differences between the Catholic and Protestant religions and views of history (a game at which Nicolai himself excelled) Stahel appealed to the Catholic-dominated Reichshofrat in a way that would never have worked before the Protestant Leipzig Book Commission. This argument laid the groundwork for the related and central argument that because Nicolai would never have found a market in Catholic regions anyway, Stahel's edition did not harm him economically.[155] This case demonstrates not only the divergent conditions in different states but also the fact that governments were chiefly interested in the economic implications of privilege and piracy, and not in conceptions of intellectual property. Until well into the eighteenth century, the general consensus was that a publisher's property rights rested on the money and effort invested in the printing of the work, and on the privilege that represented this, not on the lawful acquisition of a manuscript from the author.[156] In his study of literary property rights, Martin Vogel notes that in the course of the eighteenth century the corporative privilege granted by the authorities was gradually replaced by the legal form of the civil contract between author and publisher as autonomous and equal partners.[157] Even at the end of the century, however, in the *Allgemeines Preußisches Landrecht*, the publisher's financial investment and privilege still played a central role. A privilege was quite a different affair from a copyright with its protection against plagiarism and not merely mechanical reproduction. No consensus existed on what exactly constituted a piracy, and to what extent it could differ in form or content from the original before it had to be considered a "new" work. The definition was highly dependent on the political will of the beholder.

To illuminate some of the central issues involved, let us return to Nicolai's legal actions against Stahel, and also against the Bamberg publisher Tobias Goebhard for another piracy of Schröckh's book, and take a closer look at the lines of argumentation of the opposing parties and their lawyers.

In his successful complaint to the Leipzig Book Commission, Nicolai argued simply that he possessed a Saxon privilege and was "highly aggravated" by Stahel's pirate edition. Stahel employed a double defense to

---

155. The question of why Nicolai bothered to complain is worth asking. Nicolai and his lawyer provided no real answer to Stahel's arguments that the new edition was no financial debacle for Nicolai. J. S. Pütter, a major legal authority, saw piracy as legitimate when it did not harm the lawful publisher. It seems to have been purely a matter of principle.
156. See Vogel, "Deutsche Urheber- und Verlagsrechtsgeschichte," cols. 45–48.
157. Vogel, "Deutsche Urheber- und Verlagsrechtsgeschichte," col. 50.

this seemingly straightforward charge: On the one hand he claimed that the University of Würzburg had contracted him to print the work in question with alterations for the Catholic schools, because Schröckh's original (Protestant) version would have been useless there. Thus he had not undertaken the edition on his own behalf but on that of an official institution. On the other hand, he professed ignorance of Nicolai's possession of a privilege for the work; he had never seen the title page of the original edition on which the privilege was printed.

Nicolai answered that Stahel's excuse that the University of Würzburg had commissioned the edition was neither proven, nor could it protect him. His action remained the same. If Stahel's violation of both Saxon and imperial privileges were to go unpunished, it could set a dangerous precedent. Henceforth any publisher or printer could make slight changes to a book and, claiming differences of religion, sell it as a new work. Stahel's other claim, that he had not known of Nicolai's privilege, was untrue; at the previous book fair Stahel had bought a copy of Schröckh's book from Nicolai himself.[158]

In the meantime, Nicolai had commissioned Schröckh to write an announcement for the newspapers informing the public that Stahel's *Lehrbuch der allgemeinen Weltgeschichte zum Gebrauche katholischer Schulen eingerichtet* should be regarded as a truncated and altered piracy of the *Lehrbuch der allgemeinen Weltgeschichte*.[159] Such a work was covered by the definition of piracy under imperial law. Schröckh composed a disclaimer that was, for its time, both concise and moderate in tone. He began by describing the relationship of the book in question to his original work. It was, he said, obvious not only from the text itself; the preface actually stated that the work was based on his *Lehrbuch*. To be sure, the work was no longer identical with the one he had written. His own preface, the instructions for using the textbook, all of the questions, and the appendix on the history of Saxony and Brandenburg had been removed, as had certain entire paragraphs and footnotes. A new narrative, which even Roman

---

158. Acta Nicolai contra Stahlen, Anno 1777, in StA Leipzig, Tit. XLVI (Feud.), No. 388. Rather ironically, Stahel had been one of the signatory witnesses to the Saxon privilege for an earlier incarnation of the work in 1770. Extract from the Leipzig Book Inspector's Protocol Book, 1770, in StA Leipzig, Tit. XLVI (Feud.) No. 388.

159. As Schröckh wrote when he sent Nicolai the manuscript of his announcement, he had compared Stahel's edition with his original and found that the changes related almost exclusively to differences between Catholic and Protestant thinking. Not wishing to add fuel to Stahel's argument that a Protestant work was useless for the Catholic schools, he had refrained from noting the changes in detail. Schröckh to Nicolai, Wittenberg, 10 May 1777, in NN 69.

Catholic scholars would find faulty, had been inserted in places. As an author, he was indignant at the behavior of the Catholic edition's publisher. He could well understand that Roman Catholic readers might not agree with everything in the book. If, however, the book was considered inappropriate for use in Catholic schools, there were other ways of remedying the situation than to mutilate his text without his permission and to pirate Nicolai's property.[160]

Schröckh's announcement set out the main lines of Nicolai's case against Stahel, which focused not so much on the economic damage caused by piracy as on the unlawfulness of changing an author's work and reprinting it without his and his publisher's permission. Stahel's lawyers, however, argued on another level and avoided answering this essentially moral allegation, which was not yet regulated by law. Several months later, at the next stage of the conflict before the prince-bishopric of Würzburg, Nicolai used the Leipzig decision against Stahel to bolster his own case. He also argued that Stahel had deliberately omitted Schröckh's name from the title page in order to deceive the public and conceal his piracy. The author was not so easily duped, and Schröckh had recognized Stahel's piracy for what it was and publicly distanced himself from the new edition.[161] Stahel professed himself deeply insulted by Nicolai's allegations and Schröckh's public announcement because he by no means approved of "the vileness of malicious book piracy." He was particularly upset, he told his government, that his colleague should make such a groundless accusation not only to his sovereign but also to "the entire public in the newspapers in a quite unconscionable manner," besmirching his good name.[162]

Rather than plead ignorance of Nicolai's imperial privilege, which he had done in Leipzig to no avail, Stahel now claimed that Nicolai had none in the first place. The 1774 edition of Schröckh's *Lehrbuch*, which formed the basis of his own 1776 work, had no imperial privilege *printed in it* (not surprisingly, since the privilege was not issued until 1775). Only the later 1777 edition bore the privilege on its title page. Thus even if his edition had been a piracy rather than the much altered *new* work it was, no law could have prevented him from reprinting a book that lacked an imperial privilege. This argument must have seemed weak even to Stahel, so that he devoted some time to elaborating upon his highly plausible assertions that the original work would never have been a success in

---

160. Exhibit 12, Nicolai contra Stahel, in ÖHHStA, Bestände Reichshofrat, K848/3.
161. Koch, "Nicolai in Berlin," p. 265.
162. Ibid., p. 265.

Catholic Germany. What self-respecting Catholic school would want to hand its impressionable pupils a weapon attacking their own religion? The one copy of the original that he did have in his shop, remarked Stahel, had merely gathered dust on the shelf. Thus Nicolai lost nothing by the Catholic edition and was merely pursuing a vendetta against his Würzburg colleague motivated by envy and vengeance. Stahel demanded that Nicolai be ordered to retract his "impudent, highhanded slander of a consistently honest and decent man" as publicly as he had uttered it—in the newspapers.[163]

The arguments in the case before the Reichshofrat became increasingly complicated and longer-winded variations on the themes sketched above. Nicolai's lawyer Matolay[164] devoted much of his first brief to explaining why this was indeed a case of piracy, even if it was not as straightforward as many. What the Leipzig Book Commission seems to have taken for granted was by no means obvious in Vienna. Quoting Schröckh himself, Matolay called Stahel's book a "mutilated edition altered without permission." Stahel's oft-uttered excuse that he had printed the book for the Catholic schools was a specious one; if a Catholic edition were needed, it should not have been produced without the prior knowledge and agreement of the author and lawful publisher. Schröckh and Nicolai were quite willing to alter the text to make it palatable for the Catholic schools, he noted, but it was all too transparent that the pirate intended his own edition rather than one published by Nicolai to be sold in the Catholic lands that made up the greater part of the empire. If allowed to continue unchecked, such behavior would render imperial privileges quite worthless.

After calling Nicolai's lawsuit "inadmissible and wicked," making the obligatory attacks on his actions before the Leipzig and Würzburg authorities and his slanderous statements in the press, and repeating the excuse that Stahel had been unaware of the imperial privilege, Stahel's attorney returned to the heart of his client's defense. Nicolai and Schröckh's edition was not merely intended for Protestant youth; it was "diametrically opposed to Roman Catholic doctrines." Stahel's edition, in contrast, was intended solely for Catholic youth. The two books were as divergent as the two religions, a difference that in itself sufficed to exclude any possibility of the work being a piracy.

163. Ibid.
164. Matolay also represented Philipp Erasmus Reich in piracy trials in Vienna. See Lehmstedt, *Philip Erasmus Reich*, p. 101.

He did not rest his case there, though, and reminded the Reichshofrat that Nicolai's edition had been forbidden by the Würzburg censors[165] (surely explanation enough for Stahel's omission of Schröckh's name from the title page) and deemed by both them and the imperial censors to be anti-Catholic and thus harmful to Catholic youth. Nicolai's and Schröckh's willingness to provide a new *Catholic* edition merely substantiated the one-sidedly Protestant nature of the original.[166]

In his reply, Matolay introduced a new argument. Nicolai might not have had an *imperial* privilege for Schröckh in 1774, but he did have privileges from the Electorates of Saxony and Brandenburg and the Kingdom of Prussia. Yet, Matolay went on to argue, even if he had had no privilege of any kind, such a lack still would not have authorized anyone to reprint the book, with or without alterations (as Stahel's lawyer claimed). From the beginning, Nicolai possessed a legally grounded property right, which was subsequently further confirmed by the imperial privilege. This argument was based on an idea developed in the second half of the eighteenth century of the right to publish (*eigenthümliches Verlagsrecht*) that derived from a contract between the publisher and the author as the owner of his work. This concept was intended to prove ownership in the absence of affirmation by privilege.[167] The fact that it was not yet accepted is underlined by Matolay's use of multiple arguments based upon old and new notions of ownership rights: he still considered it necessary to point out the falseness of Stahel's claim that he had begun printing *before* Nicolai was granted an imperial privilege.

Nicolai's behavior toward Stahel, said Matolay, had at no time been excessive or vindictive. The Leipzig Book Commission had acted quite

---

165. What was Stahel doing selling (or trying to sell) a copy of a forbidden book such as Schröckh's *Lehrbuch* for which there was supposedly no local market? In 1781 he actually fell foul of the Würzburg censorship authorities when the prince-bishop ordered a visitation of the three local bookshops. Nicolai's *Sebaldus Nothanker* found itself in illustrious company when inspectors confiscated it along with works by Voltaire, Wieland, Rousseau, Ovid, and Lessing. As a bookseller, Stahel's tastes were apparently more catholic than Catholic. Goldfriedrich, *Geschichte des deutschen Buchhandels*, 3:393.

166. Interestingly enough, this does not appear to have been a hindrance to acceptance of the work everywhere. In 1780, the Société typographique de Neuchâtel agreed to publish a French translation of Schröckh's textbook. An associate in Lausanne recommended the work as "highly respected in Germany among all denominations." He believed that it would sell well in France and Switzerland as well as in Germany, the Netherlands, and northern Europe. The project eventually came to nothing, though, because of problems with the translator. Jean Pierre Berenger to the STN, 9 October 1780, quoted in Jeffrey Freedman, unpublished typescript 1987, p. vi.

167. On the right to publish, see Vogel, "Deutsche Urheber-und Verlagsrechtsgeschichte," col. 38.

correctly based on the Saxon privilege, and Nicolai had donated the fine of 50 taler to the poor. Schröckh's notice in the newspapers had not attacked Stahel's character, but merely announced that the Catholic *Lehrbuch* was a truncated and altered version of his own history text and that he disapproved of it. Such a statement was any author's good right. There was, likewise, nothing unlawful in Nicolai's complaint to Stahel's sovereign regarding the violation of his property rights.

If Stahel and the Würzburg authorities had found Schröckh's work so very inappropriate and anti-Catholic, they could have commissioned a new history textbook for the Catholic schools. The simple fact of its having been forbidden by the Würzburg censors did not give Stahel the right to pirate or mutilate a book with an imperial privilege. What was at stake here was not mere piracy, but plagiarism as well.

In his answer to Matolay's charges, Stahel's lawyer Stubenrauch defended his client both against the allegations of knowingly violating Nicolai's privilege and of plagiarizing Schröckh's work. He also differed with Matolay over his interpretation of ownership rights. The privilege of one state, he argued, was valid only within its borders. Elsewhere, anybody with the money to do so could lawfully reprint the work. Nor was Stahel's Catholic textbook a plagiarism; it did not repeat Schröckh's original "almost literally," as claimed. All that remained was the "order" of Schröckh's work, and hundreds of authors and editors acted similarly without being dragged into court. Schröckh himself had admitted that Stahel had omitted or changed much that was in his original.

In 1782 the Reichshofrat accepted Stahel's and Stubenrauch's arguments that the Catholic *Lehrbuch* was not a piracy. It fulfilled neither of the criteria set out in the current definition of piracy. It neither copied the entire text and purpose of the work, nor did it serve to reduce sales of the "genuine edition." Rather, Stahel's edition was "a reworking of a book for different ends," which would not harm sales of Schröckh's original in the Protestant countries for which the work was intended.[168] At the same time, the Reichshofrat emphasized that it did not intend to set a general precedent, or wish to be seen as encouraging piracy. For this reason, the final document was to note merely that the petitioner Nicolai's request would not be granted because of the particular nature of the case.[169] Thus

---

168. When Nicolai's lawyer informed him of the decision on 8 July 1782 (in NN 48), he remarked that he had to admit that Stahel was correct in claiming that the two editions were meant for quite different buyers and did not compete with each other.

169. Reichshofrat decision (Conclusum) of 1 July 1782, in Nicolai contra Stahel p[unc]to des Nachdrucks des Schröckischen allge[meinen] Welt-Gesch[ichte], ÖHHStA K 848/3.

Nicolai's request that Stahel's edition be banned and confiscated was not granted, but neither was Stubenrauch's request that Nicolai be required to return the 50 taler Saxon fine to Stahel, and to retract and apologize for Schröckh's notice in the newspapers labeling the Catholic *Lehrbuch* a piracy.

At the same time as he was suing Stahel, Nicolai also brought a suit against the Bamberg publisher Tobias Goebhard for another Catholic edition of Schröckh's *Lehrbuch*.[170] Although many of the arguments in the case are identical to those in the case against Stahel, the emphasis was a slightly different one and the tone more denunciatory and heated. Goebhard not only claimed ignorance of the existence of Nicolai's privilege, citing Johann Stephan Pütter to show that a privilege was valid only if made public,[171] but also attacked the privilege as a monopoly Nicolai had acquired by devious means in order to force Catholics to buy his edition. Such a viciously anti-Catholic work violated the Peace of Westphalia and thus the privilege, and should never have received an imperial privilege in the first place. Nicolai's lawyer devoted a good deal of time to contrasting Goebhard's bad reputation as a pirate with Nicolai's solid professional standing. When it came to Goebhard's word against Nicolai's there was thus every reason to believe the latter. Goebhard could easily have discovered whether Nicolai had a privilege for the *Lehrbuch* if he had wanted to, since all privileges were officially registered by the Imperial Book Commission in Frankfurt am Main. Finally, the Peace of Westphalia by no means forbade Protestants from expressing their views on the Reformation, nor were imperial privileges denied to books merely because they were written from a Protestant standpoint. Nicolai had applied for the privilege in the normal fashion, without any trickery.

Through his lawyer, Goebhard also introduced the argument, commonly used to defend the practice of piracy, that his edition was necessary because Nicolai's was too expensive. Each copy cost 12 groschen and Nicolai gave a discount of only 25 percent, which was more than consumed by transportation costs and the 20 percent loss of value through currency exchange. Goebhard's edition cost only 20 kreuzer, less than one-half that price. The greedy Nicolai only wanted to protect his own profits, a curious argument, however, if one considers that his potential sales

---

170. The documents in the case are preserved as "Nicolai contra Göbhard pcto violationis priv. über Schröckh allgemeine Weltgeschichte für Kinder de 777–780," in ÖHHStA K 848/5.

171. Goebhard's lawyer Schumann quotes Pütter in his written arguments of January 1779, in ÖHHStA K 848/5.

in Catholic areas were stated to be close to zero. Goebhard's counsel also quoted the jurist Friedrich Karl von Moser on the evils of booksellers' monopolies over widely used or necessary works.[172]

As in the suit against Stahel, the case dragged on for years, but it ended rather differently. Recognizing, no doubt, the unlikelihood of winning his case, Nicolai apparently visited Goebhard in Bamberg during his 1781 journey through southern Germany. Finding him away, he spoke to his wife to try to arrange an out-of-court settlement. After speaking to her husband, Maria Philippine Goebhard informed Nicolai that he was willing to promise never to reprint, *in any form*, so much as a page of Nicolai's publications again, and never to sell or exchange other printers' piracies of Nicolai's property. If in future he needed any books from Nicolai's list he would prefer to order them directly from him. Furthermore, Goebhard would pay all costs he had incurred through the suit himself, although he could with right demand the money from Nicolai, since he had reprinted not Nicolai's but Stahel's edition, and with the permission of the Würzburg and Bamberg authorities at that! What is more, if after reestablishing friendly relations with Nicolai he contravened this agreement, he would pay 100 ducats to the poor "as a sort of fine." Nicolai's part in the deal would be to drop his case against Goebhard, forget any previous conflicts between them (a reference to Goebhard's 1779 edition of belletristic reviews from the *ADB*),[173] and initiate friendly relations, which, she hinted, could yield substantial financial benefits. After all of these admonitions to let bygones be bygones, however, Maria Goebhard injected a not so subtle threat to sway Nicolai in the direction of compromise: "I sincerely advise you ... to reach a quick settlement, for the damage to you might otherwise be even greater and the revenge even more severe."[174]

Nicolai took Maria Goebhard's advice and dropped the case against her husband. Considering the decision in the suit against Stahel, Nicolai's lawyer applauded his wise choice.[175] Goebhard does not seem to have

---

172. "Nicolai contra Göbhard," January 1779, in ÖHHStA K 848/5.

173. Goebhard's *Litteratur der schönen Wißenschaften und klassischen Schriftsteller aus den neuesten Journalen* is mentioned in a letter of 16 October 1779 from Uz in Ansbach as a "masked" piracy of the belletristic reviews from the *ADB*. Goebhard had announced it in the Leipzig book fair catalog. When Nicolai first heard rumors of Goebhard's edition, he wrote to remind him of the imperial privilege. See Nicolai's letter of 11 October 1779 to Uz. Both letters in NN 76.

174. Maria Goebhard to Nicolai, Bamberg, 18 July 1781, in NN 25. Nicolai received it in Winterthur, Switzerland, on 31 July.

175. Matolay disagreed, however, with Nicolai's contention that it was impossible to get

kept his side of the bargain very long. He printed a second edition of the Catholic *Lehrbuch* in 1782,[176] and Nicolai and Schröckh must have relished reports of a bit of unintended symbolic justice meted out to the unrepentant but nervous pirate at the book fair that year. As Schröckh told it,

> He [Goebhard] was settling accounts with another bookseller who had also had something pirated and who, not knowing that G. also belonged to this respectable class of persons, said that he wished all pirates would be hanged from the gallows; he would gladly watch. This gave G. such a fright that he turned deathly pale, and ran out of the shop, leaving his money behind. He only retrieved it an hour later, after explaining that he had suddenly felt ill.[177]

Another method of dealing with pirates (which Nicolai attempted unsuccessfully in Würzburg against Stahel) was to appeal to local governments to stop their activities. This was a quicker and often more effective means than going through the Reichshofrat, although it was also rendered more difficult by the naturally greater sympathy pirates enjoyed on their home ground.[178]

---

satisfaction against pirates from the imperial courts. He cited a few cases he hoped to wrap up successfully soon and reminded Nicolai of his prosecution of the Frankfurt bookbinder Kämpf on his behalf some time before. He even thought he could detect some diminution in the "piracy mania." Matolay to Nicolai, Vienna, 8 July 1782, in NN 48.

176. Schröckh to Nicolai, Wittenberg, 15 May 1782, in NN 69.

177. Ibid.

178. In 1775/76, for example, with the help of his friend Bretschneider, Nicolai complained to the Frankfurt Town Council about the activities of the printer Bayrhofer who had announced a pirate edition of volume 3 of *Sebaldus Nothanker*. Members of the town council with whom Bretschneider spoke said they were not in a strong position to combat the piracy because Nicolai did not have an imperial privilege. He applied for and was granted one soon after, but he does not seem to have had any luck with the town council. On 12 June 1776, Frederick II ordered the Prussian Minister Johann Ludwig von Hochstetter to demand the confiscation of the pirated *Sebaldus Nothanker* and the punishment of Bayrhofer. He threatened the town council with other measures to protect the property and investments of Berlin publishers if they did not accede to his request. At the same period, Hochstetter made similar demands in Mainz, Hanau, Ysenburg, and other towns in the region. An investigation was begun against Bayrhofer, and Nicolai hoped that whatever the outcome, pirates might at least be chastened. The Frankfurt bookseller Johann Carl Brönner, however, seems to have argued successfully that nothing should be done to aid Nicolai because the Prussian government had not helped him when his works were pirated by Hechtel. Bretschneider to Nicolai, Usingen and Frankfurt, 13 and 29 November, and 1 December 1775, and 18 January, 5 February, and 8 and 27 March, 1776, in NN 9. See also Nicolai's letter of late August 1776 to Philipp Erasmus Reich, quoted in Buchner, *Aus den Papieren der Weidmannschen Buchhandlung*, 1:24.

This route of complaint to local authorities could also be taken in conjunction with a lawsuit before the Reichshofrat to help ensure the enforcement of decisions against pirates. A case of such a double attack on a piracy in which Nicolai actually did get satisfaction from the imperial authorities was that of the radical *Aufklärer* Carl Friedrich Bahrdt's edition of the theological articles from the *ADB*. The question of how best to combat this edition populates numerous letters to the publisher in 1777 and 1778.[179] Bahrdt's case shows the various means of public and personal pressure that could be brought to bear upon pirates. In August 1777, Nicolai complained to the Prussian government about Bahrdt's *Kritische Sammlungen der theologischen Litteratur aus der allgemeinen deutschen Bibliothek*, for which the latter had had the temerity to apply for an imperial privilege. Frederick II ordered the Prussian envoy to urge Bahrdt's sovereign, the count of Leiningen, to take action against this piracy. His efforts were at first fruitless, as the envoy reported, because the count was committed to the continuing existence of Bahrdt's school, the Philanthropin in Heidesheim, whose chief support was the printing project. The count's government must have thought better of this decision, though, noting in November that measures should be taken to keep Bahrdt from further impinging on Nicolai's property.[180] In December 1777, Nicolai brought a suit against Bahrdt before the Reichshofrat. In February 1778, that body issued a *rescriptum* to the count of Leiningen and a decree to Bahrdt himself ordering him to stop reprinting *ADB* reviews. The Frankfurt Book Commission was instructed to confiscate any further issues he did print.[181] The decision in the case was publicized in the Hamburg *Buchhändlerzeitung* of 7 May 1778.[182]

---

179. The printer Johann Philipp Ikler in Biedenkopf had also announced an edition of the theological reviews, which Nicolai was able to prevent through legal action. See letter and bill of 10 November 1783 from the lawyer Gersten in Darmstadt, in NN 24.

180. Nicolai's complaint of 22 August 1777, the king's letter to his envoy Hochstetter of 26 August, Hochstetter's letter to the king of 11 September 1777, and the *Hof- und Regierungs Canzlei Rat*'s instruction of 11 November 1777 are excerpted in DBSM Leipzig 77/27. Bahrdt began his printing venture in 1776 as a source of income for the school he directed. He himself wrote night and day to keep the presses running and viewed the edition of theological articles from the *ADB* at once as a potential gold mine for the Philanthropin and a boon to poor pastors who could not afford the original journal. See Goldfriedrich, *Geschichte des deutschen Buchhandels*, 3:173–75, and Sten Gunnar Flygt, *The Notorious Dr. Bahrdt* (Nashville: Vanderbilt University Press, 1963), pp. 161–63.

181. *Reichshofrat*, Rescriptum an den Grafen zu Leiningen, Decretum an den Doctor Bahrdt, and Rescriptum an die Kays. Bücher Commission in Frankfurth, all dated 27 February 1778, in ÖHHStA K 848/4.

182. *Buchhändlerzeitung*, no. 19 (1778): 295. Meanwhile, rumor had it that Bahrdt had failed

While waiting for the wheels of justice to grind, Nicolai also took more immediate measures to thwart Bahrdt's undertaking by making the *ADB* more attractive to the impecunious public. In November 1777, he sent flyers to his *ADB* correspondents for publication in the local press, explaining the damage Bahrdt's piracy could do and offering reduced-price sets of back issues of the journal. Until June 1778, the public had the opportunity of acquiring the first twenty-four volumes of the *ADB* for 20 taler (cash only) instead of the usual 43. Individual copies were also available at a reduced price, with extra discounts for customers buying in quantity.[183] This was a typical tactic for publishers faced with pirate editions. To the extent that pirates forced them to lower their own prices, piracy may indeed have been an effective means of making even original editions available to a wider range of customers, if only temporarily.

One of the last episodes in Nicolai's personal fight against piracy occurred in 1793. Early that year he submitted a petition to the Prussian government complaining of the activities of the publisher Samuel Friedrich Riedel in Schweinfurt, who had threatened to reprint several of his titles, including, inevitably, Schröckh's *Lehrbuch*. Minister Karl August von Hardenberg, who was busy reorganizing the newly acquired Franconian provinces for the government in Berlin, assured Nicolai that Riedel's reputation was so bad that his piracies could not really harm Nicolai. In order to discourage the notorious Reutlingen pirate printers, however, he had asked the Prussian minister for the Swabian *Kreis* to appeal to the Reutlingen town council on Nicolai's behalf.[184] The town council

---

to deliver the goods to his numerous subscribers, claiming that the packages had been lost by the post office. Plagued by creditors in Heidesheim, he was rumored to be on his way to America via Amsterdam. The truth was more prosaic, and Bahrdt reported in his autobiography that he had gone to England and Holland to seek more affluent pupils. In Amsterdam, Bahrdt received a dressing-down from Nicolai's friend and correspondent Theodor Gülcher. As the latter told Nicolai in March 1778, he had warned Bahrdt that his piracy was in danger of destroying the *ADB*, reading him a passage from one of Nicolai's letters to this effect. Bahrdt professed contrition and offered to sell Nicolai all existing copies of his edition at the printing cost if he promised to continue publishing the excerpts until volume 24 to satisfy Bahrdt's subscribers. He was also willing to consider other suggestions. Nicolai, however, was not. Walch to Nicolai, Schleusingen, 2 December 1777, in NN 79, and Gülcher to Nicolai, 17 March 1778, in NN 28. On Bahrdt's journey, see Flygt, *The Notorious Dr. Bahrdt*, pp. 184–92.

183. Individual copies cost 11 groschen up to 25 copies and 10 thereafter, the appendices 1 taler 12 groschen and 2 taler 12 groschen, respectively. Customers buying more than 80 separate copies received a discount of 6 percent; those purchasing 4 or more complete sets, 10 percent. Printed circular dated 6 Wintermonat (= November) 1777, in NN 86 [Iselin correspondence].

184. Hardenberg to Nicolai, Bayreuth, 3 February 1793, in NN 30. Riedel became known in the 1790s as a purveyor of smut (*Zotenhändler*). His name first appears in the Leipzig Book Fair catalog in 1793. Goldfriedrich, *Geschichte des deutschen Buchhandels*, 3:310, 508.

investigated the case and, finding that none of the threatened piracies had yet materialized, and that Riedel in Schweinfurt had not yet commissioned a reprint of Nicolai's titles from any Reutlingen printer, forbade the local printers to reprint any of Nicolai's books.[185] Hardenberg communicated the news to Nicolai with some of his thoughts on possible solutions to the piracy problem. He was willing to represent the cause of Prussian booksellers, if only they would unite in their own interest:

> As long as the imperial courts do not declare ... literary piracy to be theft it will be impossible to root out this evil.... Perhaps it would be possible now to effect a pact with all of the imperial estates of southern Germany to the benefit of publishers in the royal lands [i.e., Prussia], stating that they mutually agree not to reprint any book that appears with official sanction and with the name of the publisher and the place of printing. The present constellation is favorable to the Berlin booksellers, if only they can reach an agreement with one another and act in concert.[186]

The later years of Nicolai's career saw not the end of piracies but the end of his large-scale legal actions against them. Trattner in Vienna, J. G. Fleischhauer and Christian Gottlob Schmieder in Reutlingen, L.B.F. Gegel's Erben in Frankenthal, and Johann Baptist Strobl in Munich all pirated Nicolai's works in the latter half of the 1780s and the 1790s.[187] Although Nicolai had gained the support of the Prussian government in 1793, all attempts to wage a large-scale campaign against piracy were doomed to failure because of the conflicting interests of the different imperial estates and their booksellers.[188]

---

185. Mayor and Town Council, Reutlingen, to Madeweis, Prussian minister in Stuttgart, 9 March 1793, and Madeweis to Hardenberg, 22 March 1793, both letters in NN 30.

186. Hardenberg to Nicolai, Ansbach, 17 April 1793, in NN 30.

187. In 1793, Nicolai informed Eschenburg that his *Beispielsammlung* had been pirated several years before by Strobl in Munich, which had only recently come to Nicolai's attention. This explained, he believed, the decline in sales of the work and the fact that the South German booksellers were not ordering new volumes as they appeared, since they were waiting for the cheaper Munich reprint. Nicolai to Eschenburg, Berlin, 7 May 1793, in HAB, no. 146. The last mention of a piracy in Nicolai's correspondence appears to be a letter of 14 July 1805 from Nicolai to Gottfried von Ammon in Augsburg. It also refers to a work of Eschenburg's, the *Theorie der schönen Wissenschaften*. The place of publication was given as Munich, but Nicolai had reason to believe that it was actually Augsburg and asked Ammon to send any information he could gather and also to insert an announcement in the local paper warning the public of the piracy and informing them of the appearance of a new, improved edition. In SPKB Autogr. I/797.

188. See the "Auszug eines Schreibens eines Buchhändlers aus dem Reich," which Johann Friedrich Ferdinand Ganz sent to Nicolai and many other booksellers as part of his attempt to

Not all instances of piracy ended in judicial proceedings or other appeals to governmental authorities, however. Tips from correspondents could help ward off impending reprints, allowing Nicolai to make a deal with the pirate publisher. Nicolai also kept his correspondents apprised of piracies of their own works. Particularly in those cases where a work was reprinted with a noncommercial, usually pedagogical purpose in mind,[189] those responsible might be willing and even eager to negotiate with Nicolai, sometimes even coming forward of their own accord. Such piracies for a specific and limited, generally local, audience were undertaken because the book in question was either unavailable or too expensive to acquire in the quantities necessary. In 1772, for example, an improved edition of Muzell's French grammar was printed for the exclusive use of the Gymnasium in Colmar, allegedly because the original work had been unavailable for several years. Gottlieb Conrad Pfeffel, a member of the Consistorial Council, which had commissioned the edition, informed Nicolai and on behalf of the printer-publisher Decker offered him as many copies of the work as he wished at cost, "in order to remove from this reprint any appearance of an attack on your purse."[190]

---

gain support for his campaign against piracy at the election of the new emperor. Ganz to Nicolai, Regensburg, 6 June 1790. The unnamed South German bookseller complained of the continuing unfair advantages enjoyed by North German and particularly Leipzig booksellers. Ganz noted in a 10 June circular to the North German booksellers that they would indeed need to curb some of their own abuses in order to avoid a definitive split in the book trade. The booksellers were not very forthcoming, however, and Ganz complained on 13 June that only two of the two hundred booksellers he had asked for their opinions had answered. All three letters in NN 24. On Ganz's activities, see Vogel, "Deutsche Urheber- und Verlagsrechtsgeschichte," cols. 84–86. Vogel considers that the lack of interest among booksellers for Ganz's plan for an imperial prohibition on piracy may stem from the increasing disorganization, overproduction, and economic decline of the book trade in those years, but also from skepticism in more economically minded bookseller circles about centralized imperial authority. The emperor had, after all, supported piracy for years. Some booksellers may also have been wary of angering their sovereigns by seeming to favor the transfer of authority over the book trade to the imperial government. Vogel, "Deutsche Urheber- und Verlagsrechtsgeschichte," col. 86.

189. It was common practice to reprint books for a specific limited audience, but these editions sometimes found their way into the regular book trade as well. The Riga bookseller J. J. Hartknoch informed Nicolai in 1778 of a piracy of Johann Samuel Diterich's *Unterweisung zur Glückseligkeit nach der Lehre Jesu* (1st ed., 1772; 2d ed., 1776) undertaken by the printer and town councillor Lindfors in Reval (Tallinn) for the German congregation in St. Petersburg. Johann Carl Schnoor "or some other fly-by-night bookseller" in St. Petersburg had then sent the work on consignment to the Eisenach bookseller J.G.E. Wittekindt. Hartknoch to Nicolai, Riga, 17 January 1778, in NN 30.

190. Pfeffel to Nicolai, Colmar, 15 (?) March 1772, in NN 57. Along with high prices, impatience with the unavailability of a popular title could also encourage piracy. Thus in 1776, Nicolai urged his friend Isaak Iselin in Basel to send a large shipment of 50–100 copies of his journal *Ephemeriden der Menschheit* on consignment to his Leipzig warehouse. Other booksellers had

In 1778, the Austrian historian and statistician Ignaz de Luca told Nicolai of a reprint of Friedrich Gabriel Resewitz's *Gedanken, Vorschläge und Wünsche zur Verbesserung der öffentlichen Erziehung* (5 vols., 1778–86), which he himself had organized. He had distributed the edition of 600 copies for free locally, as his own modest contribution "to the complete eradication of superstition,"[191] he reported, and was surprised and hurt to discover a negative reaction to his activities in the *ADB*.[192] His self-defense echoes arguments already familiar to us from commercial pirate publishers; his intentions, he assured Nicolai, had been good, and nothing could have been further from his mind than financial gain. Indeed, his reprints of Resewitz, whom he considered "the foremost educational expert of our day," did not compete with Nicolai's edition, and harmed neither Nicolai nor the author. Not only did the volumes appear two years after the original and in a place where Resewitz's writings would never have been sold, no matter how often they were advertised in the local papers; they also awakened new interest in Resewitz's writings and consequently created demand for Nicolai's own editions: "Since I began distributing Resewitz's works at public disputations, these books are frequently demanded and purchased both in Vienna and Linz—as evidence see the flap of the second volume of my *Anzeigen*, where you will see the second volume of Resewitz's *Gedanken* etc. from your firm among the books advertised. The bookseller surely would not have placed an advertisement for the book if there were no demand for it." De Luca reminded Nicolai that it had been he who informed him of the Resewitz reprint in the first place. Nicolai had replied at the time that he expected to suffer no disadvantages from de Luca's edition. Nevertheless, De Luca promised not to reprint any more of Nicolai's titles.[193]

In some cases, a piracy could be warded off altogether by clever negotiations without involving the authorities, as we saw in the case of Nicolai's dealings with Johann Georg Scheffner over the works of Rochow and Riemann. Here Nicolai's network of correspondents played a crucial role. His friend Bretschneider wrote in January 1783 from one of a series of imperial outposts (in this case, Ofen in Hungary) that a pirate edition

---

been asking for copies, which he had been unable to provide, and this could lead to illicit reprints. Nicolai to Iselin, Berlin, 13 October 1776, in NN 86.

191. Ignaz de Luca, Linz to Nicolai, 23 July 1778, in NN 46. In 1775, de Luca had also distributed free copies of Resewitz's *Erziehung des Bürgers*, he informed Nicolai.

192. Appendix to volumes 25–36, section 4, p. 2053.

193. De Luca to Nicolai, Innsbruck, 12 September 1781, in NN 46.

of Muzell's introductory Latin grammar had recently landed on his desk as censor. Spurred to action, he informed the pirate publishers, "who are from the depths of Calvinist lower Hungary," of the dastardly attack they were waging on another's rightful property. This information, however, would have had little effect if Bretschneider had not turned to more convincing arguments. It was considered much too expensive to order the book, which was to be introduced into the local schools, all the way from Berlin. Bretschneider conferred with local firm of Weingand und Koepf, and they devised the plan of offering a 50 percent discount for large standing orders of Muzell's grammar for the local schools. Nicolai took up Bretschneider's suggestion to offer a discount to the local schools, and the piracy was nipped in the bud.[194]

Nicolai often emphasized to his authors the importance of maintaining low prices to discourage piracies, and where pirate editions already existed, he adopted the tactic of lowering prices to make the original editions more attractive, as we saw in the case of his handling of Bahrdt's edition of the theological articles of the *ADB*. In concert with the Mannheim publisher Schwan, Nicolai also devised a method for making his books readily available at more reasonable prices to South German booksellers and thus making piracy less attractive. He offered all of his publications on consignment postage-paid to Schwan at a discount of one-third on the condition that Schwan in turn sell them to other booksellers at a discount of 25 percent, thus avoiding the usual mark-ups that currency exchange and postage costs necessitated. Nicolai also agreed to take on Schwan's publications under the same conditions and to advertise and sell them in northern Germany.[195] Thus the tension between the southern and northern German book trades was not an absolute one, but contingent upon whether business partners from the South had something to offer their northern counterparts.

---

194. Bretschneider assured him that they could sell 200–300 copies a year of the work through Weingand und Koepf. Bretschneider to Nicolai, Ofen, 28 January 1783 and 24 February 1784, in NN 9.

195. Apparently, the Berlin bookseller Voß undertook similar measures. Schwan discussed the idea with Philipp Erasmus Reich and hoped to expand the project to include any North German publisher who wished to participate; in the end, however, this came to nothing. Schwan's suggestion that Nicolai might also secure those books he hoped to sell in the Southwest against pirates by printing "Berlin und Mannheim bei Nicolai und Schwan" on the title-page was likewise not taken up. Nicolai to Reich, Berlin, August 1776, and Schwan to Reich, Mannheim, 17 September 1776, quoted in Buchner, *Aus den Papieren der Weidmannischen Buchhandlung*, 1:14–15, 24–25; and Schwan to Nicolai, Mannheim, 18 October 1777, in NN 70.

Censorship

Censorship was, for the most part, less an economic factor in Nicolai's business than a continual affront to his notion of enlightened government and proper relations in the republic of letters. Although he never publicly challenged the state's basic authority to control reading matter and reserved his most scathing public remarks for far-away Austria, Nicolai maintained an unwaveringly liberal position on censorship. From his 1777 salvo against the Erfurt theological censor Johann Christoph Besler in the *ADB* to his open letter to the Austrian censors in 1780,[196] from his (albeit secret) discussions of press freedom in the Mittwochsgesellschaft in 1783/84,[197] to his remarks regarding the persecution of Fichte in his 1799 autobiography,[198] Nicolai, otherwise moderate in his political utterances and thinking,[199] took a radical position comparable to that in Carl Friedrich Bahrdt's 1787 *Ueber Preßfreyheit*, perhaps the most uncompromising essay on freedom of the press published by a German before the French Revolution.[200] In his account of his journey through Germany, Nicolai bemoaned at length the continuing reactionary censorship policies of many South German states, particularly Austria, and chided the Austrian censors for treating the entire nation like children. The censors, he believed, would render the public a better service by drawing its attention to particularly useful works rather than sniffing about for something to ban.[201] Nicolai brought forward the usual argument against the efficacy of censorship, namely, that banning a work only made people more eager to read it (in 1777 the Austrian government actually followed this to its logical conclusion and banned the catalog of forbidden books so as not to give people any wrong ideas).[202] He also went a step further, though. Even in those cases where the opinions expressed in a work might endanger the government or the welfare of the state, leading to "discord and turmoil," the authorities would do better to tackle the unrest itself rather than the books or their authors. In an "era in which philosophical opinions

---

196. *Bescheidene und freymütige Erklärung.*
197. See Hellmuth, "Aufklärung und Pressefreiheit."
198. Nicolai, *Ueber meine gelehrte Bildung*, pp. 243–50.
199. Möller, *Aufklärung in Preußen*, p. 214.
200. *Ueber Preßfreyheit und deren Grenzen. Zur Beherzigung für Regenten, Censoren und Schriftsteller* (Züllichau: Frommann, 1787).
201. *Beschreibung einer Reise*, 4:872.
202. Bodi, *Tauwetter in Wien*, p. 57.

are punished by the loss of one's livelihood, imprisonment, banishment, and so on," the next step might be to burn authors at the stake for confused theological opinions.²⁰³

Censorship was a political problem not only for the state but also for the state-within-a-state, the republic of letters. Nicolai made this very clear in his remarks to the Austrian censors of the *ADB*. He asked with mock innocence yet genuine indignation how it was possible that the appointed censors of one German land, Austria, could ban a book approved by the censors of two others, Saxony and Brandenburg. Did this not discredit the entire institution of public censorship? Should governments follow those censors who treated authors and readers as children who must not to be allowed to play with sharp sticks because they might hurt themselves, rather than those who viewed them as adults capable of handling useful tools, trusting that they would employ them for their own good and that of others? "Oh, the disgrace for Germany, Oh the disgrace for the eighteenth century ...!" if this were the case.²⁰⁴ Disturbing, however, was not simply the arbitrariness of the censors' decisions, but their unwillingness to outline the reasons for them, which violated the principle, sacred to Nicolai, of public scrutiny. Nicolai polemically compared the treatment of authors by the Austrian censors to that of prisoners of the Spanish Inquisition, who were never told the crimes of which they stood accused (p. 18). "One never learns from the Vienna censors the reasons why a book was prohibited," he complained (p. 10). As government officials in an absolutist regime, the censors were not responsible to the (re)public (of letters), nor were they obliged to justify their actions. As writers, and thus members of the republic of letters, however, they were. Contemporaries recognized the conflict between state office (that of censor) and membership in the republic of letters. We have already seen the laments of one censor, Schröckh in Wittenberg, on this account. The distinction between the "public" and "private" uses of reason, as Kant was to express it most prominently a few years later in his famous essay "What is Enlightenment?" offered one route for demanding that censors be responsible to the republic of letters. Kant's argument here was, essentially, that scholars speaking to the public through their works (as opposed to teachers or clerics, or by extension censors, who were beholden to a higher

---

203. *Ueber meine gelehrte Bildung*, p. 247.
204. *Bescheidene und freymüthige Erklärung*, pp. 16–17. The page numbers in the text refer to this pamphlet.

authority) were making a public use of their reason, and thus were entitled to absolute freedom of expression *on their own behalf*.[205] Nicolai took a related tack in approaching the Austrian censors who banned the *ADB*. He noted that the censors themselves were learned men with a reputation to preserve or lose outside of Austria. He felt that it was his prerogative, purely as an author (not as a publisher), to call upon them publicly, not as censors (that is, as servants of the state), but as *fellow writers*, on behalf of the ninety-four contributors to the *ADB*, to say why they had rejected the *ADB* and to submit the reasons to scholarly scrutiny (p. 13). "Every scholar has the right to examine another scholar's reasons" (p. 21). Nicolai expresses his critique of censorship here in terms of a critique of the behavior of writers within the republic of letters who owed certain courtesies to their fellow authors and to the "entire enlightened, honorable German public" (p. 18). As he wrote to his friend Freiherr Tobias von Gebler, "I have spoken on behalf of common sense and freedom of thought, which have been irresponsibly restricted by the power of those in high places. But I hope that I have kept within proper limits, and not violated, by speaking the truth, the respect that we owe to the decisions of rulers."[206] In such utterances as this one we see how uneasily Nicolai's essentially liberal notion of a republic of letters sat with an acceptance of absolutist authority, yet how unthinkable it was for him to challenge that authority in any fundamental way.

Nicolai's encounters with censorship outside of Prussia differed from those on his home ground to the extent that they usually involved post-publication rather than pre-publication censorship, and that they more frequently involved the actual banning of books. To be sure, he had to face the censors in towns where he had books printed, but many of these seem to have been sympathetic to him and to have acted where possible to protect his interests. In fact, local censors were a consideration for

205. Kant's "Beantwortung der Frage: Was ist Aufklärung" appeared in the *Berlinische Monatsschrift* in December 1784 and was one of several answers to the question "What is Enlightenment?" which the Berlin pastor Johann Friedrich Zöllner had raised in a footnote to an article on civil marriage in the December 1783 issue of the *Monatsschrift*. For the various contributions to this debate, see Norbert Hinske and Michael Albrecht, eds., *Was ist Aufklärung? Beiträge aus der Berlinischen Monatsschrift*, 3d ed. (Darmstadt: Wissenschaftliche Buchgesellschaft, 1981).

206. Nicolai to Gebler, Leipzig, 5 October 1780, in *Aus dem Josephinischen Wien*, pp. 101–2. After reading Nicolai's open letter to the Austrian censors, the Prussian envoy in Vienna, Johann Hermann Riedesel, assured him that he saw nothing in it that might cause offense, and hence difficulties, "since the remarks contained therein are expressed with as much modesty as truth." Should trouble nevertheless arise, it would be his pleasure to put in a good word for Nicolai. Riedesel to Nicolai, Vienna, 30 September 1780, in NN 62.

Nicolai and his authors in determining where to print a particular book.[207] In 1772, when Nicolai was deciding whether to have part of the *ADB* printed in Erfurt, he asked his friend and reviewer there, Johann Erich Springer, to investigate the situation. He was particularly concerned that nobody "leak" the fact that the *ADB* was being printed in Erfurt. Springer explained the intricacies of Erfurt censorship and the best solution to the problem of securing discreet and sympathetic treatment for the journal: "As for censorship, it poses ... no problem as long as it is in the hands of a prof[essor].... Matters are different for a continuing work; it is at least dangerous, because here as everywhere else there are different camps in which the interests of printers are also involved. In order to be as safe as possible I will ... intervene with the new governor [Erfurt belonged to Mainz] to make sure that [Johann Georg] Meusel or I become censor, or both of us at once; then we will be covered for all eventualities."[208] Such strategies of steering works toward sympathetic censors were successful only as long as regulations permitted. Springer saw his plan thwarted in 1777 because a new decree from Mainz stipulated that all works had to pass a new censorship body composed of both Catholics and Protestants. Control was threatening to slip out of Springer's hands. Somehow, word had managed to get out that the *ADB* was being printed in Erfurt, and a local professor, annoyed that he had not been entrusted with the censorship of the journal, burst into Springer's house and threatened to complain to the local government that they had by-passed him. Springer managed to placate him and convince him to wait until the journal had been printed before lodging his complaint. Despite all blandishments, he refused to show the professor even one sheet of the manuscript, pretending that it was all at the printer's. Nicolai approved of such quick thinking, scribbling "schön" in the margin of the letter. Springer was defending his project of maintaining a low profile and a minimum of outside interference for the *ADB*.

The official censor was not so easily appeased, however, and Springer and the printer had to make some last-minute changes to offending

207. Christian Wilhelm Dohm had also mentioned censorship as a reason for wanting his controversial work on Jewish emancipation, *Über die bürgerliche Verbesserung der Juden*, to be printed in Berlin. He feared that Saxon or other foreign censors might find the work a bit too daring both politically and religiously. He had already asked their mutual friend, the Enlightenment theologian Wilhelm Abraham Teller, to act as censor because the work touched on theological as well as political issues. Ludwig Geiger, "Aus Briefen Dohms an Nicolai," *Zeitschrift für die Geschichte der Juden in Deutschland* 5 (1892): 75.

208. Springer to Nicolai, Erfurt, 28 October 1772, in NN 72.

theological reviews (apparently from Nicolai's own pen). Springer described vividly his predicament, caught as he was between the local Catholic censor and his sense of loyalty to Nicolai and his army of theological reform:

> But the censorship—the censorship—was something hateful. The old *Senior*, by all appearances a chiliast, or one of their friends, or somebody trying to keep on their good side for political reasons, cut out entire half-columns several times ... the poor printer had to break everything up and bade me for God's sake to substitute something else; the pressure of time also made this necessary, but these new additions have to pass the censor as well. Imagine, my dear fellow ... the devilish predicament in which I found myself.[209]

Despite all of these problems, Springer still considered it better to print the *ADB* in Erfurt than in Wittenberg, as Nicolai was considering, because the (Protestant) censors were even stricter there.[210] Nicolai, however, decided to return to printing in Schleusingen.[211] A few months later, Springer reported that the recent censorship affair had caused quite a stir and that "everybody" would be happy to see the Erfurt theological censor given a good dressing-down in a future issue of the *ADB*. People should ponder how it was possible in a university town that censorship of the *ADB* was given to a cleric rather than a learned theologian or author.[212]

Merely knowing (or being) the censor did not always suffice. It was rarely a simple matter of good will, since the censor was responsible for the contents of the works he passed for publication and could even face legal charges. Thus the fear of sanctions sometimes outweighed friendship, loyalty, and ideological agreement. Such caution could take on exaggerated, even paranoid overtones. Schröckh in Wittenberg took the ban of the *ADB* in Prussia very much to heart and blamed careless authors for imperiling not just the journal but also his own position. He became even more timid with time, trying to outdo the authorities in orthodoxy. Schröckh was a censor who clung to his Enlightenment principles in

---

209. Springer to Nicolai, Erfurt, 20 April 1777, in NN 72. In a circular to *ADB* reviewers dated 29 May 1777, Nicolai apologized for the delay in printing, which had been caused by the new censorship regulations and the new censor, who had been happy to have the *ADB* as the first morsel into which he could sink his zealous teeth. Circular in NN 86 [Iselin correspondence].

210. Springer to Nicolai, Erfurt, 20 April 1777, in NN 72.

211. Walch to Nicolai, Schleusingen, 25 October and 2 December 1777, in NN 79.

212. Springer to Nicolai, Erfurt, 8 June 1777, in NN 72.

private but was afraid to defend them publicly. His motto at this time was "Who can swim against the current?"[213] In 1801, when the *ADB* was back in Nicolai's hands and surely out of danger so far as the Prussian government was concerned, Schröckh was still asking the theological reviewers to tone down their language and stop their attacks on received teachings. Of a review whose author had described the teaching that Christ died for the sins of humanity as "a silly and immoral Jewish notion," he noted that "I had to change and tone that down if I did not wish to bring misfortune upon myself as a censor."[214]

A few years later, he refused to approve the publication of a review of the draft judicial procedures for the courts in Electoral Saxony, once again arguing that he might compromise himself by excessive leniency. In this case, however, the Saxon government turned out to be more liberal than he suspected, and Schröckh was even reprimanded by a government minister after a reviewer complained.

Whereas only one of Nicolai's publications, the *ADB*, was forbidden in Prussia,[215] many of his publications, including his own writings, were banned abroad. Even in Saxony, where censorship had become relatively lenient by the second half of the eighteenth century, volume 2 of *Sebaldus Nothanker* was in good company when the Theological Faculty of Leipzig University banned it together with Goethe's *Sorrows of Young Werther*.[216] The chief bane of Nicolai's existence, though, was the Vienna "Bücher-Revision," the office that decided which books could or could not be sold in the Habsburg lands.[217] In the early years of Nicolai's career, the simple word "Berlin" on the title page, as a sort of code word for Protestant at best and atheistic at worst, made a book highly suspect, and works by his authors Moses Mendelssohn and Thomas Abbt, among others, featured in the 1765 imperial catalog of forbidden books.[218] In 1769 Lessing half-joked to Nicolai about a work by their mutual friend Mendelssohn, "If 'Phädon' was confiscated in Vienna it was doubtless only because it was

---

213. Schröckh to Nicolai, Wittenberg, 24 January 1805, in NN 69; and Ludwig Schneider, the brother of the *ADB* reviewer, Dresden, 24 March 1805, in NN 68. For more on this affair, see chap. 3 of Selwyn, *Philosophy in the Comptoir*.

214. Schröckh to Nicolai, Wittenberg, 11 April 1801, in NN 69.

215. That is, aside from the very brief ban of the *Litteraturbriefe*.

216. Fontius, *Voltaire in Berlin*, p. 18.

217. On the *Bücher-Revision*, see Oskar Sashegyi, *Zensur und Geistesfreiheit unter Joseph II.* (Budapest: Akademiai Kiado, 1958), pp. 67–88.

218. Mentioned by Nicolai in his discussion of the development of Austrian censorship over his lifetime in *Beschreibung einer Reise*, 4:857.

published in Berlin, and no one could imagine that anyone in Berlin would write on behalf of the immortality of the soul."[219] In later years, fewer works were singled out for disfavor. Some were banned outright, including *Johann Bunkel* and the *ADB* in the late 1770s and early 1780s, and Nicolai's novel *Die Geschichte eines Dicken Mannes*, and parts of Klügel's encyclopedia in the 1790s. Others, including the *ADB* from 1774 to 1778 and after 1783, volume 2 of *Sebaldus Nothanker* and the travel account, were available "by ticket" to certain people considered to possess the strength of character to withstand the ideological onslaught.[220] To those outside the charmed Vienna circle, it was often unclear which books were allowed when and to whom. In 1772, for example, Nicolai told Father Michael Denis in Vienna that he had hesitated to send him a copy of one of his new publications, Johann August Eberhard's *Neue Apologie des Sokrates* (which itself contained an attack on censorship)[221] for fear that it might be seized by the censors. He inquired whether such books were permitted to Denis as a professor and member of a religious order.[222]

Despite the strictness of Austrian censorship, there were loopholes even in the supposedly draconian system under Maria Theresa. The organization of the system itself allowed a certain amount of room for maneuver,[223] and the rigorousness of censorship enforcement varied from region to region. In Hungary, for example, the local system of post-publication censorship offices was less developed than in Bohemia or in Austria

219. Lessing to Nicolai, 25 August 1769, quoted in Nicolao Merker, *Die Aufklärung in Deutschland* (Munich: C. H. Beck, 1982), pp. 43–44.

220. Freiherr von Gebler's letters of 15 May 1774 and 15 July 1775 mention some numbers of the *ADB* being available with a *Passierzettel* only. He did not consider this a grave problem, however, because *ADB* subscribers belonged to those persons "from whom even heterodox books are not withheld" (15 July 1775). *Aus dem Josephinischen Wien*, pp. 54–56, 66–69. Gebler also mentions that volume 2 of *Sebaldus Nothanker* was available "by ticket" only. Letter of 9 December 1775, pp. 72–74. Nicolai's Vienna lawyer Matolay informed him of the renewed availability of the *ADB* "by ticket" in a letter of 19 March 1783, in NN 48. Officially, the censors had decided that the journal should only be available to subscribers, "but when such a ticket is brought to the *Revision* [the post-publication censorship office], nobody asks or checks up on whether the bearer is a subscriber [*continuant*] or not." Nicolai mentions the *toleratur* status of the travel account in *Beschreibung einer Reise*, 4:864–67.

221. Eberhard's book was a defense of Jean-François Marmontel's 1767 philosophical novel *Bélisaire*, which was forbidden in France, against the Dutch author Peter Hofstede.

222. Michael Denis, *Literarischer Nachlaß*, ed. Joseph Friedrich Freiherr von Retzer, 2 parts in 1 vol. (Vienna, 1801–2), pp. 163–64.

223. On censorship under Maria Theresa, see Klingenstein, *Staatsverwaltung und kirchliche Autorität*. More recently, see the section on Austria in Plachta, *Damnatur, Toleratur, Admittitur*, with documents on microfiche.

proper.²²⁴ The categorization of permitted books as *admittitur* and *toleratur*, somewhat comparable to the French distinction between *privilège* and *permission tacite*, allowed the authorities to demonstrate their disapproval of certain books without banning them altogether. While ordinary mortals had legal access only to those books designated *admittitur*, the lucky few could acquire "tickets" that allowed them to buy and subscribe to such books as the government chose to "tolerate" for their eyes only.²²⁵ They, of course, could pass these books on to the less fortunate (or those unwilling to apply openly for permission to buy non-approved books),²²⁶ expanding the circle of those with access to suspect literature. Although Joseph II's 1781 blueprint for the reform of the censorship system, the *Grund-Regeln zur Bestimmung einer ordentlichen künftigen Bücher Censur*, stipulated that books previously allowed only *erga schedam*, that is, with special permission, would now be freely available,²²⁷ the intermediate category appears to have persisted for several years at least. Thus the novelist and librarian Heinrich Gottfried von Bretschneider could still explain to Nicolai in 1784 that the common understanding of the *toleratur* was that it "allows the book to be read, but indicates disapproval of its contents." The catalog of forbidden books, reduced as it was by that time, remained a sort of "critical bibliography" that told potential readers which books were not approved by the government.²²⁸ Those with the

---

224. As part of the reform of the censorship system under Joseph II, pre-publication censorship was concentrated in Vienna and only post-publication censorship exercised in the provinces. On Hungary, see Sashegyi, *Zensur und Geistesfreiheit unter Joseph II.*, pp. 76–77.

225. How and where precisely these *Zettel* were to be obtained, what they looked like, and how they were worded remains unclear. Of the censorship status of his travel account in Vienna, Nicolai wrote in volume 4 of that work that he should be happy that it was not forbidden altogether. He noted, however, a certain incongruity in the whole system of "tolerating" books: "A peculiar inconsistency arises when a book is merely tolerated ... and yet excerpts and reviews are publicly available in Vienna itself. In my case, the Vienna *Realzeitung* contains an extensive review of this travel account, which twists and distorts everything in a spiteful manner." The censors permitted this sort of injustice, but did not allow all members of the public access to his book, so that they might judge for themselves. *Beschreibung einer Reise*, 4:867–68.

226. Nicolai notes that "some had their reasons for avoiding this formality." According to him, one had to apply in writing for permission to buy one of the "tolerated" books. *Beschreibung einer Reise*, 4:852.

227. Bodi, *Tauwetter in Wien*, p. 49.

228. Bretschneider to Nicolai, Vienna, 2 January 1784, in NN 9. The new censorship commission in Vienna revised the *Catalogus librorum prohibitorum* in 1783 and printed a new catalog in early 1784. Rather than 5,000 forbidden books, the new work contained "only" some 900. According to Leslie Bodi, these were mainly pornographic books, well-known atheistic works of the French Enlightenment, and anticlerical pamphlets. The list retained, however, Goethe's

proper contacts not only had access to books unavailable to the wider public but might also know how to get banned books past the authorities as well as have them removed from the list of forbidden works.[229] Bretschneider, for example, managed to receive the *ADB* throughout the five-year period of its banning in Austria. In 1780, however, he almost got into trouble when two copies of the *ADB* (including one for a friend who was a censor in Graz!) were addressed to him care of the bookseller Rudolph Gräffer *in* Vienna rather than *in transit via* Vienna (he lived in Ofen in Hungary). He explained to Nicolai the best way to get past the "holy censorship office": "When the books are wrapped up and addressed to some town in Hungary, they can pass through Vienna in *transito*, that is, be sent on to their destination with only a customs seal—and do not need to be examined or opened here." This time, since he had not known the books were arriving, he had not had time to tell their intermediary in Nuremberg to take precautionary measures. The Nuremberg bookseller Carl Friedrich Raspe, ignorant of the contents of the package from Nicolai, thought that he was doing Bretschneider a favor by sending the books directly to Vienna where he was spending the winter. When the package arrived, the censors wanted to open it and investigate the contents. Fearing that they would confiscate the journals and return them to Nicolai, Bretschneider had managed to stave this off. While the bales lay unopened at the censorship office, Bretschneider was trying to get them re-addressed in transit to the University Library in Ofen, where he was librarian.[230]

There were two main methods for getting books unbanned. One was to protest the censor's actions via petition and/or public pronouncements, as Nicolai had done from 1778 on in the case of the *ADB*. Another avenue opened up under the more liberal censorship regime initiated by Joseph

---

Werther, Schiller's *Räuber*, and some works forbidden for political reasons, such as Klopstock's and Lorenz Leopold Haschka's odes to Joseph II, as well as baroque devotional works considered antithetical to reform Catholicism. Bodi, *Tauwetter in Wien*, p. 51.

229. This was true not only in Vienna, of course. When post-publication censorship of foreign books was tightened in Bavaria in 1788, Nicolai's Munich reviewer Andreas Dominik Zaupser sent him instructions on the best way to get around the new vigilance without compromising himself. Nicolai was to send review copies to Zaupser, without any enclosed letters or bills, to avoid having them fall into the wrong hands. Instead, they should be sent separately with the mounted post. Packages should be sent to the bookbinder Ringer. Then the censor would not know to whom the books belonged. Zaupser continued to receive his books in this manner until at least August 1790. Zaupser to Nicolai, Munich, 4 August 1788 and 21 August 1790, in NN 84.

230. Bretschneider recounts the story in his letter of 22 January 1780, in NN 9.

II. Bretschneider, now censor for German, English, and French books in Ofen, remarked that since Joseph II had ascended the throne 886 previously prohibited books had been re-allowed by decree. More books would be unbanned if local booksellers took the initiative, ordering the works in question and pressing the censors to expedite matters and decide whether they were allowed or not.[231] Nicolai should simply send a selected group of books to Gräffer in Vienna and let him deal with the censors. "You will see, most of them will be allowed."[232] If Nicolai did try this tactic, though, it did not have any immediate effect. In May 1782, Bretschneider said he would put pressure on a new censor, Franz de Paula Rosalino, in regard to the *ADB*.[233] By early 1783, the *ADB* was allowed again, but only "by ticket."[234] In 1785, though, Bretschneider was reporting from Lemberg that Nicolai could send him any books at all, as long as he dispatched a list in a letter beforehand "so that I can make the necessary arrangements regarding censorship."[235] The books could be cleared before they were received, thus avoiding a long wait at the inspection bureau (*Revisonsamt*).

Nicolai's first personal encounter with Austrian censorship came during his 1781 journey. Upon entering Austrian waters on the Danube, a customs officer boarded his ship and surprised him by ordering that the books he was carrying for his own use be sealed and confiscated. Nicolai had recently read in the papers that foreigners were allowed free transport of books for their own use, but the customs officer cited an order from Vienna for increased vigilance. He was to let no books pass without sealing them first. The crate of books had to be sent to the nearest censor at Linz. The latter, the author and actor Benedikt Dominik Anton Cremeri, who had written a pamphlet against Nicolai's 1780 open letter to the Austrian censors (which Nicolai did not know at the time), was nevertheless obliging enough to cut through the necessary red tape and get the books released quickly. He regarded them with some interest, Nicolai reported, discovering titles that he had heard of, but never seen.[236]

Nicolai had friends and correspondents in Vienna but at least until his

---

231. Bretschneider to Nicolai, Ofen, 3 January 1782, in NN 9. See also his letter of 20 November 1781.
232. Bretschneider to Nicolai, Ofen, 17 February 1782, in NN 9.
233. Bretschneider to Nicolai, Ofen, 8 May 1782, in NN 9.
234. Matolay to Nicolai, Vienna, 19 March 1783, in NN 48.
235. Bretschneider to Nicolai, Lemberg, 16 March 1785, in NN 9.
236. *Beschreibung einer Reise*, 2:484–86; 533–34.

1781 visit, he does not seem to have had much influence among the censors there. The fact that he protested the ban of the *ADB* publicly in the journal itself and in a separate pamphlet underlines the lack of success he encountered using official channels. The situation may have improved somewhat when his friend Freiherr von Gebler gained influence over the reorganized and secularized Censorship Commission in 1781.[237] In 1783, though, Bretschneider sent Nicolai a section of the monthly censor's list showing that "even the most innocent books from your firm are merely *tolerated*, because they cannot be condemned altogether."[238] Under the stricter censorship of the 1790s, even friends in high places could not always help. In 1794, Nicolai sent a copy of his satirical novel *Geschichte eines Dicken Mannes* to Johann Melchior von Birkenstock, a Vienna censor of liberal disposition, in the hope that it would find favor.[239] Birkenstock regretted that "even before I received the copy and knew who the author was the axe had already fallen": the book was banned and there was nothing he could do about it.[240] Other letters of the period also testify to uneasiness in the book trade and republic of letters about Austrian censorship. In the summer of 1794, while the local Jacobins were being rounded up, the Vienna bookseller Joseph Stahel (not to be confused with the pirate J. J. Stahel) had strong words for the renewed strictness of Viennese censorship. "For some time now our local censorship ... has begun to rage against even learned works; the mask has been torn away, and the intentions are clear. The barbarity of the fifteenth century is to be reintroduced, and reason and freedom of thought must bend before priestly deceit and superstition." Birkenstock had been engaged for many months on a new plan for the universities and "a certain Lanser, secretary at court and a decent man of affairs, who however does not know the first thing about literature" had taken over his censorship duties.

237. On the reorganized censorship body, see Bodi, *Tauwetter in Wien*, p. 51. It was at Tobias von Gebler's instigation, for example, that Protestant scholarly books were allowed under the new censorship regulations, even when they contained some passages that might insult Catholic readers. Sashegyi, *Zensur und Geistesfreiheit unter Joseph II.*, p. 26.

238. Bretschneider to Nicolai, Ofen, November 1783, in NN 9.

239. Undated note handwritten on a printed circular, in NN 5 [Birkenstock correspondence].

240. Birkenstock to Nicolai, Vienna, 2 July 1794, in NN 5 (verso of Nicolai's printed circular used to accompany books). Eschenburg worried that the novel might displease certain censors. Eschenburg to Nicolai, Braunschweig, 20 March 1794, in NN 19. King Frederick William II was known popularly as the fat man (*der Dicke*) but it does not seem that he or the censors took offense at the fat kings or fat men mentioned by Nicolai. The main targets of the novel were disciples of Kant.

Censorship decisions were now being made on the basis of excerpts containing potentially offensive passages from books. More books were being banned daily, with "orders coming from Court to exercise stricter censorship." Birkenstock was too cowardly to protect scholarship, and no censor was willing to accept even the slightest responsibility. Learning was under attack and "booksellers were being trodden underfoot." Nicolai's *Geschichte eines Dicken Mannes* was only one of many victims of this noxious brew of incompetence and reactionary politics. Stahel, echoing in many respects Nicolai's 1780 remarks to the Vienna censors, now spiced with the rhetoric of the Revolutionary era, recommended that Germany's foremost authors band together and call those who raged against reason and freedom of thought (as Jacobins raged against property) before the "judge's bench of the nation" and demand that they account for their misdeeds. He could, he hinted, say much more about this subject if only he were sure that his letters would not be opened. He recommended that Nicolai's author Klügel publish an open letter to the censor asking him why he had recommended the banning of volumes 4 and 5 of his encyclopedia.[241] Meanwhile, Nicolai himself was suffering the burden of self-censorship imposed by the prevailing political climate. In the winter of 1794/95 he finished work on volumes 9 and 10 of his travel account, which, as he assured his friend Höpfner, "has been a highly unpleasant task ... since because of censorship I cannot say many things that I would have liked to say."[242] It is unclear from the letter whether it was the Prussian or Austrian censors he feared; in the 1790s, for the first time, they had became almost equally threatening.[243]

---

241. Stahel to Nicolai, Vienna, 9 August 1794, in NN 72. Two months later, he informed Nicolai that the Vienna censors were continuing "on their dark mysterious path" and would not stop until they had destroyed the book trade. Stahel to Nicolai, Vienna, 9 October 1794, in NN 72. Nicolai approved of the suggestion that Klügel should unite with other recently banned authors in order to demand an explanation from the Vienna censors and offered to pay any costs incurred, but it seems nothing ever came of this idea. See Klügel's letter of 30 September 1794 (with Nicolai's marginal annotations) and 17 January 1795, in which he suggests that Nicolai pen the challenge to the Vienna censor, in NN 40.

On the gradual tightening of censorship and political repression after Joseph II's death in 1790 and particularly after Leopold II's death in 1792, see Bodi, *Tauwetter in Wien*, chap. 7, "Das Ende des Tauwetters," pp. 395ff.

242. Nicolai to Höpfner, Berlin, 7 January 1795, in *Briefe aus dem Freundeskreis*, p. 333.

243. See here, for example, Nicolai's letters to Uz of 12 May 1792 (in NN 76) and to Höpfner of 14 February 1792 and 15 December 1794 complaining of Prussian censorship. In the last, he speaks of self-censorship as a sort of infanticide against his intellectual offspring. *Briefe aus dem Freundeskreis*, p. 330. For the letter of 14 February 1792, see ibid., p. 319.

The Bookseller and the State

Throughout his career, Friedrich Nicolai used both official and personal channels to negotiate the choppy waters of *ancien régime* book trade regulations. He attempted to assert influence through written reports and petitions, both alone and collectively with other booksellers, as well as through his social and professional contacts with officials (some of them his authors) for whom he was both client and patron. He took pirate printers to court with varying degrees of success, depending upon the location. And while the battle raged over whether literary piracy was "highway robbery" or a legitimate means of spreading Enlightenment and useful knowledge in those areas of Germany less blessed with authors and well-heeled customers, Nicolai's own most interesting piracy cases were fought against editions that were by no means the exact copies of the originals we usually associate with the term. Thus these lawsuits went to the heart of ideas of intellectual and not merely material property. They attempted, albeit unsuccessfully, to expand the arguments on what exactly was protected by a privilege. The conflicts in which Nicolai was entangled were, of course, no mere personal battles. Conflicts around the regulation of printed matter and its system of distribution, the book trade, reflected wider conflicts within absolutism and within the Holy Roman Empire, as well as the republic of letters: tensions between writers and censors, between Enlightenment principles and absolutist practice, between the protection of property and the spread of knowledge and ideas, among territories, estates, and the imperial government.

Publishing was always a gamble, and not only a financial one; Nicolai and his authors walked the edge separating candor from impudence, two sides of the same coin, which the authorities could flip at any time. One could improve the odds if one knew and could negotiate with the censor, as Nicolai did in Berlin, and his correspondents did in other cities. Most of the time Nicolai managed to stay on the right side, at least from the vantage point of the Prussian government, and to keep out of serious trouble. No matter what a Prussian (or Friderician) patriot he may have been, however, he had no great illusions about "German liberty." He complained bitterly against repression, mainly in letters but also, in more generalized tones, in public pronouncements. Though he abhorred the institution and not merely the abuse of censorship, he was, at bottom, a businessman, not a hero or rebel. Thus he tried to make the best use of the available possibilities in the world he knew, a world that accorded him a respectable place, a modicum of influence, and a comfortable living.

chapter
(5)

The *Allgemeine deutsche Bibliothek* as the Centerpiece of Nicolai's Program of Enlightenment and of his Firm

> German literature is perhaps the only one to
> have begun with criticism.
>
> —*Mme. de Staël, 1813*

The eighteenth century has often been called an age of criticism, a description that goes back at least to Immanuel Kant.[1] Any discussion of Friedrich Nicolai as bookseller-publisher and *Aufklärer* must consider the role of his review journal, the *Allgemeine deutsche Bibliothek* (*ADB*) in his life's work.[2] The *ADB* was Friedrich Nicolai's grandest and most widely recognized, but also most controversial, contribution to communication in, and the centralization and policing of, the German republic of letters. The French historian Henri Brunschwig once described Nicolai's critical journals as "the backbone of the *Aufklärung*."[3] If the young Schiller called Nicolai a "sovereign of literature," with all the term's implications of power, authority, and respect, but also autocracy, it was in great part because of the *ADB*.

---

1. Immanuel Kant, foreword to the first edition of *Kritik der reinen Vernunft* (Riga: Hartknoch, 1781).
2. Günther Ost recounts what he calls the "external history" of the *ADB* in his *Friedrich Nicolais Allgemeine deutsche Bibliothek*, a useful work based upon extensive research in primary sources. Ute Schneider's study of the *ADB*'s role in the republic of letters, *Friedrich Nicolais Allgemeine Deutsche Bibliothek als Integrationsmedium der Gelehrtenrepublik* (Wiesbaden: Harrasowitz, 1995), which focuses on the journal up until 1785, contains a wealth of new and interesting material, e.g., on the dissemination and readership of the *ADB* and interpretations of reviews, but suffers at times from the author's concern to fit the *ADB* into a schematic sociological model of the scientific community.
3. Brunschwig, *La Crise*, p. 106.

The *ADB* established Nicolai as a sort of Gottsched of the late Enlightenment, an arch-critic and crusader, revered, resented, and ultimately ridiculed. The Leipzig professor Johann Christoph Gottsched and the Berlin bookseller and publisher shared not so much their ideas as their reputations, particularly in old age. Their notions of the nature of literary criticism, for example, differed in a way that inspired one scholar to compare their two approaches (as ideal types) to that of the courtroom versus the coffeehouse.[4] Gottsched described the critic as someone with a philosophical grounding in the rules governing the arts, who was thus in a position to make a rational analysis and proper assessment of the "beauties and errors of all masterpieces or works of art that come to his attention on the bases of those rules."[5] Nicolai, on the other hand, called the critic a companion "who seeks to converse with me about new works, and to inspire me to investigate them more closely."[6] Despite these differences, their perceived status as dictators of taste aroused similar passions in the republic of letters.[7] Both made their names as young men with periodicals (Gottsched with the moral weeklies *Die Vernünftigen Tadlerinnen* (1725–26) and *Der Biedermann* (1727–29), Nicolai with two journals of criticism, the *Bibliothek der schönen Wissenschaften* (1757–58) and the *Briefe, die neueste Litteratur betreffend* (1759–64). Both sought to encourage writing that bridged the gap between the learned and the general reading public (what Gottsched referred to as a "middle style"). Both were patriots of German language and letters as well as organizers on a grand scale. Finally, both had long careers that spanned major changes in literary taste, which left them looking dusty and old-fashioned, obscuring their important contributions. As Gottsched scholar P. M. Mitchell succinctly remarks, "Times changed. Gottsched didn't."[8] One could say

---

4. "In Nicolai's hands Gottsched's tribunal became a democratic coffeehouse gathering," writes Barbara Maria Carvill in her study of novelist and critic Johann Karl August Musäus's reviews in the *ADB*, *Der verführte Leser*, p. 97.

5. Quoted in Carvill, *Der verführte Leser*, p. 96.

6. *ADB* 10, no. 2 (1769): 114; quoted in Carvill, *Der verführte Leser*, p. 97.

7. Gottsched and Nicolai were also on opposite sides of the debate over the relative merits of English and French literature. Gottsched had no appreciation for Milton and Shakespeare, preferring classical French literature, which adhered to the Aristotelean models he most admired. The attack on this position led to his break with the Swiss critics Bodmer and Breitinger in the 1740s, and to a smoldering conflict in the German literary world that inspired Nicolai's first two published books, the defense of Milton and the *Briefe über den itzigen Zustand*. Mitchell, "Johann Christoph Gottsched," pp. 35–61. On Gottsched as dictator, see pp. 36–37; on the feud with Bodmer and Breitinger, see p. 45.

8. Mitchell, "Johann Christoph Gottsched," p. 45.

the same of Nicolai, at least about his basic preferences and principles. The *ADB* accompanied Nicolai for most of his professional life, from 1764 to 1805. Even during those years, from 1792 to 1800, when he neither edited nor published the journal, it remained closely associated with him in the eyes of both public and governments. Nicolai published many other works, but the *ADB* was the centerpiece and linchpin of his publishing enterprise.

Holding a Mirror to the Republic of Letters

"Only now did Germany learn what was happening everywhere within it from a literary perspective; it learned to know itself, and thus came into closer contact with itself."[9] The exalted view of the unique importance of the *ADB* expressed here by Johann Erich Biester, editor of the *Berlinische Monatsschrift*, the house organ of the late Enlightenment in Berlin, reflects the patriotic fervor with which the journal began. Sometime in 1763 Friedrich Nicolai decided to end one journal and begin a new, more ambitious one. The *Briefe, die neueste Litteratur betreffend* had been, in form and style, an extension of the personal collaboration and self-education through discussion in which Nicolai, Lessing, and Mendelssohn had engaged in their early years together in Berlin.[10] The *Briefe*, he noted modestly in a letter of 1766, had been merely accounts of what the reviewers had read, and of the thoughts that had occurred to them during the reading process.[11] The *ADB* had wider aims, and moved from an intimate, epistolary style to a more impersonal one, directed at a growing, anonymous—but by no means passively receptive—public of "connoisseurs of the latest literature." These readers and writers, scattered all over Germany in small towns that often lacked a bookshop, hungered, Nicolai felt, for "reliable information on new books and their true value."[12]

The *ADB* did not, of course, appear in a journalistic vacuum. The first scholarly (review) journals in Germany had appeared in the 1660s as Latin translations of French and English models, and the *Acta Eruditorum* was founded by Otto Mencke in Leipzig in 1682 as the first original

---

9. Quoted in Göckingk, *Friedrich Nicolais Leben und literarischer Nachlaß*, p. 33.
10. Nicolai discusses the journal in his "Selbstbiographie," p. 25.
11. Nicolai to Herder, Berlin, 19 November 1766, in Nicolai, *Verlegerbriefe*, pp. 43–44.
12. "Nachricht" announcing the founding of the *ADB*, in *Briefe, die neueste Litteratur betreffend* 20 (1764): 183.

German publication of this kind, albeit in Latin. Seventeen fifteen saw the establishment, also in Leipzig, of a German-language journal, the *Neuen Zeitungen von gelehrten Sachen*, which continued until 1768, and by the mid-eighteenth century, most German cities had their own German-language "gelehrte Zeitungen," either as independent publications or as supplements to local newspapers, which reported on new books and developments at the academies and universities. Most of these publications possessed largely local significance.[13]

The *ADB* distinguished itself from other review journals in several respects. It was neither published by an academy, like its most distinguished rival in the early years, the *Göttingische Gelehrte Anzeigen*, nor was it attached to a particular town, however strongly it may have been associated, in the minds of many, with Berlin. While most scholarly journals at least attempted to review books from all over Europe, the *ADB* had a specifically German focus. It cast its net widely, setting out to review all new books appearing in the German language, in all fields, whether good or bad, weighty or trivial, and to provide information on events in the world of learning and letters. The reviewers were to be experts in their fields from all over Germany. In announcing the forthcoming journal, Nicolai admitted that the project was a difficult one, but vowed that he would not be dissuaded from an enterprise that, if properly organized, would doubtless prove useful for anyone interested in contemporary letters. With the *ADB*, he hoped that German scholarship and literature could be "surveyed each year as if in a painting."[14] With its numerous reviews of translations, an Italian member of the Berlin Academy of Sciences believed that the *ADB* provided "a general overview of European literature" as well, thus exceeding the promise of its title.[15]

It all began with Nicolai's idea to publish a German equivalent of the foremost English review journal, the *Monthly Review*, which had been

---

13. The literature on eighteenth-century German journals is relatively sparse. On mid-eighteenth-century scholarly journals, see Bernhard Fabian, "Im Mittelpunkt der Bücherwelt. Über Gelehrsamkeit und gelehrtes Schrifttum um 1750," in *Wissenschaften im Zeitalter der Aufklärung*, ed. Rudolf Vierhaus (Göttingen: Vandenhoeck & Ruprecht, 1985), pp. 249–74, esp. 257–59; more generally, see Jürgen Wilke, *Literarische Zeitschriften des 18. Jahrhunderts*, vol. 1 (Stuttgart: Metzler, 1978), and the classic Joachim Kirchner, *Geschichte des deutschen Zeitschriftenwesens*, vol. 1, *Von den Anfängen bis zum Zeitalter der Romantik*, 2d ed. (Wiesbaden: Harrassowitz, 1958), esp. chap. 4, "Auf dem Wege zur Fachzeitschrift."

14. "Nachricht," in *Briefe, die neueste Litteratur betreffend* 20 (1764): 184–85.

15. Carlo Denina, *Brandenburgische Briefe, welche der Geschichte der Litteratur zur Fortsetzung dienen*, vol. 1 (Berlin, 1786), p. 92.

founded fourteen years earlier by the London bookseller Ralph Griffiths.[16] Nicolai wrote to a number of his friends and acquaintances, but at first none of them would commit himself to joining the project.[17] C. F. Weiße, who had taken over the editorship of the *Bibliothek der schönen Wissenschaften* from Nicolai, was at first not very optimistic about the chances for success, noting that from his own experience it was very difficult to recruit reviewers for belles-lettres because the best writers were already otherwise engaged.[18] By 1764, Nicolai's vigorous letter-writing and recruitment campaign had nonetheless yielded ten authors willing to contribute to the fledgling publication.[19] He now felt ready to announce in his *Briefe, die neueste Litteratur betreffend* the founding of a new, more ambitious, review journal with the auspicious word *allgemein* (general, universal, public) in the title.[20] A year later, Nicolai could report that he had assembled twenty-two regular contributors, not counting the friends whom he had asked to furnish occasional local literary news, and now needed only four to six further contributors.[21] At this time Nicolai described himself as a "poor sinner, writing around from Copenhagen to Zurich in order to find collaborators from all the sciences.... [N]o one [with a] good mind is safe."[22] Nicolai's assiduous headhunting for likely reviewers among the most competent scholars and fluent writers in the German-speaking world prompted his correspondent Johann Heinrich Merck to quip that "the world seems to have been turned upside down; bread is pursuing genius, not genius bread."[23] Despite frequent complaints of a lack of reviewers particularly in law and belles-lettres,

16. On the 'Englishness' of Nicolai's idea for the *ADB*, see Fabian, "Nicolai and England," pp. 187–90. The *Monthly Review* existed until 1845, but its heyday was over by about 1800. Its distinguished early contributors included Richard Brinsley Sheridan, Oliver Goldsmith, and Charles Burney. *A Literary History of England*, ed. Albert C. Baugh, 2d ed. (London: Routledge & Kegan Paul, 1967), pp. 1054ff.

17. Nicolai to Uz, Berlin, 3 December 1763, in NN 76.

18. Weiße to Nicolai, Leipzig, undated letters of December 1763 or January 1764 and March 1764, in NN 81.

19. They were the theologians Wilhelm Abraham Teller, Friedrich Gabriel Resewitz, and Friedrich Germanus Lüdke, the physicians Christian Friedrich Boerner and Johann Friedrich Zückert, the jurist Georg Gottfried Boerner, Nicolai's friends Moses Mendelssohn and Thomas Abbt, and the influential Göttingen professors Christian Gottlob Heyne and Abraham Gotthelf Kästner. Ost, *Friedrich Nicolais Allgemeine Deutsche Bibliothek*, p. 14.

20. "Nachricht," in *Briefe, die neueste Litteratur betreffend* 20 (1764): 183–86.

21. Nicolai to Zimmermann, Berlin, 13 August 1765, in Nicolai, *Verlegerbriefe*, p. 35.

22. Nicolai to Herder, Berlin, 19 November 1766, in Nicolai, *Verlegerbriefe*, p. 44.

23. Quoted in Sommerfeld, *Friedrich Nicolai und der Sturm und Drang*, p. 160.

which were to continue throughout the long life of the journal, Nicolai's initial efforts were so successful that by 1768 he had assembled fifty collaborators.[24]

The very rapid development of the book market in the final third of the eighteenth century rendered the enterprise of reviewing all new German books both desirable and impossible. The 1763 Leipzig book fair catalog, which encompassed only a portion of German book production, listed 1350 new titles; in 1805 the number had risen to some 4500.[25] The production of Berlin firms alone rose from some 1080 titles in the 1760s to some 3040 in the 1790s.[26] Even if all German publications had reached the Leipzig book fair, from whence Nicolai received most of his information about new books, it would have been impossible to review all of them in the space and with the staff available.[27]

From the beginning, Nicolai intended the *ADB* as a mirror of the German republic of letters, reflecting both its beauties and its blemishes. As such, he hoped that it would furnish future historians of literature and learning with "a lively and correct tableau of recent German literature."[28] In order to serve these purposes, the *ADB* had to cover the good, the bad, and the mediocre. For posterity, which would judge the literature of the past with a less jaundiced eye, the good journals of the present had to provide an accurate chronicle. "This approximates my intention in the alg. d. Bibl.," Nicolai informed Swiss historian and new reviewer Johannes von Müller in 1772. Nicolai, soon to become an enthusiastic amateur historian himself, was keen to leave behind the right sort of record:[29] "If the chronicler selects his facts too rigorously, he leaves all too little material for the future historian. It is far better for the former to recount all of the circumstances of an event or a revolution. Although

---

24. Nicolai to Herder, Berlin, 24 December 1768, in Nicolai, *Verlegerbriefe*, p. 62. Ten years later he had eighty-five reviewers, as he remarked in a letter to Höpfner of 22 December 1778, in *Briefe aus dem Freundeskreis*, p. 161.

25. Goldfriedrich, *Geschichte des deutschen Buchhandels*, 3:248.

26. Figures in Georgi, *Die Entwicklung des Berliner Buchhandels*, p. 144.

27. Despite the growth of the *ADB* staff, Nicolai continued to lack reviewers in many fields. This was particularly true at the very beginning and after the founding of the *Allgemeine Literatur-Zeitung* in 1785. In a circular sent to reviewers in June 1786, for example, Nicolai called for new reviewers in over twenty fields from architecture to zoology. The circular is in Nicolai's correspondence with J. J. Eschenburg, in HAB, no. 64.

28. Foreword to the *ADB* 106, no. 2 (1792).

29. In the 1770s Nicolai did extensive archival research in Berlin for the new edition of his *Beschreibung der königlichen Residenzstädte*. In a letter of 13 October 1777 to Uz he describes himself as buried under "documents and dossiers." In NN 76 [Uz correspondence].

The *Allgemeine deutsche Bibliothek*

some of them may appear quite unimportant, the historian [writing] in one hundred years may recognize the influence they exerted."[30] Thus Nicolai's refusal to follow the advice of those friends and collaborators, such as Isaak Iselin and Johannes von Müller, who proposed a review journal that discussed only books of merit, was ideological as well as practical. As he told Iselin in 1769, he simply did not have the time or the staff close at hand to read and make selections among all of the new books that appeared every year. But even if he had, the bad books were as much part of German literature as the good, and they were read by the largest number of people (a theme echoed by the bookseller Hieronymus in *Sebaldus Nothanker*). Especially in the Catholic provinces, he believed, the *ADB* could play a useful part in "enlightening minds." In Austria, where the *ADB* was practically the only source of Protestant theology allowed, the spirit of free inquiry in the theological and philosophical reviews would have to have a profound effect on thinking Catholics. Truths that appeared hackneyed to Protestants, he reminded Iselin, might be new discoveries to Catholics.[31] While he hoped to leave posterity in the *ADB* a true record of the literary developments of his time, he envisioned it as part of a program of Enlightenment for the present republic of writers and readers (or teachers and learners, as he styled them in *Sebaldus Nothanker*), both Protestant and Catholic, in the German-speaking lands. Nicolai was no political nationalist, but he was a patriot of the German republic of letters. The *ADB* can be seen as the logical conclusion of thoughts he developed as a bookseller's assistant in the 1750s and put to paper in his *Briefe über den itzigen Zustand* on the necessity of creating a focal point for the republic of letters in Germany.[32] As he was later to do on a more general plane in his twelve-volume account of his journey through Germany and Switzerland, Nicolai sought to acquaint reading and writing Germans with their fellow German speakers in other regions. The *ADB*, he wrote in 1765, was intended as a point of

---

30. Nicolai to Müller, Berlin, 12 June 1772, in Nicolai, *Verlegerbriefe*, p. 78.

31. Nicolai to Iselin, Berlin, 26 December 1769, in NN 86. Most reviewers shared Nicolai's zeal for enlightening the public and agreed that the *ADB* should endeavor to present an accurate picture of the range of literary production, but nobody wanted to read the mass of dull and mediocre works. See, for example, the comments to this effect in a letter from Nicolai's long-time reviewer, author and friend J J. Eschenburg, Braunschweig, 11 July 1771, in NN 19. Similarly, Dr. Wilhelm Gottlieb Tafinger, an *ADB* reviewer in the years 1786–87, complained of being given only trivial books to review. Tafinger to Nicolai, Tübingen, 11 September 1787, in NN 74.

32. See Chapter 1, herein, on the issues raised in Nicolai's *Briefe über den itzigen Zustand*.

unification for German scholarship and letters.³³ Looking back some forty years later, he felt that this aim had been achieved: "General opinion appears to confirm that this journal made all of the German lands better acquainted with one another from a literary perspective and thus bound them more closely together."³⁴ Although a lack of faithful reporters meant that his original intention of publishing regular dispatches from all corners of Germany never came to fruition, Nicolai did institute a readers' forum, "Excerpts from Letters from Various Correspondents." Here he occasionally printed both news about the republic of letters and letters criticizing reviews, defending maligned authors, and the like. Some readers even sent in their own quite extensive reviews in the form of letters.³⁵ Thus the *ADB* was to provide at least a modicum of two-way communication, although not as much as Nicolai had originally intended.³⁶

Part of the more global project of acquainting German writers and readers with each other was the aim of assisting those who depended upon books, whether scholars, students, librarians, or the general educated public, to choose which works to buy and read in the various fields of scholarship and literature. Nicolai believed that reading intelligent reviews of both serious and trivial works, of clearly argued and muddled ones, would help train taste and the critical faculty, which was the foundation upon which all Enlightenment and useful innovation would be built. When Nicolai announced his retirement as editor and publisher of the *ADB* in 1792, it was with all the pathos of the *Aufklärer*: "I believe ... that I will not have lived in vain if this work, under my direction, has helped to disseminate new and useful ideas in the sciences, diminish one-sided and shortsighted opinions, and spread a frank and honest manner of thinking, thereby contributing to the liberation of the human mind from the chains that hierarchy, excessive piety, arrogance, shortsighted ignorance, and proud imperiousness had otherwise placed upon it."³⁷ Jochen Schulte-Sasse has described Nicolai's primary aim as the creation of a public accustomed to a critical-rational style of argumentation. From

---

33. Nicolai to Zimmermann, Berlin, 13 August 1765, in Nicolai, *Verlegerbriefe*, pp. 34–35.
34. Nicolai, "Selbstbiographie," p. 26.
35. One such review was of J. J. Eschenburg's translation of Charles Burney's biography of Handel, *Nachricht von Georg Friedrich Händel's Lebensumständen und der ihm zu London im Mai und Jun. 1784 angestellten Gedächtnißfeyer*, published by Nicolai in 1785. *ADB* 81, no. 1 (1788): 295–303.
36. In an overcrowded *ADB*, letters were allocated less space than Nicolai had hoped. On the letters rubric, see Ost, *Friedrich Nicolais Allgemeine deutsche Bibliothek*, pp. 39–40.
37. Foreword to *ADB* 106, no. 2 (1792).

this, all else would follow: "He believed that the institutionalization and universal spread of critical and rational argumentation would help to dissolve the structures of political and intellectual domination."[38] The *ADB* was thus conceived as Nicolai's primary instrument in this process of progressive enlightenment.

The *ADB* was designed to be read and reread, not merely scanned for the latest news and discarded like the literary supplement of a newspaper. Accordingly, reviews in the *ADB* went not only beyond the recitation of content that often passed for book reviewing at the time but also beyond the book in question, to address larger issues of criticism, literary politics, religious tolerance, and censorship, to name only a few frequently discussed topics. This it had in common with other serious review journals of the time, foremost among them the abovementioned *Göttingische Gelehrte Anzeigen* (founded in 1739 and still published today),[39] with which there was some overlap of staff.[40] The reviewer of *Johann Bunkel*, for example, ended his critique of the novel with a plea for religious toleration and, at least implicitly, against imperial censorship. Asserting that the novel's eponymous hero was a good Christian, despite his controversial Unitarian opinions, he remarked that the book did not deserve to be banned by the imperial censors, "for it contributes not a little to the enlightenment of humanity ... and the reformation of true Christianity when frank and loud dissent against prevailing doctrines and opinions is permitted."[41]

Some of the long reviews, often in the form of review essays, swelled into short treatises (we recall the 600-page "review" of works on the

---

38. Schulte-Sasse, "Friedrich Nicolai," p. 327.

39. The Göttingen journal, which went through several titles, was published from 1753 on by the Societät der Wissenschaften and was the work of Göttingen professors. See Margrit Rollmann, "Der Gelehrte als Schriftsteller. Die Publikationen der Göttinger Professoren im 18. Jahrhundert" (Ph.D. diss, University of Göttingen, 1988). Another notable, less strictly academic journal of the time was the *Frankfurter Gelehrte Anzeigen* (1736–73). Although long undistinguished, the journal had a short golden age in 1772, when its contributors included the young Goethe as well as the *ADB* reviewers Johann Gottfried Herder, Johann Heinrich Merck, and Ludwig Julius Friedrich Höpfner. It was published by Deinet in Frankfurt am Main. On the checkered history of this journal, see Claus Jansen, "Frankfurter Gelehrten Anzeigen (1736–1790)," in *Deutsche Zeitschriften des 17. bis 20. Jahrhunderts*, ed. Heinz-Dietrich Fischer (Pullach: Verlag Dokumentation, 1973), pp. 61–73.

40. Notable among the shared staff of the *ADB* and the *Göttinger Gelehrten Anzeigen* was the renowned classicist Christian Gottlob Heyne, professor, university librarian, and later school inspector in Göttingen.

41. Review of *Johann Bunkel*, *ADB* Supplement (Anhang) to vols. 25–36, pt. 1 (1778): 670–71.

Prussian Edict Concerning Religion). While Nicolai pleaded with reviewers to be less prolix, he encouraged them to set their criticism within a broad context. He suggested to Eschenburg, for example, that he take the opportunity of a review of a new edition of Gellert's works, and of Jakob Mauvillon's highly critical book on Gellert, to discuss the delicate problem of how best to criticize a highly popular but overrated author. With convincing examples, clarity of exposition, and the requisite modesty Eschenburg could make it clear that his aim was not to demolish the reputation of a beloved (and recently deceased) writer, but rather to improve taste for the good and the beautiful.[42]

Nicolai endeavored with the *ADB* to educate both the reading public and writers and critics. Good criticism would, he thought, raise the standard of German prose, making it more intelligible and less pedantic, and thus better suited to reaching the public. Nicolai was concerned to counteract what he described as the cabals of friends whose ill-placed praise kept writers from advancing in their craft, as well as to mitigate the isolation of provincial scholars starved for the advice of like-minded souls. To create the desired effect, however, criticism had to be detailed and, as far as possible, impartial and impersonal. In a memorandum on the future *ADB* Nicolai explained to potential reviewers what he expected of them: "Your assessments must not be ... general and flattering, but rather thorough and candid.... A timorous account of the content is not the thing." On the other hand, he hoped to introduce a more civilized and rational style of interaction in the republic of letters. Enlightenment was also a way of behaving, an attitude toward other writers, which judged them on the basis of their works, not sentiments of sympathy or antipathy: "However frank your judgments may be, you will refrain from all personal attacks."[43]

To be sure, the ideal of criticism Nicolai propounded was to remain for many reviewers just that, an ideal. "If *all* authors ... were to judge a book not by content alone, but rather to consider its overall effect, if all were capable of gaining deep insights into the progress or deviations of knowledge among our nation," remarked Nicolai to his star reviewer Herder in 1768, "this journal would doubtless be far better." Failing this, one sometimes had to make do with "mediocre workers ... who understand

---

42. Nicolai to Eschenburg, Berlin, 16 October, 1772, in HAB, no. 21.
43. Nicolai, *Verlegerbriefe*, p. 28.

their own branch of learning and whose powers of judgment are not too poor."[44]

Criticism of the work rather than the author remained a basic tenet of the *ADB*. Nicolai announced that he had stopped giving certain books to Christian Adolf Klotz, for example, when it became clear that he was using the *ADB* as a platform for personal vendettas against other writers.[45] Klotz, an infamous feuder, was himself an editor of scholarly/literary journals in Halle. Nicolai also hesitated before accepting Johann Georg Meusel as a reviewer, because he doubted his capacity for impartiality. He feared that "a man who is so provincially sensitive to praise and criticism and who is also connected ... to so many dubious people, and obviously praises them too highly out of friendship, cannot possibly be impartial, and this is the first thing I demand of a collaborator on the Bibl[iothek]."[46] That at least some reviewers took very seriously Nicolai's injunction to exercise impartiality is demonstrated by requests that Nicolai give particular books to other reviewers. Valentin August Heinze, for example, told Nicolai to find someone else to review the works of fellow Kiel historian Dietrich Hermann Hegewisch, with whom he was involved in a scholarly dispute. His opponent had recently abandoned all boundaries of "morality and moderation," and he felt unable to judge him dispassionately.[47] Even with such good intentions, however, it was difficult to keep peace on the *ADB* staff, let alone in the republic of letters. Nicolai speaks in a letter to his friend Uz of the "strangest collisions" and the difficulties of keeping on good terms with seventy or eighty reviewers, who often unwittingly criticized the work of their fellow *ADB* contributors.[48]

Several friends assisted Nicolai in the running of the *ADB*, which he kept organizationally separate from the rest of his business in order to avoid confusion. For a yearly fee of 40 (later 60) taler, the Berlin pastor Friedrich Germanus Lüdke maintained records on reviews and attended

---

44. Nicolai to Herder, Berlin, 24 December 1768, in Nicolai, *Verlegerbriefe*, p. 62. Ute Schneider examines the issue of how reviewers measured up to these standards in *Friedrich Nicolais Allgemeine Deutsche Bibliothek als Integrationsmedium*, esp. pp. 296ff.

45. Foreword, to *ADB* 8, no. 2 (1769).

46. Nicolai to Johannes von Müller, 16 March 1773, in Nicolai, *Verlegerbriefe*, p. 98. Meusel did eventually work for the *ADB*. One of the "dubious people" was Friedrich Eberhard Boysen, who threatened Nicolai after a negative review of his work in the *ADB*. Boysen to Nicolai, Quedlinburg, 16 September 1771, in NN 8.

47. Heinze to Nicolai, Kiel, 5 July 1786, in NN 31.

48. Nicolai to Uz, 26 June 1771, in NN 76.

to much day-to-day correspondence until his death in 1792.[49] Nicolai also engaged Ludwig Julius Friedrich Höpfner in Darmstadt as special editor for jurisprudence in 1774. He recommended (and offered to pay for) a secretary to keep an alphabetical register of reviews to be updated at every book fair: "My employees are too busy, I do not even entrust them with the books and papers connected with the Bibl., and I cannot burden the scholar [Lüdke] who helps me with the correspondence for the Bibl[iothek], and who does the bookkeeping, with it either."[50] Höpfner received a fee of 6 carolins, including postage and minor expenses, for his work.[51] The index and short notes on developments in the republic of letters (deaths, appointments, and so on) were compiled in the early 1770s by Georg Christoph Hamberger and then by Dr. F.W.H. Martini, a Berlin physician upon whose death in 1778 Pastor Raymund Dapp took over the index and Johann Georg Meusel the collection of career notes.[52] Albrecht Georg Walch in Schleusingen read proof and arranged for the printing of the journal for a fee of 10 taler per issue.[53]

To save time, Nicolai communicated several times a year with his *ADB* staff through printed circulars. These, along with his personal correspondence with many reviewers, served multiple functions. The circulars were pedagogical devices as well as simple communications of information and requests for favors. With their help he sought to assemble a stable of reviewers who would, ideally, practice their craft of thorough and detailed critique without either dull recitations of content or the personal attacks that plagued the book reviews of the day, and without arousing the ire of the censors. He gave them general instructions and guidelines that may now seem self-evident, but apparently were not when book reviewing was in its infancy. Reviews should meet scholarly standards. When quoting, for example, reviewers should always use quotation marks, and where paraphrasing make clear which statements and comments were their own and which the author's.[54] Nicolai's attention to material details extended to training reviewers to be orderly and methodical in keeping records and deadlines, and considerate of the poor typesetters who had to read their scrawls. In his circular of 8 November 1786, for example,

---

49. Receipts of 3 January 1770, 9 January 1784, and 20 November 1789, in NN 46.
50. Nicolai to Höpfner, Berlin, 26 July 1774, in Nicolai, *Verlegerbriefe*, pp. 103–4.
51. Nicolai to Höpfner, Berlin, 23 April 1776, in *Briefe aus dem Freundeskreis*, p. 139.
52. Ost, *Friedrich Nicolais Allgemeine Deutsche Bibliothek*, pp. 33–34.
53. Walch to Nicolai, Schleusingen, 12 April 1783, in NN 79.
54. This instruction in the circular of 12 December 1776 was repeated in that of 8 November 1786. In NN 1 [Abendroth correspondence].

Nicolai gave reviewers tips on how to read, how to get their reviews done on time, and how not to misplace books (especially easy since the works were frequently sent unbound). He also begged them—not for the first or last time—to write more legibly.[55] Providing a clean manuscript under time pressure was no easy feat in the eighteenth century, especially where good copyists were scarce. Reviewer Johann Jakob Ferber in Mitau (now in Latvia), for example, reported on the problems of finding someone to copy his reviews legibly.[56]

Nicolai's crusade to make German authors more aware of and responsible to their audience was a frequent theme in his admonitions to reviewers. In order to make the reader an active participant in the critical process, it was essential that reviews be so presented that they were comprehensible without consulting the book in question. Thus reviewers should quote the passages to which they referred, or at least explain their content.[57] They should also be more aware of the *nature* of their audience. "Do consider that the *ADB* is read by a few thousand readers of all types," Nicolai reminded Johannes von Müller. Not all readers were ready for some of Müller's satirical remarks about religious matters: "You often say things for which the noble few, but not, alas, the as yet unenlightened public, are properly prepared."[58] He also admonished Müller that his style would be more pleasant to read if he replaced the many French words he used with German ones of equal force and appropriateness.[59]

Beyond general guidelines, how meddlesome was Nicolai when it came to dictating to his contributors? The truth lies somewhere between the two extremes of his assertions that he rarely saw reviews before printing and thus had nothing to do with their contents, and some opponents' contentions that he wielded an iron hand and printed only those critiques which reflected his own opinions and prejudices. As was common practice at the time, all reviewers in the *ADB* were anonymous, so that

---

55. Copy of the circular in NN 1 [Abendroth correspondence].

56. Ferber to Nicolai, Mitau, 25 September 1777, in Johann Jakob Ferber, *Briefe an Friedrich Nicolai aus Mitau und St. Petersburg*, ed. Heinz Ischreyt, Nordost-Archiv, no. 7 (Herford: Nicolai, 1974), p. 32.

57. Circular of 12 December 1776, printed in Nicolai, *Verlegerbriefe*, pp. 113–14. See also Nicolai's complaints to Eschenburg on this subject. Nicolai to Eschenburg, 16 October 1772, in HAB, no. 21.

58. This may be an ironic reference to the orthodox Lutheran theologians who fumed at the *ADB*'s alleged irreligiosity.

59. Nicolai to Müller, Berlin, 11 October 1772, in Nicolai, *Verlegerbriefe*, pp. 87–93.

Nicolai as publisher and editor was, *de facto*, solely responsible for the journal's content. In reality, the reviewers had more control over which books were actually reviewed, and when, than did Nicolai himself. Each reviewer received a certain number of books chosen by Nicolai from the Leipzig fair catalog for review after each book fair, and they fulfilled their promises or not as time and whim allowed. Reviewers also suggested books to review of their own accord, and reviews were occasionally submitted by non-*ADB* contributors.[60] Sometimes Nicolai requested that a particular book be reviewed promptly; in 1785, for example, he sent Eschenburg a work by the Viennese poet Johann Baptist Alxinger "with the request that you review it soon and in some detail. This young poet well deserves it; he has exceeded my expectations."[61]

Nicolai also occasionally reviewed books himself. In the early years, reflecting his interests and experience in his previous journals, he wrote numerous short reviews, mainly in belles-lettres. Later he focused largely on engravings, history, and trade, but reviewed less frequently.[62] Despite remarks that he had given up writing for the *ADB* altogether in 1770,[63] he continued to stand in for negligent reviewers when necessary. Comparing himself to Hercules cleaning the Augean stables, he complained in 1775 that he had had to write some 150 reviews "for which I could find no reviewer."[64] In 1791 he even found himself reviewing some twenty works on jurisprudence that had been allocated to others years before.[65] Decisions about which reviews went into a particular issue (and thus about how quickly reviews appeared), however, were apparently often made by

60. Mieg, for example, submitted reviews by friends on two occasions. Mieg to Nicolai, Heidelberg, 19 April 1790 and 12 November 1791, in NN 50.

61. Nicolai to Eschenburg, Berlin, 24 March 1785, in HAB, no. 56. See also a letter of 21 January 1788 to Freiherr Adolph von Knigge, asking him to send in a review of Heinrich Gottfried von Bretschneider's *Heiligen-Kalendar* within two weeks and offering specific instructions. He should go into detail, quote some passages he liked, and hint that the illustrations resembled those by the Berlin engraver Meil (who had actually done them), without giving away that the work was published in Berlin. In Bayerische Staatsbibliothek Munich, Autographen. I thank Mark Lehmstedt for providing a copy of this letter.

62. Ost, *Friedrich Nicolais Allgemeine Deutsche Bibliothek*, pp. 84–85.

63. See Nicolai's letters of 20 June and 15 August 1770 to his Vienna correspondent Michael Denis, in Denis, *Literarischer Nachlaß*, pp. 158 and 162. A few months later Nicolai told Salomon Gessner that he had given up writing reviews "some time ago." Nicolai to Gessner, Berlin, November 1770, in NN 86.

64. Nicolai to Merck, Berlin, 8 December 1775, quoted in Ost, *Friedrich Nicolais Allgemeine Deutsche Bibliothek*, p. 85.

65. He remarked in a circular of 2 July 1791 that these reviews for Supplement 5, covering the years up to 1787 had cost him one day! Ost, *Friedrich Nicolais Allgemeine Deutsche Bibliothek*, p. 85n.

the printer or proofreader who was instructed merely to include a mixture of reviews from different fields.[66]

Nicolai did attempt to exercise a measure of control in several ways, the first being, of course, his choice of reviewers. From the beginning, Nicolai relied on recommendations from friends and correspondents. Only a few of his friends and earlier collaborators contributed to the new journal, notably Friedrich Gabriel Resewitz, Friedrich Germanus Lüdke, Wilhelm Abraham Teller, J. F. Agricola, and very occasionally, Moses Mendelssohn. Thomas Abbt, for whom Nicolai had had great hopes, died in 1766, and others, such as Lessing, C. F. Weiße, and Christian Ludwig von Hagedorn, had no time to give the new journal. While some reviewers were well known enough to be accepted solely on the basis of their reputations, most were either suggested to Nicolai or wrote to him at the urging of friends. Those rare reviewers who offered themselves unsolicited, however, tended to establish their credentials either by mentioning *ADB* reviewers or Nicolai's friends,[67] or emphasizing the congruency of their own principles with the journal's. One who did both was a certain Major von Wurmb,[68] who emphasized his acquaintanceship with Nicolai's close friend Elisa von der Recke and reviewers L.F.G. von Goeckingk and Gottfried Erich Rosenthal when he asked to join the *ADB* staff in 1789.[69] His description of himself was that of a man in every way after Nicolai's own heart:

> For many years I have been a devoted reader of those writings through which you seek so nobly to promote enlightenment in our German homeland, working so manfully and gloriously to combat fanaticism and prejudices of all kinds. I am, to be sure, no scholar by profession, and

---

66. Nicolai to Herder, Berlin, 24 December 1768, in Nicolai, *Verlegerbriefe*, p. 61.

67. Helmstedt chemist and professor of medicine Lorenz Crell seems to have been unusual in offering his services without mentioning that someone else had suggested he do so. He wrote to Nicolai on 13 November 1777 and was so quickly accepted that he could send in eleven reviews by 16 January 1778 (in NN 13). More common was the approach of Christian Gottfried Gruner, who mentioned that his friend Wilhelm Heinrich Bucholz in Weimar already worked for the journal when he asked to become a reviewer in 1777. Gruner to Nicolai, Jena, 4 July 1777, in NN 28. Bucholz, who covered the fields of chemistry and pharmacy, had himself been recommended by Johann Karl August Musäus, who reviewed novels, in 1770. Bucholz to Nicolai, 30 October 1770, in NN 11. Similarly, Freiherr von Knigge said that his friend, the *ADB* reviewer Hofrat Georg Ernst von Rüling in Hannover, had recommended that he offer his services to Nicolai as a reviewer of belles-lettres. Knigge to Nicolai, Hanau, 10 April 1779, in NN 41.

68. Perhaps this was Kaspar Georg Karl von Wurmb.

69. Rosenthal himself was recommended as a reviewer by Goeckingk. See Rosenthal to Nicolai, Nordhausen, 10 January 1787, in NN 64.

little known in the republic of letters. I believe nevertheless that after so many years of acquaintance with the sciences, right thinking, pure devotion to the good and the beautiful and a complete abhorrence of anything that smacks of fanaticism [*Schwärmerei*] or the mania for genius, I have been able to attain very useful knowledge conducive to the common good.[70]

With these credentials he became a reviewer soon afterward.

Occasionally, Nicolai used his circulars to call for new reviewers, asking the *ADB* staff to recommend "men whose ... skill and impartiality" they had tested themselves."[71] Many reviewers answered the call, recommending local acquaintances in particular, and not necessarily those in their own fields.[72] The jurist and garden theorist E.C.L. Hirschfeld endorsed Kiel historian Valentin August Heinze.[73] The influential Göttingen professors Christian Gottlob Heyne, Abraham Gotthelf Kästner, and August Ludwig Schlözer were particularly successful in drumming up new "Bibliothekare," as *ADB* reviewers were often called. These in turn suggested their own acquaintances as contributors to the journal. Johann Joachim Eschenburg, one of Heyne's recruits, himself recommended Johann Christian Sommer, professor of midwifery in Braunschweig, and the historian Christoph Schmidt-Phiseldeck in nearby Wolfenbüttel.[74] Another Heyne suggestion, Gotha school rector and reviewer of Greek philology, New Testament exegesis, and church history F. A. Stroth, suggested two local acquaintances, the merchant Dürfeld and the army officer von Helmold, as reviewers for, respectively, trade and finance, and agriculture.[75] Where a potential reviewer was not known to Nicolai

---

70. Rosenthal to Nicolai, Nordhausen, 27 October 1789, in NN 83.

71. Circular of June 1786, in HAB, no. 64.

72. Ost remarks that "recruitment for the *ADB* was largely conducted on a local level. A jurist might recommend a neighboring physician, etc. This in itself prevented fields from being taken over by entire cliques." *Friedrich Nicolais Allgemeine Deutsche Bibliothek*, p. 59.

73. Hirschfeld to Nicolai, Kiel, 13 May 1784, in NN 35. Heinze later recruited at least two reviewers, A. C. Gaspari of Hamburg for history and cameral science (Heinze to Nicolai, Kiel, 13 September 1786, in NN 31) and Consistorial Councillor Böttiger, his father's successor in Weimar, for editions of classical literature and philology, among other fields. Of the latter man he remarked to Nicolai, "He has a splendid mind." Hirschfeld to Nicolai, Kiel, 5 February 1792, in NN 31.

74. Eschenburg to Nicolai, Braunschweig, 16 September 1774 and 26 October 1776, in NN 19.

75. Stroth to Nicolai, Gotha, 8 May 1782, in NN 73. On the role of these Göttingen professors in the *ADB*, see Ost, *Friedrich Nicolais Allgemeine Deutsche Bibliothek*, p. 60, where he notes some of the direct and indirect connections between Heyne, Kästner, and Schlözer and numerous *ADB* reviewers.

through his writings or recommended by someone whose judgment he trusted absolutely, he requested sample reviews.[76] Particularly in those fields, such as medicine, where he could not judge for himself, he asked the advice of those more knowledgeable.[77]

Once they met his general standards, Nicolai seems to have required a genuine "party line" of *ADB* reviewers in only two, albeit very significant, areas, Catholic books and critical philosophy. In other fields he was willing to tolerate a variety of opinion. On the Catholic issue Nicolai remained adamant. The accusations (often justified) of arrogance, intolerance, and an obsession with Jesuits, which assailed him in the 1780s and 1790s, could not sway him, and he knew that he had many allies in this. A letter to a longtime collaborator, Walch in Schleusingen, who had offered to review new books coming from Würzburg, states unequivocally his attitude toward Catholics and the *ADB*'s role in their (re)education. In the *ADB*, he reminded Walch "we must view matters from a Protestant rather than a Catholic perspective." When reviewing Catholic books, one had to take into account that "considering the incredible stupidity that still prevails among Catholics, some things may be of some value to them which we, who have been cleverer for two hundred years, might consider very trivial indeed." While praising the good in such books, it was nevertheless imperative to note with care and criticize "the contradictions one finds in them ... and the horrible prejudices and errors which still prevail among all Catholic authors." If the *ADB* neglected this duty, Catholic writers might begin to imagine "they were who knows what." Even the most apparently enlightened Catholic scholars, who ingratiated themselves with Protestant colleagues through polite correspondence, persisted in writing large quantities of "nonsensical stuff," he argued. Protestants must remain vigilant lest the devious papists try to reestablish their reign of superstition and hierarchy. Michael Ignatz Schmidt in Vienna, "one of the most enlightened," had had the temerity in his history of the Germans to judge the Reformation in a most irresponsible manner, ignoring altogether its benefits for the human race. "This is unforgivable," remarked Nicolai, "and we Protestants must contradict such things, so that prejudices are not once again introduced in place of the truth."[78]

76. Nicolai to Höpfner, Berlin, 12 October 1776, in *Briefe aus dem Freundeskreis*, p. 141.

77. See his notes for an answer to a letter from "D.D." in Frankfurt am Main, received 19 February 1774, in NN 2.

78. Excerpts from a letter of 12 November 1785 in copyist hand, in NN 79 [Walch correspondence]. Walch answered on 27 November 1785: "Your reminders regarding the reviews of

Nicolai's attitude toward critical philosophy was very similar, indeed related, to his attitude toward Catholicism. A reply he wrote to a would-be philosophy reviewer in 1800 points this up nicely. Nicolai explained to Johann Baptist Schad, a former Benedictine monk who worked for the *ADB*'s arch-rival among the review journals, the Jena *Allgemeine Literatur-Zeitung* (*ALZ*), that he could not take him on as a philosophy reviewer because he was a follower of the "new" philosophy, which he found similar to Catholicism in its posture of infallibility.[79] As Nicolai's clearest statement on the ideological criteria he used in choosing *ADB* reviewers, the letter is worth quoting in detail. The *ADB* philosophy reviewers, he informed Schad,

> are devoted to a philosophy diametrically opposed to yours. Although in any good journal each reviewer is entitled to his private opinion, there is nevertheless a tendency to maintain a certain general spirit of opinion and to take it into consideration when choosing reviewers. Far be it from me to use the *ADB* to reproduce my own philosophical opinions, but I will always take serious care to ensure that the *ADB* supports the right of anyone to philosophize according to his own lights and the right of common sense not to be excluded from philosophy. All philosophical members of the *Bibliothek* have always shared this sentiment. For that reason, the *ADB* has always maintained a wise opposition to the despotism that the new and newest philosophy has sought to introduce, thus doing a greater service to the love of truth than it would have done by parroting the new or newest system, which will be displaced tomorrow by the latest system.

Nicolai extended the concept of the priesthood of all believers to the realm of philosophical inquiry: "I and all philosophical reviewers up until

---

Catholic books are well founded, and I will follow them, since in everything that I write for the A. d. B. my sole purpose is impartiality and truth." In NN 79. Schmidt's twelve-volume *Geschichte der Teutschen* was published in Ulm, 1778–97.

79. It is interesting that Schad bothered to offer his services at all. He had published three relevant works that year, *Geist der Philosophie unserer Zeit*, *Grundriß der Wissenschaftslehre*, and a study of Fichte and religion. He was also the author of "Ueber die Wichtigkeit des Studiums der kritischen Philosophie" in the *Magazin für Katholiken* (Coburg, 1796–98). One *ADB* reviewer, Karl Leonhard Reinhold, philosopher and professor in Jena and Kiel, was a follower of Kant, and it may have been for this reason that he left the journal. He was also coeditor with Wieland of the *Teutsche Merkur* from 1785 and worked for the *ALZ* from 1787, reviewing several of Kant's major works. *Die Mitarbeiter an Friedrich Nicolais Allgemeine Deutsche Bibliothek* (Berlin: Nicolai, 1842), a list of contributors compiled by Nicolai's grandson Gustav Parthey, indicates that Reinhold reviewed philosophy, literature, and Catholic books for the *ADB* well into the 1790s (pp. 22–23). Reinhold, who like Schad had fled a monastery, also wrote a defense of the Reformation against the Catholic Michael Ignaz Schmidt's *Geschichte der Teutschen* (1778).

now have treated philosophy as Protestants. We defend the rights of our own insight and thus oppose any philosophy that claims to be the only one." Immanuel Kant, he believed, had made just such a claim, and it was the duty of any lover of truth to take every available opportunity to show the absurdity of such an attitude, which was the opposite of true philosophical thinking. "Please do not take offense at my candor when I say that transcendental Idealism behaves just like the Catholic hierarchy: it seeks to be infallible" and opposes attempts to investigate its underlying premises.[80] Thus Nicolai did not consider adherence to the philosophy of Kant's followers to be a mere opinion, of which several could coexist on the *ADB* staff. For him, it was a whole attitude toward knowledge, reason, and truth that he considered antithetical to true philosophical inquiry, just as he considered Catholicism inherently antithetical to freedom of thought.[81]

In those areas outside his chief obsessions, Nicolai exhibited a willingness to accept opinions diverging from his own that contradicts the image his detractors painted of a literary dictator. For example, he printed Friedrich Arnold Klockenbring's skeptical review of Christoph Wilhelm Dohm's *Über die bürgerliche Verbesserung der Juden*, a product of his own publishing house.[82] In a letter to Isaak Iselin, Nicolai praised a review although he disagreed with his friend's position on the subject. What counted, he said, was that people had the opportunity to read "good and humanitarian principles."[83] In the literary field, where Nicolai is usually depicted as particularly philistine and dictatorial, rejecting anything new, fanciful, or imaginative, he took some pains, at least until the mid-1770s, to have opinions other than his own expressed in the *ADB*. In a letter to Graf von Borcke regarding a review of Wieland's *Amadis*, he admitted that he sometimes mistrusted his own judgment in works of the imagination, and knew that other people might have quite different reactions to Wieland. "The reviewer ... may praise the fantasy of Amadis without reserve if he sees fit."[84]

---

80. Nicolai to Schad, Berlin, 25 October 1800, in NN 65 [Schad correspondence].
81. His attitude to the more conservative Protestant theologians was somewhat more lenient, however much he may have criticized them in *Sebaldus Nothanker* and other writings. On the possible reviewer Zimmermann he told Höpfner, "The fact that Herr Z. is an orthodox theologian is of no consequence, for I love the orthodox so long as they are sensible people." Nicolai to Höpfner, 12 October 1776, in *Briefe aus dem Freundeskreis*, p. 142.
82. This example is cited in Geiger, "Aus den Briefen Dohms an Nicolai," p. 83.
83. Nicolai to Iselin, Berlin, 12 June 1772, in NN 86.
84. Nicolai to Borcke, Berlin, 19 June 1771, in NN 7.

He explained to Herder that a certain inclination toward "raisonnement" perhaps made him less susceptible than other people to the beauties of poetry. Thus Herder should not worry about Nicolai's own opinion in his review of Klopstock's works: "For I swear by God that I do not wish to use the Bibl. to reproduce my own opinions. Perhaps someone else, analyzing the matter in his own way, will come closer to the truth.... Furthermore, when I have something to criticize in the works of an otherwise famous man I vastly prefer for someone with a different opinion to review it, in order to avoid any appearance that I wish to damage anyone's reputation."[85] Whether Nicolai really believed that his "tendency toward *raisonnement*" was a handicap in judging poetry or not, he was willing to admit this as a possible shortcoming before which he was prepared to bow to the judgment of others with more developed sensibilities. For practical reasons he was also concerned that the *ADB* not seem to be too partisan in his favor.

Nevertheless, Nicolai did restrict reviewers' liberties when it seemed advisable or necessary, whether for political or literary-political reasons. This intervention could take the form of preventative general advice and guidelines in the printed circulars or specific criticisms and/or revisions of reviewers' manuscripts. On several occasions he used the circular to ask reviewers to exercise caution during politically sensitive times. During the War of the Bavarian Succession, he requested that they avoid statements that might offend any German government, following the principle that reviewers should tell the truth, but avoid strong language.[86] Thus Nicolai approved of Joachim Heinrich Campe's discretion in a review of books on Bavarian school reforms, about which the critic noted "I have considered it my duty to speak only positively of the Bavarian school reforms and to pass tacitly over their failings. Here and there, however, I have given a little hint, which may perhaps be understood and used."[87] When Prussian censorship heated up in 1791, Nicolai again asked reviewers to exercise reticence in theological-political matters affecting Prussia, reminding them that they were free to state their true opinions—cautiously.[88]

85. Nicolai to Herder, Berlin, 24 August 1772, in Nicolai, *Verlegerbriefe*, p. 82.
86. Circular of 10 November 1778, during the War of the Bavarian Succession, in NN 86 [Iselin correspondence]. He had made similar requests in his circulars of 10 April and 20 June 1778, in HAB, no. 34.
87. Campe to Nicolai, Hamburg, 4 April 1779, in NN 12. Nicolai scribbled "Correct!" in the margin.
88. Circular of 2 July 1791, in HAB, no. 116.

In general, Nicolai encouraged reviewers to abstain from careless language, not merely to appease the censors, but also to keep peace in the republic of letters. On more than one occasion he asked them to avoid slurs against the publishers of books under review, however accurate. Insulting remarks about the Leipzig bookseller Hilscher and his authors in volume 31 of the journal, he noted, had caused him "bitter trouble" and had naturally been attributed to him.[89]

Much as he admired a lively style, Nicolai appealed to Johannes von Müller not to carry the good thing of his fiery prose too far. Particularly in theological reviews the reviewer should aim to criticize while appearing as near to orthodoxy as possible.[90] Müller would only hurt his own career chances in Prussia by alienating the reformist theologians with his brash approach.[91] Nicolai suggested revisions by means of which Müller could make the same basic points, sweetened with the "calm tone of investigation rather than the loud tone of declamation" and a conciliatory introduction. He should avoid ridicule at all costs.[92]

The case of Johannes von Müller was not an isolated one and shows that Nicolai's claims to be the mere "docile publisher" of the *ADB*, who simply printed reviews as he received them[93] (or didn't receive them, because they were frequently sent directly to the printer) cannot be

---

89. The remarks were in *ADB* 31, no. 1 (1777): 126. Circular of 6 November 1777. He repeated the request in the circular of 8 November 1786, both in NN 86 [Iselin correspondence].

90. Nicolai to Müller, Berlin, 11 October 1772, in Nicolai, *Verlegerbriefe*, p. 89.

91. "The good new theologians," explained Nicolai, "are instigating a secret conspiracy against the despotism of dogmatism, and thus do not wish to admit even the best combatant to their party once they notice that he tends to seek by swordplay what they wish to attain by silent machinations." The proof of this axiom had come when, at Müller's express request, and against his own better judgment, Nicolai had shown an unpublished review of *Ein Lehrer des Naturalismus, der schädlichste Mann für Kirche und Regenten* (A Teacher of Natural Religion, the Most Harmful Man for Church and Rulers, Jena, 1772) to the prominent Berlin theologian August Friedrich Wilhelm Sack, who proceeded to discuss it with colleagues, provoking violent reactions.

92. Nicolai's letter of 11 October 1772 to Johannes von Müller, in Nicolai, *Verlegerbriefe*, pp. 87–93. Similarly, he advised Johann Joachim Eschenburg to make life easier for himself and the *ADB* by rewriting a review of Jakob Mauvillon's book on Gellert and incorporating it into a review of a new edition of Gellert's works. He feared that the review, particularly its epistolary form, "could take us too far. If we were dealing with a half-way sensible man I would accept the confidential tone, but with such an impertinent would-be wit as Mauvillon it is important to avoid him answering us in a similar tone and causing us endless trouble." Nicolai to Eschenburg, Berlin, 16 October 1772, in HAB, no. 21. Eschenburg accepted Nicolai's advice to wait with the Mauvillon review until Gellert's works appeared. Nicolai to Eschenburg, Berlin, 23 November 1772, in HAB, no. 22.

93. Nicolai to Denis, Berlin, 15 August 1770, in Denis, *Literarischer Nachlaß*, p. 162.

credited. Although he certainly did not edit or even read most of the reviews he published (much as this might have been his duty as an editor), he took some care with those reviews which fell in his chief areas of interest, or which he considered particularly important. As he informed Iselin in Basel in 1769, he had made some additions to a review of Wieland's novel *Idris* in which he touched "only quite gently" on the author's "unfortunate penchant for lascivious description." Those secure in their virtue might read such works without ill effect, but others could be harmed.[94] Five years later, he made some alterations to one of Iselin's own reviews. The *ADB* might, he said, exert little influence over the Prussian government, but that was no reason to play deliberately into its hands by questioning English liberty, thereby reinforcing the idea held by some monarchs and ministers that it was a mere chimera. Writers, he asserted, should always bravely defend liberties in other countries.[95]

Thus Nicolai sometimes altered or augmented reviews of his own accord, without prior discussion with the author. Johann Heinrich Campe remarked that Nicolai, whom he had authorized to do so, had occasionally made additions to his reviews of Lavater's works that further magnified his own negative assessments.[96] Nicolai also authorized editorial assistant Lüdke and proofreaders Walch and Johann Matthias Schröckh to make changes where necessary.[97] Although these were usually purely formal or stylistic, Schröckh, who was also censor of the *ADB* when it was printed in Wittenberg, recommended substantive alterations on several occasions, usually to avoid political difficulties for the journal or himself. The politics of the republic of letters, however, could be of equal weight. In 1785, Walch asked Nicolai to change a line in a review of Christian Gottfried Schütz's *Literary Promenades*, which remarked that there were not many flowers to pluck along the way. Schütz was the editor of the *ADB*'s new rival, the *Allgemeine Literatur-Zeitung*, and as Walch remarked, "I would not like ... to provoke him to bitterness against the A.d.B."[98]

Some reviewers welcomed these interventions, giving Nicolai carte blanche to revise as he saw fit or even actively seeking his guidance in

94. Nicolai to Iselin, Leipzig, 1769 Michaelmas fair, in NN 86 [Iselin correspondence].
95. Nicolai to Iselin, Berlin, 18 October 1774, in NN 86. He said that he hoped Iselin would not be dissatisfied with the changes.
96. Campe to Nicolai, 27 October 1788, quoted in Ost, *Friedrich Nicolais Allgemeine Deutsche Bibliothek*, p. 37n.
97. Ost, *Friedrich Nicolais Allgemeine Deutsche Bibliothek*, pp. 37–38.
98. Walch to Nicolai, Schleusingen, 18 April 1785, in NN 79.

composing their reviews.⁹⁹ One such reviewer was Johann Karl August Musäus. Upon sending Nicolai a batch of reviews in 1778, he wrote: "I present my recruits to you for inspection. Should you find a cripple among them ... I authorize you to remove the unfit ... or at least to tidy up his hair or beard."¹⁰⁰ Another, Johann Nikolaus Bischoff in Braunschweig, who had received a book to review that contained "crude attacks on the *A.d.B.*" was anxious for help in selecting the right tone for his critique.¹⁰¹

Not all reviewers took kindly to Nicolai meddling with their work, however, particularly when the changes were substantive.¹⁰² It seems that in later years Nicolai became more cavalier in his attitude to negotiating changes with reviewers, and in 1786 the Berlin Reformed theologian Johann Georg Gebhard, whom he could easily have consulted personally, complained that for some time not one of his reviews had been printed as he had written it.¹⁰³ When given the chance, some reviewers preferred to withdraw their reviews rather than submit to alterations.¹⁰⁴

The ADB and the Establishment of Nicolai's Reputation and Business

The *ADB* made Nicolai known as both a critic and publisher all over German-speaking Europe, and not only to those contemporaries who followed the kind of literary and aesthetic criticism the *Bibliothek der schönen Wissenschaften* and the *Litteraturbriefe* had offered. Friedrich Nicolai became a household word, at least among those German-speaking households with any pretense toward the intellectual. Even more than

---

99. According to Günther Ost, most reviewers authorized Nicolai, apparently at his own request, to edit their work as long as he did not change the central arguments. As one reviewer, the young jurist Carl Heinrich Geißler, put it in 1769, he could "take fire and sword to them" as he saw fit. Ost, *Friedrich Nicolais Allgemeine Deutsche Bibliothek*, p. 36.

100. Musäus to Nicolai, Weimar, 16 March 1778, printed in Carvill, *Der verführte Leser*, pp. 288–90.

101. Bischoff to Nicolai, Braunschweig, 17 December 1786, in NN 5. The book in question was titled *Litterarische Reisen durch Deutschland*.

102. As we have seen, Campe gave Nicolai the right to edit his reviews, but, as Nicolai remarked in a marginal note to Campe's letter of 27 October 1788, not every reviewer did so.

103. Gebhard to Nicolai, Berlin, 27 February 1786, cited by Ost, *Friedrich Nicolais Allgemeine Deutsche Bibliothek*, p. 37.

104. When Nicolai found Carl Friedrich Pockels's review of Vieweg's *Taschenbuch* too positive, Pockels asked him to return it and give the book to someone else. He defended in detail both his own judgment of the work in question and the genre to which it belonged, and said that he did not like the idea of someone else tinkering with his review. Braunschweig, 19 December 1801, in NN 58.

his earlier journals, the *ADB* gained Nicolai friends, allies, authors, and customers as well as enemies. Most of Nicolai's more than 2500 correspondents ended up referring to the *ADB* in one way or another. They submitted books for review, portraits for the frontispiece, recommended reviewers, apologized for late contributions, thanked Nicolai for positive reviews, or attacked him or his staff for negative critiques. Where the earlier journals had established him and his collaborators as "armed critics" before whom budding belletrists trembled,[105] the *ADB* was to widen the scope into a platform for Nicolai's concept of enlightened criticism in the service of scholarship and humanity. Heinrich Christian Boie, himself the editor of two important journals, the *Deutsches Museum* and the *Göttinger Musenalmanach*, called the *ADB* one of the most patriotic enterprises he knew.[106] It was an encyclopedic project for an age in love with encyclopedias. In fact, the nineteenth-century historian Friedrich Christoph Schlosser compared the project to that of the *encyclopédistes*.[107] A "universal library" to accompany all the universal histories, from agriculture to zoology nothing was foreign to the *ADB*. Those of more systematic inclinations, like Herder, feared that "in this way one creates imperfect polyhistors, but not men with a universal knowledge of literature."[108] The very broadness of the *ADB* was also its appeal, however, in an age when a rapid proliferation of literature began to frustrate the educated public's desire to keep abreast of developments in many branches of learning.

The principle of complete coverage of new German books had to be abandoned early on, however. Thus some works were reviewed sooner, some later, and some not at all.[109] This rather obvious fact caused a great deal of bad blood at the time. Passed-over authors assumed a deliberate snub, and those who felt unfairly criticized frequently attributed the

---

105. Schubart to Böckh, 1 June 1768, in Schubart, *Briefe*, p. 85.
106. Boie to Nicolai, Göttingen, 14 November 1773, in NN 7.
107. Friedrich Christoph Schlosser, *Geschichte des achtzehnten Jahrhunderts und des neunzehnten bis zum Sturz des französischen Kaiserreichs. Mit besonderer Rücksicht auf geistige Bildung*, vol. 2, 2d ed. (Heidelberg: J.C.B. Mohr, 1837), p. 590. In an article on the Berlin Enlightenment, Ursula Goldenbaum also speaks of the *ADB* as in "a certain sense ... the German counterpart to the French 'Encyclopédie.'" Ursula Goldenbaum, "Der 'Berolinismus': Die preußische Hauptstadt als ein Zentrum geistiger Kommunikation in Deutschland," in *Aufklärung in Berlin*, ed. Wolfgang Förster (Berlin: Akademie-Verlag, 1989), p. 350.
108. Johann Gottfried Herder, "Ueber die deutsche Literatur. Erste Sammlung von Fragmenten. Eine Beilage zu den Briefen, die neueste Literatur betreffend" (1767), in *Sämmtliche Werke*, ed. Bernhard Suphan, 33 vols. (Berlin: Weidmann, 1877–1913), 1:143.
109. Some reviewers apparently also cribbed critiques from other journals when they could not get their hands on the books in time! See Schneider, *Friedrich Nicolais Allgemeine Deutsche Bibliothek als Integrationsmedium*, esp. p. 292.

reviewer's opinions to Nicolai himself. Nicolai thus attained a powerful but much-assailed position in the German republic of letters, and the *ADB* became the journal writers loved to hate. In a way Nicolai had not quite anticipated, the *ADB* (and he with it) became a focal point not only for information and debate but also for bitter feuds, enlivening the landscape of the republic of letters. In 1788, the Comte de Mirabeau remarked of the *ADB* that "this immense collection of criticism produced the healthiest revolution in German literature. It had a crowd of detractors, and this too was a great advantage."[110] In the 1820s, F. C. Schlosser, whose sympathies lay entirely with Nicolai's adversaries, also emphasized the *ADB*'s (unintended but healthy) effect of stimulating lively opposition to the "often crude liberalism ... and critical despotism of the Berliners' oracle-like pronouncements"—and thus new thinking, "among the most original minds in every corner of Germany."[111]

While many critics of the *ADB* objected to the general tone of the journal, others disliked specific rubrics. Abbé Carlo Denina, a member of the Berlin Academy of Sciences, noted in his work on literary life in Prussia that some found the *ADB* "a bit too theological or anti-theological."[112] The young authors of the biographical *Büsten Berliner Gelehrten* thought the reviewers too zealous, and not mindful enough of the effect of the tone they employed on both public and author. Nevertheless, they accorded the *ADB* an important role in helping rid theology of musty scholasticism and dogmatism, and informing Catholics in particular about religious works both Catholic and Protestant.[113] Many Catholics, on the other hand, attacked the *ADB* for its consistently arrogant attitude toward their religion, and some Austrians thought the journal, which they associated strongly with Berlin, deliberately set out to insult them.

After his 1781 visit to Vienna, which coincided with a period of relaxed censorship and literary opening in the form of a flood of brochures there, Nicolai devoted a special rubric of the *ADB* to Viennese pamphlet literature (*Wienerschriften*). Here intense controversies between North German and Viennese writers were thrashed out.[114]

110. Mirabeau, *De la monarchie prussienne*, 5:182.
111. Schlosser, *Geschichte des achtzehnten Jahrhunderts*, 2:591.
112. Carlo Denina, *La Prusse littéraire sous Fréderic II*, 3 vols. (Berlin: Rottmann, 1790–91), 2:106.
113. [(Julius Friedrich Knüppeln, Karl Christoph Nencke, and Christian Ludwig Paalzow], *Büsten Berliner Gelehrten, Schriftsteller und Künstler* (Stendal, 1787). The three authors of this anonymous work were Berlin *Aufklärer* of the younger generation, born in the mid-to-late 1750s.
114. On avid reading of the *ADB* in Vienna in the 1780s, despite animosity toward Berlin, see Bodi, *Tauwetter in Wien*, p. 108.

Accusations of blatant partisanship, money-grubbing and corruption, intolerance, and nepotism were the order of the day. The Halle *Gelehrte Zeitungen* called the *ADB* a "wastepaper library," "bookseller's library," and "unauthorized high court," among other things.[115] With the typical invective of the age, the poet Johann Heinrich Voß railed against *ADB* reviewers as a crew of "journeymen, nameless good-for-nothings, masked bookseller's hirelings, paid nameless scribblers, serfs,[116] schoolboys, grocers, manufacturers for the Leipzig fair, in a word, men who could not even rhyme a song to Phyllis" and wrote in the "review factories"[117] purely for material gain. Nicolai himself was also portrayed as an unscrupulous entrepreneur. Given this atmosphere, even Nicolai's friends trod lightly. The Mannheim bookseller Christian Friedrich Schwan, for example, with whom Nicolai had long been on good terms, felt it necessary to accompany the first volume of his German-French dictionary in 1782 with the following explanation: "Do not believe that I have the ignoble intention of soliciting a positive review in the Bibliothek. I know that side of you too well not to realize that you are not the sort of man to sell the truth for the price of a free copy, and I hope that you will not consider me capable of such underhanded methods."[118] Nicolai was very sensitive to attacks on his and the *ADB*'s honor in this regard, and in a 1767 issue of the *ADB* he documented an attempt to bribe the editors of the *Briefe, die neueste Litteratur betreffend*. The letter in question, requesting a positive review, had been accompanied by 3 ducats, which the editors had donated to the poor. Skeptics could examine the receipt in the publisher's bookshop! Nicolai and his reviewers distanced themselves vigorously from the devious attempts of aspiring authors to see themselves praised in print, as well as from the base motives behind some of the fulsome praise that one could read in certain newspapers or magazines.[119]

The early years of the *ADB*, which coincided with a particularly nasty period in the history of feuds in the German republic of letters, were accompanied by some bizarre behavior on the part of Nicolai's enemies. Nicolai compared one of them, the erstwhile *ADB* reviewer Christian Adolf Klotz, to a drunken lout who lay in wait around every corner to

---

115. Nicolai mentions this in the Foreword to *ADB* 12, no. 2 (1770).
116. Nicolai quotes these epithets in his defense against Voß's attack (in the *Deutsches Museum*, 1781, nos. 3 and 4), in *ADB* 45, no. 1 (1781): 619.
117. Quoted in Sommerfeld, *Friedrich Nicolai und der Sturm und Drang*, p. 308.
118. Schwan to Nicolai, Mannheim, 20 June 1782, in NN 70.
119. *ADB* 4, no. 1 (1767): 307–8.

sling mud at him.[120] Poison pen letters from irate authors and satires and vendettas in journals ranging from Wieland's respected *Teutsche Merkur* to Friedrich Justus Riedel's *Bibliothek der elenden Scribenten* (Library of Miserable Scribblers) were the order of the day. Nicolai was an "evil knave" and his reviewers "Nicolaites." Wounded authors, whether named or anonymous lashed out with epistolary violence. In September 1771, for example, Consistorial Councillor Friedrich Eberhard Boysen of Quedlinburg warned Nicolai not to review any more of his books in the *ADB* or he would reveal to the public some "astounding anecdotes" about the journal.[121] A hot-blooded officer went further, threatening to visit Nicolai in Berlin "in an irksome und unpleasant manner" and boasting of his good connections with the Prince of Prussia and various generals and staff officers, which would enable him to avenge "such impolite insults"—namely, the unfavorable review of his book.[122]

Some letters objected, not to some particular review in the *ADB*, but to the entire journal and all it represented. We have seen that Catholics had good reason to suspect bias, and the many critiques of orthodox Protestant theology also encouraged attacks by Protestants on the *ADB* as a bastion of irreligion. A letter of 16 September 1768, tinged with anti-Enlightenment and anti-Jewish invective and addressed to the *ADB* staff collectively, is a good example of this genre. The anonymous correspondent purported to write in the name of numerous authors whom the journal had attacked: "I would like to write to you, if not as Christians, then as civilized philosophers, if you were such; as it is, I cannot. To be sure, I do not read your offensive work, except when some scrap of it is sent to me; the ugly opinions contained therein are also not my affair: nevertheless, I must convey a necessary warning to you on behalf of the many honest and upstanding men who have been godlessly abused therein." The letter combines themes common to many attacks on the *ADB*, accusing Nicolai and the rest of the staff of being at once anti-Christian and ignorant, incompetent and impertinent as critics: "In this scandalous work you reveal (1) a satanical enmity toward our Lord Jesus Christ; His Person,

---

120. Nicolai to Uz, Berlin, 26 June 1771, in NN 76. Klotz took every opportunity to attack the *ADB* in his *Acta Litteraria, Neue Hallische Gelehrte Zeitungen*, and *Deutsche Bibliothek der schönen Wissenschaften*. Nicolai reprinted some of the more purple passages in the *ADB*. Ost, *Friedrich Nicolais Allgemeine Deutsche Bibliothek*, p. 63. The fact that Nicolai published Lessing's *Antiquarische Briefe*, which contained a scathing critique of Klotz's works, could not have endeared him to that author.
121. Boysen to Nicolai, Quedlinburg, 16 September 1771, in NN 8.
122. O'Cahill to Nicolai, Karlsruhe, 25 May 1785, in NN 2.

His Office, and His amends for us, His word, His faith, His Sacraments, His Church, and everything that belongs to Him: thus you are *Jews*.... (2) in part a crude ignorance in matters that you judge without having understood or read what has been written about them; in part a cheeky buffoonish *petulance*: you are thus *knaves*. Together: *Jewish knaves*." Like Boysen, he threatened an impending public attack and dared them to answer with reasoned argument rather than their usual foolish exclamations. If they did not mend their ways, he hoped that a taste of the German schoolmaster's cane would teach them to follow the Eighth Commandment.[123]

Some of Nicolai's opponents devised more unusual means of revenge. Somebody, presumably from the circle around Klotz and Riedel, signed a letter in Nicolai's name inviting one *Adjunctus* Grosch in Jena to join the *ADB* staff. The unwitting object of this practical joke, probably a man who would never have dreamed of such an honor, was overjoyed at the invitation. Nicolai's answer to Grosch's letter is, alas, not recorded.[124] One insulted author, who had been sharply criticized in the *ADB*, conceived the idea of a counter-journal in which wronged authors could vent their spleen.[125] Others used the prefaces of their books to attack their anonymous reviewers.[126] The contentious Pater Alois Merz devised a particularly original means of attacking the journal when he preached a sermon against the *ADB* in the cathedral at Augsburg, in which he denounced a negative review of his sermons.[127]

123. Anonymous letter to Nicolai, signed "Von Hause," in NN 2.

124. The first letter, which Nicolai called in a marginal note "a crude forgery by Klotz or Riedel," was dated 24 December 1768. Grosch's answer is dated Jena, 2 January 1769. Both are in NN 27. Being asked to join the *ADB* was something of an honor, at least in the journal's heyday, and some people were apparently proud to announce that they had refused the invitation. See Heinze's letter in which he tells Nicolai that he had not passed on an invitation to a certain man because he would only refuse and, as he had frequently heard of others doing, boast about it afterward. Kiel, 19 May 1786, in NN 31.

125. This project is mentioned in a letter to the *ADB* from Johann Georg Friedrich Franz in Leipzig, who had been approached as a potential contributor to the anti-*ADB*, but had refused because "I do not like to involve myself in unnecessary quarrels " and because he had found the *ADB*'s criticisms of his own work helpful. Franz said that the project was conceived by Wilke, probably Christian Heinrich Wilke in Leipzig who contributed to the *Briefe der elenden Scribenten*. Franz to Nicolai, Leipzig, 11 November 1769, in NN 22. Another anti-*ADB* journal, the *Briefe wider die theologischen Recensionen der Bibliothek* (1768), is mentioned in Aner, *Der Aufklärer Friedrich Nicolai*, p. 175.

126. Carvill gives one example in *Der verführte Leser*. In the second revised edition of 1778, J. M. Miller accused the reviewer of his *Briefwechsel dreyer akademischer Freunde* of writing a negative review because his novel had criticized the *ADB*. Musäus then answered the criticism of his criticism in the *ADB* 39, no. 1 (1779): 182. Carvill, *Der verführte Leser*, p. 108.

127. The anecdote is related by Denis in Vienna in a letter of 28 December 1772 to Nicolai. Denis, *Literarischer Nachlaß*, p. 163.

Nicolai was not the only one to suffer from attacks on the *ADB*. Particularly during the "Age of Klotz and Riedel,"[128] as Walch later called the period around 1770, *ADB* contributors apparently lived in constant fear of being unmasked. "The state of affairs in the world of letters," wrote the composer Johann Adam Hiller late in 1769, "is ... so dangerous, that, in order to have peace, one should give up not only writing but even thinking."[129] For this reason, Nicolai advised Eschenburg to keep his connection with the journal a secret, "otherwise you will doubtless be exposed to the abuses of Klotz and the Klotzians. The man takes the most incredible pains to sniff out the authors of the Bibliothek."[130] Even in 1780, after the storms of the Klotzian age had abated, Johann Heinrich Campe said that if Nicolai did not keep his *ADB* contributions a secret he would be forced to leave the journal. Perhaps because he had recently founded a school, he could ill afford the enmity that being known as an *ADB* reviewer would earn him.[131]

To be sure, the *ADB* brought Nicolai and the Nicolaites not only notoriety, but also fame of a more pleasing sort. Along with the abuse came praise and gratitude, and sometimes rather outrageous flattery. When H. J. Tode sent his *Kleine Liedersammlung* for review in 1771, he remarked that he would prefer a review in the *ADB* to that in any other journal, although he frequently disagreed with the opinions expressed by the theological reviewers.[132] A young woman, who signed herself only as the "authoress of Laura's Letters," cast the *ADB* staff in the role of rescuers from a vengeful Leipzig reviewer whom she had unwittingly insulted. She addressed herself in 1799 to the "Venerable Berlin Critics," "the highest court of Literature," "the excellent and noble men, who judge each author impartially." She was, she wrote, a Prussian stranded in Saxony ("my circumstances demanded it") but the *ADB* reviewers, as her compatriots, meant more to her than "foreign" critics.[133] Her letter,

128. Walch uses the phrase "Klotz- und Riedelsche Zeitalter" in a letter on Goethe and Schiller's *Xenien*, which he saw as a revival of the earlier period of literary defamation campaigns. Walch to Nicolai, Schleusingen, 22 March 1797, in NN 79.

129. Hiller to Nicolai, Leipzig, 25 November 1769, in NN 35.

130. Nicolai to Eschenburg, Berlin, 13 June 1768, in HAB, no. 6.

131. Campe to Nicolai, Hamburg, 8 March 1780, in NN 12. Some of the damage had already been done: a Göttingen professor had discovered him to be the reviewer of a work by Christoph Meiners, editor of the *Göttingisches historisches Magazin*.

132. Tode to Nicolai, Prizier bei Boizenburg, 30 August 1771, in NN 75.

133. Letter of 1 August 1799, Eisleben, NN 2. She sent the letter to the *ADB* along with one addressed to Nicolai personally, explaining in more detail her personal circumstances, how she came to write an educational work for young ladies, and why she feared a negative review in Leipzig and hoped for an impartial one in the *ADB*.

which might seem a mere example of obsequiousness and appeals to gallantry (she refers to herself as a "defenseless girl"), although well within the conventions of the time, particularly for female writers, is interesting for several reasons. It is one of very few addressed to the *ADB* by a woman writer.[134] The journal tended to give the kind of works most frequently published by women—novels, stories, verse, and translations of fiction—short shrift. The author of *Lauras Briefe* may have felt that hers as a pedagogical book might more easily win the approval of the "Bibliothekare." She emphasized that she had written the book for the education of young minds "which carry the seeds of goodness." The letter was also written in 1799, a time when the *ADB* was in eclipse, overshadowed by several newer and more up-to-date journals, and suffering from dwindling sales. In the provinces, the *ADB* may well have maintained its standing long after writers in intellectually more vibrant cities had moved on. The letter addresses the critics as Berliners, although few of them lived in that city and the journal had been published in Kiel for seven years, showing how strongly the journal continued to be associated both with Nicolai and with Berlin long after it had ceased to be published there.

In the 1780s, Nicolai recalled that since 1757, the year he began the *Bibliothek der schönen Wissenschaften*, he had been in correspondence with an increasingly large proportion of German writers. This, he felt, had afforded him uncommon insights into the republic of letters, including its more hidden sides.[135] In his 1806 autobiographical essay, when the *ADB* was already part of the recent past, Nicolai emphasized the importance of the contacts he had made through the journal. "Through this work ... he came into closer contact with a not inconsiderable number of noble men of all ranks, which he considers the great good fortune of his life."[136]

It was a major achievement to bring together writers from so many different places. As Johann Erich Biester put it, "The task was no small one, and then quite new, to unite famous and worthy men in all German-speaking lands for one work ... [and] to solicit their judgments on the

---

134. The only other example I found was a letter from Sophie von La Roche, the most prominent German woman writer of her day, thanking Nicolai for the "favorable assessment" of her journal *Pomona*, but pointing out that the reviewer had misunderstood one of the stories. La Roche to Nicolai, Koblenz, 12 April 1784, in NN 63.

135. *Beschreibung einer Reise*, 4:901–2n. See also the remarks in his "Selbstbiographie," p. 27. The eighty-nine volumes of surviving Nicolai correspondence, with letters from well over 2000 hands, amply demonstrate the truth of Nicolai's assertions regarding his broad connections in the republic of letters of his day.

136. Nicolai, "Selbstbiographie," p. 27.

state of letters locally, such as can only be properly composed in the place itself.[137] The largest numbers of *ADB* reviewers lived in the middle-German university towns of Göttingen, Helmstedt, and Jena and the surrounding cities of Kassel, Hannover, Celle, Braunschweig, Wolfenbüttel, and Gotha, but contributors were scattered from Berne in the southwest to Memel in the northeast, with concentrations in Leipzig and Dresden in Saxony, Hamburg, Kiel, Rostock and Bützow in the north and Darmstadt, Karlsruhe, Tübingen and Erlangen in the south.[138] Although also concentrated in the Protestant regions of northern and central Germany and Switzerland,[139] the *ADB*'s readers lived in cities as far apart as Paris and St. Petersburg.[140] The journal was an important source of information for German speakers in Russia and the Baltic region.[141] However much its enemies associated the journal with Berlin and Berliners, the *ADB* was to become an organ of the German-speaking (Protestant) Enlightenment more generally.[142]

137. Quoted in Göckingk, *Friedrich Nicolais Leben und literarischer Nachlaß*, p. 33.
138. For a geographical overview of *ADB* reviewers, see the map, page viii, showing the places of residence of *ADB* contributors and Nicolai's travel route.
139. Although it is incomplete, one can get some idea of the geographical distribution of the *ADB* from a 1783 list of (bookseller) recipients compiled by *ADB* printer Christoph Günther in Schleusingen. According to this list, the largest number of copies by far went to Hamburg (184), followed by Frankfurt am Main (111), German-speaking Switzerland (70), Leipzig (64), Nuremberg (60), Göttingen (47), and the Habsburg lands (38, including 21 to Vienna). Nicolai himself spoke of 43 copies he sent to the crown lands in 1783, not counting the 5 copies he was obliged to submit to the *Reichshofrat* for privilege purposes. He thought that another 30 copies might reach Austria via other booksellers. *Beschreibung einer Reise*, 4:909–10n. Other important centers, with 20 or more *ADB* copies, were Hannover, Braunschweig, Breslau, and Mannheim. Of course, many of these copies may have been sent on by booksellers to customers living in other towns. The number of buyers in Berlin is not recorded, presumably because Nicolai took the copies he needed home with him from the book fairs. Günther's list, dated 20 November 1783, is in NN 28.
140. The German painter Georg Wille received the *ADB* in Paris. See Nicolai's letter to him of 20 October 1777, in DBSM Leipzig K123/21. The journal was also available in the German reading room (*Deutsches Lese-Kabinett*) at the corner of the rue Saint-Honoré and the rue de Richelieu. Founded around 1781 by Adrian Christian Friedel, a German tutor and translator from Berlin, this institution existed until at least 1787–88. Jürgen Voss, "Eine deutsche Lesebibliothek im Paris des späten 18. Jahrhunderts. Neue Beobachtungen und methodische Überlegungen zur Erforschung der deutschen Lesegesellschaften," *Zeitschrift für historische Forschung* 6 (1979): 466–69.
141. Ischreyt, "Buchhandel und Buchhändler im nordosteuropäischen Kommunikationssystem," in *Buch und Buchhandel*, p. 265. See also Mechthild Keller, "Nachrichtenbörse Berlin: Friedrich Nicolai und seine 'Allgemeine deutsche Bibliothek,'" in *Russen und Rußland aus deutscher Sicht. 18. Jahrhundert: Aufklärung* (Munich: Wilhelm Fink, 1987), pp. 427–32, and Annelies Lauch, "Russische Wissenschaft und Kultur im Spiegel der 'Allgemeinen Deutschen Bibliothek,'" *Zeitschrift für Slawistik* 10 (1965): 737–46.
142. See Ost, *Friedrich Nicolais Allgemeine Deutsche Bibliothek*, pp. 60ff.

The *ADB* also found its way beyond the centers of scholarship and culture to more obscure places, such as the estate of Gabriel von Pronay in Atsa, Hungary. Pronay, a rich Protestant aristocrat who signed himself "Assesseur de plusieurs contés," told Nicolai in 1776 that "The [ADB] ... continues to meet with the most universal approval, and even has a few readers in my uncultivated country." A member of "the very small company of Hungarian connoisseurs of the latest literature," he also subscribed to the *Monthly Review* and to several French journals which he ordered from Vienna.[143] In Augsburg, not renowned as a bastion of the Enlightenment, twenty-nine-year old deacon G. F. Wilhelm told Nicolai that he owed the *ADB*, which had been his favorite reading in student days, "uncommonly much light and enlightenment." Upon returning to his hometown he had joined a journal reading society and chosen the *ADB* as his contribution. "All of my fellow readers have thanked me for this decision because it required more trouble and expense than the usual journals."[144] Even in the Tyrolean backwater of Seeba there was a "devoted reader and buyer of your d[eutsche] Bibliothek." As he wrote in a 1778 letter, Father Romanus Lerchberger, chaplain of the local Benedictine convent—surely one of the most unlikely of devotees—especially enjoyed reading the journal "in such a barbarous region and in my circumstances.... It is surely an exquisite pleasure to see [expressed] so loudly one's own opinions,... which one adopted before such a [journal] even existed."[145] In 1787, another Catholic priest, Father Werkmeister, recalled his discovery of the *ADB* "in a corner of Bavaria where I was then studying theology in the monastic style.... Without flattery ... I must confess that the continual reading of this journal ... certainly opened my eyes more than everything else I read in those days taken together!"[146] These last two letters, in particular, must have given Nicolai intense satisfaction.

Typically for Nicolai, the *ADB* combined idealism with profit. Contemporaries, both pro-and anti-Nicolai, were quick to recognize and mention

---

143. Pronay to Nicolai, Atsa, 21 October 1776, in NN 58. A few years later, Pronay subscribed to Jacobsson's *Technologisches Wörterbuch* and promised to drum up more *ADB* subscribers. H. G. von Bretschneider, who knew Pronay personally, described him to Nicolai as "a man of good insights and large fortune who has much power over his neighbors" and "one of the richest Protestant squires in Hungary." Letter from Ofen, 2 July 1780, in NN 9.

144. Wilhelm to Nicolai, Augsburg, 26 January 1788, in NN 83. He also inquired as to the price of the first forty-eight volumes of the *ADB*, which he did not own. In a marginal note Nicolai mentions offering him a discount of 4 carolins over the usual price for volumes 13–47.

145. Lerchberger to Nicolai, Kloster Seeba, 5 May 1778, in NN 45.

146. Werkmeister to Nicolai, Stuttgart, 14 December 1787, in NN 82. He believed, however, that Nicolai exaggerated the danger to Protestantism and the Enlightenment from the Catholic camp.

this fact. Carlo Denina, for example, wrote in his *Prusse littéraire* that the *ADB* was "one of the best journals that has existed since the invention of this type of work and has for many years earned for its editor quite considerable sums."[147] Together with its potential usefulness for the reading and writing segment of the population, the *ADB* also helped the publishing and bookselling world to new customers. Although the intended role of the *ADB* in creating a market for good books, like those Nicolai preferred to publish and sell, went beyond mere mercantile considerations, these were not insignificant. "In regard to the book trade this work was also important, in that new books from all disciplines became known much more quickly than before.... Nicolai's own business also profited greatly in all respects from this enterprise," wrote Nicolai's friend, reviewer, and first biographer L.F.G. von Göckingk in 1820.[148] The *ADB* benefited Nicolai's business by putting him into direct contact with hundreds of scholars and writers and indirect contact with thousands more. He could advertise his own books for free and reach a wide audience of potential buyers who were already interested in his brand of Enlightenment. His stable of reviewers (and their friends and neighbors) also represented a pool of customers, as they frequently charged the books they reviewed to their accounts or ordered other books from Nicolai.[149]

Although the *ADB* was by no means the only important work Nicolai published, it was the center around which the rest of his business revolved. In terms of volumes published, the *ADB* comprised nearly 20 percent of Nicolai's production. In the early years, this proportion was even higher. In 1769, for example, the *ADB* represented two of the seven volumes we know Nicolai published that year, or almost 30 percent of his output.[150] Thus it is not surprising that the *ADB* directly or indirectly affected decisions he made regarding his business more generally. He remarked in an 1808 letter to his younger colleague Friedrich Perthes that vigorous demand for the *ADB* in the early days had led him to open a new shop in Stettin in order to provide a further outlet for the books he received from other booksellers in exchange.[151] Since the first issue of

---

147. Denina, *La Prusse littéraire*, 3:105.
148. Göckingk, *Friedrich Nicolais Leben und literarischer Nachlaß*, p. 35.
149. See, for example, Walch's letters of 28 April 1779 and 30 May 1781 from Schleusingen, in NN 79.
150. See *Friedrich Nicolai: Die Verlagswerke eines preußischen Buchhändlers der Aufklärung 1759–1811*, compiled by Paul Raabe.
151. Berlin, 4 May 1808, in NN 56. The letter is printed in "Generationskonflikt unter Buchhändlern?" pp. 13–17. In this letter, Nicolai mentions opening the Stettin branch in 1766.

the *ADB* already lists "Berlin & Stettin" as its place of publication, Nicolai's memory may have been uncharacteristically imprecise here, but he clearly associated the journal with increased trade. A 1769 letter to Lessing notes that the balance between retail sales and publishing had been upset by the strong sales of the *ADB*. The necessity of printing more issues of the journal per year to catch up with the backlog of reviews only exacerbated the problem. "The sales from my publishing company," he explained, "are no longer proportionate to sales from my shops." In order to increase the latter accordingly, he would have to embark on enterprises that would create more work than he could handle. Thus he had to cut back on publishing, taking on fewer new titles until the balance was restored.[152]

Nicolai emphasized either the lucrative or the burdensome character of the *ADB* as it suited his purposes. When he was accused of making a fortune off the journal by those who opposed him, Nicolai played down his financial interest. In a 1771 letter to Wieland, Nicolai said that his profits were only modest and noted that those who believed otherwise lacked "a proper knowledge of the state of the German book trade." He certainly had plenty of other, equally lucrative, titles, he claimed.[153] Similarly, he assured his friend and *ADB* reviewer Höpfner a few years later that the advantage the *ADB* brought him could be replaced by twenty other titles, which would require not a stroke of his own pen.[154] On the other hand, we have his statements to Perthes about booming sales and to the Prussian government about the economic importance of the *ADB* during his struggle against the ban. In his petition to the Prussian government, Nicolai spoke of gross sales of 16,000 to 18,000 taler a year (in better times up to 20,000).[155] Günther Ost calculates that in 1775, at the height of the *ADB*'s popularity and sales, Nicolai had a net profit of 1000–1200 taler for each volume of the journal, or 4000–4800 taler for the year.[156] It thus seems likely that the *ADB* contributed significantly to the solidification of Nicolai's business after the Seven Years' War, bringing in

---

152. Nicolai to Lessing, Berlin, 8 November 1769, in Lessing, *Sämtliche Schriften*, 19:325–26. This may well explain why Nicolai published very few books in 1769. On Nicolai's insistence on the balance of *Sortiment* and *Verlag*, see also his letter of 4 May 1808 to Perthes.

153. Nicolai to Wieland, Berlin, 3 December 1771, in Christoph Martin Wieland, *Briefwechsel*, ed. Annerose Schneider and Peter-Volker Springborn (Berlin: Akademie Verlag, 1979), 4:421.

154. Nicolai to Höpfner, Berlin, 26 July 1774, in Nicolai, *Verlegerbriefe*, p. 104.

155. See his letter-petition of 6 May 1794 to King Frederick William III, printed in "Actenstücke," pt. 2, pp. 256–306. The figures are cited by Ost, *Friedrich Nicolais Allgemeine Deutsche Bibliothek*, p. 27.

156. Ost, *Friedrich Nicolais Allgemeine Deutsche Bibliothek*, pp. 26–27.

a steady income that made it easier to plan for other publications of potentially less market value. He joked to Lessing in 1768 that it would be no problem to publish the latter's *Briefe, antiquarischen Inhalts*, he would merely sacrifice "a portion of the clear profits of the ... Bibliothek to ancestral portraits."[157] He mentions in his letter to Perthes that it took him seventeen years to put his firm in the black and it may well have been ten years of publishing the *ADB*, together with his bestselling novel *Sebaldus Nothanker*, that allowed him to achieve liquidity by the mid-1770s.

The popularity of the *ADB* brought Nicolai into contact with a wide range of booksellers in all parts of German-speaking Europe, from those who ordered the journal for their customers or received or procured review copies on behalf of local collaborators[158] to those who sent in their products for review. From the beginning, Nicolai urged his colleagues to ensure inclusion of their titles by providing review copies. In his announcement of the forthcoming publication of the *ADB* in the *Briefe, die neueste Litteratur betreffend*, Nicolai added that if "publishers wish to send in their new books, they will be mentioned all the sooner."[159] Although it was by no means common practice at the time for publishers to provide review copies free of charge,[160] some of Nicolai's colleagues did take up his suggestion, knowing that a review in the *ADB* carried weight and would ensure that the work came to the attention of a national audience.[161] In 1788, for example, the Berlin calendar publisher Oesfeld asked

157. Nicolai to Lessing, Berlin, 14 June 1768, in Lessing, *Sämtliche Schriften*, 19:258. The "ancestral portraits" refer to one of the topics of Lessing's work, ancestral portraits in ancient Rome. See Lessing's letter of 9 June 1768 to Nicolai, in Lessing, *Sämtliche Schriften*, 17:252.

158. Not all of Nicolai's reviewers received their review copies from him. Höpfner in Frankfurt am Main, for example, got many of his books from the Gießen bookseller Johann Christian Krieger, who dealt with Nicolai at the Leipzig fairs. Heerbrand in Tübingen also supplied books for South German reviewers, but many booksellers were reluctant to lend unbound books because they were returned in such poor condition. On this problem, see Schneider, *Friedrich Nicolais Allgemeine Deutsche Bibliothek als Integrationsmedium*, pp. 288–90. On Krieger, an interesting figure in his own right who founded a major publishing, bookselling, and lending library empire in Hesse and dealt extensively in clandestine literature, see Christine Haug, "Das Buch- und Verlagsunternehmen Krieger (1725–1825)," *Archiv für Geschichte des Buchwesens* 49 (1998): 1–170.

159. "Nachricht," in *Briefe, die neueste Litteratur betreffend* 20 (1764): 186.

160. Ost, *Friedrich Nicolais Allgemeine Deutsche Bibliothek*, p. 27.

161. See, for example, letters of 14 November 1768 from Joseph Christoph Messerer, printer in Schwäbisch Hall (in NN 49), 26 September 1770 from Schwan in Mannheim (in NN 70), 27 December 1773 from Carl Gottlob Beck in Nördlingen (in NN 3), 18 December 1781 from Johann Christian Krieger in Gießen (in NN 89), 20 January 1784 from Frommann in Züllichau (in NN 23), 8 March 1785 from Richter in Altenburg (in NN 61), 28 March 1792 from Christoph Arnold in Schneeberg (in NN 2), and July 1804 from J. S. Hammerich in Altona (in NN 30), all accompanying publications for review.

Nicolai for a quick notice of the *Heiligen-Calender*, believing that it would promote sales if it were to be reviewed before the Easter book fair.[162]

The *ADB* was also, of course, a vehicle for advertising Nicolai's own publications, through frequent announcements of new books, prenumeration offers, and discount prices on older titles, as well as the reviews themselves. In the first issues of each new year Nicolai also printed a list with prices of new books and engravings he had brought back from the Leipzig Easter Fair. In a 1789 issue of the *ADB* he published a twenty-three-page catalog of his firm's books in print, the "Verzeichniß der Bücher welche Friedrich Nicolai Buchhändler in Berlin und Stettin auf seine Kosten hat drucken lassen oder bey ihm in Menge zu haben sind."[163]

Considering his vulnerability to attack, however, he took care that reviewers did not praise his own products too extravagantly. In a letter of 1769 to Herder requesting a review of Leonhard Meister's *Romantische Briefe*, for example, Nicolai asked him to be sparing with his praise because "I prefer to avoid even the slightest appearance that a book is being praised because it comes from my publishing firm."[164] The review of the translation of Thomas Amory's controversial theological tract-cum-novel *John Buncle* under the rubric of Theology ("Gottesgelahrtheit") in 1778 is another case in point. Nicolai had been attacked for praising the novel excessively in his prenumeration announcement, and the reviewer was to provide a colder, more balanced comment: "For a novel it is too void of interesting events, is often improbable, without moving situations, without outstanding characters, indeed without variety and changes among them."[165] To be sure, the author had not written the work primarily as a novel, but rather as an exposition of a religious system. Even here, however, the reviewer did not consider it terribly successful, admitting "that many of the ideas lack maturity and firmness, and overall the author's fiery mind has not always represented them as correctly and purely as cool and settled reason might demand" (pp. 665–66). What praise there is he reserves for the translator's useful notes and additions, which might aid young theologians "in their own reflections on theological modes of

---

162. Nicolai to Knigge, Berlin, 21 January 1788, asking him to review the *Heiligen-Calender*, the anonymously published work of one of Nicolai's friends (Bretschneider), in Bayerische Staatsbibliothek Munich, Autographen.

163. *ADB* 86, no. 1 (1789): 286–310.

164. Nicolai to Herder, Berlin, 11 April 1769, quoted in Sommerfeld, *Friedrich Nicolai und der Sturm und Drang*, pp. 58–59.

165. Review of *Johann Bunkel*, *ADB*, supplement to vols. 25–36, pt. 1 (1778): 664.

thinking, and in a rational testing and consideration of the various prevailing schools of thought" (pp. 670–71).

Nicolai was particularly cautious when it came to reviews of his own writings. When Johann Heinrich Campe wrote a review of volume 2 of *Sebaldus Nothanker*, he sent the manuscript to Nicolai, hoping that he would be satisfied with both the general tenor of the review, which tried not to praise him too baldly, and the candor with which he had expressed his opinions, as if he were writing about a stranger. "The latter I considered all the more necessary, since people would otherwise not have hesitated to call my review partisan.[166] Nicolai was, however, not satisfied and asked Campe to write a "colder" review. Campe joked that one could set the motto above it "I look at it and freeze!" He submitted his revised original review to a Leipzig journal[167] and wrote a brief one for the *ADB* that manages to discuss *Sebaldus Nothanker* more as a phenomenon than as a work of fiction, thus avoiding *direct* praise or censure for the author. In fact, the review ended up as a criticism of the critics rather than of the work at hand:

> The readers of our Bibliothek will most probably not expect to find an extensive account of this work here, any more than the book itself is in need of introduction. The rapid sales of the first volume, necessitating a second printing that same year, demonstrate that it is already sufficiently well known; and that it has found no lack of judges is proven not only by the critical journals, but also by any number of brochures and leaflets published in favor of and against it. To be sure, not all of the assessments made up until now (as is generally the case at the first appearance of any work that rises above the ordinary) flow from mature reflection and healthy, unbiased powers of discernment: we may expect that time, which corrects all errors, has either already done its work, or will gradually do so.

Campe then proceeded to make general remarks about the aims of instructing and amusing the reader, and about the importance of the critic's vantage point. The author's object in *Sebaldus Nothanker*, he remarks, was to demonstrate the foibles of certain members of the clergy in the hope of remedying them, or at least acting as a warning—"a salutary but

---

166. Campe to Nicolai, Potsdam, 23 July 1775, in NN 12.
167. Campe to Nicolai, Potsdam, 31 August 1775, in NN 12.

awkward undertaking" so easily misinterpreted as a wholesale attack on the clergy or even on religion itself. The only enthusiastic praise comes at the end, and it is for Daniel Chodowiecki's illustrations, rather than Nicolai's text.[168] It is a clever review, ensuring as it does that no reader could fail to notice how important the book was.

With his early journals, but more especially with the *ADB*, we see Friedrich Nicolai as a typical powerbroker of this transitional period, at the hub of a myriad of intersecting networks of information and influence. He received a steady stream of news and gossip about literature, both informal and in the guise of printed publication announcements, and about the progress of careers in the republic of letters. Nicolai's reviewers and readers, who together comprised a significant portion of the educated German public, afforded him one of the widest information networks of any man in Germany. Although some of the most important contacts made during the early years of the *ADB*—most notably Herder—abandoned Nicolai in the pitched literary battles of the 1770s, the growing and changing staff of reviewers was to provide him not only with book authors but also with a wide range of literary allies and informants. In an age of slow and expensive communications and a weakly developed infrastructure in banking and the book trade, Nicolai depended upon a veritable army of correspondents to carry on his business effectively. From Amsterdam to Zwickau, *ADB* reviewers formed a network of loyal assistants and in many cases friends, who also afforded Nicolai access to their local connections. Nicolai used the printed circulars to reviewers to request services that could best be organized regionally, particularly the collection of subscriptions and prenumerations or the recruitment of collectors and the placement of advertisements for his books in local newspapers and journals. Along with the circular of 29 May 1777, for example, Nicolai sent his staff copies of the prenumeration advertisement for *Johann Bunkel* requesting their help in soliciting subscriptions. "If you prefer not to do so yourself, I ask you to appoint another appropriate person to do the collecting and disseminate the advertisement, for which I will be deeply grateful."[169]

Nicolai took a similar tack with Johann Karl Gottfried Jacobsson's *Technologisches Wörterbuch*.[170] When he asked reviewers to distribute announcements of Raymund Dapp's *Predigten für christliche Landleute* "particularly

---

168. Review of *Sebaldus Nothanker*, *ADB* 26, no. 2 (1775): 479–81.
169. The circular is in NN 86 [Iselin corrspondence].
170. Circular of 4 November 1780, in HAB, no. 38.

among the country pastors of your acquaintance," it was doubtless a good way to reach such clerics all over Germany.[171]

Nicolai also enlisted his reviewers in the fight against piracy. When he decided to reduce the price of the first twenty-four volumes of the *ADB* for a time, "in order to inhibit to some extent Dr. Bahrdt's scandalous piracy of the theological reviews," he asked his reviewers to distribute his notice "in the form of excerpts in the newspapers ... and to promote my efforts."[172] Nicolai's *ADB* correspondents served a multitude of other functions as well. They paid bills, dispatched letters and book packets to friends in remote towns and villages, warned of pirate editions, suggested authors, recommended booksellers' apprentices, relayed gossip and literary and political news, provided Nicolai's family with Braunschweig sausage and North Sea salmon, and not least, bought books. The many review copies of books that, to Nicolai's dismay, some contributors kept for years at a time, also brought new works into circulation in areas where they might otherwise have been unavailable.[173]

ADB reviewers also wrote books. Before the advent of the *ADB*, Nicolai had published books written or translated by a handful of friends, and by authors he had inherited from his father. The *ADB* opened a whole new world of potential authors. Of the German writers whose books, including translations and editions, Nicolai published, some 40 percent were also *ADB* reviewers. Of his firm's more important authors (those who published three or more titles), 57 percent were *ADB* contributors. In the end, 16 percent of the approximately 430 writers who contributed to the *ADB* over the years also became authors of Nicolai's publishing firm. Many more submitted manuscripts or proposals for works that were never published. Readers, too, sent in manuscripts, attracted by Nicolai's reputation as the editor and publisher of the *ADB*. Prince Moritz of

---

171. Circular of June 1786, in HAB, no. 64. Nicolai also sent prenumeration announcements with the circulars of 17 April 1781 (in NN 86 [Iselin correspondence]) and 2 July 1791 (in HAB, no. 116).

172. Circular of 6 November 1777, in NN 86 [Iselin correspondence].

173. See for example, Nicolai's complaints in his printed circular dated 20 June 1775 (in NN 86 [Iselin correspondence]) that approximately four hundred reviews were outstanding, some of them of books distributed three or four years previously, and in that of 8 Wintermonat (November) 1786 (in NN 1 [Abendroth correspondence]) that reviewers were often extremely dilatory and tended to "mislay" the books in their own libraries. In 1789 Johann Erich Springer still had not returned some books he had received for review before 1781. See Springer to Nicolai, Rinteln, 26 March 1789, in NN 72. During those eight years Springer certainly had ample opportunity to lend out the books to his friends. Whether he did so is another question.

Isenburg, for example, sent Nicolai his translation of Bolingbroke's *Reflections upon Exile* in 1779, "after having read a large portion of your *Allgemeine deutsche Bibliothek*."[174]

The Decline and Fall of the *ADB*

In 1792, in the face of the growing theological repression and censorship in Prussia and his own ill-health and overwork, Friedrich Nicolai sold the *ADB* to Hamburg bookseller Carl Ernst Bohn for the sum of 6000 taler and eighty free copies of each future issue of the journal.[175] This move only confirmed and consolidated the loss of sales and influence the journal had experienced since the mid-1780s. Changing literary and intellectual fashions and the foundation of new (review) journals, both general and specialized, had thrust the *ADB* from its onetime pinnacle as central arbiter of German taste. In 1783, perhaps not coincidentally also the year when the *Berlinische Monatsschrift* was founded as the central organ of the late Enlightenment in Berlin, Nicolai reduced the *ADB*'s edition for the first time, from 2500 to 2200 copies.[176] As faithful reviewer and proofreader Walch reported in a letter of 1784, the announcement of the founding of the *Allgemeine Literatur-Zeitung* (*ALZ*) in Jena boded ill for the *ADB*, particularly as regarded potential new readers. The *ALZ* approached numerous *ADB* reviewers, including Walch, to contribute to the new journal. Although Walch refused, pleading lack of time and access to a good bookshop,[177] ultimately more than a hundred *ADB* reviewers worked for the *ALZ*. This served to exacerbate Nicolai's problems in attracting and keeping reviewers, making it more difficult to get out reviews on time, which in turn favored the competition.[178] When Bohn

---

174. Prince Moritz to Nicolai, Birstein, 24 March 1779, in NN 37. The work was published that year as *Von der Verbannung*, with a frontispiece illustration by J. W. Meil.

175. The negotiations between Nicolai and Bohn over the sale of the *ADB* are documented in a number of letters from Bohn to Nicolai (in NN 7), and in Ost, *Friedrich Nicolais Allgemeine Deutsche Bibliothek*, pp. 72ff. and 90ff. At the Leipzig Easter Fair of 1791, Nicolai had also apparently asked the Gotha bookseller Ettinger whether he would be interested in publishing the *ADB*. Ettinger's letter of 6 July 1791 mentions that he was unsure whether Nicolai had said this in jest or earnest, in NN 20.

176. From 1783 sales declined irrevocably. In 1798, Bohn complained that they had fallen to barely 750 copies. Bohn to Nicolai, Hamburg, 12 July 1798, in NN 7.

177. Walch to Nicolai, Schleusingen, 1 October 1784, in NN 79. Five months later, Walch told Nicolai that considering the competition from the *ALZ* it was more important than ever to keep the presses occupied and dispatch the journal (which was running behind schedule) promptly. Walch to Nicolai, Schleusingen, 11 March 1785, in NN 79.

178. Ost, *Friedrich Nicolais Allgemeine Deutsche Bibliothek*, p. 66. It is against this background that we must see Nicolai's call in a circular of June 1786 for new reviewers in some twenty-four

reproached Nicolai in 1800 that the journal had already been sinking when he bought it, he called the *ALZ* "the first significant rival."[179]

The *ALZ* shared the *ADB*'s program of reviewing all new German publications but also covered important foreign works. It was much more current, written daily and available to subscribers either weekly or monthly, while the *ADB* was published monthly, with the issues usually only distributed around the time of the book fairs at Michaelmas and Easter. *ALZ* editor Friedrich Justin Bertuch managed to keep prices low while luring reviewers with significantly higher fees than the *ADB* paid.[180] The *ALZ* cost 6 taler (8 with postage and packing) a year in 1785, while the *ADB*, sold by the volume rather than the year, could cost anywhere from 6 taler (for four volumes) to 15 taler (for ten volumes) a year, including postage.[181] When the *ALZ* was paying many reviewers a generous 15 taler a sheet, Nicolai's staff had to make do with an average of 5 to 7 taler.[182] Eschenburg seems to have been the highest-paid *ADB* reviewer at 10 taler per sheet in 1789.[183] Unlike the *ALZ* staff, however, all *ADB* reviewers, received a free copy of the journal. At a price of 1 taler 12

---

disciplines. The circular is in HAB, no. 64. For a comparison of the *ADB* with the *ALZ*, as well as with some of the specialist scholarly journals that emerged in the 1780s, see Schneider, *Friedrich Nicolais Allgemeine Deutsche Bibliothek als Integrationsmedium*, pp. 314–43.

Although the *ADB* and the *ALZ* represented different attitudes and trends in the literary and philosophical fields, theologically conservative contemporaries placed them in the same anti-orthodox, deist camp. In 1794, Johann Georg Müller wrote to his brother, the historian Johannes von Müller, that the *ALZ* continued in the same spirit as the *ADB*, whose chief purpose he saw as working to diminish the reputation of the Bible. If anything its influence was more deleterious because it launched its assaults more frequently. Letter of 29 January 1794, in *Der Briefwechsel der Brüder J. Georg Müller und Joh. von Müller, 1789–1809*, vol. 1, 1789–99 (Frauenfeld: J. Huber, 1891), pp. 48–49.

179. Bohn to Nicolai, Hamburg, 18 March 1800, in NN 7. Nicolai had accused Bohn of mismanagement, and Bohn replied that the decline had begun even before he bought the journal. He implied that Nicolai had not been completely frank with him on this account.

180. Ost, *Friedrich Nicolais Allgemeine Deutsche Bibliothek*, pp. 65–66.

181. In 1800, Bohn referred to the price as 10–12 taler a year, which was too expensive for many people considering the multiplicity of journals on the market. Bohn to Nicolai, Hamburg, 18 March 1800, in NN 7. The number of titles reviewed per year in the *ADB* rose from 215 in 1765 to 1500 in 1789, not including supplement volumes. The larger the number of volumes per year (reflecting both the rising publication of books and the backlog of unreviewed works from earlier years), the more expensive the *ADB* became and the lower its sales figures fell. Ost, *Friedrich Nicolais Allgemeine Deutsche Bibliothek*, pp. 107–8.

182. Ost, *Friedrich Nicolais Allgemeine Deutsche Bibliothek*, p. 27. His statements coincide with my own calculations based upon mentions of honoraria in correspondence with reviewers. The issue of honoraria is discussed in the chapter on relations between Nicolai and his authors.

183. He asked for and received a raise that year, arguing that he had made a substantial contribution to the journal for more than twenty years, and that the print had become very small (a measure undertaken by Nicolai to squeeze more reviews into the same number of sheets). Eschenburg to Nicolai, Braunschweig, 9 May 1789, in NN 19.

groschen per volume, of which a varying number were published each year, this was a significant supplement to the modest honoraria, particularly for those reviewers who produced little.[184]

Precisely because the *ADB*'s position had become more precarious by 1792, reviewers worried that Nicolai's decision to give up his dual role as editor and publisher would lead to an even greater loss of influence and prestige.[185] Nicolai's day-to-day involvement with the *ADB* by no means ended with its sale to Bohn, though. Nicolai continued, for example, to supply the portraits of authors that decorated the frontispiece of the *ADB*.[186] His consistent interest in the journal's welfare extended to asking to see certain reviews in advance to ensure that they did not cause trouble with the censors.[187] Since Bohn was paying the purchase price in installments and provided a large number of free copies of each issue, Nicolai maintained a strong financial as well as an ideological stake in the journal's prosperity. He also literally kept a foot in the door, in that he sent his son Carl August to work for Bohn after Michaelmas 1791, at the time of the transfer of the journal.[188] Whether Carl August, Nicolai's problem child, was intended specifically to help with the *ADB* is unclear.

The *ADB* had always been something of an albatross around Nicolai's neck,[189] dominating many of his waking hours, and this changed less than he had hoped after the transfer to Bohn. The new publisher and editors

---

184. Ost, *Friedrich Nicolais Allgemeine Deutsche Bibliothek*, p. 23. Despite rising printing and paper costs and reviewers' fees, Nicolai was able to keep the cost per volume at the same level throughout the journal's life. Ost, *Friedrich Nicolais Allgemeine Deutsche Bibliothek*, p. 26. Bohn continued to supply old *ADB* reviewers with free copies, but new reviewers had to pay 5 taler a year for the journal. Walch to Nicolai, Schleusingen, 1 June 1793, in NN 79. To save money, Bohn also cut off reviewers, such as Nicolai's Berlin friend Friedrich Gedike, who had not submitted a review in years but continued to receive their free copies. Bohn to Nicolai, Hamburg, 16 April 1794, in NN 7.

185. The faithful Walch expressed just such misgivings to Nicolai. Walch to Nicolai, Schleusingen, 13 November 1792, in NN 79.

186. Bohn thanks him for this service in a letter of 1 February 1794 and expresses the hope that he will continue to send them, in NN 7.

187. The most prominent example was Nicolai's concern about Henke's review essay on the Prussian Edict Concerning Religion, which Bohn discusses in letters of 20 and 27 September 1793, in NN 7.

188. Nicolai mentions in a letter to Eschenburg that he was sending his son to Bohn "for a while." Nicolai to Eschenburg, Leipzig, 13 October 1791, in HAB, no. 120. Bohn reported on 12 November 1791 that he was satisfied with the young man (in NN 7).

189. Among many examples is a letter to Salomon Gessner, in which Nicolai complains of the indescribably tedious work of managing the journal. "The most unpleasant part of it for me," he remarked, "is that it embroils me in constant quarrels." Nicolai to Gessner, Berlin, November 1770, in NN 86.

frequently asked for Nicolai's advice, particularly on prospective reviewers and potentially controversial reviews.[190] When Adam Christian Gaspari vacated the *ADB* editorship at the end of 1794, it was Nicolai and not Bohn whom Martin Gottfried Hermann approached to ask for the position, taking it for granted that he would still make such important decisions as the choice of a new editor.[191] When Nicolai convinced him of the contrary, he asked for and received Nicolai's recommendation and Bohn took him on.[192] Reviewers also used him as a sounding board for their dissatisfaction with the new *ADB* regime. Walch complained that the books Bohn gave him to review were the dregs of the book fair. As one of the oldest *ADB* reviewers, he felt that he deserved better[193] and was even beginning to regret having rejected an offer from the *ALZ*. Only the desire to earn his free copy, he wrote, kept him reviewing for the *ADB*.[194] Valentin August Heinze, too, contemplated abandoning the journal. He complained to Nicolai that Bohn had incorporated (Nicolai's) revisions into a review without informing him beforehand. He did not object as such to Nicolai making changes, but he wanted to know about them first. Bohn's behavior was making him, too, lose any desire to write for the *ADB*.[195]

Nicolai remarked to Count von Schmettow in 1792 that he would have more peace and quiet if the editors of the *ADB* left him alone, although he was naturally prepared to do anything in his power to keep such a

---

190. Examples are Bohn's letters of February/March 1793 (received 5 March), in which he asked Nicolai's opinion of a potential reviewer in Heilbronn and sent a copy of the circular he had written on Nicolai's model, and of January 1795 (received 16 January) and 10 March 1797, in which he sent Nicolai reviews he thought might cause problems, in NN 7.

191. Hermann to Nicolai, Hamburg, 15 October 1794, in NN 33. Hermann, a classical scholar who had studied under Christian Gottlob Heyne in Göttingen and ran a school in Hamburg, was already a Nicolai author.

192. Hermann to Nicolai, Hamburg, 27 October, 10 November, 14 November, and 21 December 1794, in NN 33. Bohn came to regret his decision and fired Hermann two years later. In September 1796, Hermann asked Nicolai to let him know the true reason for Bohn's action and to help him change his mind. Letter of 17 September 1796, in NN 33. In a letter of 18 March 1800, Bohn remarked that Hermann had been miserably unsuited to the job of editor, in NN 7.

193. Walch to Nicolai, Schleusingen, 15 November 1792, in NN 79.

194. Walch to Nicolai, Schleusingen, 6 March 1793, in NN 79. Walch also objected to the meagreness of the gazetteer Bohn had added to the *ADB* to attract more readers. It robbed each volume of the journal of several sheets for reviews without being of any great interest. Walch to Nicolai, Schleusingen, 22 March 1797, in NN 79.

195. Heinze to Nicolai, Kiel, 8 February 1795, in NN 31. Bohn was able to tempt Heinze to stay by offering to let him review all books on the French Revolution. Heinze to Nicolai, Kiel, 12 December 1796, in NN 31.

useful work in print.[196] In 1800, when Bohn finally decided to abandon the *ADB* before it ruined him financially,[197] Nicolai tried, in a somewhat desultory way, to find another publisher for the journal. Considering dropping sales and Bohn's financial losses, however, the *ADB* was hardly an attractive proposition, particularly because Nicolai wanted the new publisher to commit himself to printing the journal for another fifteen years.[198] Rather than let the journal die or put it into uncertain hands, Nicolai decided to make a final effort to revive it. As he told Eschenburg, "I did not have the heart to let the Bibl[iothek] go under." Assuming a martyrlike tone, Nicolai asserted that he had "decided to sacrifice myself in order to serve scholarship."[199] Times being what they were, it would be a great shame to abandon the *ADB* now. It was important, he told Karl August Böttiger, editor of the *Neue teutsche Merkur*, "to put in a good word for common sense these days, when so many people take unreason for truth."[200]

Reviewers and the public were informed by personal letter, circulars, and advertisements of the changes at the *ADB*. In language recalling the literary wars of the period around 1770, Nicolai's brothers-in-arms applauded his decision to resume personally the struggle against unreason. "It is with pleasure," wrote one, "that I continue the literary militia ... begun years ago under your command."[201] An anonymous society of "learned friends" announced that they were glad that Nicolai would be leading the journal into the new century "now that terrorism has once again gained the upper hand in literature, and bias even in the pompous and yet very small-minded Alg[emeine] Lit[eratur] Zeit[ung]."[202] Another reviewer congratulated the new century on regaining Nicolai's *ADB* because "it is indeed high time that someone put a stop to philosophical nonsense."[203]

---

196. Nicolai to Schmettow, Berlin, 30 October 1792, in NN 67.
197. Bohn to Nicolai, Hamburg, 18 March, 11 April and 22 April 1800, in NN 7.
198. See Nicolai's letters of 15 July, 9 August, and 2 September 1800 to the publisher C. G. Fleckeisen in Helmstedt, who offered to take over the *ADB* (in *Verlegerbriefe*, pp. 172–76) and of 22 July 1800 to Eschenburg (in HAB, no. 209) and Fleckeisen's letters of 2 August and 20 September 1800, in NN 22.
199. Nicolai to Eschenburg, Berlin, 22 July 1800, in HAB, no. 209.
200. Nicolai to Böttiger, Berlin, 28 November 1800, in Nicolai, *Verlegerbriefe*, pp. 180–81.
201. Gruner to Nicolai, Jena, 10 October 1800, in NN 28. Walch also expressed pleasure at the news, saying that he had long wished for Nicolai to resume publication of the *ADB*. Walch to Nicolai, Schleusingen, 28 September 1800, in NN 79.
202. Letter received 18 October 1800, in NN 2.
203. Stöver to Nicolai, Hamburg, 23 December 1800, in NN 73.

Bohn reported that he had felt "a very heavy burden" fall from his shoulders when he passed the journal back to Nicolai.[204] After resuming publication in 1801, Nicolai complained to friends and family that the work and worries associated with the *ADB* were ruining the last years of his life. As he lamented to his daughter Minna, upon learning of the death of the *ADB*'s printer Christian Wilhem Melzer, "How gladly I would extricate myself, if I could do so with honor!"[205] Whatever leisure he had had was now lost, and various writing projects had to be abandoned because of the massive paperwork associated with the journal.[206] He had imagined his old age differently.[207]

Finally, in order to preserve the sight of the eye he had left, Nicolai resolved to give up the *ADB* at the end of 1805, as he informed his correspondent and author of nearly forty years' standing, Ludwig Heinrich von Nicolay, in February of that year. Convinced to the end of the salutary effects of the *ADB* on German letters, he declared, "I proceed unwillingly, for I know that this will truly leave a lacuna in our literature that cannot be beneficial. But I cannot think of another solution. German literature is growing ever broader, rendering the editing of this work ever more laborious. The correspondence alone is astoundingly taxing and leaves me scarcely a moment of rest."[208] In his last *ADB* circular, dated 11 February 1805, Nicolai explained to the reviewers his reasons for giving up the journal, emphasizing the loss of his eyesight and general overwork, with twelve-hour days and little rest. He had considered turning the *ADB* over to another editor and publisher, but this was not practicable: "If I knew of a learned editor whom I could trust sufficiently, and who was willing to take on such a laborious work, and of a bookseller living in the same town who wanted to publish it, I would gladly turn it over to them, and be pleased to see it continued. Because I know of no one at present,

---

204. Bohn speaks of his relief in a letter of 27 October 1800, in NN 7. His misfortunes continued, however, with the death of his seventeen-year-old son and the decline in business brought about, as he saw it, by the increasing number of new bookshops in Hamburg—four of them founded by his former employees.

205. Nicolai feared that Melzer's heirs would have to give up the printing shop, leaving him without a reliable printer at a difficult time. Nicolai to his daughter Minna, Klein Schönebeck, 15 February 1801, in LAB, Rep. 200 Acc. 450, vol. 9.

206. Nicolai to H.K.A. Eichstädt, Berlin, 31 October 1800, in *Verlegerbriefe*, pp. 182–83; Nicolai to L. H. von Nicolay, Berlin, 15 April 1801 and 10 March 1804, in *Die beiden Nicolai*, p. 426 and pp. 522–24; and Nicolai to Eschenburg, Berlin, February 1802 and 7 February 1804, in HAB, nos. 211 and 213.

207. Nicolai to Eschenburg, Berlin, February 1802, in HAB, no. 211.

208. Nicolai to L. H. von Nicolay, Berlin, 16 February 1805, in *Die beiden Nicolai*, pp. 536–38.

though, and have good reasons for not making suggestions to certain people,[209] the only possibility ... is to end publication of the *Allgemeine deutsche Bibliothek* with the reviews of books from 1804." He thanked the many reviewers who had held the *ADB* aloft over the years and regretted only "that I must end my closer connection with so many worthy and noble men of letters."[210]

Nicolai's farewell elicited a flurry of responses, full of pathos and elegiac pronouncements. For long-time reviewers, the end of the *ADB* represented the end of an era, both of their own lives and that of the republic of letters. "It was with regret that I learned of the end of the ... Bibliothek, an institution that since 1765—for nearly half a century—has spread light and truth with a high degree of frankness,"[211] wrote the educator Carl Friedrich Pockels from Braunschweig. Walch in Schleusingen, who had devoted most of his adult life to the journal, struck a particularly melancholy note: "Such a sudden separation after so many years of connection with my most valued friend, and from an activity that offered relaxation from the toil and annoyances of school work, appears to me a mere prelude to the more general separation upon which no other follows." Fiercely loyal to the end, he mourned the passing of an institution that, he believed, had acted "almost alone up until now to salvage common sense and good taste."[212]

Nicolai's publishing career neither began nor ended with the *ADB*, but the years of the "old" *ADB*, 1764 to 1792, mark the central period of his life and fame. Nicolai and the *ADB* persisted into the nineteenth century. They were, however, with both their ideological bent and their encyclopedic aspirations, very much of the eighteenth. With the *ADB*, Nicolai and his anonymous colleagues had put their stamp on the German republic of letters in the last third of the eighteenth century, helping to set the terms of debate in many fields, but most particularly in theology.[213] The *ADB* became less literary as time went on, and more a journal addressing

---

209. Nicolai did try to find a successor, but to no avail. Two long-time contributors were willing to take over as editor, but Gebrüder Hahn in Hannover, whom Nicolai had offered the work, decided against publishing. Aner, *Der Aufklärer Friedrich Nicolai*, p. 179.

210. Promemoria to the *ADB* reviewers, 11 February 1805, in Nicolai, *Verlegerbriefe*, pp. 193–94.

211. Pockels to Nicolai, Braunschweig, 23 February 1805, in NN 58.

212. Walch to Nicolai, Schleusingen, 18 May 1805, in NN 79.

213. Walter Sparn speaks of the *ADB* under Nicolai and his assistant Lüdke as the most important instrument for connecting German Enlightenment theologians with the rest of the educated world, which was an essential goal of their project of (re)connecting religion with practical life. See his "Vernünftiges Christentum," pp. 18–57, 41.

religious, educational, and social issues, as well as more narrowly scholarly ones, within the context of book reviews. Thus reviews also touched on such subjects of public interest as new laws, schoolbooks, hymnals, and catechisms, which were at the heart of practical Enlightenment pedagogy and theology. This reflected the developments in Nicolai's own interests, and in his publishing activities after the 1760s. With the loyal assistance of a wide network of *ADB* writers and readers, Nicolai succeeded as well in broadening his publishing and book-selling business and becoming known throughout German-speaking Europe.

chapter

(6)

Literary-Mercantile Relations

Nicolai and His Authors

Fortunately, I know that I do not speak to you as a mere merchant.

—*Wilhelm Friedrich Hermann Reinwald, 1800*

Over the past century of histories of German literary life, a few studies have charted the sometimes stormy relations between publishers and authors in the late eighteenth century. From Karl Buchner in the 1870s to Alexander von Ungern-Sternberg in the 1980s,[1] authors have tended, in large part because of the availablity of sources, to focus on famous literary figures. Thus there remains a certain gap between our knowledge of the published debates of the time on authorial versus publishers' rights and prerogatives and the broader day-to-day practice from which they emerged.[2] The rich material in Friedrich Nicolai's correspondence can help to fill in some of these lacunae in the everyday history of author-publisher relations.

Nicolai was well aware of the contradictory nature of the relations between author and publisher, characterized, as his fictional alter ego Hieronymus had said, by two often diametrically opposed approaches to a given literary work. How were authors at once to maintain their integrity and produce something booksellers were willing to buy? A letter

---

1. Karl Buchner, *Aus der Korrespondenz der Weidmannschen Buchhandlung mit ihren Autoren*, 2 vols. (Berlin: Weidmann, 1871–73), and *Wieland und die Weidmannsche Buchhandlung. Zur Geschichte deutscher Literatur und deutschen Buchhandels* (Berlin: Weidmann, 1871); Wolfgang von Ungern-Sternberg, "Christoph Martin Wieland und das Verlagswesen seiner Zeit. Studien zur Entstehung des freien Schriftstellertums in Deutschland," *AGB* 14 (1974): cols. 1211–1543.

2. For a recent consideration of the situation of authors in eighteenth-century Germany, see John A. McCarthy, "Rewriting the Role of the Writer: On the 18th Century as the Age of the Author," *Leipziger Jahrbuch zur Buchgeschichte* 5 (1995): 13–37.

that Nicolai wrote to a young writer in the year that the first volume of *Sebaldus Nothanker* was published reflects this dilemma. The aspiring author Friedrich August Clemens Werthes, later professor in Stuttgart and Ofen and a distinguished translator from the Italian, had offered Nicolai his services as translator or writer as well as a drama from his own pen. He hoped in Berlin to mix with the literati and broaden his horizons.[3] Nicolai answered him more as an older and wiser member of the republic of letters and a citizen than as a publisher pursuing financial interests. "The seeds of talent" recognizable in Werthes's letter moved Nicolai to offer him some friendly advice, which is worth quoting in detail here because it reveals many of Nicolai's attitudes on the matter.

> You seem inclined to make yourself dependent upon publishers, to write and to translate what they ask of you. Believe me, nothing is more harmful to genius.... You would do better to choose the most difficult state office, where you will at least come to know people and not misuse your talent. If the writer is not impelled by an inner drive ..., the book will always be bad, whether it be commissioned by a king, a minister, or a publisher.... I am sorry for anyone who must deny his dearest inclinations ... because I have long been in this position myself. There are, however, but two paths—if one feels a burning desire for learning ... one should follow it. But this is a discipline in which one must remain steadfast. He who does not possess the necessary steadfastness would do better to seek his living in the world along the well-trodden path, and to live unnoticed among millions ... to acquire as much knowledge as he can, and to use it as best he can for the good of the human race.[4]

Nicolai's ideal of authorship, as expressed in this advice to Werthes to keep out of the hands of publishers who only wanted to hire his pen, as well as in the programmatic writings on literature, was bound to collide with his economic interests as a publisher. His correspondence with his authors and especially translators is full of references to works that were written not out of an "inner" drive, let alone a "burning desire" for learning, but rather for money. To be sure, a passion for scholarship or literature and a desperate need for cash were not mutually exclusive. Nicolai was also not as averse to hiring writers to produce to order as his

---

3. Werthes to Nicolai, 11 January 1773, in NN 82. I am grateful to Rita Unfer-Lukoschik for drawing my attention to this letter and Nicolai's reply.

4. Copy of a letter from Nicolai to Werthes, 2 February 1773, in NN 82.

statements in *Sebaldus Nothanker* and his letter to Werthes might lead us to believe. Rather, the development of projects to be carried out by others was central to Nicolai's sense of himself as an organizer of the republic of letters and as a publisher. "I myself am satisfied to be a midwife, without myself giving birth," Nicolai wrote to Freiherr von Gebler in November 1771.[5] A letter to Georg Christoph Lichtenberg repeats the metaphor in a less contented tone, "It is easy to tell a midwife: 'Be fruitful!' when she has to go out every night and assist the births of others, and is either too busy to conceive or too weary to feel any desire."[6] In his letters and published autobiographical writings Nicolai fluctuated between these poles of regretting his lot as an amateur scholar and expressing his contentment with being of use to others. Of course, Nicolai was his own firm's most prolific author, managing in a few weeks of rural seclusion that he snatched in dead periods of the winter to produce numerous novels, polemics, and his massive travel account. But the public role he claimed for himself was that of literary midwife. The topos of the midwife is of course a very common one in the republic of letters, and an ancient one as well,[7] but it could have been a description of the function of the ideal publisher. Nicolai, however, was a rather interfering midwife at times. He attempted in numerous cases to affect the product of the intellectual labor he supported, and sometimes it was he who suggested the pregnancy in the first place. Occasionally, he tried to find authors to carry to term ideas he had no time to bring to fruition himself, though these efforts often proved abortive, as we saw in the case of the "Library for Amateurs of Learning."

In his relations with authors, Friedrich Nicolai wore many hats. He and his authors could approach each other as charitable institution and client, as partners in the enterprise of edifying the public and spreading Enlightenment, or as teacher and pupil. To some extent, Nicolai accepted the role of benefactor, publishing certain works at least partially as a means of supporting their authors.[8] Nicolai once said that he had experienced most aspects of human existence, except poverty, and this may have strengthened a sense of responsibility rooted in ideas of Christian

---

5. *Aus dem Josephinischen Wien*, p. 26.
6. Quoted in Nicolai, "Selbstbiographie," p. 55 n. 18.
7. In Plato's *Theaetus*, for example, Socrates refers to himself as a midwife, who, though skilled in bringing forth the children of others and recognizing their talents, is incapable of child-bearing himself. Quoted in Peter Gay, *The Enlightenment: The Rise of Modern Paganism* (New York: Vintage, 1966), p. 144.
8. See Nicolai's correspondence with Friedrich Bothe, in NN 7.

charity.⁹ In keeping with this, though, he expected a certain measure of gratitude and objected to those who took his largesse, such as it was, for granted. At the same time he also occasionally published works that he knew (or at least strongly suspected) would not sell well, because he considered them useful and important or, as he put it "for love of the subject" (or "love of scholarship").¹⁰ As he told Ludwig Heinrich von Nicolay in 1809, however sad the times might be, and however unlikely the chances of good sales, he could not refuse to publish his friend's ballads, since he regarded the publication of the earlier volumes of poems as a monument to their friendship.¹¹ In such cases, Nicolai's behavior serves to underline Reinhard Wittmann's injunction to be skeptical of those sociologists who characterize profit maximization as the sole motor of publishing in the developmental phase of the modern literary market.¹² Georg Joachim Göschen may have said that " a shopkeeper cannot be a patron," and Nicolai that "the bookseller can regard books only as wares,"¹³ but we should not take this too literally as a description of their own practices. As York-Gothart Mix has argued more recently, publishers retained an interest in symbolic representation and acted to maximize *both* their material and symbolic profits.¹⁴ This is particularly true of publishers like Nicolai, who have a strong ideological investment in many of their products.

As a writer and critic in his own right, Nicolai played an active role in selecting and shaping most of the books he published. He and his authors believed him capable of judging manuscripts on both their intrinsic

---

9. Nicolai to Lavater, 24 April 1774, quoted in Sommerfeld, *Friedrich Nicolai und der Sturm und Drang*, p. 359. Throughout his life, Nicolai frequently donated or loaned money to those in need. When Nicolai died in 1811, the neighborhood gathered to catch a glimpse of his coffin, and his grandson described the Luisenkirche during his funeral as "packed full of an incredible mob" who remembered his charitable acts. Parthey, *Jugenderinnerungen*, p. 151.

10. Nicolai uses the phrases, respectively, in a letter of 22 May 1790 to J. J. Eschenburg regarding a biographical and bibliographic lexicon of English literature which was later published as *Das Gelehrte England* (in HAB, no. 90) and in his annotations on a letter of 1 February 1796 from W. F. H. Reinwald regarding a second volume of his *Hennebergisches Idiotikon*, in NN 60.

11. Nicolai to L. H. von Nicolay at Monrepos in Finland, Berlin, 12 December 1809, in *Die beiden Nicolai*, pp. 544–46. As Nicolai told Elisa von der Recke in 1794, L. H. von Nicolay's collected works, of which the *Balladen* represent the eighth and final volume, had been selling poorly. Nicolai to Recke, Berlin, 30 December 1794, in NN 288.

12. "Zur Verlegertypologie der Goethezeit," p. 117. Wittmann refers here specifically to Lutz Winkler's *Kulturwarenproduktion* (Frankfurt a. M.: Suhrkamp, 1973).

13. Göschen, who made this statement in a 1796 letter to C. A. Böttiger, is quoted in Wittmann, "Zur Verlegertypologie der Goethezeit," p. 117. Nicolai is quoted in Voigtländer, "Das Verlagsrecht," p. 18.

14. York-Gothart Mix, "Buchwissenschaft in der Postmoderne. Probleme, Prämissen und Perspektiven, *Leipziger Jahrbuch zur Buchgeschichte* 8 (1998): 13–32, 19–20.

merits and their potential as products for the market. He combined the qualities of what Johann Christian Gädicke has called trained (*gelernte*) and learned (*gelehrte*) booksellers,[15] despite his lack of a university education. Other "gelernte" publishers who concentrated most of their own energies on the business side of things established a greater division of labor. Nicolai's Leipzig friend and colleague Philipp Erasmus Reich, the leading literary publisher of the period, left all or most decisions about accepting and editing manuscripts to a group of advisers.[16] Nicolai, in contrast, generally read the sketches or manuscripts offered to him for publication himself (although, as with the *ADB*, he frequently did not see the final manuscript before it went to the printer),[17] sometimes commenting upon and revising them in detail, discussed subjects for illustrations with the author, suggested and provided reference works and other aids, and imparted his own ideas on how to organize research. He also commissioned numerous new works and revised editions of old titles he had inherited from his father.

The Regulation of Author-Publisher Relations

The twenty years after the Seven Years' War were a period of great struggle between German-speaking authors and publishers. As the literary market, and the opportunities for profit therein, expanded, many of the more successful authors became exasperated at publishers' unwillingness to share their substantial earnings by paying higher fees. Publishers countered that the constant risk of piracy prevented them from doing so. Unconvinced, some authors undertook a sort of strike, vowing to avoid the professional book trade and publish their own works for a fair profit.

15. Gädicke, *Der Buchhandel von mehreren Seiten betrachtet*, esp. chap. 2, "Der gelernte und der gelehrte Buchhändler," pp. 4–9, and chap. 3, "Ist es also nöthig, dass ein Buchhändler gelehrt sey, oder dass Gelehrte Buchhändler werden?" pp. 10–17. Gädicke argues that book trade training and a good basic education were quite sufficient, and indeed more useful, for a successful bookseller than academic learning.

16. Hazel Rosenstrauch remarks that Reich's authors rarely discussed the content of their works with him. "Buchhandelsmanufaktur und Aufklärung," p. 102. For more detail, see Lehmstedt, *Struktur und Arbeitsweise*, esp. chap. 4, "Die Lektoren des Verlages," which discusses the role of Reich's adviser-editors in developing his list, recruiting authors, and generally giving Weidmanns Erben und Reich the illustrious profile it enjoyed from the 1760s to the 1780s. Reich's division of labor may have been an extreme example.

17. Johann Christian Gädicke remarks that it was very common at the time for authors to send their manuscripts sheet by sheet directly to the printer, thus by-passing the publisher. *Der Buchhandel von mehreren Seiten betrachtet*, pp. 14–15.

Some, notably Klopstock, published their books by subscription, while others turned to collective self-help projects like the Buchhandlung der Gelehrten and the Verlagskasse für Gelehrte und Künstler in Dessau. Lack of publishing and bookselling experience combined with the opposition of the regular book trade meant that most of these projects, as Nicolai and others had prophesied, were short-lived.[18] By the mid-1780s it had become clear to most writers that self-publication enterprises were not the hoped-for solution to dependence on the book trade. The pitfalls of self-publication are illustrated by the case of an unnamed author who, via an intermediary, offered Nicolai volume 2 of a little work on divine justice. He had printed volume 1 at his own expense and given it to the Buchhandlung der Gelehrten. Distribution had been so poor, however, that the book never found its way into the bookshops and only became known after a review appeared in the *ADB*. Now he wanted a "famous publisher" for his work.[19] Because of such experiences, authors placed a more vigorous emphasis on improving conditions within the existing system. In the last quarter of the eighteenth century, many were indeed able to wrest higher fees from their publishers, as well as more influence over the appearance of their books and decisions about new editions.

What had not changed, however, was that, legally speaking, authors in Germany had almost no rights vis-à-vis their own intellectual and literary products. In 1791, Christoph Martin Wieland, one of the most prominent German writers of his day, lamented, "It is, alas, one of the deficiencies of our legislation that we in Germany do not have a generally valid positive law that stipulates exactly what is proper in all cases of dispute between author and publisher.... Thus no law remains but the basic rules of universal justice and fairness."[20] In a system of privileges

---

18. The idea of self-publication itself predated the eighteenth century. For general accounts of the self-publication projects, see Bettmann, "Die Entstehung buchhändlerischer Berufsideale," esp. pp. 43–48; Helmut Kiesel and Paul Münch, *Gesellschaft und Literatur im 18. Jahrhundert. Voraussetzungen und Entstehung des literarischen Marktes in Deutschland* (Munich: Beck, 1977), pp. 149ff.; and Ungern-Sternberg, "Schriftsteller und literarischer Markt," pp. 180–85.

19. Walch to Nicolai, Schleusingen, 1 December 1784, in NN 79. Walch had reviewed the first volume of the work in question in the *ADB*. The author apparently wanted Nicolai to buy the first volume and reimburse him for the printing costs. Otherwise he expected only a certain number of free copies but no cash payment.

20. Wieland, "Grundsätze, woraus das merkantilische Verhältnis zwischen Schriftsteller Verleger bestimmt wird," § 17. This essay, dated 5 November 1791, was printed by Karl Buchner in *Wieland und die Weidmannsche Buchhandlung*, pp. 135–45, and reprinted in *Gelehrsamkeit ein Handwerk? Bücherschreiben ein Gewerbe?, Dokumente zum Verhältnis von Schriftsteller und Verleger im 18. Jahrhundert in Deutschland*, ed. Evi Rietzschel (Leipzig: Reclam, 1982), pp. 185–97.

bestowed in a corporate context, the author as a free-floating citizen of the republic of letters had no official status. The bookseller possessed a privilege to buy, sell, and publish books. The printer belonged to a guild. The author had nothing but the right to sell his or her manuscript for a predetermined sum, no matter what profits the publisher might draw from the work in subsequent years or from later editions.[21] A *privilegium impressorium* at least theoretically protected publishers from the economic losses of piracy in those states where it was prohibited, but not the author from plagiarism. Johann Matthias Schröckh had no legal recourse when Stahel hired some local writer to "Catholicize" his history textbook while using his research and ideas and retaining the basic structure of his book. All he could do was to publish a complaint in the newspaper and back up Nicolai in his piracy suit. Most authors who called for strict laws against piracy did so from the pragmatic standpoint of persons deprived of the just fruits of their labor, arguing that piracy diminished the sales of the lawful edition, and thus also the chance that a book might go into a second or third edition (for which the author could receive an additional fee).[22] Others, such as Kant and Fichte, attacked piracy from a legal-philosophical position, arguing that reprinting was unlawful regardless of whether it actually harmed writers because the pirate appropriated the author's speech without the permission to do so that the lawful publisher possessed.[23] Authors had no recognized collective place in a set of economic and legal relations; they were individuals in a society composed of estates. In legal terms, their productions were viewed not as the unique

---

21. On the development of literary property rights, particularly in Germany, see Walter Bappert, *Wege zum Urheberrecht. Die geschichtliche Entwicklung des Urheberrechtsgedankens* (Frankfurt a. M.: Klostermann, 1962); Ludwig Gieseke, *Die geschichtliche Entwicklung des deutschen Urheberrechts*, Göttinger rechtswissenschaftliche Studien 22 (Göttingen: Otto Schwarz, 1957); and Vogel, "Deutsche Urheber- und Verlagsrechtsgeschichte." See also Herbert G. Göpfert, "Zur Geschichte des Autorenhonorars," in *Vom Autor zum Leser. Beiträge zur Geschichte des Buchwesens* (Munich: Hanser, 1977), pp. 155–64; Ungern-Sternberg, "Schriftsteller und literarischer Markt," pp. 173ff.; and more recently, Martha Woodmansee, "The Genius and the Copyright: Economic and Legal Conditions of the 'Author,'" *Eighteenth-Century Studies* 17, no. 4 (Summer 1984): 425–48, and John A. McCarthy, "Literatur als Eigentum: Urheberrechtliche Aspekte der Buchhandelsrevolution," *MLN* 104, no. 3 (April 1989): 531–47.

22. See, for example, Rudolph Zacharias Becker, *Das Eigenthumsrecht an Geisteswerken mit einer dreifachen Beschwerde über das Bischöflich-Augsburgische Vikariat wegen Nachdruck, Verstümmelung und Verfälschung des Not-und Hülfsbüchleins von Rudolph Zacharias Becker* (Frankfurt and Leipzig, 1789).

23. Immanuel Kant, "Von der Unrechtmäßigkeit des Büchernachdrucks," *Berlinische Monatsschrift* 5 (1785): 403–17; Johann Gottlieb Fichte, "Beweis der Unrechtmäßigkeit des Büchernachdrucks," *Berlinische Monatsschrift* 21 (1793): 443–74.

result of personal characteristics, as intrinsically their own property, but rather as objects to be sold once and for all like cloaks, cabinets, or cartwheels. Implicit in Joseph II's phrase that no more knowledge was needed to sell books than to sell cheese was the comparison between an author and a cheesemaker. Even the 1794 *Allgemeines Preußisches Landrecht*, the first German legal code to discuss author-publisher contracts, failed to anchor authors' property rights in law. For this, German writers had to wait nearly a century.[24]

The fact that publishers maintained the upper hand over authors in the new Prussian legal code was to a great extent a result of Friedrich Nicolai's vigorous intervention and revisions to the draft of new laws on publishing. Nicolai was able to present his revisions at the very last minute in December 1790, thanks to the good offices of Ernst Ferdinand Klein and, no doubt, Carl Gottlieb Svarez, members of the commission drafting the new legal code.[25] Most of his suggestions were adopted, and they shed a good deal of light on his notion of author-publisher relations.

Friedrich Nicolai was author and publisher in personal union, but when it came to Prussian public policy, he defended his estate as a merchant rather than the individual denizens of the republic of letters. These economic interests were of course portrayed as patriotic interests, and his defense of the publisher was couched in terms of the common good, because practitioners of the book trade were, he believed, more productive citizens than writers, and thus more deserving of state protection and support.

The image of author-publisher relations—and of writers—that emerges from Nicolai's suggested revisions to the *Allgemeines Preußisches Landrecht* is not a pretty one. If we had nothing else to go on, we might believe that Nicolai's experiences with his authors consisted of one fearful chicanery after another. The drafter of the proposed publishing regulations had been influenced by proponents of author's rights. The object of Nicolai's revisions was, of course, to strengthen the position of publishers by

---

24. Evi Rietzschel, "Nachwort," in *Gelehrsamkeit ein Handwerk?* pp. 249–76, p. 275.

25. Klein reminds him to send in his comments soon in a letter of 1 December 1790, in NN 39. Klein was connected to Nicolai by multiple ties, as friend, author, fellow member of the Mittwochsgesellschaft, and as the father of Nicolai's daughter-in-law, the widow of his favorite son Samuel Friedrich. Svarez also belonged to the Mittwochsgesellschaft. He was chiefly responsible for drafting the segment of the Prussian civil code on publishing law. Why Nicolai only submitted his objections at such a late date is unclear. The draft legislation in question had already been published and initial opinions solicited in December 1787. Voigtländer, "Das Verlagsrecht," p. 40.

anchoring their interests in positive law. He was very consciously voicing collective interests. As he said, "I speak on behalf of ... an important branch of trade, which feeds many families and which, were it to be battered by the heavy restrictions outlined here, would be difficult to reestablish."[26] He was at pains to explain why what might seem the legitimate complaints of the economically weaker party, the author, were actually attempts to tie publishers' hands, in order to relieve them all the more easily of their money. Where discussions of the book trade in *Sebaldus Nothanker* had unmasked the nefarious practices of booksellers, Nicolai now pointed the finger at unscrupulous writers.

Nicolai begins with the premise, popular at the time among critics of literary life, that most writers were not true scholars or men of letters but mere hacks. Their main interest was making money with as little intellectual effort as possible. If they could start with an idea from the fertile minds of their publishers, who also provided them with reference books and advance payments, so much the better. "Writing," he lamented, "has unfortunately become a trade." Many writers sought to live by their pens and wrote just to fill as many sheets as possible, sell them to the highest bidder, and wallow in idleness and independence (p. 10). Such authors often mistreated their publishers. All too frequently they broke with booksellers, tried to press more money out of them than was stipulated in the contract, or engaged in vengeful chicaneries, driven by an exalted opinion of their works' value or ignorance of the true nature of the sale of books (p. 21).

Writers were not merely a vain and contentious lot, ignorant of the book trade and the relative worth or worthlessness of their products, they were also fickle and disorderly. Pity the poor bookseller who, in his own interest, suggested a written contract, particularly to a famous author. According to Nicolai, many writers shunned formalities and were "disorderly in their dealings and often stubborn." They were only too glad to keep a back door open for advance payments and the like. In nine cases out of ten, he said, it was the author, not the publisher, who wronged the other party in economic arrangements (p. 10).

The state thus had good reason not to encourage such unscrupulous scribblers. Echoing his advice to Werthes many years before, he noted that "it would be far better for the state and the progress of literature if the greater part of these people either endeavored to serve in state offices

---

26. Ibid., p. 37. All page numbers in the text refer to this article.

or to engage in some handicraft" (p. 10). Bookseller-publishers, in contrast, were truly useful citizens, whose business required support, encouragement, and protection in order to flourish, for the benefit of the state, the public, and the republic of letters (pp. 10–11). "The general good of the public," he wrote in another context, "demands the preservation of publishers, and consequently of the publisher's property rights [*Verlagseigenthum*]. The private advantage of the author's heirs cannot be accorded the same value."[27]

Nicolai's suggestions for a new law regulating the relations between authors and publishers arose from these basic presuppositions. What he most objected to in the draft law was its failure to distinguish between real authors and the allegedly more numerous hired pens, who were not the actual creators of their works. As a consequence, the law gave much more power and influence to the latter than he believed circumstances warranted.

Although the new law touched on various problems, including piracy and the use of false places of publication, the central issue was that of property rights between authors and their publishers. The law sought to secure the rights of authors to their productions and its main stipulations were that

1. No publisher could acquire the rights to a work without the author's or heirs' consent (§713);

2. Contracts between author and publisher should be made in writing (§714);

3. In most cases, publishers only acquired the rights to the first edition of a work; when the edition sold out, the rights reverted to the author and further editions must be renegotiated (§715);

4. The size of the edition should be set out in the contract between author and publisher (§717).

Nicolai suggested revisions in all four areas. Concerning point 1, Nicolai asserted that authors should only have the rights to those books

---

27. E. M. Gräff (who took over Weidmanns Erben und Reich after the death of Philipp Erasmus Reich) quotes Nicolai in his *Versuch einer einleuchtenden Darstellung des Eigenthums und der Eigenthumsrechte der Schriftsteller und Verleger* (Leipzig: Weidmann, 1794), p. 100. Gräff and the other booksellers he cites all shared this viewpoint. Heinrich Bosse, *Autorschaft ist Werkherrschaft: Über die Entstehung des Urheberrechts aus dem Geist der Goethezeit* (Paderborn: Schöningh, 1981), p. 35 and p. 166 n. 121.

based upon their own ideas and not those commissioned and paid for by a publisher. In all other cases, the rights rested with the publisher, and the author had nothing to say about it. He provided several examples of publishers in Berlin and Leipzig hiring writers to carry out their own concepts, including his own project (never realized) of a guide for travelers, for which he had collected travel accounts, maps, postal reports, and the like at great expense over the years. He intended to hire somebody to carry out the idea, providing all the necessary materials. Given this fact, "would it not be unheard-of for the writer to refuse to consent to my right of publication [*Verlagsrecht*]?" (pp. 8–9). If authors were to maintain full property rights in such cases they could use the occasion of conflicts with their publishers to steal the idea, run off with the manuscript, and sell it to a higher bidder, or at least threaten to do so in order to obtain a higher fee, a method of petty extortion "of which we have sufficient examples" (pp. 22–23). The writer, Nicolai believed, risked nothing, being paid, usually in advance, to do a job. In such cases, it was the publisher's felicitous idea or the familiar title in a series that made the book. A mere instrument of another's idea, the writer could never expect to hold "the full property right." The bookseller, on the other hand, "risks everything if he does not retain the right to the enterprise initiated and conceived by himself." In such cases, in fact, publishers needed laws to protect *them*, particularly when they spent time and money helping the author to produce the work in question (p. 7). This also applied to most translations, a category of literature not mentioned specifically in the draft legislation, but which comprised about one-half of the new German books appearing at each Leipzig fair, often surpassing original German works in their value as commodities. Translators, Nicolai asserted, could not be compared to original authors and did not deserve the same rights to their work. The vast majority only translated to earn money. In most cases, the publisher commissioned the translation and provided a copy of the foreign-language work. Translators often produced sloppy work, and the publisher had no recourse against them. If they owned the rights, they could sell the work to another publisher, who would reap the benefits of the original bookseller's investment (p. 26).

Nicolai agreed in principle with the need for contracts, but laid the blame for the frequent lack of written agreements firmly with the authors. It would be useful, he believed, to require authors to protect themselves with written contracts. While the law itself would emphasize the protection of the publisher's property rights, writers would remain free to secure better conditions for themselves through individual contracts (p. 11).

Nicolai disagreed violently with point 3, that publishers acquire the rights to one edition only. He countered that in order to have a "solid business," the publisher depended upon the proceeds from the few good sellers that went into second or third editions. These were necessary to counterbalance the losses on other books, particularly "in the present dismal state of the book trade" (p. 12). He suggested retaining the current German, Dutch, and French custom of a perpetual right of publication (*ewiges Verlagsrecht*). As long as the authors and their immediate heirs lived, the publisher had to come to a fair agreement with them regarding new editions. After their death, property rights remained with the publisher.[28]

Nicolai objected that the stipulation of edition size (point 4) was purely a business matter, which writers little understood. He had never specified the number of copies in *his* contracts, and it was not common practice. The proper edition size could also not always be determined with certainty at the time when the contract was made, as he illustrates with an example. He had intended to print 750 copies of a particular book, but after inquiring about paper and printing costs, found a printer who charged the same price for 1000 copies as others did for 750. Naturally he decided to print 1000. Thus he retained a certain flexibility. He suggested that the law be changed to read that *when it is specified* beforehand, the publisher may not print more copies than stated in the contract.

What particularly impressed the legal code commission were Nicolai's lengthy remarks about the important role publishers played in initiating and fostering the writing of books, and his comments were incorporated into §§1021 and 1022. Nicolai's ideas as expressed here are far removed from the theoretical discussions of the time. Whether or not the publisher had furnished the original idea, the work's final form was still the product of the author's mind, even in the case of a translation. He ignored such philosophical questions about property rights in works of intellect and imagination as outlined, for example, by Immanuel Kant in the *Berlinische Monatsschrift* in 1785.[29] Instead, he presents, in the simple economic terms he no doubt believed would most influence the legal code commission, his concept of what would be fair to booksellers and publishers, given current conditions and practices in the German literary

---

28. Voigtländer, "Das Verlagsrecht," p. 29. The problem, however, which the draft law addresses, was that some publishers did not consult authors about new editions of their works, let alone pay them—a source of great bitterness.

29. "Von der Unrechtmäßigkeit des Büchernachdrucks," pp. 403–17.

marketplace. Some years later, Friedrich Perthes was to enunciate the idea that part of the publisher's function was to compensate the author on behalf of society, fulfilling its obligation to remunerate "the discoveries and inventions provided, the enlightenment, depictions, edification, uplift, [and] amusement," because authors sacrificed to the arts and sciences time they might have used to the advantage of themselves and their families, "in state office, commerce or crafts."[30] Nicolai might have added here that the state was obligated to assist bookseller and publishers in fulfilling this useful social function by solidifying their property rights, which kept the book trade and thus also the compensation of authors afloat.

With over thirty years of personal experience, Friedrich Nicolai spoke to the commission with the voice of authority. His own experiences with authors, however, were usually not quite as grim as those he describes as typical. To be sure, he received letters from a fair number of hacks, but he seems to have known how to protect himself well enough. He did on numerous occasions hire authors to translate or write for him, but most of these were friends of his or *ADB* reviewers, or otherwise people for whom he harbored intellectual respect, even if they did write for money. His old friend from Frankfurt an der Oder, Samuel Patzke, for example, translated numerous works from the French for Nicolai in the late 1750s and early 1760s when he was a theology candidate and then a country cleric, but his demands were exceedingly modest, and their relations, to judge from the letters, warm. Other "hired pens" were the university professors Georg Simon Klügel, Johann Matthias Schröckh, Jeremias David Reuss, and Valentin August Heinze; the apothecary and chemical author Johann Christian Wiegleb; and the well-known literary theorist and Shakespeare translator Johann Joachim Eschenburg. In the category of hacks we might place Friedrich Bothe, a classical scholar who eked out a living doing English translations to support his mother, or the young Ludwig Tieck, who churned out tales and novels with his sister Sophie and her fiancé August Ferdinand Bernhardi in a little house by the Rosenthal Gate in Berlin. There were authors who gave Nicolai trouble, but most of his experience with the truly low life of literature was not in his own publishing company.

30. Friedrich Perthes, *Der deutsche Buchhandel als Bedingung des Daseyns einer deutschen Literatur* (Gotha, 1816), pp. 5–6. Particularly in the days before royalties, the publisher did in a very real sense take a financial risk on behalf of the public, paying the author the same amount whether the book sold 100 or 1000 copies.

The Author Approaches

To become an author, one had first to find a publisher, and over the years hundreds of writers in towns from Aurich to Zurich laid their egos and their ideas before Friedrich Nicolai in the hope of persuading him either to launch their careers or to promote them further. "Sir, your name on the title-page of a book is a greater and more certain recommendation than the most voluminous praise of most reviewers," wrote Dr. J.J.H. Ribock of Lüchow near Salzwedel to Nicolai in 1780.[31] As a famous author and editor as well as a respected publisher, Nicolai exercised a certain magnetism over (would-be) members of the republic of letters, who approached him, usually by letter, with varying degrees of obsequiousness or bravura. Some found favor, some fatherly advice, and others summary rejection. Who were these people, how did they approach Nicolai, and why did they offer their manuscripts or their willing pens to him in particular? What factors led Nicolai to accept or reject a manuscript or, more frequently, the outline for or excerpt from a work in progress?[32]

Nicolai's correspondence reveals, if not exactly a German Grub Street, nevertheless a large number of impecunious people of the middle ranks of society who in the course of the eighteenth century increasingly came to regard writing as a source of income. Even that large majority of Nicolai's authors with secure positions, whether in the Protestant church, government service, or the secondary schools and universities, depended upon authors' fees to supplement their salaries. Johann Karl August Musäus, for example, had a tenured position at the Wilhelm-Ernst-Gymnasium in Weimar from 1769 until his death. His salary of 300 taler a year (for teaching eight hours a day), however, was insufficient to support his family of four in a fashion commensurate with their status, and he depended upon private pupils and lodgers as well as fees for reviews, books, and occasional poetry.[33] To most, income from writing may not have meant

---

31. Ribock to Nicolai, 28 April 1780, in NN 61. Ribock was a physician and well-known amateur flautist.

32. Authors often sent not a completed manuscript but a sketch or outline. Sometimes they did this to save postage, but often the work they offered was not yet written. As Nicolai's colleague Johann Christoph Gädicke noted in 1803, "For many men of letters nowadays an idea . . . an easily sketched outline, suffices to make a contract with a publisher." *Der Buchhandel von mehreren Seiten betrachtet*, pp. 13–14.

33. Carvill, *Der verführte Leser*, p. 37. Musäus could not afford to visit Nicolai in Berlin, which was apparently a dream of his. Three hundred taler yearly was the salary of a middling civil servant. This was more than most artisans or shop assistants or country schoolteachers would have earned, but men like Musäus, particularly if they had contact with the court, as he

the difference between starvation and satiety, but it did make it possible for authors to buy books, marry off their daughters, send their sons to the university, finance moving expenses, or even buy houses of their own.[34]

For the most part, such authors did not leave home to seek their fortunes in the metropolis as they might have been tempted to do in France or England.[35] Instead, aided by the relatively decentralized nature of the German book trade, they stayed at or close to home and tried to integrate literary labor into their everyday lives. Two typical examples may stand in for many others. In August 1792, Immanuel Gottfried Rothe, pastor in a village near Görlitz in Upper Lusatia, screwed up his courage, "despite the improbability of success," and asked Nicolai for the "admittedly unhappy work of a translator." Like Nicolai's fictional Sebaldus Nothanker, he had come down in the world through various misfortunes and persecutions. He had managed to send his two sons to the university, but was now hard pressed to pay off his debts and secure his family's future. "The fervent desire to die a solid man, paternal feelings toward my promising children who ... keenly feel their father's persecution, grateful concern for a wife who has done much for me, compel me to seek any means of saving myself and them. I have no choice but to earn something in the field of letters."[36]

The young Emmanuel Friedrich Wilhelm Ernst Follenius was less desperate but still badly needed money for his state law examinations in Berlin in 1800. "Where to get it," he asked rhetorically in a letter to Nicolai, "I do not wish to borrow, but am ashamed to beg and be a burden to my father." Marrying for money was, he said, against his principles. Writing for money was not, and selling his latest "novelette" to Nicolai seemed the best solution to his financial problems.[37] Both of these men were already published authors.

---

did in Weimar, were expected to maintain a high standard of dress and general representation. For an overview of salaries at the period and authors' earnings, see Rolf Engelsing, "Wieviel verdienten die Klassiker?" *Neue Rundschau* 87, no. 1 (1976): 124–37, esp. pp. 129–30.

34. Hazel Rosenstrauch makes a similar observation about Philipp Erasmus Reich's authors. Rosenstrauch, "Buchhandelsmanufaktur und Aufklärung," p. 99.

35. There was, of course no metropolis like London or Paris in Germany, but there was a good deal of literary piece-work available particularly in Leipzig, which is probably the reason why there was one published writer to every 170 inhabitants of that city in 1790. In the two largest German cities, Berlin and Vienna, in contrast, the ratios were 1:675 and 1:800, respectively. In Germany as a whole the ratio has been estimated at 1:4000. Goldfriedrich, *Geschichte des deutschen Buchhandels*, 3:249.

36. Rothe to Nicolai, Sohra bei Görlitz, 16 August 1792, in NN 64.

37. Follenius to Nicolai, Magdeburg, 14 January 1800, in NN 22. Nicolai rejected the novel, but ended up advancing Follenius 200 taler for "some novel or other" to help defray the

From the proverbial poor students, underpaid country parsons, and retired Prussian noncommissioned officers to well-born widows struggling to raise families on incomes incommensurate with their station and genteel female orphans facing the rent collector, many individuals who negotiated the cracks of estate society looked to publishers as potential benefactors, and Nicolai never lacked for offers of manuscripts. In hundreds of letters to the "sovereign of letters," would-be authors alternated woeful tales worthy of three-volume novels with assurances of potential good sales, assuming or hoping that the former as well as the latter would commend their works or services to Nicolai.[38]

Other authors, settled in professorships or more lucrative ecclesiastical livings, struck a more positive note in their approaches, emphasizing their admiration for Nicolai's works and merits, and their hope for a partnership for the good of learning (*Gelehrsamkeit*). Sometimes they sought his advice and criticism of their outlines, since he was knowledgeable both in many branches of learning and in the market value of intellectual products.

Although most authors appear to have spoken on their own behalf, some, either out of timidity or because they desired to remain anonymous,[39] approached Nicolai through an intermediary, frequently one of Nicolai's friends, authors, or *ADB* reviewers. One such intermediary was Friedrich Germanus Lüdke, a Berlin pastor and long-time *ADB* collaborator. He not only arranged in 1791 for Nicolai to publish a religious work by the army chaplain Christian Samuel Ludwig von Beyer, but also edited the work and read the final proofs. Lüdke presented himself very much as Nicolai's ally and agent in this enterprise. As he reported, he had

---

expenses of his examinations. Mentioned in his annotations on Follenius's letter of 17 February 1800, in NN 22. In 1798–99, Nicolai had published Follenius's novel *Die Milchbrüder Ferdinand und Ernst*. Follenius had previously written a two-volume continuation of Schiller's *Geisterseher*.

38. A particularly (melo)dramatic example was Julie von Penz, who regaled Nicolai with her family misfortunes and tried on four occasions between 1793 and 1800 to convince him to publish her poetry by subscription. In a letter of 17 May 1800 she spoke of her grandfather, an officer killed in the Thirty Years' War, of her father, who was forced by a duel to forsake friends and fatherland and enter Swedish service, then brought down by a cabal, and of her mother, who had died of sorrow. She herself had gone deaf suddenly at the age of eight. Now she was so far in debt that she could not even pay for rent and fuel. Rather than publish her poetry, Nicolai sent her 10 taler. Nicolai's note on her letter of 17 May 1800, in NN 56.

39. Even if they wrote themselves, many authors made their first approach to Nicolai anonymously, asking him to write to them care of a friend, perhaps to save themselves embarrassment if Nicolai rejected the work. NN 2, a volume of anonymous letters, is full of such offers, which Nicolai rarely accepted.

informed the author that Nicolai, although not keen to take on the work, would do so out of respect for Beyer and his brothers. He should not expect much payment, but leave this up to Nicolai's discretion. According to the loyal Lüdke, to be published by Nicolai was honor enough: "He will doubtless be pleased," he wrote, "to have the best publisher in the Holy Roman Empire for his first foray into the literary world."[40]

Other authors used intermediaries as a means of insuring their anonymity. The author of a sensitive work of political geography on Rhenish trade must have been very afraid of discovery. His intermediary, Franz Anselm von Benzel, asked Nicolai to mention the manuscript and his correspondence to no one, and to burn all his letters.[41] This was only one of a number of anonymous works Nicolai published where the author's name was not mentioned even in the correspondence.[42] It appears that Nicolai only published works by anonymous authors when he knew at least the intermediary.

The rhetorical approaches used by those authors who mentioned their motivations for approaching him reveal both the various public images of Friedrich Nicolai and some of the problems authors faced in getting their works published. They tend to emphasize the following points, in various combinations: Nicolai's participation in particular ideological battles or scholarly disputes; acquaintance with and admiration for his writings more generally; the fact that he was not a "mere" bookseller; the desire for a "solid" or "famous" publisher; dissatisfaction with previous publishers or

40. Lüdke to Nicolai, Berlin, 21 March 1791, in NN 46. The book was *Betrachtungen über einige wichtige Gegenstände der christlichen Religion und Moral.* For further examples, see Selwyn, *Philosophy in the Comptoir*, p. 230 and nn. 51–53.

41. Benzel to Nicolai, Mainz, 9 February and 1 March 1785, in NN 4. The work was *Betrachtungen über die Folgen der Eröffnung der Schelde, in Absicht auf den Rheinischen Handel und den Handel von Franken, Schwaben und der Schweiz.* Benzel, Nicolai's informant on the counter-Enlightenment in Mainz, also asked him to memorize his handwriting so that he did not have to sign his letters in future. The fact that Benzel had been forced to leave Mainz for eight years after the 1774 death of Elector Emmerich Joseph because of his association with the secularization of the schools and other Enlightenment activities must have increased his trepidation. He was called back to Mainz in 1782 by Elector Frederick Karl as *Curator* of the universities of Mainz and Erfurt. See F. G. Dreyfus, *Société et mentalités à Mayence dans la seconde moitié du dix-huitième siècle* (Paris: Armand Colin, 1968).

42. Another was the bizarrely titled *Des alten Kauz Meditationen über Besenstiele, Stiefelknechte, Schuhbürsten, Schlafmützen etc. : Ein Buch zur Beförderung der Humanität*, which has sometimes been attributed to Nicolai but was actually submitted by the cameralist Karl August Noeldechen, allegedly on behalf of an acquaintance. Noeldechen to Nicolai, Berlin, 14 June 1799, in NN 54. Noeldechen sent the *Alte Kauz* along with a second manuscript on hunting, which Nicolai rejected.

with conditions in the local book trade; and Nicolai's reputation for humanitarianism and charity.

Although one might assume that many authors who approached Nicolai felt at least some ideological kinship or commonality of interests with him, whether it was a general allegiance to the idea of Enlightenment or a shared taste for linguistics, surprisingly few said so in their letters. One who did was the Zurich poet, artist, and bookseller Salomon Gessner, who in 1777 sent Nicolai an anonymous manuscript against current intellectual fads in Switzerland, calling him the chief apothecary against the epidemic of "dreamers" and "fools" that was currently afflicting the nation.[43] In 1806, toward the end of Nicolai's career, one Georg Friedrich Wehner thought he had found a kindred spirit in Nicolai in regard to the failings of current philosophy and literature. "Sir, you are renowned as an opponent of the pompous tone that dominates philosophy, poetry, etc. at present, and I, who share the same sentiments, which are rooted in my innermost being, thus dare to place myself under your protection."[44] The late 1790s found Nicolai embroiled in numerous unfortunate philosophical disputes, and other authors were eager to join the fray. An anonymous correspondent from southwestern Germany believed Nicolai just the man to publish a work he had been writing for years against the philosophy of Kant, Reinhold, Fichte, and Schelling. He knew Nicolai's works and recognized in him a fellow enemy of the new philosophy, particularly of the excesses of the "Pseudo- and Extra- and Ultra-Kantians."[45] Wilhelm Traugott Krug, in contrast, thought that it would be an effective strategy for his *Bruchstücke aus meiner Lebensphilosophie* if Nicolai, his apparent philosophical opponent, were to publish the book. Written "by a so-called Kantian and published by a so-called anti-Kantian," his book "might gain all the more credence," and such a partnership might even presage an eventual reconciliation of the two camps. At any rate Krug claimed to have absolute faith in Nicolai's impartiality and in the services

---

43. Gessner to Nicolai, Zurich, 8 August 1777, in NN 86. The author and his intermediary Gessner apparently hoped that publishing the manuscript in Berlin would mask the work's Swiss origins. Nicolai did not publish it.

44. Wehner to Nicolai, Auerbach in the Saxon Vogtland, April 1806, in NN 80.

45. Letter of 2 March 1799, probably from Heilbronn, in NN 2. Imitation being the sincerest form of flattery, the unnamed author said he wanted to call his work *Gundibert der Zweyte*, after Nicolai's *Leben und Meinungen Sempronius Gundibert's eines deutschen Philosophen* (1798). In his notes, Nicolai expressed the hope that he would at least change the title, although he could not demand this. Similarly, Christian Gottfried Gruner offered Nicolai a "pièce du temps" against their mutual antagonist Fichte. Gruner to Nicolai, Jena, 14 July 1799, in NN 28.

he had rendered true Kantian philosophy by criticizing the excesses of certain overzealous followers.[46] Nicolai followed his logic and published the book.

The would-be authors who professed a more diffuse admiration for Nicolai and his works were, naturally, legion. They mentioned his "invaluable efforts and services on behalf of German literature"[47] or " the veneration that I owe to your enlightenment and merits."[48] One, the aspiring theologian August Ludwig Ummius, said that he had been raised by his father to be a great admirer of Nicolai's work.[49] Follenius, who had just finished his legal studies, described Nicolai as "the man who earned Germany's respect in so many directions." Unlike many other aspirants, flattery got Follenius somewhere; Nicolai accepted his novel.[50]

Several authors appealed to Nicolai as a man with feet in both the literary and business worlds. Marie Josephe de Monbart (née de l'Escun), a Parisian exiled to the wilds of Pomerania, said that she wished to entrust her "contes vrais" to a publisher "in a position to judge them, and who, an author himself, can appreciate the work of others."[51] Master soapmaker Johann Karl Lieber, who had written a geometry for everyday life, even referred to Nicolai's fictional bookseller Hieronymous and asserted that he was "seeking a publisher ... who acts ... not solely as a merchant (cf. Sebaldus Nothanker!) but also as a promoter of true Enlightenment and humanity."[52] Others emphasized the business side of things. "The well-known solidity of your firm," wrote Johann Christoph Erich Springer, "has made me desirous of offering one or another of my works to you for publication."[53] Christian Cajus Lorenz Hirschfeld was looking

---

46. Krug to Nicolai, Wittenberg, 29 October 1799, in NN 42. Krug was to become Kant's successor at Königsberg University.

47. Wiegleb to Nicolai, Langensalza, 24 October 1775, in NN 82.

48. Anonymous letter received on 31 March 1775, accompanying a "Lettre sur Mr Voltaire," in NN 2. See also the letter of 8 August 1793 from Weimar from the former actress Caroline Schulze-Kummerfeld offering Nicolai her memoirs, in NN 42.

49. Ummius to Nicolai, Boitzenburg, 29 August 1800, in NN 76. He was a former student of the famous classicist Heyne in Göttingen, an *ADB* collaborator, and asked Nicolai to publish his new edition of Sophocles' *Oedipus tyrannus*.

50. Follenius to Nicolai, Magdeburg, 11 January 1798, in NN 22. The novel was *Die Milchbrüder Ferdinand und Ernst* (Berlin, 1798–99).

51. De Monbart to Nicolai, Stolp, 28 March 1783, in NN 50.

52. Lieber to Nicolai, Buttstadt, 1 November 1801, in NN 45. Lieber was the author of several practical works around 1800.

53. Springer to Nicolai, Göttingen, 20 March 1767, in NN 72. Although Nicolai did not publish these works he invited Springer to join the *ADB*.

for "a considerable publishing house such as your own "to publish his *Gartenkalender*.⁵⁴

Some authors also referred to problems with their previous publishers or with the local book trade as reasons for seeking another publisher. Their letters reveal a panoply of troubles, complaints, and abuses, real or imagined. Johann Jakob Ferber, for example, was actually advised by his Mitau publisher Jacob Friedrich Hinz to look elsewhere. "His bookselling business," Ferber reported to Nicolai, "appears to be going nowhere ... and he consequently has no money for new books or publishing projects."⁵⁵ Heinrich Wilhelm Lawätz was encouraged by a friend to approach Nicolai after his publisher Johann Justinus Gebauer decided at the last minute not to bring out a selective bibliography he had prepared. Rather than take Gebauer to court for breach of contract he hoped to secure another publisher.⁵⁶ The eccentric novelist Johann Karl Wezel, one of whose plays Nicolai had already published, wrote that he was looking outside Saxony because he was convinced that the Leipzig booksellers were all slaves to his persecutors, the local university professors and censors,⁵⁷ and a young poet, who called himself "an unknown admirer of the Muses," lamented in 1769 that he lived in the most unliterary of places "where nothing is printed but postils and hymnals.... The jocular Muse is a vagrant there, banished from the land."⁵⁸ While Tileman Dothias Wiarda noted that he was sending Nicolai his study on the origins of German first names because he could get neither good type nor

---

54. Hirschfeld to Nicolai, Kiel, 29 November 1785, in NN 35. Nicolai seriously considered taking on Hirschfeld's popular *Gartenkalender*, but in the end the editor entrusted it to the Buchhandlung der Gelehrten in Dessau, a writers' self-publication project.

55. Ferber to Nicolai, Mitau, 9 September 1779, in Ferber, *Briefe an Friedrich Nicolai*, p. 70.

56. Lawätz to Nicolai, Altona, 18 September 1792, in NN 44. The friend who recommended Nicolai was the well-known political journalist Johann Wilhelm von Archenholtz, editor at the time of *Minerva*. The book was entitled *Bibliographie interessanter und gemeinnütziger Kenntnisse*.

57. Wezel to Nicolai, Leipzig, 8 September 1787, in NN 82. The play was *Die komische Familie*. To what extent the paranoid tone of Wezel's letter is justified is unclear, but the work he offered Nicolai was never published, and neither was anything he wrote thereafter. According to some accounts, Wezel had gone insane by 1787. Phillip S. McKnight believes that there *was* a campaign against Wezel by the Leipzig censors, quoting from the letter to Nicolai as evidence. *The Novels of Johann Karl Wezel: Satire, Realism and Social Criticism in Late 18th-century Literature* (Berne: Peter Lang, 1981), pp. 37–38.

58. Anonymous letter received 17 September 1769, in NN 2. Although the man did not give his own address, he asked that Nicolai write to him c/o a Herr Abt, director of a theatrical troupe in Bayreuth, which suggests that he lived somewhere in the area. Nicolai returned the packet of poems there, rather than follow the author's melodramatic suggestion that he burn them if they were unworthy of publication.

accurate printing in his remote corner of northwestern Germany,[59] Captain Alphons Heinrich Traunpaur d'Ophanie said that he preferred to entrust his collected works to a foreign publisher rather than the "literary Arabs of Vienna."[60] Johann Friedrich Herz in Hamburg could (or dared) not publish his pamphlet against Lessing's old opponent, the Hamburg cleric Johann Melchior Goeze, locally.[61] Finally, a penniless law student wrote in 1798 that he feared falling into the clutches of the translation factories, as depicted by Nicolai and others, evidence of the continuing influence of Nicolai's remarks on the book trade in *Sebaldus Nothanker* more than twenty years after its initial publication.[62]

Authors, particularly when they were in financial straits or just beginning their careers and seeking protection, frequently sought to flatter Nicolai by mentioning his reputation for humanitarianism and magnanimity.[63] Johann Friedrich von Werner, a disabled army officer serving a four-year sentence in a fortress, commended himself and his geography to Nicolai's "philanthropic attitudes."[64] August Friedrich Ernst Langbein, a popular Berlin novelist and short story writer, was looking for a novel to translate and/or adapt and said that he had found the courage to write as a stranger after hearing Nicolai praised as a man who "gladly helped anyone with his wealth of knowledge."[65]

These by no means exhaust the possible motivations and strategies of the authors who approached Nicolai as a potential publisher. With his reputation as writer and critic, one obvious reason for submitting a work to him was to obtain his opinion and suggestions for revisions, as well as his stamp of approval.[66] Prince Moritz of Isenburg, an avid *ADB* reader,

---

59. Wiarda to Nicolai, Aurich in Ost Friesland, 5 January 1799, in NN 82.

60. D'Ophanie to Nicolai, Vienna, 30 December 1788, in NN 75. The fact that his eyesight had grown too poor for him to proofread his own works removed one of the chief reasons for publishing locally.

61. Herz to Nicolai, Hamburg, 24 August 1784, in NN 34. Herz, whose dates were unavailable, was a theologian turned classical translator and writer.

62. Chr. Karl Lehmann to Nicolai, Frankfurt an der Oder, 24 August 1798, in NN 45.

63. Salomo Gottlob Unger, a pastor in the Thuringian village of Colleda a. d. Loß, to Nicolai, 26 February 1793, in NN 76. Unger offered Nicolai a theological work in exchange for some volumes of the *ADB*, suggesting that the ideas contained therein would thus come into circulation in his region. Although Nicolai said he could not accept the manuscript, he could give Unger the volumes of the *ADB* he wanted at auction-level prices. Nicolai's annotations on Unger's letter of 26 February 1793. Unger replied on 21 April 1793 that he could not afford even auction prices.

64. Werner to Nicolai, Fort Pillau, 9 January 1787, in NN 82.

65. Langbein to Nicolai, Berlin, 30 April 1807, in NN 43.

66. Johann Bernouilli, for example, sent him some manuscripts for possible publication as a

asked Nicolai for an honest opinion, "which I would expect in vain from my best friends," of his translation of Lord Bolingbroke's *Reflections upon Exile*. Nicolai had often declared his desire to judge works "without regard to person or rank," and Prince Moritz wanted him to apply this precept now. If he found the work worthy, he should print it, making any corrections or improvements he saw fit.[67]

Recommendations from friends were important,[68] and a personal meeting with Nicolai could also make it easier to approach him in his professional capacity. Friedrich August Müller, whose epic poem on Richard the Lionheart Nicolai accepted for publication in 1789, had met the publisher in Dessau several years before. Nicolai had invited Müller, the brother-in-law of his Vienna lawyer Matolay,[69] to visit him in Berlin. Having no contacts to local publishers in Halle, where the young Viennese writer was living temporarily, he naturally thought of Nicolai.[70] The amateur scientist and prominent Hamburg merchant Nikolaus Kirchhoff, whom one might have expected to offer his works to a local bookseller, turned to Nicolai to publicize his electrical experiments because he had seen and shown interest in them during a visit to Hamburg.[71]

Finally, some authors mentioned that they were writing to Nicolai in order to avail themselves of his network of bookseller contacts, hoping that he would help them reach another, preferably well-known, publisher if he declined. Thus with his famous name he could serve as a conduit

---

periodical. After getting his works back accompanied by Nicolai's sometimes severe criticisms, the author thanked him for the useful suggestions and confessed "that I sent you the whole pile in part with the intention and hope of receiving your judgment of various pieces." Bernouilli asked Nicolai to keep him in mind if he needed a geographical writer. He was well traveled, and possessed a good book collection and much experience in the area. Nicolai noted that he would come back to Bernouilli when he had something for him. Bernouilli to Nicolai, Berlin, 28 October and 22 November 1784, in NN 4.

67. Prince Moritz to Nicolai, Birstein, 18 December 1778, in NN 37. Nicolai edited the translation himself and published the little pamphlet with a frontispiece by Johann Wilhelm Meil. Prince Moritz's letter explaining that he had undertaken the translation because Bolingbroke's work had so comforted him during his own exile served as a preface.

68. This was also the case, for example, with Dr. Johann Kaspar Philipp Elwert in Hildesheim, who told Nicolai that he was writing on the suggestion of his friend *Sanitätsrat* Joachim Friedrich Brandis, an *ADB* reviewer. Elwert to Nicolai, Hildesheim, 25 December 1790, in NN 18. Elwert and Nicolai entered into serious negotiations on the latter's biographical lexicon of the medical professions, and it seems that they came to an initial agreement but for some reason the book appeared elsewhere.

69. Müller mentions Matolay in a letter of 16 November 1790 from Vienna, in NN 51. The poem was titled *Richard Löwenherz*.

70. Müller to Nicolai, Halle, 13 June 1789, in NN 51.

71. Kirchhoff to Nicolai, Hamburg, 6 November 1780, in NN 38. Nicolai and Kirchhoff met in the summer of 1780.

to colleagues less in the public eye. Georg Michael Weber, for example, who lived in Bamberg (not known as a center of Enlightenment, particularly in the dark days of 1795), was anxious for his translation of Locke's *Two Treatises Concerning Government* and *Essay on Tolerance* to be published in northern Germany. Whether or not Nicolai himself consented to publish, said Weber, he hoped for Nicolai's advice, and that his connections would help him to find a publisher in Berlin or Leipzig. Nicolai recommended that Weber offer his translation to the Leipzig publishers Georg Joachim Göschen, Weidmanns Erben, or Johann Gottlob Feind.[72] As we shall see, he frequently recommended other possible publishers when offered a worthwhile work that he could not accept, whether the author requested this or not.

The reasons that led Nicolai to accept or reject a work for publication are not always easy to reconstruct, particularly in the absence of his own letters. In most cases, he had only the author's reputation (if any) and an outline of the work, rather than a complete manuscript, on which to base his decision. From the evidence of the reply dates he scribbled on the letters he received, he very often answered authors' queries within a few days. A combination of financial, practical, and intellectual factors doubtless played a role in any deliberation. A key consideration was, of course, the probability of profit, and more particularly how well the work in question might correspond to the demands and tastes of Nicolai's own habitual customers. Timing was also important, in two respects: One of Nicolai's chief business precepts was the necessity of balancing publishing and retail sales (*Verlag* and *Sortiment*), so that he was reluctant, except in a few special cases, to accept too many titles at one time and risk overextending himself. The number of titles which might be "too many" varied, of course, but Nicolai was particularly cautious during hard economic periods such as wartime. The proximity of the next Easter book fair was also important. Nicolai preferred not to publish new titles at the less well attended Michaelmas fair,[73] but for various reasons, authors sometimes refused to wait until the following Easter fair.[74]

---

72. Weber to Nicolai, Bamberg, 14 September 1795, in NN 80. Weber taught law and politics at the University of Bamberg.

73. For an example, see his letter of 10 May 1781 from Leipzig to Isaak Iselin, in NN 86. Because few booksellers attended the Michaelmas fair, and because of the flood of titles, which made booksellers reluctant to pay cash for potentially unsalable books, by the end of the eighteenth century, new works that appeared before Easter were often sent out "à condition" with the option to return them, usually at the next Easter fair. Nicolai to Eschenburg, Berlin, 24 June 1796, in HAB, no. 185.

74. This was the case, for example, when the work was highly topical or when two similar

Authors' honorarium demands do not appear to have been a major factor in deciding whether or not to publish.[75] Usually, Nicolai determined whether or not he was interested in a manuscript before financial matters were discussed, and negotiations followed acceptance of the work. In a few cases, however, probably those in which he was skeptical about potential sales, Nicolai said that he needed to know the honorarium before making a decision.[76]

Apart from the more intangible question of quality, the subject of the work and its seriousness could also be important factors. Nicolai was by no means a specialized publisher; he took on manuscripts in most branches of literature and learning. His reputation, particularly in the latter part of his career, was as a publisher of solid nonfiction. If literature in the narrow sense of the word comprises the largest number of volumes he published, this is because of his own works and those of a small handful of authors. He accepted very few works in the field of belles-lettres from authors he did not already know. The author who offered him a forestry and hunting almanac in 1796 had heard correctly that Nicolai "did not like to publish novels and little stories, but welcomed scholarly practical works."[77]

It is easier to know why Nicolai rejected works (or at least why he said he did) than why he accepted them, because the former usually required more comment than the latter. The reasons Nicolai offered for *not* publishing will shed some light on his relations with authors and his

---

works had been announced and the author wanted a jump on the competition. An example of the former problem was Eschenburg's planned pamphlet on Samuel William Henry Ireland's Shakespeare forgeries. Nicolai thought that the topic had cooled off to the extent that Eschenburg could incorporate this text into his larger work on Shakespeare and wait for some forthcoming new works from England and France, including Ireland's defense of his edition, as well as new German Shakespeare translations, which he could discuss in his own study. Eschenburg, however, decided to publish in the *Berlinische Monatsschrift* rather than wait until the 1797 Easter book fair as Nicolai suggested. Nicolai to Eschenburg, Berlin, 24 June 1796, in HAB, no. 185, and Eschenburg's response of 8 July 1796, in NN 19.

75. In the case of Hirschfeld's *Gartenkalendar* (which must have interested the gardening enthusiast in Nicolai), for which he went so far as to make cost calculations, the editor's demands of 200 taler per volume (more than 22 taler per sheet, about twice the amount he paid for anything else) and 100 free copies may have swayed him against it. The fact that he could not take it on that year, as Hirschfeld requested, may have been equally decisive, however. Nicolai's annotations on Hirschfeld's letter of 29 November 1785, in NN 35.

76. For example, he told Martin Gottfried Hermann that he needed his honorarium demands before deciding whether to publish his work on the origins of the constellations. Historical works, he said, were currently not very popular with the public. Note on Hermann's letter of 17 September 1796, in NN 33.

77. Günther to Nicolai, Halle, 30 July 1796, in NN 28.

publishing policies more generally.⁷⁸ In *Sebaldus Nothanker*, Nicolai self-ironically cited the "usual" arguments booksellers used with authors: "that he is overloaded with titles, that trade has declined, that printing and paper were becoming ever dearer."⁷⁹ Indeed, his own most frequently expressed reason for not taking on a new work was that he was already publishing too many books at the coming book fair. In many cases, of course, this may simply have been a polite means of refusal. Nicolai, however, was not known for his excessive diplomacy, except perhaps with women correspondents. If we take into account his financial caution and near-religious belief in the tenet of balancing publishing and sales, and the fact that he frequently gave authors other reasons for rejecting their works, we may be more inclined to accept these pronouncements at face value. In 1767, for example, he refused several works by the cameralist Johann Erich Springer, ranging from a historical essay on the plow to a handbook on German law, explaining "I am so overwhelmed with titles that I must restrict myself against my will, and thus cannot publish even those books that I like very much."⁸⁰ If we look at Nicolai's publications during this period, we find that 1767–68 were indeed years of relatively high productivity within the half-decade 1765–1770. Nicolai used this explanation repeatedly throughout his career, however, telling even his friend and faithful author J. J. Eschenburg in 1791 that he was publishing too much, and expressing relief that he had found another publisher, Herold in Hamburg, for a translation of Edward Gibbon's *Essai sur l'étude de la littérature*.⁸¹ There were other purely practical reasons for refusing to publish a book. Bad timing could refer not only to the proximity of the book fair but also to economic hard times. In the 1790s and early 1800s, Nicolai was not the only bookseller to lament frequently the dire situation of the book trade and the excessive risks involved in taking on large new projects. "I must confess," he told Heinrich Wilhelm Lawätz in 1792, "that given the current critical condition of the book trade, it is

78. The following comments are based mainly upon annotations Nicolai scribbled in the margins of letters from would-be authors, and in a few cases upon copies of Nicolai's own letters preserved in his papers. They concern 119 works by 84 authors, representing a sample of the unsolicited outlines and more rarely manuscripts sent to him over the years.

79. *Sebaldus Nothanker*, p. 391.

80. Nicolai's annotations on Springer's letter of 20 March 1767 from Bückeburg, where he was employed by the local imperial nobility, the counts of Schaumburg-Lippe-Bückeburg, in NN 72. To show his good will, however, he invited Springer to review for the *ADB*. Springer accepted, and Nicolai published his *Ökonomische und kameralische Tabellen* in 1771.

81. Nicolai to Eschenburg, Berlin, 17 February 1791, in HAB, no. 111. Eschenburg had offered him the work on 24 January 1791, in NN 19.

increasingly hazardous to take on multivolume works." Much as he regretted not being able to accept his useful bibliography, he feared, "(as I must candidly say) that a work such as yours would probably not find enough readers." Such works of literary reference, alas, enjoyed decreasing popularity. He went on at such length, he said, because he wanted Lawätz to know the reasons why a publisher might refuse his work, despite its excellence.[82]

Lawätz was only one of several authors whose manuscripts Nicolai explicitly rejected because of trepidation about sales. In 1794 he told his friend and author Elisa von der Recke that he could not publish her friend "R's" poems because "This is no time for poetry in Germany." In two years he had sold only 160 copies of the new edition of L. H. von Nicolay's poetry, and thus had not yet recovered his costs.[83] Similarly, he refused Follenius's offer of a new novel in 1804 because his last novel had not yet covered costs.[84] The problem with sales might not be a general one, but rather specific to Nicolai's own customers. He informed the abovementioned Johann Erich Springer in 1781 that his brand of "juridical-political works" did not sell well among his circle of customers.[85] Similarly, he told Adam Christian Gaspari that his collection of documents on the political history of the Nordic countries would not sell in Prussia, particularly at the cost of almost 1 louis d'or for a work five alphabets long (some 1800 pages in octavo).[86]

Just as often, however, to judge from his notes, Nicolai stated that he preferred not to publish a work because he found it bad or objectionable according to his critical standards (particularly clear writing and awareness of audience) or moral precepts. Johann Ernst Plamann's tract on the evils of female coquetry, for example, he described in his notes as "a vapid thing in the form of verbose letters."[87] *Winter Evenings*, a periodical,

---

82. Copy of a letter of 24 September 1792 to Lawätz, in NN 44. Lawätz found another publisher, Gebauer in Halle.

83. Nicolai to Recke, Berlin, 30 December 1794, in NN 288. Nicolai published his old friend L. H. von Nicolay's *Vermischte Gedichte und prosaischen Schriften* in seven volumes from 1792 to 1795. An eighth volume followed in 1810.

84. Out of an edition of 750, only 250 copies of the novel *Eduard Humber, oder die Folgen allzurascher Handlungen* had been sold in the first year. That was apparently too slow a rate for such perishable merchandise.

85. Springer to Nicolai, Bückeburg, mentioning Nicolai's response to his own offer of a work for publication, 8 April 1781, in NN 72.

86. Nicolai's annotations on Gaspari to Nicolai, Hamburg, 5 November 1784, in NN 24.

87. Nicolai's annotations on Plamann to Nicolai, Berlin, 21 November 1802, in NN 57. Plamann was a Berlin educator and follower of the Swiss pedagogue Johann Heinrich Pestalozzi.

warranted a slightly more detailed comment. Although the author obviously had some talent, Nicolai thought little of the journal itself: "The lewd passages displease me and I see no purpose in the work."[88] With authors he knew and respected, Nicolai was more explicit in his criticisms. He took his editorial duties seriously and was not afraid to point out unpleasant truths. In short, he sought to follow his own precepts as a critic. When Freiherr Adolf von Knigge sent him an outline and an extract from an epistolary novel he was writing, Nicolai made extensive notes on both, and commented upon the characters. Regarding the sixth and eleventh letters, for example, he believed that the people told their life histories too early on, which might lead the reader off on a tangent. Knigge also needed to make clear why the characters decided to confide their stories to each other in letters. The outline Knigge had sent was insufficient to give an idea of the whole, but from what he had seen, the novel did not seem to be "particularly new or rich." Tinkering with others' outlines for novels was rarely fruitful; it was generally best to leave them as they were or reject them altogether. "Improvement on the advice of others is usually mutilation. If the plan is simple, the beauties of detail are most important. But I must admit that I find the sample too ordinary and particularly too *contrived*. Contrivedness is one of the commonest faults in epistolary novels."[89] *Lenchen* and *Palibu*, two novels by Nicolai's English translator of the period around 1800, Friedrich Bothe, were also subjected to an extensive critique. Of *Lenchen*, the reader[90] complained that "one sees the author, who lives in a great city and forgets the provincial town." Much in the novel would be incomprehensible to most readers, and the author tended to forget the audience for whom he was supposedly writing, a cardinal sin in the Nicolai canon: "How can novel-readers know who the handsome Eutomisius is? I myself do not.... In some other passages too much is expected of the reader. In short, the

---

88. Nicolai's annotations on an anonymous letter of 8 June 1780, in NN 2. The reference to lewdness is typical for Nicolai, who preferred high-minded to racy literature.

89. Notes in NN 41 [Knigge correspondence]. The novel was titled *Begebenheiten aus meinem und anderer Leute Leben*. Adolf Franz Friedrich Ludwig von Knigge, who is best known for his 1788 primer on human relations, *Über den Umgang mit Menschen*, accepted these criticisms with good humor. He thanked Nicolai in a letter of 29 September 1780 and said that he would wait until he had something better to offer him. He does not seem to have done so, however.

90. It is unclear whether Nicolai himself wrote the critique (like most everything of the period it is not in his own hand) or whether he had solicited a written opinion from someone else. The sentiments are similar to those he has expressed elsewhere, particularly concerning the importance of the audience.

author reveals himself too much and too often as a learned man, a bel esprit, a belletrist, and too rarely as a popular novelist, or a middle-class novelist, which is what he is supposed to be." The book's two good chapters could not compensate for these flaws. *Palibu* suffered from quite another ill, a lack of originality. The novel was "a very unsuccessful imitation of Jean Paul. I discovered no wit in it, however, nor what the author was trying ... to say."[91]

Finally, Nicolai might reject a work, or at least hesitate to accept it, if he feared that it might involve him in unnecessary disputes, either with the censors or with private persons who felt themselves maligned. Still smarting from the banning of the *ADB* in Prussia, in 1796 Nicolai told his old comrade-in-arms, the educational reformer Friedrich Gabriel Resewitz, that he would publish his *Schulreden* only on the condition that they contain "no allusions to the local [i.e., Prussian] schools."[92] He must have expressed his fears quite vividly in his letter, because Resewitz withdrew the offer forthwith, saying that he did not wish to cause problems for either of them. To be sure, his speeches were politically blameless, "but the spirit of the times is such that one can suck poison from even the finest flowers."[93] During those same politically delicate times Nicolai dismissed a manuscript that critically analyzed the situation in Saxony with the words, "I do not wish to make trouble for myself."[94] Trouble came in numerous varieties. When Nicolai refused to publish Ernst August Anton von Goechhausen's treatise on oaths in 1793, the overextension of his publishing budget and the unavailability of printers were not his only considerations. Goechhausen mistakenly believed himself to be taking Nicolai's side in a dispute recently aired in the *Berlinische Monatsschrift*. Nicolai emphasized that he was not the journal's publisher, as Goechhausen implied, although such confusions of his activities as author and bookseller-publisher were frequent. If he were to publish a book discussing his opponents in this way, people might think he was seeking a new dispute, which was not the case. Goechhausen could publish whatever he

---

91. Undated note, probably from May 1800, in NN 7. Bothe had offered Nicolai the two novels with a letter of 26 April 1800, in NN 7.

92. Nicolai's annotations on Resewitz to Nicolai, 26 December 1796, in NN 60. Resewitz, who was the abbot of Kloster Bergen, a boys' school near Magdeburg, had contributed to all of Nicolai's critical journals and published several books with him.

93. Resewitz to Nicolai, Kloster Bergen, 9 January 1797, in NN 60.

94. Nicolai's annotations on a letter of 13 July 1795 (or 1796) from Heun on behalf of the author, an anonymous Saxon official. Heun's exact identity and full name cannot be ascertained from this letter.

liked, but Nicolai wanted no part of it.⁹⁵ He also shied away from works that might be considered insulting to individuals (at least unless he wrote them himself). Of Goethe's "Possenspiele," short comic plays offered to him by their mutual friend Ludwig Julius Friedrich Höpfner in July 1774, Nicolai remarked, "I want no part in such personal satires. I must admit to you privately that I do not approve of them at all.... As it is, impertinent mockery has already been taken ... too far." Someday, when he had a literary reputation to defend, Goethe might regret his unbridled tone, Nicolai believed.⁹⁶

Nicolai's interest in a work offered to him did not necessarily end when he rejected it. When he could or would not take on a work, but considered it worthy of the public, he sometimes arranged for its publication elsewhere. In other cases he suggested the author try another bookseller or means of publication. In 1774, for example, he arranged for the printing of *Timorus*, the first book by the Göttingen physicist and *Aufklärer* Georg Christoph Lichtenberg. Although he did not publish it himself, Lichtenberg referred to Nicolai as "the midwife at its birth."⁹⁷ Their mutual friend Heinrich Christian Boie, editor of the important journal *Deutsches Museum*, had sent Nicolai the pamphlet for possible publication in April 1773. The author, who asked only for twenty to twenty-five copies and good printing, wished to remain anonymous.⁹⁸ As Boie had suspected, Nicolai liked the satirical pamphlet, but preferred not to publish it himself. He may have felt that publishing the satire on the Zurich pastor Johann Kaspar Lavater (with whom he was still on reasonably good terms at that point) and his appeals to Moses Mendelssohn to convert to Christianity might cause more trouble than it was worth. At any rate he passed the work on to another publisher, and it appeared a few

---

95. Copy of Nicolai to Goechhausen, Berlin, 15 January 1793, in NN 25. Goechhausen, a former Prussian military officer, was Geheimer Kammerrat in Eisenach and author of numerous political works.

96. Nicolai's letter of 26 July 1774 is printed in *Briefe aus dem Freundeskreis*, pp. 101–2. The plays were published in 1774 by Weygand in Leipzig as *Götter, Helden und Wieland* and *Moralisch-politisches Puppenspiel*. Once Goethe had a literary reputation to lose (and his *Leiden des jungen Werther* was published that same year), he became even more inclined to poke fun at others, particularly at Friedrich Nicolai, and he does not appear to have regretted it.

97. Lichtenberg to Nicolai, Göttingen, 3 April 1774, in Lichtenberg, *Briefe*, p. 196. The work's full title was *Timorus, das ist Vertheidigung zweyer Israeliten, die durch die Kräftigkeit der lavaterischen Beweisgründe und der Göttingischen Mettwürste bewogen den wahren Glauben angenommen haben* (Defense of two Israelites who, moved by the power of Lavater's proofs and Göttingen sausages, accepted the true faith).

98. Boie to Nicolai, Göttingen, April and 10 May 1773, in. NN 7.

months later under the simple (and probably false) imprint "Berlin 1773."[99] Around the same time, Nicolai also found a publisher for Johann Christian Wiegleb's pamphlet against the alchemists. Wiegleb was perfectly content for Nicolai to give the work to a colleague because he was anxious to remain anonymous and feared detection if the book appeared under Nicolai's name.[100]

In cases where he was less personally engaged but nevertheless desirous of helping the author or the work to reach the public, Nicolai made suggestions rather than taking action himself. Thus even while they were negotiating, Nicolai suggested to Christian Gottfried Gruner that if things did not work out between them, the translation of Galen (which had been Nicolai's idea in the first place) might be an appropriate work for the Leipzig publishers Engelhard Benjamin Schwickert, Johann Friedrich Junius, or Weidmanns Erben und Reich.[101] Some works, he believed, might do better in another form. He suggested that both Friedrich Christian Karl Krebs and Adam Christian Gaspari publish their works as articles rather than books[102] and encouraged J.G.M. Poppe to bring his history of clockmaking up to present times and submit it for inclusion in a history of the sciences that another author was preparing.[103] He advised Friedrich Bothe to try to get his plays performed before attempting to publish them, since untried plays rarely found readers. Nicolai recommended he offer them to the director of the National Theater in Berlin, August Wilhelm Iffland.[104]

Thus Nicolai saw his role in dealing with authors and would-be authors not only from the standpoint of his own publishing company but also from that of the republic of letters and the public interest more generally. Unlike his evil creation Mynheer van der Kuit, he did not pretend that works that did not belong to him did not exist.

99. In a letter to Ramberg, Lichtenberg reported that the book had been printed in Königsberg, and it is unlikely that a Berlin publisher would have gone so far afield to print if the author was in Göttingen. *Briefe,* p. 301. Lichtenberg gave Boie permission to reveal his identity to Nicolai in June 1773. Boie to Nicolai, Göttingen, 5 June 1773, in NN 7.
100. Wiegleb to Nicolai, Langensalza, 24 October 1775, in NN 82.
101. Gruner mentions this suggestion in his letter of 27 August 1778 from Jena, in NN 28.
102. Krebs to Nicolai, Blankenburg, 3 May 1791, in NN 42; Nicolai's annotations on Gaspari to Nicolai, Altona, 16 September 1783, in NN 24.
103. Nicolai's annotations on Poppe to Nicolai, Göttingen, 30 May 1799, in NN 58.
104. His edition of the popular English satirist Samuel Foote's plays, which had apparently never been performed in Germany, had sold poorly, he told Bothe. Nicolai's annotations on Bothe to Nicolai, Berlin, 9 January 1806, in NN 7. It seems that it was very common for publishers to turn down plays that had not yet been performed. Helmut Hiller, *Zur Sozialgeschichte von Buch und Buchhandel,* Bonner Beiträge zur Bibliotheks- und Bücherkunde, vol. 13 (Bonn: Bouvier, 1966), pp. 75–76.

Literary-Mercantile Relations

Doing Business: Agreements, Contracts, Payment

Few of Nicolai's authors were writers by profession in the modern sense, and most entertained varying degrees of ambivalence about writing "for bread." The classical scholar and compiler Martin Gottfried Hermann doubtless summed up the feelings of many when he noted in 1795, "as fate would have it ... authorship is to become a line of business for me, as much as I hate it to be so."[105] Even fewer authors, however, refused payment for their work, whether in cash or books. There was an important distinction between writing for money and accepting remuneration for one's writing. The extent to which authors actively negotiated and defended their own financial interests differed markedly, though.

After the first step, when Nicolai informed the lucky author that he would accept the manuscript or proposal for publication, there was much to be decided and negotiated. Details were usually settled in an exchange of letters, a sort of gentlemen's agreement, rather than a formal contract. Such business tended to be conducted in a polite and friendly matter, with much protestation on both sides of the distastefulness of financial dealings. As Wilhelm Traugott Krug put it, "The negotiations regarding my fee cannot be more unpleasant for you than for me. The honorarium will be the ruin of our literature."[106] Nicolai was of a similar mind, as he told another author: "I can assure you, Sir, that nothing is more irksome to me than negotiating with an author as a bookseller. For my own self-preservation, I must deny my other sentiments and calculate coolly as a mere merchant."[107] Some authors had to be forced to even name a fee.[108] Others were considerably more assertive, but Nicolai's authors were never

---

105. Hermann to Nicolai, Hamburg, 30 July 1795, in NN 33.
106. Krug to Nicolai, Wittenberg, 4 December 1799, in NN 40. Paradoxically, the man who found honoraria the ruin of literature had just asked to have his raised, from the paltry 4 taler Nicolai suggested (Krug had left this up to him) to a still modest 5 taler a sheet. His reasoning shows the ambivalence with which literary fees were still regarded by some writers: "I must admit that, whenever I am supposed to demand or receive a fee, I feel a secret aversion to this not very honorable so-called honorarium, whose name is perhaps only an antiphrasis, but ... necessity and prevailing custom ... are a pair of tyrants in the face of which both scholastic philosophy and a philosophy of life are powerless."
107. Copy of a letter of 24 November 1792 to E.J.W.E. von Massow, whose demands he had had to disappoint drastically, in NN 48.
108. A case in point was Jeremias David Reuß. Nicolai had to ask him numerous times, but each time Reuß either ignored the question or said he would be satisfied with whatever Nicolai, who was more experienced in such matters, offered. Finally Nicolai gave up and suggested that the fee be no less than 5 taler per sheet, and one-half of that for any new editions. Reuss declared himself grateful and wholly satisfied. Quoted in Fabian, "Die erste Bibliographie," pp. 16–43, 32.

the greedy and brazen primadonnas of letters about whom publishers or critics of literary life complained.

At first glance, Nicolai appears somewhat tight-fisted when we contrast the sums he paid his authors to the lavish figures on late-eighteenth-century honoraria cited by literary sociologists such as Hans J. Haferkorn. Images of a sharp rise in honoraria in the last third of the century, in particular, have been colored by the focus on a handful of bestselling authors who were particularly good at looking after their own interests and seeking out generous publishers. In his study of the development of authorship, Haferkorn indicates that the *average* per sheet honorarium rose from 3 taler at midcentury to 12–40 taler around 1800.[109] The latter figure seems vastly exaggerated for anything but popular belletrists. Rolf Engelsing was probably closer to the truth when he estimated that at the end of the eighteenth and the beginning of the nineteenth century honoraria per sheet ranged from 3–5 taler on the low end to 20–40 taler on the high end of the scale. Thus while the highest honoraria were incomparably better than they had been at midcentury, there was a much more modest increase at the lower end of the scale. Two large categories of books, translations and scholarly works, however (and here, sadly, not much has changed), continued to be remunerated at the low end of the scale.[110] The Hamburg publisher Benjamin Gottlob Hoffmann may have paid the poet Johann Heinrich Voß some twenty taler a sheet for his works in 1785, but most of his authors received only 4 or 5.[111] Even Philipp Erasmus Reich, of whom it has been claimed that he paid an average honorarium of 12½ taler per sheet,[112] paid top fees of 12, 15, or

---

109. Hans J. Haferkorn, "Der freie Schriftsteller," *AGB* 5 (1964): col. 642. He gets his figures from Walter Krieg, *Materialien zu einer Entwicklungsgeschichte der Bücher-Preise und des Autoren-Honorars vom 15. bis zum 20. Jahrhundert* (Vienna: Herbert Stubenrauch, 1953).

110. In 1781, Immanuel Kant, already a well-known author, received the modest fee of four taler per sheet for his *Kritik der reinen Vernunft*. Engelsing, "Wieviel verdienten die Klassiker?" p. 131.

111. Ueding and Steinbrink, *Hoffmann und Campe*, pp. 137–38.

112. Hans J. Haferkorn, "Der freie Schriftsteller Müller und seine Einkünfte. Zur wirtschaftlichen Situation der Autoren in der zweiten Hälfte des 18. Jahrhunderts," in *J. G. Müller von Itzehoe und die deutsche Spätaufklärung*, ed. Alexander Ritter (Heide in Holstein: Westholsteinische Verlagsanstalt Boyens, 1978), p. 256 n. 35. One must be a bit skeptical of Haferkorn's figures when he calculates a sheet at eight pages when referring to novels, which were doubtless printed in either the octavo format, with sheets of sixteen pages, or duodecimo, with twenty-four pages per sheet. Much of the information on honoraria during this period comes either from Johann Goldfriedrich's *Geschichte des deutschen Buchhandels* or from Krieg, *Materialien zu einer Entwicklungsgeschichte*. The lack of scholarly apparatus in the latter makes it a rather shaky source, however. A recent addition to the scholarly literature on author's fees, which unfortunately came

even 25 taler to only a few authors such as Gellert and Wieland, more recent research has revealed. In the 1740s, he paid honoraria of 2–3 taler for both original works and translations, and by the 1780s most of his authors were still only receiving 4–6 taler per sheet for original works and 2–4 taler for translations.[113] The well-known poet Karl Wilhelm Ramler, for example, earned only 6 taler per sheet for his 1783 *Fabellese*.[114] A large proportion of the books Reich published were translations, so that he not only paid honoraria within the normal range for large North German publishers of the period, but on the whole got off rather cheaply.[115] Viewed against this background, Nicolai appears less penurious. What is striking, however, is the narrow range of the honoraria he paid his authors. Where Reich ranged from 2 to 25 taler per sheet from the 1740s to 1780s, Nicolai paid honoraria from 1 taler 16 groschen for a translation in the 1760s[116] to 10 taler for original works in the 1790s and after.[117] Reviewer's fees at the *ADB* also rose from 2–5 taler in 1765 to 6–10 taler in 1800.[118] The payments he offered increased, but not sharply, from 2 taler for translators and 3–5 for original authors in the 1770s to 3–4 taler for translators and 4–7 for original authors in the 1780s and 3–6 taler for translators and 4–10 taler a sheet (usually 5–7) in the 1790s and 1800s. Unlike Reich, he had no stars who commanded honoraria greatly in excess of those accorded to other authors. Such fees as he paid rewarded work,

---

to my attention too late to be used here, is Harald Steiner, *Das Autorenhonorar—seine Entwicklungsgeschichte vom 17. bis 19. Jahrhundert* (Wiesbaden: Harrassowitz, 1998).

113. Lehmstedt, *Struktur und Arbeitsweise*, pp. 49–50.

114. Karl Buchner, *Aus dem Verkehr einer deutschen Buchhandlung mit ihren Schriftstellern* (Berlin: Weidmann, 1873), p. 83.

115. Lehmstedt, *Struktur und Arbeitsweise*, p. 50.

116. This fee was paid to Jünger for the German translation of the Marquis d'Argens' *Lettres juives* in 1764. Weiße, who negotiated with the translator in Leipzig for Nicolai, mentions the fee in a letter of 5 July 1764, in NN 81. The same translator received 2 taler from Reich and other Leipzig booksellers, Weiße remarks.

117. Some authors who received the highest fees were Wiegleb for his *Geschichte ... der Chemie* (1790), Eschenburg for his *Lehrbuch der Wissenschaftskunde* (1791) and his *Theorie der schönen Wissenschaften* (3d ed., 1804), Svarez and Goßler for their *Unterricht über die Gesetze für die Einwohner der Preussischen Staaten* (1793), and Nöldechen for his *Über den Anbau der sogenannten Runkelrüben* (1799–1802).

118. Carl Ernst Bohn reported in 1799 that many of the old *ADB* reviewers had recently raised their fees to 10 taler per sheet, citing the high honoraria paid by the *ALZ*. Bohn to Nicolai, Hamburg, 4 January 1799, in NN 7. After Nicolai resumed publication J. J. Eschenburg even asked for a raise from 10 to 15 taler a sheet, but it is unlikely that Nicolai assented. In his illegible annotations scribbled on Eschenburg's letter the word "Debit" (sales) stands out, and it is probable that Nicolai refused Eschenburg's request because of the journal's poor sales. Eschenburg to Nicolai, Braunschweig, 23 April 1801, in NN 19.

not genius or fame. None of his authors amassed riches from the sums he paid them. His most popular and prolific author received no honorarium at all, although he reaped the most profits. He was, of course, Nicolai himself.

Once Nicolai had accepted a work for publication, a number of practical issues had to be settled. Essentially, Nicolai left only two questions up to the author's discretion: the fee and the number of free copies. In most instances, the size of the fee was set early on, although in a few cases, where Nicolai knew the author well, the subject was not even broached until the manuscript had been sent to the printer. Nicolai and his old friend Samuel Patzke, for example, did not discuss financial matters in advance at all. Only after Patzke had sent Nicolai the manuscripts for eight separate works, mainly translations from the French, did he mention the matter of money and ask to know how their accounts stood. "You may set whatever fee you wish," Patzke told Nicolai.[119] Frequently, authors named a price in their initial letter. Where this was not the case, Nicolai's invariable method was to ask them to set the honorarium. Many authors did so readily, but others demurred modestly and insisted that Nicolai name a price. So it went back and forth until one or the other gave in and suggested an amount. Nicolai usually accepted the figure demanded, but sometimes considered it too high or even too low and made another suggestion. Despite authors' occasional complaints and threats to seek another, more generous, publisher, Nicolai always managed to come to terms with them. After the issue of the honorarium was settled, Nicolai needed to know the number of free copies the author required, since most wanted at least some of them on fine paper, which—paper always being in short supply—needed to be ordered well in advance. The number of free copies was left up to the author's discretion and ranged from 4 to 40 copies, usually 15 to twenty-five. In some cases, the method of payment was discussed, namely, whether in cash or in books, or both, whether in advance or upon delivery of the manuscript or completion of printing, in a lump sum or in installments. Payment in advance was common, particularly for large works.

---

119. Patzke to Nicolai, Magdeburg, 18 June 1764, in NN 56. Letters from Eschenburg and Wiegleb provide further examples. Eschenburg's *Handbuch der klassischen Litteratur* was begun in late 1778 but he and Nicolai did not discuss the honorarium until 1782. Eschenburg to Nicolai, Braunschweig, 5 June 1782, in NN 19. Similarly, Wiegleb did not name his price until the *Chemische Versuche über die alkalische Salze* appeared at the Easter book fair in 1774, over a year after Nicolai had accepted the work for publication. Wiegleb to Nicolai, Langensalza. 23 April 1774, in NN 82.

Among other practical matters was the exact title of the book, so that Nicolai could announce it under the forthcoming works in the next Leipzig book fair catalog. Generally, authors chose their own titles, although they occasionally gave Nicolai the option of changing them if he wished.[120] If the work appeared by subscription, he needed to know how many sheets and how many volumes it would contain so that he could set a price. This could become a very sore point between author and publisher as works expanded beyond the original size and time frame and disgruntled subscribers spurned later volumes.[121] Authors were also frequently asked to compose a prenumeration brochure or announcement for journal and newspaper advertisements, and to aid in advertising their own books, sending round flyers and placing notices in the local papers at Nicolai's expense.[122] If the work was to contain illustrations or maps Nicolai needed to know how many, what the subjects would be, and whether the author knew of an appropriate engraver. In the case of novels, in particular, the authors provided detailed descriptions of possible scenes to be illustrated.[123]

Timing, of course, was also important. Although strict schedules were a rarity, Nicolai was naturally anxious to know when the manuscript would be delivered, either to him or to the printer, and thus at which book fair it could appear. It was essential to know this so that a printer could be engaged and paper ordered in time. The place of printing also had to be decided. Some authors insisted upon local printing so that they could read the proofs, and in such cases Nicolai might ask them to speak to printers, order paper and printing samples, and compare prices.[124] For most authors, the correctness of their works was a burning issue, and

---

120. One such changed title was Wilhelm Traugott Krug's *Bruchstücke aus meiner Lebensphilosophie* (Fragments of my Philosophy of Life) changed apparently at Nicolai's request from the original "Rhapsodien aus meiner Lebensphilosophie." Krug to Nicolai, Wittenberg, 10 November 1799, in NN 42.

121. This was the case, for example, with Rosenthal's Supplement to the *Technologisches Wörterbuch*. He promised on 6 June 1790 that it would not be more than two volumes but it grew to four. Rosenthal to Nicolai, Nordhausen, 6 June 1790, in NN 64.

122. Rosenthal, for example, composed a brochure for his Supplement to the *Technologisches Wörterbuch* and sent it to Nicolai, asking for several hundred copies which he would give the editor of the *Handlungszeitung* in Gotha to be inserted into the newspaper. Rosenthal to Nicolai, Nordhausen, 6 June 1791, in NN 64.

123. On authors' growing influence on and interest in illustrations for their works see Ungern-Sternberg, "Schriftstelleremanzipation und Buchkultur," esp. p. 88.

124. Friedrich August Müller, for example, insisted that his poem *Richard Löwenherz* be printed in Halle and visited several local printers at Nicolai's request. Müller to Nicolai, Halle, 24 June 1789, in NN 51.

they preferred if possible to read their own proofs, however tedious the task. Friedrich August Bothe, for example, even considered giving up the promise of a position in Copenhagen so that he could finish reading the proofs of his Euripides translation, a job he did not trust anyone else to do properly. If his two best friends had missed numerous mistakes, what could he expect from "common hirelings ... who care neither for me nor for a work whose correct presentation means so much to me!"[125] Where authors could not read the proofs, because postage was too expensive or time too short, they had to find someone else in the printer's vicinity with the requisite knowledge. Martin Gottfried Hermann admonished Nicolai to select "a good, exact and skillful proofreader" because of the many Greek quotations in his handbook of mythology.[126] When someone in Nicolai's shop jotted down printing instructions, they translated this into "a good philosophical knowledgeable proofreader."[127] Some authors even went so far as to pay a proofreader personally to ensure correctness.[128]

Whether or not the author wished to be named on the title page, and if so, by name only or with titles, was also an important question. Not all authors whose names are absent from the title page were truly anonymous. Some are mentioned by name in the preface.[129] Although most authors' names included their professional titles, some felt that modesty dictated their name appear unadorned.[130] Those many authors who chose

---

125. Bothe to Nicolai, Berlin, 3 March 1801, in NN 7. In the end, however, poor health and later the amputation of his leg forced him to turn the task over to his schoolmaster friends Georg Gustav Samuel Köpke of the Gymnasium zum Grauen Kloster and August Gottlieb Spilleke of the Friedrichswerder Gymnasium. Bothe's letters of 18 May and 17 December 1801 and his mother's letter of 13 January 1802, in NN 7.
126. Hermann to Nicolai, Hamburg, May 1789, in NN 33.
127. Sheet of paper with notes dated 18 December 1789, in NN 33.
128. Wilhelm Mila, for example, the French Reformed pastor in Köpenick near Berlin who offered Nicolai an abridged French version of his description of Berlin (which appeared in 1793 as *Guide de Berlin, de Potsdam et des environs*) engaged a teacher at the French Gymnasium in Berlin to read the proofs. Mila told Nicolai that he wanted 15 ducats honorarium, which he thought fair because he was paying the proofreader. Mila to Nicolai, Berlin, 9 March 1793, in NN 50. This must have been a fairly modest per sheet honorarium of 1 ducat (= ca. 3 taler) or less, even assuming that the French translation was considerably shorter than the abridged German version (some 18 1/2 sheets).
129. Karl Wilhelm Hennert, for example, is mentioned in Nicolai's preface to the former's 1778 *Beschreibung des Lustschlosses und Gartens Sr. Königl. Hoheit des Prinzen Heinrichs ... zu Reinsberg*.
130. One such was Tileman Dothias Wiarda, who requested that his name appear without titles on his *Ueber deutsche Vornamen und Geschlechtsnamen*. Wiarda to Nicolai, Aurich, 1 October 1799, in NN 82.

to remain anonymous had various reasons for doing so. Modesty or notions of social propriety might be considerations for women or nobles.[131] Most authors, of course, were not afraid of appearing as authors per se, but rather of being associated with particular works, especially those that were politically (and this included theologically) sensitive. One of Nicolai's correspondents underlined this problem when he proposed the idea of a "literary foundling hospital" where persecuted authors who might otherwise have to abort their intellectual offspring could bring them safely into the world under the cover of anonymity.[132] Fear of reprisals from the censors, however, was not the only reason for wishing to remain anonymous. Philipp Engel Klipstein, author of the *Patriotische Phantasien eines Kameralisten*, echoed a common argument of the time that people were more likely to accept suggestions from an anonymous author, and to judge a work on its own merits. He also feared that certain powerful men who knew of his position in government might misconstrue his intentions.[133] Knigge argued in a letter to Nicolai that it was better to remain anonymous, because once the public knew the author of a novel, they attributed to him evil motives and began searching among his acquaintances for the characters' real-life models.[134] Another author preferred not to be named, he said, because he already had several works appearing at one book fair and feared that people would think him a scribbler (*Vielschreiber*).[135] Nicolai usually accepted the author's decision in this matter, but in this last case he did not, perhaps

---

131. Wilhelmine Singer, for example, asked to remain anonymous as the author of *Emiliens Reise nach Paris, oder die Macht der Verführung*, "in part in order not to be known as an authoress." Singer to Nicolai, Berlin, 6 January 1791, in NN 71. The female translator of Fanny Burney's *Camilla* also wished to remain anonymous, as her intermediary with Nicolai, Johann Reinhold Forster, informed him. Forster to Nicolai, Halle, 25 May 1797, in NN 22. Prince Moritz of Isenburg wanted his name removed from the title page of his translation of Bolingbroke, *Von der Verbannung* (1779), because he feared people might think he was trying to put himself on the same plane as that great man. Letter of 24 March 1779, in NN 37. Nicolai, however, refused to bow to this modesty and left Prince Moritz's name where it was. The works of Empress Catherine, although by no means anonymous, appeared with only initials on the title page: "Von I [hro] K [aiserliche] M [ajestät] d [er] K [aiserin] a [ller] R [ussen]."

132. J.C.C. Rüdiger, *Cammersecretaire* in Halle, to Nicolai, 27 January 1781, in NN 51. He wrote on behalf of two friends, "staff officers in the theological army" who feared losing their livings in Bohemia if they published their "heretical" works openly.

133. Klipstein to Nicolai, 30 November 1789, in NN 39. Klipstein held the rank of *wirklicher Rat* in the Darmstadt administration.

134. Knigge to Nicolai, Kassel (?), undated letter (late 1780), in NN 41.

135. Negotiations between Nicolai and C. P. Funke over the latter's *Ökonomisches Lexicon* ultimately broke down because of Funke's insistence on anonymity. Funke to Nicolai, Dessau, 9 April 1797, in NN 23.

because of tightened censorship in the 1790s. The 1788 Edict Concerning Censorship forced the publishers of anonymous works into the unpleasant position of either naming the author or assuming sole responsibility if problems arose. Heinrich Gottfried von Bretschneider accordingly asked for his name to be left off the title page of his 1793 novel *Georg Wallers Leben und Sitten*, which dealt with Freemasonry, but authorized Nicolai to name him in case of legal action.[136] In this case, both author and publisher remained anonymous: the imprint on the title page read "Köln: Peter Hammer, 1793."[137]

Other issues that arose between Nicolai and some, but not all of his authors, concerned the physical appearance of the books, namely, format, paper quality, type fonts, and occasionally, illustrations. Edition size and the book's retail price might also be mentioned. This area was not, in general, open to much negotiation. Nicolai considered these matters his prerogative, but he did occasionally consult those authors with whom he worked most closely regarding paper and type. When making plans for Friedrich August Bothe's translation of the complete works of Euripides, obviously a title of some weight, he asked at the outset which format and font he would prefer. Bothe answered diplomatically, but specifically, that although he trusted Nicolai's wealth of experience, he believed that the median octavo and font used for Friedrich Leopold von Stolberg's edition of Sophocles would be appropriate. Nicolai agreed to Bothe's suggestion.[138] Many authors took a keen interest in their books' physical presentation, especially in the correctness and sharpness of printing and the

---

136. Bretschneider to Nicolai, Lemberg, 22 February 1793, in NN 9. Nicolai kept Bretschneider's secret so well that many people thought *Georg Waller* his own work. Knigge, for example, was convinced of this. Knigge to Nicolai, Bremen, 31 August 1794, in NN 41.

137. The use of this traditional false name, which first appeared as Pierre Marteau in the 1660s in both French and German works, probably accounts for the fact that Paul Raabe's catalog does not attribute the novel to Nicolai's firm. According to censorship historian H. H. Houben, it became particularly popular in the 1790s for political pamphlets, with such variants as "Hammers Erben" or "P. Hammer der Ältere." Books with false places of publication were forbidden by the Prussian Edict concerning Censorship. *Der ewige Zensor*, pp. 41–42, 53.

138. Bothe to Nicolai, Berlin, 13 December 1797, with Nicolai's annotations, in NN 7. Another author whom Nicolai frequently consulted on typographical matters was Eschenburg. For example, he sent him printing samples and asked him to choose the font he preferred for his *Entwurf einer Theorie und Literatur der schönen Wissenschaften*. Eschenburg to Nicolai, Braunschweig, 14 November 1781, 20 December 1782, in NN 19. He also sent samples of Solbrig's "clean Burgis type" which Eschenburg had requested for his *Beispielsammlung zur Theorie und Literatur der schönen Wissenschaften*. Nicolai to Eschenburg, Berlin, 5 September 1787, in HAB, no. 74.

quality of paper.[139] More rarely they tried to influence the work's price[140] or the size of the edition, which Nicolai did not believe was the author's affair.[141] With a few exceptions he also disapproved of authors trying to dictate format or type fonts. Format (usually median or large octavo) and the size of fonts were, however, important to authors not only for aesthetic reasons but also because they determined the proportion of manuscript to printed sheet and thus the final fee, since this was almost always calculated per printed sheet.[142] In a world where paper was expensive and scarce, the surest way to keep costs down was to use a small font closely

139. Of the authors' correspondences I read regarding some eighty separate titles, one-half mention issues of paper, format, and typography.

140. This was generally the case when the work was intended for a wide audience, such as the schools. Eschenburg, for example, chose a small font for his *Entwurf einer Theorie und Literatur der schönen Wissenschaften* to keep the price low for his less affluent students. Eschenburg to Nicolai, Braunschweig, 20 December 1782, in NN 19. Friedrich Rambach, who also intended his *Odeum. Eine Sammlung deutscher Gedichte* for the schools, said he would leave all matters of typography up to Nicolai, so long as the work was cheap. Rambach to Nicolai, Berlin, 9 October 1799, in NN 59. Heinrich Gottlob Zerrenner asked Nicolai to lower the price of his journal *Der neue teutsche Schulfreund* because of the poverty of schoolteachers, his intended audience. Nicolai agreed that a lower price would be preferable but considered it impossible at present because of the small edition size and unsure sales. Zerrenner to Nicolai, Derenburg, 8 November 1801, and Nicolai's annotations, in NN 84. Carl Gottlieb Svarez and Christoph Goßler likewise asked Nicolai to set a low price for their *Unterricht über die Gesetze für die Einwohner der Preussischen Staaten*, a work explaining the new legal code for the layperson. Svarez to Nicolai, Berlin, 5 January 1793, with Nicolai's annotations, in NN 73.

141. In 1786, Valentin August Heinze set out conditions for his (never published) "Grundriß der Europäischen Staatenkunde," and suggested an edition of 750. Nicolai agreed to all of his conditions except this last one, saying that he could not allow him to dictate the matter of print runs, which "must be left to my own convenience." Nicolai's letter of 25 April 1786, quoted in Heinze's reply of 1 May 1786, in NN 31. A year later, when Eschenburg asked for an honorarium of 5 taler per sheet for an edition of 1000 of his *Beispielsammlung*, Nicolai gave a similar answer. Nicolai to Eschenburg, Berlin, 16 October 1787, in HAB, no. 75. Eschenburg was disappointed, saying that a larger edition would mean "a disproportion in the remuneration of my efforts." He probably meant that a larger edition would make it unlikely that a new edition, for which he would be paid, would be needed soon. In a suggestion very unusual for one of Nicolai's authors, at least, he asked whether Nicolai might not prefer to share costs and profits with him in this instance. Eschenburg to Nicolai, Braunschweig, 21 October 1787, in NN 19. Moses Mendelssohn had also offered to pay half of the costs for Thomas Abbt's French translation of his *Recherches sur les sentiments moraux*, which Nicolai published. Mendelssohn to Nicolai, Berlin, July 1764, in Mendelssohn, *Neuerschlossene Briefe*, pp. 21–22.

142. A few authors asked for flat fees for their manuscripts, e.g., Wilhelm Mila for his abridged French version of Nicolai's *Beschreibung der königlichen Residenzstädte* and E. J. W. E. von Massow for his *Handbuch der Litteratur, angehenden Justizbedienten vorzüglich den Kgl. preußischen Justizreferendare gewidmet*. Mila to Nicolai, Köpenick, 9 March 1793, in NN 50; Massow to Nicolai, Stettin, 29 June 1792, in NN 48. Journal editors also tended to take flat per-issue fees, which they then distributed among the contributors.

spaced and thus squeeze more words onto a printed sheet. Nicolai frequently used this tactic, especially in the *ADB* where the short reviews were printed very small indeed. For this reason, some reviewers demanded different fees for small- and large-type reviews.[143] Authors, who were concerned to know in advance approximately how much they would earn from a manuscript, occasionally asked that it be printed in the same style as another work for which they knew the proportion of manuscript pages to printed sheets.[144] For Nicolai, though, low price remained an important factor in most cases, which meant that he often scrimped on printing and paper unless the author demanded little or no remuneration. He disagreed with those of his authors who maintained that good paper attracted readers[145] and firmly believed throughout his career—despite all evidence to the contrary from other publishers' luxury editions—that Germans were not willing to pay for fancy books. This cannot have been a *mere* hobby-horse of Nicolai's, but a reflection of his own customers' relative lack of means or desire for "your fine writing paper ... *quarto format* ... red lines ... vignettes by Meil, und ... a thousand other devilries" as Nicolai had put it in a 1768 letter to Lessing. He saved fine paper, exquisite illustrations by Johann Wilhelm Meil or Daniel Chodowiecki, and elegant printing for a few select works—many of them his own—and these often happened to be those where he also had to pay no honorarium.[146] Little as it endeared him to some of his more aesthetically minded

---

143. Joachim Heinrich Campe, for example, requested higher per sheet fees for his small print reviews. Letter in NN 12.

144. When Follenius submitted the manuscript of his novel *Eduard Humber*, he asked that it be printed "in the same format as Johnson." Nicolai apparently objected that this would be too expensive. Follenius to Nicolai, Magdeburg, 22 and 30 January 1802, in NN 22. Follenius had already had one disappointment when small type shrank his earnings on the first novel he published with Nicolai. Diplomatically, he attributed this to a printer's error and asked Nicolai to make up the difference, which Nicolai did only in part. Letter of 21 May 1798, in NN 22. Heinrich Ludwig Manger also asked that the printing of his *Baugeschichte von Potsdam* be like that of his previous works (published by Junius in Leipzig, Haller in Brandenburg, and Horvath in Potsdam), and larger than Nicolai's *Beschreibung der königlichen Residenzstädte* because he could not read such small type anymore. Manger to Nicolai, Potsdam, 7 April 1788 and 4 October 1788, in NN 47.

145. Follenius remarked in a letter of 22 January 1802 (in NN 22) that without a frontispiece illustration no book was successful, and that many people only bought books for the pictures and the woven paper.

146. Nicolai to Lessing, Berlin, 14 June 1768, quoted in *Sämtliche Schriften*, 19:284. Although many of his works contain illustrations, Nicolai seldom used the quarto format. He made exceptions for T. D. Wiarda's translation of the *Asega-Buch*, because it had to be printed in three columns (and perhaps also because Wiarda had not requested an honorarium), the collected works of L. H. von Nicolay (for which he also paid no honorarium, and which were doubtless

authors, for Friedrich Nicolai price usually went before beauty. Thus his friend Johann Jakob Engel complained to Johann Christoph Adelung, who had asked him to recommend a Berlin publisher, that Nicolai had been so frugal in printing his work that it crawled with typographical errors, and the paper was so porous that the compositor could scarcely read his corrections.[147] Similarly, Johann Karl August Musäus was appalled by the ugly cramped printing of the *Strausfedern*, with scarcely any margins at all. He managed to complain to the printer in time, however, and obtained a more satisfactory result. Of course, some authors were quite satisfied with the appearance of their works.[148] Rarely, however, did they overflow with praise for the handsome printing and paper in which Nicolai had chosen to clothe their products. More often they admonished him not to make the type *too* small or the paper *too* gray. Still, most expressed understanding that if the book's price were to be kept down, appearance would have to be sacrificed.

Hans J. Haferkorn has suggested that relations between authors and publishers became increasingly formalized as the century wore on, with written contracts replacing earlier agreements based in customary law, a development he attributes to the widespread philosophical and legal discussions of author's and publisher's property rights that emerged from

---

among the rare works he aimed at an aristocratic audience), Eschenburg's translation of Charles Burney's life of Handel, because of the size of the engravings, and his own 1803 lecture before the Academy of Sciences in Berlin, "Ueber Abstraktion, ihre nothwendigen Unvollkommenheiten, und ihren öftern Missbrauch," perhaps because it was a separate printing of an Academy publication in that format.

On Nicolai's relationship with Chodowiecki, which was both personal and professional, see Willi Geismeier, *Daniel Chodowiecki* (Leipzig: E. A. Seemann, 1993), esp. pp. 115ff. Among Chodowiecki's most celebrated illustrations for Nicolai were those for the novels *Sebaldus Nothanker* and *Johann Bunkel*. He also provided portraits of authors for the *ADB*, including the first published portrait of Goethe in 1776. Meil provided illustrations for, among other books, Nicolai's *Geschichte eines dicken Mannes* (1794) and for the 1799 edition of *Sebaldus Nothanker*.

147. The work in question was the *Anfangsgründe einer Theorie der Dichtungsarten aus deutschen Mustern*, a poetry textbook for the schools, which probably explains Nicolai's cost-cutting efforts. School books had a better chance of being adopted for use if they were cheap. Engel to Adelung, Berlin, 2 November 1779, in *Johann Jakob Engel. Briefwechsel aus den Jahren 1765 bis 1802*, ed. Alexander Košenina (Würzburg: Königshausen und Neumann, 1992), p. 67.

148. Nikolaus Kirchhoff, for example—who perhaps not incidentally asked for no payment—was pleased with the printing of the third edition of his *Astronomie nach Newtons Grundsätzen erklärt*. Kirchhoff to Nicolai, Hamburg, 11 June 1793, in NN 38. Johann Samuel Patzke found that his sermons were "neatly printed." Patzke to Nicolai, Lietzen, 26 February 1760, in NN 56. Eschenburg was well satisfied with the printing of both text and illustrations to his translation of Burney's life of Handel. Eschenburg to Nicolai, Braunschweig, 10 September 1785, in NN 19. Friedrich Heinrich Bothe thanked Nicolai for the "very pleasing appearance" of his translation of Euripides. Bothe to Nicolai, Berlin, 20 September 1802, in NN 7.

the piracy struggles of the 1770s and 1780s.[149] As in the case of authors' fees, Nicolai's correspondence provides no conclusive basis for such an assertion. To be sure, more authors asked for, or at least mentioned, contracts in the last decade of the century than previously, but their numbers remained small.[150] On the other hand, Nicolai's father and grandfather had drawn up formal written contracts with their authors at least as early as 1716.[151] The publisher Georg Joachim Göschen noted in 1802 that "all too often, one neglects to make contracts with authors, which serve, through the precise definition of the reciprocal duties and rights of writer and publisher, to seal off the sources of chicanery."[152] In 1800, as in 1760, Nicolai reached agreements with most of his authors without formal contracts. This does not mean that the substance of agreements remained unchanged, or that authors did not become more self-assertive with time, but merely that formal written contracts did not become the norm. Equally, there is little evidence for Friedrich Nicolai's assertion in his

---

149. Haferkorn, "Der freie Schriftsteller," col. 631.

150. Of the fifty-one authors' correspondences I read, only seven even mention formal contracts, and only one contains an actual signed contract. Unless these were only coincidentally the authors who did not make contracts, which seems unlikely, it appears that contracts were the exception for Nicolai, even at the end of the eighteenth century. A discussion with Mark Lehmstedt, who has studied the publishing practice of Philipp Erasmus Reich, revealed that the latter also only drew up contracts when authors specifically requested them.

151. In 1716 Christoph Gottlieb Nicolai and the lawyer and notary Johann Georg Job signed and sealed an agreement on Job's *Anleitung zu den curiösen Wissenschaften*. The contract stipulated not only which subjects the work was to cover, but also the maximum number of sheets, a delivery date for the manuscript, and the author's responsibility to see that the work was presented to the Berlin censor. It set the honorarium at 1 taler 12 groschen per sheet and five free copies. Contract dated 31 July 1716, in NN 285. Gottfried Zimmermann's contract of the same year with Professor Johann Christoph Beckmann not only set down when the manuscript had to be delivered, the honorarium of 1 taler 12 groschen per sheet and six free copies on ordinary paper and 8 on writing paper (to be paid for by the author) but also the font and type of paper. In addition, it stated that the publisher could reprint the work as often as he wished, "and thus do whatever he wished with it as his property," and that both parties' heirs would be bound by the contract if one of them should die (which Beckmann did in 1717). Contract dated 23 September 1716, in NN 285. The latter contract demonstrates that even at the beginning of the eighteenth century, long before the widespread debates over intellectual property, the question of the publisher's rights to later editions was enough of an issue to be mentioned in writing. Otherwise, what is most striking about these documents is that they dictate a delivery date for the manuscript. Although the authors were clearly to be paid for their work, "pro Studio et labori" as the typical phrase ran, the remuneration was modest, and they had to pay extra for the better paper used to print a portion of their "free" copies.

152. Georg Joachim Göschen, *Meine Gedanken über den Buchhandel und dessen Mängel, meine wenige Erfahrungen und meine unmaßgeblichen Vorschläge, dieselben zu verbessern. Bloß abgedruckt für die Herren Vorsteher und meine übrigen Herren Kollegen zur Prüfung, Verbesserung und Ergänzung* (Leipzig, 1802), p. 17; quoted in *Gelehrsamkeit ein Handwerk?* pp. 158–59.

remarks to the legal code commission that authors frequently *refused* to make contracts. On the contrary, the impetus for written contracts seems to have come, when at all, from authors. In 1773, for example, when Nicolai asked Johann Beckmann what he wanted for his translation of J. G. Wallerius's *Mineralsystem*, the latter sent him a contract to sign, "which I ask of every publisher for the sake of good order."[153] In at least two cases, authors did explicitly state that no contract was necessary, but this does not appear to have come in response to Nicolai's request for one. Gottfried Erich Rosenthal, who had been the one to request a contract in the first place because he did not know when or if his supplements to Johann Karl Gottfried Jacobsson's *Technologisches Wörterbuch* would ever see the light of day, found this formality unnecessary when it became clear after Jacobsson's death that the work would indeed be published.[154] Carl Gottlieb Svarez and Christoph Goßler thought a contract superfluous, since their letters served the same purpose.[155] As jurists and Prussian officials they felt themselves on solid legal ground with the conditions they and Nicolai set down informally. Such written agreements in letter form appear to have taken the place of formal contracts between Nicolai and his authors. They offered certain advantages to both parties, leaving flexibility to renegotiate fees, fonts, or edition size (so far as these were points of discussion), the length of manuscripts, and the number of volumes and publication dates without recourse to new contracts or legal disputes. Informality could, however, also foster confusion and conflict about what constituted an agreement to publish or to pay a certain honorarium. In general, though, the system seems to have worked, in large part because of the respectful and cordial relations between Nicolai and most of his authors, which allowed them to settle conflicts through rational discussion rather than the exceedingly slow-grinding legal system.

When authors did request contracts, what issues did they wish to see covered in them, and how did these differ from informal agreements? Three draft contracts and one signed contract in Nicolai's correspondence provide some answers. When Nicolai and Gottfried Erich Rosenthal agreed that the latter would begin collecting supplements for a

---

153. Beckmann to Nicolai, Göttingen, 4 April 1773, in NN 3. When they decided several months later to abandon the project, Beckmann reported that he had destroyed the contract. Beckmann to Nicolai, Göttingen, 28 September 1773, in NN 3.

154. Rosenthal sent Nicolai a draft contract on 18 March 1789. On 6 December 1789 (letter in NN 64) he said that a contract would no longer be necessary, unless Nicolai wanted one. The matter never comes up again in the letters.

155. Svarez to Nicolai, Berlin, 8 January 1793, in NN 73.

future continuation of Jacobsson's popular *Technologisches Wörterbuch*, they also agreed to draw up a contract for the work. Although Rosenthal said that he would leave the drafting to Nicolai, he wanted certain provisions included. The most important of these were (1) a fee of 4 taler per sheet plus some amount in books (to be left to Nicolai's discretion) per printed sheet in the same format and type as the original work, with half of the sum in advance; (2) in the event of Rosenthal's death, Nicolai would take his manuscripts and have two printers estimate the number of printed sheets and pay the honorarium to his heirs; (3) in the event of Nicolai's death, his heirs were obligated to fulfill Rosenthal's contract and continue the work or to pay for the remaining manuscript; (4) since it was not yet certain when (and if) the work would be published, they would say that the manuscript was due at the 1796 Easter book fair and that they would settle their accounts then. If the work could not appear at that date, they would set a new one; (5) if the author was in the publisher's debt at his death, the sum would be subtracted from the honorarium due him for any manuscript left behind; and (6) the publisher promised to send the author all books necessary for his writing postage-paid. If the author did not return said books within one year, they would be debited to his account.[156] Nicolai agreed in principle with all of the stipulations and promised to draw up a contract that would protect both parties and their heirs in the case of the other's death.[157]

E.J.W.E. von Massow thought it a waste of time to write back and forth between Stettin and Berlin, and set out his ideas for a contract in his very first letter offering Nicolai his outline of a training handbook for aspirants to the Prussian judicial service. The conditions were (1) an honorarium of 120 Friedrich d'or (ca. 600 taler) plus the books on a list 2½ pages long, to be delivered to him postage-paid no later than four weeks after the signing of the contract; (2) 40 Friedrich d'or by post at the 1793 Easter fair; (3) the same format and type as his previous book (also published by Nicolai), with paper thick enough to make notes on without the ink bleeding through; and (4) printing must be completed by the 1793 Easter book fair.[158] Negotiations were protracted, and Nicolai agreed to neither the cash nor the book honorarium. The final contract that Massow drafted, which Nicolai promised in November 1792 to read and sign soon, has not survived.[159]

---

156. Rosenthal to Nicolai, Nordhausen, 18 March 1789, in NN 64.
157. Copy of Nicolai to Rosenthal, Berlin, 11 May 1789, in NN 64.
158. Massow to Nicolai, Stettin, 29 June 1792, in NN 48.
159. Copy of Nicolai to Massow, Berlin, 24 November 1792, in NN 48.

Ernst Ferdinand Klein's contract for his periodical collection *Noteworthy Legal Opinions of the Halle University Faculty of Law* was shorter and simpler, but also more formal in style. Point 3 reflects the keen interest at the time in the issue of the author's consent in decisions about later editions: (1) the periodical would be printed in the same style as the editor's previous journal; (2) his fee would be 7 reichstaler per sheet; (3) a new contract would be made for each new printing or edition, which neither publisher nor editor could undertake without the other's agreement; and (4) the editor would receive thirty-five free copies.[160]

Nicolai's agreement with yet another jurist, Johann Anton Ludwig Seidensticker of Göttingen, is interesting as a rare surviving contract that Nicolai actually signed, and thus an embodiment of what he considered to be a proper example of the genre. It is neatly divided between the obligations of the author and the publisher: The author, having delivered his manuscript, which had been approved by the Berlin censor, turned it over to the publisher as his property and left entirely up to Nicolai the choice of font, paper, and format as well as the number of copies to be printed. He also promised to deliver the two missing supplements and the preface within four weeks, postage paid. The publisher in turn promised to pay Seidensticker twenty Friedrich d'or in cash (ca. 5½ reichstaler per sheet) in a lump sum as soon as he received the supplements and preface. Once printing was completed he would send the author twenty free copies on fine paper. He would also ensure that the author received the galleys for proofreading, three sheets at a time, together with the manuscript. The publisher would cover the postage.[161]

In this case, unfortunately, we know nothing of the earlier negotiations, if any, between Seidensticker and Nicolai, nor whose idea the formal contract was. At any rate it reflects Nicolai's belief that it was the publisher alone who decided on the externals of the work. No mention was made of possible later editions (there were none) or of payment for them. Nicolai clearly acquired the work outright, with no question of a reversion of ownership to Seidensticker, or any mention of his heirs.

Formal contracts and informal written accords differed little from each other when it came to their provisions. As time went on, however, more authors did become concerned with securing their positions, whether through a contract or a simple agreement. In the first half of Nicolai's

---

160. Klein to Nicolai, Halle, 6 January 1796, in NN 39. The title was *Merkwürdige Rechtssprüche der Hallischen Juristen-Facultät*.

161. Contract dated Berlin, 11 February 1797. Copy in NN 71 [Seidensticker correspondence]. The book in question was *Italien und die kaiserlichen Staaten insbesondere Wien*.

career, authors did not often mention property rights as part of their conditions. One who did was Friedrich Eberhard von Rochow, who although he asked no money for his schoolbook for peasant children, hoped to use profits from further editions for the good of his village school. When in 1772 a certain Herr Gillet sent Nicolai the manuscript on Rochow's behalf, he asked whether he agreed "that the author could regard the work as his own property again after the first edition."[162] Nicolai refused to relinquish the publishing rights of later editions, even for a good cause. Using Nicolai's usual arguments, Gillet succeeded in convincing his friend Rochow that it was unfair to rob a publisher of the opportunity to make money from good books to compensate him for those that did not sell.[163] In the 1790s, though, the hot debates about authors' rights combined with bad economic conditions and war-induced inflation to make authors worry more about secure agreements and the need to protect their heirs. Literature was a free market, and authors had to protect themselves as best they could. The fact that, under the circumstances, so many of Nicolai's authors appear to have relied on informal agreements is a measure of the trust they placed in his probity. We have seen that Ernst Ferdinand Klein (1796) wanted to ensure his consultation over future editions of his work, and Gottfried Erich Rosenthal (1789) raised the issue of protecting both parties in case of death. Similarly, Friedrich August Bothe asked in 1804 for a retroactive contract for his Euripides translation in case it went out of print, apologizing for bothering Nicolai so late in the game with something he should have asked for in the beginning. To be sure, "such a measure would be superfluous between us, but you never know whose hands the business might fall into in future." All of Bothe's other publishers had accorded him such contracts, he said.[164] Around the same time, when he was preparing the third edition of his encyclopedia, Georg Simon Klügel expressed the wish to provide for his family after his death. He asked that his widow and children receive one-half of his own per sheet honorarium of 1 Friedrich d'or for each future edition of the work.[165]

162. Gillet to Nicolai, Berlin, 10 June 1772, in NN 25. The work was the *Versuch eines Schulbuches für Kinder der Landleute*.
163. Gillet to Nicolai, Berlin, 6 July 1772, accompanying Rochow's manuscript, in NN 25. The work in question seems to have been a good investment. New editions appeared in 1776, 1790 and 1810. It was only the first of five books by Rochow that Nicolai published, so they must have come to a mutually satisfactory arrangement. Rochow also provided the prefaces for several other works on education that Nicolai published.
164. Bothe to Nicolai, Berlin, 28 February 1804, in NN 7.
165. Klügel to Nicolai, Helmstedt, 17 May 1803, in NN 40. Nicolai refused, but the rest of his answer has unfortunately been cut away.

Nicolai refused his request. Klügel made another attempt, explaining that his Leipzig publisher Schwickert had made such an agreement with him, as had Röhl in favor of Franz Christian Lorenz Karsten's heirs.[166] Nicolai's response is not recorded, but the third edition was in any case the last one. It appears to have been a matter of principle with Nicolai to regard his obligation to authors as fulfilled once he had paid the full fee. From that point on property rights remained with the publisher.[167]

In the absence of a contract, misunderstandings could easily arise over what constituted a promise to publish. In fact, it is surprising that this did not happen more often. The case of Nicolai's abortive association with Christian Gottfried Gruner demonstrates which areas needed to be settled before he considered their informal agreement binding. In 1777, Nicolai told *ADB* reviewer Gruner that he was considering a new edition of Galen in Greek and Latin with a commentary. If Gruner was interested, he would have at least until the Easter book fair of 1779 to complete the work.[168] Gruner waited some nine months before expressing his interest and naming his conditions, which included an estimate that the work would be about five alphabets long.[169] Nicolai was taken aback, since he had calculated the book to be much shorter. Under the circumstances it would be too expensive, particularly since it was now wartime. He also emphasized that they had not yet reached an accord. Thus Gruner was free to offer the work to another publisher, perhaps Reich, Schwickert, or Junius in Leipzig. Gruner disagreed with this assessment of the situation. As far as he was concerned, Nicolai's inquiries, which the publisher had thought merely a preliminary testing of the waters, were "binding enough ... for an honest man to keep his word, even if it was not in black and white." If he had been less convinced of Nicolai's honesty, he would have demanded everything in writing. If Nicolai refused to publish now, all of his work would be lost, work he had only undertaken at Nicolai's request. As to the other publishers, he did not know them and considered it beneath his dignity to go forth hat in hand to strangers. Under the circumstances, the least Nicolai could do was to compensate

---

166. Klügel to Nicolai, Helmstedt, 23 July 1803, in NN 40.
167. In only one case does he appear to have offered to relinquish those rights, and that was during a dispute with Christian Wilhelm Dohm over the honorarium to be paid for the second edition of a work. If Dohm insisted on such a high fee, he said, he was welcome to publish elsewhere. Nicolai's annotations on Dohm to Nicolai, Berlin, 4 November 1782, in NN 15. The case will be discussed in more detail below.
168. Nicolai's notes to an answer to Gruner's letter of 15 September 1777, in NN 28.
169. Gruner to Nicolai, Jena, 23 July 1778, in NN 28.

him for his labor and cash outlays so far.[170] Nicolai replied at some length on the series of misunderstandings between them, revealing his notions of what constituted a binding agreement. He had, to be sure, intended to publish the Galen edition, but his letter to Gruner was only provisional and "as long as there is not the slightest agreement between author and publisher regarding the book and its contents, or the honorarium, one cannot say that the publisher has made any promise to publish." Gruner should have told him how he planned to organize his edition before he began work on it. They also had no agreement on the fee, "and naturally nobody is bound to accept a work for which no price has been set." Once Gruner had provided more details about his ideas for the commentary, and a more exact estimate of the work's size from the printer,[171] and once they had discussed an honorarium, then he would be able to say if and under what conditions he would publish the work. If he decided not to publish, he would reimburse Gruner for his actual cash outlays, but not for the work itself, since he had neither known whether Gruner was interested nor set an honorarium on which to base any payment.[172] Thus in order to consider an accord as binding, Nicolai and the author needed to agree on the nature of the work, its approximate size, and the honorarium. In Gruner's case, the necessity of precise financial calculations was underlined by the projected extent of the work (nearly 2000 pages in octavo) and the fact of the war.

It was a rare case in which so many factors were contested. Not surprisingly, issues of honoraria, including agreements on advance payments, were the chief object of negotiation and conflict between Nicolai and his authors. How did authors justify their honorarium demands, and how did Nicolai react to those demands? When financial conflicts arose, how, and to whose benefit, were they settled?

It was a commonplace of eighteenth-century thought that one could never adequately remunerate intellectual labor.[173] Nicolai himself had noted in a letter of 1776, "I know ... that what the bookseller gives the author only rarely compensates him for the effort and value of his

---

170. Gruner to Nicolai, Jena, 27 August 1778, in NN 28.
171. He also asked Gruner to have the Jena printer Fickelscher give samples of his Greek and Latin Burgis type to Nicolai's *Diener* at the coming Leipzig Michaelmas fair, and to let him know in writing the prices for printing and paper of an edition of 1000 and 1500 copies. Copy of Nicolai to Gruner, Berlin, 28 September 1778, in NN 28.
172. Ibid.
173. See Göpfert, "Zur Geschichte des Autorenhonorars," pp. 156–57.

work."[174] Most authors nevertheless asked for, and received, payment. As Philipp Erasmus Reich put it, "The products of the mind are wares just as much as any material ones worked by hand. Just as one cannot demand these without payment, it would be unjust to expect men of letters to work for free and to offer up the fruits of their reflections and ... sleepless nights without regard for themselves and their livelihood."[175] In answering the question of how to decide on a fee, Christoph Martin Wieland suggested that the author take into account "how much intellectual effort and consequently also vital energy and how much time the work might have cost him."[176] Some of Nicolai's authors appear to have followed Wieland's rule of thumb, but it was by no means the only justification they provided for setting or raising an honorarium. While Friedrich August Bothe explained the price for his translation of Euripides in terms of the complexity of the task,[177] and Martin Gottfried Hermann in terms of the tediousness and unpleasantness of the work,[178] Johann Christian Wiegleb emphasized both the time and the expense he had put into the scientific experiments upon which his books were based. When deciding upon a fair honorarium, he said that Nicolai should take into account that his *Chemische Versuche über die alkalische Salze* had been "no fleeting product, but instead had cost him much precision, hard work and expense."[179] For him, the fee appears mainly as a means of financing his experiments. After subtracting these costs, he assured Nicolai, "only an almost insignificant amount remains for the honorarium proper."[180] He also mentioned the expenses incurred in another work as the reason for the size of his fee. After the death of the local artist who was doing the illustrations for his *Natürliche Magie*, Wiegleb had had to

---

174. Nicolai to Höpfner, Berlin, 23 April 1776, in *Briefe aus dem Freundeskreis*, p. 139.
175. Quoted in Rosenstrauch, "Buchhandelsmanufaktur und Aufklärung," p. 78.
176. Quoted in Haferkorn, "Der freie Schriftsteller," col. 580.
177. Considering the difficulty of translating Euripides well, Bothe hoped Nicolai would not think the price too high. Bothe to Nicolai, Berlin, 13 December 1797, in NN 7. According to Nicolai's notes they reached a verbal agreement of 5 taler per sheet.
178. "The work is one of the most laborious, exhausting and unpleasant imaginable," he said of the *Handbuch der Mythologie*. He asked for 5 taler rather than the 4 he had received for the previous volume, and Nicolai agreed. Hermann to Nicolai, Hamburg, 7 February 1788, in NN 33.
179. Wiegleb to Nicolai, Langensalza, 17 April 1774, in NN 82.
180. Wiegleb to Nicolai, Langensalza, 23 April 1774, in NN 82. He named a modest honorarium of 4 taler per sheet, plus the first 14 volumes of the *ADB*. When it came time for a new edition he asked for 2 taler per sheet, "since I received far too little for the first edition." Wiegleb to Nicolai, Langensalza, 20 September 1780 and 6 May 1781, in NN 82.

hire a man from Gotha and to house and feed him for eight days while he worked in Langensalza. Thus he felt that the sum of 6 taler per sheet was justified.[181]

The second most common argument was that the author had received a certain amount from previous publishers. Rather than demand a particular honorarium, authors might simply tell him that another publisher was in the habit of paying them a certain fee per printed sheet in a certain font.[182] Similarly, they might mention the honorarium another, similar author had received from Nicolai himself. Thus the philosophical essayist Johann August Eberhard requested the same fee for his 1781 *Sittenlehre der Vernunft* as Nicolai had paid Ernst Christian Trapp for a pedagogical work a year earlier.[183] "I know," he told Nicolai, "that you certainly do not wish to treat me less well than him."[184]

Other, less frequently used arguments, fall into three main categories. The first is that of need, that is, that the author must live at least in part from writing. Martin Gottfried Hermann, for example, tried to get Nicolai to raise his honorarium from 5 to 6 taler per sheet, and to throw in a copy of each of his new publications, by painting a grim picture of his circumstances. If he did not earn more, he hinted, he would have to seek more lucrative projects than the handbook of mythology. Working four to six hours daily, it took him more than two weeks to produce one printed sheet, for which he earned a mere mark in Hamburg currency. With inflation as it was he could not survive long at this rate.[185] Similarly, Friedrich August Bothe complained of poverty and the high cost of living in Berlin, despite his mother's thrifty housekeeping. Anticipating potential

---

181. Wiegleb to Nicolai, Langensalza, 5 May 1785, in NN 82. He also asked Nicolai to take into account the "very numerous and costly experiments" necessary for his *Handbuch der allgemeinen und angewandten Chemie* when considering his request for 5 taler per sheet (Nicolai agreed to it). Wiegleb to Nicolai, Langensalza, 20 September 1780, in NN 82.

182. See, for example, Manger to Nicolai, Potsdam, 7 April 1788, in NN 47. Manger mentions receiving 1 louis d'or from Junius in Leipzig, Haller in Brandenburg, and Horvath in Potsdam. The translator Johann Andreas Engelbrecht wrote that he received 2 1/2 rt. per sheet for regular octavo and 3 rt for large octavo, plus six free copies from Reich, Junius, Voss, Pauli, and others. Engelbrecht to Nicolai, Bremen, 12 July 1787, in NN 18. Eschenburg set his honorarium for the new edition of Lessing's *Briefe antiquarischen Inhalts* (part of Lessing's collected works, of which Nicolai was publishing four volumes) by referring to the amount the work's main publisher Voß had paid him for another volume of the *Vermischte Schriften*. Nicolai noted "I'll have to" in the margin of Eschenburg's letter of 24 August 1792, in NN 19.

183. Trapp to Nicolai, Halle, 23 May 1780, in NN 16. Trapp's book was the *Versuch einer Pädagogik*.

184. Eberhard to Nicolai, Halle, 14 October 1780, in NN 16.

185. Hermann to Nicolai, Hamburg, 30 July 1795, in NN 33.

objections, he remarked, "I could live in smaller quarters. Granted! But also less healthfully, especially for my ailing mother, and more sadly for me, for whom pure air and a cheerful view are necessities." Surely Nicolai could give him 5 taler rather than the usual 4 for his English translations.[186] Curiously, this argument could also be inverted. Karl August Noeldechen argued that precisely because he did not *need* the money, he would not work for a hack's wage of 4 taler a sheet.[187]

Many authors felt that they were underpaid, but Friedrich August Bothe's lament that miserable scribblers made more than he did, and that he thus deserved a raise was clearly inspired by the debates about trivial literature and author's emancipation at the end of the century. "When I see how much many literary idlers are paid, I cannot suppress a painful feeling of vexation. One truly need not be vain to believe that one does better work than such hermaphrodites. And yet they are better paid. And is it credible that those who support them fail to profit?"[188]

Similarly flavored by the debates of the day was the argument that Nicolai should raise the honorarium for subsequent editions in order to pass on some of his profits to the author, at a time when royalties were as yet unknown. Christian Wilhelm Dohm expressed dismay when Nicolai refused to pay him 1 louis d'or per sheet for the second edition of his *Über die bürgerliche Verbesserung der Juden* and 2 louis d'or per sheet for new additions. He had asked a mere ducat (ca. 3 taler) per sheet for the first edition, which had sold very well, and he had expected that Nicolai would let him share in the book's good fortune now. He had thought "this one of the rare instances in which a decent bookseller and even more a man of letters ... who must be sensible of the substantial disproportion between the usual fee and works such as my own, would be pleased to grant the author a fair share of his profits for a second edition."[189] Similarly, Martin Gottfried Hermann felt he deserved a higher honorarium for the second edition of volume 1 of his *Handbuch der Mythologie*. He apparently believed, however, that it was not merely Nicolai's moral but also his legal obligation. When Nicolai refused, and offered him the sum of 60 taler for his additions (ca. 2 taler per sheet),

---

186. Bothe to Nicolai, Berlin, 15 June 1798, in NN 7.
187. Noeldechen to Nicolai, Berlin, 2 October 1799, in NN 54. Noeldechen received 10 taler per sheet for his *Über den Anbau der sogenannten Runkelrrüben* (3 vols., 1799–1802). Noeldechen to Nicolai, Berlin, 9 May 1799, in NN 54.
188. Bothe to Nicolai, Berlin, 15 June 1798, in NN 7.
189. Dohm to Nicolai, Berlin, 15 November 1782, in NN 15.

Hermann answered that he had a legal right to that amount whether he made any revisions or not. Nicolai noted, "According to what law?"[190] Hermann had received 4 taler per sheet for the first edition, making 2 taler the customary, but by no means mandatory, fee.

Nicolai's answers to his authors' financial demands ranged from assent to violent disagreement. On occasion he even gave the author more than he asked for.[191] Where he refused, his arguments were, as is to be expected, almost exclusively economic in nature. General statements about hard times and the critical state of the book trade abounded,[192] particularly in the 1790s, often in tandem with other reasons. A typical argument, one difficult to gainsay and which authors therefore were obliged to accept, was that a higher honorarium would make the work in question too expensive and hurt sales with the target audience—in such cases almost invariably the schools.[193] It was particularly important to keep school books cheap, lest they be pirated or replaced by less expensive works.[194]

Potential sales were, of course, an important consideration in setting the honorarium. Generally, this meant that Nicolai cited projected sales as an argument for keeping the fee low.[195] In the case of the second volume of Wilhelm Friedrich Reinwald's *Hennebergisches Idiotikon*, a dialect

190. Hermann to Nicolai, Hamburg, 29 April and 2 May 1800, and Nicolai's annotations, in NN 33.

191. The modest Hermann Andreas Pistorius, for example, asked only 2 taler per sheet for his notes to *Johann Bunkel*, and Nicolai insisted on giving him 4 taler. Pistorius to Nicolai, Poseritz, 25 February 1777, and Nicolai's annotations, in NN 89.

192. Wilhelm Traugott Krug paraphrased Nicolai's reason for suggesting an honorarium of only 4 taler, which Krug considered "somewhat disproportionate" compared to what other publishers paid him. Krug to Nicolai, Wittenberg, 10 November 1799, in NN 40.

193. For example, when Friedrich Andreas Stroth requested 1 louis d'or (5 taler) per sheet for his school edition of Cicero's letters, Nicolai remarked that they had to keep the price low and he could thus pay only 4 taler. Stroth to Nicolai's son Samuel Friedrich, Gotha, 10 August 1783, and Nicolai's marginal annotations, in NN 73. Similarly, Nicolai said that he hoped Eschenburg would accept 5 taler rather than the 1 1/2 pistoles (7 taler 12 groschen) he had requested because paper and printing had become prohibitive and he was reluctant to raise the price of the *Lehrbuch der Wissenschaftskunde*. Nicolai to Eschenburg, Berlin, 22 March 1799, in HAB, no. 199.

194. Nicolai to Eschenburg, Berlin, 22 May 1800, in HAB, no. 204. In the end, however, Nicolai ended up paying what Eschenburg asked, although not in gold coins, which he claimed were unavailable.

195. Johann Jakob Ferber, who told Nicolai that he would be satisfied with whatever he saw fit to pay for the *Physikalisch-Metallurgische Abhandlungen*, was nevertheless disappointed with the offer of ½ louis d'or. Nicolai responded that he could not give more because the work was unlikely to make money. In the end it appears Nicolai gave Ferber the full ducat per sheet he requested in order to help pay the copyist. Ferber to Nicolai, Mitau, 9 September 1779 and 28 October 1779, in Ferber, *Briefe an Friedrich Nicolai*, pp. 70–74 and p. 93.

dictionary of obviously limited appeal, Nicolai even said initially that he would publish it only if he had to pay no honorarium, since he had only managed to sell one hundred of the three hundred copies of the first volume. Reinwald assented, remarking without irony that the circulation of ideas among scholars was as important as the circulation of money among merchants.[196] There were exceptions, however. When Ernst Ferdinand Klein asked for 200 taler per volume of his *Annalen der Gesetzgebung*, Nicolai replied that under ordinary circumstances that would be too high, but if Klein saw to it that the work was recommended to all state judicial offices, and that he could refer to this publicly in his advertisements, he would gladly pay it.[197] In the case of a pet project, the biographical (and bibliographical) lexicon of English authors titled *Gelehrtes England*, he insisted on paying the same honorarium for the supplement as for the first volume despite poor sales, telling his author Jeremias David Reuß, "I undertook this work, like so many others, purely out of love for the subject, and I do not wish to penalize you for the probably meager sales."[198]

In retrospect, the most curious reason Nicolai gave for refusing an honorarium request was to his friend Dohm, in the abovementioned case of the second revised edition of *Über die bürgerliche Verbesserung der Juden*. Dohm's book, he said, was a topical work of only ephemeral value (it was occasioned by a request to present the grievances of Alsatian Jews to the French government)[199] and it thus would be absurd to pay even more for the second edition than the first.[200] With the benefit of hindsight this judgment seems very ironic, since, of all the books Nicolai published, aside from his own, Dohm's is one of the few still frequently cited today.

196. Reinwald to Nicolai, Meiningen, 18 September 1800, in NN 60. Reinwald had first suggested the second volume in a letter of 1 February1796, in NN 60. Reinwald's selfless devotion to learning must have softened Nicolai's heart, and he noted on the letter that he would pay something after all.
197. Nicolai's annotations on Klein to Nicolai, 14 July 1787, received in Bad Pyrmont, in NN 39.
198. Nicolai to Reuß, Berlin, 16 March 1804, quoted in Fabian, "Die erste Bibliographie," p. 43.
199. A group of Alsatian Jews had approached Moses Mendelssohn in 1781 with the request that he compose a *Mémoire sur l'État des Juifs en Alsace*, requesting an improvement in their extremely unfavorable legal, economic, and social position. Mendelssohn was able to convince Dohm to take on the task. In the end the *Mémoire*, which apparently had little or no effect in France, grew into a book that inspired debates in Germany. Julius H. Schoeps, *Moses Mendelssohn* (Königstein/Ts.: Jüdischer Verlag, 1979), pp. 136–38.
200. Nicolai's annotations on Dohm to Nicolai, Berlin, 4 November 1782, in NN 15.

Although disagreements about honoraria were frequent, they usually remained minor. Where they did erupt into unpleasantness, this was invariably short-lived and the two parties arrived at some kind of compromise. Authors might threaten to take their works elsewhere, or Nicolai might challenge them to do so, but this does not actually appear to have happened. How precisely the serious difference of opinion between Nicolai and Dohm was resolved, for example, is unknown. Nicolai had been adamant in his refusal to pay what Dohm asked, and Dohm had been equally adamant in his refusal to go to another publisher, because it would look very bad for both of them and lead to unpleasant gossip. He gave Nicolai a choice. His final word on the subject was that Nicolai should pay him either the same fee as for the first edition or nothing at all, as long as he published the second edition. As regarded the continuation of the work, however, he could not lower his price, because it would absorb all of his free hours that winter and his economic circumstances did not permit him to work for nothing. In case they could not agree, he would have to seek another publisher who was in a position to remunerate him proportionately.[201] Dohm did not have to find another publisher, though, so they must have come to some arrangement. The two men remained friends and close associates, but Nicolai never again acted as Dohm's publisher.

This conflict, as well as many others over fees, highlights the issue of agreements about and payments for further editions, which were a subject of much discussion at the time. One author, Christoph Girtanner, even went so far as to launch a newspaper attack on his Göttingen publisher Johann Christian Dieterich because the latter had made a second printing of one of his works without consulting him.[202] Most of the new editions Nicolai published were revised ones, so that there was no question of not informing the author.

There were no hard and fast rules about honorarium payments beyond the first edition. Carl Gottlieb Svarez and Christoph Goßler even indicated in their written demands that they would ask no honorarium at

---

201. Dohm to Nicolai, Berlin, 15 November 1781, in NN 15. For a number of additional examples of disputes between Nicolai and his authors over fees, see Selwyn, *Philosophy in the Comptoir*, pp. 264–67.

202. See *Mein scharmantes Goldmännchen: Gottfried August Bürgers Briefwechsel mit seinem Verleger Dieterich*, ed. Ulrich Joost (Göttingen: Wallstein, 1988), commentary, p. 254. Gottfried August Bürger made similar complaints in letters of 3 and 7 April 1791 to Dieterich, who defended himself by saying it was only an edition on cheap paper to prevent piracy. Bürger, however, claimed to have seen copies on fine paper as well (p. 168).

all for a second edition as long as the text of their book was not changed significantly.[203] When it came to remuneration for further editions, the usual rule-of-thumb was one-half of the original fee. Where revisions were extensive, however, the author might receive the full honorarium again, or even more. Such a pattern was almost invariably the case with Eschenburg, most of whose books went into numerous editions and thus must have been quite successful. Nicolai paid him 2 ducats (6 taler) per sheet for the first and second editions of his *Handbuch der klassischen Literatur*. When Eschenburg asked for the same amount for the third edition, Nicolai replied, "As to the honorarium, I will accept whatever you decide, but ask you to consider ... that this third edition will sell somewhat more slowly."[204] Eschenburg replied that he would be satisfied with 5 taler. He received 7 taler, however, for the fourth edition in 1800.[205] In the case of his *Entwurf einer Theorie der schönen Wissenschaften* he also received 6 taler for the first and second editions, but 10 taler for the third.[206]

Nicolai almost always agreed to advances if the author asked, and sometimes even offered them unsolicited, as in the case of Svarez and Goßler[207] or of Follenius, who professed to being "deeply touched ... by your noble offer, which banishes many a worry."[208] As part of a practice that at times combined the roles of publisher and patron, he also continued in some cases to pay advances even when the authors were years behind with their manuscripts. In one case, that of Martin Gottfried Hermann, he paid several advances "with pleasure," including one for a work that never appeared at all.[209] When the author requested yet another advance, as well as a higher honorarium, without setting any date for delivery of the manuscript, though, Nicolai finally began to lose his

---

203. Svarez to Nicolai, Berlin, 5 January 1793, in NN 73. The work was the *Unterricht über die Gesetze*, a layperson's guide to the new Prussian legal code.

204. Nicolai to Eschenburg, Berlin, 21 June 1791, in HAB, no. 115.

205. Nicolai's note of 23 May 1800, in NN 19.

206. Nicolai to Eschenburg, 12 February 1782 and 8 October 1788, in HAB, nos. 41 and 82, and Eschenburg to Nicolai, Braunschweig, 31 August 1804, in NN 19.

207. In his letter of 13 January 1793, Svarez acknowledged receipt of the full honorarium of 200 taler in advance, saying that he had not requested it, in NN 73.

208. Follenius to Nicolai, Magdeburg, 27 February 1800, in NN 22. Follenius said that he would have been too timid to ask for an advance himself, and that he especially appreciated the fact that Nicolai put him under no pressure to write the book quickly. In 1802, however, he had enough courage to ask for an advance himself, which Nicolai appears to have granted. Follenius to Nicolai, Insterburg, 31 December 1802, in NN 22.

209. Hermann to Nicolai, Hamburg, 20 June 1793, 17 September 1793, 24 January and 12 June 1794, and 6 May 1795, and Nicolai's annotations, in NN 33. The work in question was volume 4 of Hermann's *Handbuch der Mythologie*.

patience. He agreed to the raise but at first refused an advance. He later relented, saying that it would be the last time.[210] Hermann continued to postpone publication, professing all the while that he wanted to see the book finished as much as Nicolai did.[211] By 1800, when Hermann asked him to pay the full (and higher) honorarium for a new edition of volume 1 of the same work upon delivery, without subtracting the advances already paid, Nicolai had already given up on the idea of a volume 4. It was, after all, more than five years overdue. This time, he felt, Hermann had gone too far. His remark that "you are a rich man and can fulfill this request without the slightest hardship" touched a raw nerve, and an epistolary altercation ensued.[212] Nicolai did not like having his generosity taken for granted. He replied that at this late date he did not intend to publish any further volumes, because the third had sold poorly and people had forgotten the book by now. He was only printing a small new edition of volume 1 so that he could offer customers complete sets, and certainly would not pay an additional honorarium under these circumstances. The peremptory tone of Hermann's requests also displeased him:

> Excuse me for remarking that you are badgering an advance out of me in a rather rude manner, as if I were doing you an injustice by not paying it. Then, as now, you referred in your letter to my wealth. I do not know what conceptions you have of that alleged wealth. Be that as it may, just because someone [acquires] something through industry and frugality does not give others the right to make demands as they please. However, this has happened to me so often that I am almost determined not to pay advances of this kind, which only lead to irksome explanations.[213]

Not surprisingly, Hermann adopted a defensive tone in his reply, even denying having requested an advance. It was, he said, perfectly normal for booksellers to pay advances. As to Nicolai's wealth, of course he had no claims on it, "but it was neither insult nor impudence to ask the help of a wealthy man in time of need when one was going to repay the advance with hard work." He professed himself deeply wounded by Nicolai's unfair accusations, while Nicolai felt that Hermann had treated

---

210. Hermann to Nicolai, Hamburg, August 1795, and Nicolai's annotations, in NN 33.
211. Hermann to Nicolai, Hamburg, 2 January 1796 and [received] 26 January 1797, in NN 33. Illness and failing eyesight, as well as the hope of contributions from other scholars, were the reasons Hermann gave for the delays.
212. Hermann to Nicolai, Hamburg, 29 April 1800, in NN 33.
213. Nicolai's draft response to Hermann's letter of 29 April 1800, in NN 33.

him "wrongly and impolitely." As he said in his notes to a reply to Hermann, "I would like to bring the matter to a swift conclusion." He promised that once the manuscript for the new edition of volume 1 was in his hands, "we will forget that we ever had dealings with each other."[214] In the end, Hermann had an outstanding debt of twenty louis d'or (100 taler), which Nicolai apparently preferred to the uncertain prospect of publishing volume 4 at some future date. Thus ended one of the most unpleasant conflicts between Nicolai and one of his authors, in bitterness, to be sure, but at least not in court.

The case of Hermann points up the image, touched on earlier, of publishers as benefactors, whose financial stability and power represented a well to be drawn upon, sometimes rather shamelessly, by needy authors. Nicolai was quite willing to accept this role up to a point, as long as authors asked politely and kept their end of the bargain by delivering their manuscripts. In one extreme case, that of Gottfried Erich Rosenthal, Nicolai paid advances fairly regularly over a period of at least fourteen years, from 1788 to 1802.[215] Rosenthal spoke of Nicolai as an instrument sent by providence "to put my shattered finances back in order."[216] When Rosenthal called the *Natürliche Magie* the project that "nourished me so maternally," he meant it rather literally. Regular advances allowed Rosenthal's wife to buy the grain for her malt business, one of the mainstays of the family income. Over the period between 1789 and 1805 the work earned him some 2015 taler, or an average of 126 taler a year, apparently just about the amount Frau Rosenthal needed.[217] The supplements to Jacobsson's *Technologisches Wörterbuch* also represented a substantial contribution to Rosenthal's income over the years. He continued to collect material for new supplements in the hope that Nicolai would reconsider his decision to end the work with volume 4. Now that his son was studying in Jena "his support is turning my hair gray," he lamented. He clearly

---

214. Hermann to Nicolai, Hamburg, 2 May 1800, and Nicolai's annotations, in NN 33.

215. Rosenthal to Nicolai, Nordhausen, 10 August and 23 November 1788, 19 May and 6 December 1789, 1 June and 3 October 1791, 1 August and 7 October 1792, 14 April 1793, 8 June 1794, 1 June 1795, 17 May 1796, 8 October 1797, 15 November 1798, 22 December 1799, 16 July 1800, and 27 January 1802, in NN 64.

216. Rosenthal to Nicolai, Nordhausen, 1 November 1788, in NN 64. Rosenthal was a brewer who had lost his business. The family was supported by three pensions, one of 60 taler from the duke of Gotha, one of 50 taler from the governor (*Statthalter*) of Erfurt, and one of 2 louis d'ors monthly from Count von Borcke, as well as the proceeds from his writing and his wife's malt business.

217. The eighteen volumes of the *Natürliche Magie* Rosenthal wrote contained ca. 6400 pages or 403 sheets, which were remunerated at 5 taler per sheet.

saw a continuation of the supplements and the further payment of advances as a way to secure his livelihood. For the first time, however, Nicolai refused to pay an advance, since he had no idea whether the book would ever appear.[218] Rosenthal repeated his request, not so subtly pressuring Nicolai by saying that he could not afford to send his son, who was home on holiday, back to Jena until he got the money. Again, Nicolai refused.[219] G.F.H. Plieth, a friend of Rosenthal's, relayed pathetic tales of the author's recent misfortunes and begged Nicolai to reconsider and to send 100–200 taler before Rosenthal succumbed to despair, adding dramatically "Oh, do it soon." The refusal of the advance "had shattered him so that heart and energy have all but left him." His health was suffering. Rosenthal had placed all his hopes in Nicolai. Perhaps significantly, Rosenthal's importunings occurred at the same time as Hermann's, adding to Nicolai's sense of authorial bombardment. Nicolai eventually gave in and sent Rosenthal an advance of 100 taler, not, as he emphasized, for the *Technologisches Wörterbuch*, but for the next volume of the *Natürliche Magie*.[220] Rosenthal was dissatisfied and requested regular payments of 60 taler per year (in four installments) for collecting material for the supplements. Nicolai, however, was willing to commit himself neither to paying Rosenthal nor to publishing the supplements. Rosenthal refused to abandon the idea, reporting that he placed all his hopes for the future in the *Technologisches Wörterbuch*. His letters reached new depths of pathos as he pleaded with Nicolai not to abandon him.[221] Three hundred taler in debt, Rosenthal prophesied his impending arrest and the reduction of his wife and children to beggars. "I fall upon my knees before you," he wrote in a shaky hand, "You ... must save me—my entire existence in this world depends upon you. Only you can keep me among the living." Among the factors contributing to his downfall, he said, was "a penchant for writing."[222] Nicolai remained obdurate in his determination not to commit himself to any further supplements to the *Technologisches Wörterbuch* and told Rosenthal so in no uncertain terms.[223] He continued, however, to pay

218. Rosenthal's letter of 19 March 1800 from Nordhausen, and Nicolai's annotations, in NN 64.
219. Rosenthal to Nicolai, Nordhausen, 6 May 1800, in NN 64.
220. G.F.H. Plieth to Nicolai, Nordhausen, 12 June 1800, and Nicolai's annotations, in NN 58.
221. Rosenthal to Nicolai, Nordhausen, 4 October 1801, in NN 64.
222. Rosenthal to Nicolai, Nordhausen, 22 October 1801, in NN 64.
223. In his letter of 27 January 1802 (in NN 64), Rosenthal complained that Nicolai's sharply worded letters, which dashed all his hopes of new supplements, were making matters worse at a time when he was suffering from "griefs and cares [and] black phenomena in my head."

advances for the *Natürliche Magie*, so that its completion in 1805 came as a grave disappointment to the author.[224]

The latter stages of communications with Hermann and Rosenthal were the exception rather than the rule in Nicolai's relations with his authors. Few writers were so persistent; and when confronted with Nicolai's arguments and his expert status, most accepted (or at least professed to accept) his arguments about the vagaries of publishing, his own economic hardships, and his reasons for not publishing a particular work, paying higher honoraria, or ordering finer paper. They could cite all the examples they liked of other authors who were better paid, of expensive and lavishly produced books that sold well. Even where they disagreed with him, as in the above-cited case of Dohm, they could not gainsay his statements that a publisher needed a cushion for all the works that failed even to cover costs, let alone make a profit. They were quite a different breed from authors like Goethe, who, as his friend Schiller described him, dictated to his publishers and cared nothing for the niceties of business. As Schiller warned the publisher Johann Friedrich Cotta, "you cannot bargain with Goethe." He knew his own worth only too well, "and he cares nothing for the fortunes of the book trade, about which he has only the vaguest notions.... Generosity toward his publishers is not his way."[225] Nicolai's authors, many of whom were his friends and allies, were much inclined to compromise. Perhaps they lacked Goethe's legendary self-confidence. More than that, though, most subscribed to a very different notion of authorship, which emphasized work rather than genius. Martha Woodmansee has rightly emphasized the close connection between changing ideas of originality and genius and author's demands for property rights and higher remuneration for their work.[226] Such ideas were by their very nature more suited to belles-lettres, which were no longer the focus of Nicolai's publishing program after the 1760s. Thus just as notions of authors' emancipation were gaining ground, Nicolai was shifting to those areas of literature less touched by it. Looked at this way, it is less surprising that Nicolai's authors were so relatively modest in their demands. Perhaps more knowledge of non-literary authors

---

224. Rosenthal to Nicolai, Nordhausen, 6 June 1805, in NN 64. Nicolai did not abandon Rosenthal altogether; later in 1805 he tried to help him get a position in the Prussian civil service by writing him a letter of recommendation. Rosenthal to Nicolai, Nordhausen, 28 August 1805, and Nicolai's annotations, in NN 64.

225. Schiller to Cotta, Weimar, 18 May 1802, quoted in *Gelehrsamkeit ein Handwerk?* p. 184.

226. Woodmansee, "The Genius and the Copyright," pp. 425–48.

and their relations with their publishers will put a different slant on the struggle for authors' rights than we have gained so far from the study of a handful of belletristic authors.

A Collective Portrait of Nicolai's Authors: A Cross-Section of the Enlightenment Republic of Letters?

Nicolai's authors were not, for the most part, those who have come down to us as the luminaries of eighteenth-century German literature. Nicolai rejected, for example, manuscripts by Hamann, Goethe, and Lenz,[227] and for various reasons was not the main publisher of his more famous friends such as Lessing and Moses Mendelssohn.[228] He rarely courted illustrious writers, except as reviewers for the *ADB*. Neither does he seem to have indulged in the practice, complained of by some critics of publishing practice, of luring authors away from other publishers with hefty honoraria or other promises.[229] As publisher and editor of the *ADB* Nicolai was already in contact with a large percentage of the important writers in Germany. Thus although he did not have paid scouts, he had a large number of correspondents on the lookout for manuscripts that might

---

227. For an account of Nicolai's attitudes toward *Sturm und Drang* literature, see Sommerfeld, *Friedrich Nicolai und der Sturm und Drang*. The rejection of Hamann's manuscript is discussed on pp. 134–36, that of Lenz's translation in alexandrines of Pope's "Essay on Criticism" is mentioned on p. 276. In 1776, Nicolai told Isaak Iselin that he was beginning to lose patience with "the nonsense of our geniuses." Nicolai to Iselin in Basel, 13 October 1776, in NN 86. He mused about writing a parody of a "newfangled tragedy" filled with seances, ghosts, and energetic geniuses in which the hero and heroine were stabbed to death in the first act and married in the last. Nicolai to Eschenburg, Berlin, 4 October 1776, in HAB, no. 33.

228. Beginning a communication to Nicolai with a quotation from Cicero that "letters don't blush," Mendelssohn explained that he wouldn't offer his translation of the Psalms to him or any other publisher he knew personally because his conditions were too "shameless." "You in particular," he told his friend, "have so many publications, and such expensive ones, that you will certainly not grant my conditions." He intended to ask for an honorarium of 5 louis d'or (ca. 25 taler) for each sheet of poetry, and 2 1/2 louis d'or for each of prose, which although not unheard of at the time for top literary authors, was about five times what Nicolai normally paid. Mendelssohn wanted to be compensated somewhat for the 1000 taler he had paid out of his own pocket for printing. When the translation was published by Friedrich Maurer in 1783, Mendelssohn received 100 louis d'or. Mendelssohn to Nicolai, Berlin, 27 May 1782, printed in Mendelssohn, *Neuerschlossene Briefe*, pp. 68–69, 120 n. 51. Other friends may also have decided to publish elsewhere in order to command higher fees. Loyalty to their old publishers and the desire not to mix business with friendship also no doubt played a role.

229. Nicolai's bookseller colleague Schwan, for example, wrote in Isaak Iselin's journal *Ephemeriden der Menschheit* in 1786 that certain booksellers had begun to eye other publishers' books with envy and to try to lure away their authors. Quoted in Haferkorn, "Der freie Schriftsteller," col. 649 n. 416.

interest him. Like a famous printer-publisher of an earlier age, the soliciting of authors was not Nicolai's usual method. "As a rule," Martin Lowry has written of Aldus Manutius, "it was not necessary, since the men concerned beat their own path to his door and the publisher could make his choices according to his own very personal criteria."[230]

A detailed prosopography of Nicolai's authors would require more biographical research than was feasible within the context of this study, but three particularly relevant variables help to provide an overview of the kind of writers he published—profession, geographical origins, and age/generation.[231]

Scholars of the German, and more particularly of the Prussian, Enlightenment have frequently remarked that it was dominated by men in state service.[232] Anthony LaVopa, for example, has observed that while literary men in "trendy but extremist Paris ... might prefer to live off sinecures or from the earnings their writings commanded;... in a soberly progressive society—the kind of society [Friedrich] Gedike's Berlin seemed to anticipate—the security of office was a solid foundation for the critical, reform-oriented posture of a 'republic of letters.'"[233] How do authors published by Nicolai, that arch-exponent of the Prussian Enlightenment (though himself a member of the commercial classes) fit this mold?

For the majority of Nicolai's authors, writing was not in itself a vocation, but part of a vocation that usually included public office in the broad sense of the word. In his book on "poor students" and article on Nicolai's Berlin crony Friedrich Gedike,[234] La Vopa explores eighteenth-century German ideas of vocation and public service. He speaks of the "tensions

---

230. Martin Lowry, *The World of Aldus Manutius* (Ithaca, N.Y.: Cornell University Press, 1979), p. 223.

231. The main source of biographical information, particularly on the less well known authors, is the invaluable *Deutsches Biographisches Archiv*, a microfiche compilation of more than two hundred biographical reference works published in Germany and Austria in the eighteenth and nineteenth centuries. At least rudimentary entries are available for some 90 percent of Nicolai's authors.

232. See, for example, Hans Erich Bödeker, "Prozesse und Strukturen politischer Bewußtseinsbildung der deutschen Aufklärung," in *Aufklärung als Politisierung—Politisierung der Aufklärung*, ed. Hans Erich Bödeker and Ulrich Herrmann (Hamburg: Meiner, 1987), pp. 10–31. This stimulating article notes that "the decisive social foundation of the German Enlightenment was ... its closeness to the State" (p. 10).

233. Anthony La Vopa, "The Politics of Enlightenment: Friedrich Gedike and German Professional Ideology," *JMH* 62 (March 1990): 51.

234. Friedrich Gedike was director of the Friedrichswerdersche Gymnasium, and editor of the *Berlinische Monatsschrift*.

within eighteenth-century ideologies of vocation, talent and merit," which "lay precisely in the fact that they sanctioned individual self-determination without relaxing an overriding insistence on collective imperative."[235] In his case study of Gedike, this collective imperative was translated into the notion "that a cluster of educated and peculiarly 'public' professions" constituted the "moral conscience" of the political arena.[236] A new ideal of scholarship in the public service lay at the heart of Gedike's conception of political participation and of the republic of letters. This reflected a transition in the second half of the eighteenth century to an ideal of the republic of letters that emphasized practical as well as learned expertise and moved its focus away from the traditional university disciplines and, for a time at least, away from the universities.[237] Among Nicolai's authors, some 17.4 percent were professors at universities or other institutions of higher education (such as the medical college in Berlin). Another 9 percent taught in a Latin school or Gymnasium. Together, these comprise a healthy percentage but by no means an overwhelming one when we consider that, after the early years and aside from Nicolai's own works, his publishing company was known more for scholarly, informational, and pedagogical works than for belles-lettres.

If we look at public service in the broadest sense and include the church and the educational establishment as well as the legal profession, state administration, and the military, nearly 68 percent of Nicolai's authors were in public service. Except for the military men, almost all of these had at least some university training. Twenty-one percent were members of the clergy, ranging from village pastors to urban consistorial councillors; 17.4 percent were university professors; 12 percent administrative and 4.8 percent judicial officials; 9 percent schoolteachers; and 3.6 percent military officers. The remaining 30 percent were members of the medical professions (physicians, surgeons, and apothecaries), 9.6 percent; "private scholars" (both men of independent means and those living from

---

235. Anthony La Vopa, *Grace, Talent and Merit: Poor Students, Clerical Careers and Professional Ideology in Eighteenth-Century Germany* (Cambridge: Cambridge University Press, 1988), p. 14.

236. La Vopa, "Politics of Enlightenment," p. 51.

237. On the demise of the traditional learned estate (*Gelehrtenstand*) and the creation of the nineteenth-century educated middle class (*Bildungsbürgertum*), see R. Steven Turner, "The *Bildungsbürgertum* and the Learned Professions in Prussia, 1770–1830: The Origins of a Class," *Histoire sociale–Social History* 13, no. 25 (May 1980): 105–35, and Rudolf Vierhaus, "Umrisse einer Sozialgeschichte der Gebildeten in Deutschland," in his *Deutschland im 18. Jahrhundert. Politische Verfassung, soziales Gefüge, geistige Bewegungen* (Göttingen: Vandenhoeck & Ruprecht, 1987), pp. 167–82.

their pens), 8.4 percent; librarians or archivists, 3 percent; private tutors, 1.2 percent; private secretaries, 1.2 percent; and merchants and commercial employees, 2.4 percent. Others were (one each) a titled noble without office, a student, a house dramatist for a theatrical troupe, an astronomer, an agricultural manager (*Oekonom*), an architect, a ship's captain, and a brewer. Four were women.[238]

The fathers of these authors present a more differentiated picture, but professions of public service dominate here as well.[239] The idea of the Protestant parsonage as the cradle of the German Enlightenment is borne out by the figures: nearly one-third of the fathers belonged to the clergy. Of these, about one-half were pastors in villages or small towns, as opposed to only roughly one-third of the sons. Only 5 percent taught at universities and only 3 percent are listed as schoolteachers, although many of the pastors may have taught as well. In other professions, 3.9 percent were military officers. 15.5 percent were administrative and 3.9 percent judicial officials, and one was a petty official. Including the 7.8 percent who were city officials such as mayors—a category of the traditional urban middle class almost completely absent from the sons' biographies—some 72 percent were in public service. Of the remaining fathers, 8.7 percent were artisans (2 wigmakers, a linen weaver, a gardener, a cook, a confectioner, a ropemaker, and a hosier), 5.9 percent belonged to the medical professions, and 4.9 percent were in trade (some of these, however, began as artisans, such as a furrier who became a merchant), 3.9 percent were farmers, 3 percent were titled nobles without office, two were castle stewards, and one each was a private tutor, a church musician (cantor), a ship's captain, a manufacturer, and an unskilled laborer. Thus although more than two-thirds of both fathers and sons depended upon public service for their livelihood, more of the fathers exercised traditional occupations, and the sons appear to have had more academic training, as witnessed by the larger percentage of university professors, Latin school

238. These figures are based on biographical information for 167 authors. Horst Möller's analysis of three hundred contributors to the *Berlinische Monatsschrift*, a journal with which Nicolai was closely associated, from 1783 to 1796, shows a similar overall pattern, with some 67 percent in public professions. He found that 26.7 percent were university and Gymnasium professors, 20 percent higher civil servants, 16.7 percent clergy, 3 percent military officers, 1.7 percent merchants and bankers, and ca. 3–4 percent private scholars. The main difference between the two groups is that in Möller's figures the medical profession is absent and the number of private scholars or "freie Schriftsteller" is even smaller than among Nicolai's authors. Möller, *Aufklärung in Preußen*, p. 252.

239. These figures are based on biographical information for 103 authors where the father's occupation was available.

and Gymnasium teachers, and physicians. One should not exaggerate the significance of the figures, because there are a number of authors for whom the father's occupation is unavailable. It may be that those cases where the father was a professor, high official, or other respected personage were more likely to be known and thus recorded. Thus it may be that the father's occupations are skewed toward the upper end of the educational and social scale, and that there were more artisans and peasants than the figures indicate. The general trends, however, remain of interest, and indicate a certain shift of sons from the clergy into academic teaching; the approximately 10 percent difference in the number of clergyman between the generations is almost matched by the difference, in the opposite direction, in the percentage of university professors.

Geographically speaking, Nicolai's authors present no great surprises.[240] Nicolai was a staunchly Protestant publisher, and only 11.4 percent of his authors were born in the predominantly Catholic regions of Bavaria, Austria, the Palatinate, and Silesia.[241] None came from the Catholic Rhineland. Nearly 66 percent of his authors originated in predominantly Protestant northern and north central Germany and the Baltic region (including Courland, northern Poland, and southern Sweden), with another 17 percent from the south central regions of Hesse, Franconia, Saxony, and Thuringia. Some 10 percent came from the also largely Protestant German Southwest and Switzerland. One was born in Ireland.

If we break down the overwhelmingly northern origins of Nicolai's authors, it is particularly striking that nineteen of them, or 13 percent, were born in Berlin (plus one in neighboring Potsdam). No other city comes even close to this number. Magdeburg is next as the birthplace of five authors, followed by Hamburg with four, Lübeck and Braunschweig with three each, and Erfurt, Halberstadt, Helmstedt, Leipzig, Osnabrück, Quedlinburg, Stendal, and Vienna with two each. Twenty-six cities and towns of some importance, from Zurich in the south to Stargard in the north, provided one author each. Together with the aforementioned cities, these account for seventy-five or almost exactly half of the authors for whom a birthplace is available. The other half were born in small towns and villages scattered across the German-speaking region. Thus as a group, Nicolai's authors were predominantly of northern and, by the standards of the time, urban origins.

---

240. These figures are based on biographical information for 149 authors.
241. I do not include here the birthplaces of authors whose works Nicolai only had translated.

Contemporaries and literary historians alike regarded Nicolai's publishing company as one that specialized in the literature of the Enlightenment. The company existed under Nicolai's proprietorship from 1758 until January 1811, a period that saw the waxing and waning of the Enlightenment movement, and of the prestige of its leaders. In this context, it may be interesting to take a brief look at the birth dates of his authors. Can one see them as a generation of writers who shared common experiences? Nicolai and his original collaborators were born in the 1730s and 1740s, participated in the literary revival of the 1750s and 1760s, and experienced the Seven Years' War as young men. Of the authors Nicolai published over the years, a substantial portion, 45 percent, were born in those decades.[242] Twenty percent were born in the 1750s. Almost equal percentages were born before 1730 (mostly in the 1720s) and after 1760: approximately 18 percent. Thus although Nicolai's publishing company was to continue for more than fifty years after 1759, 82 percent of his future authors had already been born when he began his career. The 18 percent who had not been, however, show that Nicolai (and all he stood for) was not anathema to everybody below middle age, even in the 1790s.

Lest we get the impression that Nicolai's authors simply grew old with their publisher, we should examine the figures from another angle, that of the age at which authors were first published by Nicolai. Regarded in this light, we can see that although Nicolai by no means ignored young authors (7.6 percent were under twenty-six), some 63 percent were over thirty-five when he first published them. The largest group, at 32 percent, was that of the thirty-six to forty-five-year-olds. Thus Nicolai tended to publish those authors who had already established themselves in some way. This is very much in keeping with the nature of his business as a publishing company, which, from the mid-1760s on, increasingly emphasized practical and specialist literature rather than belles-lettres. Significantly, Nicolai's youngest authors, with the exceptions of popular philosopher Thomas Abbt and the chemists Sigismund Friedrich Hermbstaedt and Wilhelm August Lampadius, wrote or translated novels, stories, and dramas, typical work for younger writers.

While Nicolai, by virtue of his independence as a merchant, wielded economic power over most of his authors, they were his superiors in

---

242. Horst Möller's study of contributors to the *Berlinische Monatsschrift* also found that the largest number were born in the 1730s and 1740s. Möller, *Aufklärung in Preußen*, p. 253.

formal education. In other ways, however, they were peers. Like Nicolai himself they tended to be Protestants who were born and lived in northern Germany, mature men with positions in the world. Eighteen were fellow Berliners. As such, they were, in the main, authors after his own heart, without aspirations to live in a world "solely of thought and imagination."

Nicolai the Publisher: Midwife, Meddler, Manufacturer?

The two central images of the publisher in late eighteenth-century Germany were those of the midwife and the manufacturer. The former carried positive and the latter largely negative connotations, even if some publishers liked to emphasize the active role they took in conceiving plans for new works. Nicolai professed to be the former, but was accused of being the latter. The truth, as usual, lies somewhere in between, or perhaps in the flexibility of definitions.

The publisher-as-midwife was a partner to authors, coaxing out their productions in order to present them to a waiting world. Johann Christian Wiegleb, for example, emphasized this notion of partnership when, maintaining the ubiquitous parenthood metaphor, he told Nicolai, "I have lavished much industry upon this literary child and hope that you will do your part to ensure that it appears with honor among the other citizens of the world."[243] In another instance he referred to Nicolai as the foster father and asked him to prevent the compositor from turning his offspring into a freak of nature.[244] Nicolai's role in the majority of works he published was that of an intermediary between author and public, who for reasons of time and practicality sometimes never even saw the finished manuscripts of books before they went to the printer.[245] Nevertheless, he also took a very active role in the development of certain works, particularly those he initiated himself. Nicolai's authors, like those of the humanist printer Aldus Manutius, "not only condoned, but expected a large amount of intervention from their publishers."[246] Nikolaus Kirchhoff asked Nicolai to look at his essay on his electrical experiments, "and correct any errors, or give it a different appearance.... I ask only that you

243. Wiegleb to Nicolai, Langensalza, 20 September 1780, in NN 82.
244. Wiegleb to Nicolai, Langensalza, 10 June 1773, in NN 82.
245. His contemporary, the bookseller J. C. Gädicke, remarked in 1803 that the publisher often did not see the manuscript itself, which the author sent directly to the printer, sometimes sheet by sheet. Gädicke, *Der Buchhandel von mehreren Seiten betrachtet*, p. 12.
246. Martin Lowry gives the example of Erasmus, who "was quite content to admit alterations to his translations from Euripides." *The World of Aldus Manutius*, p. 227.

not change the essence of the description."²⁴⁷ It was this acceptance of Nicolai's critical authority which led some authors to approach him in the first place. Nicolai's failure to exercise his editorial prerogatives could even be a source of disappointment to some. Franz Anselm von Benzel, for example, complained in 1785 that Nicolai had not made use of the editorial carte blanche he had offered.²⁴⁸

In general, Nicolai readily dispensed advice and criticism on both form and content to authors he published as well as those he did not. He tried, if not always successfully, to practice in his publishing company what he preached in his early theoretical works and in the *ADB*, encouraging authors to write appropriately for the public by taking their audience into account and developing a clear and pleasing style. For example, he told the young Ludwig Tieck: "Allow me to note that the writer must consider his reader, and not only himself. The art of depiction is the true writer's art, and the effect of a work is that which it has, and can have, upon the reader. It appears from some of your recent writings that you take pleasure in following the leaps of your imagination without plan or context. That may amuse you, but I doubt whether it will amuse your readers, who truly do not know from what vantage to view what they read." Only his high regard for Tieck's talents, he said, led him to give such advice.²⁴⁹

In the period during which most of Nicolai's authors had received their education, German composition, if taught at all, was not a major school subject.²⁵⁰ The literary language was still very much in flux as regarded

247. Kirchhoff to Nicolai, Hamburg, 6 November 1780, in NN 38.
248. Benzel to Nicolai, Mainz, 21 May 1785, in NN 4. When Benzel sent Nicolai the manuscript of the *Betrachtungen über die Folgen der Eröffnung der Schelde* on 9 February on behalf of an unnamed friend, he said that the author authorized Nicolai to change whatever he saw fit, particularly as regarded the improvement and correction of language and style. A month later he again admonished Nicolai to edit the style before printing, but time must have been too short, with little more than three months elapsing between the initial sending of the manuscript from Mainz and the arrival of the printed copies, presumably direct from the Leipzig Easter book fair. Benzel to Nicolai, Mainz, 9 February, 11 March, and 21 May 1785, in NN 4.
249. Nicolai to Tieck, Berlin, 19 December 1797, in *Briefe an Ludwig Tieck*, 3:58–62. While he chafed at Nicolai's criticisms of his flights of fancy, and at having to write in the style of his predecessors Musäus and Müller, Tieck enjoyed smuggling little digs at Enlightenment orthodoxies into his stories for the *Strausfedern*. For Tieck's relationship with and remarks about Nicolai, see *König der Romantik*, pp. 132–33, 145–47, 170.
250. In 1771, for example, the curriculum of the Latin school in Hannover included no German or other modern languages, a state of affairs common for the so-called *gelehrte Schulen* (academic schools). Margot Kraul, *Das deutsche Gymnasium 1780–1980* (Frankfurt a. M.: Suhrkamp, 1984), pp. 13–21. The reform pedagogues began to emphasize the teaching of German in the last third of the century, an interest reflected in such works as Johann Christoph Adelung's

spelling, punctuation, grammar, and vocabulary. Use of Latinisms and Gallicisms was rampant, even where German equivalents existed. Thus Nicolai saw himself faced with a number of authors whose writing skills he felt needed improvement. One of the first was his friend Thomas Abbt, the editing of whose works Nicolai compared to plowing a stony field. Much of Abbt's style, he assured him, was excellent. He could not attain perfection on his own, however, because "you have ... become accustomed to writing so peculiarly ... that you no longer notice it."[251] He pointed out examples of Abbt's faulty grammar and incorrect word usage and suggested many stylistic changes. When preparing a new edition of Abbt's 1765 *Vom Verdienste*, Nicolai told the author that he had carefully examined a section of the work and made detailed notes in order to give him a clear idea of what several readers had objected to in his style. Once Abbt understood this, he could correct himself, for the problems were minor ones. Abbt's chief failing was giving words meanings "that only half belong to them." He also employed too many French words, which should be avoided "because they lend *German style* an *alien*, or rather *precious appearance*."[252] Nicolai also provided a detailed critique of Johann Georg Heinrich Bretschneider's novel *Georg Waller's Leben und Sitten*, as requested.[253] Somewhat to the author's dismay, however, he sent the manuscript to the printer without allowing him to make the necessary corrections and changes personally.[254] The fact that Bretschneider lived so far away (in what is now the Ukraine) with the mail often taking many months to arrive may have contributed to Nicolai's unusual decision not to send him his own manuscript for revisions.

As we have seen in the case of the *ADB*, Nicolai's editorial intervention could reach well beyond the stylistic and structural realm, particularly when it came to sensitive political issues. In 1799, for example, he suggested to Wilhelm Traugott Krug that he remove the chapter on the aristocracy from his *Bruchstücke aus meiner Lebensphilosophie*. Krug took this in good humor, remarking philosophically that "the salvation of the

---

Deutsche Sprachlehre. Zum Gebrauche der Schulen in den Königlich-Preussischen Landen (Berlin: Voß, 1781) which was frequently reprinted into the nineteenth century.

251. Nicolai to Abbt, Berlin, 23 February 1765, in Nicolai, *Verlegerbriefe*, pp. 29–31.

252. Nicolai to Abbt, Berlin, 20 May 1766, in Nicolai, *Verlegerbriefe*, pp. 38–42.

253. In a letter of 23 May 1792 (in NN 9), Bretschneider said that he would like Nicolai's "Censur" before the work was printed. He had written the novel, he said, upon Nicolai's advice that he seek distraction through writing.

254. Bretschneider to Nicolai, Lemberg, 22 February 1793, in NN 9. Nicolai and Bretschneider nevertheless remained on good terms.

world does not depend upon its knowing my opinion on this topic, and you are doubtless right to note that this subject has something spiteful about it at present." Although he still believed that one could question the legitimacy of the aristocracy and its privileges without casting doubt on the legitimacy of hereditary monarchy, he agreed that readers might easily misconstrue his intentions.[255]

In one case at least, that of the *Technologisches Wörterbuch*, Nicolai took the authors in hand to such an extent that he told them how to write the book. The story is an interesting one for the light it sheds on the genesis and development of a work from the initial idea, and Nicolai's involvement in it. It also illustrates nicely both the latitude of his editorial authority and the limited means he had of enforcing it. As Nicolai described him, Johann Karl Gottfried Jacobsson, a noncommissioned officer in the Prussian army, was a man of great energy and ambition but no learning, quite incapable of writing anything unsupervised.[256] When he first presented his idea to Nicolai, he thought it was absolutely novel, although he had read little and was thus in no position to know what had or had not been written before. In the eighteenth century, technology referred to the study of the crafts and trades, but Jacobsson had had only a vague notion of what he meant by a dictionary of technology and had given little thought to which subjects belonged in such a work. Nicolai, however, recognized a good idea when he saw one and set Jacobsson to work like a student assistant. "I first had him compile a list of all the crafts and trades according to the three kingdoms of nature, which was initially very muddled, so that it took me an entire day to revise it together with him, after which he reworked it again. I myself then did additional research and made various improvements." He then proceeded to lay out a work schedule for his author. Jacobsson was to make careful excerpts from all compendia and monographs dealing with crafts and trades. Then he was to write each article on a separate piece of paper, ready for printing, and place it in the appropriate slot of an alphabetical *Repositorium* or file divided into twenty-four sections, which Nicolai provided. In order to make sure that all subjects were covered, Jacobsson was to make a list of the crafts and trades for which he had complete written information and those for which he did not. The latter would have to be "more carefully

---

255. Krug to Nicolai, Wittenberg, 10 November 1799, in NN 42.

256. Jacobsson and Nicolai had already worked together on the *Beschreibung der königlichen Residenzstädte*, for which the former provided materials on local manufactures and on the military. Denina, "Jacobsson (Jean Charles Godefroi)," in *La Prusse littéraire*, vol. 2.

investigated and described." He had instructed Jacobsson to interview a competent local artisan in each craft or trade about the tools and technical terms used in their work. Again, he was to keep exact records of what was lacking, and use the new information to correct any mistakes in the articles already collected. At this stage, Jacobsson was to recheck all his materials for any gaps, "letter by letter ... consulting all available lexica ... and supplementing whatever is missing." He admonished him to be concise and exact in his writing. "Everything," he wrote "must be precise and ready to print, but not written in an overly verbose manner, merely to fill the page. Only that which is technological about each trade should be described, and everything else left out." Jacobsson promised to follow this plan but in the end was either unwilling or unable to work systematically. Nicolai had collected information from knowledgeable metallurgists and provided Jacobsson with all the books he needed, but believed that he had not read them, finding it easier to use lexicons and works containing indexes. He was, however, most diligent in speaking to informants personally. The editing process was a trying one because everything Jacobsson wrote had to be revised. Matters were made worse by the fact that the first editor, Pastor Otto Ludwig Hartwig, also refused to adhere to the original plan and allowed all sorts of subjects to slip in that did not belong to technology. He was so enthralled with agriculture that, as Nicolai recalled, "I had to fight tooth and nail to prevent him from putting all of agricultural science back into the already rambling work." The editor of the second volume, Raymund Dapp, knew nothing of technology but was adept at smoothing out Jacobsson's jumbled style, sometimes jettisoning entire pages of nonsense written to extend the work (and presumably to earn more money).[257] After Jacobsson's death, Nicolai had many of the same problems with the author of the four supplements, Gottfried Erich Rosenthal, despite his much greater experience as a writer. In their initial discussion on the supplements, Nicolai told Rosenthal that he would be glad to have someone truly knowledgeable weed out the many unnecessary articles in Jacobsson. Rosenthal was quick to agree to greater self-restraint, but long disagreements ensued about the proper scope of a technological dictionary. Rosenthal's definition of technology seems to have been a very broad one, which included trade, agriculture, and hunting, as well as such bizarre items as the technical

---

257. Draft of a letter to Gottfried Erich Rosenthal from the Easter book fair, 1788, in NN 64.

terms used by cooks for frying cod in butter.[258] Nicolai became exasperated, scribbling phrases such as "technology only" and "God forbid" in the margins of Rosenthal's letters.[259] He feared that the supplements would become just as long as Jacobsson's original work (four volumes), which in the end they were, and that nobody would buy them (prenumerations indeed fell precipitously). Nobody would look for methods of frying cod in such a work; at most they might seek information on fancy banquet dishes, but such recipes alone could fill two quarto volumes and would only annoy those readers seeking edification on technology. As far as Nicolai was concerned, he informed Rosenthal, technology included the knowledge of tools and mechanical instruments and the explanation of the technical terms employed in the crafts and mechanical arts. Trade, agriculture, gardening, hunting, forestry, architecture, mining engineering (*Markscheidekunst*), and cooking did not belong in a dictionary of technology. It was also not intended as a guide to the practice of the crafts and mechanical arts themselves, but only to their tools and terminology. In this sense, he explained to Rosenthal, one could describe the double plow as a machine, but did not need to list the types of grain or manure used in planting fields. If one spoke of distilling, one described the apparatus, not the types of liqueurs it produced. He went on at great length to drive this point home, adding that he wanted a supplement of one volume only.[260] Rosenthal promised to remove all extraneous matter and start again from scratch. As the publication date approached, though, he was making excuses for the expansion of the work, saying that certain expectations had been raised by the wide coverage in Jacobsson's volumes which he had to meet as well.[261] Nicolai had the Göttingen professor Johann Beckmann, the father of technology as a discipline, write a critique of the manuscript in which he deplored its inflation with all manner of subjects that did not belong there and said that at this rate the work would never be finished. "Any deviation from the original plan," he warned, "is detrimental to the public and the publisher."[262] Nicolai sent this (unsigned) critique to Rosenthal in the hopes of curbing him, but instead of taking the suggestions to heart, the latter accused Beckmann

---

258. Rosenthal to Nicolai, Nordhausen, 18 March 1789, in NN 64.
259. Nicolai's annotation on Rosenthal to Nicolai, Nordhausen, 18 March 1789, in NN 64.
260. Copy of Nicolai to Rosenthal, Berlin, 11 May 1789, in NN 64.
261. Rosenthal to Nicolai, Nordhausen, 19 May 1789 and 17 May 1791, in NN 64.
262. Beckmann to Nicolai, Göttingen, September 1792, in NN 3.

(he had seen through his anonymity) of jealousy and resentment.²⁶³ The material itself demanded an extensive treatment, and the more complete it was, the more likely it was to become a classic.²⁶⁴ At this point Nicolai seems to have given up trying to enforce his original plan. A few years later Rosenthal delivered the bibliography, confessing, "I never tire of writing" to which Nicolai noted, perhaps with resignation, "That is true indeed."²⁶⁵ His attempts to tease out of the prolix Rosenthal a strictly systematic treatment of a limited subject rather than a baroque compendium had been in vain. Nicolai may have had some very firm ideas about the books that he published, but he knew when he was defeated.

Most of Nicolai's authors were openly appreciative of his assistance, whether they actually followed his advice or not. The recalcitrant Jacobsson, for example, wrote in his preface that he had been fortunate in a publisher "who with his broad knowledge was in a position to determine the plan ... more precisely with me, and to provide me with the printed sources that I needed to tap when writing about subjects I could not investigate in person."²⁶⁶ Similarly, when Carl Martin Plümicke submitted the final section of manuscript to his essay on the history of the Berlin theater, he told Nicolai, "How gratefully I acknowledge your many efforts up until now on behalf of my work." Given his respect for Nicolai's insights and judgments, the influence of his critical remarks would be all too obvious in many passages of the book. He admitted that he had sometimes gotten carried away, but Nicolai had revised and corrected his prose in such cases: "If only all publishers were like you, how immeasurably many authors and their works would benefit!" The only way he could truly show his appreciation was to state publicly, in the preface, that the work owed anything good or useful to the publisher's "cooperative assistance." "No! No! It is his work and must remain such," exclaimed Nicolai in the margin of a letter.²⁶⁷ Plümicke was correspondingly sparing in his mentions of him in the preface. As he wrote in his next letter, "in accordance with your wishes I have spoken as little as possible in the preface of your kind influence. Please consider, however, that I could not

---

263. Rosenthal to Nicolai, Nordhausen, 7 October 1792, in NN 64. Rosenthal even went so far as to visit Beckmann in Göttingen and set the critique before him, but Beckmann denied having written it. Nicolai heartily disapproved of this rash visit, as he noted in the letter's margin.
264. Rosenthal to Nicolai, Nordhausen, 20 November 1792, in NN 64.
265. Rosenthal to Nicolai, Nordhausen, 1 June 1795, in NN 64.
266. Preface to volume 1 of the *Technologisches Wörterbuch*, pp. 13–14.
267. Plümicke to Nicolai, Berlin, 2 March 1781, in NN 58.

remain altogether silent, since some people who suspect the true circumstances might otherwise believe me ungrateful."[268] In the preface to his *Entwurf einer Theatergeschichte von Berlin* he merely expressed gratitude to Nicolai for making available materials from his own researches in the Royal Archives.

In most cases, Nicolai's role began after the author offered him a manuscript or outline and consisted in providing reference works, suggestions, encouragement, and stylistic improvements, but he also commissioned works. This activity, which he shared with many of his bookseller colleagues, was what prompted Immanuel Kant to speak of him disparagingly as a "bookmaker," a mere manufacturer of books. Although spurning this designation, Nicolai also devoted a good deal of attention to publishers' initiative in his remarks on the draft of the new Prussian legal code, as we have seen. What was the difference between a manufacturer and an initiator of books? In Nicolai's eyes, it seems to have been one of quality, usefulness, and integrity. Nicolai defended himself against Kant's accusations by characterizing "bookmaking" as slavery to the "genius saeculi." Its most prominent symptoms, he said, were the shameless exploitation of political scandal and gossip and the proliferation of imitations of popular gothic novels.[269] The books he commissioned were, by contrast, sober and solid: mainly works of reference or new, updated editions of the pedagogical perennials he inherited from his father. A significant proportion of the commissioned works, however, were of a less weighty, if harmless, nature: literary translations. During the early years of Nicolai's career the emphasis was on French literature, while in the 1780s and 1790s he commissioned numerous translations or adaptations of English novels and plays. The most extensive literary project developed by Nicolai and carried out by hired authors was *Strausfedern, oder Sammlung unterhaltender Geschichten* (8 vols., 1787–98), a lighthearted anthology of French tales adapted and edited first by Johann Karl August Musäus, then by Johann Gottwerth Müller (both of them popular authors), and finally by the novice Ludwig Tieck. As Tieck described it, Nicolai sent him reams of French trivial literature and left it up to him to select stories to rework for the German public.[270] Helmut Hiller has noted in a more general context that publishers' opportunities to initiate

---

268. Plümicke to Nicolai, Berlin, 29 March 1781, in NN 58.
269. Nicolai, *Ueber meine gelehrte Bildung*, pp. 178–80.
270. Ludwig Tieck described the work some years later. Quoted in *König der Romantik*, pp. 146–47. He soon tired of adapting existing tales and invented some of his own.

new works extend chiefly to handbooks, lexicons and dictionaries, periodicals, biographies and memoirs, new editions of older works, anthologies, translations, school textbooks, anthologies, and series,[271] a description that amply covers Nicolai's own sphere of activities.

Translations aside, the commissioning of a new work usually involved more than merely hiring an author. After the initial inquiry, Nicolai and the author developed a plan for the work together. The best documented example of such a collaboration is that of Jeremias David Reuß's *Das gelehrte England* (1791, 1804).[272] As Nicolai reported to J. J. Eschenburg in the spring of 1789, he had long wished for a biographical and bibliographic companion to English literature. When he came upon the English original of this work, he immediately staked his claim by announcing a forthcoming German translation in the book fair catalog, although he had as yet no candidate to carry out the project. He hoped Eschenburg could recommend a diligent young man with a good command of English who could freely translate the work and bring it up to date under his supervision in Braunschweig.[273] Eschenburg recommended that Nicolai write to the university at Göttingen where the necessary English journals and other reference works were most likely to be available. He also sent a preliminary sketch of how the translation project might be carried out.[274] Nicolai provided his Göttingen correspondent, Jeremias David Reuß, with his own ideas as well as Eschenburg's suggested plan, outlining in detail the method and sources to be used. The compilation, for example, should be organized with each book title on a separate sheet of paper so that additions could be easily made. Reuß decided to take on the project himself rather than turn it over to a student and warned Nicolai that it would be more complicated than he anticipated, requiring a revision and not merely a translation of the English work. In the end, Reuß's work encompassed 3700 authors as against the original's 500! Throughout the

---

271. Hiller, *Zur Sozialgeschichte von Buch und Buchhandel*, p. 9.
272. For a more detailed account, see Fabian, "Die erste Bibliographie," pp. 16–43.
273. Nicolai to Eschenburg, Berlin, 8 and 22 May 1789, in HAB, nos. 89 and 90.
274. Eschenburg to Nicolai, Braunschweig, 6 June 1789, in NN 19. At that time the University of Göttingen had the best library of English books in Germany, not least because Göttingen belonged to Hannover. On the library, see Bernhard Fabian, "Die Göttinger Universitätsbibliothek im 18. Jahrhundert," *Göttinger Jahrbuch* 28 (1980): 109–23, and "Göttingen als Forschungsbibliothek im 18. Jahrhundert," in *Öffentliche und private Bibliotheken im 17. und 18. Jahrhundert. Raritätenkammern, Forschungsinstrumente oder Bildungsstätten?* ed. Paul Raabe (Bremen and Wolfenbüttel: Jacobi, 1977), pp. 209–39.

process, Nicolai offered advice, bibliographical references, and encouraging words to move Reuß along. He borrowed journals for him from other people, as well as sending works from his own library. Thus the work, although carried out by Reuß, grew from seeds provided by Nicolai and Eschenburg.

The at least partially collective nature of this work was characteristic of many of the books Nicolai commissioned, as well as others he published. In some cases he brought in outside editors and advisers as well as scholars to write prefaces, compile indexes, and the like. Jacobsson's *Technologisches Wörterbuch* was such a collective effort, and if we include the very numerous prenumeration collectors, a great many men were involved in both its production and distribution.[275] Georg Simon Klügel's revised edition of Benjamin Hederich's *Kurze Anleitung zu den vornehmsten ... Sprachen und Wissenschaften*, which Nicolai commissioned in 1778 and which began appearing in 1782, was another such collaborative project. The *Encyklopädie, oder zusammenhängender Vortrag der gemeinnützigsten Kenntnisse* grew from four to six volumes in its three editions, and Klügel brought in such colleagues as Matthias Christian Sprengel, Julius August Remer, and Paul Jakob Bruns to help him cope with the mammoth task.[276] Nicolai's own description of Berlin and account of his travels through Germany were also the product of contributions from many correspondents and local experts. Even in the most straightforward instances of authorship, as in Friedrich August Bothe's translation of Samuel Foote's dramatic works, Nicolai enlisted the frequent aid of Carl G. Küttner, a Leipzig acquaintance who had spent many years in England. Küttner acted as a consultant on all questions of English literature, language, and place names arising during the project.[277] This was a necessity,

---

275. Both Jacobsson and Beckmann discuss the evolution of the project and the various participants in their respective prefaces to volume 1 of the *Technologisches Wörterbuch*. See also Jacobsson's preface to volumes 2 and 4, in which he underlines the collective nature of the project by asking readers to send in remarks on any mistakes or omissions they had discovered so that they might be incorporated into the supplements. Nicolai outlines his own version of events in a draft of a letter to Gottfried Erich Rosenthal, written at the Easter book fair of 1788, in NN 64.

276. Klügel to Nicolai, Helmstedt, 26 August 1778 and 8 October 1781, and Halle, 14 December 1793, in NN 40.

277. Küttner to Nicolai, Leipzig, several letters over the years 1795–96, in NN 42. He and Nicolai met frequently at the book fairs, introduced perhaps by their mutual friend, the Leipzig literary theorist Christian Friedrich von Blankenburg. They appear to have corresponded from 1795 to 1802.

given pressures of time as well as the frequent inaccessibility of libraries and specialized books, but it was also part of the ethos of communication in the republic of letters. Hazel Rosenstrauch has spoken of the material aspects of the eighteenth-century cult of friendship, which included "mutual aid in getting books published and finding jobs, in proofreading poems and improving one's financial situation,"[278] and Nicolai's publishing endeavors provide ample evidence of this.

Friedrich Nicolai was, then, more a midwife than a manufacturer, although he did sometimes hire authors to carry out his ideas. Within the context of his day and its struggles, he can be accused neither of running a factory nor of actively championing the emancipation of authors or the beautification of the German book. He paid what he thought fair, no more but also no less. He supported authors when they were in financial distress, but more out of humanitarian concern than to nurture genius. When he advanced money to Follenius and Rosenthal, Klügel or Hermann, or even Ludwig Tieck, it was to help them make it through the next few months, not to allow them to produce great works free of the cares and worries of the real, unpoetic world. Follenius would have to pay back his debt with a novel, but Nicolai did not give him the money *in order to allow him to write that novel*. There was a distinction, at least in theory, between giving authors (writing) work so that they could live and giving them money so they could write. Nicolai tended toward the former practice. He believed that if a great work was in an author, it would emerge whether a publisher paid for it or not.

278. Rosenstrauch, "Buchhandelsmanufaktur und Aufklärung," p. 93.

(afterword)
===

Some ten years have passed since the *Frankfurter Allgemeine Zeitung*, Germany's establishment newspaper par excellence, brought Friedrich Nicolai to the attention of a broader (German) public. Marcel Reich-Ranicki, former chief critic of that bastion of cultural orthodoxy and serious prose, and a man whose combative and curmudgeonly stance bears a certain spiritual kinship to Nicolai's own, bestowed this belated honor upon his predecessor, whom he referred to as the "founder of our literary life."[1] Blithely ignoring Horst Möller's excellent monograph on his subject (as well as the publications and exhibitions occasioned by the 250th anniversary of Nicolai's birth in 1983), Reich-Ranicki proclaimed Friedrich Nicolai ripe for (re)discovery. His appeal to plunder the untouched riches of the Nicolai papers for a study, perhaps even a biography, of the arch-critic and *Aufklärer* may raise a smile among those who have surreptitiously forced back the red and Prussian-blue bindings of the correspondence housed in Berlin's Staatsbibliothek to read Nicolai's scrawled marginal notes.

The present book—neither a biography nor an intellectual history—has nevertheless been an attempt to "rediscover" a Nicolai well known to at least some of his contemporaries but lost in the shuffle of grand literary histories and analyses. In order to do so, I have adopted a very particular view, looking at Nicolai largely through what other people wrote to him, and what remarks he noted in the margins of their letters. Since the account books of his shop and publishing company no longer exist, I adopted this "ant-like" approach (as Anthony Grafton described it) in order to reconstruct what I could of his hitherto underexposed life in the

---

1. "Der Gründer unseres literarischen Lebens: Über den unermüdlichen Aufklärer Friedrich Nicolai," *Frankfurter Allgemeine Zeitung*, 2 December 1989, no. 280.

Afterword

book trade. Following Jules Michelet's notion of "letting the silences of history speak," I have devoted a good deal of attention to people who do not generally figure much in histories of German literary life, such as booksellers' assistants and unsuccessful authors—influenced no doubt in part by my own experiences as a professional translator. The results of this undertaking have taken up several hundred pages, and it is perhaps time to say what, after all these years of reading his correspondence, I think about Friedrich Nicolai. Those who have read this far will realize that I believe that he was neither the shallow philistine of the nineteenth-century literary histories nor the salvation of German letters from the rampaging egos of the *Stürmer* and *Dränger* and the *Schwärmerei* of a Lavater that his friends and *ADB* colleagues believed him to be. He was a shrewd businessman, an upright *Hausvater*, a charitable if not very pious Christian, and a sometimes pompous and schoolmasterly critic. He was also the doughty old *Aufklärer* and disbeliever in the immaterial cruelly lampooned by Goethe in the "Walpurgisnacht" scene in *Faust* as the "Proctophantasmist," because he not only thought that applying leeches to his anus had cured him of apparitions (of his beloved dead son Samuel Friedrich, among others), but also lectured on the subject to the Berlin Academy of Sciences in 1799.[2]

Nicolai was a burgher's burgher, who believed that Enlightenment and notions of right living would trickle down from the middle class to the lower classes, and up to the nobility. A prolific author and a dedicated retail bookseller, who went to great lengths to make good books better known to his own circle of customers and a wider public through personal contact and catalogs, he never doubted that books and periodicals were the central medium for the circulation of new and useful ideas in a fragmented Germany. After he died, his old friend Göckingk went through his papers and collected his notes and aphorisms. One of them was, "We Germans are book people, a writing nation. All sentiments are lost to us, or only imperfectly expressed, if they cannot be read."[3]

Nicolai was, by all accounts, a man of great integrity but rather less charm, tall, raw-boned, and often humorless. His long-windedness was legendary, and his friend Elisa von der Recke, who harbored only the

---

2. This lecture, held on 28 February 1799, was published that same year as a pamphlet, *Beispiel einer Erscheinung mehrerer Phantasmen, nebst einigen erläuternden Anmerkungen* (An Example of a Manifestation of Several Phantasms, with Some Explanatory Notes), occasioning much ridicule.

3. No. 22 of Nicolai's "Einzelne Gedanken," collected after his death by Göckingk, in his *Friedrich Nicolais Leben und literarischer Nachlaß*, pp. 128–29.

Afterword

deepest admiration for him (she referred to him as "Father Nicolai"), was relieved to find that her aristocratic friends in Bad Pyrmont, who were initially bored by Nicolai's pontificating, now found him interesting, "and are no longer put off by his prolix way of speaking."[4] To be sure Nicolai's almost racist anti-Catholicism (his travel account contains physiognomic portraits of ridiculous-looking priests, for example) is tiresome in the extreme. He also had some peculiar notions about women, including that two ladies of high rank could never be truly close friends, because such a friendship required the gratitude of the woman of lower rank to the other for laying aside her prejudices.[5] On the other hand, he had numerous extremely loyal life-long friends among both women and men, and left monuments to some of these friends in biographical essays. Most of those he so honored were fellow *Aufklärer* and men of distinguished accomplishments. Despite a tendency to priggishness and moralizing, however, he could still write a sympathetic and affectionate account of the misspent life of the companion of his apprentice days, Johann Joachim Ewald, a penniless itinerant *bon vivant* who abused the kindness and hospitality of J. J. Winckelmann in Rome, converted to Catholicism (both naturally aroused Nicolai's disapproval) and was last heard from in 1762, when he apparently embarked for North Africa.[6]

Nicolai is a man who benefits from closer scrutiny and longer acquaintance. His patience with inept authors; his acts of generosity, often performed in secret[7] (unlike most other things he did); his opposition to censorship and serfdom and support for Jewish emancipation; his rejection of mystification in all its guises; his love of archives, music, and dancing; his curiosity about strange subjects such as the history of wigs; and his desire to make German writing clearer and less pedantic (a battle still being fought to this day, to the vexation of German-English translators) all speak in his favor. He may have been fanatical in opposing fanaticism and intolerant in defending tolerance, but there are far worse things to

---

4. Diary entry for 4 September 1791, in Recke, *Tagebücher und Selbstzeugnisse*, p. 130.
5. Recke, *Tagebücher und Selbstzeugnisse*, p. 203.
6. Nicolai's sketch of the known facts of Ewald's life was published in the *Neue Berlinische Monatsschrift*, November 1808, pp. 257–72. Ewald was the son of an innkeeper in Spandau near Berlin and was working as a private tutor in Frankfurt an der Oder when Nicolai met him. He was a close friend of the officer-poet Ewald von Kleist under whose influence he occasionally wrote poetry.
7. For example, when he donated to collections of money for impoverished Jewish widows, he asked that his name not be publicized. This is mentioned in the correspondence (1788–1809, in NN 46) of Christine Sophie Ludwig (née Fritsche), a friend whom Nicolai saw regularly when he went to Leipzig.

be fanatical and intolerant about. He may have been a *philosophe* in the broad sense sketched in the introduction, but he was no philosopher; for he was insufficiently critical, perhaps, of his own categories—particularly of the limits of reason. He may well have been wrong about the possibilities of gradual enlightenment and reform through education, reading, and debate. Yet we have not really developed any better alternatives, and enlightenment, whether with a small or a capital "e," is alive and well in many parts of the world today, and as necessary now as it ever was.

In his later years, Nicolai expended a good deal of energy on a losing battle: the attempt to stave off the emerging radical split in German literature between the trivial and the highbrow, a chasm that persists today in a way that it does not in either French or English. This, together with resentment of his (in their eyes) unwarranted position of economic and ideological power in the republic of letters, was at the root of his acrimonious feuds with Goethe and Schiller and the early Romantics, notably Friedrich and August Wilhelm Schlegel and Ludwig Tieck. Nicolai refused to relinquish his conviction that literature should be understandable to the many, and that its aim should be the common good of society. He thus could not approve of the autonomy of the aesthetic sphere propagated by the Romantics. What appeared to many literary historians as mere stupidity or stubbornness at least arose from a genuinely egalitarian belief that the products of the printing press should, ideally, be accessible to people of all classes and levels of education. Nicolai was far from grasping the implications of the French Revolution, and the same may doubtless be said of his assessment of the epochal significance of the so-called Wars of Liberation against Napoleon, part of which he experienced at first hand. That the world of 1810 would never again be the world of 1760 was something that he was apparently unwilling to accept, a common enough attitude for a man in his late seventies. He died less than fifteen years before the founding of a German book trade organization, the Börsenverein für den Deutschen Buchhandel, which he had mistakenly believed would never come about because German booksellers could not agree on anything.

In the spring of 1793, in a letter to his old friend, the poet Johann Peter Uz, who had abandoned the muses for a life in the Ansbach bureaucracy, Nicolai expressed his depression over the retreat of Enlightenment, a cause to whose advancement he felt he had devoted his entire life.[8] This was to remain his refrain for the next seventeen years, during

---

8. Nicolai to Uz, Berlin, 27 April 1793, in NN 76.

Afterword

which he continued to write and publish. Friedrich Nicolai may have seemed a rather prosaic publisher to younger contemporaries, but he remained a passionate one to the end, thriving on controversy and debate. He fought on several fronts in his campaigns on behalf of Enlightenment. We see this in its purest form in his own writings, whether critical, satirical or historical. His second front was the *ADB*, described by friends and foes alike as a sort of army. The bookshop and the publishing company represent a third front, the nature of whose battles were mediated by the financial exigencies of business. The bookseller, try as he might to arouse interest in the best he had to offer, could not force people to buy, let alone to read. As has been said of one of Nicolai's publishing forefathers, "idealism constantly interacted with shrewd commercial calculation."[9] Nicolai believed to the end that both his intellectual contributions—disdained though they might be, particularly by the younger generation—and his economic activities provided valuable services to state and society, well beyond the republic of letters. In publishing and selling works, including many from his own pen, which he hoped would contribute to the spread of critical thinking and discussion among the middle and upper classes, and eventually the popular classes as well, Nicolai was both an intellectual and a merchant. As such, he helped to blaze a possible path for such energetic and patriotic publishers as Friedrich Perthes and Johann Cotta, who successfully combined the promotion of new ideas and their own fortunes into the next century.

Rudolf Vierhaus has written of the "atmosphere of the sober, Protestant, practically oriented, prosaic Prussian-Berlin Enlightenment"[10] of the period between 1750 and 1780, and it is there that we must situate Nicolai. In the last year of his life, he offered the following assessment of his own contributions to German letters as critic, bookseller, and publisher: "Incidentally, I am by no means the high priest in the temple of literature, but at most the sexton of many years' standing, who faithfully maintained the locks and occasionally drove out the moneychangers and other folk who desecrated the sacred altar."[11] With its characteristic mixture of modesty and self-importance, this statement is the very quintessence of Friedrich Nicolai.

9. The third element in Martin Lowry's characterization of Aldus, "a degree of divine disorder," was however quite lacking in the fastidious Prussian. *The World of Aldus Manutius*, p. 147.

10. "Daniel Chodowiecki und die Berliner Aufklärung," in *Daniel Chodowiecki (1726–1801). Kupferstecher, Illustrator, Kaufmann*, ed. Ernst Hinrichs and Klaus Zernack, Wolfenbütteler Studien zur Aufklärung 22 (Tübingen: Max Niemeyer, 1997), p. 8.

11. *Der Briefwechsel zwischen Friedrich Nicolai and Carl August Böttiger*, ed. Bernd Maurach (Berne: Peter Lang, 1996), p. 73.

(appendix)

Nicolai's Shop Employees

Nicolai's first *Diener* appears to have been August Mylius, who served him until he set up his own shop in Berlin in 1763.[1] Other employees in the Berlin shop were Johann Eberhard Zehe, a native of Uffenheim near Frankfurt, who was trained by Gebhard in Frankfurt am Main and joined the firm in June 1765,[2] followed in November 1768 by Johann Andreas Schäfer, who was recommended by Franz Heinsius of Gotha.[3] In the winter of 1769 Carl Gottfried Amende, trained by Johann Ernst Meyer in Breslau, went to work in the Berlin shop and remained until around 1773, at which point he joined the firm of Hartknoch in Riga.[4] A certain Herr Müller was *Diener* in the Berlin shop from around 1770 until his death in 1777 or 1778.[5] His successor was J.C.D. Schneider, who came to Nicolai in September 1778 from Frommann in Züllichau.[6] Like Mylius, he eventually became an independent bookseller, with a business in Göttingen until at least 1818. Müller and Schneider's Berlin coworker was Georg Emanuel Beer, who had apprenticed in Nicolai's Stettin shop and set up his own business in Leipzig in 1785 after a short stint as *Diener*

---

1. Meyer, "Die geschäftlichen Verhältnisse," p. 245.
2. Zehe to Nicolai, Frankfurt am Main, 2 and 9 February, 1 March, and 25 April 1765, and Uffenheim, 30 May 1765, in NN 65.
3. Schäfer to Nicolai, Gotha, 12 October 1768, in NN 65, and Heinsius to Nicolai, Gotha, 31 October 1768, in NN 31.
4. Amende to Nicolai, Breslau, 25 November 1769, in NN 1, and Hartknoch to Nicolai, Riga, 31 July 1773, in NN 30.
5. Johann Friedrich Agricola to Nicolai, Berlin, 15 May 1770, in NN 1; Hartknoch to Nicolai, Riga, 17 January 1778, in NN 30; and Johann Adam Stein to Nicolai, Nuremberg, 27 June 1788, in NN 72.
6. Frommann to Nicolai, Züllichau, 15 June, 9 July, and 17 September 1778, in NN 25, and Schneider to Nicolai, Züllichau, 3 July 1778, in NN 68.

to Joseph von Kurzböck in Vienna.[7] Nicolai's son Samuel Friedrich, who also learned the trade in the Stettin shop in the late 1770s and early 1780s, managed his father's Berlin establishment from the early 1780s until his death in 1790. F.C.C. Steinfurth was the third Berlin *Diener* (from 1781) to serve an apprenticeship in Stettin. He later worked for Frommann in Züllichau and Korn in Breslau.[8] The most faithful employee was Johann Christoph Kraehe, who started in the Berlin shop around 1780 and was still working there in January 1807.[9] Of Bube we know only that he worked in the Berlin shop until 1788.[10] Lotter, who came to Nicolai from J. F. Korn in Breslau, was *Diener* from around 1787 until at least 1794.[11] F.C.F. Francke had been apprenticed to Johann Rudolph Cröcker in Jena, served three years as a *Diener* there, seven years as *Diener* to Hanisch in Hildburghausen, and then one year with Stahel in Würzburg. At thirty-one he was probably only willing to accept the lowly position of fourth *Diener* in Nicolai's shop in order to get a foot in the door in Berlin. After about a year and a half, in 1792, he set up his own business there, which survived until at least 1825.[12] His superiors in Berlin at the time were Carl August Nicolai (presumably the third *Diener*), who worked for his father from 1789 to 1795 after an apprenticeship in Stettin, and the above-mentioned Lotter and Kraehe. Francke's successor was Messerschmidt, while Carl August was replaced by Carl Zolling, son of the Langensalza bookseller Johann Siegmund Zolling. The younger Zolling had served his apprenticeship in Stendal in the firm of Franzen und Große. The book trade was not to his taste, however, and in 1796 or 1797 he left Nicolai's employ to become private secretary to Count von Dohna, the adjutant to General von Knobelsdorff.[13] Johannes Ritter, a former apprentice and

7. Joseph Lorenz von Kurzböck to Nicolai, Vienna, 12 June and 2 November 1784, in NN 42. Kurzböck was extremely pleased with Beer, whom he considered an ideal *Diener*. He asked Nicolai to encourage him to stay despite the current bad state of business; Kurzböck would make it worth his while. He was accordingly disappointed and bitter when Beer gave notice in November 1784, claiming that the air in Vienna did not agree with him.

8. Frommann to Nicolai, Züllichau, 8 January 1781, in NN 25, and Steinfurth to Nicolai, Breslau, 14 January 1801, in NN 73.

9. Kraehe to Nicolai, Berlin, 26 June 1781, in NN 89, and Hane to Nicolai, Stettin, 2 April 1807, in NN 87.

10. Andreä to Nicolai, Frankfurt am Main, 30 June 1788, in NN 1.

11. J. F. Korn to Nicolai, Breslau, 14 November 1787, in NN 42, and Carl August Nicolai to his sister Wilhelmine, Leipzig, 14 May 1794, in NN 289.

12. Francke to Keyser (in Erfurt), Hildburghausen, 15 January 1789; Francke to Nicolai, Würzburg, 27 June, 13 August, and 10 October 1789; and Francke to Nicolai, Berlin, 5 February 1792, all letters in NN 22. On Francke's later career, see Georgi, *Die Entwicklung des Berliner Buchhandels*.

13. Joh. Siegmund Zolling to Nicolai, Langensalza, 12 July, 24 November, and 29 December

Appendix: Nicolai's Shop Employees

Diener to Georg Adam Keyser in Erfurt, replaced Zolling and stayed with the firm until the 1820s.[14] Another Keyser employee, Stechmesser, also worked for Nicolai around this time, until his death in 1802.[15] The last *Diener* to enter Nicolai's employ in Berlin was Johann Wilhelm Richardi. Like several others, he had first learned the book trade in Nicolai's Stettin branch before working in Berlin from 1808 to 1810. From 1811 to 1812, when he entered Prussian military service, Richardi managed the Stettin shop. At the end of the war he returned to Berlin to carry on under Nicolai's son-in-law Friedrich Parthey.[16]

The Stettin shop was a considerably smaller operation than that in Berlin, managing as it did only the retail side of the business, and thus required fewer employees. Aside from apprentices, of whom the names of Georg Emanuel Beer, Samuel Friedrich Nicolai, F.C.C. Steinfurth, Carl August Nicolai, and Johann Wilhelm Richardi are recorded, the shop appears to have had at most two *Diener* at a time, and that only during the late 1780s and early 1790s. The shop's managers were Gohl (until 1784); Harrer (1784–86), who had trained under Frommann in Züllichau for six years;[17] Hane (1786–1811), who came from Korn Senior in Breslau,[18] and Johann Wilhelm Richardi (1811–12). Christian Friedrich Schmidt, who was a clerk from outside the book trade, served under Harrer and Hane from around 1786 until at least 1791.[19]

1794 and 17 January 1795; Carl Zolling to Nicolai, Langensalza, 13 July 1794; and Stendal, 30 March 1798, all letters in NN 84; Dr. Friedrich Christian Stöller to Nicolai, Langensalza, 17 January 1795, in NN 73; and Wiegleb to Nicolai, Langensalza, 18 January 1795, in NN 82.

14. Keyser to Nicolai, Erfurt, 12 June 1796, in NN 38, and Ritter's stepfather Pastor Zerrenner to Nicolai, Calbe a. d. Saale, 24 June 1796, in NN 84. According to *275 Jahre Nicolaische Buchhandlung: Eine Chronik* (Berlin: Nicolai 1988), Ritter stayed with the firm until 1827 (pp. 24 and 32). This work states incorrectly, however, that Ritter entered the shop in 1792 (p. 24).

15. Keyser to Nicolai, Erfurt, 8 July 1802, in NN 38.

16. Hane to Nicolai, Stettin, 31 December 1807 and 1 October 1808, in NN 87, and Richardi to Nicolai, Stettin, 12 June 1808, in NN 87.

17. Frommann to Nicolai, Züllichau, 26 August, 16 October, and 28 October 1784, in NN 23.

18. Hane may have gone to work for Nicolai as early as 1783. A letter of 31 October 1783 (in NN 42) from Korn Senior answers Nicolai's query about "Hahn" calling him "loyal, hardworking, and knowledgeable."

19. Schmidt, a native Stettiner who had served as Contoir Diener to Royal Manufactures Inspector Forckel at his factory at Amalienhof bei Neustadt, was twenty-six when he went to work for Nicolai. He had the misfortune of being both eligible for Prussian military service and tall enough to be of particular interest. He begged Nicolai to help get him exempted from further service by claiming that he was indispensable to the shop. He did not wish to repeat his previous experience of the "agonizing soldier's life," which had begun when he was dragged out of bed in the middle of the night of 1 April 1780. Carrying heavy weapons, he said, had permanently ruined his health. Schmidt to Nicolai, Stettin, 21 September (received) and 15 October 1786, in NN 67.

(bibliography)

ARCHIVES

Berlin
  Archiv der Evangelischen Kirche der Union, Berlin
    Kirchenbuchstelle
    Berlin, Kartei der Taufen
    Berlin, Sophiengemeinde, Kirchenbücher
  Landesarchiv Berlin (LAB)
    Familiennachlaß Nicolai-Parthey
    Rep. 200, Acc. 450, vols.1, 8, 10, 11
  Staatsbibliothek Preußischer Kulturbesitz (SPKB), Handschriftenabteilung
    Nachlaß Nicolai (NN), vols. 1–89, 90 (index), 284–89, 292
    Autogr. I/1590-1-26 & I/1622: Letters from Nicolai to Philipp Erasmus Reich
    Autogr. I/796, 797, 799: Letters from Nicolai to Anton Graff
    Nachlaß 141 (Slg. Adam), K. 2, K. 3
    Nachlaß Decker

Hamburg
  Staats- und Universitätsbibliothek (SUB), Handschriften-Abteilung
    Letter of 3 June 1772 from Nicolai to P. E. Reich

Leipzig
  Deutsche Bücherei, Deutsches Buch und Schrift Museum (DBSM)
    H 8d 90/8, 90/47
    K 123/21
    Sig. Ctf 20/215
    Sig. 20/191–192
    Sig. 17/124
    Sig. 77/27
    BöV Archivalien 95/1–2
  Universitätsbibliothek
    II A IV 1281
    L 467
    25 zh 7

MS 01321
Slg. Chlodius
Stadtarchiv (StA)
Tit. XLVI, No. 144, 388

Neuchâtel
Sociéte Typographique (STN)
MS 1187, fols. 98–105
MSS 11–19

New Haven
Yale University, Beinecke Library
Zg. Winkler
Speck Coll. N54b G 801 1:26

Paris
Bibliothèque Nationale
Ms. allem. tome viii (199), Nos. 218, 219
Letters of 21 November 1784 and 9 May 1805 from Nicolai to Jeremias Jacob Oberlin

Vienna
Österreichisches Staatsarchiv
Haus-, Hof- und Staatsarchiv (ÖHHStA)
Bestand Reichshofrat, Impressorien

Wolfenbüttel
Herzog August Bibliothek (HAB)
Cod. Guelph 622 Nov
Letters from Nicolai to Johann Joachim Eschenburg

PRINTED MATERIALS

Primary Sources

Acta Borussica. Die Behördenorganisation und die allgemeine Staatsverwaltung Preußens im 18. Jahrhundert. Vols. 7–12. Berlin: Paul Parey, 1904–26.

Acta Borussica. Die Handels-, Zoll- und Akzisepolitik Preußens 1740–1786. Vol. 3, pt. 1. Berlin: Paul Parey, 1928.

"Actenstücke zur Geschichte der preußischen Censur- und Preßverhältnisse unter dem Minister Wöllner." Ed. Friedrich Kapp. Part 1, 1788–93, *AGDB* 4 (1879): 138–214. Part 2, 1794–96, *AGDB* 5 (1880): 256–306.

Allgemeine deutsche Bibliothek. Berlin and Stettin: Nicolai, 1765–92; Kiel: Bohn, 1792–1800. Continued as *Neue allgemeine deutsche Bibliothek* (Berlin and Stettin: Nicolai, 1800–1805).

Allgemeines Landrecht für die Preußischen Staaten von 1794. Textausgabe. Frankfurt a. M. and Berlin: Alfred Metzner, 1970.

Allgemeines Verzeichniß derer Bücher, welche ... entweder ganz neu gedruckt, oder sonst verbessert, wieder aufgelegt worden sind (Leipzig Book Fair Catalog). Microfiche reprint. Hildesheim: Olms, 1977–81.

"Alphabetisches Verzeichniß aller Buchhändler und Buchdrucker, die die Leipziger

Bibliography

Messen besuchen, oder deren Verlag daselbst zu bekommen ist." *Buchhändlerzeitung auf das Jahr 1779*, 15 April 1779, 223–32. Hamburg: Herold, 1779.
Annalen der Gesetzgebung und Rechtsgelehrsamkeit in der Preussischen Staaten. Ed. Ernst Ferdinand Klein. 24 vols. Berlin and Stettin: Nicolai, 1788–1807.
Aus dem Josephinischen Wien. Geblers und Nicolais Briefwechsel während der Jahre 1771–1786. Ed. R. M. Werner. Berlin: Hertz, 1888.
"Auserlesene Bibliothek von allerhand zur Ergötzlichkeit und zum Unterricht dienlichen Büchern in deutscher und französischer Sprache welche unter nachstehenden Bedingungen dem Publico zum Gebrauch dargebothen wird von Friedrich Nicolai Buchhändlern in Berlin auf der Stechbahne im Schaarschmidischen Hause." Berlin, 1763. [Pamphlet announcing a lending library]
[Bahrdt, Karl Friedrich.] *Ueber Preßfreyheit und deren Grenzen. Zur Beherzigung für Regenten, Censoren und Schriftsteller.* Züllichau: Frommanns Erben, 1787.
Die beiden Nicolai. Briefwechsel zwischen Ludwig Heinrich Nicolay in St. Petersburg und Friedrich Nicolai in Berlin (1776–1811). Ed. Heinz Ischreyt. Lüneburg: Nordostdeutsches Kulturwerk, 1989.
Berliner Leben 1648–1806. Erinnerungen und Berichte. Ed. Ruth Glatzer. Berlin: Rütten & Loening, 1956.
Bertuch, Friedrich Justin. "Gedanken über den Buchhandel." *Archiv für Geschichte des Buchhandels* 7 (1967): cols. 1797–1810.
Briefe aus dem Freundeskreis von Goethe, Herder, Höpfner und Merck. Ed. Karl Wagner. Leipzig: Ernst Fleischer, 1847.
Briefe, die neueste Litteratur betreffend. Berlin: Nicolai, 1759–65.
Der Briefwechsel der Brüder J. Georg Müller und Joh. v. Müller, 1789–1809. Vol. 1, 1789–99. Ed. Eduard Haug. Frauenfeld: J. Huber, 1891.
Der Briefwechsel zwischen Friedrich Nicolai und Carl August Böttiger. Ed. Bernd Maurach. Bern: Peter Lang, 1996.
Der Briefwechsel zwischen der Kaiserin Katharina II. von Russland und Joh. Georg Zimmermann. Ed. Eduard Bodemann. Hanover and Leipzig: Hahn, 1906.
Buchhändlerzeitung. Hamburg: Herold, 1778, 1779, 1784.
"Bücher Inquisition in Prag. Ein Schreiben aus Prag, 3 Mai 1779." In *Schlözers Briefwechsel meist historischen und politischen Inhalts.* 2d ed., vol. 5, no. 25 (1779): 51–68. Göttingen: Vandenhoeck & Ruprecht, 1780.
Catalogue de Plusieurs Livres François Latins Italiens et Anglais qui se vendent au Prix Marque à Berlin chez Frederic Nicolai.... Berlin, 1761.
Catalogus von Allerhand Büchern, welche in der Franckfurter und Leipziger Ostermesse 1752 angeschaffet und um beygesetzten billigen Preiß zu bekommen sind bey Christoph Gottlieb Nicolai, Buchhändler in Berlin. Berlin, 1752.
Catalogus von allerhand Büchern, welche in der Frankfurter und Leipziger Oster-Messe 1758 angeschaffet und um beygesetzten billigen Preise, nebst vielen andern zu bekommen sind, bey Gottfried Wilhelm Nicolai, Buchhändler in Berlin. Berlin, 1758.
Catalogus von allerhand Büchern, welche in der Frankfurter und Leipziger Oster-Messe 1759 angeschaffet und um beygestezten billigen Preise, nebst vielen andern zu bekommen sind, bey Friedrich Nicolai, Buchhändler in Berlin. In der Brüder Strasse im du Fourschen Hause. Berlin, 1759. The catalogues in Deutsche Staatsbibliothek, now SBPK Aq 8791a continue only until Michaelmas [late September / early October] 1764.

Catalogus von Alten und Neuen Büchern welche vor beygesetzten billigen Preiß zu haben sind bey Christoph Gottlieb Nicolai Buchhändlern in Berlin. SPKB Aq 8791a. Berlin, 1737.

Chodowiecki, Daniel. *Briefwechsel zwischen ihm und seinen Zeitgenossen.* Ed. Charlotte Steinbrucker. Vol. 1, 1736–86. Berlin: Carl Duncker, 1919.

"Collectiveingabe an Herzog Karl Eugen von Württemberg gegen die Tübinger Nachdrucker vom 10. Februar 1779." *AGDB* 14 (1891): 150–54.

Denina, Carlo, Abbé. *La Prusse littéraire sous Fréderic II.* 3 vols. Berlin: Rottmann, 1790–91.

Denis, Michael. *Literarischer Nachlaß.* Ed. Joseph Friedrich Freiherr v. Retzer. 2 parts in 1 vol. Vienna: A. Pichler, 1801–2.

Ferber, Johann Jakob. *Briefe an Friedrich Nicolai aus Mitau und St. Petersburg.* Ed. Heinz Ischreyt. Nordost-Archiv, No. 7. Herford & Berlin: Nicolai, 1974.

Fichte, Johann G. *Friedrich Nicolai's Leben und sonderbare Meinungen: Ein Beitrag zur Litteratur Geschichte des vergangenen und zur Pädagogik des angehenden Jahrhunderts.* Ed. August Wilhelm Schlegel. Tübingen: Cotta, 1801.

[Francke, Friedrich Chr.] *Ueber den jetzigen Verfall des Buchhandels in Teutschland überhaupt und in den Preußischen Staaten insbesondere. Nebst einigen Vorschlägen die obwaltenden Mißbräuche zu heben.* Teutschland [Berlin?], 1802. Reprinted in *Quellen zur Geschichte des Buchwesens,* vol. 9 (Munich: Kraus, 1981).

Franklin, Benjamin. *Benjamin Franklin's Autobiography.* Ed. J. A. Leo Lemay and P. M. Zall. New York: Norton, 1986.

"Frömmichen." "Einige Bemerkungen welche sich über den Meßkatalogus machen lassen." *Deutsches Museum* 2 (August 1780): 176–87.

[Gädicke, Johann Christian.] *Der Buchhandel von mehreren Seiten betrachtet für solche Leser, die denselben näher kennen lernen, oder sich als Buchhändler etabliren wollen.* Weimar, 1803. 2d ed. Greiz: C. H. Henning, 1834.

Gelehrsamkeit ein Handwerk? Bücherschreiben ein Gewerbe? Dokumente zum Verhältnis von Schriftsteller und Verleger im 18. Jahrhundert in Deutschland. Ed. Evi Rietzschel. Leipzig: Reclam, 1982.

Gellert, Christian Fürchtegott. *Briefwechsel.* Vol. 2, 1756–59. Ed. John F. Reynolds. Berlin and New York: de Gruyter, 1987.

"Ein Generationskonflikt unter Buchhändlern? Der deutsche Buchhandel im Briefwechsel zwischen Friedrich Perthes und Friedrich Nicolai im Frühjahr 1808." Ed. Pamela E. Selwyn. In *Börsenblatt für den deutschen Buchhandel* (Leipzig), no. 24 (1990), Beiheft 2, pp. 13–17.

Göckingk, Leopold F. G. v. *Friedrich Nicolais Leben und literarischer Nachlaß.* Berlin: Nicolai, 1820.

Göschen, Georg Joachim. *Meine Gedanken über den Buchhandel und dessen Mängel, meine wenigen Erfahrungen und meine unmaßgeblichen Vorschläge dieselben zu verbessern. Bloß abgedruckt für die Herren Vorsteher und meine übrigen Herren Kollegen zur Prüfung, Verbesserung und Ergänzung,* p. 17. Leipzig, 1802. Reprinted in *Quellen zur Geschichte des Buchwesens,* vol. 9 (Munich: Kraus, 1981).

Heine, Heinrich. *Beiträge zur deutschen Ideologie.* Frankfurt a. M.: Ullstein, 1971.

Heinzmann, Johann Georg. *Appell an meine Nation über Aufklärung und Aufklärer; über Gelehrsamkeit und Schriftsteller; über Büchermanufakturen, Rezensenten, Buchhändler; über moderne Philosophen und Menschenerzieher; und auch über mancherley anderes, was Menschenfreyheit und Menschenrechte betrifft.* Bern 1795. Reprint. Hildesheim: Gerstenberg, 1977.

Jacobi, Johann Georg. *Ungedruckte Briefe von und an Johann Georg Jacobi.* Ed. Ernst Martin. Strasbourg: K. J. Trübner, 1874.

Jacobsson, Johann Karl Gottfried. *Technologisches Wörterbuch oder alphabetische Erklärung aller nützlichen mechanischen Künste, Manufacturen, Fabriken und Handwerker, wie auch aller dabey vorkommenden Arbeiten, Instrumente, Werkzeuge und Kunstwörter, nach ihrer Beschaffenheit und wahrem Gebrauche.* Ed. Otto Ludwig Hartwig. 8 vols. Vols. 5–8 continued by Gottfried Erich Rosenthal. Berlin and Stettin: Nicolai, 1781–84 and 1793–95.

Kant, Immanuel. *Über die Buchmacherey. Zweiter Brief an Herrn Friedrich Nicolai, den Verleger. Kants Gesammelte Schriften,* vol. 8. Berlin: Reimer, 1912.

Klein, Ernst Ferdinand. "Selbstbiographie." In *Bildnisse jetztlebender Berliner Gelehrten mit ihren Selbstbiographien.* Ed. M. S. Lowe. 3d collection. [Berlin, 1806.]

———. "Ueber Denk- und Druckfreiheit. An Fürsten, Minister und Schriftsteller." *Berlinische Monatsschrift* 3 (1784): 316ff.

[Knüppeln, J. F., C. C. Nencke, and C. L. Paalzow.] *Büsten Berliner Gelehrten, Schriftsteller und Künstler.* Stendal, 1787.

Die Leihbibliothek der Goethezeit. Exemplarische Kataloge zwischen 1790 und 1830. Ed. Georg Jäger, Alberto Martino, and Reinhard Wittmann. Hildesheim: Gerstenberg, 1979.

Lessing, G. E. *Sämtliche Schriften.* Ed. Karl Lachmann, rev. Franz Muncker. Vols. 17, 18, 19. Leipzig: Göschen, 1904–5.

Lichtenberg, Georg Christoph. *Briefe.* Vol. 4 of *Schriften und Briefe.* Ed. Wolfgang Promies. Munich: Hanser, 1967.

Linguet, Simon Nicolas Henri. *Des Herrn Linguets Betrachtungen über die Rechte des Schriftstellers und seines Verlegers.* Ed. Philipp Erasmus Reich. Leipzig: Weidmanns Erben & Reich, 1778.

[Mallinckrodt, Armin.] *Über Deutschlands Litteratur und Buchhandel.* Dortmund: Mallinckrodt, 1800.

Marperger, Paul Jacob. *Getreuer und Geschickter Handels-Diener, In welchem vornehmlich Was ein Handels-Diener sey, was derselbe vor Qualitäten und Wissenschaften an sich haben müsse....* Nuremberg and Leipzig: Peter Conrad Monath, 1715.

Mein scharmantes Geldmännchen: Gottfried August Bürgers Briefwechsel mit seinem Verleger Dieterich. Ed. Ulrich Joost. Göttingen: Wallstein, 1988.

Mendelssohn, Moses. *Gesammelte Schriften. Briefwechsel.* Ed. Alexander Altmann. 3 vols. Stuttgart-Bad Canstatt: Frommann-Holzboog, 1976–77.

———. *Neuerschlossene Briefe Moses Mendelssohns an Friedrich Nicolai.* Ed. Alexander Altmann and Werner Vogel. Stuttgart: Frommann-Holzboog, 1973.

Mirabeau, Honoré Gabriel de Riqueti. *De la monarchie prussienne sous Frédéric le Grand.* Londres, 1788.

Neues Archiv für Gelehrte, Buchhändler und Antiquare. Erlangen: Palm, 1795.

Nicolai, Friedrich. *Bescheidene und freymüthige Erklärung an das Deutsche Publikum betreffend das Verbot der allgemeinen deutschen Bibliothek und vieler sonst allgemein erlaubten Bücher in den Kaiserl. Königl. Erblanden.* Berlin: Nicolai, 1780.

———. *Beschreibung der königlichen Residenzstädte Berlin und Potsdam, aller daselbst befindlichen Merkwürdigkeiten, und der umliegenden Gegend.* 3d rev. ed. 3 vols. Berlin and Stettin: Nicolai, 1786.

———. *Beschreibung einer Reise durch Deutschland und die Schweiz im Jahre 1781.* 12 vols. Berlin: Nicolai, 1783–96.

———. *Briefe über den itzigen Zustand der schönen Wissenschaften in Teutschland.* Berlin: Kleyb, 1755.

———. *Leben und Meinungen des Herrn Magister Sebaldus Nothanker.* Frankfurt a. M.: Ullstein, 1986.

———. *Noch ein paar Worte betreffend Johann Bunkel und Christoph Martin Wieland.* Berlin and Stettin: Nicolai, 1779.

———. *Ein paar Worte betreffend Johann Bunkel und Christoph Martin Wieland.* Berlin and Stettin: Nicolai, 1779.

———. "Review" of G. E. Lessing's *Hamburgische Dramaturgie* and of the pirate edition by "Dodsley & Comp." *ADB* 10, no. 2 (1769).

———. "Selbstbiographie." *Bildnisse jetztlebender Berliner Gelehrten mit ihren Selbstbiographien.* Ed. M. S. Lowe. 3rd collection. [Berlin, 1806.]

———. *Ueber meine gelehrte Bildung.* Berlin and Stettin: Nicolai, 1799.

———. *Friedrich Nicolai: Verlegerbriefe.* Selected and edited by Berhard Fabian and Marie-Luise Spieckermann. Berlin: Nicolai, 1988.

[Perrin, Antoine.] *Almanach de la librairie.* 1781. Reprint. Aubel: P. M. Gason, 1984.

[Perthes, Friedrich.] *Der deutsche Buchhandel als Bedingung des Daseyns einer deutschen Literatur.* [Gotha: Perthes,] 1816.

Recke, Elisa v. d. *Tagebücher und Selbstzeugnisse.* Ed. Christine Träger. Munich: C. H. Beck, 1984.

[Riem, Andreas.] *Geschichte einiger Esel oder Fortsetzung des Lebens und der Meynungen des Weltberühmten John Bunkels.* 3 vols. Hamburg and Leipzig, 1782–83.

[Roch, Johann Christian Friedrich.] *Materialien zu einer Geschichte des Buchhandels.* Leipzig: Johann Gottlob Feind, 1795.

Schattenriß von Berlin. Amsterdam, 1788. Reprint. 2 vols. Berlin: Berliner Handpresse, 1974–75.

Schiller, Johann Christoph Friedrich v. *Briefwechsel. Schillers Briefe, 1772–1785.* Vol. 23 of *Werke. Nationalausgabe.* Ed. Walter Müller-Seidel. Weimar: Hermann Böhlaus Nachfolger, 1956.

Schlosser, Friedrich Christoph. *Geschichte des achtzehnten Jahrhunderts und des neunzehnten bis zum Sturz des französischen Kaiserreichs. Mit besonderer Rücksicht auf geistige Bildung.* Vol. 2. 2d ed. Heidelberg: J.C.B. Mohr, 1837.

Schubart, Christian Friedrich Daniel. *Briefe.* Ed. Ursula Wertheim and Hans Böhm. Leipzig: Dieterich, 1984.

Schulz, Günter. "Christian Garve im Briefwechsel mit Friedrich Nicolai und Elisa von der Recke." *Wolfenbütteler Studien zur Aufklärung* 1 (1974): 222–305.

Verlags-Katalog der Nicolaischen Buchhandlung in Berlin. Bis zum Schluß des Jahres 1846. Berlin: Nicolai, 1846.

Wieland, Christoph Martin. *Briefwechsel.* Vol. 4. Ed. Annerose Schneider and Peter-Volker Springborn. Berlin: Akademie Verlag, 1979.

Secondary Literature

Albrecht, Wolfgang. "Berliner Spätaufklärung offensiv. Friedrich Nicolais Kontroverse mit den Klassikern and Frühromantikern (1796–1802)." In *Das Angenehme und*

Bibliography

das Nützliche. Fallstudien zur literarischen Spätaufklärung in Deutschland. Tübingen: Max Niemeyer, 1997.
Altenkrüger, Ernst. *Friedrich Nicolais Jugendschriften.* Berlin: C. Heymann, 1894.
Aner, Karl. *Der Aufklärer Friedrich Nicolai.* Studien zur Geschichte des neueren Protestantismus, 6. Giessen: A. Töpelmann, 1912.
Barber, Giles. "Books from the Old World and the New: The British International Trade in Books in the Eighteenth Century." *Studies on Voltaire and the Eighteenth Century* 151 (1976): 185–224
———. "Pendred Abroad. A View of the Late 18th-Century Book Trade in Europe." In *Studies in the Book Trade.* In Honour of Graham Pollard. Oxford: Oxford Bibliographical Society, 1975.
———. "Who Were the Booksellers of the Enlightenment?" In *Buch und Buchhandel,* pp. 211–24.
Barker, Nicolas. "Typography and the Meaning of Words: The Revolution in the Layout of Books in the Eighteenth Century." In *Buch und Buchhandel,* pp. 127–65.
Bender, Thomas. *New York Intellect. A History of Intellectual Life in New York City from 1750 to the Beginnings of Our Own Time.* New York: Knopf, 1987.
Bettmann, Otto. "Die Entstehung buchhändlerischer Berufsideale im Deutschland des XVIII. Jahrhunderts." Ph.D. diss., Universität Leipzig, 1927.
Birtsch, G. "Religions- und Gewissensfreiheit in Preußen von 1780 bis 1817." *Zeitschrift für historische Forschung* 11 (1984): 177–204.
Bodi, Leslie. *Tauwetter in Wien: Zur Prosa der österreichischen Aufklärung 1781–1795.* Frankfurt a. M.: S. Fischer, 1977.
Bödeker, Hans Erich. "Prozesse und Strukturen politischer Bewußtseinsbildung der deutschen Aufklärung." In *Aufklärung als Politisierung—Politisierung der Aufklärung.* Ed. Hans Erich Bödeker and Ulrich Herrmann. Hamburg: Felix Meiner, 1987.
Books and Society in History. Papers of the Association of College and Research Libraries Rare Books and Manuscripts Conference, June 24–28, 1980. Ed. Kenneth E. Carpenter. New York and London: Bowker, 1983.
Bosse, Heinrich. *Autorschaft ist Werkherrschaft: Über die Entstehung des Urheberrechts aus dem Geist der Goethezeit.* Paderborn: Schöningh, 1981.
Breuer, D. *Geschichte der literarischen Zensur in Deutschland.* Heidelberg: Quelle & Meyer, 1982.
Bruford, W. H. *Germany in the Eighteenth Century: The Social Background of the Literary Revival.* Cambridge: Cambridge University Press, 1935.
Brunschwig, Henri. *La Crise de l'état prussien à la fin du xiiie siècle et la genèse de la mentalité romantique.* Paris: Presses Universitaires, 1947.
Buch und Buchhandel in Europa im achtzehnten Jahrhundert. The Book and the Book Trade in Eighteenth-Century Europe. Proceedings of the Fifth Wolfenbütteler Symposium, November 1–3, 1977. Wolfenbütteler Schriften zur Geschichte des Buchwesens, vol. 4. Ed. Giles Barber and Bernhard Fabian. Hamburg: Hauswedell, 1981.
Buchner, Karl. *Aus den Papieren der Weidmannschen Buchhandlung.* 2 vols. Berlin: Weidmann, 1871–73.
Bürger, Thomas. "Der redlichste Buchhändler seit Adams Zeiten." In *Maler und*

Dichter der Idylle: Salomon Gessner 1730–1788, ed. Martin Bircher et al. Wolfenbüttel: Herzog August Bibliothek, 1982.

Carvill, Barbara Maria. *Der verführte Leser: Johann Karl August Musäus' Romane und Romankritiken*. Canadian Studies in German Language and Literature, no. 31. Frankfurt a. M.: Peter Lang, 1985.

Cosentius, Ernst. "Die Berliner Zeitungen während der Französischen Revolution." *Preußische Jahrbücher* 117 (1904): 449–88.

———. "Friedrich der Große und die Zeitungs-Zensur." *Preußische Jahrbücher* 115 (1904): 220ff.

Dann, Otto. "Die Lesegesellschaften des 18. Jahrhunderts und der gesellschaftliche Aufbruch des deutschen Bürgertums." In *Buch und Leser*, ed. Herbert G. Göpfert. Schriften des Wolfenbütteler Arbeitskreises für Geschichte des Buchwesens, 1. Hamburg: Hauswedell, 1977.

———, ed. *Lesegesellschaften und bürgerliche Emanzipation: Ein europäischer Vergleich*. Munich: C. H. Beck, 1981.

Darnton, Robert. *The Business of Enlightenment: A Publishing History of the Encyclopédie, 1775–1800*. Cambridge: Harvard University Press, 1979.

———. "What Is the History of Books?" *Books and Society in History*. New York and London: Bowker, 1983.

Dreyfus, F. G. *Sociétés et mentalités à Mayence dans la seconde moitié du dix-huitième siècle*. Paris: Armand Colin, 1968.

Duncker, Dora. "Zweihundert Jahre Nicolaische Buchhandlung, 1713–1913." *Festschrift zur Zweihundert-Jahr-Feier zum 3. Mai 1913*. Berlin: Nicolai'sche Buchhandlung Borstell and Reimarus, 1913.

Eichler, Helga. "Berliner Buchdrucker, Buchhändler und Verleger am Ende des 18. Jahrhunderts." Typescript.

Eisenhardt, Ulrich. *Die kaiserliche Aufsicht über Buchdruck, Buchhandel und Presse im heiligen Römischen Reich Deutscher Nation (1496–1806): Ein Beitrag zur Geschichte der Bücher- und Pressezensur*. Studien und Quellen zur Geschichte des deutschen Verfassungsrechts, series A, vol. 3. Karlsruhe: C. F. Müller, 1970.

Engelsing, Rolf. *Der Bürger als Leser: Lesergeschichte in Deutschland, 1500–1800*. Stuttgart: Metzler, 1974.

———. "Hanseatische Lebenshaltungen und Lebenshaltungskosten im 18. und 19. Jahrhundert." *Zur Sozialgeschichte deutscher Mittel- und Unterschichten*. Göttingen: Vandenhoeck and Ruprecht, 1973.

———. "Wieviel verdienten die Klassiker?" *Neue Rundschau* 87, no. 1 (1976): 124–37.

———. "Die wirtschaftliche und soziale Differenzierung der deutschen kaufmännischen Angestellten im In- und Ausland 1690–1900." In *Zur Sozialgeschichte deutscher Mittel-und Unterschichten*. Göttingen: Vandenhoeck and Ruprecht, 1973.

Epstein, Klaus. *The Genesis of German Conservatism*. Princeton, N.J.: Princeton University Press, 1966.

Fabian, Bernhard. "The Beginnings of English-Language Publishing in Germany in the Eighteenth Century." In *Books and Society in History*. New York and London: Bowker, 1983.

———. "Die erste Bibliographie der englischen Literatur des achtzehnten Jahrhunderts: Jeremias David Reuss' *Gelehrtes England*." In *Das Buch und sein Haus*,

Festschrift Gerhard Liebers, vol. 1, ed. Rolf Fuhlrott and Bertram Haller. Wiesbaden: Reichert, 1979.
———. "Der Gelehrte als Leser." In *Buch und Leser*, ed. Herbert G. Göpfert. Hamburg: Hauswedell, 1977.
———. "Die Meßkataloge des achtzehnten Jahrhunderts." *Buch und Buchhandel*, pp. 321–42.
———. "Im Mittelpunkt der Bücherwelt. Über Gelehrsamkeit und gelehrtes Schrifttum um 1750." In *Wissenschaften im Zeitalter der Aufklärung*. Aus Anlaß des 250jährigen Bestehens des Verlages Vandenhoeck and Ruprecht. Ed. Rudolf Vierhaus. Göttingen: Vandenhoeck and Ruprecht, 1985, pp. 249–74.
———. "Nicolai und England." In *Friedrich Nicolai. Essays zum 250. Geburtstag*, ed. Bernhard Fabian. Berlin: Nicolai, 1983.
Feather, John. *A History of British Publishing*. London: Croom Helm, 1988.
———. *The Provincial Book Trade in Eighteenth-Century England*. Cambridge: Cambridge University Press, 1985.
Flygt, Sten Gunnar. *The Notorious Dr. Bahrdt*. Nashville: Vanderbilt University Press, 1963.
Fontius, Martin. *Voltaire in Berlin*. Berlin: Rütten & Loening, 1966.
Friedel, Ernst. *Zur Geschichte der Nicolai'schen Buchhandlung und des Hauses Brüderstraße in Berlin*. Berlin, 1891.
Friedrich Nicolai: Essays zum 250. Geburtstag. Ed. Bernhard Fabian. Berlin: Nicolai, 1983.
Friedrich Nicolai: Leben und Werk. Compiled by Peter Jörg Becker. Catalog of the exhibition for his 250th birthday, 7 December 1983–4 February 1984, at the Staatsbibliothek Preußischer Kulturbesitz. Berlin: Nicolai, 1983.
Friedrich Nicolai: Die Verlagswerke eines preußischen Buchhändlers der Aufklärung 1759–1811. Compiled by Paul Raabe. Catalog of the exhibition at the Herzog August Library. Wolfenbüttel: Herzog August Bibliothek, 1983.
Fromme, Jürgen. "Kontrollpraktiken während des Absolutismus (1648–1806)." In *Deutsche Kommunikationskontrolle des 15. bis 20. Jahrhunderts*. Ed. H. D. Fischer. Munich: K. G. Saur, 1982.
Furstner, Hans. *Geschichte des Niederländischen Buchhandels*. Wiesbaden: Otto Harrassowitz, 1985.
Gay, Peter. *The Enlightenment: The Rise of Modern Paganism*. New York: Vintage, 1966.
Geiger, Ludwig. "Aus Briefen Dohms an Nicolai." *Zeitschrift für die Geschichte der Juden in Deutschland* 5 (1892): 75–91.
———. *Berlin: Geschichte des geistigen Lebens der preußischen Hauptstadt*. 2 vols. Berlin, 1893–95.
Georgi, Arthur. *Die Entwicklung des Berliner Buchhandels bis zur Gründung des Börsenvereins der deutschen Buchhändler 1825*. Berlin: Paul Parey, 1926.
Gerth, Hans H. *Bürgerliche Intelligenz um 1800: Zur Soziologie des deutschen Frühliberalismus*. Göttingen: Vandenhoeck and Ruprecht, 1976.
Giese, Ursula. *Johann Thomas Edler von Trattner: Seine Bedeutung als Buchdrucker, Buchhändler und Herausgeber*. AGB 3 (1961): cols. 1013–1454.
Glas, Christine. *Johann Jacob Palm (1750–1826). Ein Erlanger Verleger und Buchhändler*. Erlanger Studien, no. 78. Erlangen: Palm and Enke, 1988.

Göbel, Wolfram. "Lektoren- die geistigen Geburtshelfer: Marginalien zu Praxis und Geschichte eines jungen Berufsstandes." *Gutenberg Jahrbuch* 61 (1986): 217–80.

Göpfert, Herbert G. "Bemerkungen über Buchhändler und Buchhandel zur Zeit der Aufklärung in Deutschland." *Wolfenbütteler Studien zur Aufklärung* 1 (1974): 69–83.

———. "'Welcher Fürst könnte mir ... Arbeit verbieten?' Zur Publikationsgeschichte der 2. Auflage von Jean Pauls 'Siebenkäs.'" In *Vom Autor zum Leser: Beiträge zur Geschichte des Buchwesens*. Munich: Hanser, 1977.

———. "Zur Geschichte des Autorenhonorars." In *Vom Autor zum Leser: Beiträge zur Geschichte des Buchwesens*. Munich: Hanser, 1977.

Goldenbaum, Ursula. "Der 'Berolinismus': Die preußische Hauptstadt als ein Zentrum geistiger Kommunikation in Deutschland." In *Aufklärung in Berlin*, ed. Wolfgang Förster. Berlin: Akademie-Verlag, 1989.

Goldfriedrich, Johann. *Geschichte des deutschen Buchhandels*. Vol. 2, *Vom Westfälischen Frieden bis zum Beginn der klassischen Litteraturperiode (1648–1740)*. Vol. 3, *Vom Beginn der klassischen Litteraturperiode bis zum Beginn der Fremdherrschaft (1740–1804)*. Vol. 4, *Vom Beginn der Fremdherrschaft bis zur Reform des Börsenvereins im neuen Deutschen Reiche (1805–1889)*. Leipzig: Börsenverein, 1908, 1909, 1913.

Gut, Albert. *Das Berliner Wohnhaus: Beiträge zu seiner Geschichte und seiner Entwicklung in der Zeit der landesfürstlichen Bautätigkeit*. Berlin: W. Ernst, 1918.

Guthke, Karl S. *Literarisches Leben im achtzehnten Jahrhundert in Deutschland und in der Schweiz*. Bern and Munich: Francke, 1975.

Habermas, Jürgen. *Strukturwandel der Öffentlichkeit: Untersuchungen zu einer Kategorie der bürgerlichen Gesellschaft*. 1962. 13th ed. Darmstadt: Luchterhand, 1982.

Haferkorn, Hans Jürgen. "Der freie Schriftsteller." *AGB* 5 (1964): cols. 523–711.

———. "Der freie Schriftsteller Müller und seine Einkünfte: Zur wirtschaftlichen Situation der Autoren in der zweiten Hälfte des 18. Jahrhunderts." In *J. G. Müller von Itzehoe und die deutsche Spätaufklärung*. Ed. Alexander Ritter. Heide i. Holstein: Boyens, 1978.

Hansers Sozialgeschichte der deutschen Literatur. Vol. 3, *Deutsche Aufklärung bis zur Französischen Revolution*. Ed. Rolf Grimminger. 2d ed. Munich: dtv, 1984.

Heier, Edmund. *Ludwig Heinrich v. Nicolay (1737–1820) as an Exponent of Neo-Classicism*. Bonn: Bouvier, 1981.

Hellmuth, Eckhart. "Aufklärung und Pressefreiheit. Zur Debatte der Berliner Mittwochsgesellschaft während der Jahre 1783 und 1784." *Zeitschrift für historische Forschung* 9 (1982): 315–45.

———. "Ernst Ferdinand Klein: Politsche Reflexion im Preußen der Spätaufklärung." *Aufklärung als Politisierung—Politisierung der Aufklärung*. Ed. Hans Erich Bödeker and Ulrich Herrmann. Hamburg: Felix Meiner, 1987.

———. "Zur Diskussion um Presse- und Meinungsfreiheit in England, Frankreich und Preußen im Zeitalter der Französischen Revolution." *Grund- und Freiheitsrechte im Wandel von Gesellschaft und Geschichte*. Ed. Günter Birtsch. Göttingen: Vandenhoeck and Ruprecht, 1981.

Hermsdorf, Klaus. *Literarisches Leben in Berlin: Aufklärer und Romantiker*. Berlin: Akademie-Verlag, 1987.

Bibliography

Hesse, Franz Hugo. *Die Preußische Preßgesetzgebung, ihre Vergangenheit und Zukunft.* Berlin: E. H. Schroeder, 1843.
Hiller, Helmut. *Zur Sozialgeschichte von Buch und Buchhandel.* Bonner Beiträge zur Bibliotheks-und Bücherkunde, vol. 13. Bonn: Bouvier, 1966.
Holmsten, Georg. *Die Berlin-Chronik: Daten. Personen. Dokumente.* 2d rev. ed. Düsseldorf: Droste, 1987.
Houben, H.H. *Der ewige Zensor: Längs- und Querschnitte durch die Geschichte der Buch- und Theaterzensur.* 1926. Reprint. Kronberg i. Ts.: Athenäum, 1978.
Ischreyt, Heinz. "Buchhandel und Buchhändler im nordosteuropäischen Kommunikationssystem (1762–1797)." In *Buch und Buchhandel,* pp. 249–69.
———. "Die Königsberger Freimaurerloge und die Anfänge des modernen Verlagswesens in Rußland (1760–1763)." In *Rußland und Deutschland.* Festschrift für Georg von Rauch. Ed. Uwe Liszkowski. Kieler Historische Studien 22. Stuttgart: Klett, 1974.
Jentzsch, Rudolf. *Der deutsch-lateinische Büchermarkt nach den Leipziger Ostermeßkatalogen von 1740, 1770 und 1800 in seiner Gliederung und Wandlung.* Beiträge zur Kultur- und Universalgeschichte, 22. Leipzig: R. Voigtländer, 1912.
Kiesel, Helmut, and Paul Münch. *Gesellschaft und Literatur im 18. Jahrhundert: Voraussetzungen und Entstehung des literarischen Markts in Deutschland.* Munich: C. H. Beck, 1977.
Kirchhoff, Albrecht. "Der ausländische Buchhandel in Leipzig." *AGDB* 14 (1891): 155–82.
———. "Lesefrüchte aus den Acten des Städtischen Archivs zu Leipzig. Klagen und Mißstände im Anfang des 18. Jahrhunderts.—Vertrieb." *AGDB* 14 (1891): 196–269.
Kirsop, Wallace. "Les mécanismes éditoriaux." In *Histoire de l'édition française.* Vol. 2, *Le livre triomphant.* N.p: Promodis, 1984.
Kleinschmidt, John R. "Les imprimeurs et libraires de la République de Genève 1700–1798." Ph.D. diss., University of Geneva, 1948.
Klingenstein, Grete. *Staatsverwaltung und kirchliche Autorität im 18. Jahrhundert. Das Problem der Zensur in der theresianischen Reform.* Munich: Oldenbourg, 1970.
Knudsen, Jonathon. "Friedrich Nicolai's 'wirkliche Welt': On Common Sense in the German Enlightenment." In *Mentalitäten und Lebensverhältnisse: Beispiele aus der Sozialgeschichte der Neuzeit.* Rudolf Vierhaus zum 60. Geburtstag. Göttingen: Vandenhoeck and Ruprecht, 1982.
———. *Justus Möser and the German Enlightenment.* Cambridge: Cambridge University Press, 1986.
Knufmann, Helmut. "Das deutsche Übersetzungswesen des 18. Jahrhunderts im Spiegel von Übersetzer- und Herausgebervorreden." *AGB* 9 (1969): cols. 491–572.
Kobuch, Agatha. *Zensur und Aufklärung in Kursachsen.* Weimar: Hermann Böhlaus Nachfolger, 1988.
Koch, Adolf. "Nicolai in Berlin contra Stahel in Würzburg: Ein Nachdruckstreit aus dem Jahre 1777, nach Papieren des Königlichen Kreisarchivs in Würzburg." *AGDB* 13 (1890): 264–68.
König der Romantik: Das Leben des Dichters Ludwig Tieck in Briefen, Selbstzeugnissen und Berichten. Ed. Klaus Gunzel. 2d ed. Berlin: Verlag der Nation, 1986.

Koselleck, Reinhard. *Kritik und Krise: Zur Pathogenese der bürgerlichen Welt.* 1959. First paperback edition. Frankfurt a. M.: Suhrkamp, 1973.

Krauss, Werner. "Über den Antheil der Buchgeschichte an der literarischen Entfaltung der Aufklärung." *Studien zur deutschen und französischen Aufklärung.* Berlin: Rütten and Loening, 1963.

Krieg, Walter. *Materialien zu einer Entwicklungsgeschichte der Bücher-Preise und des Autoren-Honorars vom 15. bis zum 20. Jahrhundert.* Vienna: Herbert Stubenrauch, 1953.

Kühlmann, Wilhelm. *Gelehrtenrepublik und Fürstenstaat: Entwicklung und Kritik der deutschen Späthumanismus in der Literatur des Barockzeitalters.* Tübingen: Niemeyer, 1982.

Kuhnert, Reinhold P. *Urbanität auf dem Lande. Badereisen nach Pyrmont im 18. Jahrhundert.* Publications of the Max-Planck-Institut für Geschichte, 77. Göttingen: Vandenhoeck and Ruprecht, 1984.

La Vopa, Anthony. *Grace, Talent and Merit: Poor Students, Clerical Careers and Professional Ideology in Eighteenth-Century Germany.* Cambridge: Cambridge University Press, 1988.

———. "The Politics of Enlightenment: Friedrich Gedike and German Professional Ideology." *JMH* 62 (March 1990): 34–56.

Lehmstedt, Mark. "Die Geschichte einer Übersetzung. William Robertsons 'Geschichte von Amerika' (1777)." *Jahrbuch des Leipziger Arbeitskreises zur Buchgeschichte* 1 (1991): 265–97.

———. *"Ich bin nicht gewohnt, mit Künstlern zu dingen ...": Philipp Erasmus Reich und die Buchillustration im 18. Jahrhundert.* Leipzig: Deutsche Bücherei, 1989.

———. *Philipp Erasmus Reich (1717–1787): Verleger der Aufklärung und Reformer des deutschen Buchhandels.* Exhibition catalog, Karl-Marx-Universität Leipzig. Leipzig, 1989.

———. *Struktur und Arbeitsweise eines Verlages der deutschen Aufklärung: Die Weidmannische Buchhandlung in Leipzig unter der Leitung von Philipp Erasmus Reich zwischen 1745 und 1787.* Ph.D. diss., Karl-Marx-Universität Leipzig, 1989.

Lösel, Barbara. *Die Frau als Persönlichkeit im Buchwesen. Dargestellt am Beispiel der Göttinger Verlegerin Anna Vandenhoeck (1709–1787).* Wiesbaden: Harrassowitz, 1991.

Lowry, Martin. *The World of Aldus Manutius: Business and Scholarship in Renaissance Venice.* Ithaca, N.Y.: Cornell University Press, 1979.

McCarthy, John A. *Crossing Boundaries: A Theory and History of Essay Writing in German, 1680–1815.* Philadelphia: University of Pennsylvania Press, 1989.

———. "Literatur als Eigentum. Urheberrechtliche Aspekte der Buchhandelsrevolution." *MLN* 104, no. 4 (1989): 531–47.

———. "Rewriting the Role of the Writer: On the 18th Century as the Age of the Author." *Leipziger Jahrbuch zur Buchgeschichte* 5 (1995): 13–37.

Martens, Wolfgang. "Die Geburt des Journalisten in der Aufklärung." *Wolfenbütteler Studien zur Aufklärung* 1 (1974): 84–98.

Martin, Henri-Jean, Roger Chartier, et al. *Le livre triomphant, 1660–1830.* Vol. 2 of *Histoire de l'édition française.* N.p.: Promodis, 1984.

Martin, Henri-Jean. "Publishing Conditions and Strategies in Ancien Régime France." *Books and Society in History.* New York and London: Bowker, 1983.

Merker, Nicolao. *Die Aufklärung in Deutschland.* Munich: C. H. Beck, 1982.

Bibliography

Meyer, F. H. "Der Außenhandel deutscher Buchhändler im 18. Jahrhundert." *AGDB* 14 (1891): 183–95.
———. "Der deutsche Buchhandel gegen Ende des 18. und zu Anfang des 19. Jahrhunderts." *AGDB* 7 (1882): 199–249.
———. "Die geschäftlichen Verhältnisse des deutschen Buchhandels im 18. Jahrhundert." *AGDB* 5 (1880): 175–255.
———. "Die Leipziger Büchermesse von 1780 bis 1837." *AGDB* 14 (1891): 288–316.
Milstein, Barney M. *Eight Eighteenth-Century Reading Societies: A Sociological Contribution to the History of German Literature.* German Studies in America, no. 11. Berne and Frankfurt a. M.: Herbert Lang, 1972.
Minor, Jacob, ed. *Lessings Jugendfreunde: Chr. Felix Weiße, Joh. Friedr. v. Cronegk, Joach. Wilh. v. Brawe, Friedrich Nicolai.* Deutsche National-Litteratur, vol. 72. Berlin: W. Spemann, [1883].
Mitchell, P. M. "Johann Christoph Gottsched." *Deutsche Dichter des 18. Jahrhunderts. Ihr Leben und Werk.* Ed. Benno v. Wiese. Berlin: Erich Schmidt, 1977.
Mittenzwei, Ingrid. *Friedrich II. von Preußen.* 2d ed. Berlin: Deutscher Verlag der Wissenschaften, 1987.
———. *Preußen nach dem Siebenjährigen Krieg: Auseinandersetzungen zwischen Bürgertum und Staat um die Wirtschaftspolitik.* Berlin: Akademie-Verlag, 1979.
Möller, Horst. *Aufklärung in Preußen: Der Verleger Publizist und Geschichtsschreiber Friedrich Nicolai.* Publications of the Historische Kommission zu Berlin, vol. 15. Berlin: Colloquium, 1974.
———. *Fürstenstaat oder Bürgernation: Deutschland 1763–1815.* Berlin: Siedler, 1989.
———. *Vernunft und Kritik: Deutsche Aufklärung im 17. und 18. Jahrhundert.* Frankfurt a. M.: Suhrkamp, 1986.
Mollenhauer, Peter. "Friedrich Nicolai." *Dictionary of Literary Biography.* Vol. 97, *German Writers from the Enlightenment to the Sturm und Drang, 1720–1764.* Ed. James N. Hardin and Christoph E. Schweitzer. Detroit: Gale, 1990.
———. *Friedrich Nicolais Satiren: Ein Beitrag zur Kulturgeschichte des 18. Jahrhunderts.* Amsterdam: John Benjamins B.V., 1977.
Moran, Daniel. *Toward the Century of Words: Johann Cotta and the Politics of the Public Realm in Germany, 1795–1832.* Berkeley and Los Angeles: University of California Press, 1990.
Ost, Günther. *Friedrich Nicolais Allgemeine Deutsche Bibliothek.* Germanistische Studien, 63. Berlin: E. Ebering, 1928.
Parthey, Gustav. *Jugenderinnerungen: Handschrift für Freunde.* Ed. Ernst Friedel. Berlin: Privatdruck-Ernst Frensdorff, 1907.
———. *Die Mitarbeiter an Friedrich Nicolais Allgemeine Deutsche Bibliothek.* Berlin: Nicolai, 1842.
Paulin, Roger. *Ludwig Tieck: A Literary Biography.* Oxford: Oxford University Press, 1985.
Perthes, Clemens Theodor. *Memoirs of Frederick Perthes.* 2 vols. Edinburgh: Constable, 1856.
Philips, F.C.A. *Friedrich Nicolais literarische Bestrebungen.* Den Haag: W. P. van Stockum and Son, 1926.
Pröhle, Heinrich. "Der Dichter Günther v. Göckingk über Berlin und Preußen unter Friedrich Wilhelm II. und Friedrich Wilhelm III." *Zeitschrift für preußische Geschichte und Landeskunde,* 1877, pp. 1–89.

Bibliography

Quedenbaum, Gerd. *Der Verleger und Buchhändler Johann Heinrich Zedler 1706–1751: Ein Buchunternehmer in den Zwängen seiner Zeit.* Hildesheim and New York: Georg Olms, 1977.

Raabe, Mechthild. *Leser und Lektüre im 18. Jahrhundert. Die Ausleihbücher der Herzog August Bibliothek Wolfenbüttel 1714–1799.* 4 vols. Munich: K. G. Saur, 1989.

Raabe, Paul. "Die Aufklärung und das gedruckte Wort: Die Entfaltung neuer Ideen mit Hilfe Berliner Verleger." In *Digressionen: Wege zur Aufklärung. Festgabe für Peter Michelsen.* Ed. G. Frühsorge, K. Manger and Fr. Strack. Heidelberg: Winter, 1984.

———. *Bücherlust und Lesefreuden: Beiträge zur Geschichte des Buchwesens in Deutschland.* Stuttgart: Metzler, 1984.

———. "Der Buchhändler im 18. Jahrhundert." In *Bücherlust und Lesefreuden*, pp. 21–35, 287–88.

———. "Der Buchhändler im achtzehnten Jahrhundert in Deutschland." In *Buch und Buchhandel*, pp. 271–92.

———. "Der Verleger Friedrich Nicolai, ein preussischer Buchhändler der Aufklärung." In *Bücherlust und Lesefreuden*, pp. 141–64.

———. "Die Zeitschrift als Medium der Aufklärung." *Wolfenbütteler Studien zur Aufklärung* 1 (1974): 99–136.

———. "Zum Bild des Verlagswesens in der Spätaufklärung: Dargestellt an hand von Friedrich Nicolais Lagerkatalog von 1787." In *Bücherlust und Lesefreuden*, pp. 66–88.

Rachel, Hugo. *Das Berliner Wirtschaftsleben im Zeitalter des Frühkapitalismus.* Berlin: Rembrandt, 1931.

Rachel, Hugo, and Paul Wallis. *Berliner Großkaufleute und Kapitalisten.* Vol. 2, *Die Zeit des Merkantilismus 1648–1806.* Berlin: privately printed, 1938.

Randow, Andreas M.G.H.H. v. *Öffentlichkeit Erfahrung und Beschreibung: Hausväterrepublik und Gelehrtenrepublik als Möglichkeiten kultureller Partizipation der Bürger Nicolai und Chodowiecki im friderizianischen Berlin.* Ph.D. Diss., Universität Bonn, 1984.

Reill, Peter Hanns. *The German Enlightenment and the Rise of Historicism.* Berkeley and Los Angeles: University of California Press, 1975.

Riethmüller, Brigitte. "1596–1971. Die Geschichte der Osianderschen Buchhandlung." *Osiander 1596–1971: Buchhandel in Tübingen.* Ed. Konrad-Dietrich Riethmüller and Brigitte Riethmüller. Tübingen: Osiander, 1971.

Roche, Daniel. "Censorship and the Publishing Industry." *Revolution in Print: The Press in France 1775–1800.* Ed. Robert Darnton and Daniel Roche. Berkeley and Los Angeles: University of California Press, 1989.

Rodenberg, Julius. "Die Nicolaische Buchhandlung." In *Beiträge zur Kulturgeschichte von Berlin. Fs. zur Feier des fünfzigjährigen Bestehens der Korporation der Berliner Buchhändler.* Berlin: Korporation der Berliner Buchhändler, 1898.

Rollka, Bodo. "Tageslektüre in Berlin (1740–1780)." *Mendelssohn-Studien* 4 (1979): 47–80.

Rosenstrauch, Hazel. "Buchhandelsmanufaktur und Aufklärung. Die Reformen des Buchhändlers und Verlegers Ph. E. Reich (1717–1787). Sozialgeschichtliche Studie zur Entwicklung des literarischen Marktes." *AGB* 26 (1986): 1–129.

Bibliography

———. "Philipp Erasmus Reich—Bourgeois und Citoyen." *Karl-Marx-Universität Leipzig. Wissenschaftliche Zeitschrift.* Gesellschaftswissenschaftliche Reihe 1 (1989): 96–107.
Rosenstrauch-Königsberg, Edith. *Freimaurerei im Josephinischen Wien. Aloys Blumauers Weg vom Jesuiten zum Jakobiner.* Wiener Arbeiten zur Deutschen Literatur, 6. Wien and Stuttgart: Braumüller, 1975.
Ruppert, Wolfgang. *Bürgerlicher Wandel. Die Geburt der modernen Gesellschaft im 18. Jahrhundert.* Frankfurt a. M.: Campus, 1983.
Ruprecht, Wilhelm. "Göttinger Gelehrtenbuchhandlungen: Pläne aus der Frühzeit der Georg Augusts-Universität." *AGDB* 21 (1930): 195–231.
Rychner, Jacques. "Alltag einer Druckerei im Zeitalter der Aufklärung." In *Buch und Buchhandel*, pp. 53–80.
———. "Le travail de l'atelier." *Histoire de l'édition française.* Vol. 2, *Le livre triomphant.* N.p.: Promodis, 1984.
Sashegyi, Oskar. *Zensur und Geistesfreiheit unter Joseph II.* Budapest: Akademiai Kiado, 1958.
Schenda, Rudolf. *Volk ohne Buch: Studien zur Sozialgeschichte der populären Lesestoffe 1770–1910.* Munich: dtv, 1977.
Schmidt, Frieder. "Die Internationale Papierversorgung der Buchproduktion im deutschsprachigen Gebiet vornehmlich während des 18. Jahrhunderts." In *Deutschland und der europäische Buchhandel im 18. Jahrhundert.* Ed. Mark Lehmstedt. Wiesbaden: Harrassowitz, 1999.
Schmitt, R. *Deutsche Buchhändler, deutsche Buchdrucker.* Eberswalde, 1902–8.
Schneider, Ute. *Friedrich Nicolais Allgemeine Deutsche Bibliothek als Integrationsmedium der Gelehrtenrepublik.* Wiesbaden: Harrassowitz, 1995.
Schnelle, Kurt. *Aufklärung und klerikale Reaktion: Der Prozeß gegen den Abbé Henri-Joseph Laurens. Ein Beitrag zur deutschen und französischen Aufklärung.* Berlin: Rütten & Loening, 1963.
Schürmann, August. *Der deutsche Buchhandel der Neuzeit und seine Krisis.* Halle: Buchhandlung des Waisenhauses, 1895.
Schulte-Sasse, Jochen. "Friedrich Nicolai." In *Deutsche Dichter des 18. Jahrhunderts: Ihr Leben und Werk.* Ed. Benno v. Wiese. Berlin: Erich Schmidt, 1977.
Selwyn, Pamela E. "Daniel Chodowiecki. Der Künstler als Kaufmann." In *Daniel Chodowiecki (1726–1801). Kupferstecher, Illustrator, Kaufmann.* Ed. Ernst Hinrichs and Klaus Zernack. Wolfenbütteler Studien zur Aufklärung 22. Tübingen: Max Niemeyer, 1997.
———. "A *Philosophe* in the *Comptoir*: The Bookseller-Publisher Friedrich Nicolai." *Histoires du Livre. Nouvelles Orientations.* Ed. Hans Erich Bödeker. Paris: IMEC Éditions, 1995.
———. "Philosophy in the Comptoir: The Berlin Bookseller-Publisher Friedrich Nicolai 1733–1811." Ph.D. diss., Princeton University, 1992. Ann Arbor: Michigan: University Microfilms, 1992.
Sichelschmidt, Gustav. *Friedrich Nicolai: Geschichte seines Lebens.* Herford: Nicolai, 1971.
Siegert, Reinhard. "Aufklärung und Volkslektüre: Exemplarisch dargestellt an Rudolph Zacharias Becker und seinem 'Noth-und Hülfsbüchlein.'" *AGB* 19 (1978): cols. 565–1348.
Siemann, Wolfram. "Ideenschmuggel: Probleme der Meinungskontrolle und das Los

der deutschen Zensoren im 19. Jahrhundert." *Hist. Zeitschrift* 245 (1987): 71–106.
Siemers, Victor-L. "Die Förderung der Papiermühlen durch Herzog Karl I. (1735–1780) von Braunschweig. Ein Beispiel für merkantilistische Wirtschaftspolitik in einem deutschen Kleinstaat des 18. Jahrhunderts." *Leipziger Jahrbuch zur Buchgeschichte* 8 (1998): 79–113.
Sommerfeld, Martin. *Friedrich Nicolai und der Sturm und Drang.* Halle: M. Niemeyer, 1921.
Sondermann, Ernst Friedrich. *Karl August Böttiger: Literarischer Journalist der Goethezeit in Weimar.* Mitteilungen zur Theatergeschichte der Goethezeit, vol. 7. Bonn: Bouvier, 1983.
Stanescu, Heinz. "Vertriebsformen der Hochmeisterschen Buchhandlung in Hermannstadt im letzten Viertel des 18. Jahrhunderts." *Buch- und Verlagswesen im 18. und 19. Jahrhundert: Beiträge zur Geschichte der Kommunikation in Mittel- und Osteuropa.* Ed. Herbert G. Göpfert, Gerard Koziełek, and Reinhard Wittmann. Berlin: Camen, 1977.
Steiner, Harald. *Das Autorenhonorar—seine Entwicklungsgeschichte vom 17. bis 19. Jahrhundert.* Wiesbaden: Harrassowitz, 1998.
Strauss, Walter. *Friedrich Nicolai und die kritische Philosophie.* Stuttgart: W. Kohlhammer, 1927.
Stroup, John. *The Struggle for Identity in the Clerical Estate. Northwest German Protestant Opposition to Absolutist Policy in the Eighteenth Century.* Leiden: E. J. Brill, 1984.
Tortarolo, Edoardo. *La ragione sulla Sprea. Coscienza storica e cultura politica nell'illuminismo berlinese.* Bologna: il Mulino, 1989.
Turner, R. Steven. "The *Bildungsbürgertum* and the Learned Professions in Prussia, 1770–1830: The Origins of a Class." *Histoire sociale—Social History* 13, no. 25 (May 1980): 105–35.
275 Jahre Nicolaische Verlagsbuchhandlung. Eine Chronik. Berlin: Nicolai, 1988.
Ueding, Gert, and Bernd Steinbrink. *Hoffmann und Campe: Ein deutscher Verlag.* Hamburg: Hoffmann und Campe, 1981.
Ungern-Sternberg, Wolfgang v. "Christoph Martin Wieland und das Verlagswesen seiner Zeit. Studien zur Entstehung des freien Schriftstellertums in Deutschland." *AGB* 14 (1974): cols. 1211–1534.
———. "Schriftstelleremanzipation und Buchkultur im 18. Jahrhundert." *Jahrbuch für internationale Germanistik* 8 (1976): 72–98.
van Dülmen, Richard. *Die Gesellschaft der Aufklärer. Zur bürgerlichen Emanzipation und aufklärerischen Kultur in Deutschland.* Frankfurt a. M.: Fischer, 1986.
Vierhaus, Rudolf. "Chodowiecki und die Berliner Aufklärung." *Daniel Chodowiecki (1726–1801). Kupferstecher, Illustrator, Kaufmann.* Ed. Ernst Hinrichs and Klaus Zernack. Wolfenbütteler Studien zur Aufklärung 22. Tübingen: Max Niemeyer, 1997.
———. *Deutschland im 18. Jahrhundert. Politische Verfassung, soziales Gefüge, geistige Bewegungen.* Göttingen: Vandenhoeck and Ruprecht, 1987.
———. *Deutschland im Zeitalter des Absolutismus (1648–1763).* Göttingen: Vandenhoeck and Ruprecht, 1978. Translated by Jonathon B. Knudsen under the title *Germany in the Age of Absolutism* (Cambridge: Cambridge University Press, 1988).

Vogel, Martin. "Deutsche Urheber- und Verlagsrechtsgeschichte zwischen 1450 und 1850: Sozial- und Methodengeschichtliche Entwicklungsstufen der Rechte von Schriftsteller und Verleger." *AGB* 19 (1978): cols. 1–190.
Voigtländer, R. "Das Verlagsrecht im Preußischen Landrecht und der Einfluß von Friedrich Nicolai darauf." *AGDB* 20 (1898): 4–66.
Voss, Jürgen. "Eine deutsche Lesebibliothek im Paris des späten 18. Jahrhunderts. Neue Beobachtungen und methodische Überlegungen zur Erforschung der deutschen Lesegesellschaften." *Zeitschrift für historische Forschung* 6 (1979): 461–70.
Ward, Albert. *Book Production, Fiction and the German Reading Public 1740–1800.* Oxford: Oxford University Press, 1974.
Weber, Ernst. "Sortimentskataloge des 18. Jahrhunderts als literatur- und buchhandelsgeschichtliche Quellen." In *Bücherkataloge als buchgeschichtliche Quellen in der frühen Neuzeit.* Ed. Reinhard Wittmann.Wolfenbütteler Schriften zur Geschichte des Buchwesens, 10. Wiesbaden: Harrassowitz, 1984.
―――. "J. G. Müllers Wochenschrift 'Der Deutsche': Ein Modell aufklärerischer Publizistik." In *J.G. Müller von Itzehoe und die deutsche Spätaufklärung.* Ed. Alexander Ritter. Heide i. Holstein: Westholsteinische Verlagsanstalt Boyens, 1978.
Weiß, Wisso. *Zeittafel zur Papiergeschichte.* Leipzig: Fachbuchverlag, 1983.
Welke, Martin. "Das Pressewesen." In *Panorama der Fridericianischen Zeit. Friedrich der Grosse und seine Epoche. Ein Handbuch.* Ed. Jürgen Ziechmann. Bremen: Edition Ziechmann, 1985.
Widmann, Hans. *Geschichte des Buchhandels. Vom Altertum bis Gegenwart.* 2d ed. Wiesbaden: Harrassowitz, 1975.
Willnat, Elisabeth. "Johann Christian Dieterich. Ein Verlagsbuchhändler und Drucker in der Zeit der Aufklärung." *AGB*, 39 (1993): 1–254.
Wittmann, Reinhard. *Buchmarkt und Lektüre im 18. und 19. Jahrhundert. Beiträge zum literarischen Leben 1750–1880.* Tübingen: Niemeyer, 1982.
―――. "Ein Doppeldruck des 'Sebaldus Nothanker.'" *Wolfenbütteler Notizen zur Buchgeschichte* 2, no. 3 (August 1977): 127–28.
―――. "Die frühen Buchhändlerzeitschriften als Spiegel des literarischen Lebens." *AGB* 13 (1973): cols. 613–932.
―――. *Geschicte des deutschen Buchhardels. Ein Überblick.* Munich: C. H. Beck, 1991.
―――. *Ein Verlag und seine Geschichte. Dreihundert Jahre J. B. Metzler Stuttgart.* Stuttgart: Metzler, 1982.
―――. "Zur Verlegertypologie der Goethezeit." *Jahrbuch für internationale Germanistik*, 8, no. 1 (1976): 99–130.
Woodmansee, Martha. "The Genius and the Copyright: Economic and Legal Conditions of the Emergence of the 'Author.'" *Eighteenth-Century Studies* 17, no. 4 (Summer 1984): 425–48.

(index)

Abbt, Thomas (1738–66), 45, 58, 337 n. 141, 366
 as ADB contributor, 255 n. 19, 265
 Vom Verdienste, 33, 186, 217, 221 n. 148
 works of on index of forbidden books, 216, 243
ADB. See *Allgemeine deutsche Bibliothek*
Adelung, Johann Christoph (1732–1806), 87 n. 199, 339, 365–66 n. 250
advertising, 72–75, 78, 333. *See also* subscription
Aelianus, Claudius (third century), *Varia historia*, 45
Agricola, Johann Friedrich (1720–74), 265
Ahl, Rudolf A. W., 65 n. 109, 68, 71 n. 138
Albrecht, Johann Gottlieb (b. 1755), 141 n. 186
Allgemeine deutsche Bibliothek (ADB), 12, 31, 33, 34, 37, 197, 216, 217, 217 n. 32, 241, 252–53 n. 2, 274, 275, 278, 278 n. 125, 280, 281
 administrative and editorial staff, 261–62
 advertising in, 73, 286
 associated with Berlin, 275, 279, 281
 attacks on, 276–78
 ban on: in Austria, 34–35, 200, 216, 217, 239–40, 247; in Prussia, 38, 197 n. 56, 207–10
 as a bastion of irreligion, 277–78, 291 n. 178
 compared to other review journals, 254, 291
 and Enlightenment, 258, 260, 274, 281
 founding of, 253–57
 geographical dissemination of, 281, 281 n. 139
 and German book production, 254, 256, 257, 274–75
 and Nicolai, 40, 264, 269–70, 273–74, 283, 292–93, 293 n. 190; aims in, 257–59, 260; benefits of for his business, 283–86; cautions reviewers, 200, 206, 270–71; complaints by, 292, 292 n. 189, 293–95; legal responsibilities for, 210–11, 263; sells to Carl Ernst Bohn (1792), 38, 205, 290; tries to find a new publisher for (in 1800), 294, 294 n. 198, (in 1805), 295–96, 296 n. 209
 "party line" in, 267–69
 price of, 153, 233
 printing of, 66–68, 67 n. 118
 readers, 258, 258 n. 35, 282, 289–90
 reviewers, 152, 255 n. 19, 262–63, 264, 264 n. 61, 266, 267, 272–73, 289; distribution of, 76, 281, 288–89; fears and complaints of, 257 n. 31, 279, 293, 293 n. 194; payment of, 291–92, 331, 331 n. 118; recruitment and choice of, 255–56, 256 n. 27, 265–66, 290–91 n. 178
 reviews, 199, 200, 241–42, 259–60, 263, 264, 264 n. 61, 265, 267, 272, 273, 274 n. 109, 276, 285–86, 285 nn. 158, 161, 287–88, 291 n. 181
 sales of, 284, 290, 290 n. 176, 291 n. 179
 and scholarly feuds, 261, 276–79
 success of, 98, 283–85
Allgemeine Literatur-Zeitung (ALZ), 211, 294
 comparison to ADB, 291, 331 n. 118
 as competition to ADB, 256 n. 27, 268, 272, 290, 291
Allgemeines Preußisches Landrecht
 censorship law in, 192, 213

Index

and literary property, 185, 223, 306
Nicolai influences publishing law in, 26, 189, 189 n. 30, 306–11, 371
Alxinger, Johann Baptist (1755–97), 264
Amende, Carl Gottfried, 166, 170, 170 n. 297, 176 n. 317, 381
Ammon, Gottfried von, 234 n. 187
Amory, Thomas (?1691–1788), *Life and Opinions of John Buncle, Esquire*. See *Johann Bunkel*
Anderson, James (1739–1808), 56
Anières, Friedrich Benjamin de, 187, 196–97, 198
anonymity, authors' desire for, 334–35, 335 n. 131
Archenholtz, Johann Wilhelm von (1743–1812), 114, 318
Argens, Jean-Baptiste de Boyer, Marquis de (1704–71), 119, 119 n. 79, 187
Arnold, Christoph (1763–1847), 285 n. 161
Aufklärer, 2, 142, 142 n. 195, 359–60, 377
  defined, 1
  and French Revolution, 37, 202, 202 n. 74
  Nicolai as, 4, 14–15, 54–55, 97, 265
  Prussian, 359–60
Austria, 183, 184, 185. *See also* censorship: in Austria
authors, 303–4, 305, 333–34, 339, 339 n. 148, 358, 364–65
  anonymous, 315, 335
  attitudes of, 329–30, 347, 348–49
  contemporary critiques of, 193, 307
  fees, 330–31, 322, 322 nn. 75–76, 337, 337 n. 142; advance payment of, 332, 353 nn. 207–8, 354–56; disputes over, 345 n. 167, 349–52; literature on, 330–31, 330–31 n. 112; negotiation of, 322 nn. 75–76, 329, 332, 347–57; for subsequent editions, 349, 351, 352–53, 354
  and Nicolai, 314, 320, 320 nn. 68, 71, 358–64
  on piracy law, 305
  relations with publishers, 299–300, 303–11, 346–47

Bad Freyenwalde, Nicolai visits, 108, 134
Bad Pyrmont, 98, 108, 140 n. 183, 141, 141 n. 188
Bage, Robert (1720–1801), 85, 92
Bahrdt, Carl Friedrich (1741–92), 192, 217, 232–33, 232 n. 180, 238
barter system, 40, 102

in the German book trade, 17, 42, 107
role in international book trade, 124, 124 n. 103, 132
Basedow, Johann Bernhard (1723–90), *Geschenk an Bürgerschulen*, 154–55
Bassompierre, J. F., 121 n. 84, 123 n. 97
Bayle, Pierre (1647–1706), 4, 7, 131
Beck, Carl Gottlob, (1732–1802), 285 n. 161
Becker, Rudolf Zacharias (1751–1822), 117, 305 n. 22
Beckford, William (1760–1844), 92
Beckmann, Johann (1739–1811), 156, 341, 369–70 , 373 n. 275
Beckmann, Johann Christoph (1641–1717), written contract with Nicolai's grandfather, 340 n. 151
Beer, Georg Emanuel, 23, 23 n. 63, 176 n. 319, 381–82, 382 n. 7
Beguélin, Nicolas (1714–89), 125
Behn, Georg Heinrich, 36
Bel, Carl Andreas (1717–82), 217 n. 133, 220 n. 148, 221
Belitz, J. C., 105–6
belles-lettres, Nicolai as publisher of, 48–50
Benekendorf, Karl Friedrich von, 54
Ben Israel, Menasse, 89–90
Bensel, W. G. (d. 1835), 142 n. 192
Benzel, Franz Anselm von (1738–86), 315, 315 n. 41, 365, 365 n. 248
Berlin, 93 n. 213, 185, 243, 313 n. 35
  book trade in, 8–9, 103–6, 106 n. 26, 133, 133 n. 144, 166 n. 277;
  intellectuals in, 92, 93 n. 213
Berlinische Monatsschrift, 81 n. 167, 192, 212 n. 115, 253, 290, 310, 322 n. 74, 326
  attacked by: J. A. Starck, 202 n. 74; J. C. Wöllner, 203
Berlockenbücher, 32, 32n. 11
Bernhardi, August Ferdinand (1769–1820), 311
Bernouilli, Johann (1741 or 1744–1807), 319–20 n. 66
Beroldingen, Franz von (1740–98), 56
Bertuch, Friedrich Justin (1747–1822), 29, 291
Besler, Johann Christoph (1712–91), 238
Beyer, Christian Samuel Ludwig (after 1730–after 1808), 314–15
Bibliothek der elenden Scribenten, 277
Bibliothek der schönen Wissenschaften. See Nicolai, (Christoph) Friedrich: periodicals
Biester, Johann Erich (1749–1816), 193, 203, 253, 280–81

Index

Birkenstock, Johann Melchior von (1738–1809), 59 n. 90, 248
Bischoff, Johann Nikolaus (1756–1833), 273
Bismarck, Levin Friedrich von (d. 1774), 191
Blankenburg, Christian Friedrich (1744–96), 119, 373 n. 277
Blumauer, Alois (1755-98), 80
Bode, Johann Elert (1746–1826), 76
Bode, Johann Joachim Christoph (1728–93), 116
Bodmer, Johann Jakob (1698–1783), 9, 252 n. 7
Böhme, Adam Friedrich, 84, 160
Boerner, Christian Friedrich (1736–1800), 255 n. 19
Boerner, Georg Gottfried (1734–1804), 255 n. 19
Böttiger, Karl August (1760/1762–1835), 266 n. 73, 294
Bohn, Carl Ernst (1749–1827), 40, 114, 128 n. 121, 205 n. 83, 290, 291 n. 179, 293, 294, 295, 295 n. 204, 331n. 118
Bohn, Johann Carl (1712–73), 101
Boie, Heinrich Christian (1744–1806), 127, 274, 327, 328 n. 99
Bolingbroke, Henry St. John, Viscount (1678–1751), 290, 320
Bonnet, Charles (1720–93), 89 n. 206
book fair, 107–11, 120
  catalogs of, 179, 179 n. 332
  Frankfurt, 107
  Leipzig, 39, 101 n. 8, 107–11, 110 nn. 43–44, 120–21, 121 n. 84, 321, 321 n. 73
  book prices, authors try to influence, 337, 337 n. 140. *See also* discounts
book titles, 333
book trade, xii, 105 n. 22, 120–21, 256, 323–24
  accounts and records kept, 174–75
  changes in, 24–25, 40, 42, 102, 108
  characterized, 15–16, 108
  contemporary attitudes toward, 25–26, 30 nn. 3, 4
  and Edict on Censorship, 210
  honor in, 16–19, 116
  ideologization of, 25–26
  Nicolai on, 28, 30, 100–102
  state control of, 181–84; in Prussia, 184–213
books as collective projects, 373–74
bookseller-publishers, 3, 16, 26, 209, 210, 308

Borcke, Adrian Heinrich, Graf von (1715–88), 269, 355 n. 216
Bothe, Friedrich Heinrich (1771–1855), 85–86, 85 n. 185, 311, 328, 348–49
  Nicolai rejects novel by, 325–26, 325 n. 90
  translation of Euripides, 68, 334, 334 n. 125, 336, 339 n. 148, 344, 347, 347 n. 177
  translation of works of Samuel Foote, 373
Bourdeaux, Etienne de, 133
Boysen, Friedrich Eberhard (1720–1800), 261 n. 46, 277
Brandis, Joachim Friedrich (1762–1826), 320 n. 68
Brandt, J. C., 163 n. 266
Braunschweig, 35, 204–5
Breitinger, Johann Jakob (1701–76), 252 n. 7
Breitkopf, Johann Gottlob Immanuel (1719–94), 72, 88 n. 205
Bretschneider, Heinrich Gottfried von (1739–1810), 68, 81, 137, 137 n. 164, 146–47 n. 213, 152, 219 n. 142, 231 n. 178, 236–37, 245–48, 282 n. 143
  Georg Wallers Leben und Sitten, 336, 336 n. 136, 366, 366 n. 253
  Heiligen-Kalendar, 264 n. 61, 286 n. 162
Briefe, die neueste Litteratur betreffend. See Nicolai, (Christoph) Friedrich: periodicals
Brömel, Wilhelm Heinrich (1754–1808), 84–86
Brönner, Heinrich Ludwig (1702–69), 119, 121, 121 n. 86
Brönner, Johann Carl (1738–1812), 186, 231 n. 178
Brüder Straße in Berlin, 36
Bruns, Paul Jakob (1743–1814), 373
Brunswick, dowager duchess of, 140, 140 n. 181
Brunswick, duke of, 204
Bruyset, Jean-Marie (1749–1817), 121 n. 84
Bube, Nicolai's *Diener*, 163 n. 269, 382
Buchholtz, privy councilor and Berlin censor, 191 n. 38
Bucholz, Wilhelm Heinrich (1734 or 1735–93), 67, 265 n. 67
Buchhandlung der Gelehrten, 304, 318 n. 54
Buchhandlungsgesellschaft, 99, 186–87, 187 n. 23, 220
Bürger, Gottfried August (1747–94), 352 n. 202
Büsching, Anton Friedrich (1724 or 1727–93), 140 n. 179

Index

Büsten Berliner Gelehrten, 1, 275
Burney, Charles (1726–1814), 58, 127, 339 nn. 146, 148
Burney, Frances (Fanny, 1752–1840), 92, 335 n. 131

Cagliostro, Alessandro, Count (1743–95, pseud. of Giuseppe Balsamo), and Elisa von der Recke, 35 n. 21
Calve, Johann Gottfried, 163
Campe, Johann Heinrich (1746–1818), 141 n. 190, 279
  as ADB contributor, 270, 272, 287–88, 338 n. 143
Carl August, Grand Duke of Saxe-Weimar-Eisenach (1757–1828), 5 n. 8
Carlyle, Thomas (1795–1881), 23
Carmer, Johann Heinrich Casimir von (1721–1801), 75, 119, 207
catalogs, Nicolai's, 136–39, 138 n. 172
Catherine II of Russia (1729–96), 22, 49, 140, 149, 149 n. 218, 335 n. 131
  and Nicolai 35, 131, 149–50, 149 n. 221, 150 n. 222
Catholicism, 275
  Nicolai's views on, 3, 257, 267–68, 377
censors, 187, 192, 198–202, 212, 238–40, 248
censorship, 240–42
  defined, 182
  in Austria, 216, 238, 243, 244–45, 245 nn. 225, 228, 247
  in Bavaria, 202, 246 n..229
  in Hungary, 244–45
  in Mainz/Erfurt, 241–42
  Nicolai's experiences with, 34, 195–202, 239–49
  in Prussia, 38, 39, 189–213, 190 n. 36, 336
  in Russia, 212 n. 115
  in Saxony, 2 n. 3, 212 n. 115, 214, 243
  in Wittenberg, 242
Chodowiecki, Daniel (1726–1801), xiv, 78 n. 160, 111, 117, 133, 136, 288, 338, 339 n. 146
classical literature, 94 n. 216
Cocceji, Samuel von (1679–1755), 191
commissionaires, work of, 108–12
consignment (*à condition*), books sold on, 321 n. 73
contracts, 227, 309, 340, 340 nn. 150, 151, 341–44
Conybeare, John (1692–1755), 51

Corrodi, Heinrich (1752–93), 50, 51 n. 69
Cotta, Johann Friedrich (1764–1832), 357, 379
Cotta, Johann Georg, 220 n. 147
Courland, Dorothea, duchess of (née von Medem, 1761–1823), 131, 136, 136 n. 155, 140, 144 n. 201, 148, 148 n. 217
Crell, Lorenz Florens Friedrich (1744–1816), 265 n. 67
Cremeri, Benedikt Dominik Anton (1752–95, pseud. of Joseph von Reinberg), 247
Crichton, Alexander (1763–1856), 150, 150 n. 223
critical philosophy, 90, 268–69, 316
critics and criticism, 12–13, 252, 260–61
Cröcker, Johann Rudolph, 382
Crusius, Siegfried Lebrecht (1737–1824), 117 n. 74, 168 n. 288, 172 n. 304
"crypto-Catholics," 35, 35 n. 21
Curas, Hilmar, 43, 186, 217
customers, Nicolai's, 136, 140–58, 142 nn. 192–94, 194, 338

Danckelmann, Carl Ludolph (1699–1764), 191
Danzig, 134, 134 n. 148
Dapp, Raymund (1744–1819), 50 n. 69, 52, 81, 108, 262, 288–89, 368
Dauling, Johann Gustav (b. 1715), 69
debts and debtors, 103 n. 11, 177, 177n. 325
Decker, Georg Jacob (1732–99), 71 n. 140, 106 n. 26, 118–19, 133, 235
Deinet, Johann Konrad (1735–97), 123, 259 n. 39
Denina, Carlo (1731–1813), 275, 283
Denis, Johann Michael Kosmas (1729–1800), 244, 264 n. 63, 278 n. 127
Destouches, (Philippe) Néric(ault) (1680–1754), 31
Deutsches Museum, 74, 274, 327
Diderot, Denis (1713–84), 45, 49
Dieterich, Johann Christian (1722–1800), 72, 127, 352, 352 n. 202
discounts, 153, 152–53 n. 235, 233, 237
  between booksellers, 113–15, 115 n. 65
  for non–book trade customers, 73 n. 146, 152, 152 n. 134, 153, 319 n. 63
Diterich, Johann Samuel (1721–97), 50 n. 69, 235 n. 189
dogmatic symbols, 51, 207, 207 n. 90
Dohm, Christian Wilhelm (1751–1820), 193, 198

Index

Über die bürgerliche Verbesserung der Juden, 89, 241 n. 207, 268, 349, 351–52, 351 n. 199, 357
Dohna, Graf von, 382
Doll, Jan, 123–24
Dürfeld, merchant in Gotha, 266
Dürr, Carl Christian, 65 n. 109, 68
Durand, J. M., 129
Dusch, Johann Jakob (1725–87), 32
Dyck, Johann Gottfried, 88 n. 205, 122

Eberhard, Johann August (1738–1809), 50 nn. 68, 69, 58, 93, 141 n. 187, 150, 152, 157, 201 n. 7, 202 n. 74, 348
  Neue Apologie des Sokrates, 98, 244
Edict Concerning Religion, 193, 204–5, 206 n. 85
editing and editors, 83–87
edition sizes, 42, 42 n. 42, 43, 310, 336, 337 n. 141
Efendi, Ahmed Resmi, 48 n. 60
Eichhorn, Johann Gottfried (1752–1827), 48 n. 57
Eichmann (d. 1829), 57 n. 81
Eisenberg, collaborator of Ernst Ferdinand Klein, 75
Elsner, Jakob (1692–1750), as Prussian censor, 191 n. 38
Elwert, Johann Kaspar Philipp (1760–1827), 320 n. 68
Emmerich Joseph, elector of Mainz (1704–74), 315 n. 41
employees in the book trade (*Diener*), 30, 157–78, 172 n. 304
  and Nicolai, 163, 163 nn. 266–68, 165–69, 171–72, 171 n. 302, 174–78, 178 n. 330, 381–83
  Philipp Erasmus Reich's, 159–60, 167 n. 287
  salaries, 167–69, 168 nn. 288–90
Engel, Johann Jakob (1741–1802), 58, 217, 339, 339 n. 147
Engelbrecht, Johann Andreas (1733–1803), 56, 348 n. 182
England, 4, 8
English, 8, 31, 33, 34, 126 nn. 113–14, 127, 129
Enlightenment, 12, 147
  German and French compared, 1–3
  Nicolai and, 88–90, 92, 363, 378
  popular (*Volksaufklärung*), 2, 12, 52, 93
  practical, 15, 54–55, 297

Prussian, 359, 379
  See also *Aufklärer*
Ensslin, Johann Matthias, 168–69
Ephemeriden der Menschheit, 219, 235 n. 190, 358 n. 229
Erasmus, Desiderius (1466–1536), 364 n. 246
Eschenburg, Johann Joachim (1743–1820), 53, 58, 93, 94, 130, 136 n. 154, 137, 150, 152, 153, 158, 204, 257 n. 31, 294, 311, 322 n. 74, 323, 331 nn. 117–18, 336 n. 138, 337 n. 141, 348 n. 182
  as ADB contributor, 260, 264, 266, 271 n. 92, 291
  Beispielsammlung, 234 n. 187
  Entwurf einer Theorie und Literatur der schönen Wissenschaften, 95 n. 221, 234 n. 187, 337 n. 140
  Handbuch der klassischen Litteratur, 43, 74, 94 n. 216, 332 n. 119
  Lehrbuch der Wissenschaftskunde, 350 nn. 193, 194
  and Nicolai, 71 n. 138, 84 n. 183, 279, 372
Esslinger, Friedrich, 164
Esslinger, Johann Georg, 109 n. 35
Ettinger, Carl Wilhelm, 69 n. 134, 290 n. 175
Euripides, 94 n. 216
Everth, sends Nicolai English books, 128
Ewald, Johann Joachim (1727–after 1762), 8, 9–10, 377, 377 n. 6

Faber, L. G., 186, 186 n. 21
Fauche, Pierre-François, 122
Feind, Johann Gottlob, 321
Ferber, Johann Jakob (1743–90), 263, 318, 350 n. 195
Ferguson, Adam (1723–1816), 12
Ferdinand, Prince of Prussia (1762–1813), 140 n. 182, 156
feuds, literary and scholarly, 316. See also specific authors
Fichte, Johann Gottlieb (1762–1814), xi, 37, 96, 316
  and Nicolai, 14–15, 238
  Philosophisches Journal, 212 n. 115
  on piracy and literary property, 303, 310
Finck von Finckenstein, Karl Friedrich Ludwig von (1743–1803), 196
Fischbach, Friedrich Ludwig Joseph (b. 1752), 62–64
Fleckeisen, C. G., 294 n. 198
Fleischer, Wilhelm (1767–1820), 161, 161 n. 260

Index

Fleischhauer, J. G., 234
Follenius, Emmanuel Friedrich Wilhelm
    Ernst (1773–1809), 92, 338 n. 145, 353,
    374
  Eduard Humber, 324, 324 n. 84, 338 n.
    144
  and Nicolai, 217, 313, 313 n. 37
  font size, 337–38, 338 n. 144
Foote, Samuel (1722–77), 91–92, 328 n. 104
formats, 95, 338, 336, 337, 338–39 n. 146
Formey, Jean Henri Samuel (1711–97), 45,
    93 n. 213
Forster, (Johann) Georg (1754–94), xi, 335 n.
    131
Forster, Johann Reinhold (1729–98), 127
Franck, Christian Gottlieb, 220 n. 147
Francke, Franz Christian Friedrich (b. 1758),
    162, 167, 171, 382
Frankfurt am Main, 186. *See also* book fair
Frankfurt an der Oder. *See* Nicolai, book
    trade apprenticeship
Frankfurter Gelehrte Anzeigen, 259 n. 39
Franklin, Benjamin (1706–90), 7
Francis II of Austria (1768–1835), 207 n. 90
Franz, Johann Georg Friedrich (1737–89),
    278 n. 125
Frederick II of Prussia (1712–86), 2, 23, 24,
    203, 231 n. 178, 232
  and censorship, 185, 189–90, 190 n. 36,
    191, 201, 213
  death of, 35, 56, 203
  and German writing, 2, 93 n. 213, 184
  and Nicolai, 2, 197
  Oeuvres du philosophe de Sans Souci, 158
Frederick Karl Joseph, elector of Mainz
    (1719–1802), 315 n. 41
Frederick William II of Prussia (1744–97), 22
    n. 61, 28, 62, 203–4, 248 n. 240
  censorship practice under, 206–7, 208
  death of, 212
Frederick William III of Prussia
    (1770–1840), 212 n. 113
freemasonry, 5, 336
French books, 121–23. *See also* translations,
    from the French
French booksellers, 122–23
French Revolution, 36, 37, 202
Friedel, Adrian Christian (b. 1753), 181 n.
    140
Friedel, Johann (1755–89), *Briefe über die
    Galanterien von Berlin*, 157, 157 n. 249
Fritsch, Caspar, 186

Frommann, N. G., 102, 102 n. 10, 160 n.
    257, 169–70, 285 n. 161, 381, 382, 383
Funke, C. P., 335 n. 135

Gädicke, Johann Christian (1763–1837), 27
    n. 82, 88 n. 205, 303, 303 n. 15, 312, 364
    n. 245
Gandersheim, abbess of, 130, 142 n. 193, 156
Ganz, Johann Friedrich Ferdinand
    (1741–95), 189, 189 n. 29, 234–35 n. 188
Gaspari, Adam Christian (1752–1830), 266,
    293, 324, 328
Gebauer, Johann Jacob (d. 1819), 65 n. 109,
    318, 324 n. 82
Gebhard, Johann Christian, 116, 121, 121 n.
    87, 381
Gebhard, Johann Georg (1743–1807), 273
Gebler, Tobias Philipp von (1726–86), 240,
    248, 301
Gedike, Friedrich (1755–1803), 203, 292 n.
    184, 359–60, 359 n. 234
Gegels Erben (L. B. F.), 234
Geißler, Carl Heinrich (1742–89), 273 n. 99
Das Gelehrte England, 127, 302 n. 10, 351,
    372–73
Gellert, Christian Fürchtegott (1715–69), 10,
    221 n. 151, 260, 271 n. 92, 330–31
genius, 12, 357
Georg, Prince of Waldeck-Pyrmont, 140 n.
    183
Gerhardt, Widow, housekeeper to Nicolai,
    173, 173 n. 309
German, as a literary language, 365–66
Gersten, lawyer in a piracy case, 232 n. 179
Gessner, Salomon (1730–88), 33, 45, 49, 264
    n. 63, 292 n. 189, 316
Gibbon, Edward (1737–94), *Essai sur l'etude
    de la littérature*, 323
Giese, Carl Gottfried, 65 n. 109
Gillet, Friedrich Wilhelm? (1762–1829), 344
Girtanner, Christoph (1760–1800), 352
Gjörwell, Carl Christoffer (1731–1811), 131,
    131–32 n. 141
Gleim, Johann Wilhelm Ludwig
    (1719–1803), 12 n. 38
Goebhard, Maria Philippine, on settlement
    with her husband, 230
Goebhard, Tobias, (pirate) publisher in Bamberg, 114, 223, 229, 230, 231
Goechhausen, Ernst August Anton von
    (1740–1824), 326, 327 n. 95
Göckingk, Leopold Friedrich Günther von

Index

(1748–1828), 38, 41 n. 37, 149 n. 221, 265, 283, 376
Görling, Johann Chr., 65 n. 10
Goeschen, Georg Joachim (1752 or 1756–1828), 91, 152, 302, 321, 340
Goethe, Johann Wolfgang von (1749–1832), 5 n. 8, 34, 82, 259 n. 39, 327 n. 96, 357
and Nicolai, xi, 327, 358, 376
Göttingen university library, 372, 372 n. 274
Göttinger Musenalmanach, 274
Göttingische Gelehrte Anzeigen, 254, 259, 259 nn. 39, 40
Götz, Gottlieb Christian, 167 n. 287
Goeze, Johann Melchior (1717–86), 319
Gohl, Mlle., Nicolai's cousin by marriage, 134 n. 149
Gohl, Daniel August (d. 1784), 134, 134 n. 149, 383
Goldhagen, Hermann (1714 or 1718–94), 218
Gosse, Pierre, 116, 124, 124 n. 103
Goßler, Carl Christoph (1752–1817), 48, 57, 146, 331 n. 117, 352
Gottleber, née Gross, mother of Carl August Nicolai's illegitimate child, 38 n. 30
Gottsched, Johann Christoph (1700–1766), 9, 10 n. 30, 251–52, 252 n. 7
Gräff, Ernst Martin (1760–1802), 179, 308
Gräffer, Rudolph (1734–96), 246, 247
Grävemeyer, Frau von (née von Hugo), 141 n. 188
Grävesmühlen, merchant in Altona, 32 n. 11
Gransee, Nicolai's manservant, 178 n. 330
Griffiths, Ralph (1720–1803), editor of the *Monthly Review*, 255
Gronau, Nicolai's commissionaire in Danzig, 134 n. 148
Grosch, *Adjunctus* in Jena, 278
Grosse, Friedrich (pseud. Eduard Romeo, Count Vargas), 94 n. 216
Gruner, Christian Gottfried (1744–1815), 265 n. 67, 316 n. 45, 328, 345–46
Gülcher, Theodor, 71, 123, 144, 150–51, 233 n. 182
Günther, Christian Friedrich (d. 1839), 168 n. 290, 172
Günther, Christoph, printer in Schleusingen, 65 n. 109, 66, 68, 69 n. 134, 281 n. 139
Güth, Johann Wilhelm, 162

Hagedorn, Christian Ludwig von (1712–80), 265

Halberstadt, 9
Halle, and ADB, 209, 210, 276
Haller, publisher in Brandenburg, 348 n. 182
Haller, Albrecht Emmanuel, 125
Hamann, Johann Georg (1730–88), xi, 358
Hamberger, Georg Christoph (1726–73), 96 n. 223, 262
Hammer, Peter, fictitious publisher's name, 336, 336 n. 137
Hammer-Purgstall, Joseph von (1774–1856), 48 n. 60
Hammerich, Johann Friedrich (1763–1827), 285 n. 161
Hane, Nicolai's shop manager in Stettin, 173, 173 n. 309, 174, 176–77, 178, 383
Hardenberg, Karl August von (1750–1822), 75, 141 n. 186, 233, 234
Harrer, Nicolai's shop manager in Stettin, 170–71, 171 n. 300, 177, 383
Hartknoch, Johann Friedrich (1740–89), 88 n. 205, 115–16, 131, 235 n. 189, 381
Hartwig, Otto Ludwig (1740–1802), 368
Haupt und Grisson, paper merchants in Hamburg, 71
Hechtel, Daniel Christoph, 32 n. 11, 186, 220–21 n. 148, 231 n. 178
Hederich, Benjamin (1675–1748), 93, 93 n. 214, 373
Heerbrandt, Jacob Friedrich, 220 n. 147, 285 n. 158
Hegewisch, Dietrich Hermann (1746–1812), 261
Heine, Heinrich (1797–1856), 24, 37
Heiniccius of the Seehandlungssocietät in Berlin, 130
Heinius, Dr., censor in Berlin, 195, 196 n. 49
Heinsius, Franz, 381
Heinsius, Johann Samuel, 163 nn. 266, 268, 169 n. 292
Heinze, Valentin August (1758–1801), 261, 266, 266 n. 73, 293, 293 n. 195, 311, 337
Helmold (von), army officer in Gotha, 266
Henke, Heinrich Philipp Conrad (1752–1809), 207–9, 207–8 n. 94, 211, 292 n. 187
Hennert, Karl Wilhelm (1739–1800), 334 n. 129
Herder, Johann Gottfried (1744–1803), xi, 5 n. 8, 34, 259 n. 39, 260, 270, 274, 286, 288
Hermann, Benedikt Franz Johann (1755–1815), 144, 148 n. 216

Index

Hermann, Martin Gottfried (1754–1822), 94 n. 216, 293, 293 nn. 191, 192, 322 n. 76, 329
   Handbuch der Mythologie, 334, , 347, 347 n. 178, 348, 349, 353, 353 n. 209, 354–55, 374
Hermbstädt, Sigismund Friedrich (1760–1833), 54
Hermes, Hermann Daniel (1734–1807), 206, 208, 210
Hermes, Johann August (1736–1822), 51 n. 69, 217
Hermes, Johann Timotheus (1738–1821), 78 n. 160
Hertzberg, Ewald Friedrich von (1725–95), 188 n. 26, 196, 205 n. 84
Hervey, Frederick Augustus, Earl of Bristol, 140–41, 141 n. 184
Herz, Henriette (née de Lemos, 1764–1847), 90 n. 207
Herz, Johann Friedrich, 319, 319 n. 61
Herz, Markus (1747–1803), 90 n. 207
Hesse, S. F., 106
Heun, sends Nicolai a manuscript, 326 n. 94
Heyne, Christian Gottlob (1729–1812), 255 n. 19, 259 n. 40, 266, 293 n. 191, 317 n. 49
Heyne, Christian Leberecht (pseud. Anton-Wall, 1752–1821), 50
Hiller, Johann Adam (1728–1804), 279
Hillmer, Gottlob Friedrich (1756–1835), 206, 208, 210, 211, 212
Hilscher, Christian Gottlob, 126
Himburg, Christian Friedrich (d. 1801), 137
Himmes, Nicholas, 162, 172 n. 305
Hinz, Jacob Friedrich (d. 1787), 318
Hirsch, Abraham, 57 n. 82
Hirschfeld, Christian Cajus Lorenz (1742–92), 266, 317–18, 318 n. 54, 322 n. 75
Histoire de la Vie Privée de Louis XV, 22–23, 23 n. 62
history, Nicolai as publisher of, 57–59
Hochmeister, Martin (1767–1837), 138
Hochstetter, Johann Ludwig von (b. 1742), 178, 231 n. 178, 232
Höpfner, Ludwig Julius Friedrich (1743–97), 207, 249, 259 n. 39, 262, 284, 285 n. 158, 327
Hoffmann, Benjamin Gottlob (1748–1818), 109, 114, 330
Hoffmann, Johann Jacob, 7, 8

Hohenleiter, Lucas, 144 n. 203
Holle, bookseller's *Diener*, nephew of Johann Samuel Heinsius, 169 n. 292
Holy Roman Empire, 183, 234
Homer, 94 n. 216
Die Horen (Goethe and Schiller), 95–96
Horst, Julius August Friedrich von der (d. 1791), 141 n. 187, 201
Horvath, Carl Christian (1752–1837), 146 n. 212, 338 n. 144, 348 n. 182
Hoym, Karl Georg Heinrich von (1739–1807), 74, 201, 201 n. 72

Ibn-Tufail, Abu-Bakr Muhammad, 48 n. 57
Ikler, Johann Philipp (1753–1819), 232 n. 179
Iffland, August Wilhelm (1759–1814), 328
Illuminati, 5 n. 8
illustrations, 333, 338, n. 146
Im Hof, Johann Rudolph und Sohn, 125, 126
Imperial Book Commission, 215, 218, 219, 229, 232
Iselin, Isaak (1728–82), 125, 129, 219, 269, 272
Isenburg, Prince Moritz of (1739–99), 158, 289–90, 319–20, 320 n. 67, 335 n. 131

Jacobsson, Johann Karl Gottfried (1725–89), 288, 367–68, 367 n. 256, 370, 373 n. 275. See also *Technologisches Wörterbuch*
Jesuits, Nicolai obsessed with, 23, 267
Jewish emancipation, 5, 89–90, 241 n. 205, 377
Job, Johann Georg, 340 n. 151
Johann Bunkel, 51, 76, 124, 216, 288, 286–87
   banned in Austria, 20, 34–35, 217–19
   complaints about, 19, 78, 78 n. 160, 79
Joseph II of Austria (1741–90), 3, 25, 25 n. 73, 184, 306
   censorship under, 189, 216, 245, 245 n. 224, 246–47
journals, literary and scholarly (*gelehrte Zeitungen*), 73–74, 253–54
Jünger, ?Christian Friedrich (1724–94), translator, 331 n. 116
Junius, Johann Friedrich, 328, 338 n. 144, 345, 348 n. 182
jurisprudence and administration, books on, 56–57
Justi, Johann Heinrich Gottlob von (1720–71), 195, 195 n. 48

Kämpf, bookbinder in Frankfurt am Main, 231 n. 175

Index

Kästner, Abraham Gotthelf (1719–1800), 255 n. 19, 266
Kahle, Ludwig Martin (1712–75), 192 n. 40, 198
Kant, Immanuel (1724–1804), xi, 37, 90, 251, 268 n. 79, 316
  and Nicolai, 21–22, 239–40, 248 n. 240, 269, 305, 310, 316–17, 330 n. 110, 371
Kanter, Johann Jakob (1738–86), 88 n. 205, 131
Karl Eugen, duke of Württemberg (1728–93), 220 n. 147
Karsten, Franz Christian Lorenz (1751–1829), 345
Karsch, Anna Luisa (née Dürbach, 1722–91), 12, 12 n. 38
Kehr, Ludwig Christian (1775–1848), 164–65, 164 n. 271, 168
Keyser, Georg Adam (1743 or 1746–1814), 162 n. 262, 383
Kirchhoff, Nikolaus (1725–1800), 320, 320 n. 71, 339 n. 148, 364–65
Klein, Ernst Ferdinand (1744–1810), 36, 57, 75, 192, 210, 351
  and Nicolai, 36, 306, 306 n. 25, 343, 344
Kleist, Ewald Christian von (1715–59), 9, 58, 377 n. 6
Kleyb, Johann Christian, 6–8, 160
Klipstein, Philipp Engel (1747–1808), 70 n. 134, 335, 335 n. 133
Klockenbring, Friedrich Arnold (1742–95), 269
Klopstock, Friedrich Gottlieb (1724–1803), 78, 270, 304
Klopstock, Johann Christoph Ernst, 167 n. 287
Klotz, Christian Adolf (1738–71), 261, 276–77, 277 n. 120, 279, 278
Klügel, Georg Simon (1739–1812), 75, 249, 311, 374
  Enzyklopädie, 54, 75, 77, 79 n. 162, 98, 217, 344, 373
Knigge, Adolf Franz Friedrich Ludwig von (1752–96), 264 n. 61, 265 n. 67, 286 n. 162, 325, 325 n. 89, 335, 336
Knüppeln, Julius Friedrich (1757–1840), 275 n. 113
Koch, Friedrich Albrecht von (d. 1800), 131, 147–48, 147 nn. 214–15
Kochendorster, bookshop employee in Frankfurt am Main, 163 n. 269

Koehler, Konrad Friedrich (1752–1838), 81, 109
Köpke, Georg Gustav Samuel (1773–1837), 334 n. 125
Köppen, ADB reviewer, 169 n. 292
Korn, (Johann) Friedrich, 131, 382
Korn, Johann Jakob, 88 n. 205
Korn, Wilhelm Gottlob (1739–1806), 116, 131
Kraehe, Johann Christoph, 167, 174, 176 n. 319, 178 n. 330, 382
Krebs, Friedrich Christian Karl (1757–93), 328
Kresel von Guatenberg, Franz Karl (1720–1801), 81
Krieger, Johann Christian (1746–1825), 285 nn. 158, 161
Krug, Wilhelm Traugott (1770–1842), 316–17, 317 n. 46, 329, 329 n. 106, 333 n. 120, 350 n. 192, 366–67
Kümmel, Carl Christian, 163
Küster, Karl Daniel (1724–1804), 59
Küttner, Carl Gottlob (1755–1805), 373, 373 n. 277
Kulmus, Johann Ludwig (b. 1745), 84 n. 183
Kummer, Paul Gotthelf (1750–1835), 111, 163, 169 n. 291, 179
Kunst, Christian Ludwig, 65 n. 109, 69
Kurzböck, Joseph Lorenz von (1736–92), 381

Lagarde und Friedrich, publishers, 88
Lamottraye, Aubry de, 55–56
Lampadius, Wilhelm August (1772–1842), 363
Langbein, August Friedrich Ernst (1757–1835), 319
Langer, Ernst Theodor (1743–1820), 153
Lanser, censor in Vienna, 248
La Roche, (Marie) Sophie von (1730–1807), 280 n. 134
Latin books, 46–47
Lavater, Johann Kaspar (1741–1801), 34, 50, 50 n. 68, 89, 327
  Physiognomische Fragmente, 136, 150
Lawätz, Heinrich Wilhelm (1748–1825), 318, 323–24
Leibniz, Gottfried Wilhelm (1646–1716), 12 n. 35
Leiningen, Graf von, 232
Leipzig, 313 n. 35. *See* book fair, Leipzig
Leipzig Book Commission, 213, 214, 215, 221, 223, 226, 227

lending libraries, 145–46, 145 n. 210, 195
　founded by Nicolai, 34, 135–36, 135–36 n. 154
Lenz, Johann Michael Reinhold (1751–92), 358, 358 n. 227
Leopold II of Austria (1747–92), 207 n. 90
Lerchberger, Romanus, 142 n. 19, 282
Lesage, Alain-René (1668–1747), *Gil Blas*, 91
Lessing, Gotthold Ephraim (1729–81), xi, 14 n. 44, 20 n. 57, 30 n. 4, 35 n. 21, 265, 284, 285, 319, 338, 358
　Briefe antiquarischen Inhalts, 58, 86, 118, 277 n. 120, 348 n. 182
　and Mendelssohn, 33, 243–44, 253
Lichtenau, Wilhelmine, Countess (née Enke, 1753–1820), 22, 22 n. 61
Lichtenberg, Georg Christoph (1742–99), xi, 301, 327, 328 n. 99
Lieber, Johann Karl (b. 1774), 317
Lieder, town councilor in Berlin, 105 n. 22
Lindfors, town councilor in Reval (Tallinn), 235 n. 189
Linguet, Simon Nicolas Henri (1736–94), 214
livres philosophiques, 125, 125 n. 107, 157, 176
Locke, John (1632–1704), *Two Treatises Concerning Government*, 321
Logan, Johann Zacharias, 168 n. 290, 171–72
Lohmann, Christoph Wilhelm, 169, 169 n. 292
Lombard, Johann Wilhelm (1767–1812), 41
Lorenz, Johann Gotthilf (1755–91), *Kurze Anleitung für Lehrer*, 154–55
Lotter, Nicolai's *Diener*, 163 n. 269, 382
Luca, Ignaz de, 236
Ludwig, Christine Sophie (née Fritsche, 1764–1815), 377 n. 7
Lück, D. F. von, 143 n. 197
Lüdke, Friedrich Germanus (1730–92), 50, 52, 255 n. 19, 261, 265, 272, 296 n. 213, 314–15

Malesherbes, Chrétien-Guillaume de Lamoignon de (1721–94), 199
Malthé, Johann Chr. von, 140 n. 185
Maltzow (Petr Malcev?), 131
Manger, Heinrich Ludwig (1728–90), 338 n. 144, 348 n. 182
Manutius, Aldus (1450–1515), 359, 379, 379 n. 9
Maria Theresa of Austria (1717–80), 146–47 n. 213, 184, 244

marketing. *See* advertising and subscription
Marlow, Harriet, (pseud.). *See* William Beckford
Marsh, Herbert (1757–1839), 128–29
Martini, Friedrich Heinrich Wilhelm (1729–78), 262
Martiny, Friedrich Wilhelm, 162 n. 261, 163 n. 269, 169 n. 292
Marx, David Raphael, 146 n. 210
Massow, E.J.W.E. von (1750–1816), 337 n. 142, 342
Matolay, Bernhard Samuel, 218, 226, 227, 230–31 n. 175, 320
Mauke, Johann Michael, 65 n. 109
Maurer, Friedrich (d. 1825), 358 n. 228
Mauvillon, Jakob (1743–94), 260, 271 n. 92
Mechau, book inspector in Leipzig, 217
Mechel, Christian von (1737–1815), 130
Meierotto, Johann Heinrich Ludwig (1742–1800), 53 n. 75
Meil, Johann Wilhelm (1733–1805), xiv, 264 n. 61, 320 n. 67, 338, 339 n. 146
Meinecke, Johann Albrecht Friedrich August, 53 n. 75
Meiners, Christoph (1747–1810), 279 n. 131
Meister, Leonhard (1741–1811), *Romantische Briefe*, 286
Melzer, Chr. Wilhelm, 65 n. 109, 295, 295 n. 205
Mencke, Otto (1644–1707), editor of *Acta Eruditorum*, 254
Mendelssohn, Moses (1729–86), xi, 5, 32, 35, 45, 58, 89, 93, 327, 337 n. 141, 351, 351 n. 199
　as ADB contributor, 255 n. 19, 265
　translations by, 90, 358 n. 228
　and Nicolai, 33, 91, 176 n. 319, 253
　Phädon, 34, 98, 186, 217, 221 n. 148
　works in index of forbidden books, 216, 243
Mercier, Louis-Sébastien (1740–1814), 46 n. 49
Merck, Johann Heinrich (1741–91), 255, 259 n. 39
Merz, Pater Alois (1727–92), 278
Messerer, Joseph Christoph, 285 n. 161
Messerschmidt, Nicolai's *Diener*, 382
Meß-Relationen, 39
Meusel, Johann Georg (1743–1820), 38, 96 n. 223, 241, 261, 261 n. 46
middle classes, 5, 376
Mieg, Johann Friedrich (b. 1744), 264 n. 60

Index

Mila, Wilhelm (1764–1833), 334 n. 128, 337 n. 142
Milton, John (1608–74), Nicolai and, 4, 10, 10 n. 30, 252 n. 7
Mirabeau, Honoré Gabriel, Comte de (1749–91), 14, 36, 53, 133, 141 n. 185, 275
Mittwochsgesellschaft, 4–5, 36, 54, 57, 198, 238, 306 n. 25
Möller, Johann Georg Peter (1729–1807), 78 n. 159
Möller, W., opens bookshop in Hamburg, 129
Möser, Justus (1720–94), 58, 91, 118
Monbart, Marie Josephe de (née de l'Escun, b. ca. 1758), 317
Montagsklub, 10
Monthly Review, 19, 255, 255 n. 16, 282
Moser, Johann Jakob (1701–85), 182
Moser, Karl Friedrich von, 230
Moufle d'Angerville, Barthélemy-François-Joseph, 58
Müchler, Johann Georg Philipp (1724–1809), 53
Müller, bookseller's assistant in Berlin, 105–6
Müller, Nicolai's *Diener*, 381
Müller, Friedrich August (1767–1807), 92
   Richard Löwenherz, 65 n. 110, 95 n. 211, 320, 333 n. 124
Müller, Johann Georg (1759–1819), brother of Johannes von Müller, 291 n. 178
Müller, Johann Gottwerth (1743–1828), 39, 49, 365 n. 249, 371
Müller, Johannes von (1752–1809), 145, 256, 263, 271, 291 n. 178
Munnikhuisen, J. H., 124, 124 n. 101
Musäus, Johann Karl August (1735–87), 78, 265 n. 67, 273, 312, 312 n. 33, 339, 365 n. 249, 371
Muzell, Friedrich (1684–1753), 237
Mylius, August, 29, 30 n. 2, 141, 381

Nagel, Johann Samuel (d. 1775), employee of Philipp Erasmus Reich, 160 n. 256
Nencke, Karl Christoph (d. 1811), 275 n. 113
Neues Archiv für Gelehrte, Buchhändler und Antiquare, 164, 165
Neue Zeitungen von gelehrten Sachen (Leipzig), 254
Nicolai, Carl August (1769–99), Nicolai's son, 30 n. 5, 38, 38 nn. 28, 30, 40, 92 n. 212, 165, 166, 174, 292, 292 n. 188, 377–78

Nicolai, (Christoph) Friedrich (1733–1811), ix–xiii, 54–55, 249, 280, 280 n. 135, 269 n. 81, 300, 378, 379
   as bookseller-publisher, xiv, 13, 20–22, 26, 44, 45, 79–80, 92–95, 94 n. 219, 99, 100, 115–16, 121–32, 153–54, 157, 173 n. 313, 174, 179, 189–90, 196, 284, 301–3, 306–11, 320 n. 66, 321–27, 336–37, 336 n. 138, 338, 355–56, 364, 367–71, 378
   contemporary assessments of, 23–24, 316
   education and training, 6–8, 9–10, 94 n. 216, 160
   family and personal life, xiv, xiv n. 22, 35, 36, 41 n. 37, 133, 133 n. 145, 174 n. 310, 302 n. 9, 376, 377; charity, 301, 302 n. 9, 319, 377 n. 7; children, 33, 34, 56–57 n. 81, 98, 98 n. 224 (*see also by name*)
   ideas and attitudes: on booksellers and the book trade, 16–19, 22, 26–28, 30, 44, 308; compares German to French and English literature and authors, 11, 18; explains his business principles, 100–101; on German writers, 11–13, 91, 94 n. 216, 95–97, 263, 365, 366; political views, 5–6, 239–40, 272, 377 (*see also* press freedom, Nicolai and); skepticism toward book trade reforms, 99–100, 179; on writing as a profession, 13–14, 18, 300–301, 307, 365
   negative assessments of, x–xii, xii n. 18
   periodicals: *Bibliothek der schönen Wissenschaften*, 12, 122, 252, 255, 273, 280; *Briefe, die neueste Litteratur betreffend*, 12, 31, 33, 195–96, 252, 253, 255, 273, 276; *Neue Berlinische Monatsschrift*, 40. See also *Allgemeine deutsche Bibliothek*
   writings: almanac of folk songs, 34, 90; anecdotes on Frederick II, 23, 58, 88; biographical essays on his friends, 58; *Briefe über den itzigen Zustand der schönen Literatur in Teutschland*, 10–13, 11 n. 32, 252 n. 7, 257; description of Berlin, 9, 59, 217, 256 n. 29; defense of Milton, 4, 10, 10 n. 30; *Freuden des jungen Werthers*, 34, 90; *Geschichte eines Dicken Mannes*, 90, 244, 248, 249; *Sempronius Gundibert*, 21, 90; travel account, 52, 55, 79–81, 216, 249, 257; *Ueber meine gelehrte Bildung*, 6, 13, 21. *See also* periodicals; *Sebaldus Nothanker*
Nicolai, Christoph Gottlieb (1690–1752),

Index

Nicolai's father, 8, 8 nn. 21–22, 24, 45, 93, 104 n. 19, 136, 138, 340 n. 151
Nicolai, Elisabeth Macaria (née Schaarschmidt, 1744–93), Nicolai's wife, 33, 36 n. 22, 38, 94 n. 216, 176, 176 n. 319, 205
Nicolai, Gottfried Wilhelm (d. 1758), Nicolai's brother, 9, 29, 31
Nicolai, Johann David (1771–1804), Nicolai's son, 57 n. 81
Nicolai, Maria Justina (née Zimmermann, d. 1738), Nicolai's mother, 8
Nicolai, Samuel Friedrich (1762–90), Nicolai's son, 33, 137 n. 161, 376
　death of, 38, 38 n. 27, 174, 205
　as *Diener* and shop manager, 165, 382
　marries Juliane Sophie Eleonore Klein, 36, 57 n. 81
Nicolai, Wilhemine (Minna, 1767–1803), Nicolai's daughter, 57 n. 81, 110 n. 44, 295
Nicolaische Buchhandlung, 8–9, 36–37, 104
　Berlin shop, 132–33, 133 n. 145
　branch in Danzig, 134
　branch in Stettin, 34, 134
　and Nicolai, 8, 29–31, 136
　output of the firm, 42, 33–59, 90–91
　trends in book production, 43–59
Nicolay, Ludwig Heinrich von (1737–1820), 50, 68, 86–87, 140 n. 180, 295, 302
　collected works, 48 n. 62, 302 n. 11, 324 n. 83, 338–39 n. 146
Nicolovius, Friedrich (1768–1836), 22, 118, 131
Niebuhr, Carsten (1733–1815), 78 n. 159
Noeldechen, Karl August (1745–1808), 54, 315 n. 42, 331 n. 117, 349, 349 n. 187
Nolde, von, inquires about books, 141 n. 190
Norberg, Samuel, 117, 117 n. 73
Nouffer, Jean Abraham, 125

Oberlin, Jeremias Jakob (1735–1806), 149 n. 220
O'Cahill, Baron (b. 1746), army officer, 277 n. 122
Oemigke, Wilhelm, 152 n. 234, 177, 177 n. 326
Oesfeld, Berlin calendar publisher, 285–86
Olivarius, Holger de Fine (1758–1838), 131, 131 n. 135
Osterloh, Friedrich, 169 n. 292
Ott, Russian embassy in Vienna, 147 n. 214

Paalzow, Christian Ludwig (1755–1824), 275 n. 113
Palatinate, regulations for the book trade in, 214 n. 120
Palm, Johann Jakob (1750–1826), 165, 168, 168 n. 290
paper, 59–62, 65–66, 69–71, 184
Parthey, Friedrich (1745–1822), Nicolai's son-in-law, 57 n. 81, 166, 174 n. 313, 383
Parthey, Gustav (1798–1872) Nicolai's grandson, 174 n. 310
Patzke, Samuel (1727–86), 8, 12 n. 38, 32, 32 n. 11, 31, 311, 332, 339 n. 148
Paul, Grand Duke, later Paul I of Russia (1754–1801), 140 n. 180
Pauli, Joachim, 71 n. 140, 120, 186, 187, 348 n. 182
pedagogy and school texts, 52, 92
Pelloutier, Simon (1694–1757), 191 n. 38
Penz, Julie von (1763 or 1768–1817), 314 n. 38
Perthes, Friedrich Christoph (1770–1843), 100–101, 110, 160–61, 179, 283, 284, 285, 311, 379
Pestalozzi, Johann Heinrich (1746–1827), 324 n. 87
Pfeffel, Gottlieb Conrad (aka Théophile Conrad, 1736–1809), 235
Pfeil, Christian Karl Ludwig von (1712–84), 222
philosophe, 1–2
Pilati di Tassulo, Carlo Antonio (aka Karl Anton, 1733–1802), 56
piracy, literary, 28 n. 83, 187, 233, 236, 305
　Catholic editions of Protestant works and, 222–23, 224, 226, 228
　contemporary views of, 250, 305
　dealing with out of court, 220 n. 142, 231, 231 n. 178, 233, 235–37
　definition of, 228
　and Nicolai on, 28, 186, 216, 219, 220–37
　plagiarism and, 228
　political obstacles to combating, 219, 234
　Prussian policy on, 185–89
　Saxon policy on, 188, 189, 214
Pistorius, Hermann Andreas (1730–98), 50 n. 69, 350 n. 191
Plamann, Johann Ernst (1771–1834), 324, 324 n. 87
Plieth, G. F. H., 356
Plümicke, Carl Martin (1749–1804), 72 n. 144, 370

Pockels, Carl Friedrich (1757–1814), 273 n. 104, 296
Pope, Alexander (1688–1740), ix, 31–32, 49, 126
Poppe, Johann Heinrich Moritz (b. 1776), 328
press freedom, 192, 238
　Nicolai and, 5, 196, 197, 204–5, 207, 219, 238–40
　See also censorship
Priestley, Joseph (1733–1804), 51
printers, 63, 64–69, 106 n. 26
　used by Nicolai's firm, 65 n. 109
privileges, publishing, 182, 214, 214 n. 120, 217, 223, 229, 230, 305
　acquisition of, 106 n. 26, 215–19, 220–21, 227
Pronay, Gabriel von (1748–1811), 81, 137, 282, 282 n. 143
proofreading and proofreaders, 86, 87, 88 nn. 202–4, 333–34
property, literary and intellectual
　contemporary views of, 223, 304–6
　Kant and Fichte on, 305, 310
　Nicolai on, 26–27, 308–11
Prussian Legal Code Commission, 4, 144, 146. *See also* Allgemeines Preußisches Landrecht
public scrutiny, Nicolai and principle of, 239–40
publishers' property rights, basis of, 223
publishing companies, division of labor in, 303
publishing rights, conflicts and agreements concerning, 116–20
Pütter, Johann Stephan (1725–1807), 223 n. 155, 229

Rabener, Gottlieb Wilhelm (1714–71), 10
Rabenhorst, Christian Gottlieb, 118
Radecke, Friederike von, 142 n. 193
Rambach, Friedrich (1767–1826), 53 n. 75, 337 n. 140
Ramler, Karl Wilhelm (1725–98), 58, 86–87, 331
Raspe, Carl Friedrich, 163 n. 269, 246
reading, 169
　popularization of as a pastime, 25, 25 n. 70
　societies and clubs, 144–45, 144–45 nn. 205–8
Rebmann, Andreas Georg Friedrich von (1768–1824), on censorship under Frederick II, 189

Recke, Charlotte Elisabeth Konstanze (Elisa) von der (née von Medem, 1754–1833), 35, 35 n. 21, 36, 110 n. 44, 141 n. 188, 148, 265, 302 n. 11, 324, 376–77
Reclam, Pierre Christian Frédéric (1741–89), 111 n. 47
Regnard, Jean-François (1655–1709), 31
Reich, Philipp Erasmus (1717–87), 25, 29, 30 n. 3, 48, 91, 95 n. 221, 107, 116, 120 n. 83, 123, 140, 152 n. 234, 167, 173, 179, 186, 187, 221 n. 151, 222, 237, 308, 313, 345, 347
　decision making on manuscripts, 84, 303, 303 n. 16
　fees paid to authors, 330–31, 348 n. 182
　and Nicolai, 100, 111–13, 119–20
Reichshofrat (imperial aulic council), 213, 215, 217, 221–23 passim, 226–28 passim, 231, 232
Reim, Johann Christian Benjamin, 159–60, 167 n. 287
Reinhold, Karl Leonhard (1758–1823), 316, 268 n. 79
Reinwald, Wilhelm Friedrich Hermann (1737–1815), 299
　Hennebergisches Idiotikon, 43, 302, 350–51, 351 n. 196
Remer, Julius August (1738–1803), 373
republic of letters, Nicolai and, 10, 238–40, 271, 272
Resewitz, Friedrich Gabriel (1729–1806), 53, 65, 236, 255 n. 19, 265, 326, 326 n. 92
retail sales, 140. *See also* customers
Reuß, Jeremias David (1750–1837), 38, 129, 311, 329, 372. See also *Das Gelehrte England*
Rey, Marc-Michel, 123
Ribock, J. J. H. (d. 1785 or 1787), 312
Richardi, Johann Wilhelm, 160, 167, 178 n. 330, 383
Richter, asks Nicolai's help, 146 n. 212
Richter, Johann Paul Friedrich (1763–1825), 326
Riedel, Friedrich Justus (1742–85), 277, 278
Riedel, Samuel Friedrich, 233, 234
Riedesel, Johann Hermann (1740–85), 240 n. 206
Riem, Andreas (1749–1807), 204
Riemann, Carl Friedrich, *Versuch einer Beschreibung der Rekahnschen Schuleinrichtung*, 154–55
Ringer, bookbinder in Munich, 246 n. 229

Index

Ritter, Johannes, 169 n. 292, 178 n. 330, 382–83
Robinson, Henry Crabb (1775–1867), 24
Robinson, Mary Darby (1748–1800), 92
Rochow, Friedrich Eberhard von (1734–1805), 36, 38, 52–53, 154–55, 344, 344 n. 163
Rode, (Christian) Bernhard (1725–97), 111 n. 47, 222 n. 152
Röhl, publisher, 345
Rosalino, Franz de Paula (1736–93), as Austrian censor, 247
Rosenbusch, Johann Georg, 65 n. 109
Rosenthal, Gottfried Erich (1745–1814), 82, 265, 265 n. 69, 355 n. 216, 356 n. 223, 357 n. 224
    continues Wiegleb's *Natürliche Magie*, 55, 356
    continues Jacobsson's *Technologisches Wörterbuch*, 241 n. 154, 333 nn. 121, 122, 342, 344, 355–56, 368–70, 370 n. 263, 374
Roßnagel, Franz, 146 n. 210
Rostock, bookshop employee in Breslau, 163 n. 269
Rothe, Immanuel Gottfried (1737–1809), 313
Rüdiger, Johann Christian Christoph (1751–1822), 335 n. 132
Rüdiger, Johann Heinrich, 133 n. 14, 190 n. 36
Rüling, Georg Ernst von (d. 1807), 265 n. 67
Ruhkopf, Friedrich Ernst (1760–1821), 84 n. 183

Saalbach, Ulrich Christian, 65 n. 109
Sack, August Friedrich Wilhelm (1703–86), 271 n. 91
Sailer, Johann Michael, (1750–1832), 208 n. 94
Sammlung vermischter Schriften zur Beförderung der schönen Wissenschaften und der freyen Künste, 33
Sander, Johann Daniel (1759–1825), 115, 115 n. 65
Sanders, Charlotte Elizabeth, 85
Savioli Corbelli, Ludovico Aurelio, 148 n. 217
Schaarschmidt, Madame, Nicolai's mother-in-law, 133, 133 n.145
Schaarschmidt, Samuel, father of Nicolai's wife, 33
Schad, Johann Baptist (1758–1834), 268, 268 n. 79

Schäfer, Johann Andreas, 170, 381
Schaumburg-Lippe-Bückeburg, counts of, 323 n. 80
Scheffner, Johann Georg (1736–1820), 236, 154–55, 155 n. 246, 236
Schelling, Friedrich Wilhelm Josef (1775–1854), 316
Scherer, A. M., 153
Scheve, Adolf Friedrich von (1752–1837), 212
Schiller, Friedrich von (1759–1805), xi, 23, 23 n. 65, 251, 357
Schiller, Johann Friedrich, 120 n. 83
Schink, Johann Friedrich (1755–1835), 50
Schirach, Peter Elias (1742–after 1790), 65 n. 109, 67, 70
Schlegel, August Wilhelm (1767–1816), 15, 96
Schlözer, August Ludwig (1735–1809), 266
Schlüter, ?Joachim André (b. 1723), 200–201, 205 n. 84
Schmettow, Karl Friedrich Wilhelm, Graf von, 293
Schmid, Konrad Arnold (1716–89), 49
Schmidt, dealer in fancy goods, 32 n. 11
Schmidt, Christian Friedrich, 165, 173, 177, 383, 383 n. 19
Schmidt, Michael Ignatz (1736–94), 267
Schmidt-Phiseldeck, Christoph (1740–1801), 266
Schmieder, Christian Gottlob, 234
Schneider, J. C. D., 160 n. 257, 166, 381
Schnoor, Johann Carl, 235 n. 189
Schramm, Wilhelm Heinrich, 220 n. 147
Schreuder, Johann, 121 n. 84, 123
Schröckh, Johann Matthias (1733–1808)
    censors ADB in Wittenberg, 211–12, 242–43, 272, 311
    Lehrbuch der allgemeinen Weltgeschichte, 43, 58, 216, 222, 224, 224 n. 159, 305
Schubart, Christian Friedrich Daniel (1739–91), 24, 189–90
Schütz, Christian Gottfried (1747–1832), 272
Schulz, Widow, Nicolai's landlady, 134, 134 n. 149
Schulze-Kummerfeld, Caroline (1743–1821), 317 n. 48
Schumann, lawyer, 229 n. 171
Schwab, Johann Christoph (1743–1821), 21 n. 59
Schwager, Johann Moritz (1738–1804), 51 n. 69, 52

Index

Schwan, Christian Friedrich (1734–1815), 15, 109, 220, 276, 285 n. 161, 358 n. 229
 on piracy, 214 n. 120, 237, 237 n. 195
Schwarz, papermaker, 69
Schweighauser, Johann (d. 1806), 116, 125, 126, 130
Schweppe, Carl Christian Friedrich, 163 n. 269
Schwickert, Engelhard Benjamin (1741–1825), 328, 345
Sebaldus Nothanker, 16–19, 22, 34, 48, 79, 86, 90, 108, 149, 216, 221, 227 n. 165, 243, 257, 287–88, 300
 depictions of book trade in, 16–19, 307, 319, 323
 piracy of, 186, 231 n. 178
 and Nicolai, 51, 207, 207 n. 91
 success of, 48 n. 62, 98, 285
 translations of, 116, 117, 117 n. 71
Seidensticker, Johann Anton Ludwig (1766–1817), 56, 343
Seven Years' War, 29, 33
Seyberth, bookshop employee, 172 n. 304
Shakespeare, William (1564–1616), 33 n. 14, 252 n. 7, 322 n. 74
 Nicolai's plans to publish, 32 n. 9, 33
Siebmann, Christian Ludwig (1748–1802), , 205 n. 84
Simon, Berlin Jew, 106, 106–7 n. 27
Sinapius, Johann Christian (d. 1807), 201–2
Singer, Wilhelmine (1774–after 1827), 92, 335 n. 131
Société typographique de Bâle, 126
Société typographique de Berne, 125
Société typographique de Neuchâtel, 227 n. 166
Socrates, on himself as a "midwife," 301 n. 7
Solbrig, Christian Friedrich, 65 n. 109, 336 n. 138
Sommer, Johann Christian (1741–1802), 266
Spilleke, Gottlieb August (1778–1841), 334 n. 125
Splitgerber und Daum, bankers, 167 n. 285
Splittegarb, Karl Friedrich (1753–1802), 53
Sprengel, Matthias Christian (1746–1803), 373
Springer, Johann Christoph Erich (von) (1727–98), 55, 153, 323 n. 80, 324
 as ADB reviewer, 289 n. 173, 317 n. 53, 323 n. 80
 and Nicolai, 72, 317, 323
 oversees printing of ADB, 67–69, 241–42

Staël, Anne-Louise-Germaine de (1766–1817), 251
Stahel, Johann Jacob (d. 1789), printer and publisher, 162, 221–29, 227 n. 165, 382
Starck, Johann August von (1741–1816), 21, 202 n. 74
Steck, Johann Christoph Wilhelm von (1730–97), 36, 46, 192 n. 40, 200, 200 n. 69
Steckmesser, Nicolai's *Diener*, 174, 382
Steele, Richard (1672–1729), 15
Steinfürth, F. C. C., 163 n. 269, 382
Stettin, 173. *See also* Nicolaische Buchhandlung
Stöver, Johann Hermann (1764–96), 73–74
Stolberg-Stolberg, Friedrich Leopold Graf zu (1750–85), 336
Straube, Josef Jacob Friedrich, 65 n. 109, 67, 68, 69
Strobl, Johann Baptist, 234
Stroth, Friedrich Andreas (1750–85), 266, 350 n. 193
Stubenrauch, Christian Ludwig (1748–1844), lawyer, 228, 229
Sturm und Drang, Nicolai on, 90, 91, 371
subscription and "prenumeration," 75–83, 288–89
Süßmilch, Johann Peter (1707–67), 191 n. 38
Sulzer, Johann Georg (1720–79), 58 n. 89, 93 n. 213, 192 n. 40, 198, 218
Svarez, Carl Gottlieb (1746–97), 48, 57, 75, 119, 130, 306, 306 n. 25, 331 n. 117, 337 n. 140, 341, 352–53

Tafinger, Wilhelm Gottlieb (1760–1813), 257 n. 31
Technologisches Wörterbuch (Jacobsson and Rosenthal), 54, 69, 79, 373, 373 n. 275
 advertising of, 74, 81–82, 288
 and Nicolai, 367–70
 subscribers to, 82–83, 83 nn. 177–80, 282 n. 143
Teller, Wilhelm Abraham (1734–1804), 58, 255 n. 19, 265
 as Prussian censor, 192, 197, 198, 212, 218, 241 n. 207
Teutsche Merkur, 19, 74, 268 n. 79, 277
theology and theologians (Protestant)
 in the ADB, 3, 275, 296, 296 n. 213
 and Nicolai, 3, 40, 50–52, 271
Thilo, Louise (née Lots), 154, 154 n. 245
Thomasius, Christian (1655–1728), 12 n. 35

Index

Thorn, P. N., 172 n. 305
Thurneysen, Emmanuel, 125, 126
Tieck, Ludwig (1773–1853), 38, 92, 92 n. 212, 365 n. 249, 371 n. 270, 365, 374
  and the *Strausfedern* collection, 311, 365 n. 249, 371, 371 n. 270
Tieck, Sophie (1775–1833), 311
Tindal, Mathew (1653–1733), 51
Tode, Heinrich Julius (1733–97), 279
translations, 91–92
  competition over rights to, 116, 119–20
  from the French, 37–38, 47
  from the English and other languages, 47
translators, Nicolai on, 309
Trapp, Ernst Christian (1745–1818), 53, 348
Trattner, Thomas Edler von (1717–98), 88 n. 205, 185, 185 n. 216, 219, 219–20 n. 144
  pirates Nicolai's publications, 216 n. 128, 221, 234
Traunpaur d'Ophanie, Alphons Heinrich (b. 1734), 319
travel accounts, 55–56
Treumann, Georg Heinrich (d. 1823), 50 n. 69, 52, 53
Treuttel, Karl Friedrich, 168 n. 288, 169 n. 292
Troschel, Christian Ludwig (1735–1802), 50 n. 69, 103 n. 11
Troschel, Ferdinand, 103 n. 11
Troschel, Jakob Elias (1735–1807), 50 n. 69
Trost, Karl Friedrich (1740–1807), 23 n. 62, 56, 119
typography, typefaces, 336, 336 n. 138, 338 n. 144

Uhden, Johann Christian von (d. 1783), 196 n. 49
Uhrlandt, Carl Friedrich, 153, 153 n. 242
Ummius, August Ludwig (b. 1769), 317, 317 n. 49
Unger, Johann Friedrich (1750–1804), 65 n. 109, 68, 106 n. 26, 194 n. 46
Unger, Salomo Gottlieb (1752–1818), 319 n. 63
Utrecht, Friedrich Wilhelm (b. 1740), 128
Uz, Johann Peter (1720–96), 82, 94, n. 216, 207, 378

Van Cleef, Isaak, 119, 124, 124 n. 105
Van Scheben, Franz Xaver, 218
Vanselow, J. J., wine merchants, 134 n. 149

Veltheim, Friedrich Wilhelm von (d. 1803), 143
Verlagskasse für Gelehrte und Künstler, 304
Vienna, 243, 247, 313 n. 35
Vieweg, Friedrich (1761–1835), 65 n. 109, 71 n. 140, 209
Villaume, Peter (1746–1806), 53 n. 75
Voltaire, François Marie Arouet de (1694–1778), 13, 45, 57 n. 82
Voß, Christian Friedrich (1724–95), 29, 71 n. 140, 86, 107, 113, 113 n. 56, 118, 158 n. 250, 187, 237 n. 195, 348 n. 182
Voß, Johann Heinrich (1751–1826), 276, 330

Wachter, Georg, 148 n. 217
Walch, Albrecht Georg (1726–1822), 152, 157, 212–13, 279
  and ADB contributor, 66, 67, 69–70 n. 134, 75, 87–88, 209, 262, 267, 290, 290 n. 177, 296, 304 n. 18
  and Nicolai, 272, 294 n. 201
War of the Bavarian Succession, 219, 270
Weber, author of articles on papermaking, 61
Weber, Georg Michael (b. 1768), 321
Wehner, Georg Friedrich, 316
Weidmann, Marie Luise (1714–93), 159
Weidmanns Erben (und Reich), 44, 46, 47, 71, 121–22, 129, 308, 321, 328. *See also* Philipp Erasmus Reich
Weikard, Melchior Adam (1742–1803), 58, 148
Weiße, Christian Felix (1726–1804), 121 n. 86, 255, 265, 331 n. 116
Weißhaupt, Adam, 5 n. 8
Wendland, Chr. Friedrich, 153–54, 154 n. 243
Werkmeister, Benedikt Maria Leonhard von (1745–1823), 282, 282 n. 146
Werner, Johann Friedrich von, 319
Werthes, Friedrich August Clemens (1748–1817), 300, 307
Wever, Arnold, 115 n. 65
Weygand, Johann Friedrich (1743–1806), 101, 327 n. 96
Wezel, Johann Karl (1747–1819), 50, 318, 318 n. 57, 331 n. 117
Wiarda, Tileman Dothias (1746–1826), 318–19, 334 n. 130, 338 n. 146
Wiegleb, Johann Christian (1732–1800), 136, 311, 328, 364
  Chemische Versuche über alkalische Salze, 332 n. 119, 347, 347 n. 180
  Natürliche Magie, 55, 347

Index

Wieland, Christoph Martin (1733–1813), 34, 268 n. 79, 269, 284, 304, 330–31, 347
  and Nicolai, 19–21, 272
  See also *Teutsche Merkur*
Wilhelm, Gottlieb Tobias (1758–1811), 282
Wilke, Christian Heinrich (d. 1776), 278 n. 125
Wilkinson, Tate (1739–1803), 58
Wille, Georg, 281
Williams, David, 53
Winckelmann, Johann Joachim (1717–68), 58, 130, 377
Wittekindt, J. G. E., 235 n. 189
Wöllner, Johann Christian (1732–1800), 203–4, 210, 212 n. 113
  and tightened censorship, 203–4, 211, 212
Wolf, Johann Christoph (1730–85), 56
Wolff, Christian (1679–1750), 4, 12 n. 35
women, Nicolai's notions about, 377
women authors, 314 n. 38, 317, 317 n. 48, 335, 335 n. 131
  reviews of works in the ADB, 279–80, 280 n. 134
writing, as a source of income, 193, 312–13, 329
Würzburg, prince-bishop of, 222, 225
Würzer, Heinrich, 206 n. 85
Wurmb, Major v., 265, 265 n. 68

Xenien (Goethe and Schiller), xi n. 17, 279 n. 128

Zahn, Johann Christian (1767–1818), 133 n. 143
Zaupser, Andreas Dominik (1746 or 1747–95), 246 n. 229
Zedlitz, Karl Abraham von (1731–93), 62, 74
Zehe, Johann Eberhard, 172, 172 n. 306, 381
Zehetmayer, J. M., and B. Kiermayr, 145 n. 210
Zeller, C., 125 n. 106
Zerrenner, Heinrich Gottlob (1750–1811), 53, 169 n. 292, 337 n. 140
Zimmermann, Gottfried (Nicolai's grandfather), 8, 340 n. 151
Zimmermann, Johann Georg (1728–95), 150 n. 222, 220
Zöllner, Johann Friedrich (1753–1804), 50 n. 69, 240 n. 205, 382
Zolling, Carl, 382
Zolling, Johann Siegmund, 109
Zückert, Johann Friedrich (1737–78), 255 n. 19
Zumbrock, Henry, 128

www.ingramcontent.com/pod-product-compliance
Lightning Source LLC
Chambersburg PA
CBHW032126010526
44111CB00033B/131